THE HOOVER LIBRARY ON WAR, REVOLUTION, AND PEACE

———————————————PUBLICATION No. 25———————————————

Soviet Russia and the East
1920–1927

PUBLISHED under the authority of the Publication Committee
of the Hoover Library on War, Revolution, and Peace

SOVIET RUSSIA and the EAST

1920-1927
A Documentary Survey

by
XENIA JOUKOFF EUDIN
and
ROBERT C. NORTH

1957
STANFORD UNIVERSITY PRESS / Stanford, California

STANFORD UNIVERSITY PRESS, STANFORD, CALIFORNIA
London: Oxford University Press
© 1957 by the Board of Trustees of the Leland Stanford Junior University
Printed in the United States of America
Library of Congress Catalog Card Number: 56-8690

FOREWORD

This volume on *Soviet Russia and the East, 1920–1927* is one of two companion studies of Soviet foreign policy in this period. The second, published simultaneously, presents the relations of the Soviet Union with the West. Both volumes are composed principally of documents. In each, brief introductory narratives provide the historical setting for the documents.

The Hoover Institute and Library is following a long-established policy in making these documents, drawn almost entirely from its own collections, available in English. The intention is to serve scholars and a broader public by placing at their disposal the source materials upon which understanding and interpretation of Soviet foreign policy in the years 1920–27 must be based. Every effort has been made by the authors and editors to present a representative and objectively chosen selection of documents. It goes without saying that the Institute and Library does not assume responsibility for the views contained in these documents.

A few words about the author-editors of these volumes are in order. Mrs. Xenia Joukoff Eudin has been associated with the Hoover Institute and Library since 1932. Earlier she was a student at the University of London, and before the revolution she attended Moscow University. She is coeditor of two other volumes in the series of Hoover Library Publications: *Features and Figures of the Past: Government and Opinion in the Reign of Nicholas II* (1939), and *The Life of a Chemist: Memoirs of V. N. Ipatieff* (1946).

Robert Carver North has been a staff member of the Institute and Library since 1948. He is the author of two of the Hoover Institute Studies: *Kuomintang and Chinese Communist Elites* (1952), and a longer work, *Moscow and Chinese Communists* (1953).

Much of the preliminary research for this volume was conducted under the Slavic Fellowship Program made possible by a grant from the Rockefeller Foundation in 1946. Additional research and editorial assistance, together with the costs of publication, have come from the private gift funds of the Hoover Institute and Library and from those of Stanford University. It is understood that the Rockefeller Foundation, despite its generous contribution to the preparation of this volume, bears no responsibility for its contents.

Stanford University   C. EASTON ROTHWELL
November 1956   *Director, Hoover Institute*
                                 and Library

PREFACE

This volume presents a documentary survey and narrative of seven crucial years in the history of Soviet relations with Asia—a period during which Russian communist leaders formulated and first sought to implement the fundamental principles that have guided them ever since in their relations with Eastern peoples. All the documents it includes are available in Hoover Library collections.

In seeking to describe and document the main lines of Soviet policy and action during these years, we have found it necessary to confine ourselves within severe limitations of purpose and scope, and we are fully aware of vast areas left untouched.

Since the record of Soviet relations with the East is extensive and intricate, our account of it is necessarily selective rather than comprehensive. Restrictions of space largely dictated our decision to confine ourselves in this volume to the period beginning in 1920 and ending in 1927, when the failure of the Chinese revolution, the break in official Russo-Chinese relations, and the severing by Great Britain of diplomatic relations with the U.S.S.R. forced Russian communist leaders to modify their tactics in Asia and to stiffen their strategy in the Western countries. We trust the published survey of these years will serve as a foundation for further investigations into later phases of Soviet policies toward countries of Asia.

Most of the documents here presented originated with the Soviet government or the Russian Communists. Except for a very few, they have been translated from the Russian language. They thus cover only one side of the record of Soviet relations with the East during the period in question, and they do not cover that completely. Any comprehensive presentation of the Soviet and communist documentation on relations with Asia will require a careful integration of Russian sources with those in Chinese, Japanese, Indian, Persian, and other languages. To present also the appropriate documents of the Asian peoples who were the objects of Soviet foreign policy, in order that the record may be complete, is a task of such magnitude that it could not be undertaken in the present project.

Within this volume, however, we have been careful to combine with the official records of Soviet diplomacy the documents which reveal unofficial and extralegal activities throughout Asia of the various organs of the Russian Communist Party and the Communist International. The two must be studied together because the officials of the Soviet government were, at the same time, leaders in the Party and dominating figures in the newly formed Comintern. Their unofficial and extralegal activities in the latter capacities were carried on side by side with their official diplomacy.

Our purpose, then, has been to present for the period 1920–27 English translations of Soviet and communist documents which would be of particular value to readers who do not have access to the original sources. We have drawn materials from Soviet newspapers and periodicals, and from files of the Communist

International, as well as from official Soviet sources available in the Hoover Library. In difficult choices, we have tried to select the materials which, from the perspective of today, appear best to document the genesis of Soviet theories concerning relations with Eastern countries, the main lines of action that emerged from these theories, and the chief tactical shifts that occurred within the broad range of Russian communist political strategy toward Asia.

We wish to convey our gratitude to Dr. Harold H. Fisher, Mrs. Rosemary Jones, and Mr. Richard Sorich for their generous assistance during preliminary stages of the undertaking. We are indebted to the late Eleanor Bisbee for her deep interest in the study and valuable suggestions. We also wish to thank Mrs. Priscilla T. Lee and Dr. Raymond H. Fisher for having read the manuscript and for their corrections and many useful comments, Dr. Travers Edgar Durkee for permitting us to use his doctoral dissertation as a basic source for the section on Japan, and Dr. Merrill T. B. Spalding for valuable suggestions and generous advice in the preparation of our historical introduction. To the staff of the Hoover Library, and to Mrs. Arlene Paul in particular, we are grateful for patient and unstinting assistance provided us in our search for materials. Laura M. Bell has prepared the index.

XENIA J. EUDIN
ROBERT C. NORTH

Stanford, California
October 1956

CONTENTS

DOCUMENTS

PART I

PART II

Historical Introduction

HISTORICAL INTRODUCTION

Russia is not only in Europe, it is also in Asia; and a Russian is not only a European, but also an Asiatic. Moreover, there is more hope for Russia in Asia than in Europe. Perhaps Asia is the best outlet for us in the future.

DOSTOEVSKY, *The Diary of a Writer, January 1881*

When the Bolsheviks came to power in October 1917, they hastened to repudiate the foreign associations and commitments of the Imperial regime and the Provisional Government. Within months, however, they discovered that this either could not or should not be done. For strategic or other reasons, the Soviet leaders reversed their initial position and decided to hold the territories acquired by their predecessors, although presumably upon a federative rather than an imperial basis.

True, the Bolsheviks were obliged, because of the Soviet state's weak military position, to yield western borderlands of Russia to Austro-German armies of occupation, and two years later to make peace with these borderlands, which had meanwhile declared their independence. The Soviet leaders fought desperately, however, to retain other Russian territories, particularly those on the vast Asian continent. They were strikingly successful in holding the Eurasian heartland acquired by Imperial Russia in its eastward drive "against the sun."[1]

The revised approach of the Soviet government — and therefore of the party—toward relations between Russia and Asia was expressed in ideological terms eighteen months after the establishment of the Soviet regime by Chicherin, the People's Commissar of Foreign Affairs. After quoting the 1856 opinion of Prince Gorchakov (the foreign minister of Imperial Russia) that the future of Russia was in Asia, he added:

If the imperialist representative of tsarist policy was completely justified in saying that the future of Russia was in Asia, now, in the proletarian period of human history which has just begun, this unity in the history of the Russian and Asian toiling masses will be expressed in the joint revolutionary struggle against the international yoke of the imperialist oligarchy, and in support of an international socialism under which there will no longer be exploiting and exploited countries or any sharp differences between Europe and Asia.[2]

Asiatic Russia: Its Geography, Peoples, and Resources

The territory in Asia which the Communist regime inherited from Imperial Russia is vast. It is half the size of all Europe and two and one-half times that of European Russia. Extending to the Pacific, it makes Russia an Asian as well as a European power, a neighbor of China, Japan, Persia, Afghanistan, and

[1] For a graphic description of this drive, see G. V. Vernadsky, "Protiv solntsa; rasprostranenie russkogo gosudarstva k Vostoku" (reprint from *Russkaia Mysl*, 1914).

[2] G. V. Chicherin, "Rossiia i aziatskie narody," *Vestnik Narodnogo Komissariata po Inostrannym Delam*, No. 2, August 12, 1919, p. 7.

3

Turkey. Within this huge Asian area there is great mineral wealth and an abundance of timber. Traditionally the region produced food and fur, but in more recent years industry and mining have come to the fore.

The peoples and languages of this huge territory are varied. Outside the Caucasus area, with its mixture of many ethnic and linguistic elements, the population of Russian Asia is divided among five major groups: (1) the Finno-Ugrians, who inhabit the northern part of Western Siberia; (2) the Tungus or Evenki in Eastern Siberia; (3) the Buriats and other Mongolian people who live in the Transbaikal and Irkutsk region; (4) the Paleo-Asiatic tribes inhabiting the northeastern sector of Siberia; and (5) the Turkic peoples, of whom the largest group inhabit Russian Central Asia.

Russian contact with the peoples of Asia began as early as the tenth century. It was the period of Tatar or Mongol invasion from the thirteenth to fifteenth centuries, however, that brought the Russians into close association with Asian customs and methods of government and reinforced to some extent the various autocratic tendencies of the Muscovite state.[3]

The Dynamism of Russian Expansion

Russian expansionist tendencies had three main goals: (1) to exploit the economic potential of Asia; (2) to enhance the power and prestige of the Russian state both militarily and politically; and (3), in addition to these not uncommon imperialist impulses, to obtain badly needed warm-water ports.

A fourth motive has been suggested by Kliuchevsky to explain the "continuous" and "spontaneous colonization" of new regions by the Russian people: the desire for better living conditions and freedom from government pressure.

Many Russians of the eighteenth and nineteenth centuries were conscious, too, of a civilizing and Christianizing mission to be carried out in Asia. Not only was infidel-held Constantinople to become a Christian city, but as one publicist put it, an expanded Russian state would stretch "from the Nile to the Neva, from the Elbe to China, from the Volga to the Euphrates, and from the Ganges to the Danube."[4] Belief in this "mission" found vigorous expression through S. Iu. Witte, the guiding spirit of Russia's modern economic and industrial development at the end of the nineteenth century:

Situated on the boundary line of two completely different worlds, Russia at the same time contributes a world of her own. Her independent position in the family of nations and her special role in world history have been determined by her geographical position, that is, by her direct proximity to both European and Asiatic peoples . . . Russia has long been a bearer of the Christian ideal among Asiatic peoples and

[3] After freeing itself from Tatar domination, Muscovite Russia continued for some time to defend itself against Tatars who held power in adjacent regions, as well as against its Western neighbors. Consequently, as Professor Vernadsky has stated, "the regimentation of the social classes which started during the Mongol period and was originally based on the Mongol principles of administration, was carried further and completed by the Muscovite government. Autocracy and serfdom were the price the Russian people had to pay for national survival." (George Vernadsky, *The Mongols and Russia*, p. 390.)

[4] F. I. Tiutchev, "Russkaia geografiia," *Polnoe sobranie sochinenii*, II, 190. Tiutchev was a well-known Russian poet and publicist of Pan-Slavic tendencies in the nineteenth century.

has tried to spread among them the principle of Christian enlightenment . . . not under the banner of Europeanism, but under Russia's own banner.[5]

There were three Asiatic areas of special interest to Russia: one comprising Central Asian khanates and extended from there to Afghanistan, Sinkiang, and Tibet; a second which included Transcaucasia, Asiatic Turkey, and Persia; and a third, North Asia—that is, Siberia and the Maritime Provinces—which provided connecting links between European Russia and Manchuria, Korea, Outer Mongolia, China, and Japan.

Central Asia

Muscovite attention was focused centuries ago on the Central Asian khanates of Kokand, Khiva, and Bukhara and on faraway India; fabulous tales were told of the riches of these countries. The attempt of Peter the Great to reach India through the Central Asian khanates failed, however, and it was not until the second half of the nineteenth century that Russia finally conquered them. Thereafter, an almost continuous Russian advance toward the frontier of Afghanistan—by then a British protectorate—and toward the Pamirs, together with the tsarist seizure of the Merv oasis, appeared as a threat to British India. For a while Great Britain and Russia were on the brink of war.[6]

The Russian occupation of Central Asia resulted in active commercial relations with the Chinese province of Sinkiang, as well as in a lively Russian interest in Tibet.[7]

The Anglo-Russian agreement of 1907 brought tsarist expansion in Central Asia to an end. From 1907 to 1917 there were no further frontier incidents, and the "buffer states" separating India from the Russian territory were able

[5] V. P. Semennikov (ed.), *Za kulisami tsarizma; archiv tibetskogo vracha Badmaeva.* The attitude of Russian Communists toward the subjugation of non-Russian nationalities has undergone several changes since the Bolsheviks assumed power. The Pokrovsky school treated such conquests as *naibolshee zlo* (the greatest evil of all). After 1937, this term was replaced by *naimenshee zlo* (the least evil of all). Finally, in 1951, the Soviet historian Nechkina questioned the word *zlo,* believing it to have a negative and harmful connotation. In reality, the assimilation of Russian and non-Russian peoples within the Russian state, Nechkina said, was a positive and beneficial development (M. Nechkina, "K voprosu o formule naimenshee *zlo*," *Voprosy Istorii*, No. 4, 1951, pp. 44–48). Quite recently there appears to be a return to the term "the least evil of all."

[6] Russian resentment over British policy at the Congress of Berlin inspired various loose proposals for "lowering the British crest" by threatening the British Empire at one of its supposedly vulnerable points, and Russian military men made a number of appropriately inflammatory speeches. The Tsar, however, and other high Russians apparently stood opposed to action of so aggressive and risky a nature.

[7] Russian interest was stimulated by the reports of two famous Russian explorers of Tibet, N. M. Przhevalsky and P. K. Kozlov. A certain Dorji (Dorjieff), who was at once a Buriat, a Buddhist lama, and a Russian subject, also visited Tibet for a number of years and was one of the young Dalai Lama's teachers. On returning to Russia in 1898, Dorji was invited by the Russian government to serve as a Russian agent in Lhasa. During his second visit to Tibet, Dorji succeeded in persuading the Dalai Lama to seek protection from the Russian "White Tsar" in order to escape the pressure of China and the designs of Great Britain. A Tibetan mission to St. Petersburg brought back with it the draft of a projected treaty between Russia and Tibet and a proposal that a member of the Russian imperial family serve as Russia's representative in Lhasa. This move aroused British suspicions and gave rise to Colonel Younghusband's famous march to Lhasa, which he reached on August 3, 1904. Thereupon both Dorji and the Dalai Lama fled from Tibet to Urga, the capital of Outer Mongolia.

to attend to their own internal problems without any interruption from the thrusts and counterthrusts of Russian and British foreign policies. Unlike Europe, approaching its great World War, Central Asia had become an area of relative peace.

The Caucasus

Ivan IV's conquest of the khanate of Astrakhan in 1556 was an important step toward the Caspian regions, where the benefits to be derived from any new annexation were considerable. Even a relatively small Russian acquisition in this area would provide greater accessibility to the overland trade routes from eastern Russia to Persia, Central Asia, and India, a convenient base for the protection of Christian peoples of the Caucasus and of western Asia from religious persecution, and numerous new opportunities for exploiting the rich mineral deposits that were then known to exist. Beyond this, the Russians, impelled by their "urge to the sea," might force a way through Turkish Armenia to the eastern Mediterranean or through Persia to the Persian Gulf.

Yet formidable obstacles stood in the way. The rugged Caucasian area was difficult to conquer, and the two great Muslim states south of the Caucasus, the Ottoman Empire and the Persian monarchy—which had fought over and intermittently ruled the Caucasus peoples—held sufficient military power to make a Russian advance extremely costly, if not impossible.

Tsarist expansion in this direction was consequently slow, but by the latter part of the nineteenth century Russia was in possession of all the Caucasus, the local Mountaineers having accepted a Russian government system which allowed them to maintain their religious beliefs and social customs.[8] In Transcaucasia, Christian Georgians and Armenians, who had been under the Muslim rule of Persia and Ottoman Turkey, enjoyed during the reign of Tsar Alexander II what is often spoken of as a "golden age" in their cultural development.[9]

Under Alexander III, the policy of russification which affected all national minorities of the Russian Empire led first to embitterment and then to the awakening of national spirit among these nationalities. The result was an upsurge of radical and national aspirations, with the Georgians at the same time embracing Marxism and insisting on constitutional and social reforms rather than political independence. In the 1890's Armenian leaders formed a nationalist party under the name of Dashnaktsutiun ("Union") which demanded liberation for fellow Armenians still subject to the Sultan, the unification of all Armenian people, and the creation of a Greater Armenia. The Azerbaijani Turks, on their part, organized in 1912 a nationalist party, Musavat ("Equality"), with Pan-Turkic tendencies.

The Ottoman Empire and Persia

Beyond Russian Transcaucasia lay territories long held by the Turkish Sultan and the Persian Shah. The Turks had been traditional foes of the Rus-

[8] For a descriptive account of Russia's struggle for the Caucasus, see W. E. D. Allen and Paul Muratoff, *Caucasian Battlefields, a History of the Wars on the Turco-Caucasian Border, 1828–1921;* also John F. Baddeley, *Russia's Conquest of the Caucasus.*

[9] The famous statesman M. T. Loris-Melikov, whose project for a constitutional order in Russia might have been accepted but for the death of Alexander II at the hands of a revolutionary assassin, was an Armenian.

sians ever since the sixteenth century, when Russians first began to think of wresting control of the Sea of Azov and the Black Sea from the Sultan. From 1801 to 1917 Russian objectives in this area included the Christian-inhabited regions of the Balkan peninsula and the city of Constantinople, with its adjacent water route to the Mediterranean.[10]

In Persia Russian interests had collided with those of Great Britain as early as the seventeenth and eighteenth centuries. In 1818 Persia signed a treaty with Britain which called for mutual assistance against aggression by any third power, and which obligated the Shah to use his influence with Central Asian rulers to block any attempt to attack India. Russia, not to be outdone, forced Persia in 1828 by the Treaty of Turkmanchai[11] to grant her exclusive rights on the Caspian Sea and to place Russian merchants in Persia as well as Persian employees in Russian service under the jurisdiction of tsarist diplomats.

Anglo-Russian rivalry continued unabated throughout the nineteenth century, and by 1903 Russia's growing economic domination of the Shah's territory had become so pronounced that the tsarist foreign minister, Count Lamsdorff, felt justified in stating : "Our task is to make Persia an obedient and useful but sufficiently strong tool in our hands and to retain for our own economic interest a large Persian market."[12]

England's growing fear of Germany and Russia's military and political difficulties in the years after 1904 paved the way for a satisfactory understanding between these two supposedly irreconcilable antagonists. In 1907, a series of agreements embracing Afghanistan and Tibet, as well as Persia, provided for a Russian sphere of interest in northern Persia, a British sphere in the south, and a kind of no man's land in between. Persia, whose "independence" the two countries pledged themselves to respect, was no party to this agreement, and Persian liberals who had imposed a constitutional regime on the Shah that same year were bitter in disapproval.

Siberia and the Far East

The first Russian attempts to penetrate into Siberia grew out of the commercial activities of the city of Novgorod. As early as the eleventh century Novgorodian merchants had begun to trade with the Finno-Ugrian peoples inhabiting both slopes of the Ural Mountains, and in the twelfth century the Russians temporarily conquered Obdoria, the trans-Ural region bordering on the river Ob. The Tatar khanate of Sibir, a state from which the whole Siberian

---

[10] For more detailed comments on Imperial Russia's nineteenth-century policies favoring either maintaining the integrity of the Ottoman Empire as a weak but friendly neighbor or partitioning the "sick man" of Europe, and for a discussion of the final Russian effort to obtain control of the Straits and Constantinople in the last period of the tsarist regime, see the companion volume, Eudin and Fisher, *Soviet Russia and the West, 1920–1927: A Documentary Survey.*

[11] This important treaty actually laid the foundation for the rapid ascendancy of Russian political and economic influence in Persia. The text appears in Ali-Akhsar Bina, *La Question au debut du XIX siècle des traités de Gulistan et de Turkman-Tchai (1813–1828)*, pp. 268–76.

[12] "Tsarskaia Rossiia i Persiia v epokhu russko-iaponskoi voiny," *Krasnyi Arkhiv,* No. 53, 1932, pp. 14–15; see also A. Popov, "Stranitsa iz istorii russkoi politiki v Persii," *Mezhdunarodnaia Zhizn,* No. 4-5, 1924, pp. 132–64, and "Anglo-russkoe sopernichestvo v Persii v 1890–1906 gg.," *Krasnyi Arkhiv,* No. 56, 1933, pp. 33–64.

region took its name, was conquered next. Advancing by waterways and portages and subduing one tribe after another, Russian pioneer detachments reached the Pacific Ocean approximately half a century after the conquest of Sibir.

During their drive to the Pacific, the Russians came in contact with the Chinese, who responded rather coolly to a proposal for trade between the two countries. In 1689, however, representatives of the two empires signed the Treaty of Nerchinsk, which ended certain frontier disputes and permitted the tradesmen of each country to enter the other country's territory. Subsequent treaties brought further rapprochement between the two countries, while Russia acquired territory west of the Amur River and east of the Ussuri.

Russia, meanwhile, had made contact with Japan. Three visits to the Japanese islands by Russian fleets in 1792, 1804, and 1810 met with rebuffs. In 1853, however, after Commodore Perry had used American naval pressure to "open up" Japan, the Russian admiral Putiatin succeeded in signing a treaty with the Japanese government which called for "permanent peace" and "sincere friendship" between the two countries, for recognition of the Kurile Islands as a Russian possession, and for the opening of Japanese harbors to Russian ships. The question of the ownership of Sakhalin Island was left unsettled for several years. Eventually Russia took possession of it in return for ceding the Kuriles to Japan.

The late nineteenth century saw Russia focusing her attention more and more on the Far East as a field for commercial and political expansion. The Trans-Siberian Railroad, begun in 1890, was the spearhead of the drive, with Count Witte serving as its most distinguished advocate. In his report to Tsar Alexander III in 1892, Witte pointed out that thanks to this "great change in communication between Europe and the Asian East" Russia would emerge not only as the essential middleman in expanding East-West trade, but also as a producer and consumer "standing closer to the peoples of Asia than other countries."[13]

The defeat of China by Japan in the war of 1894–95 opened up new and highly promising opportunities, of which Witte was to take quick advantage. According to Witte's ambitious program, Russia was not, at least in the immediate future, to annex any additional Chinese territory. Instead, the tsarist government would pose as the friend of the enfeebled Manchu Empire, extend its influence in China by railroad concessions and bank loans, and use its troops wherever necessary to defend China from Japanese attack. That Witte was

---

[13] B. A. Romanov, *Russia in Manchuria (1892–1906)*, p. 58. An American traveler in Central Asia observed that "the Russians have always displayed a certain facility in dealing with half-civilized peoples . . . There is not that feeling of the vast difference which separates, or which in the opinion of some should separate, an inferior from a superior and ruling race." (Eugene Schuyler, *Turkistan, Notes of a Journey in Russian Turkistan, Khokand, Bukhara and Kuldja,* p. 233.) Russian understanding of the Asian people was also noted, perhaps somewhat romantically, by a Russian publicist of the late nineteenth and early twentieth centuries, E. E. Ukhtomsky: "There is nothing easier for the Russians than to get along with the Asians . . . To any Volga or Viatka man who formerly moved east with the seekers of freedom, the Finno-Turkic unclean spawn [*griaznoe otrodie*] he met appeared as a younger brother, whom his own conscience as well as his self-interest would not allow him to treat unkindly." E. E. Ukhtomsky, *Ob otnoshenii Zapada i Rossii k Vostoku,* pp. 82, 90.

not averse to some future partition of Chinese territory is clear from a number of statements he made during this period. He urged, however, that for the time being Russia should act as the big brother to a weak China, just as during the early reign of Nicholas I the St. Petersburg government had adopted an aggressively protective attitude toward an even weaker Turkey. In Witte's opinion, shared by many influential Russians, the economic and political rewards of such a policy would be substantial, and for a short while Russian activities in the Far East were brought in line with his ideas. But two jarring developments soon affected the strategy of Russian and, indeed, of all European imperialism in the Far East: in 1898 Germany seized Liaotung, touching off a series of demands by other powers for territorial compensation, and in 1900 the Boxer Rebellion flared up.

As a consequence, Witte's plan for co-operating with a dependent but friendly China was replaced by the more aggressive policy of converting Manchuria—and perhaps adjacent territories—into a tightly controlled Russian sphere of influence. This policy and some unfortunate Russian undertakings in Korea led in 1904 to the Russo-Japanese conflict and the defeat of tsarist forces.[14] However, in spite of the Treaty of Portsmouth, Japan did not succeed in driving Russia from northern Manchuria. The secret conventions between Russia and Japan which soon followed (1907, 1912, and 1915) led to the improvement of Russo-Japanese relations and the consolidation of Russia's position in Manchuria and in Outer Mongolia.[15]

Outer Mongolia

Outer Mongolia had long been an area with which Russia desired to promote trade relations. Early in the twentieth century these commercial interests became more pronounced, and Mongolian demands for independence after the Chinese revolution of 1911 gave the tsarist government an excellent pretext for intervening in Mongolian affairs. A secret gathering of Mongolian lamas and princes in July of that year decided to send a delegation with a special message to "the powerful and merciful White Tsar of the great Russian people who is the embodiment of virtue and the protector of the yellow race," and to seek his assistance against China. The message enumerated the wrongs suffered by the Mongolian people from the Chinese and ended by "humbly begging for immediate assistance and patronage."[16]

Since the tsarist government did not desire any diplomatic complications with China, Japan, or the Western powers, the Russian reply was cautious. On December 16, 1911, nevertheless, Outer Mongolia proclaimed its inde-

[14] Although the Russian government adopted a more aggressive attitude during this period, there were efforts by Witte and Count Lamsdorff to reach an amicable understanding with Japan. At one time—in 1901—a satisfactory agreement regarding both Korea and Manchuria seemed possible. For a detailed and scholarly discussion of this problem, see W. L. Langer, *The Diplomacy of Imperialism*, Vol. II, chaps. xiv, xxi, and xxiii, and Romanov, *Russia in Manchuria (1892–1906)*, pp. 223 ff.

[15] See Ernest Batson Price, *The Russo-Japanese Treaties of 1907–1916 Concerning Manchuria and Mongolia*.

[16] S. Shoizhelov, "Mongolia i tsarskaia Rossiia," *Novyi Vostok*, No. 13-14, 1926, pp. 353, 354. The Tsar of Russia, as the successor of the khans of the Golden Horde, better known to Asians as the White Horde, was spoken of by the Asian people as the White Khan or White Tsar.

pendence. How much actual support Russia furnished the Mongols in their revolt against China is difficult to determine. In any case, an agreement was soon concluded between the Russian government and the newly proclaimed independent Mongolian state. The preamble of this agreement stated that "the old relations between Mongolia and China" had come to an end, and Article I provided that the Russian government should assist Outer Mongolia in maintaining an autonomous regime and a national army.[17]

Russian influence in Mongolia rapidly increased. A Russo-Mongolian Bank was formed, and a Russian financial adviser was stationed at Urga. The tsarist government guaranteed loans, cleared the way for an agreement to construct a telegraphic line between Kosh-Agath and Kobdo,[18] outlined projects for the construction of a railway, and arranged for Russian instructors to train the Mongolian armed forces.[19]

China, although naturally apprehensive about the Mongolians' declaration of independence, was too weak to undertake drastic measures toward bringing the country back into the Chinese fold. A Chinese protest, followed by further negotiations, led to a tripartite agreement signed by China, Russia, and Mongolia on June 7, 1915, which recognized Chinese suzerainty over the country. This agreement also specified that "autonomous Mongolia had no right to conclude international treaties with foreign powers respecting political and territorial questions," and that China and Russia would not interfere in the system of autonomous internal administration existing in Outer Mongolia.[20]

The political significance of this agreement is clear. Although Outer Mongolia now officially became an autonomous state within the Chinese Empire, Chinese weakness and Russian strength made tsarist political and economic domination of the country almost inevitable. Outer Mongolia, in fact, became a new Russian sphere of influence, thus providing the tsarist government with some compensation for the failure of Witte's larger and more ambitious projects in the Far East.

The Impact of the Revolution of 1917 upon Russia's Position in Asia

The Provisional Government, which assumed control over Russia after the February revolution of 1917, was officially committed to three political objectives: (1) ending the war between the Entente and the Central Powers on the basis of no annexations and no indemnities; (2) maintaining the unity of the Empire until a constitution should be adopted; and (3) eventually having Russia's relationship to its national minorities determined by a democratically elected Constituent Assembly. The more influential moderate socialists in the newly established soviets shared this desire for Russian political unity. As a result, a determined effort was made to hold the various parts of the Empire together despite certain vigorous demands for political autonomy, as in the Ukraine, and despite some strong separatist talk, as in Finland.

[17] Text appears in John van Antwerp MacMurray, *Treaties and Agreements with and Concerning China*, II, 992–96.
[18] Text in MacMurray, II, 1038–39.
[19] "Tsarskaia Rossiia i Mongoliia," *Krasnyi Arkhiv*, No. 37, 1929, pp. 53, 62.
[20] MacMurray, II, 1229–43.

When the Russian Constituent Assembly met, in January 1918, the Provisional Government had been overthrown and the Bolshevik regime was consolidating its control. Nevertheless, the Constituent Assembly followed essentially the policies laid down at the time of the February revolution. It voted for "a universal democratic peace" and for the defense "of the interests of Russia." Its final act was to proclaim the new Russian state a "Democratic Federative Republic and an indissoluble union of peoples and territories, each sovereign within the limits laid down by the federal constitution."[21]

Generally speaking, the national minorities in Russian Asia seemed ready to accept the liberal program originally formulated by the Provisional Government. This was markedly true in Georgia, where the Menshevik-controlled soviets vigorously upheld the leadership of the Provisional Government, in which a Georgian Menshevik, Irakly Tseretelli, participated. It was also true of Armenia, where the Anatolian massacres committed by the Turks in 1915 had created a feeling of dependence upon and strong loyalty to the Russian government—as long as it remained anti-Turkish in its policy.

The Muslim peoples of Russia also seemed, on the whole, ready to cooperate with the Provisional Government. To be sure, some Islamic leaders had tried during the war to provoke Pan-Turkic or Pan-Islamic agitation aimed at uniting all Muslims of the Russian Empire into one great Islamic state. However, the vast majority of Russian Muslims did not respond to this appeal. From February to October, 1917, they stirred up little trouble and appeared to be satisfied with projects for cultural and territorial autonomy within the new Russian republic.[22]

The relations of the Provisional Government with neighboring Asian states were reasonably amicable, except for Turkey, a World War I enemy, and Persia, which had involuntarily become a theater of military operations in the Anglo-Russian campaign against the Turks. Russia maintained its protectorate over Mongolia as well as its control over North Manchuria and the Chinese Eastern Railway. China, more concerned after February 1917 with Japanese aggression than with Russian, seemed ready to wait for Russia's new regime to translate itself into a liberally constructive foreign policy. And Japan, an ally of Russia against Germany, was much more interested in recently conquered Kiaochow and the Shantung peninsula than in Russia's Manchurian sphere of influence.

The relative peace in Russian Asia during the period of the Provisional Government was followed by three stormy years of Bolshevik attempts to dominate Russia's Asian territory and anti-Bolshevik efforts to resist the extension of Soviet rule. These years witnessed almost kaleidoscopic changes in the political status of various Russian territories in Asia: there were, for example, (1) the successful revolt of Siberian liberals against the Bolsheviks,

21 James Bunyan and H. H. Fisher, *The Bolshevik Revolution, 1917–1918*, p. 379.

22 An All-Russian Congress, convened at Moscow May 1–11, 1917, resolved in favor of national and cultural autonomy for Muslim groups within a federated Russian state and established a central Muslim organization to foster this aim. In July of the same year, a second All-Russian Muslim Congress, meeting concurrently with a congress of the Muslim clergy and one of Muslims in army service, organized an All-Muslim Military *Shuro* (Council). This council was to serve as the supreme authority for all Muslim combatants, whom the Congress sought to have put into separate Muslim units.

followed by the overthrow of this democratic movement by Russian militarists; (2) the attempt of Japan to push its way into Eastern Siberian territory during the period of Allied intervention in the Russian Far East; (3) sweeping changes in the administration of the Chinese Eastern Railway, over which American railway engineers, Chinese and Japanese soldiers, and a few old tsarist officials competed for control; (4) a reassumption by the Chinese republic of its sovereign rights over Outer Mongolia; (5) a revolt of the Muslims of Central Asia against Bolshevik rule, leading to the temporary establishment of an autonomous Turkestan republic (the Kokand Autonomy) as a component part of a Russian democratic federation; and (6) the occupation of almost all of Persia by British forces, followed by British attempts to challenge German-Turkish designs upon Transcaucasia and, later, to impose a short-lived protectorate over nominally independent Georgia and Azerbaijan.

All these episodes in the Russian civil war turned Russian Asia into an area of widespread suffering and immense confusion, and the principles underlying the new Soviet foreign policy made the confusion even greater. Bolshevik repudiation of treaties concluded by the tsarist government and Bolshevik reinterpretation of international law in terms of Marxist-Leninist ideology swept away all the guideposts of conventional diplomacy. As a result, the Soviet republic faced a Herculean task when it embarked on its campaign to reunite the former territories of the tsarist Empire, to establish its new political and economic system in Russian Asia, and to promote relations with neighboring Asian countries.[23]

Despite all the difficulties confronting them in Asia, the Russian Communists were confident that they would succeed in carrying out their revolutionary mission. They were relying upon two weapons to win the approval of the Asian people, one of them revolutionary, the other traditional. They hoped to appeal with revolutionary doctrines to the "downtrodden and subjected masses" of a continent which the imperialist powers had exploited. And they planned to rely upon the long-established Russian capacity for doing business with Asian peoples and for maintaining successful diplomatic and trade relations with their governments. Using these weapons in combination, the Bolsheviks set about converting their Asian neighbors to communism and simultaneously restoring the shattered influence and power of the Russian state on the Asian continent.

[23] The Russian Communist reinterpretation of international law which furnished the theoretical foundation of Soviet foreign policy is discussed in the Historical Introduction to the companion volume, Eudin and Fisher, *Soviet Russia and the West, 1920–1927: A Documentary Survey.*

PART I

The Nationality and Colonial Policies of the Russian Communists

Revolutionary Task in the East

The political strategy and tactics which Lenin and other communist leaders devised for Asia and the Near East were from the beginning an integrated part of a larger drive for world domination. At the First Congress of the Communist International, March 6, 1919, Lenin concluded a speech with this warning: "Let the bourgeoisie of the world rage, let them drive away, imprison, and even kill the . . . Bolsheviks. All this is of no avail. It will lead only to the enlightenment of the masses, to their liberation from the old prejudices, and to their tempering for the struggle. The victory of the proletarian revolution throughout the world is assured. The foundation of the International Soviet Republic is at hand."[1]

Later, at a meeting of party cell secretaries, November 26, 1920, Lenin sought to dispose of any lingering doubts among his followers concerning the inherent antagonism between the new Russian government and the capitalist world: "As long as capitalism and socialism last," he declared, "we cannot live in peace: in the end one or the other will triumph—a funeral dirge will be sung either over the Soviet Republic or over world capitalism."[2]

How, then, did Lenin and other Bolshevik leaders view this struggle for the world as developing?

The basic rules had been formulated much earlier by Karl Marx, and it was his fundamental theory concerning both the economic structure of modern society and the proximity of interest between workers in the industrial countries and toilers of the backward regions that Lenin and his collaborators developed as the underlying premise of their policies toward colonial areas.

Considering Ireland as an object of colonial exploitation by Great Britain, Marx had outlined the tasks of the British workers toward the exploited Irish toilers, mainly the peasants. He emphasized the similarity of their aims as well as their dependence on each other. Writing to S. Meyer and A. Vogt in April 1870, Marx said:

Ireland is the bulwark of the English landed aristocracy. The exploitation of this country is not only one of the main sources of that aristocracy's material welfare; it is its greatest moral strength. . . . Ireland is therefore the great means by which the English aristocracy maintains its domination in England itself.[3]

Since the task of the revolutionary workers was to hasten the social revolution in England, they were also to bring about the revolution in Ireland:

The sole means of hastening it [the revolution in England] is to make Ireland independent. Hence it is the task of the International everywhere to put the conflict between England and Ireland in the foreground, and everywhere to side openly with

[1] V. I. Lenin, *Sochineniia*, XXIV, 22.
[2] *Ibid.*, XXV, 512.
[3] *Karl Marx and Frederick Engels on Britain*, p. 505.

Ireland. And it is the special task of the Central Council in London to awaken a consciousness in the English workers that for them the national emancipation of Ireland is no question of abstract justice or humanitarian sentiment but the first condition of their own social emancipation.[4]

So positive was Karl Marx about the interdependence of the political situation of the two countries, that he remarked: "The overthrow of the English aristocracy in Ireland involves and has as a necessary consequence its overthrow in England."[5] But in addition to the existing struggle between Great Britain and Ireland, another great conflict, according to Marx, was apparent in the modern world: "Society is more and more splitting into two great hostile camps, into two great classes directly facing each other: Bourgeoisie and Proletariat."[6]

Expanding on Marx's views, Lenin wrote in 1916 that with the rise of large industrial combines, syndicates, and trusts, free enterprise was giving way to monopoly and to the great concentration of individual capital in the hands of a few capitalists. The superabundance of capital in the industrial countries called for its investment in the underdeveloped regions, such as the Eastern colonies and semicolonies. This process, on its part, was leading to a struggle among the capitalists for a new redistribution of the colonies, and to the intensification of the efforts of the "younger" capitalist powers for further expansion. It also meant the aggravation of living conditions in the colonial and exploited regions,[7] and the growth of dissatisfaction among the people inhabiting them.

But to what profit was this accumulation of capital in the hands of a few industrial magnates as far as the workers were concerned? They had no share in the capitalist profits, and, therefore, the overthrow of the existing capitalist regime must still be their aim. And just as Karl Marx urged the unification of the British and Irish workers' revolutionary efforts, so Lenin and his collaborators urged the industrial workers to support the colonial people in their efforts to free themselves from imperialist domination:

Every party which is desirous of belonging to the Third International is duty-bound to mercilessly expose the deeds of "their own" imperialists in the colonies, to support not in words only but in deeds every movement of liberation in the colonies.[8]

Meantime, the Communists were to make use of existing antagonisms among the Great Powers in their efforts to redistribute the colonies. These antagonisms represented, according to the Bolsheviks, the Achilles heel of the capitalists. Stalin made this clear in a statement February 22, 1919. The world had been split into two camps decisively and finally, he said. In the imperialist camp lay the United States, Great Britain, France, and Japan, with their capital, their agents and administrators, and their armaments; in the Bolshevik camp lay Soviet Russia and the young soviet republics, with no armaments and no

---

[4] *Ibid.*, p. 507.

[5] *Ibid.*, p. 505.

[6] Karl Marx, *Manifesto of the Communist Party by Karl Marx and Friedrich Engels*, p. 13.

[7] Lenin, *Imperialism, the Highest Stage of Capitalism*, pp. 76 ff.

[8] Condition No. 8 of the "Twenty-one Conditions for Joining the Communist Party" resolved upon by the Second Congress of the Comintern (*Vtoroi Kongress Kominterna, iiul-avgust, 1920*, p. 502). (Cited hereafter as *Vtoroi Kongress Kominterna*.)

"experienced agents or administrators," but with "experienced agitators capable of arousing the toilers with enthusiasm for liberation."[9]

The Russian Communists saw also that between these two camps lay a decisive element, the peasant areas of the East (some within Russian borders, many more beyond). The outcome of the struggle between the two camps depended to a considerable degree upon which side gained control of these areas, with their raw materials, their markets, and their enormous population.

Some of these peasant regions—even within historical Russian borders—were under the control of the Western Entente. The borderlands, so the Russian Communists believed, had but two choices: liberation under the auspices of Soviet Russia, or subjection under the imperialists. There was no third way.[10]

Through infiltration of various Asian nationalist movements the Russian Communists hoped, over the succeeding years, to make political advances on three primary fronts: from Tashkent into Afghanistan and India; through the Buddhist regions of Tibet and Mongolia; and by direct negotiations with and subversion of China.

In 1920, *Zhizn Natsionalnostei*, the official organ of the People's Commissariat of Nationalities, published an article entitled "The New Period of the Revolution and the New Revolutionary Tasks," which stated in part:

It is necessary to break and to destroy the capitalist front by means of organizing the revolution and the revolutionary fighting forces behind the capitalist line. This means calling to revolutionary life the peoples and countries which have been so far the prey of capitalist vultures. . . . This new field of revolutionary work will mean striking a blow in the rear of the rapacious Entente, and this in turn will clear the way for the triumphant march of the proletariat of the West.[11]

By this time Bolshevik leaders were already initiating a two-pronged attack upon "the rear of the rapacious Entente," first by hastening the settlement of Russia's own nationalities problem, second by inciting colonial and dependent peoples beyond Russian borders to revolt.

Geographically and ethnically the Russian Communists were well situated for an attempt to gain revolutionary leadership among the Asian peoples. The enormous domains of the Russian Empire contained a number of non-Russian nationalities, many of them related both ethnically and religiously to the Muslims and Buddhists of the Asian world. Properly handled, these nationalities, in addition to serving as an example of conversion to communism, could be used to expound their new beliefs before the Asian colonial and semicolonial peoples, who were already in a state of turmoil and were dissatisfied with their dependency upon the great imperialist powers. As we shall perceive later, such a program was outlined in some detail at the Second Congress of the Communist International in July 1920.

Lenin had already foreseen the importance of separating the Western powers from the raw materials and markets of their colonies and "semicolonies" in the East. In 1916 he had said:

Not only socialists must demand the unconditional and immediate liberation of the

[9] I. Stalin, *Sochineniia*, IV, 232; see Document 2.
[10] See Document 7.
[11] "Novyi period revoliutsii i novye revoliutsionnye zadachi," *Zhizn Natsionalnostei*, No. 27 (84), September 2, 1920, p. 2.

colonies without compensation—and this demand in its political ramification signifies nothing more or less than the recognition of the right to self-determination—but they must render determined support to the more revolutionary elements in the bourgeois-democratic movements for national liberation in these countries and assist them in rebellion, and, if need be, in their revolutionary war *against* the imperialist powers that oppress them.[12]

The two-edged program developed by Lenin (and modified by M. N. Roy) at the Second Congress of the Communist International was essentially a projection of this statement. It was designed primarily to drive a wedge between the Western powers and the resources and peoples of the East, and to bring the latter over to the side of the Russian Communists.

The Theory of Self-Determination

Long before the Bolsheviks attained power in Russia, Lenin had devoted considerable attention to the problem of self-determination of national minorities in multinational states such as the Russian Empire; but he and his colleagues made it quite clear that their platform of national self-determination differed profoundly from what they called the "bourgeois" interpretation of that principle. In order to "solve the national question openly and by socialist methods," they said, "it is necessary to approach it from the Soviet viewpoint, subordinating it entirely and finally to the interests of the toiling masses organized into soviets. Thus, and only thus, can we knock from the bourgeoisie's hands its last spiritual weapon. . . ."[13]

The program was as follows:

Point One: Self-determination of the Russian national minorities, and for that matter self-determination in general, was to be the exclusive prerogative of the workers, and the national bourgeoisie was to have no voice in the matter.[14]

Point Two: Self-determination (including secession) was temporary in nature. Eventually all self-determined nationalities would unite in a single, centralized, indivisible proletarian state which was to pursue one common task, namely, the establishment of a socialist order. In other words, the Russian Bolsheviks desired, although they did not actually say so, to preserve the old territorial framework of the Russian state.[15]

Point Three: The future proletarian state was not to be organized according to federation along ethnic lines, a principle advanced by some European "bourgeois" scholars. In their interpretation of the party structure (and later of the state structure) the Bolsheviks were for a strong unitary centralized party (or state) organization. Consequently, when they spoke of the party or of the state, they meant a system of regional autonomy, with authority vested in the proletarian groups within the region rather than in the predominant ethnic group as such.[16]

As early as 1903, the Second Congress of the Russian Social Democratic Labor Party had incorporated within the party program a statement declaring

---

[12] Lenin, *Sochineniia*, XIX, 44; also *Selected Works*, V, 276.
[13] Stalin, *Sochineniia*, IV, 91; see Document 3.
[14] See Document 6.
[15] See Documents 7 and 13.
[16] See Documents 13, 15, 17.

"the right of self-determination for the nationalities which form composite parts of the state."[17]

Insight into the restricted meaning of this plan in the party platform was provided by Stalin in an article published in a Georgian newspaper:

According to Article Nine, the "non-Russian" nationalities have the right to arrange their national affairs as they wish. But we, on our part, and on the basis of this same article, are duty-bound to see to it that the wishes of these nationalities are truly social-democratic, and that their wishes correspond to the class interests of the proletariat. Therefore, it becomes necessary to educate the proletariat of these nationalities in the spirit of social democracy.[18]

As early as March 1916, Lenin had emphasized the temporary nature of self-determination in the communist scheme, terming it a means of achieving the final unification of all nationalities within a communist society. He wrote:

The goal of socialism is not only to do away with the separation of mankind into small states and with every kind of isolation of nations, not only to bring nations closer together. The goal of socialism is also their fusion. . . . Just as mankind can reach the state when classes no longer exist only through a transitional period of the dictatorship by the oppressed class, so can this inevitable fusion of nations be reached only through a transitional period of the complete liberation of all oppressed nations, i.e., through their freedom to secede.[19]

Interpreting Lenin's point of view on self-determination at the Sixteenth Party Congress in 1930, Stalin remarked:

Lenin sometimes expressed the thesis of national self-determination in the form of a simple formula, "disunion for the purpose of union." . . . It even smacks of the paradoxical. And yet this "self-contradictory" formula reflects the living truth of Marxian dialectics which enabled the Bolsheviks to capture the most impregnable fortresses in the sphere of the nationality question.[20]

That the right to self-determination was not the final communist goal, and that at best such a right was to apply only to the proletariat, were clearly indicated by Lenin in 1917 in the following statement:

If we assumed power we would at once recognize the right [of separation] of Finland, the Ukraine, Armenia, and any other nationality which had been oppressed by tsarism (and by the Great Russian bourgeoisie). But we, on our part, do not at all wish for this separation. No. We want the largest possible state, the closest possible union, the largest possible number of nations who are neighbors of Great Russia. We desire this in the interests of democracy and socialism, in the interests of bringing into the struggle of the proletariat the largest possible number of workers of all nations. We desire a *revolutionary proletarian* unity, a *unification*, and not the separation of peoples. We desire a *revolutionary* unification, and therefore we do not advance the slogan of the unification of all and every state in general. The immediate task advanced by the social revolution is the unification *only* of the states which have passed over or are passing over to socialism, of the colonies which are

[17] Article Nine of the Program of the Russian Social Democratic Labor Party. *Vsesoiuznaia Kommunisticheskaia Partiia (B) v rezoliutsiiakh i resheniiakh sezdov, konferentsii i plenumov TS. K.*, Part I, p. 22. (Hereafter cited as *V.K.P. v rezoliutsiiakh.*)
[18] Stalin, *Sochineniia*, I, 52. (Originally published in *Proletariatis Brdzola* ["The Struggle of the Proletariat"], Tiflis, No. 7, Sept. 4, 1904.)
[19] Lenin, *Sochineniia*, XIX, 40.
[20] Stalin, *Sochineniia*, XII, 370.

freeing themselves, and so forth. Desiring a *free* unification, we are duty-bound to recognize the freedom of separation (otherwise free unification would have no meaning). We are duty-bound to recognize this freedom of separation all the more because tsarism and the Great Russian bourgeoisie with their oppression have left a heritage of great irritation and distrust toward most Great Russians. Only by *action*, and not by words, can we conquer this distrust. Nonetheless, unification means much to us, and this must be stated and emphasized in the program of the party of such a motley state [as Russia]. . . . Contrary to the bourgeois democrats, we advance the slogans of the fraternity of the *workers* of all nationalities, and not the fraternity of peoples, because we distrust the bourgeoisie of every country, and we consider them to be our enemies.[21]

In April 1917, Stalin declared:

Our views on the national question reduce themselves to the following propositions: (a) the recognition of the right of peoples to secede; (b) regional autonomy for peoples that remain within the given state; (c) specific laws guaranteeing freedom of development for national minorities; (d) a single, indivisible, proletarian collective body, a single party for the proletarians of all nationalities in the given state.[22]

The Communist Principle of Self-Determination as Applied in Practice

In so far as minorities were concerned, then, the Bolsheviks proceeded on the basis of three clearly defined principles: (1) self-determination for revolutionary workers only; (2) the temporary nature of the right of self-determination (and secession); and (3) organization according to regional workers' and *not* ethnic autonomy. From these premises they set about transforming the polyglot Russian Empire into the communist state they envisaged.

The problem was complicated at the time by a bitter civil war and by Allied intervention on various fronts. The minority peoples, moreover, had already begun to take "self-determination" into their own hands, and consequently had slight enthusiasm for the rather restricted Bolshevik interpretation of the principle. Needless to record, the Bolsheviks adapted their tactics to the circumstances. Whereas in the colonies and dependencies of capitalist countries they urged support for the national bourgeoisie against the ruling European imperialists, in Russian possessions they did not hesitate to use military force *against* the national bourgeoisie.[23]

The Communists had theories to explain this apparent inconsistency. In a colony or semicolony in which a struggle was still being waged against "feudalism" or "medievalism" and in favor of bourgeois democracy, the national-democratic bourgeoisie might legitimately exercise the right of self-determination, including secession; but in countries in which the struggle against "feudalism" had been won and a new struggle was being waged to transform bourgeois democracy into soviet or proletarian democracy, as was the case in Russia, there only the proletariat could legitimately exercise the right of self-determination and secession. Since a communist party under Moscow control was considered the

[21] Lenin, *Sochineniia*, XXI, 316–17.
[22] Stalin, *Sochineniia*, III, 55.
[23] See Document 6.

only legitimate spokesman for the proletariat, there was no possibility that a proletarian party would vote to secede.

In further discouraging the desire of the Russian national minorities for self-determination, the Russian Communists stressed the fact that this right was actually subordinate to the interest of socialism and the working class as a whole. Thus, on January 20, 1918, Lenin spoke in reference to the conditions of peace made to Russia by the Germans in the following terms:

Objectively, we should now struggle for the liberation of Poland, Lithuania, and Kurland. But no Marxist, unless he wishes to break with the very basis of Marxism and socialism in general, can deny that the interests of socialism are above the interests of the nations and their rights to self-determination."[24]

Later, on May 14, 1918, speaking of the international situation, Lenin added: "We affirm that the interests of socialism, the interests of world socialism, are above the national interests, above the interests of [individual] states."[25]

That the aspirations for self-determination of many of the national bourgeoisie were ignored and resented by the Russian Communists was made apparent soon after the October Revolution, when the Soviet government became involved in conflicts with the Finnish and Ukrainian governments. In each case the Soviet government maintained that the incumbent government failed to express the will of the masses it governed and declared that this will could find expression only if the toiling masses, led by the Communists, deposed their respective bourgeois governments.

Similar situations arose in Estonia, Lithuania, Belorussia, and Transcaucasia; in all these areas the Communists attempted to set up, and in some cases succeeded in setting up, soviet regimes. Speaking on January 15, 1918, Stalin denounced all opposition offered by the borderland countries to the Soviet government as a bourgeois attempt to gain power, and as unrelated to communist-defined self-determination. He then went on to say:

All this demonstrates the necessity of interpreting the principle of self-determination as the right of self-determination for the toiling masses of a nation and not for its bourgeoisie. The principle of self-determination must be a weapon in the struggle for socialism, and it must be subordinated to the principles of socialism.[26]

In expressing these views, Bolshevik leaders were adhering to and developing their earlier theory of self-determination. In one respect, however, they made a concession which professedly was of a temporary nature and which actually was of little practical importance. On January 18, 1918, they proclaimed Soviet Russia a federated state, based to a considerable degree on the ethnic principle which they had earlier condemned. The resolution of the Third Congress of Soviets stated that "the All-Russian Republic is formed on the basis of a free union of the nations as a federation of soviet national republics.[27] However, the Communist Party continued to be based upon the strictly centralistic principle. This fact was made clear in the program of the All-Russian Com-

---

[24] Lenin, *Sochineniia*, XXII, 198.

[25] *Ibid.*, XXIII, 14.

[26] Stalin, *Sochineniia*, IV, 31–32.

[27] *Treti Vserossiiskii Sezd Sovetov, Rabochikh, Soldatskikh i Krestianskikh Deputatov*, p. 90.

munist Party[28] adopted at the Eighth Congress of the party in March 1919, which stated:

There exist at the present time special Soviet republics of the Ukraine, Latvia, Lithuania, and Belorussia. This is the manner in which the question of state structure [of former Russia] has been resolved. This, however, does not mean that the Russian Communist Party must likewise be organized on the basis of a federation of independent communist parties. The Eighth Congress of the Russian Communist Party resolves: It is imperative to have a single centralized Communist Party with a single Central Committee to direct the entire work of the party in all sectors of the R.S.F.S.R. [sic]. All the decisions of the Russian Communist Party and its leading institutions are absolutely obligatory for all sections of the party, irrespective of their national composition. The central committees of the Ukrainian, Latvian, and Lithuanian Communists enjoy the rights of regional committees of the party, and are fully subordinate to the Central Committee of the Russian Communist Party.[29]

Because the highly centralized Communist Party tightly controlled the entire mechanism of the state organization which it created, such autonomy as materialized within the Soviet federation was at best cultural rather than political. Moreover, this structure of the Soviet state was expected from the first by the communist leaders to be only transitional and to last merely until such time as a centralized structure might be practical. In April 1918, Stalin said of this:

[In Russia] coercive tsarist unitarianism is giving way to the principle of federation, which is voluntary. This is done in order that in the course of time the principle of federation may give place to the similarly voluntary fraternal union of the toiling masses of all nations and tribes in Russia. Federalism in Russia . . . is destined to play a transitional role in order to give way to the future *socialist* unitarianism.[30]

Somewhat later, this view of the transitional role of federalism within Russia was broadened to include a projected transitional role for federalism throughout the world. The "Theses on the National and Colonial Questions" of the Second Congress of the Communist International accordingly declared federation to be "a transitional stage toward the complete union of the toilers of all nations."[31]

The Activities of the People's Commissariat of Nationalities

To combat the separatist tendencies of the Russian national minorities and to bring them into the soviet orbit—either as independent soviet republics or as autonomous republics and regions federated with the Russian Soviet Federated Socialist Republic—the Communists set up the People's Commissariat

[28] The All-Russian Communist Party or Vserossiiskaia Kommunisticheskaia Partiia (V.K.P.) was sometimes referred to as the Russian Communist Party or Rossiiskaia Kommunisticheskaia Partiia (R.K.P.). The two terms were identical in their usage. When the Union of Soviet Socialist Republics or Soiuz Sovetskikh Sotsialisticheskikh Respublik was formed in 1923, the term Vserossiiskaia or Rossiiskaia was changed to Vsesoiuznaia (All-Union), and the party was then called Vsesoiuznaia Kommunisticheskaia Partiia (All-Union Communist Party).

[29] *V.K.P. v rezoliutsiiakh,* Part I, p. 313.
[30] Stalin, *Sochineniia,* IV, 73.
[31] *Vtoroi Kongress Kominterna,* p. 492. See Document 18.

of Nationalities, known also as the Narkomnats. Each national group had a corresponding national commissariat or section within the framework of the central commissariat. The national commissariats and sections, in turn, acted on instructions from their respective local communist parties, each of which was affiliated with and subordinated to the All-Russian Communist Party. By the autumn of 1918 a total of seven national commissariats and eleven national sections had been set up. Through these national commissariats and sections the People's Commissariat of Nationalities immediately took up the struggle against the antisoviet nationalist groups in the borderlands.

In addition to its political activity, the People's Commissariat of Nationalities was also charged with the organization of national units in the Red Army. This work was at first concerned primarily with the absorption into the Red Army of existing military formations, i.e., national units formed during the regimes of the tsarist and Provisional governments, and with the disbanding of units regarded as undesirable. This military phase of the Commissariat's work was undertaken particularly in regard to the nationalities of the Russian western borderlands and even before the establishment of soviet governments in the regions concerned, that is, at the time when most of these regions were under German occupation. Consequently, when, after the defeat of Germany by the Allies on the western front, German forces of occupation began their retreat from the Russian western borderlands, the native armed forces assisted by the Russian Red Army moved swiftly upon the heels of the retreating Germans. Almost immediately thereafter five so-called independent soviet republics were set up, this time in the western borderlands: a Ukrainian S.S.R., a Belorussian S.S.R., a Latvian S.S.R., an Estonian S.S.R., and a Lithuanian S.S.R.

Russian Bolshevik leaders soon perceived the desirability of bringing these new governments into closer relationship with the Soviet Union. According to a decree of the All-Russian Central Executive Committee, June 1, 1919:

The forces of the international imperialism which cherish the insane hope of conquering the world and which aim at unlimited exploitation of these republics, have united against the international movement of the toilers, have ignored the peace offers of the toiling masses of Russia, the Ukraine, Latvia, Lithuania, and Belorussia. These forces now strain their energies to the utmost in order to suppress the soviet government wherever it has been organized by the revolutionary movement of the workers' and peasants' masses. World capital has mobilized against the soviet governments all the forces of the monarchist and capitalist counterrevolution, and it is now trying by means of an all-out offensive on all fronts to destroy the government of workers and peasants. The need to resist this attempt to enslave once more scores of millions of Russian, Ukrainian, Latvian, Lithuanian, Belorussian, and Crimean workers and peasants, necessitates a close union of their military forces and the centralization of leadership in a hard life-and-death struggle.[32]

The Sovietization of Transcaucasia

In Transcaucasia, meanwhile, civil war and intervention temporarily precluded the possibility of overt Soviet attack upon the three national republics

[32] *Sobranie Uzakonenii i Rasporiazhenii Rabochego i Krestianskogo Pravitelstva*, No. 21, June 6, 1919, pp. 264, 280–81 (hereafter cited as *Sobranie Uzakonenii i Rasporiazhenii*); also *Obrazovanie S.S.S.R. Sbornik dokumentov, 1917–1924*, p. 126 (hereafter cited as *Obrazovanie S.S.S.R.*).

which had been set up in that area in May 1918: Georgia, Armenia, and Azerbaijan. On May 7, 1920, the Soviet government went so far as to sign a peace treaty with the Menshevik government of Georgia, recognizing the sovereign independence of the state of Georgia and guaranteeing that Russia would abstain from interference in its internal affairs.

Georgia, in return, agreed to prevent the residence or activity upon its territory of groups or organizations "pretending to the role of the Government of Russia or part of it, as well as any groups or organizations aiming to overthrow the Government of Russia." Also included in the treaty, however, was a special secret supplement by which the government of Georgia agreed to permit throughout its territory and without interference the activity of communist organizations.[33] This permission was duly used by the Communists in Georgia to strengthen their position there.

The conclusion of the civil war and the withdrawal of Allied forces from Transcaucasia made it possible for the Russian Communists to resort to the tactics which they had already used in late 1918 and early 1919 when they attempted to sovietize the Russian western borderlands. According to Stalin, three years of this civil war had shown that victory for the revolution was "impossible without mutual assistance between Central Russia and its borderlands." He continued: "Of course, the borderlands of Russia, . . . just as any other nation, have the absolute right to separate from Russia. . . . But just now we are not discussing the question of the right of nations [to separation], . . . but rather the interests of the masses. . . . The interests of the masses indicate that in the present stage of the revolution the demand for separation of the borderlands is deeply counterrevolutionary."[34]

The Russian Commissariat of Nationalities applied political pressure from within while the Red Army brought persuasive force to bear from without, and thus the national governments of Azerbaijan and Armenia were overthrown and soviet regimes created in their place. A communication of April 28, 1920, regarding the establishment of a soviet regime in Azerbaijan (received by Lenin from the Revolutionary War Council of the Eleventh Russian Soviet Army, active in the Caucasus) declared: "On April 27 the advance detachment and armored trains of our army reached Baku. The Azerbaijan toiling masses deposed the bourgeois government with the help of the Red Army and established soviet authority."[35]

Toward the end of 1920, the Armenian national government also was overthrown. At that time Armenia was threatened once more with a Turkish invasion; several of the Armenian provinces had already been occupied by the Turks. The Armenian government was powerless to cope with the situation, which appeared to the Communists as most opportune for the overthrow of that government.[36] On November 29, local communists proclaimed a soviet government in Armenia and formed a revolutionary committee. This committee, in conjunction with troops of the Russian Red Army, entered Erivan, the capital of Armenia. "Fraternal help rendered to Armenia by the troops of the Red

---

[33] The full text of this treaty including the secret clause appears in L. Shapiro, *Soviet Treaty Series,* Vol. I, pp. 44–46. (Hereafter cited as Shapiro, I.)

[34] Stalin, *Sochineniia,* IX, 351, 353–54; see Document 7.

[35] *Leninskii Sbornik,* XXXIV, 292; see Document 9.

[36] For more information on the Armenian-Turkish war, see Part II.

Army directed by Comrade Ordzhonikidze played an important role in the liberation of that country," writes a Soviet historian. "Comrade Stalin was very much interested in the situation in Armenia and constantly sent instructions to Ordzhonikidze. On November 27, 1920, i.e., two days before the proclamation of soviet government in Armenia, Comrade Stalin talked by direct wire with Sergo Ordzhonikidze. Comrade Stalin pointed out that it was necessary to give more careful consideration to all measures that were to be taken immediately to help Armenia."[37]

Georgia was now the only Transcaucasian national state that had remained unsovietized. To strengthen its position the Georgian government welcomed the occupation of Batum by Allied troops, although by that time the Allied intervention in the Caucasus was practically over. This gave an occasion to the Soviet government to appeal on November 18, 1920, to the workers of all Entente countries against the Entente's designs on Batum.[38] Soviet occupation of Georgia now appeared to be only a question of time. "The fate of Menshevik Georgia," writes a Soviet historian, "was already sealed. The Bolshevik Caucasus Bureau, directed by Sergo Ordzhonikidze, launched preparations, upon the directions of Lenin and Stalin, for an armed rising by the [Georgian] masses."[39]

Once more the Russian troops were set in motion, this time to help the Georgian Revolutionary Committee. On February 17, 1921, the Georgian government was obliged to flee Tiflis; on February 25, Ordzhonikidze was able to telegraph to Moscow that the red banner of the soviet government had been hoisted there.[40]

Documents 10 and 11 suggest that Communist Party leaders in Georgia were expected (1) to win the sympathy and trust of the Georgian masses, (2) to arm the workers and poorest peasants, (3) to grant concessions to petty traders and the intelligentsia, and (4) to seek compromise with relatively broad sections of the bourgeoisie generally. The reasoning behind the formulation of these tactics appears in Document 12.

Communist Policy Regarding the Muslims of Russia

The Commissariat of Nationalities was particularly concerned with the Muslims of southern and eastern Russia, since they were a natural link between Communists of the West and the colonial and dependent peoples of the East. Referring to the Soviet Muslim policy in a speech delivered in May 1918, Stalin remarked:

Allow me to state in the name of the Central Soviet government that the Council of People's Commissars has always believed and still believes that it is its sacred

---

[37] S. I. Iakubovskaia, *Obedenitelnoe dvizhenie za obrazovanie S.S.S.R. (1917–1922)*, p. 99. (Hereafter cited as Iakubovskaia, *Obedenitelnoe dvizhenie*.) "Sergo" was a nickname for Grigorii Konstantinovich Ordzhonikidze, as was "Koba" for Stalin.

[38] Text appears in Iu. V. Kliuchnikov and A. V. Sabanin, *Mezhdunarodnaia politika noveishego vremeni v dogovorakh, notakh i deklaratsiiakh*, III, 72–73. (Hereafter cited as Kliuchnikov and Sabanin.)

[39] E. B. Genkina, *Obrazovanie S.S.S.R.*, p. 66.

[40] G. B. Khachapuridze, *Bolsheviki Gruzii v boiakh za pobedu sovetskoi vlasti*, p. 235; for a detailed account of the establishment of soviet regimes in Azerbaijan, Armenia, and Georgia, see Firuz Kazemzadeh, *The Struggle for Transcaucasia (1917–1921)*.

duty to meet halfway the movement of liberation of the oppressed and exploited masses of the East, and first of all, of the most wronged Muslim East. The entire character of our revolution, the very nature of the Soviet government, the general international situation, and finally even the geographical position of Russia, situated between imperialist Europe and oppressed Asia—all these necessarily prompt the Soviet government to pursue the policy of fraternal support of oppressed peoples of the East in their struggle for their own liberation.[41]

In order to implement Soviet policy in regard to the oppressed Asian peoples as outlined by Stalin, it became imperative to draw the Muslims of Russia into the Soviet orbit. A Muslim Commissariat was organized by the Commissariat of Nationalities in late 1917, and it immediately set about undermining the Muslim nationalist organizations and governments that had sprung up in 1917. This task did not prove difficult. Although various Muslim nationalist groups continued to resist Bolshevik domination by aiding the anti-Bolshevik White forces in the civil war, nevertheless, in the early months of 1918, the Tatars of the Crimea, the Alash-Orda government in Kirghizia, the Kokand Autonomy in Turkestan, the Volga Muslims were all defeated by Red forces with the help of some Muslim groups that were fighting on the Soviet side.

To replace these defeated national organizations, the Soviet government, and the Commissariat of Nationalities in particular, had plans for setting up the Muslim nationalities in Russia in autonomous soviet republics within the R.S.F.S.R. One of the earlier attempts to cut the ground from under the anti-soviet national groups was the regulation worked out by the Commissariat of Nationalities and published March 23, 1918, regarding the formation of the Tatar-Bashkir Autonomous Soviet Republic. In this document the territory of the South Ural region and the Middle Volga was declared to be the Tatar-Bashkir Autonomous Soviet Republic within the R.S.F.S.R.[42]

On May 10–16, 1918, the Conference for the Convocation of the Constituent Congress of the Tatar-Bashkir Autonomous Soviet Republic met in Moscow with Stalin as the chief speaker. Outlining the difference between soviet autonomy and the "bourgeois" form of autonomy, Stalin characterized the latter by references to the Ukrainian *Rada*[43] and the Transcaucasian national formation at that time. This form, he said, precluded any interference by the central authority; it was purely nationalist and, so to speak, extraterritorial.

We offer a different kind of autonomy, that is, the type of autonomy of an area in which one or several minorities are in the majority. . . . This autonomy must be a soviet autonomy based on a soviet of deputies. This means that the division of people in a given autonomous region will proceed along lines of class and not national distinction.[44]

Civil war and the Allied intervention in southern and eastern Russia delayed somewhat the realization of the Soviet plan for establishing soviet republics for the Muslims and national minorities of Russia in general. Nonetheless, in 1918 Turkestan was proclaimed an autonomous republic within the R.S.F.S.R.,

---

[41] Stalin, *Sochineniia,* IV, 90–91 ; see Document 3.

[42] *Obrazovanie S.S.S.R.,* pp. 38–39.

[43] The *Rada* (Council) was the Ukrainian national government, which was in opposition to the Russian Soviet regime.

[44] Stalin, *Sochineniia,* IV, 88; see also Document 3.

and this autonomy was confirmed by a constitution in 1921. In 1919 and 1920 separate Bashkir and Tatar soviet republics were proclaimed as autonomous entities within the general framework of the R.S.F.S.R. At the conclusion of the civil war other autonomous republics and *oblasts* (regions) were set up, among them Chuvash, Kirghiz, Yakut, Buriat-Mongol, Caucasian Mountaineers', and Daghestan. All in all, by early 1923, ten autonomous soviet republics and eleven oblasts had been created within the R.S.F.S.R.[45] But at no time did the Soviet leaders wish to bring several Muslim nationalities together and risk the threat of an exterritorial and Pan-Muslim unification.

In dealing with borderland Muslims, moreover, the Russian Communists learned valuable lessons in how to infiltrate and subvert Islamic groups. Bolshevik agitators were to assert that they were not conducting a struggle against religion, but were only stating their personal—if atheistic—views; only Communists of Muslim origin were to be allowed to carry on antireligious propaganda among Islamic groups; Communists were to make their personal conduct serve as favorable propaganda, i.e.: "It is necessary for every Muslim to get well acquainted with an atheist and to form a good opinion of him."[46]

On the basis of these techniques, the Russian Communists were able to make considerable headway, not only among the Muslims of Russia, but in colonial areas as well.

The Russian Communists and the Muslims of Turkestan

Developments in Turkestan during early years of soviet rule are particularly important in view of the significance of this area and its Muslim population to the Russian Communists' plan for the infiltration of Afghanistan, India, and other parts of Asia.

Almost immediately upon the seizure of power by the Bolsheviks in Russia and until September 1919, Turkestan was cut off from all communication with the Central Soviet government by the front line of the civil war. The Orenburg and the Ural Cossacks refused to recognize the Soviet government in Moscow and raised arms against it. The Turkestan Communists—few in number and almost exclusively Russian—were left, therefore, to work and to carry out their own communist policies.

In January 1918, the Fourth Regional Congress of Turkestan Soviets proclaimed Turkestan an autonomous republic and declared its intention of maintaining close co-operation with the Soviet government in Central Russia. The Council of People's Commissars of Turkestan, which, in addition to the Russian Communists, included some Socialist-Revolutionaries, but no Muslim natives, established its residence in Tashkent. A few months later both the Turkestan regional government and the regional communist party of Turkestan resolved to draw into the work of the government the poor Muslim natives, the *dekhans*.

But difficulties continued to plague the Russian Communists in their dealings with the native Muslim population in Turkestan. The misrule of local soviet organs made the natives skeptical of the communist autonomy officially

[45] Iakubovskaia, *Obedenitelnoe dvizhenie*, p. 77.
[46] M. Sultan-Galiev, *Metody anti-religioznoi propagandy sredi musulman*, p. 6; see Document 4.

announced for their region. Even the Muslim nationals whom the Russian Communists had succeeded in recruiting for membership in the party manifested Pan-Turkic tendencies, desiring the unification of all Turkic nationals into one autonomous republic rather than the separation of these nationals into smaller administrative groups.

Aware of the situation in Turkestan, the government at Moscow dispatched a special so-called Turkestan Commission to Tashkent to investigate the apparent difficulties there. This commission, consisting of Eliava, Frunze, Kuibyshev, Rudzutak, and Goloshchekin, arrived in Tashkent in November 1919 and set about (1) enforcing the laws which promised the native people freedom from the illtreatment and illegal exactions of the local soviet organs, and (2) curbing the Pan-Turkic national aspirations of the Turkestan Muslims.[47]

That the second part of this task was pressing was demonstrated in late January, 1920, when delegates to the Third Conference of the Regional Muslim Bureau of the Russian Communist Party[48] came out openly in support of a Pan-Turkic movement.[49] The resolution adopted at this conference was indicative of the mood that prevailed among the Muslim Communists in Turkestan. It read as follows: "Be it resolved that we shall oppose by means of communist agitation the desire of Turkic nationals to separate into various national groups, such as Tatars, Kirghiz, Bashkirs, Uzbeks, and so forth, and that we shall strive instead for the unification into a single state of all the Turkic nationals which so far have not become members of the R.S.F.S.R., in order that these nationals may be united into one Turkic Soviet Republic."[50]

Following up this apparent "deviation" from the communist standpoint, the native delegations that took part in the Fifth Regional Conference of the Communist Party of Turkestan (which met in the same month) changed the name of the Turkestan Section of the Russian Communist Party to the Turkic Communist Party, and the name of the Turkestan Republic to the Turkic Republic. This move was in complete disagreement with the Russian Communist concept of a single centralized communist party for the Russian Republic as a whole (the All-Russian Communist Party) and no independent regional communist parties whatever. Nor could the Russian Communists condone either Pan-Turkic or Pan-Islamic tendencies.

The Fifth Congress of the Turkestan branch of the Russian Communist Party, which met on September 12–18, 1920, had to take drastic measures to do away with these nationalistic deviations. A new course of soviet policy in Turkestan was outlined. The Turkestan regional party organization was officially designated the Communist Party of Turkestan. The Congress advocated centralistic organization of the party, iron discipline, and a purge of undesirable elements. A registration of all party members was planned. The Congress likewise outlined a policy for organizing the semiproletarian and poor elements

[47] See Document 5.

[48] This was a subsidiary organization of the Russian Communist Party of Turkestan, and it developed the so-called Muslim organizations of the Russian Communist Party of Turkestan.

[49] The idea of such a movement had been popularized by a former Turkish officer, Efendiev, who had been sent to Turkestan as a prisoner of war during World War I, and who gradually acquired strong influence among the local Muslims.

[50] S. Muraveisky (V. Lopukhov), "Ocherki po istorii revoliutsionnogo dvizheniia v Srednei Azii," p. 30. (A typewritten copy, partly translated into English in the Hoover Library, Stanford University.) Also G. Safarov, *Kolonialnaia revoliutsiia*, p. 110.

of the native population. "The Union of Toiling Dekhans" was now formed. The basic tasks of this union were to effect a class division among the *kishlak* (village) population by antagonizing the poor villagers toward those who were more prosperous.

Difficulties in handling the native problem in the Turkestan region (designated by a decree of the Moscow government as the Turkestan Autonomous Soviet Socialist Republic on April 11, 1921) continued to exist for some time. According to some Soviet writers, the situation was far from satisfactory even as late as 1925–26. These authors maintain (1) that the soviet government was forced upon the natives of Turkestan from above by a small group of Russian Communists, and (2) that up to 1926, and even later, strong chauvinistic tendencies were being shown in the former Turkestan region by both the Russian and native members of soviet institutions and even by the Communist Party.[51]

The Establishment of People's Soviet Republics in Bukhara and Khiva

The semi-independent khanates of Bukhara and Khiva, conquered by Russia in the nineteenth century, were drawn, likewise, into the orbit of soviet infiltration. In February 1919, *Zhizn Natsionalnostei* referred to the need for the overthrow of the Emirate in Bukhara, concluding: "Bukhara represents a very important place for the development of the revolution in Central Asia. Either it will serve as a bulwark of reaction led by the British . . . or it will become the vanguard for a number of Central Asian and Indian revolutionary movements."[52]

In the events that occurred in Bukhara after the fall of the tsarist regime in Russia, the subsequent overthrow of the Emir of Bukhara, and the establishment of a soviet republic in that territory, the so-called Young Bukharan Party was active and in many ways instrumental.

The revolutionary upheaval which took place in Russia in 1905–6 had its repercussions even in remote Bukhara. There, through contacts with the advanced Muslims inhabiting the Volga region, the Crimea, and the Caucasus,

---

[51] "It may sound paradoxical, but in Turkestan it was not the *Bolshevik party that created the soviet government. On the contrary, the soviet government led to the organization of the Bolshevik and Left S.R. parties.* The inevitable consequence was that from its inception the Bolshevik and Left S.R. parties became harbors of a large number of adventurers, careerists, and plain criminals. It is worth noting that in Turkestan the 'Bolsheviks' gave themselves the name of 'the Bolshevik government' party, and that, on the other hand, when Turkestan was a tsarist colony, membership in the industrial proletariat was the *national privilege of the Russians.* Consequently the proletarian revolution in Turkestan acquired from the outset a typical colonial character. The Russian workers assumed 'the administration of the peoples of Turkestan.' Inasmuch as these workers were unorganized, had no definite class program based on revolutionary experience and had no revolutionary tradition, they were bound to accept into their midst many 'former men' [i.e., men in sympathy with the old regime] . . ." (G. Safarov, *Kolonialnaia revoliutsiia,* p. 71).

"Strictly speaking during this period [up to 1926] there did not exist a single united party organization in Kazakhstan. The Kazakh party organization was broken up into groups led by such 'leaders' as Khodzhaev, Ryskulov, Sadvokasov, Mendeshev, Seifulin, and others. . . . Between the Kazakh and the European sections of the party disagreements and national squabbles prevailed; the necessary Bolshevik unity was lacking" (F. I. Goloshchekin, *Partiinoe stroitelstvo v Kazakhstane,* p. 9) ; see also Documents 5, 6, and 7.

[52] *Zhizn Natsionalnostei,* No. 6 (14), February 23, 1919, p. 2.

and also through the influence of the Turkish revolution, a progressive party came into being known as the Djadids or Jadids ("Innovators").

The Russian revolution of 1905 had dealt an ineffaceable blow to Russian tsarism in the East. Its seemingly invincible strength had been shaken in the eyes of the oppressed people. Consequently, the Russian revolution revolutionized even the most backward borderland peoples, kindling among them the hope for a possible national liberation.

[Similarly] the Turkish revolution—the revolution of an advanced Muslim country having close affinity with the ideology and the way of life of the native peoples of Turkestan—provided an equal impetus for the appearance of political organizations among the Muslim bourgeoisie, which directed their efforts against the sultans, khans, and other representatives of Eastern absolutism.[53]

According to another Soviet historian, "The greatest influence [on the young, revolutionary Bukharans] was that of the Russian and Turkish revolutions, and also partly of Tatar nationalism and Pan-Islamism."[54]

In the beginning the Djadids' program called for progressive reforms in the Bukharan khanate, the return to the rules of *Shariat* (the Muslim law), and the curtailment of unnecessary expenditures by the Emir and by rich Bukharans in general. After the revolutionary events in Russia in 1917, however, a Young Bukharan Party headed by Faizulla Khodzhaev was organized side by side with the Djadids. It was upon this Young Bukharan Party that the interests of the Turkestan Communists were now concentrated, and contacts with its representatives were soon made.

The first steps taken by the Turkestan soviet were cautious; the chairman of the soviet, Broido, even negotiated an agreement with the Emir whereby the latter was to legalize the Young Bukharan Party, an agreement the Emir never kept. Somewhat later, in March 1918, after the successful campaign against the Kokand Autonomy, Kolesov, the chairman of the Council of People's Commissars in Tashkent, was urged by the Young Bukharans to send help, and he ordered the Red forces of Tashkent into Bukhara with the intention of bringing about a *coup d'état* there. This, as it turned out, was a serious miscalculation, for although the Young Bukharans supported the Red troops, the campaign failed. The Red troops were forced back in disorder, and the Young Bukharans were decimated. The Turkestan soviet was obliged to sign an agreement with the Emir pledging to refrain from interference in the internal affairs of Bukhara. This agreement, known as the peace of Kizyl-Tepe, "was actually the defeat of the revolution," in the words of a Soviet writer.[55]

This overt attack upon the Emir's domain was one of the first examples of the Soviet technique—used shortly thereafter in the Baltic, in Transcaucasia, and in Mongolia—of sending Red Army units into an area to overthrow a local government upon the pretext of rendering assistance to local national revolutionary groups.

The unsuccessful campaign undertaken by Kolesov resulted in an almost complete physical destruction of the Young Bukharan Party on Bukharan territory. Those who remained, about 150–200 in number, emigrated to Soviet

[53] G. Skalov, "Khivinskaia revoliutsiia 1920 g.," *Novyi Vostok,* No. 3, 1923, p. 244.

[54] M. N., "Pod znakom Islama," *Novyi Vostok,* No. 4, 1923, p. 92; see also Faizulla Khodzhaev, *K istorii revoliutsii v Bukhare.*

[55] O. Glovatsky, *Revoliutsiia pobezhdaet,* p. 24. For an account of Kolesov's campaign, see F. Kolesov and A. Bubnov, "Vosstanie v Bukhare," in *Voina v peskakh,* pp. 233–75.

Turkestan and created two political centers, one in Samarkand and one in Tashkent. In the course of the months that followed, an ideological difference developed among the Young Bukharans, and some of them split off to form the Bukharan Communist Party. This group became very active, secretly agitating in Bukhara for the overthrow of the Emir. Nor were Russian Communist efforts to that end abandoned. In August 1920 an uprising against the Emir was engineered and once again the Red Army moved into Bukhara. On August 28, 1920, M. V. Frunze, then Soviet commander on the Turkestan front, wired Tashkent:

A revolutionary uprising occurred in a number of localities in Bukhara. The hour of a decisive struggle by the suppressed and enslaved masses of Bukhara against the bloody government of the Emir and the *bekhs* has struck. The regiments of the Bukhara Red Army which are being organized have marched on to help their own people. The Red regiments of Workers' and Peasants' Russia are duty-bound to stand by them. I therefore order our troops to give their powerful armed assistance to the Bukharan people in this decisive hour.

Red Soldiers, Commanders, Commissars! All people of Soviet Russia look upon you, expecting you to fulfill your revolutionary duty. Onward in defense of the interests of the toilers of Bukhara and Russia! Long live the resurging people! Long live the coming Bukharan Soviet Republic![56]

This time Soviet aid to Bukhara had a decisive effect. On September 2, Frunze wired Lenin that Bukhara had been captured by the joint efforts of Bukharan and Soviet Russian units, and that the Emir and his retinue had fled.[57] Commenting on the part played by the Red Army forces in overthrowing the Emir's regime, a Soviet historian remarked:

There is no need for us to keep silent . . . on the active role played by the Red Army in the struggle against the Emir. The powerful support given from outside in order to win over the Emirate in the revolution in Bukhara was inevitable, not only to fulfill the international obligations of the victorious working class toward an oppressed people who launched a struggle against their exploiters, but also to guarantee peaceful reconstruction in Turkestan and an end to counterrevolution within the soviet land. The international situation, likewise, did not permit Soviet Russia to assume a waiting or indifferent attitude to the coming revolutionary events in Bukhara which had finally broken out.

In the South of Russia stood Wrangel; in the West, the White Poles. In India the first wave of the revolutionary movement was rising. That is why the problem that was being settled under the wall of Old Bukhara was not only of local significance. The victory of the revolution in Bukhara was a necessary and important stage in the great struggle of the proletariat and the oppressed people of the world against capitalism.[58]

Thereupon a People's Soviet Republic was proclaimed in Bukhara, and on March 4, 1921, the new Republic signed a treaty of alliance and an economic agreement with the R.S.F.S.R.

In Khiva the Young Khivan Party, like the Young Bukharan Party, was active in preparing the downfall of the Khivan Khan. On February 1, 1920, he was deposed and killed, and the Khorezm People's Soviet Republic was proclaimed by the Young Khivan Committee.

[56] M. V. Frunze, *Sobranie sochinenii*, I, 136.
[57] "M. V. Frunze na Turkestankom fronte," *Krasnyi Arkhiv*, No. 3 (100), 1940, p. 77.
[58] O. Glovatsky, *Revoliutsiia pobezhdaet*, p. 32.

The influence of the Committee was short-lived, for in the spring a communist party was organized in Khiva and it soon thereafter captured power. In the autumn of 1920 the Khorezm People's Soviet Republic entered into agreements with the R.S.F.S.R. similar to those that were signed between Bukhara and the R.S.F.S.R. in 1921. The texts of these agreements were similar in a general way to the agreements between the R.S.F.S.R. and the independent Baltic states of Estonia, Latvia, and Lithuania signed in 1920—with this important difference, that they provided for military agreements as well.[59]

The establishment of the formally independent soviet republics of Bukhara and Khorezm and the autonomous republic of Turkestan did not bring pacification to these regions of Central Asia. The so-called Basmachi movement[60] continued to exist, and in fact drew an increasing number of followers. The deposed Emir of Bukhara, who had fled to Afghanistan, gave his support to this movement, and a number of Young Bukharans who had become disillusioned with the soviets also joined it.

The Basmachi movement flared up with greater intensity when it came to be led by Enver Pasha, the colorful and once powerful Turkish leader, who appeared in 1922 in the new Bukharan People's Soviet Republic professing his deep sympathy with the new government there. Soon, however, he left the western sector of Bukhara for the eastern sector, which was not yet sovietized. There he re-established the old Emirate, and from there he attempted several times to penetrate Communist-held western Bukhara. His immediate aim was to unite all Basmachi groups in Turkestan, his over-all goal to unify the Muslim people as a whole. The latter intention is evident from his appeal to all Muslims, which read in part:

I have been appointed by the Caliphate of the Islamic world to liberate you from bondage and to bring you together. For this purpose and for geographical reasons I have found eastern Bukhara the most suitable field of action, and I have established my headquarters there.[61]

In spite of his apparent popularity, Enver Pasha was unable to arouse sufficient forces either to defeat the Red forces or to make much headway with the unification of all Islamic peoples. He was defeated and killed in a skirmish with Red troops in 1922. His successor continued to harass the Soviets for several years to come.

The Unification of the Soviet Republics and the Official Formation of the Soviet Union (U.S.S.R.)

It still remained for the Communists to bring about a union of the different soviet republics which had been created on the territory of the former Russian

[59] For texts, see *Obrazovanie S.S.S.R.*, pp. 251–55 and 245–47.

[60] Originally the Basmachi were Muslim insurgents loosely organized into bands to fight the Soviet government in Tashkent. The mistakes which the Soviet officials frequently made in their treatment of the natives caused the ranks of the Basmachi to swell tremendously, and they remained a source of trouble to the Soviet government for years to come.

[61] M. N., "Pod znakom Islama," *Novyi Vostok*, No. 4, 1923, p. 95. For more information on the Basmachi movement see S. Ginsburg, "Basmachestvo v Fergane," *Novyi Vostok*, No. 10–11, 1924, pp. 175–202; F. Khodzhaev, *K istorii revoliutsii v Bukhare;* and J. Castagné, *Les Basmatchis.*

Empire, as well as to establish a number of autonomous republics within the R.S.F.S.R. To this they applied themselves carefully and systematically.

In 1919, while the Russian civil war was still in progress, the leaders in Moscow, true to their original theories, proceeded to transform the process of self-determination "out" into self-determination "in." The unification of the so-called independent soviet republics advanced from stage to stage, and "voluntarily" at that.

Once the opposition of the non-Russian groups claiming national independence had been broken, the Russian Communists' next move was to establish close co-operation, and particularly military and economic co-operation, between the R.S.F.S.R. and the non–Russian soviet republics such as the Ukrainian S.S.R. and the Belorussian S.S.R., thereby tipping the scales in favor of the Red Army in its bitter struggle against the antisoviet armed forces.

In May 1919, the Central Committee of the Russian Communist Party outlined a draft for a military alliance of the soviet republics,[62] and on June 1, 1919, the All-Russian Central Executive Committee of Soviets decreed a close alliance of the soviet republics:

(1) in military organization and military command
(2) in the work of the Councils of National Economy
(3) in railway management and economy
(4) in finance, and
(5) in the work of the Commissariats of Labor of the Soviet Socialist Republics of Russia, the Ukraine, Latvia, Lithuania, and Belorussia, so that the management of these branches of national activities shall be concentrated in unified collegiate bodies.[63]

As events developed, only two of these western soviet republics were to survive, the Ukrainian and the Belorussian. The Latvian, Estonian, and Lithuanian soviets were soon overthrown and superseded by independent national governments. Following their usual practice of adapting their tactics to the circumstances, the Russian Communists in 1920 recognized these new governments as sovereign in their respective territories.[64] Thereafter they waited more than twenty years to absorb them into the Soviet Union.

But the trend was unmistakable: Soviet Russia could not tolerate the independence of even soviet republics along its borders; each must be incorporated, if possible, under the central government in Moscow. Over the years this pattern of absorption was to become a familiar one.

When the Azerbaijan and the Georgian soviet republics were set up in 1920 and 1921, they too signed military and economic alliances with the R.S.F.S.R.[65]

The next step was to bring together the three soviet republics that had been organized in Transcaucasia. Stalin, as head of Narkomnats, undertook, with the approval of Lenin, an intensive campaign to bring about their unification into a single Transcaucasian federation.

---

[62] Text appears in *Leninskii Sbornik,* XXXIV, 120–21, and in *Obrazovanie S.S.S.R.,* pp. 124–25.

[63] Text of this decree appears in *Obrazovanie S.S.S.R.,* p. 126.

[64] See the companion volume, *Soviet Russia and the West, 1920–1927.*

[65] E. B. Genkina, *Obrazovanie S.S.S.R.* Texts of the two agreements appear in *Obrazovanie S.S.S.R.,* pp. 247–48, 257–58.

Such a union was vigorously opposed by certain local Communists, notably some of the Georgian Communist Party leaders. In 1921 Stalin personally visited his native Georgia, and while there (and thereafter through his lieutenant, Ordzhonikidze) dealt summarily with the recalcitrant elements.[66] The opposition having been removed, Stalin's campaign was successful, and on March 12, 1922, the Transcaucasian republics were proclaimed the single Transcaucasian Soviet Federated Socialist Republic.[67]

It appears that Lenin became outraged by the methods Stalin used in this matter and intended that Stalin should be reprimanded by the Twelfth Party Congress in 1923. But before that Congress met, Lenin was incapacitated by his last stroke, and accordingly Stalin was able to maneuver the affair in his own way.[68]

An additional move preliminary to the union of all the soviet republics was a proclamation issued by representatives of the Ukraine, Belorussia, Georgia, Azerbaijan, Armenia, Bukhara, Khorezm, and the Far Eastern Republic,[69] which empowered the R.S.F.S.R. to act for them at the Genoa Conference of 1922.[70]

Moscow, meanwhile, had unloosed a propaganda barrage urging general union of all soviet republics. Typical of the arguments were the theses on the "Current Tasks of the Party in Regard to the National Question" prepared by Stalin for the Tenth Congress of the Party, which met in March 1921. These stated in part:

Not one soviet republic taken separately can consider itself safe from economic exhaustion and military defeat by international imperialism. Therefore, the isolated existence of separate soviet republics has no firm basis in view of the threats to their existence from the capitalist states. The common interests of the defense of the soviet republics on one hand, the task of reconstructing the productive forces destroyed by the war on the other, and the necessary help with food for the nonproductive soviet republics from the productive ones, all strongly call for a political union of the separate soviet republics, which alone can save them from the imperialist yoke and national oppression. The national soviet republics, which have freed themselves from their "own" and from "foreign" bourgeoisie, will be able to defend their existence and conquer the united forces of imperialism only by joining in a close political union. Otherwise they cannot achieve victory.[71]

Again, in an interview with a *Pravda* correspondent in November 1922, Stalin declared:

In order actually to unite the economic efforts of separate republics and make them into a single economic union, it is necessary to create the proper active agencies within the union which will direct the economic life of these republics along one definite channel. That is why the old economic and commercial treaties between these republics are no longer sufficient. That is why the movement for the union

[66] See Document 14.

[67] Text of the proclamation appears in *Obrazovanie S.S.S.R.*, pp. 288–89.

[68] See Documents 14 and 17. The Georgian opposition to Stalin is discussed at some length by Trotsky in his volume *Stalin, An Appraisal of the Man and His Influence*.

[69] The Far Eastern Republic was created by the decision of the Congress of the Toilers of the Baikal Region, Verkhneudinsk, April 6, 1920. For details see below.

[70] Text in Kliuchnikov and Sabanin, III, 168–69.

[71] Stalin, *Sochineniia*, V, 21–22.

of the republics has overgrown these treaties and has put forward the question of the unification of the republics.[72]

The combined agitation and pressure for union soon had their effect. By December 1922, congresses of soviets in each of the soviet republics had passed resolutions urging union. At the first session of the Tenth Congress of Soviets of the R.S.F.S.R., December 23, 1922, these resolutions were duly noted, and a further resolution was passed which declared the unification of the R.S.F.S.R., the Ukrainian S.S.R., the Belorussian S.S.R., and the Transcaucasian S.F.S.R.

The First Congress of Soviets of the U.S.S.R. was convened one week later.[73] At that Congress a Central Executive Committeee for the U.S.S.R. was elected. In the months immediately following, the newly elected Central Executive Committee drafted a constitution and worked out the organization of the new government.[74] On January 31, 1924, the Second Congress of Soviets of the U.S.S.R. met and adopted the constitution, thereby formally establishing the Union of Soviet Socialist Republics.[75]

In addition to the four constituent republics of the Union, there were also established under the jurisdiction of the union republics the so-called autonomous republics and oblasts. As already indicated, the establishment of such units was begun in 1919; by the time the U.S.S.R. came into being there were ten autonomous soviet republics and eleven oblasts within the R.S.F.S.R. From 1922 to 1936 the number of autonomous republics within the U.S.S.R. rose only to seventeen.

During World War II, five autonomous units were dissolved or reorganized, allegedly because of collaboration with the Germans. These units were: (1) the Crimean Autonomous S.S.R.; (2) the Kabardino-Balkar Autonomous S.S.R.; (3) the Chechen-Ingush Autonomous S.S.R.; (4) the Karachai Autonomous Oblast; and (5) the Volga German Autonomous S.S.R., created in 1919.

Numerous changes took place also in regard to the constituent republics, especially in Central Asia, when the so-called *razmezhevanie* (territorial distribution) took place in 1924–25. The Turkestan A.S.S.R. was dissolved, and out of its territories and those of the Kirghiz (later Kazakh) A.S.S.R.[76] and the Khorezm and Bukhara People's Soviet Republics new republics were formed on an ethnic basis. These were: (1) the Uzbek S.S.R., with its capital at Tashkent, which was admitted into the Union on May 13, 1925 (since then, its boundaries have been modified twice, in 1929 and 1936); (2) the Turkmen S.S.R., with Ashkhabad as its capital, bordering on Persia and Afghanistan and admitted into the Union on May 13, 1925; (3) the Kazakh Autonomous S.S.R., with its capital at Alma-Ata (formerly Vernyi); (4) the Tadzhik Autonomous Oblast within the Uzbek S.S.R., which became a separate constituent republic in 1929, with its capital at Stalinabad (formerly Diushambe) and bordering on Afghanistan, Pakistan, and China; and (5) the Kara-Kirghiz Au-

[72] *Ibid.*, pp. 139–40.
[73] See Document 15.
[74] See Document 16.
[75] Text appears in *Obrazovanie S.S.S.R.*, pp. 422–34.
[76] The Kirghiz A.S.S.R. was formed by the decree of the Russian Central Executive Committee, August 26, 1920. Its name was changed to Kazakh A.S.S.R. in 1925, and to Kazakh S.S.R. in 1936, when it became a union republic.

tonomous Oblast, with Frunze as its capital. The last-named became the Kirghiz Autonomous Oblast in May 1925, the Kirghiz Autonomous S.S.R. in February 1926, and the Kirghiz S.S.R. in 1936.

In late 1920 the First Congress of the Soviets of the Kirghiz (Kazakh) A.S.S.R. took note of that Republic's special geographical situation and declared in part: "In joining the ranks of the Russian Soviet Federation, the Kirghiz [Autonomous] Soviet Socialist Republic hopes to become the school of revolution for the entire East . . . and in that way to hasten the approach of the last hour of capitalism."[77] If the area never fully achieved this distinction, at least the declaration was in complete harmony with Moscow's plans for the infiltration and eventual subversion of Asia.[78]

Communist Tactics Among the Colonial and Dependent Nations

Simultaneously with the incorporation of various borderland nationalities into the Soviet Union, Bolshevik leaders pushed their program for separating colonial people from European ruling powers.

Lenin envisaged that communist work among colonial and dependent nations would consist of rendering support to the national-liberation movements, which would be led by the national bourgeoisie then rising to prominence in Asian countries. A theoretical basis for Lenin's arguments in favor of a bourgeois revolution in the colonies could be found in his earlier writings, including his statements supporting the bourgeois-democratic revolution in Russia.

Lenin's Characterization of the Russian Revolution as a "Bourgeois Revolution"

As early as 1894 Lenin had argued for a revolutionary union of the Russian workers (representing the proletariat) and the Russian peasants (representing the petty bourgeoisie) as the chief means for overthrowing tsarism and the bourgeoisie.[79] Somewhat later in his "Dve taktiki sotsial-demokratii v demokraticheskoi revoliutsii" ("Two Tactics of the Social Democrats in the Democratic Revolution"), published in Geneva in 1905,[80] Lenin advanced the theory that the proletariat not only could, but must, become the leader, the "hegemon" in the bourgeois-democratic revolution. Lenin never denied, however, that the 1905 revolution in Russia was, or could have been, anything but a bourgeois revolution.

Lenin's View on the Role of the Bourgeois Revolution

In "Dve taktiki" Lenin expressed himself as favoring Social Democratic participation in the bourgeois government, categorically stating that in a period

---

[77] *Obrazovanie S.S.S.R.,* p. 180; see Document 8.

[78] For a detailed and up-to-date account of the regional organization of the U.S.S.R., see Theodore Shabad, *Geography of the U.S.S.R., A Regional Survey.*

As for the Transcaucasian S.F.S.R., it was dissolved by the constitution of 1936, and replaced by three constituent republics of the Union: Georgia, Azerbaijan, and Armenia. All in all through the constitution of 1936 the number of constituent republics rose to eleven.

[79] "Chto takoe 'druzia naroda' i kak oni voiuiut protiv sotsial-demokratov?" ("Who Are the Friends of the People and How Do They Fight the Social Democrats?"). Text appears in Lenin, *Sochineniia,* I (4th ed.), 115–83; also Lenin, *Selected Works,* I, 1–63.

[80] Lenin, *Sochineniia,* IX (4th ed.), 3–119; also, Lenin, *Selected Works,* III, 39–133.

of democratic revolution, and with a given correlation of class forces, the participation of the representatives of the Social Democratic Party (i.e., Bolsheviks) in a provisional government was in principle not only possible but necessary, and was to be undertaken for the purpose of struggle against counterrevolution and for the defense of the particular interests of the working class.

In "Dve taktiki" Lenin further declared that bourgeois revolution would be but a stage, a steppingstone in the general revolution, which would eventually turn into a socialist revolution. Therefore, he argued, the sooner and more complete the victory of the bourgeois-democratic revolution, the sooner the complete liberation of the proletariat and other exploited masses from political and economic oppression.

Complete victory of the bourgeois revolution, Lenin asserted, would be the end of the democratic revolution and the beginning of the decisive struggle for socialism. "Our business," he wrote in March–April, 1905, "i.e., the business of a social democracy, is *to push* the bourgeois revolution as far forward as possible, never forgetting the *main* task, namely, the independent organization of the proletariat."[81] And a little later (September 1905) in his "Otnoshenie sotsial-demokratii k krestianskomu dvizheniiu" ("Attitude of the Social Democrats Toward the Peasant Movement") he added: "From the democratic revolution we shall immediately pass on—in the measure of our strength, the strength of the class-conscious and organized proletariat—toward the socialist revolution. We are for the uninterrupted revolution. We shall not stop halfway."[82]

Elaborating upon the attitude the Social Democrats should take toward the bourgeois revolutionary government in its first stage, Lenin stated in his "Dve taktiki":

The *bourgeois* revolution is in the *highest degree advantageous to the proletariat*. The bourgeois revolution is *absolutely* necessary in the interests of the proletariat. . . . Marxism teaches the proletariat not to keep aloof from the bourgeois revolution, not to refuse to take part in it, not to allow the leadership of the revolution to be assumed by the bourgeoisie, but, on the contrary, to take a most energetic part in it, to fight resolutely for consistent proletarian democracy, to fight for the revolution to its completion. We cannot jump out of the bourgeois-democratic boundaries of the Russian revolution, but we can enormously extend those boundaries, and within those boundaries, we can and must fight for the interests of the proletariat, for its immediate needs and for the prerequisites for training its forces for the complete victory that is to come.[83]

Lenin went on to say:

One of the objections raised to the slogan "the revolutionary democratic dictatorship of the proletariat and the peasantry" is that dictatorship presupposes a "unified will" . . . and that there can be no united will between the proletariat and the petty bourgeoisie. This objection is fallacious, for it is based upon an abstract "metaphysical" interpretation of the term "united will." Will may be united in one respect and not united in another. The absence of unity on the questions of socialism and the struggle for socialism does not prevent unity of will on the question of democracy and the struggle for a republic. To forget this would be tantamount to forgetting the local and

---

[81] Lenin, "Revoliutsiia tipa 1789 ili tipa 1848 goda?" ("Revolution of the Type of 1789 or 1848?"), *Sochineniia*, VIII (4th ed.), 229.

[82] Lenin, *Sochineniia*, IX (4th ed.), 213.

[83] *Ibid.*, pp. 34, 35–36; also Lenin, *Selected Works*, 75, 77.

historical difference between a democratic revolution and a socialist revolution. To forget this would mean forgetting the *national* character of the democratic revolution: if it is "national" it means that there *must* be "unity of will" precisely in so far as this revolution satisfies the national needs and requirements. Beyond the boundaries of democracy there can be no unity of will between the proletariat and the peasant bourgeoisie. Class struggle between them is inevitable, but on the basis of a democratic republic, this struggle will be for the most far-reaching and extensive struggle of the people for *socialism*.[84]

Envisaging the revolutionary democratic dictatorship of the proletariat and the peasantry as but a transient stage in the development of the revolution, Lenin nevertheless said of it:

A Social Democrat must never, even for an instant, forget that the proletarian class struggle for socialism against the most democratic and republican bourgeoisie and petty bourgeoisie is inevitable. This is beyond doubt. From this logically follows the absolute necessity of a separate and independent party with socialist and democratic membership. From this logically follows the provisional character of our tactics to "strike together" with the bourgeoisie and the duty to carefully watch "our ally as if he were our enemy," etc. All this is beyond doubt, but it would be ridiculous and reactionary to deduce from this that we must forget, ignore, or neglect those tasks which, although transient and temporary, are vital at the present time. The struggle against autocracy is a temporary and transient task of the Socialists, but to ignore or neglect this task would be tantamount to betraying socialism and rendering a service to reaction. Certainly, the revolutionary democratic dictatorship of the proletariat and the peasantry is only a transient, provisional task of the Socialists, but to ignore this task in the period of a democratic revolution would be simply reactionary.[85]

The Stages of the Russian Revolution as Envisaged by Lenin

In summing up the stages through which he expected the Russian revolution to pass and the role which he believed the Social Democratic Party (Bolshevik) should play in these various stages, Lenin wrote in early 1906:

1. Under the leadership of the Russian Social Democratic Labor Party the workers' movement at once arouses the proletariat and *awakens* the liberal bourgeoisie, 1895-1901-1902;

2. The workers' movement passes on into an open revolutionary political struggle, and it *attracts* the politically awakened elements of the liberal and radical bourgeoisie and petty bourgeoisie, 1901-1902-1905;

3. The workers' movement develops into the direct *revolution,* while the liberal bourgeoisie, now organized into a Constitutional Democratic Party, plans to halt the revolution by means of an agreement with tsarism. Meanwhile, the radical elements of the bourgeoisie and petty bourgeoisie change over and favor an alliance with the proletariat for the *continuation of the revolution, 1905* (especially the end of the year);

4. The workers' movement wins in the *democratic* revolution under the condition of passive waiting by the liberals, while the *peasantry* actively support it. In addition, radical republican intelligentsia and the corresponding elements among the petty bourgeoisie in the cities support it. The rising of the peasants is victorious, the authority of the *pomeshchiks* [landlords] is broken;

5. The liberal bourgeoisie, which was hesitant in the third period and passive

[84] Lenin, *Sochineniia*, IX (4th ed.), 66; also Lenin, *Selected Works*, III, 98-99.
[85] Lenin, *Sochineniia*, IX (4th ed.), 67-68; also Lenin, *Selected Works*, III, 100.

in the fourth, now becomes directly counterrevolutionary and organizes itself in order to snatch from the proletariat the achievements of the revolution. Likewise, all well-to-do peasantry and a considerable number of the middle peasantry "grow wiser," quiet down, and join the side of the counterrevolution in order to knock the authority out of the hands of the proletariat and the village poor, who are sympathetic to the proletariat;

6. On the basis of the new relationship which came into being in the fifth period, a new crisis develops as well as a new struggle, while the proletariat is already struggling for the retention of the democratic achievements of the socialist revolution . . .[86]

Discussion of the Principle of Temporary Alliance with Colonial Bourgeois Democracy at the Second Congress of the Communist International, 1920 (Lenin's and Roy's Views)

These earlier utterances of Lenin's are important in view of the disagreements which arose at the Second Congress of the Communist International when Lenin came out in favor of supporting the national revolutionary movements led by the bourgeoisie in the colonial countries. Opposition to his insistent demands in this regard came mainly from non-Russian Communists. The Russian Communists did not, of course, find an absolute similarity between the Russian situation of 1905 and the situation in China and India in 1920. (Their chief qualification was that the colonial and dependent countries were subjected to the oppression of foreign imperialist powers, as the old Russian Empire had not been.) Nevertheless, in 1920 and later they favored supporting "nonproletarian" revolutionary movements in colonial and dependent countries oppressed by imperialist powers, such as China and Turkey, just as in 1905 they had favored supporting the revolutionary democratic dictatorship of the proletariat and the peasantry (the latter representing petty bourgeois tendencies) in Russia.

When the Second Congress of the Communist International met in July 1920, it discussed at some length the strategy and tactics to be followed by the Communists in their work among the colonial and dependent nations. The problem was threshed out thoroughly at sessions of the specially appointed Commission on the National and Colonial Questions, as well as at sessions of the Congress itself on July 26 and 28. The outcome of these discussions was the adoption of the extremely important "Theses on the National and Colonial Questions,"[87] which expressed Lenin's views slightly modified by the proposals introduced in the "Supplementary Theses"[88] by M. N. Roy, an Indian representative at the Congress and a high-ranking member of the Communist International.

Roy questioned Lenin's contention that the Communist International should make temporary alliances with bourgeois elements in the colonies.[89] He urged that the Communist International determine more specifically the relationship

---

[86] Lenin, *Sochineniia,* X (4th ed.), 73–74; also Lenin, *Selected Works,* III, 134–35.

[87] See Document 18.

[88] See Document 19.

[89] Point Eleven of Lenin's preliminary theses stated in part: "The Communist International must be ready to establish a temporary alliance with the bourgeois democracy of the colonies and backward countries. It must not, however, amalgamate with it. It must retain the independent character of the proletarian movement even though this movement be in the embryonic stage" (Lenin, *Sochineniia,* XXV, 290).

between itself and the revolutionary movements in the countries dominated by capitalist imperialism, such as China and India. "Two distinct movements which grow further apart every day are to be found in the dependent countries," Roy's theses stated. One was the bourgeois-democratic national movement aiming at the establishment of a bourgeois order. The other was "the mass struggle of the poor and ignorant peasants and workers for their liberation from various forms of exploitation."

Since the bourgeoisie were attempting, often with success, to control the masses, it was the duty of the Communist International to devote itself to the organization of the broad masses, to develop their class-consciousness, to prepare them for the revolution and the establishment of soviet republics. Roy acknowledged that no immediate communist revolution was possible in the colonies, and that in the first stages of the colonial revolution a petty bourgeois program of reforms might be necessary. From the outset, nevertheless, the leadership of the revolution in the colonies should be assumed by a communist vanguard.

Roy's other contention was that the success of world communism depended on the triumph of communism in the East. He pointed out (1) that world capitalism was drawing its main resources and most of its income from the colonies, and principally from Asia; (2) that European capitalists could in an emergency give their entire surplus profit to the workers in order to attract them to their side and to destroy revolutionary tendencies in the colonies.[90] In that case the capitalists would be in a position to continue, with the aid of the proletariat, to exploit Asia. Hence, unless the communist revolution triumphed in the East, the communist movement in the West would be powerless.

Lenin disagreed. Roy, he said, had gone too far in declaring that the destiny of the West would depend exclusively upon the degree of development and the strength of the revolutionary movement in Eastern countries.[91] In so far as keeping aloof from all national liberation movements in the colonies was concerned, Lenin referred to the Bolsheviks' support of the democratic movement of liberation in Russia under tsarism, and in doing so confirmed his earlier views on this subject.[92]

A. Sultan-Zade, representing the Persian Communists, commented on and partially supported Roy's views. He agreed with Lenin, he said, that the destiny of world communism did not depend on the socialist revolution in the East. But he added:

The passage in the theses [of Lenin] in which support is pledged for the bourgeois-democratic movement in the backward countries, appears to me to be applicable only to those countries where the movement is still in an embryonic stage. But in those countries where the movement has already been going on for ten years and more,

---

[90] The concept of the colonies as the chief resource of European capitalists, and the possibility of the workers' being "bribed" by capitalists, were central theses in Lenin's earlier *Imperialism, the Highest Stage of Capitalism.*

[91] This interpretation of the Lenin-Roy dispute is based upon evidence in *Vtoroi Kongress Kominterna,* pp. 105–7 and 496–99, and *Vestnik 2-go Kongressa Kommunisticheskogo Internatsionala,* No. 2, July 29, 1920, pp. 1–2; and upon statements made by M. N. Roy in an interview with Robert C. North at Dehra Dun, India, October 15, 1951. For a detailed analysis of the Lenin-Roy controversy and its circumstances, see Allen S. Whiting, *Soviet Policies in China, 1917–1924,* pp. 42–58.

[92] See our p. 36.

or in those countries where, as in Persia, the bourgeois democracy is the basis and the prop of the government, there such a support would mean leading the masses to counterrevolution. In such countries we must create a purely communist movement in opposition to the bourgeois tendencies. Any other attitude might bring deplorable results.[93]

Maring (real name, H. Sneevliet), a Dutchman, who represented Indonesia at the Second Congress of the Communist International, tried to reconcile Lenin's and Roy's views by stating that he found "no distinction between the theses of Comrade Lenin and those of Comrade Roy":

They are alike in essence. The difficulty lies only in finding the precise formula for the relationship between the revolutionary national and the socialist movements in the backward countries and colonies. This difficulty does not exist in reality. In actual practice we find it necessary to work together with the revolutionary national-ist elements, and our work would be half done if we should ignore the national-revo-lutionary movements and play dogmatic Marxists. . . . We must realize that the colonies can bypass capitalist development.[94]

In the same speech Maring brought out two important points which, as the later activities of the Communist International indicate, must have been taken into account by the Congress. Maring proposed that the theses adopted by the Second Congress be published in the oriental languages, and that a Bureau of Propaganda of the Communist International be organized for the Far East similar to the one organized for the Near East. Such a bureau, he believed, would unify the work which had already been started in the Far East and which could not be easily directed from Moscow.

Maring also proposed that the Communist International organize in Russia special facilities for training the leaders of the Far Eastern revolutionary move-ments in communism. "Moscow and Petrograd," he said, "have become a new Mecca for the East, . . . and we must give the Eastern Communists the oppor-tunity to obtain a theoretical education in communism here, in Russia, so as to help make the Far East an active member of the Communist International."[95] We shall see in Part II that Maring's suggestions were duly followed by the Executive Committee of the Communist International.

Agreement on the Wording of the "Theses on the National and Colonial Ques-tions"

In his subsequent speech to the Congress on July 26, Lenin referred to the above-described disagreements among the participants of the Congress. "We argued," he said, "over whether it is proper theoretically and in principle to declare that the Communist International and the communist parties are bound to support the bourgeois-democratic movements in the backward countries"; it was unanimously decided "that we should speak of the national-revolutionary and not of the 'bourgeois-democratic' movements."

"The meaning of the above change," Lenin concluded, "is that we, as Com-munists, should support the bourgeois movements of liberation in the colonies only if these are really revolutionary, when those who represent these move-

93 *Vtoroi Kongress Kominterna,* p. 120.
94 *Ibid.,* p. 138.
95 *Ibid.,* pp. 138–39.

ments would not oppose us in our efforts to educate and organize the peasantry and the masses of exploited people in general, in the revolutionary spirit. When this is impossible, the Communists must oppose the reformist bourgeoisie [in those countries]."[96]

Pak Chin Shum, the Korean representative at the Congress, echoed Lenin's theses in an article in *Petrogradskaia Pravda* on July 27:

To our great joy, the majority of the nationals with ideas have proved to be on the side of the revolution. Of course, there are elements among the revolutionists themselves who will join us, the internationalists, only for the purpose of national political liberation. We shall utilize their revolutionary spirit for combating world capital and for the triumph of social revolution throughout the world; but if the revolution requires it, we will know how to turn our weapons on the "allies" of yesterday, and the victory undoubtedly will be ours. . . . Therefore, while we are fighting along with the above-named elements, we cannot regard them as comrades with whom we might go to the end without danger. Without tiring for a minute, we must explain to the broad masses of toilers of the East that national political enfranchisement alone will not give them what they are fighting for, and that *only social liberation can give them the full guarantee of freedom.*[97]

Stalin's comments on the Lenin theses pertained to Points 6 and 7 and the problem of federation. Nationalities which had existed as independent entities, he maintained, could not be expected to join in an organization so damaging to their sovereignty. The need was for a soviet *confederation* in which not only advanced countries of the West, but also "backward" though independent states like Persia and Turkey, might take their place at the time of their sovietization.[98]

Peasant Soviets in Backward Countries

Speaking to the Congress on July 26, Lenin referred to two other important points which, according to him, aroused lively discussions in the Commission on the National and Colonial Questions, namely the problem of peasant soviets, and the possibility of the backward countries' bypassing the capitalist stage of development.

Lenin spoke of the experience of the Russian Communists in such backward regions as Turkestan, in which precapitalist relations still prevailed, and in which, therefore, there could be no question of a purely proletarian movement:

The idea of soviet organization is a simple one, and it can be applied not only to proletarian conditions but also to feudal and semifeudal relations. . . . We must base the theses of the Communist International on the assumption that the peasant soviets, the soviets of the exploited, are applicable not only to capitalist countries but also to the countries of precapitalist conditions, and that it is the absolute duty of the communist parties and of their sympathizers to propagate the idea of peasant soviets, the soviets of the toiling people everywhere, including the backward and colonial countries, and to try, wherever conditions permit, to create peasant soviets or soviets of the toilers.[99]

In the same speech Lenin affirmed that once the first proletarian state had been established in Russia, the backward and colonial peoples could throw off

[96] Lenin, *Sochineniia*, XXV, 352 and 353; see Document 21.
[97] *Petrogradskaia Pravda*, No. 164, July 27, 1920, p. 1.
[98] See Document 20.
[99] Lenin, *Sochineniia*, XXV, 353–54; see Document 21.

imperialist rule, provided they were helped by the advanced proletariat. They could then bypass the capitalist stage of development and move on directly from the feudal or semifeudal stage to socialism.

On July 26, 1920, Lenin, reporting to the Congress on the work of the Commission on the National and Colonial Questions, remarked:

There can be no argument about the fact that the proletariat of the advanced countries can and must assist the backward toiling masses, and that the development of the backward countries can emerge from its present stage when the victorious proletariat of the soviet republics stretches out a helping hand to these masses, and when it is able to render them its assistance.

We had rather lively debates on this point in the Commission, not only in connection with the theses which I signed, but even more so in connection with the theses of Comrade Roy, which he will defend here, and into which certain corrections were unanimously introduced.

The question raised was this: Can we recognize as correct the assertion that the capitalist stage of development of national economy is inevitable for those backward nations which are now liberating themselves, and among which a movement toward progress is now, after the war, being observed? We replied to this question in the negative. If the revolutionary victorious proletariat carry on systematic propaganda among these people [i.e., backward colonial people], and if the soviet governments come to their assistance with every means at their disposal, then it would not be correct to suppose that the capitalist stage of development is inevitable for the backward nationalities.

In all colonies and backward countries, we must not only form independent cadres of fighters and party organizations, we must not only carry propaganda for the organization of peasant soviets, and try to adapt them to the precapitalist conditions in these countries. The Communist International must [also] outline and theoretically explain the thesis that, with the help of the proletariat of the more advanced countries, the backward countries can proceed to a soviet regime, and by definite stages of development, to communism, bypassing the capitalist stage of development.[100]

The Problem of Pan-Muslimism

Lenin's "Theses on the National and Colonial Questions" also touched upon the problem of Islam and Pan-Muslimism:

In regard to the more backward countries and nations, with prevailing feudal or patriarchal and patriarchal-peasant relations, it is necessary to bear in mind especially as follows: . . . A struggle must be carried on against reactionary and medieval influences of the clergy, Christian missions and other similar elements.

[100] Lenin, *Sochineniia*, XXV, 354; see Document 21. For a detailed analysis of the discussions which followed at the Congress on July 26 and 28, see Whiting, *op. cit.*, pp. 42–48. At an earlier date Lenin's views on the backward countries' chances of bypassing capitalism were somewhat different. In an article of July 1912, entitled "Demokratiia i Narodnichestvo v Kitae" ("Democracy and Populism in China"), Lenin spoke of the Narodniks' (Populists') hopes that capitalist development could be bypassed by backward countries or prevented as "socialist dreams." Stating that Sun Yat-sen shared such dreams, Lenin added: "This theory [i.e., the theory that capitalism could be bypassed by backward countries] . . . is a theory of a petty bourgeois 'socialist' reactionary, because the dream that capitalism can be 'prevented' in China, that 'social revolution' is easier in China because it is a backward country, is a reactionary dream" (Lenin, *Sochineniia*, XVI, 29). It is true, of course, that when Lenin made this statement, there was not as yet a soviet proletarian government in Russia ready to come to China's assistance.

It is also necessary to combat the Pan-Islamic and Pan-Asiatic movements and similar tendencies which aim at combining the cause of the liberation movements directed against the European and American imperialists with the efforts to consolidate the power of Turkish and Japanese imperialism, or the power of large-scale landowners, clergy, etc.[101]

As we shall see in the subsequent chapters, the problem of Pan-Muslimism came to the foreground more than once in years that followed.

Importance of the Second Congress of the Communist International

The Second Congress of the Communist International held its last session on August 6, and its decisions set the stage for intensive work in the colonial and semicolonial countries. A leading article in *Izvestiia* summarized the results of the Congress in the following manner: "A new world is awakening to life and to struggle—the world of the oppressed nationalities which has been comprehended by us, though not quite correctly under the name of the East. For here are found not only the peoples of Asia, but also those of Africa and America."

The article spoke with scorn of the platonic protests of the Second International against imperialist colonial policies, and pointed out that the Communist International acted quite differently. Not only did it stand in close solidarity with the revolutionary uprisings of oppressed peoples against capitalist domination, but it also required that the communist parties of all countries, and particularly the countries that were doing the oppressing, give active support to colonial revolutionary movements directed against imperialist bourgeoisie. The article concluded:

When the news of the decisions of the Second Congress of the Communist International reaches the hundreds of millions of Indians, Chinese, Negroes, Malays, and other oppressed peoples, it will be happy tidings for them, and also the call for a new and greater struggle against the capital that exploits them. . . . The fact that the Communist International was the first openly to raise the banner of the struggle, and to call to this banner all the oppressed peoples and the organized proletariat, will stand to its eternal credit.[102]

We shall deal in succeeding pages with the practical measures taken by the Executive Committee of the Communist International—the general staff of world revolution[103]—to develop and intensify this struggle.

[101] *Vtoroi Kongress Kominterna,* p. 494; see Document 18.
[102] *Izvestiia,* No. 176, August 11, 1920, p. 1.
[103] See Document 22.

DOCUMENTS

1

Lenin on Colonial Revolts and Civil War
in Imperialist Countries

[Excerpt from an Article "On the Caricature of Marxism" (1916)][1]

. . .

A social revolution cannot be a joint action of the proletariat of *all* countries simply because the majority of the countries and of the population of the globe have not even reached the capitalist stage or are only in the beginning of it. . . . *Only* the advanced countries of the West and North America are ripe for socialism. . . .

Socialism will be realized by the joined actions of the proletariat of a small number of countries, and not of all countries, i.e., of the countries which have reached the degree of development of *advanced* capitalism. . . . In *these* advanced countries (Britain, France, Germany, and so forth) the national problem has been settled long ago, the national unity has long outlived itself, so that *objectively* there exist there no longer any "common national tasks." Therefore, it is only in such countries that it is possible *now* to "blow up" the national unity and to establish a class unity.

Quite a different situation exists in undeveloped countries, . . . that is, in the countries of eastern Europe and in all colonies or semicolonies. There, one *still* finds, as a rule, oppressed and capitalistically undeveloped nations. Such nations *still* have, *objectively* speaking, general national tasks, namely, the *democratic* tasks, the tasks of *overthrowing the alien oppression*. . . . [Meantime] while the proletariat of the advanced countries is overthrowing the bourgeoisie and repulsing its counterrevolutionary attempts, the backward and oppressed nations do not wait, do not stop living, do not disappear. If they utilize even such a small crisis of the imperialist bourgeoisie as the war of 1915–16 (small in comparison with the social revolution) in order to raise revolts (for example in the colonies and in Ireland), then there is not the slightest doubt that they will make even more use for their revolts of such *a great crisis* as civil war in the advanced countries.

Social revolution can occur only in an entire epoch in which the civil war of the proletariat against the bourgeoisie in the advanced countries is joined with the *whole number* of revolutionary democratic and national-liberation movements in the backward and oppressed nations.

Why is it so? Because capitalism does not develop evenly, and because the actual situation proves that side by side with the highly developed capitalist nations there exist a number of nations which are little developed or not developed at all. . . .

2

Stalin on the Two Camps and the Doom of Imperialism

[An Article in *Izvestiia*, February 22, 1919][2]

The world has been split into two camps decisively and finally: the camp of imperialism and the camp of socialism. There, in *their* camp, are the United States and

[1] Lenin, *Sochineniia*, XIX, 220–22.
[2] Stalin, *Sochineniia*, IV, 232–35.

Britain, France, and Japan with their capital, with their armaments, with their experienced agents and equally experienced administrators.

Here, in *our* camp, are Soviet Russia with the young soviet republics, and the growing proletarian revolution in the European countries. [Soviet Russia has no] capital, no experienced agents or administrators; instead it has experienced agitators capable of arousing the toilers with enthusiasm for liberation.

The struggle between these two camps characterizes the present world situation; it influences the foreign and domestic policies of the leaders of the old and the new worlds.

Estonia and Lithuania, the Ukraine and the Crimea, Turkestan and Siberia, Poland and the Caucasus, and finally Russia itself are not the goals by themselves; they are only the arena of the struggle, of a death struggle between the two forces: imperialism, which is trying to strengthen the yoke of servitude, and socialism, which is struggling to throw off that yoke.

The strength of imperialism lies in the backwardness of the masses, who provide wealth for their masters and thus forge chains for themselves. But backwardness is a passing stage which has a tendency to disappear as time goes on, as the discontent of the masses grows and the revolutionary movement spreads. As for the capital of the imperialists, who does not know that capital is helpless before the inevitable? It is exactly because of this that the dominance of imperialism is not permanent and is not secure.

The weakness of imperialism lies in its inability to put an end to wars *without* experiencing catastrophes, *without* increasing unemployment, *without* new robberies of their own workers and peasants, *without* new seizures of other people's land.

.   .   .

Is it necessary then to say that the above facts widen the base of the revolution, undermine the foundation of imperialism, and hasten the inevitable catastrophe?

.   .   .

The world has been divided into two irreconcilable camps: the camp of imperialism and the camp of socialism. Imperialism, which is breathing its last, seizes its last straw, namely the "League of Nations," and tries to save the situation by bringing about an alliance among all robbers of all countries. But all these efforts are in vain because the situation and time work against it; and they work for socialism. The waves of socialist revolution are rising and beating against the fortresses of imperialism. Their roar is heard in the countries of the oppressed East. The ground under the feet of imperialism is shaking. Imperialism is headed for its inevitable doom.

3

A Beacon for the Muslims of the World

[Stalin's Remarks at the Closing Session of the Conference for the Convocation of the Constituent Congress of the Tatar-Bashkir Autonomous Soviet Republic, May 16, 1918][3]

Allow me to state in the name of the Central Soviet government that the Council of People's Commissars has always believed and still believes that it is its sacred duty to meet halfway the movement of liberation of the oppressed and exploited masses of the East, and first of all, of the most wronged Muslim East. The entire

[3] Stalin, *Sochineniia,* IV, 90–92.

character of our revolution, the very nature of the Soviet government, the general international situation, and finally even the geographical position of Russia, situated between imperialist Europe and oppressed Asia—all these necessarily prompt the Soviet government to pursue the policy of fraternal support of oppressed peoples of the East in their struggle for their own liberation.

From among the various forms of oppression which exist now, national oppression is the most subtle and also the most dangerous. It is subtle because it very conveniently conceals the rapacious designs of the bourgeoisie. It is dangerous because it very dextrously wards off popular discontent against the bourgeoisie, and leads instead to clashes between national groups. If the European vultures have succeeded in making the workers fight one another in the arena of international slaughter, if they have succeeded in going on with this slaughter even now—this is owing, among other things, to the fact that the influence of bourgeois nationalism which has dimmed the vision of the European workers has not yet been overcome. Nationalism is the last position from which the bourgeoisie must be dislodged in order finally to be defeated.

However, to bypass the national question, to ignore it or deny it, as some of our comrades do,[4] is not defeating nationalism. Far from it. National nihilism only harms the cause of socialism, and it plays into the hands of nationalists. In order to destroy nationalism it is imperative, first of all, to raise and to solve national questions. But in order to solve the national question openly and by socialist methods, it is necessary to approach it from the soviet viewpoint, subordinating it entirely and finally to the interests of the toiling masses organized into soviets. Thus, and only thus, can we knock from the bourgeoisie's hands its last spiritual weapon. The autonomous soviet republic of the Tatar-Bashkirs which is now planned provides a practical solution for this general problem which is so important for our entire revolution. Let then this autonomous republic serve the peoples of the Muslim world, as a shining beacon which lights their way toward liberation. . . .

4

Methods for Antireligious Propaganda Among the Muslims[5]

The question of the methods of antireligious propaganda among the Muslims is a very complicated and delicate one. It is complicated on one hand by the position which Islam occupies in the lives of the Muslim peoples, and on the other hand by the social and political conditions of the Muslim peoples in general.

The question of the necessity of antireligious propaganda among the Muslims, not only in Russia but far beyond Russia's borders, arouses, of course, no disputes or disagreements among us, the Communists. For us, all religions are alike . . . What concerns us is choosing the methods by which to carry through this task painlessly and successfully. . . .

We must acknowledge that there are a number of reasons for adopting methods absolutely different from those used among other peoples. . . . Among the "great" religions of the world, Islam is of comparatively recent origin, and therefore it possesses particular strength and vigor. . . . In addition it provides—more than any

---

[4] This may be a reference to the point of view of Rosa Luxemburg and her supporters.

[5] M. Sultan-Galiev, *Metody anti-religioznoi propagandy sredi musulman*, pp. 3–7. Sultan-Galiev was criticized by the Moscow Communists in the twenties for his allegedly Pan-Islamic tendencies.

other faith—rules of political and civil behavior, and in that way it differs from other religions, in which spiritual and ethical motives predominate. *Shariat,* or the Muslim law, represents a code of laws and legal norms which regulate the entire life of a Muslim. . . .

The second important fact which complicates antireligious propaganda is the social and economic position of the Muslim people during recent centuries. The defeat dealt to the Arab culture on one hand, and to the Turko-Tatar culture on the other (the expulsion of Arabs from Spain and the Turko-Tatars from southeastern Europe, the conquest by the Europeans of North African and Near Eastern Muslim possessions, and the subjugation by the Russians of the Tatars, the Bashkirs, the Mountaineers of the Caucasus, and the Turkic peoples of Central Asia) resulted in the political, social, and economic enslavement of almost the entire Muslim world of 300 million people. . . .

The above fact was bound to have a repercussion on the Muslim people's faith. The first encroachments of Western European imperialism on the Muslim countries took the form of Crusades, but in recent years the struggle has become purely economic. Nevertheless, in the view of the Muslims, or at least of the majority of them, this struggle is still interpreted as a political struggle, i.e., the struggle against Islam as a whole. Such an attitude can be easily explained because, according to the Muslims, the entire Muslim world, without distinction of nationality and tribe, represents one undivided whole.

Consequently, Islam is even today, in the eyes of the Muslim peoples, a religion which is oppressed and which must be defended. [Hence the difficulty of antireligious propaganda among the Muslims.] . . .

Speaking of obstacles to antireligious propaganda among the Muslims, we must also mention that these peoples are very backward. . . .

What, then, are the methods that should be used?

First, a very careful and dextrous approach. . . . Our program should be of the nature of antireligious propaganda, and not of antireligious struggle. We must knock from the hands of our enemies the weapon they use against us: We must openly say to those concerned that we do not conduct any struggle against any religion, but only propagandize our own atheistic views—which we have an absolute right to do.

Second, we must clearly indicate that we have no connections whatsoever with the former missionary groups, and we must have only Communists of Muslim origin to carry on antireligious propaganda. . . .

Third, we must conduct effective propaganda, and make our own conduct an example of it. . . . It is necessary for every Muslim to get well acquainted with an atheist and to form a good opinion of him. [It is desirable to carry on discussions on religious subjects among the Muslim workers in towns and in factories, and gradually pass the information on to the villages.]

But when we conduct antireligious propaganda among the Muslims, we must not forget for a moment that their cultural backwardness and their position as a politically and morally downtrodden people are their main evil. . . . Even since the formation of the autonomous republics, the Muslims have very often stayed away from participation in the political life of their republics. As long as we do not break these chains [of political backwardness], as long as we do not make these peoples truly free and equal citizens of the Soviet republic, no antireligious propaganda can be successful. The improvement in the education of the Muslim peoples; the extensive drawing of these people into economic and administrative, and also political, organs of the government, whenever that is possible; the widening of party work among them—these are the tasks of the day in the work among the Muslim peoples. . . .

5

Communist Difficulties in Turkestan, 1920

[Statement by M. V. Frunze, Member of the Turkestan Commission][6]

1. The Communist Party of Turkestan never experienced unity. It was divided into two groups:

(a) European Communists, mainly railway workers, who maintained the principle of pure dictatorship of the proletariat and attempted to apply this principle to life in spite of the fact that this actually meant the dictatorship of a small group of the local European population over the Muslim masses, and

(b) a group of Muslim worker-communists who considered as unacceptable the position taken by the Europeans, and who emphasized instead the significance of the national problem.

2. The above disagreement took the form of an open or concealed struggle within the party; it brought about disintegration in the party, and made any constructive work impossible. On the other hand, Turkestan's peculiar situation [i.e., its isolation from Moscow] caused this struggle to take a most ugly form: petty intrigue, baiting, attempts to damage the position of another, and so forth.

3. At the time when the Turkestan Commission arrived, the European wing of the party was the most belligerent. In order on the one hand to weaken the nationalist tendencies of the Muslims, and on the other hand to do away with the opinion held by the European section [of the party] that the European Communists were the only legal aspirants for authority, the Turkestan Commission launched a struggle against the European wing, and by sending back [to European Russia] the most irreconcilable representatives of the above tendencies was able to put an end to the existing [party] struggle.

4. The Turkestan Commission was also faced with the urgency of doing away with the petty bourgeois nationalist deviation on the part of some Muslim members of the party.

5. The above deviation was expressed:

(a) In the decision of the party conference [held by Muslims] to form a Turkic republic and a Turkic communist party;

(b) in the concealed refusal [by the Muslim communists] to adopt the class point of view and to struggle against colonialism and bourgeois relations among the Muslims. . . .

6

The Necessity and the Meaning of Soviet Autonomy

[People's Commissariat of Nationalities to the Soviets of Kazan, Ufa, Orenburg, Ekaterinburg, the Council of People's Commissars of Turkestan, etc., April 1918, signed by Stalin][7]

. . .

After considerable delay, the revolution which was begun in the center has spread to the borderlands, especially to the East.

[6] M. V. Frunze, *Sobranie sochinenii*, I, 119–20. Material found in Frunze's papers; probably an outline for one of his speeches.

[7] *Politika sovetskoi vlasti po natsionalnym delam za tri goda, 1917 - XI - 1920*, pp. 8–9.

The way of life, the language differences, and the economic backwardness of these borderlands have somewhat complicated the task of the consolidation of soviet authority there. In order to make the masses of the people the bearers of this authority, it becomes necessary to use special means to draw the toilers and exploited masses of these borderlands into the current of revolutionary development. It is necessary to raise the masses to the level of soviet authority and to draw the best native representatives into it. Such measures can be taken only if autonomous rule is enjoyed in these regions, that is, if native schools, native courts, native administration, native organs of authority, and local, public political and educational institutions are established, and if the use of the native tongue is permitted in all spheres of public and political activity.

To this end, the Third Congress of Soviets has proclaimed a federative order for the Russian Soviet republic. The bourgeois autonomous groups which came into existence in the borderlands last November and December . . . are being gradually exposed in the process of the revolution in order that the native masses may be finally drawn away from these groups and rallied around the soviets.

It is imperative to take away from the bourgeois groups the principle of autonomy, to cleanse it of all bourgeois filth, to propagate instead the principle of soviet autonomy. The bourgeois nationalist groups desire autonomy as a weapon for the enslavement of their own masses; it is for this reason that these groups recognize the Central Soviet government, but at the same time refuse to recognize local soviets and insist on noninterference by the Central government in their local affairs.

In view of all this, some soviets have decided not to tolerate any local autonomy, but to settle national differences by force of arms. However, this method of settling the national problem is absolutely unacceptable to the Soviet government. Such a policy will only rally the masses around the bourgeois national leaders. The Soviet government does not wish these leaders to appear to be the saviors of their country and the defenders of their nation. Not the denial of autonomy, but its recognition—this is the immediate task of the Soviet government. But it is imperative to build autonomy on the basis of local soviets because only under such conditions can the government become national and close to the masses. In other words, it is imperative that this autonomy guarantee the power to the lower strata of the population and not to the upper one. This is the essence of the problem, and this is the reason why the Soviet government has introduced autonomy for the Tatar-Bashkirs. The Soviet government intends to declare autonomy also for Kirghizia, the Turkestan region, and other national territories. . . .

7

Stalin on the Mutual Dependence of Central Russia and the Russian Borderlands, October 1920[8]

The three years of revolution and civil war in Russia have shown that victory for the revolution is impossible without mutual assistance between Central Russia and its borderlands, just as it is impossible without such assistance to liberate Russia from the clutches of imperialism. Central Russia, which is the center of the world revolution, cannot hold on for a long time without assistance from the borderlands, which are rich in raw materials, fuel, and food supplies. The Russian borderlands, on their part, are destined to become inevitably enslaved by imperialists unless they

8 Stalin, *Sochineniia*, IV, 351–55, 360.

are given political, military, and organizational assistance by the better developed Central Russia.

If it is true that the more developed proletarian West cannot put an end to the world bourgeoisie without the support of the peasant East (which is less developed, but is rich in raw material and fuel), it is equally true that the more developed Central Russia cannot bring the revolution to its final goal without the support of the less developed borderlands of Russia, which are rich in natural resources.

The above facts must undoubtedly have been taken into account by the Entente from the first days of the appearance of the Soviet state, when it (the Entente) carried out the plan of an economic encirclement of Central Russia by separating it from its most important borderlands. The plan of the economic encirclement of Russia remained unchanged throughout the entire period of the Entente's campaigns against Russia, i.e., from 1918 to 1920, including its present machinations in the Ukraine, Azerbaijan, and Turkestan.

In view of the above, a lasting alliance between the center and the Russian borderlands has become particularly important. Hence follows the necessity of establishing definite relations, definite connections between the center and the borderlands which will ensure a close and permanent union between them.

What should be the nature of these relations, and what forms should they take? In other words, what is the policy of the Soviet government in regard to the nationality question in Russia?

There must be no insistence that the relations between Russia and the borderlands should take the form of a separation of the one from the other, not only because such a separation would interfere with the establishment of a union between the center and the borderlands, but mainly because it would go radically against the interests of the masses of the people, both in the center and in the borderlands. The separation of the borderlands will undermine the revolutionary power of Central Russia, which represents a driving force in the liberation movement in both the West and the East. Besides, the separated borderlands themselves would inevitably be enslaved by international imperialism. It is sufficient to look at Georgia, Armenia, Poland, Finland, and other countries which have separated from Russia to see that they have retained only the semblance of independence, and actually have become vassals of the Entente. It is sufficient finally to remember the recent happenings in the Ukraine and Azerbaijan—the first plundered by the Germans, and the latter by the Entente—in order to understand the counterrevolutionary nature of the insistence on secession of the borderlands under existing international conditions. Owing to the growing mortal struggle between proletarian Russia and the imperialist Entente, the borderlands have only two choices:

Either with Russia, which means the liberation of the toiling masses of the borderlands from the imperialist yoke. *Or* with the Entente, which means the inevitable imperialist yoke. There is no third way.

The so-called independence of the so-called independent Georgia, Armenia, Poland, Finland, and so forth, is only a façade which conceals the complete dependence of these so-called states on one or the other imperialist group.

Of course, the borderlands of Russia, the nations and tribes inhabiting these borderlands, just as any other nation, have the absolute right to separate from Russia, and if some of these nations should press a demand by the majority of the population to separate from Russia, as Finland did in 1917, Russia probably would have to accept and sanction the separation. But just now we are not discussing the question of the right of nations [to separation], which, of course, cannot be disputed, but rather the interests of the masses of the people both in Central Russia and in the borderlands. The question is: What sort of propaganda, according to these interests, must be carried on by our party if it does not wish to repudiate itself, if it desires to influence the will of the toiling masses and nationals in a certain direction? The interests of the masses indicate that in the present stage of the revolution the demand for separation of the borderlands is deeply counterrevolutionary.

We must likewise refuse to support the so-called cultural-national autonomy as a form of union between the center and the borderlands of Russia. The practical experience of Austria-Hungary (the birthplace of cultural-national autonomy) has shown during the last ten years that this autonomy is ephemeral and impractical as a form of a union among the toiling masses of the nationalities inhabiting a multi-national state.

.   .   .

There remains only a *regional* autonomy of the borderlands which are distinguished by special ways of life and special natural composition. This is the only expedient form of a union between the center and the borderlands, an autonomy which will bind together the Russian borderlands with Russia's center by the ties of a federative union. This is the soviet autonomy which has been proclaimed by the Soviet government from the first days of its existence, and which is now being applied in the borderlands in the form of administrative communes and autonomous soviet republics.

Soviet autonomy does not mean something static and established once and for all; it permits various forms and degrees of development. From narrow administrative autonomy (the Germans of the Volga region, the Chuvash, the Karelians) it extends to the broader political autonomy (the Bashkirs, the Tatars of the Volga region, the Kirghiz), then to a still broader form (the Ukraine, Turkestan), and finally from the Ukrainian type of autonomy to the still higher form, that of relations by agreement (Azerbaijan). This elasticity of soviet autonomy is also its particular merit, since it permits the inclusion of the various borderlands of Russia which vary in their cultural and economic development.

.   .   .

One of the serious obstacles in the realization of soviet autonomy is the lack of educated forces among the local population of the borderlands, the lack of instructors in every branch of soviet and party work. This lack is bound to delay both education and revolutionary constructive work in the borderlands. It is exactly for this reason that it will be unwise and harmful to the work to reject the few groups of local intelligentsia who can and wish to work for the cause of the masses, but who are unable to do so, perhaps because they are not Communists, because they believe they are not trusted, and because they fear repression. There can be well applied to these groups the policy of drawing them into soviet work, of recruiting them for industrial, agrarian, food supply, and other posts so that they may be eventually sovietized. It is hardly right to say that these cultural groups are less reliable than, let us say, the counterrevolutionary military specialists whom we drew to work in spite of their counterrevolutionary views, and whom we later sovietized in order to give them the most important positions. . . .

A no less serious obstacle to the application of soviet autonomy is haste, which often expresses itself in crude and tactless actions by some of the comrades who try to sovietize the borderlands. These comrades desire to apply "heroic measures" to instill "pure communism" in regions which lag behind Central Russia by one whole historical period, regions whose way of life is still feudal. One can definitely say that nothing good can come from such a cavalry invasion and from such "communism." It would not be amiss to remind such comrades of the well-known clause in our program which states:

"The R.K.P. supports the historical class point of view, and takes into account the stage of historical development of each nation: that is, whether such a nation stands between feudal practices and bourgeois democracy, or between bourgeois democracy and soviet or proletarian democracy, and so forth.

"In any case, it is imperative that the proletariat of the nations which were the oppressors use special caution and special consideration for the still existing national sentiments among the toilers of the nations who were oppressed and enjoyed no equal rights in the past. . . ."

8

A School of Revolution for the East

[Declaration of the First Congress of the Soviets of the Kirghiz (Kazakh) Autonomous Soviet Socialist Republic to All Autonomous Republics and Oblasts of the Russian Soviet Federation, October 4, 1920][9]

. . .

We wish to point out the special task which results from the location of the Kirghiz republic. Being situated in the Asian borderland, and having close contact with the peoples of the East, we, the Kirghiz, will be the instrument for spreading the revolutionary influence of Russia in the East. We declare that the revolutionary East is passing from unorganized actions to active struggle against the world vultures. In the course of this struggle the ideas of communism will penetrate into all Eastern countries, and will arouse the people of these countries to struggle for their own liberation.

The toiling population of Soviet Kirghizia rallies closely around the red banner of the revolution. In joining the ranks of the Russian Soviet Federation, the Kirghiz [Autonomous] Soviet Socialist Republic hopes to become the school of revolution for the entire East. In this great hour we declare that we shall do everything we can in order to spread the ideas of the communist revolution to the East, and in that way to hasten the approach of the last hour of capitalism. . . .

9

The Red Army "Liberates" Azerbaijan and Imposes Soviet Rule

[Telegram of the Revolutionary War Council of the Eleventh Russian Soviet Army Concerning the Liberation of Baku, April 28, 1920][10]

On April 27 the advance detachment and armored trains of our army reached Baku. The Azerbaijani toiling masses deposed the bourgeois government with the help of the Red Army and established soviet authority. In the course of a few days the valiant units of the Eleventh Army have marched 200 versts[11] and with a lightning blow have prevented the infamous intention of the [Azerbaijani] bourgeoisie to destroy, in retreating, the oil wells. This is our special task to commemorate the First of May. Many million puds[12] of crude oil have been captured from the international bourgeoisie and have become the property of the proletariat. The toiling masses of Azerbaijan are greeting the Red Army with joy as their liberator from the yoke of capital. The Red soldiers behave as the worthy sons of the proletarian state.

Long live Soviet Azerbaijan!
Long live the Red Army!

[9] *Obrazovanie S.S.S.R.*, p. 180.
[10] *Leninskii Sbornik*, XXXIV, 292.
[11] One verst is equivalent to 0.66 mile.
[12] One pud is equivalent to 36.11 pounds.

10

Directives to the Red Army in Menshevik Georgia

[Lenin's Wire to the Revolutionary War Council of the Eleventh Army,
March 1921][13]

In view of the fact that the units of the N army[14] are now stationed on the
territory of Georgia, you are advised to establish full contact with the Revolutionary
Committee of Georgia and follow strictly the directives of this Committee. You are
advised not to resort to any measures which might go against the interests of the
population, without first making contact with the Georgian Revolutionary Committee; you must treat with particular respect the sovereign institutions of Georgia and
behave with courtesy and respect toward the Georgian population. You must immediately issue corresponding directions to all institutions of the [Red] Army, including
the Special Section. Make all persons who break these directives responsible [for
their actions]. Inform us of every such case of transgression, or of even the smallest
difficulty and misunderstanding with the local population.

11

Directives to Communist Party Leaders in Menshevik Georgia

[Lenin's Letter of G. K. Ordzhonikidze, March 2, 1921][15]

Please convey to the Georgian Communists, and particularly to all members of
the Georgian Revolutionary Committee, my hearty welcome to Soviet Georgia. I ask
you particularly to let me know whether you have reached an agreement on these
three points:

First, it is imperative immediately to arm the workers and the poorest peasants
for the organization of a strong Georgian Red Army.

Second, a special policy of concessions to the Georgian intelligentsia and petty
traders is absolutely necessary. It is imperative to understand that it is not profitable
to nationalize them [i.e., their enterprises], and it is necessary to sacrifice [certain
principles] to improve their position and keep their trade alive.

Third, it is extremely important to seek an acceptable compromise with Zhordaniia[16] and other Georgian Mensheviks who, before the revolt, were not absolutely
hostile to the idea of a soviet order in Georgia under certain circumstances.

I ask you to remember that the internal and international situation of Georgia
demands from the Georgian Communists an efficient and pliable organization and
tactics based on greater complaisance with all sorts of petty bourgeois elements [than
is permitted in Russia], and not on the application of standard Russian rules.

Awaiting your answer,

LENIN

[13] Lenin, *Sochineniia*, XXVI, 188.
[14] Russian N stands for English *x*.
[15] Lenin, *Sochineniia*, XXVI, 187–88.
[16] N. N. Zhordaniia was leader of Georgian Mensheviks and president of the Georgian
Menshevik government, 1918–21.

12

Lenin's Instructions for Cautious Sovietization of Transcaucasia

[Letter to the Communist Comrades of Azerbaijan, Georgia, Armenia, Daghestan, and the Mountaineers' Republic, April 14, 1921][17]

In sending heartfelt greetings to the soviet republics of the Caucasus, I take the opportunity to express the hope that their close union will provide an example of peace among nationalities as yet unknown and impossible under the bourgeois regime.

But although peace among the workers and peasants of the Caucasian nationalities is extremely important, the preservation and development of the Soviet government as a transitory state to socialism is still more important. The task is difficult but realizable. In order to accomplish it the Communists of Transcaucasia must understand the *peculiarity of the situation of their republics, which is different from the situation and conditions of the R.S.F.S.R.* It is imperative for our Transcaucasian Communists *to understand that they should not copy our tactics, but should carefully modify them to conform to their conditions.*

[First:] The Soviet republic in Russia was not given any political or military support; on the contrary, she fought for years against the armed invasions and blockades of the Entente.

The soviet republics of the Caucasus have received political and some military support from the R.S.F.S.R. This makes the situation completely different.

Second: There is no need now to fear that the Entente's intervention will be launched and military support will be given to the Georgian, Azerbaijani, Armenian, Daghestani, or Mountaineers' White Guardists. The Entente has "burned its fingers" in Russia, and for the time being it will be more careful.

Third: The Caucasian republics, even more than Russia, are peasant countries.

Fourth: Economically Russia has to a considerable extent been cut off from the advanced capitalist countries; *the Caucasus is able to make "contact" and to exchange goods with the capitalist West more quickly and easily.*

These are not all the differences, but they are enough to show that new tactics must be applied.

. . .

This policy should be pursued on a broad scale, efficiently and cautiously. Side by side with it there should be an improvement in the position of the workers and peasants, and the intelligentsia should be attracted to the building up of the country's economy. The exchange of commodities with Italy, America, and other countries must serve for the extensive development of the productive forces, such as white coal and irrigation, of the rich region. *The development of irrigation is particularly important in order at any cost to raise the level of agriculture and cattle breeding.*

A slower, more careful, more systematic transition to socialism should be the policy of the Caucasian republics, in contradistinction to the R.S.F.S.R. This policy must be understood and carried out.

We have been the first to force a breach in world capitalism. This primary task has been accomplished. We have succeeded in defending ourselves by conducting a terrible, unnatural, and extremely difficult and painful war against the Whites, the S.R.'s, the Mensheviks, who were supported by the Entente's military assistance and blockade.

You, comrades, Caucasian Communists, are not expected to make a breach, but you must create carefully and systematically new conditions, making use of the ad-

[17] Lenin, *Sochineniia*, XXVI, 191–92.

vantageous international situation of this year (1921). The situation in Europe and in all countries of the world is not the same now as it was in 1917 and 1918.

* * *

[Lenin repeats his admonition not to copy Soviet tactics, to make use of the capitalists, and to improve the situation of the peasants by electrification and irrigation.]

I apologize for the careless manner in which this letter is written, but I was obliged to write it hastily, in order to send it with Comrade Miasnikov. I send once more my best greetings and wishes to the workers and peasants of the soviet republics of the Caucasus.

N. LENIN

13

Independence and Interdependence of the Transcaucasian and Russian Republics

[Explanation by Ordzhonikidze at the Meeting of the Tiflis Organizations of the Communist Party of Georgia, December [?], 1921][18]

* * *

Under the tsarist government a struggle went on here [in the Caucasus] between Russia and Britain for the right to control and to exploit the peoples of the East. Under Soviet Russia, a struggle is taking place here between revolution and counterrevolution for influence over the Eastern peoples. . . . The inexorable march of history calls for a clear answer: either with the counterrevolution or with the revolution. There is no middle course.

We are likely to be asked: What kind of independence is there under the soviet government? Does it not mean from what has been said that there can be no question of Georgian independence under the soviet government? And if this is so, why all this talk about independent Georgia? Whom are you trying to deceive, and why?

We declare most sincerely and most emphatically that we are for the independence of the workers and peasants of Georgia, as well as of all Transcaucasia. We are irreconcilably hostile to every act of oppression of the toiling masses of Georgia and to dependence on counterrevolution. We are for the fullest development of the nationalities of Transcaucasia—of Georgians, Armenians, and Azerbaijani. We are in favor of the development of their language, their native culture, and their liberties. We sincerely desire these peoples to organize their own internal life as they wish. We are ready to defend the independence of these peoples with our own blood in case their frontiers are threatened. . . .

We understand the independence of these republics as an absolute independence from counterrevolution. At the same time, we consider that independence of the soviet republics from each other, and from the world revolution, is absolutely impossible.

The interests of the soviet republics are inseparably intermixed. A small blow given to a small soviet republic is a blow to all soviet republics. Soviet republics form an unbreakable revolutionary union of the toiling masses encircled by foes. Without mutual economic and military assistance the soviet republics cannot exist. It would be enough for certain soviet republics to become isolated for only twenty-four hours, and they would be crushed immediately by the encircling enemies.

Let us take Soviet Georgia. Can it possibly exist without Russian bread? Can it exist without Azerbaijani oil? Can it defend its frontiers without the Russian

---

[18] *Zhizn Natsionalnostei,* No. 31 (129), No. 31 (129), December 31, 1921, p. 2.

Red Army? Can it organize its own Georgian army without the help of the Russian Red Army? Can Armenia and Azerbaijan exist without the port of Batum and Russian bread? Does not Soviet Russia need Baku oil as man needs air? Can we possibly speak of the re-establishment of our industries while the Donets Basin is in a ruinous state, without Baku oil? And if now, in the Donets Basin, the output of coal has increased from nine million puds in August to forty-six million, is this increase not due to Baku oil, which we have been using temporarily as fuel? And is not the rise in the output of Baku oil from ten million puds in the summer to fourteen and fifteen million now due to Russian bread and gold? How can one speak of the absence of economic ties between the soviet republics of Transcaucasia and Russia? . . . Thousands of similar examples could be given. But even these few demonstrate clearly enough that once Georgia had thrown off the shameful yoke of world counterrevolution and had become a soviet country, it had irrevocably bound its destiny with the soviet world. Besides, Georgia is completely independent in the domain of its own internal organization, in the use of its native language, literature, and culture; it is completely independent of counterrevolution, while there is an unbreakable political and economic connection between it and all existing soviet republics. This connection is absolutely necessary and inevitable. The common lot, the common misfortune, and the common fortune of all soviet republics must be shared by Georgia if it does not wish to find itself again in the dark camp of counterrevolution.

That is how we understand independence . . . The above-mentioned considerations have brought us to the decision of creating a federation of Transcaucasian republics among themselves and also with Russia. [He goes on to speak of the animosity which had existed between the three peoples of Transcaucasia during the rule of the national governments recently overthrown, and of the necessity of doing away with all signs of national chauvinism.] . . .

There is still another objection which the S.R.'s and Mensheviks advance: How is it that this [i.e., the federation of the three Transcaucasian republics] has been announced by the Caucasian Bureau of the V.K.P. [i.e., the All-Russian Communist Party], and not by the Central Committee of [the Communist Party of] Georgia? And some people loudly say: "How is it that we are being ordered about by the Caucasian Bureau, since the latter is the organ of the Central Committee of the V.K.P.? Does this not mean that the directives come from the Russian Communist Party, that no attention is paid to us, and that we are being ordered about? How can you then talk about an independent republic of Georgia?"

Allow me now to explain. We are all members of the Russian [*rossiiskaia*] Communist Party, and the Communist parties of Georgia, of Azerbaijan, and of Armenia are composite parts of the Russian Communist Party. We take part in the All-Russian congresses of the party; we are an integral part of the R.K.P. The Central Committee of the R.K.P. is the supreme party organ of our party. And if the Central Committee were to give a directive regarding the federation of the Transcaucasian republics, the Georgian Communists would, of course, consider it neither an offense nor a humiliation. However, I declare that the Central Committee of the R.K.P. has not given any directive on this point, and that it has not as yet been informed of the decision of the Caucasian Bureau. [On the other hand] the Caucasian Bureau consists of the Caucasian people only . . . [Here he gives names, and goes on to argue that if a directive for federation had been issued by the Georgian Central Committee of the Communist Party, the Azerbaijani and Armenian nationalists would immediately have objected to it.]

Why then all this idle talk; and is this really the crux of the matter? The crux of the matter lies in the nature of the federation. The nationalists of all three republics hate each other; they are bitterly against federation. But we, the Communists, the Georgians, Armenians, and Azerbaijani who are the members of the Russian Communist Party, must be proud that our Russian Communist Party is the founder of the Third International, the headquarters of the world revolution, and that in spite of the hissing and howling of the nationalists of Azerbaijan, Armenia, and Georgia, we shall firmly and undeviatingly carry out the will of our party, and of the toiling masses of all the soviet republics.

14

Stalin Answers Georgian Communist Opposition Complaints

[Excerpt from Speech at the Twelfth Party Congress, April 19, 1923][19]

. . . [Comrade Mdivani] spoke here of the vacillations of the Central Committee [in the solution of the problem of the organization of the Transcaucasian soviet republics] : that is to say, today a decision is made to unify the economic efforts of the three republics of Transcaucasia; tomorrow a decision is made to join these republics in a federation; and the day after, a third decision is made, namely, to unite all the soviet republics into a union of republics. This is called vacillation on the part of the Central Committee. But is this vacillation? No, comrades, this is not vacillation; this is a system. At first the independent republics were brought together on an economic basis. This step was undertaken as early as 1921. After the results of such co-operation among the republics proved beneficial, a second step was made, namely, unification into a federation. In a region such as Transcaucasia, a special organization to maintain national peace is absolutely necessary. You know that in Transcaucasia Azerbaijani-Armenian massacres took place under the Tsar, and that under the regime of Mussavats, Dashnaks, and Mensheviks, a war was fought. To end this wrangle, an organization of national peace was needed, i.e., a supreme authority which could say the last word. The creation of such an organization of national peace without the Georgian nationality would be absolutely impossible. Consequently, a few months after the economic unification the next step was taken, namely, the federation of the republics, and a year later, a third and final measure, the creation of the union of republics. Where do you see vacillations in this procedure? This is our national policy system. Although he considers himself an Old Bolshevik, Comrade Mdivani has simply failed to understand the essence of our national policy.

He put a number of questions, implying that the most important questions pertaining to the national problems of Transcaucasia, and especially Georgia, are being decided not by the Central Committee but by separate individuals. The basic question for Transcaucasia is the question of federation. Allow me to read some brief documents which will tell you the history of the directive of the Central Committee of the Russian Communist Party in regard to Transcaucasian federation.

On November 28, 1921, Comrade Lenin sent me a draft of his plan for the formation of the federation of Transcaucasian republics. This draft stated: (1) "To consider the federation of the Transcaucasian republics absolutely correct in principle, and absolutely necessary, but in so far as its immediate application, to consider it untimely and requiring several weeks for discussion and propaganda, and for carrying it out from below; (2) To instruct the Central Committee of Georgia, Armenia, and Azerbaijan to carry out this decision." Thereupon I wrote to Comrade Lenin and suggested that he not hurry with this plan, but wait, to give the local workers a certain period of time in which to carry out the proposed federation. I wrote to

[19] Stalin, *Sochineniia,* V, 227–30.

him: "Comrade Lenin, I have nothing to say against your resolution if you agree to introduce the following amendment: instead of the words 'requiring several weeks for discussion,' to state 'requiring a certain period of time for discussion,' etc. The fact of the matter is, that 'to carry out' federation in Georgia 'from below' in a 'soviet manner' in 'several weeks' is impossible since the soviets in Georgia are just beginning to be organized. They are as yet not fully constructed. A month ago there were none, and to convene a Congress of Soviets there within 'several weeks' is impossible, while federation without Georgia would be a federation on paper. I believe that we must take two to three months in order that the idea of federation might win the broad masses of Georgia. STALIN." Comrade Lenin, on his part, replied: "I accept your amendments." A day later this resolution was passed by Lenin, Trotsky, Kamenev, Molotov, and Stalin. Zinoviev was away, and Molotov replaced him. This decision was taken by the Politburo in late 1921, as you see, unanimously. The struggle of the group of Georgian Communists headed by Comrade Mdivani against the directive of the Central Committee on federation started after that time. You see, comrades, that the point here was not as Comrade Mdivani tried to represent it. . . .

15

The Formation of the Union of Soviet Socialist Republics as a Step Toward a World Soviet Socialist Republic

[Declaration Passed by the First Congress of Soviets of the U.S.S.R., December 30, 1922][20]

Since the formation of the soviet republics, the states of the world have been divided into two camps—the camp of capitalism, and the camp of socialism.

In the camp of capitalism we find national animosity, inequality, colonial servitude and chauvinism, national oppression, pogroms, and imperialist brutalities.

Here, in the camp of socialism, we find mutual trust and peace, national freedom and equality, peaceful coexistence and fraternal co-operation among peoples.

For scores of years the capitalists have attempted to settle the problem of minorities, and to combine the free development of peoples with the exploitation of man by man; but their attempts have proved futile. Instead, the web of national contradictions has grown more and more tangled and now threatens the very existence of capitalism itself. The bourgeoisie has proved incapable of organizing co-operation among peoples.

Only in the soviet camp, only under the dictatorship of the proletariat, which has rallied the majority of the population, have the uprooting of national oppression, the creation of conditions of mutual trust, and the laying down of a foundation for fraternal co-operation among peoples proved possible. Solely because of these circumstances were the soviet republics successful in repelling the attacks of the imperialist world, both foreign and domestic; solely because of these circumstances were they successful in bringing the civil war to a victorious conclusion, in making their own existence secure, and in starting peaceful economic reconstruction.

But the years of war did not pass without leaving a deep imprint. Fields have been devastated, factories closed, productive facilities destroyed, and economic re-

[20] Kliuchnikov and Sabanin, III, 225–26; this declaration was incorporated as Section One into the Constitution of the U.S.S.R., which was confirmed and put into force by the Central Executive Committeee of the U.S.S.R., July 6, 1923, and finally made law by the Second Congress of the Soviets of the U.S.S.R., January 31, 1924. The text of the Constitution appears in *Obrazovanie S.S.S.R.,* pp. 422–34.

sources exhausted. This heritage of war has made insufficient the separate efforts of the individual republics to plan their economic reconstruction. The re-establishment of the national economy has proved to be impossible during the separate existence of these republics. At the same time, the instability of the international situation and the danger of new attacks have made the creation of one united front among the soviet republics inevitable, if capitalist encirclement is to be averted. Furthermore, the construction of the soviet government itself, international in its class nature, leads the toiling masses of the Soviet republics to join together in one socialist family.

All these circumstances make imperative the unification of the soviet republics into one union state capable of guaranteeing safety from foreign attack, and capable of guaranteeing well-being at home, as well as freedom for the national development of the peoples.

The peoples of the soviet republics met recently at the congresses of their respective soviets and unanimously adopted resolutions to form a Union of Soviet Socialist Republics. Their will serves as reliable proof of the voluntary nature of the union of the peoples exercising equal rights. The resolutions ensure to every republic the right of free secession from the union, and indicate that membership in the union is open to all other soviet socialist republics, present and future. This unanimous will of the peoples likewise shows that the new union state will prove to be a worthy expression of the basic principles of peaceful coexistence and fraternal co-operation among peoples laid down in October 1917. The union will serve as a true bulwark against world capitalism and will be a new and decisive step on the path to the unification of the toilers of all countries into a World Soviet Socialist Republic.

While making this declaration to the peoples of the world—and while solemnly proclaiming the inviolability of the principles of the soviet government which have found expression in the constitutions of the soviet socialist republics whose representatives we are—we, the delegates of these republics, by authority vested in us, sign the treaty decreeing the formation of the Union of Soviet Socialist Republics.

16

The Causes of the Unification of the Soviet Republics and the Purposes of the Union

[Declaration of the Central Executive Committee of the U.S.S.R. to All Peoples and All Governments of the World, July 13, 1923][21]

From the first day of their existence, the soviet republics were united in close co-operation and mutual assistance, which later took the form of treaties of alliance. The governments of workers and peasants were bound together by a common need to repulse the attacks of the capitalist states from without, and the counterrevolutionary attempts on the soviet regime from within. The solidarity of the toilers welded them together in the common task of bringing about fraternal collaboration of the liberated peoples. Together they emerged from the victorious proletarian revolution by which the authority of landlords and capitalists was overthrown. These republics likewise bore together the heavy historical trials of intervention and blockade, and withstood them victoriously. Later, after a period of unprecedented calamity, they began together a tremendous task—to reconstruct their national economy on the basis of the new economic regime.

[21] Kliuchnikov and Sabanin, III, 278–80.

For a long time, though rendering continual mutual fraternal assistance with all the forces and means at their disposal, the republics remained separate states united by treaties of alliance. But the development of their relations, and the requirements resulting from the international situation, have brought them to unite in one union state.

The growth of world reaction, the aggressive designs of the imperialist governments, and the danger of new attacks deriving therefrom, have made inevitable the unification of the defensive forces of all the soviet republics under one union leadership.

The economic reconstruction of the soviet republics, which have been devastated by war, intervention, and blockade, is too strenuous a task unless the efforts of all are united. Success will be possible only under the planned leadership of one economic center for the whole union. The nature of the workers' and peasants' government, during the gradual development and consolidation of the new regime in the soviet republics, has prompted them in ever-increasing measure to unite and to join their efforts, directed as they are at one and the same goal.

The peoples of these republics decided recently and unanimously, at their respective congresses, to form a Union of Soviet Socialist Republics—i.e., one union state. This union of the peoples, all exercising equal rights, is a voluntary union in which there is no room for national oppression—a union which cannot compel any separate peoples to remain within the fold, and which leaves to each republic the right to secede. This union is open to the voluntary inclusion of any other soviet socialist republic which now exists, or which, in the future, may come to exist.

On July 6 [1923], the declaration and the treaty adopted by the soviet republics, which had decided to form a union, were confirmed and put into force by the Central Executive Committee of the Union.

In view of the necessity for the soviet republics to unite their efforts in defense against outside attack, one All-Union War and Navy People's Commissariat has been formed.

In view of the similarity of tasks and needs of the soviet republics, against which the capitalist states are aligned, one All-Union People's Commissariat of Foreign Affairs has been formed.

Because in their trade with foreign countries the soviet republics need complete centralization on the basis of state monopoly in order to defend themselves from the attempts of the capitalist states to enslave them, it has been necessary to create our All-Union People's Commissariat for Foreign Trade. [An All-Union People's Commissariat of Ways and Communications was likewise to be formed. The national economy, finance, and workers' and peasants' inspection were to be controlled both by an all-union center and locally.]

The unity of the will of the toiling masses of the whole union is expressed in its supreme organ, the All-Union Congress of Soviets; but at the same time, each nationality is given special representation in the Council of Nationalities, which, in its work, collaborates on an equal basis with the Union Council elected by the Congress.

A union state, created in this way on the basis of fraternal co-operation among the peoples of the soviet republics, has as its goal the maintenance of lasting peace among its peoples. The nationalities all exercising equal rights, hand in hand, in close co-operation and with joint effort, will progress in the development of their own culture and well-being while fulfilling the tasks of the toilers' government.

As the natural ally of all oppressed peoples, the Union of Soviet Socialist Republics seeks peaceful and fraternal relations and economic co-operation with all peoples. The Union of Soviet Socialist Republics has as its aim the promotion of the interests of the toilers throughout the world. In the huge territory which stretches from the Baltic, Black, and White Seas to the Pacific, the Union is applying the principle of fraternity among peoples and of prosperity for labor. At the same time, it is seeking to promote fraternal co-operation among the peoples of the whole world.

17

The Right of National Self-Determination Is Subordinate to the Right of the Workers to Unite and Consolidate Their Dictatorship

[Excerpts from Speeches by Stalin at the Twelfth Party Congress, April 23 and 25, 1923][22]

. . .

As to the international significance of the national question, you know, comrades, that we, the Soviet federation, by the will of historical destiny, now represent the vanguard of the world revolution. You know that we were the first to break through the general capitalist front. You know that by the will of destiny we found ourselves at the forefront [of the revolution]. You know that in our advance we went as far as Warsaw, that we then retreated, entrenching ourselves in the positions we considered strongest. From that moment we passed to the New Economic Policy, from that moment we realized that the international revolutionary movement was slowing down, and from that moment our policy changed from an offensive to a defensive policy. We could not advance after we had failed at Warsaw (we shall not hide the truth) ; we could not advance, for we would have risked being cut off from our base, which in our case is a peasant base; and, lastly, we would have risked advancing too far ahead of the reserves of the revolution with which destiny has provided us, the reserves of the West and the East. That is why we made a turn within the country toward the New Economic Policy, and outside the country toward a slower rate of advance; for we decided that we needed a breathing space, that we must heal our wounds, the wounds received by the vanguard, the proletariat; that we must establish contact with the peasant base, and continue to prosecute our work among the reserves, which had fallen behind us—the reserves of the West and the reserves of the East, the heavy reserves which form the main rear-line reserves of world capitalism. It is of these reserves—the heavy reserves [of the East], which at the same time continue to be the rear-line of world imperialism—that we must speak when discussing the national question.

Two things are possible; either we succeed in stirring up and revolutionizing the far imperialist rear—the colonial and semicolonial countries of the East—and thereby hasten the fall of capitalism, or we fail and thereby strengthen imperialism and weaken the force of our movement. That is how the question stands.

The fact of the matter is that the whole East regards our union of republics as an experiment station. Either we shall, within the union, find a correct solution for the national problem in its practical application and establish truly fraternal relations and true collaboration between the peoples—in which case the entire East will see that our federation is the banner of its liberation, an advance guard, in whose steps it must follow—and that will be the beginning of the collapse of world imperialism; or we, the federation as a whole, shall commit errors, undermine the confidence of the formerly oppressed peoples in the proletariat of Russia, and deprive the union of republics of that power of attraction which it possesses in the eyes of the East—in which case imperialism will win and we shall lose.

. . .

[22] Stalin, *Sochineniia,* V, 236–38 ; 264–66.

It is clear to us, as Communists, that the basis of all our work must be to strengthen the power of the workers; and only then do we address ourselves to the other question—a very important question, but subordinate to the first—the national question. . . . It is clear that the political basis of the dictatorship of the proletariat consists mainly and primarily of the central, the industrial regions, and not the border regions, which are peasant countries. If we overemphasize the peasant border regions at the expense of the proletarian districts, a fissure in the system of the dictatorship of the proletariat may result. This is dangerous, comrades. . . .

It should be borne in mind that besides the right of nations to self-determination there is also the right of the working class to consolidate its power, and to this latter right the right of self-determination is subordinate. There are occasions when the right of self-determination conflicts with the other, the higher right—the right of the working class that has assumed power to consolidate its power. In such cases—this must be said bluntly—the right to self-determination cannot and must not serve as an obstacle to the exercise by the working class of its right to dictatorship. The former must give way to the latter. That, for instance, was the case in 1920, when in order to defend the power of the working class we were obliged to march on Warsaw.

It must not, therefore, be forgotten, when showering all sorts of promises upon nationals and bowing before the representatives of nationalities, as some comrades have done at this Congress, that the sphere of action in the national question, its competence, so to speak, is limited—in view of our external and internal conditions—by the sphere of action and competence in the "workers' question," which is the basis of all questions. . . .

In examining Marx's letter on the national question in his article on self-determination, Comrade Lenin draws the following conclusion:

"In comparison with the 'workers' question,' the subordinate position of the national question is, in the opinion of Marx, unquestionable."

Here are only two lines, but they solve everything. And this should be well remembered by our overzealous comrades. . . .

18

Excerpt From the Theses on the National and Colonial Questions

[Final Draft of Lenin's Theses Adopted at the Second Congress of the Communist International, July–August, 1920][23]

. . . .

3. The imperialist war of 1914–18 has clearly demonstrated to all nations and to all the oppressed classes of the world the deceitfulness of bourgeois-democratic phraseology. The war that was carried on by both sides under the false slogan of the liberation of peoples and the right of nations for self-determination, has shown through the Brest-Litovsk and Bukharest treaties on the one hand, and the Versailles and Saint-Germain treaties on the other, how unceremoniously the victorious bourgeoisie determine "national" boundaries in conformity with their own economic interests. "National" boundaries are, to the bourgeoisie, nothing but market com-

---

[23] *Vtoroi Kongress Kominterna,* pp. 491–95; also appeared in English: *The Second Congress of the Communist International; Report of Proceedings of Petrograd Session of July 17th and of Moscow Sessions of July 19th–August 7th, 1920,* pp. 571–75. (Hereafter cited as *Second Congress of the Communist International.*)

modities. The so-called "League of Nations" is nothing but an insurance policy in which the victors mutually guarantee each other their prey. The striving for the restoration of national unity and for the "reunion of alienated territories" is, according to the bourgeois notion, nothing but an attempt of the vanquished to gather forces for new wars.

The reunion of nationalities artificially torn apart also corresponds to some extent to the interests of the proletariat, but real national freedom and unity can be achieved by the proletariat only through revolutionary struggle and the overthrow of the bourgeoisie. The League of Nations, as well as the entire policy pursued by the imperialist Entente since the end of the war, demonstrates this even more clearly and definitely, intensifying everywhere the revolutionary struggle of both the proletariat in the advanced countries and all the toiling masses in colonial and dependent countries. The imperialist policy speeds the breakdown of the Philistine nationalist illusions concerning the possibility of peaceful collaboration and the equality of nations under capitalism.

4. From the fundamental principles laid down above, it is apparent that the chief emphasis in the Communist International in regard to national and colonial questions must be to draw together the proletariat and the toiling masses of all nations and countries for a joint revolutionary struggle which will lead to the overthrow of landowners and bourgeoisie, for only such a union can assure that victory over capitalism without which national inequality and oppression cannot be abolished.

5. The political situation of the world at the present time has placed the question of the dictatorship of the proletariat in the foreground, and all the events in world politics are inevitably concentrated around one central point—namely, the struggle of the world bourgeoisie against the Russian Soviet republic. This republic is inevitably bound to gather around itself the soviet movements of the advanced workers of all countries, as well as all the national-liberation movements of the colonial and oppressed peoples. These people have been learning through bitter experience that there can be no salvation for them except in a union with the revolutionary proletariat and in the triumph of soviet power over world imperialism.

6. Consequently, we must not content ourselves now with a mere recognition or declaration concerning the unity of the toilers of different nations; we must carry out a policy designed to bring about the closest union between Soviet Russia and all the national and colonial liberation movements. We must determine the structure of this union in accordance with the stage of development of the communist movement among the proletariat of each country, or of the revolutionary liberation movements of backward countries and backward nationalities.

7. Federation is a transitional stage toward the complete union of the toilers of all nations. Federation has already proved its efficacy in practice in the relations of the R.S.F.S.R. and the other soviet republics (Hungarian, Finnish, and Latvian in the past, and Azerbaijani and Ukrainian at present). Within the R.S.F.S.R., federation has also been effective for those nationalities which had had neither national existence nor autonomy (for example, the autonomous republics of Bashkirs and Tatars which were formed within the R.S.F.S.R. in 1919 and 1920).

8. It is the task of the Communist International in this regard to study and to test by experience these federations which have arisen out of the soviet order and the soviet movement, as well as to develop them further. Recognizing federation as a transitional stage toward complete union, we must strive for ever closer federative connection, bearing in mind first, that without a close union of the soviet republics it will be impossible to defend them, surrounded as they are by the imperialist nations of the world, which are much more powerful militarily; second, that without a close economic union of the soviet republics, the restoration and development of the productive forces which were destroyed by imperialism and the ensuring of the

welfare of the workers are impossible. Third, we must strive for the creation of a unified world economy based on a general plan and regulated by the proletariat of all the nations of the world. This tendency has already appeared under capitalism, and must certainly be developed and brought to final completion under socialism.

. . .

11. In regard to the more backward countries and nations, with prevailing feudal or patriarchal and patriarchal-peasant relations, it is especially necessary to bear in mind the following:

(a) All communist parties must give active support to the revolutionary liberation movements in these countries. The type of support shall be studied by the party in every country where there is one. This duty of giving active support is to be imposed, in the first place, on the workers of those countries on whom the subject nation is dependent in a colonial or financial way;

(b) A struggle must be carried on against reactionary and medieval influences of the clergy, Christian missions and other similar elements;

(c) It is also necessary to combat the Pan-Islamic and Pan-Asiatic movements and similar tendencies which aim at combining the cause of the liberation movements directed against the European and American imperialists with the efforts to consolidate the power of Turkish and Japanese imperialism, or the power of nobility, large-scale landowners, clergy, etc.;

(d) In backward countries it is especially important to support the peasant movements against the landowners, large-scale land ownership, and all feudal survivals. One must strive to give the peasant movements the most revolutionary character by organizing in so far as possible the peasants and all the exploited into soviets, and by doing so bring about the closest possible union between the communist proletariat of Western Europe and the revolutionary peasant movements of the East, in the colonies, and in the backward countries in general;

(e) It is likewise necessary to fight the attempts to cloak with communist garb the revolutionary movements for liberation in the backward countries which are not truly communist. It is the duty of the Communist International to support the revolutionary movements in the colonies and in the backward countries, for the exclusive purpose of grouping together the various elements of the future proletarian parties (those who are communist in more than name) in all the backward countries, and educating them to the consciousness of their specific tasks—i.e., the tasks of fighting the bourgeois-democratic tendencies within their respective nationalities. The Communist International must be ready to establish temporary relationships and even alliances with the bourgeois democracy of the colonies and backward countries. It must not, however, amalgamate with it. It must retain the independent character of the proletarian movement, even though this movement be in the embryonic stage. . . .

19

Supplementary Theses on the National and Colonial Questions Presented to the Second Congress of the Communist International by M. N. Roy[24]

1. One of the most important questions before the Second Congress of the Third International is to determine more specifically the relationship of the Communist

[24] *Vtoroi Kongress Kominterna*, pp. 496–99; also *Second Congress of the Communist International*, pp. 576–79.

International to the revolutionary movements in countries dominated by capitalist imperialism—for example, China and India. The history of the world revolution has entered a phase in which a proper understanding of this relationship is imperative. The great European war and its results have demonstrated clearly that because of the centralization of world capitalism, the masses in the non-European dependent countries are inseparably connected with the proletarian movement in Europe. This was demonstrated, for example, by the sending of colonial troops as well as whole armies of workers to the battlefront during the war, etc.

2. One of the main sources from which European capitalism draws its basic strength is in the colonial possessions and dependencies. Without control of the extensive markets and vast areas for exploitation in the colonies, the capitalist powers of Europe would not be able to exist even for a short time. . . . By enslaving the hundreds of millions of inhabitants of Asia and Africa, English imperialism has succeeded in keeping the British proletariat under the domination of the bourgeoisie.

3. Super-profit obtained from the colonies is the mainstay of modern capitalism. It will not be easy for the European working class to overthrow the capitalist order until the latter is deprived of this source of super-profit. . . . By exploiting the masses in the colonies, European imperialism is in a position to make concession after concession to the labor aristocracy at home. . . .

4. The breakdown of colonial rule, together with the proletarian revolution in the home countries, will overthrow the capitalist system in Europe. Consequently, the Communist International must widen the sphere of its activities. It must establish contact with those revolutionary forces which are working for the overthrow of imperialism in the politically and economically subjugated countries. In order to ensure the final success of the world revolution, the co-ordination of these two forces is imperative.

5. The Communist International is the concentrated will of the world revolutionary proletariat. Its mission is to organize the working class of the whole world for the overthrow of the capitalist order and for the establishment of communism. The Third International is a fighting organization which must assume the task of uniting the revolutionary forces of all the countries of the world. . . .

6. Foreign imperialism, by imposing its will on the Eastern peoples, has prevented them from developing socially and economically along with the peoples of Europe and America. Because of the imperialistic policy of preventing industrial development in the colonies, a proletarian class, in the strict sense of the word, could not come into existence there until recently. . . .

7. Two distinct movements which grow farther apart every day are to be found in the dependent countries. One is the bourgeois-democratic nationalist movement, with a program of political independence under the bourgeois order. The other is the mass struggle of the poor and ignorant peasants and workers for their liberation from various forms of exploitation. The former endeavor to control the latter, and often succeed to a certain extent. But the Communist International and the constituent parties must struggle against such control, and help develop the class-consciousness of the working masses in the colonies. In order to overthrow foreign capitalism, which is the first step toward a revolution in the colonies, it would be profitable to make use of the co-operation of the bourgeois national-revolutionary elements.

But the foremost and immediate task is to form communist parties which will organize the peasants and workers and lead them to the revolution and to the establishment of soviet republics. Thus the masses in the backward countries may reach communism not through capitalist development, but through the leadership of the class-conscious proletariat of the advanced capitalist countries.

8. The revolutionary strength of the liberation movements in the colonies is no

longer confined to the narrow circle of bourgeois-democratic nationalists. In most of the colonies there already exist organized revolutionary parties which try to keep in close contact with the working masses. . . .

9. In its first stages, the revolution in the colonies is not going to be a communist revolution. But if, from the outset, the leadership is in the hands of a communist vanguard, the revolutionary masses will be on the right road toward their goal, and they will gradually achieve revolutionary experience. Indeed, in many of the Eastern countries, it would be extremely unwise to try to solve the agrarian problem according to pure communist principles. In its first stages, the revolution in the colonies must be carried on under a program which will include many petty bourgeois reforms, such as the division of land, etc. But from this it does not in the least follow that the leadership of the revolution will have to be surrendered to the bourgeois democrats. On the contrary, the proletarian parties must carry on vigorous and systematic propaganda for the idea of soviets, and must organize peasants' and workers' soviets as soon as possible. In co-operation with the soviet republics established in the advanced capitalist countries, these soviets will work for the coming final overthrow of the capitalist order throughout the world.

20

Stalin on Confederation as a Step in the Transition to a World Union of Toilers

[Stalin's Remarks on the Theses on the National and Colonial Questions Drafted by Lenin and Adopted by the Second Congress of the Communist International, July–August, 1920][25]

On June 11, I received your draft of the theses on the national and colonial questions for the Second Congress of the Communist International. I am not able (have no time) at the present moment to comment on the theses in detail, but I would like to comment briefly on one weakness. I mean the absence of any mention of confederation in the theses—confederation as a transition step toward bringing together the toilers of all countries.

For the nations which were a part of old Russia, our (soviet) type of federation can and must be considered as expedient and as leading toward international unity. The reasons for this are self-evident: those nationalities either had no statehood of their own in the past, or lost it long ago, and therefore can be grafted to the soviet (centralized) type of federation without particular difficulties.

This cannot be said, however, of those nationalities which were not a part of the old Russia, but existed as independent entities and developed their own statehood, and which, if they become soviet, will be obliged to adopt one or another type of political relations (connections) with Soviet Russia. For example, consider the future Soviet Germany, Poland, Hungary, Finland. It can hardly be expected that these nations, which have their own sovereignty, their own military and monetary systems, will immediately agree, once they become soviet, to enter into a federation with Soviet Russia on the same basis as the Bashkirs or Ukrainians. In your theses, by the way, you note a difference between the Bashkir and the Ukrainian type of federated connection, whereas actually there is no such difference, or it is so insignificant that it amounts to nothing. But the others [i.e., the formerly independent states] would be inclined to consider a federative union as belittling their political independence, as a threat to that independence.

[25] Lenin, *Sochineniia*, XXV, 624.

I have no doubt that for these latter nationalities a confederation (that is, an alliance of independent states) will be the most acceptable form of union. I do not even mention the backward nationalities, such as, for example, Persia or Turkey, to whom soviet federation, and federation in general, is still less acceptable.

In view of all this, I believe that the paragraph of your theses concerning the means of bringing together different nations must also include (along with federation) *confederation*. Such a correction would make the theses more elastic, and would provide still another transitional step toward bringing together the toilers of different nations. It would also help the nationalities which were not part of old Russia to form a political connection with Soviet Russia.[26]

21

The Decision to Use "National-Revolutionary" Instead of "Bourgeois-Democratic" to Describe Liberation Movements in the Colonies. The Importance of Soviets and the Possibility of Transition from Precapitalism to Communism

[Lenin's Explanations at the Second Congress of the Communist International, July 26, 1920][27]

· · ·

I wish to lay special stress on the question of the bourgeois-democratic movement in the backward countries. This matter was the subject of some controversy. We argued [in the Commission on the National and Colonial Questions] over whether it is proper theoretically and in principle to declare that the Communist International and the Communist parties are bound to support the bourgeois-democratic movements in the backward countries. The result of the discussion was that we came to the unanimous conclusion that we should speak of the national-revolutionary and not of the "bourgeois-democratic" movements.

There is no doubt that every national movement can be only a bourgeois-democratic movement, for the great masses of population in the backward countries are peasants, who represent the bourgeois-capitalist relations. It would be Utopian to suppose that proletarian parties—as far as there is a chance of forming them in such countries—will be in a position to pursue communist tactics and communist

---

[26] The points in Lenin's theses to which Stalin specifically refers read as follows:

6. . . . We must not content ourselves now with a mere recognition or declaration concerning the unity of the toilers of different nations; we must carry out a policy designed to bring about the closest union between Soviet Russia and all the national and colonial liberation movements. We must determine the structure of this union in accordance with the stage of development of the communist movement among the proletariat of each country, or of the revolutionary liberation movements of backward countries and backward nationalities.

7. Federation is a transitional stage toward the complete union of the toilers of all nations. Federation has already proved its efficacy in practice in the relations of the R.S.F.S.R. and the other soviet republics (Hungarian, Finnish, and Latvian in the past, and Azerbaijani and Ukrainian at present). Within the R.S.F.S.R., federation has also been effective for those nationalities which had had neither national existence nor autonomy (for example, the autonomous republics of Bashkirs and the Tatars which were formed within the R.S.F.S.R. in 1919 and 1920). *Vtoroi Kongress Kominterna*, p. 492.

[27] Lenin, *Sochineniia*, XXV, 352–55.

policies without maintaining definite relations with the peasant movement and without supporting it in these countries.

The objection was raised that in speaking of the bourgeois-democratic movement we lose the sense of difference between the reformist and the revolutionary movement. This difference, however, has been made very clear recently in the backward and colonial countries since the imperialist bourgeoisie has been doing everything in its power to create a reformist movement among the oppressed peoples. A certain understanding has been reached between the bourgeoisie of the exploiting countries and that of the colonial countries, so that most often—or rather in the majority of cases—the bourgeoisie of the oppressed countries, though supporting the national movement, nevertheless has collaborated with the imperialist bourgeoisie, that is, has waged a joint struggle with it against all revolutionary movements and revolutionary classes. This was clearly proved in the Commission, and we decided that the only correct move would be to take note of this difference, and to replace the expression "bourgeois-democratic" by the term "national-revolutionary."[28]

The meaning of the above change is that we, as Communists, should support the bourgeois movements of liberation in the colonies only if these are really revolutionary, when those who represent these movements would not oppose us in our efforts to educate and organize the peasantry and the masses of exploited people in general, in the revolutionary spirit. When this is impossible, the Communists must oppose the reformist bourgeoisie, to which, likewise, belong the "heroes" of the Second International. There are already such reformist parties in the colonial countries, and sometimes they call themselves Social Democratic or Socialist. The above distinction has been made clear in all our theses, and therefore, I believe, our point has now been formulated with much more precision.

Another remark I wish to make concerns the question of the peasant soviets. The practical work of the Russian Communists in the former tsarist colonies, in such backward countries as Turkestan and others, has put us face to face with the question of how communist tactics and policies are to be applied to precapitalist conditions. For the most important feature of these countries is that the precapitalist relations still prevail there and that, therefore, there can be no question of a purely proletarian movement in them. There is almost no industrial proletariat in those countries. Nevertheless we assumed and were compelled to assume leadership in these backward regions. Our work there has shown that there are enormous difficulties to be overcome, but the results of our activities have likewise shown that it is possible, in spite of these difficulties, to awaken independent political thought and activity even in the countries where there is almost no proletariat. Our task has been harder for us than it would have been for the comrades of the Western European countries, because the Russian proletariat has been overburdened with problems of state. It goes without saying that peasants who are in a state of semifeudal dependence are quite able to grasp the idea of soviet organization, and also to act upon this idea. It is clear that the oppressed masses in these countries who are exploited not only by commercial capital, but also by the feudal relations of the state, are able to use this weapon, this form of organization [i.e., the soviets] under their own conditions. The idea of soviet organization is a simple one, and it can be applied not only to proletarian conditions but also to feudal and semifeudal peasant relations. Our experience in this field has not been very great, but the discussions in the Commission [on the National and Colonial Questions], in which many representatives of the colonial countries were present, have proved to us quite definitely and absolutely that we must base the theses of the Communist International on the assumption that the peasant soviets, the soviets of the exploited, are applicable not only to capitalist countries but also

[28] It should be noted that in the final text of the "Theses on the National and Colonial Questions" the word "national" was omitted; see our p. 65, Point 11(a).

to the countries of precapitalist conditions, and that it is the absolute duty of the communist parties and of their sympathizers to propagate the idea of peasant soviets, the soviets of the toiling people everywhere, including the backward and colonial countries, and to try, wherever conditions permit, to create peasant soviets or soviets of the toilers.

The above task provides us with a very interesting and important field of practical activity. Our experience is not large as yet, but we shall accumulate more and more material. There can be no argument about the fact that the proletariat of the advanced countries can and must assist the backward toiling masses, and that the development of the backward countries can emerge from its present stage when the victorious proletariat of the soviet republics stretches out a helping hand to these masses, and when it is able to render them its assistance.

We had rather lively debates on this point in the Commission, not only in connection with the theses which I signed, but even more so in connection with the theses of Comrade Roy.[29] . . . [Actually] the question raised was this: Can we recognize as correct the assertion that the capitalist stage of development of national economy is inevitable for those backward nations which are now liberating themselves, and among which a movement toward progress is now, after the war, being observed? We replied to this question in the negative. If the revolutionary victorious proletariat carry on systematic propaganda among these people [i.e., backward colonial people], and if the soviet governments come to their assistance with every means at their disposal, then it would not be correct to suppose that the capitalist stage of development is inevitable for the backward nationalities.

In all colonies and backward countries, we must not only form independent cadres of fighters and party organizations, we must not only carry propaganda for the organization of peasant soviets, and try to adapt them to the precapitalist conditions in these countries. The Communist International must [also] outline and theoretically explain the thesis that, with the help of the proletariat of the more advanced countries, the backward countries can proceed to a soviet regime, and by definite stages of development, to communism, bypassing the capitalist stage of development.

It is impossible to indicate beforehand the means to be used for that purpose; practical experience will show the way. But it has been firmly established that all toiling masses, including those of the remotest nationalities, are close to the idea of soviets, that these soviet organizations must be adapted to precapitalist relationships, and that the work of the Communist parties must start at once in this direction all over the world. . . .

22

The Communist International—General Staff of World Revolution—and Its Colonial Reserves

[Statement by L. B. Kamenev on the Occasion of the Second Congress of the Communist International, July 1920][30]

Bourgeois governments throughout the world have long been accustomed to frightening their Philistine citizens with [accounts of] underground revolutionary conspiracies to bring about a socialist revolution. A conspiracy of the socialist proletariat against world capitalism is unquestionably here. But how different is this

---

[29] For the text of Roy's theses see Document 19.
[30] *Krasnaia Gazeta*, No. 158, July 18, 1920, p. 1.

conspiracy from the pictures drawn by the frightened imagination of petty bourgeois Philistines.

Not in the artificial light of a dark cellar but in the clear light of day, with full publicity from an international tribune, in the face of all mankind, the international proletariat through its best representatives is now discussing plans and tactics for the overthrow of the bourgeois governments of Europe and America. The oppressed masses of all countries are taking part in this conspiracy.

Helpless against this conspiracy, the governments cannot do anything to prevent the general staff of world revolution from calmly discussing the plan of war. The conference is taking place in that fortress of the proletariat which is inaccessible to the old world—that is, in Soviet Russia, which guards the Congress and its work against all attack by a steel circle of proletarians armed and hardened by three years of fighting.

Through its imperialist war and its imperialist peace, world capital unleashed a civil war of the proletariat against the bourgeoisie of all countries of the world. The Communist International takes civil war as the point of departure for all its acts and for all its tactics.

It intends to win this war. It must win this war if it does not wish to be destroyed physically and morally. Victory in this war can mean only one thing—the replacing of the dictatorship of capital, which prevails throughout the world, by the dictatorship of the proletariat.

To win, one must be strong. To be strong, one must be organized. Inasmuch as the war has been declared on an international scale, in order to win, the proletarian army must be organized on an international scale.

But this international organized army of the progressive proletariat of Europe and America has enormous reserves. These reserves are the people of the Orient, oppressed by colonial imperialistic slavery, who have come to understand clearly and feel deeply that they can be liberated from slavery only with assistance and under the flag of the Third International. The Third International is the general staff of this world army, which is on the move and is marching to victory.

Yes, this is a conspiracy. But it is a conspiracy that cannot be crushed, one in which millions participate, which is supported by tens of millions—a conspiracy which embodies the law of history, and which, therefore, is destined to triumph in the end.

PART II

Reopening the Diplomatic and Revolutionary
Window to Asia, 1920–1923

A. COMMUNIST REVOLUTIONARY STRATEGY AND TACTICS FOR ASIA

Soviet Two-Edged Policy in Asia

Lenin saw the colonial East as a vast area vulnerable to communist penetration, an area through which major blows could be struck against the capitalist West. His *Imperialism, the Highest Stage of Capitalism,* together with the "Theses on the National and Colonial Questions" for the Second Congress of the Communist International, laid the theoretical foundation for a practical drive to win the East. This drive took three main lines: from Tashkent toward Afghanistan and India; through Buddhist regions of Mongolia; and by unilateral negotiations with China on both legal and subversive levels. The Russian Communists dealt also with Turkey and Persia, both diplomatically and through the Communist Party apparatus.

Initially the Communist International turned toward Afghanistan and India with the hope of training and employing Russian Muslim agents and "special battalions" to spearhead an eventual communist assault on British colonies and areas of influence in South Asia and the Middle East. It was toward this same end, moreover, that Moscow sought to conclude treaties with Turkey and Persia.

When this approach failed, Russian leaders shifted their emphasis to Mongolia and China, where they met with considerable success. Their strategy in these latter areas resulted (by 1950) in the alienation of all Mongolia, Sinkiang, China, and Tibet to communist control.

But the task of infiltrating the East was complicated by certain realities in the Soviet position. Direct and open incitement was not entirely expedient. There were advantages in arriving at temporary understandings with existing governments in the East. Friendly relations with the more powerful of them were sought in order to gain temporary peace and to facilitate commerce—both of which the Russian Communists badly needed. In the short term, too, such governments, weak or strong, could be used as pawns in diplomatic struggles with Western capitalist powers. Thus, Soviet policy in the East, as in the West, maintained a delicate balance, governed largely by expediency, between legalism and subversion. Meanwhile, of course, the long-range goal was kept always in sight: the undermining and eventual overthrow of the incumbent Eastern governments and the substitution for them of communist-controlled regimes.

India: The Early Communist Goal

The revolutionary importance of the East and the practical tasks to be undertaken in order to bring about revolutions in the Eastern countries were emphasized by various Soviet leaders almost immediately upon their coming to power. Stalin, for example, urged his fellow-communists: "It [the East] must not be forgotten for the reason that it provides inexhaustible reserves and is the most reliable rear for world imperialism. . . . The task of communism is to do away with the century-old slumber of the oppressed peoples of the East, to infect the workers and peasants of these countries with the liberating spirit of the revolution."[1]

It seemed at that early stage that India was to be the first target of communist propaganda. The official organ of the People's Commissariat of Nationalities spoke of it in the following manner: "Marx had foreseen the development of the present events when he said that the communist revolution must be preceded by a number of national revolutions of the oppressed peoples, first of all of India, and the peoples of the East."[2] The Russian Communists believed that the stage had been set for such a national revolution in India.

A certain A. Mashitsky, writing in the official organ of the People's Commissariat of Foreign Affairs, declared:

India is aflame with revolution. Continuous strikes, frequent risings, revolutionary tendencies of various tribes, political work of a newly formed revolutionary party which is definitely leaning toward communist ideology, strong unrest among the people [of India] which often appears like the [beginning of a] revolution—all this indicates that India will play in the near future not the last, but, on the contrary, the most important role in the task of winning the international victory over imperialism by the Great Revolution.[3]

A noted Soviet student of the East emphasized the great power opposition facing Soviet tasks in the East. He wrote of the long-standing antagonism between Russia and Great Britain in Asia and said that Soviet Russia appeared to Great Britain to be even more formidable than the old Russian Empire. Referring to the British fear of a strong and united Russia as a threat to the British hegemony in Persia, in Afghanistan, and especially in India, M. L. Pavlovich wrote: "If the gigantic Russia of the tsars, whose possessions in Asia were continually growing, appeared to Beaconsfield to be the greatest threat to the British Empire, the Russia of the workers' and peasants' soviets is bound to appear all the more dangerous to the present-day British ministers . . . for Soviet Russia enjoys tremendous prestige among the awakening peoples of the East, including those of British India."[4]

The Importance of Turkestan

The Turkestan Muslim population was assigned the task of spreading the revolutionary movement to India and to other Asian countries dominated by Great Britain: "Cossacks' spears appearing on the Himalayan summits," wrote *Zhizn Natsionalnostei*, "were Britain's nightmare in the past. Now these will

[1] *Zhizn Natsionalnostei*, No. 3, November 24, 1918, p. 1; see Document 23.

[2] Paliukaitis [? pseud.], "Turkestan i revoliutsii Vostoka," *Zhizn Natsionalnostei*, No. 19 (27), May 26, 1919, p. 2.

[3] A. Mashitsky, "K istorii revoliutsii v Bukhare," *Vestnik Narodnogo Komissariata po Inostrannym Delam*, No. 3–4, May 15, 1921, pp. 24–25. For more on the Indian revolutionary situation, see our pp. 280–86.

[4] M. L. Veltman (M. Pavlovich), *Sovetskaia Rossiia i kapitalisticheskaia Angliia*, p. 21; see Document 24.

be the spears of the Russian proletarian Muslims who will be coming to the rescue of their brothers in Persia, India, and Afghanistan."[5]

It was in view of the geographical position of Turkestan and the task assigned to this region that Lenin wrote an official letter to the Communists of Turkestan in November 1919, in which he said in part:

The establishment of satisfactory relations with the peoples of Turkestan is for the Russian Socialist Federated Soviet Republic, without exaggeration, of tremendous and world-wide historical significance. The attitude of the Soviet workers' and peasants' republic toward weak and formerly oppressed peoples will have practical effect upon all the peoples of Asia, upon the colonies of the world, upon hundreds of millions of people.[6]

Another Soviet student of the East, S. M. Dimanshtein, said in 1919 of the loss of the Ukraine by the Reds to the Russian White forces: "Our temporary loss of the Ukraine has been offset by an advance in the southeast[7] and by a penetration of the ring of hostile forces which surround us. Our frontiers now touch Khiva, Bukhara, and Afghanistan. From Afghanistan the road leads to Hindustan, the possible key to world revolution, for it is from India that Britain draws a great deal of her strength."[8]

The Role of the Muslims of Russia and the First Congress of the Muslim Communists

The Muslims of Russia were among the primary targets of the Soviet Eastern drive. Because they occupied a pivotal geographical position, it was hoped that their conversion would open the way for the communization of the promised lands of the Near East, India, Southeast Asia, and the Far East. We have noted how, as early as January 1918, a Muslim Commissariat had been established in the Commissariat of Nationalities to direct work among the Muslims of Russia, to counter the antisoviet national movements among them, and to enlist them into the Red Army.[9]

In November 1918, the Communist Party made an official appeal to the Muslims, calling them to a Congress of Muslim Communists in Moscow, which met in the same month. Stalin addressed the gathering, stressing the importance which the Communist International attached to the spread of communism among the Muslims:

No one can erect a bridge between the West and the East as easily and quickly as you can. This is because a door is opened for you to Persia, India, Afghanistan, and China. The liberation of the peoples of these countries from the yoke of the imperialists would ensure freedom for your own country and at the same time would undermine imperialism at its very foundation. That is why I believe that the socialist educa-

---

[5] Paliukaitis, "Turkestan i revoliutsii Vostoka," *Zhizn Natsionalnostei*, No. 19 (27), May 26, 1919, p. 2; see Document 25b.

[6] Lenin, *Sochineniia*, 531; see Document 25a.

[7] This refers to the success of the Red troops against anti-Soviet forces in southeastern Russia which made it possible to establish a junction between Moscow and Communist Turkestan.

[8] S. M. Dimanshtein, "Nashi protivorechiia i Vostok," *Zhizn Natsionalnostei*, No. 36 (44), September 21, 1919, p. 1; see Document 25c.

[9] See our pp. 25–26.

tion of the peoples of the East must be your first task. The Central Committee of the party does not doubt that your conference and your workers locally will honorably fulfill their historic mission.[10]

The Muslim delegates passed resolutions stating that their organizations would call upon the Muslim peoples of the East to rise against international imperialism and declaring their intention to prepare for the revolutionary movement in the East.[11] They also elected a Central Bureau of the Muslim Organizations of the Russian Communist Party (B), i.e., Tsentralnoe Biuro Musulmanskikh Organizatsii Rossiiskoi Kommunisticheskoi Partii (B).

This bureau hastened to issue an appeal to the Muslim Communists emphasizing that their duty was to take active part in the "sacred work" of spreading revolutionary ideas among backward peoples of the East. "With the above in view," the appeal stated, "the Central Bureau of the Muslim Organizations of the Russian Communist Party (B) has decided to organize a Department of International Propaganda." The appeal ended with a statement that "the Central Bureau hopes to spread the ideas of communism quickly in the East and to draw all oppressed peoples into the world laboring family."[12]

The organization of the Department of International Propaganda was entrusted to a Turkish revolutionary, Mustafa Suphi, who was interned in Russia during World War I as an alien, and later became an active organizer of the Turkish Communist Party. This Department soon had twelve sections: Arab, Persian, Turkish, Azerbaijani, Bukharan, Kirghiz, [Caucasus] Mountaineers', Kalmuk, Chinese, Korean, Japanese, and Indian.[13]

In September 1919, the First Congress of the Muslim Communists, meeting in Turkestan, sent a telegram to G. E. Zinoviev, Chairman of the Executive Committee of the Communist International. This dispatch was, in fact, a resolution passed at the Second Extraordinary Conference of the Muslim Communists of Turkestan (September 12, 1919) in connection with the union effected between Central Russia and Turkestan through efforts of the Red Army. Signed by a number of prominent Turkestan Communists including T. R. Ryskulov, the resolution declared: "Soviet Turkestan is becoming a revolutionary school for the whole East. Revolutionaries of neighboring states are coming to us in droves; they are becoming convinced adherents of communism; through them and with their help we are taking all measures for the spread of the communist idea in the East."[14]

The Second Congress of the Muslim Communists

In November 1919 a second Muslim congress was convened in Moscow. This time Stalin declared that the mission of awakening the oppressed people

[10] *Zhizn Natsionalnostei*, No. 3, November 24, 1918, p. 2. The text of the above speech does not appear in Stalin's *Sochineniia*.

[11] *Zhizn Natsionalnostei*, No. 3, November 24, 1918, p. 2.

[12] *Zhizn Natsionalnostei*, No. 5, December 8, 1918, p. 8; see Document 26. The Central Bureau of the Muslim Organizations changed its name in March 1919 to the Central Bureau of the Communist Organizations of the Peoples of the East (Tsentralnoe Biuro Kommunisticheskikh Organizatsii Narodov Vostoka) (*Kommunisticheskii Internatsional*, No. 4, August 1919, pp. 563–64).

[13] See Document 27.

[14] *Kommunisticheskii Internatsional*, No. 5, September 1919, p. 702.

of the East undertaken by the first congress had been accomplished and that imperialism was already in the process of being undermined.[15]

Lenin also addressed the assembled delegates, calling upon them for more intensive and extensive struggle against the imperialist powers and declaring that the civil war of the workers against the exploiters was already beginning to merge with the national wars against international imperialism. He reminded his audience that because the masses in the East were peasants, the struggle in the East would be against remnants of the feudal order and not against capitalism directly, and went on to stress the importance of directing appeals to the masses in each country in terms and in a language which they could understand:

It goes without saying that the final victory can only be gained by the proletariat of all advanced countries of the world; and we, the Russians, are beginning the task which will be consolidated later by the English, French, and German proletariat. However, we must realize that they will not be able to be victorious unless the toilers of all oppressed colonial peoples, in the first place the peoples of the East, render them help. We must clearly understand that the vanguard alone cannot achieve communism. The task is to awaken the revolutionary activity and the sense of independence of the toiling masses and to organize them irrespective of their cultural level. You must interpret for them the true communist teaching which has been actually drawn for the communists of the more advanced countries in the language of each people, applying into life the practical tasks which are to be accomplished immediately, and uniting with the proletariat of all countries in a common struggle. These are the tasks, the solution of which you will not find in any communist book, but rather in a common struggle begun by Russia.[16]

Resolutions passed by the second Muslim congress called for the formation in the Eastern countries of communist parties as sections of the Third International, and directed that for a period of time party work in the East should support the national-liberation movements as a means of overthrowing the rule of Western European imperialism.[17]

The Baku Congress of the Peoples of the East

The Comintern sponsored an even more elaborate attempt to reach the Asian masses. In early July, 1920, the Executive Committee of the Communist International issued an appeal in the name of the European and American workers to the "enslaved peoples of Persia, Armenia, and Turkey," inviting them to a congress in Baku to be held in September of the same year for the purpose of discussing "together with you the question of how the forces of the European proletariat can be united with your forces for the struggle against the common enemy."

The appeal explained why such a congress was necessary:

The workers and peasants of Europe and America who are struggling against capitalism, apply to you because you are suffering in a similar manner under the yoke of world capitalism, and because you, too, are forced to fight the world exploiters. Your joining the workers and peasants of Europe and America will accelerate the end of world capitalism, and will guarantee the liberation of all workers and peasants throughout the world.

---

[15] See Document 28.   [16] Lenin, *Sochineniia*, XXIV, 550–51.
[17] *Zhizn Natsionalnostei*, No. 47 (55), December 14, 1919, p. 2; see Document 29.

Enumerating the ills suffered by Persian, Armenian, and Turkish toilers from the domination of British, Italian, and French capitalists, the appeal added :

We turn first of all to the workers and peasants of the Near East, but we shall be glad to see among them also delegates of the enslaved masses living farther from us—the representatives of India, and also the representatives of the Muslim peoples living in free union with Soviet Russia. . . .

Workers and peasants of the Near East, if you organize yourselves, if you form your own workers' and peasants' army, you will defeat the British, French, and American capitalists, you will liberate yourselves from your oppressors, you will secure freedom, you will be able to form a free world republic of working masses, and you will use the wealth of your own land in your own interests and the interests of the international proletariat, which will be glad to exchange your wealth against their own products, and will be glad to send you their help.[18]

The congress held its sessions from September 1 to September 8, 1920. It was attended by 1,891 persons representing various nationalities inhabiting the former Russian Empire as well as independent Near Eastern states. The chief speakers representing the Russian Communist Party were Zinoviev and Pavlovich. These communist dignitaries exhorted the delegates to declare a holy war against the British and French capitalists and to join with Soviet Russia in a common struggle.

"We are waging a battle to the death against those persons," declared Zinoviev, "who forget, even for a moment, their duty to the oppressed nations, to the toiling masses of those countries which are plundered and exploited by capital. . . . The European proletariat cannot help seeing now that the course of historical development has bound the toilers of the East to the workers of the West. We must conquer or perish together."[19]

Karl Radek pressed the same argument : ". . . your destiny and ours is one; either we and the peoples of the East shall be united and consequently shall hasten the victory of the Western European proletariat [over capital], or we shall perish, and you will become slaves. . . ."[20]

A discordant note was introduced by a nonparty member from Turkestan, Narbutabekov, when he condemned the manner in which soviet policy was being carried out in Turkestan. But the general mood was expressed by Pavlovich, who said :

The transitional step toward the full unity of the toiling masses of the different nations lies in a federation of the soviet republics of the East for the struggle against both the expansionist plans of the imperialist powers and the machinations of their own domestic enemies. . . . Arise, then, peoples of the East ! The Third International calls you to a sacred war against the capitalist rabble. Comrade delegates, develop the class-consciousness of the masses; organize them into peasant soviets, soviets of toilers; call all the toilers to union with Soviet Russia; propagate the idea of the federation of the oppressed nations; and finally, create a union of the proletarians and peasants of all countries, religions, and languages.[21]

Thus, it is apparent that the Russian Communists controlled the entire procedure of the congress and were its main speakers, while the non-Russian repre-

---

[18] *Izvestiia,* No. 144, July 3, 1920, p. 1.
[19] *Pervyi sezd narodov Vostoka. Baku, 1–8 sentiabria 1920 g., Stenograficheskie otchety,* pp. 35–36. (Hereafter cited as *Pervyi sezd narodov Vostoka.*)
[20] *Pervyi sezd narodov Vostoka,* p. 70.   [21] *Ibid.,* pp. 151, 152.

sentatives not only kept in the background but very likely failed to understand what their illustrious leaders were so vehemently trying to convey to them.

Meantime in seeking to explain the reasons for Turkey's being drawn into the Communist International, Enver Pasha, who claimed to represent the Turks, spoke about "the similarity of our ideas." It appeared, indeed, that Enver claimed even a greater responsibility than that of a Turkish delegate. "Comrades," he said, borrowing extensively upon his own imagination, "I wish to declare that the union of the revolutionary organizations of Morocco, Algeria, Tunisia, Tripolitania, Egypt, Arabia, and Hindustan, which has sent me here as its representative, is in complete agreement with you."[22]

But Enver's declaration of Turkish sympathy with the Communist International was coldly received by the communist leaders in the congress, who introduced and passed a resolution on the Turkish national movement. In this document the congress expressed its sympathy with the Turks in their struggle against international imperialism, but added:

However, the Congress wishes to state that the national revolutionary movement in Turkey is directed only against foreign oppressors, and that the success of this movement will not necessarily mean that the Turkish peasants and workers will be freed from oppression and exploitation. . . . The Congress finds it necessary to approach with particular caution the leaders of this movement, for in the past they have led Turkish peasants and workers to the slaughter in the interests of an imperialist group, and in this way, in the interests of a small group of rich high-ranking Turkish officers, have exposed the masses [of Turkey] to the danger of destruction. The Congress recommends that these leaders now prove by their actions that they are prepared to serve the toilers and to redeem past mistakes.[23]

Under the supervision of the Moscow Communists, certain theses on soviet government in the Eastern countries were adopted at the sixth session of the congress. They stated in part:

The revolution of the peoples of the East against their foreign and domestic oppressors . . . makes the question of the future government of all the countries of the East the vital problem of the day.

The establishment of soviet government in the Eastern countries was the only way of settling this problem.

The soviet government and the soviet organization [of society] not only represent the [best] organization for the industrial proletariat; they are also the only suitable type of organization for the toiling masses in general. . . . Only the soviet government will surrender authority exclusively to the toiling poor.

The organization of soviet governments in the Eastern countries would lead also to peaceful collaboration among them and would "destroy by common effort the rule of foreign and local oppressors." This, in turn, would facilitate mutual assistance in economic relations between the proletarian West and the East. "All the interests of the toiling peoples of the East," the theses concluded, "indicate clearly that the creation of a soviet government [in the East] is imperative."[24]

22 *Ibid.*, pp. 111–12.
23 *Ibid.*, pp. 116–17.
24 *Ibid.*, pp. 183, 184–86; see Document 30, and also Document 31.

Communist Organizations for Propaganda in Asia

An immediate outgrowth of the Baku congress was the setting up of a permanent Council for Propaganda and Action of the Peoples of the East as an auxiliary for the Third International. The first session of the Council for Propaganda and Action was held in October 1920 when a presidium was elected, including Pavlovich, Stasova, Eliava, Narimanov, Narbutabekov, and others. Pavlovich and Stasova were given the right of veto on all matters. The Council was soon broken up into three departments: (1) agitation and propaganda, (2) organization and control, (3) administration. The publication of a periodical, *Narody Vostoka* ("The Peoples of the East"), in Russian, Turkish, Persian, and Arabic was outlined, and plans were made to organize propaganda and establish contact with various Eastern countries.

The Council for Propaganda and Action felt, however, that it could not possibly cover all Eastern countries. Therefore, as a first step a special department of the Council was organized for Turkestan with G. Ia. Sokolnikov at its head.[25] Then, in October 1920, a delegation from the Baku Council came to Moscow with a proposal for additional councils. Its proposal read in part:

In order to do more efficient and successful work in the East it is imperative to organize—instead of one—three Councils for Propaganda and Action: in Baku, Tashkent, and Irkutsk. In that way the entire East will be divided into three separate spheres of influence: (1) The Near East, including Turkey, Arabia, Syria, Egypt, Armenia, Georgia, Persia, Azerbaijan, Daghestan, and Terek; (2) Middle Asia, including India, Afghanistan, Turkestan, Kirghizia, Bashkiria, West Chinese Turkestan, Kashmir, and Altai; and (3) the Far East, including China, Korea, Mongolia, Manchuria, Siberia, and Japan.

It was proposed that all three councils of propaganda be placed directly under the Comintern.[26] Subsequent communist activities indicate that this proposal must have been followed, but probably with some modifications. The Baku Council for Propaganda and Action, for example, was soon abolished and no other congress of the Eastern peoples was convened in Baku, despite the plans made at the first congress.

The geographical position of Baku, Tashkent, and Irkutsk made them convenient starting points for a three-directional communist penetration into Asia: Baku served as a center for communist activities in Persia and Turkey; Tashkent in Turkestan housed institutions assigned for work in India; Irkutsk became the center for propaganda and organizational work in the Far East.

Since India was at first the object of particular interest for Moscow, the office of the Commissariat of Foreign Affairs in Tashkent assumed at an early date the task of reaching revolutionary-minded Indians, and in due course a special training school was set up there. Later the Turkestan Bureau of the Communist International, a three-man organization including M. N. Roy, carried on the work. "The Indian revolutionaries have already made contact with the Communist International," wrote G. I. Safarov in July 1920. "Al-

---

[25] *Pravda*, No. 232, October 17, 1920, p. 3.

[26] T. R. Ryskulov, "Komintern i rabota na Vostoke," *Zhizn Natsionalnostei*, No. 46, (96), December 15, 1920, pp. 1–2.

though their organization is mainly of a national revolutionary nature, the Left radical movement has also taken root."[27]

In May of the previous year there had come to Moscow an unofficial Afghan mission under Professor Barakatullah, a member of the Muslim League in Delhi and of the National Indian Congress. "I am not a Communist or a socialist," Barakatullah stated in an interview with *Izvestiia*. "My political program has been so far that of driving the Britons from Asia. I am an unreconcilable foe of European capitalism in Asia, which is represented largely by the British. In this attitude I stand close to the Communists, and in that respect you and I are natural allies."[28]

The chief of the Eastern Department of the People's Commissariat of Foreign Affairs, A. Voznesensky, declared: "The Afghan delegation which is now in Moscow is not an official one. Professor Barakatullah is a personal friend of the new Emir, and as far as we are concerned is a private individual so far not officially connected either with us or with the new Afghan government. . . . Afghanistan is very important for the cause of [our] propaganda in Asia. Situated in the center of the Asiatic mainland, it touches upon India, Persia, China, Bukhara, and Russia. Historically and geographically, Afghanistan is a steppingstone from India to Central Asia; through Afghanistan passes the trade route to Bukhara (the defile of Paropamisus). Ethnographically Afghanistan is closely connected with India, and as an independent country professing the same religion as that of India, it exercises a tremendous influence on the seventy-million population of Muslim India. Any movement in Afghanistan has always a repercussion in India. . . ."[29]

Ironically, the Russian Communists made their first direct contact with Indian revolutionaries through the Pan-Islamic Muhajirun movement which had started in India as an offshoot of the Caliphate movement launched in 1919 to pressure the British government into restoring Constantinople to the Caliph of Islam. The nationalist crusade of the Indian Gandhiists made the Caliphate movement one of its main issues, the purpose being to use Muslim fanaticism for nationalist ends.

Amanullah, Emir of Afghanistan, being thoroughly anti-British, invited the Indian Muslims of the Muhajirun movement to settle in Afghanistan if and when they found themselves unable—as a result of their protests against the Afghan War of 1919—to perform their religious duties in British-occupied India. In actuality, Amanullah's invitation appears to have been a political maneuver designed to squeeze some advantageous concessions from the British government in the struggle for Afghan sovereignty. Like Kemal Pasha in Turkey and Riza Shah Pahlavi in Persia, Amanullah tried to introduce and enforce a number of reforms to modernize his country. But his reforms were resented by a number of Afghan tribes and led in some cases to armed uprisings. Soviet spokesmen, making the most of the opportunity, asserted that these insurrections were inspired by the British government.[30]

[27] G. I. Safarov, "Vostok i sotsialisticheskaia revoliutsiia," *Pravda*, No. 155, July 16, 1920, p. 1.

[28] *Izvestiia*, No. 95, May 6, 1919, p. 1. See Document 37.

[29] *Izvestiia*, No. 96, May 8, 1919, p. 1.

[30] I. M. Maisky, *Vneshniaia politika R.S.F.S.R. 1917–1922*, p. 145.

In May 1920, an initial group of Muhajiruns left India—the first steps in a migration which lasted until the end of the year and finally included thousands of Indian Muslims. Over immediately succeeding years large numbers of students in the Punjab, United Provinces, the Northwestern Frontier Province, Delhi, and several of the Indian states (Bhopal, Patiala, Bikaner) joined the organization — as did several thousand veteran Indian revolutionaries — and there was talk of forming bands for the purpose of going to Soviet Russia. For the news of Soviet aid to Turkey had gradually seeped into India, and this word aroused considerable Indian Muslim interest in and sympathy for the new Russian government.

In October 1920, a group of thirty-six Indians (including one Shaukat Osmani) reached Tashkent, where they were met by Roy and enrolled in a training course for revolutionaries.[31] After ten months of training at Tashkent, three members of this group (Shaukat Osmani, Abdul Majid, and Abdul Kabir Sehrai) were selected for further instruction in Moscow. Somewhat later (March 1921) the Tashkent school was closed (a result of conditions laid down by the British in concluding the Soviet-British agreement of March 16, 1921),[32] and most of the remaining Indian revolutionaries enrolled there were also shifted to Moscow, where they were admitted to the Communist University of the Toilers of the East.[33]

In June 1921, another deputation of Indian revolutionaries reached Moscow. This group (led by Virendranath Chattopadhyaya and including Bhupen, C. P. Dutt, G. A. K. Luhani, Agnes Smedley, Khankhoji, and Nalini Gupta) represented Indian revolutionaries who had organized themselves in Berlin during World War I, their object being, of course, to exploit that conflict to the detriment of British rule in India.

At about this time fifteen or so Indian students from the University of the Toilers of the East returned to India, where they were arrested in 1922, tried at Peshawar, and sentenced to imprisonment in proceedings of the Tashkent Conspiracy case.[34]

During the course of these developments no clear distinction was made between the responsibilities of the Comintern, the Commissariat of Foreign Affairs, and the Russian Communist Party.

The revolutionary work among the Far Eastern peoples was at first directed by the Regional Bureau of the Russian Communist Party in Siberia, which soon instituted in Irkutsk a Section for the Eastern Peoples, known later as the Asian Bureau. In 1920 a Special Department of the Far Eastern Secretariat of the Comintern (Osobyi Otdel pri Dalnevostochnom Sekretariate Kominterna) was also established there.[35]

---

[31] [Saumyendranath Tagore,] *Historical Development of the Communist Movement in India,* edited and published by the Politbureau of the Central Committee of the Revolutionary Communist Party of India, p. 3. (Cited hereafter as Tagore, *Historical Development of the Communist Movement in India.*)

[32] For more on this agreement see the companion volume, *Soviet Russia and the West, 1920–1927.*

[33] Kommunisticheskii Universitet Trudiashchikhsia Vostoka (KUTV). For more on it see below.

[34] Tagore, *Historical Development of the Communist Movement in India,* p. 5. See also Alexandre Barmine, *One Who Survived, the Life Story of a Russian Under the Soviets,* pp. 100–101.

[35] I. I. Genkin, "Konets Ungerna i nachalo novoi Mongolii," *Severnaia Aziia,* No. 2 (20), 1928, p. 81. Cited hereafter as Genkin, *Severnaia Aziia,* No. 2 (1928).

In Irkutsk the Special Department of the Far Eastern Secretariat began publication of a weekly bulletin, *Biulleten Dalnevostochnogo Sekretariata Kominterna* ("Bulletin of the Far Eastern Secretariat of the Comintern"), the first issue being dated February 27, 1921. The last number came out on May 29, 1921, after which the bulletin gave way to a regular journal, *Narody Dalnego Vostoka* ("The Peoples of the Far East"), beginning probably in May 1921. Its chief editor was B. Z. Shumiatsky, of whom more will be said later. This journal was published in Russian and English.

In addition to the Special Department of the Far Eastern Secretariat of the Comintern, there was also established in Irkutsk a section of the Far Eastern Department of the Commissariat of Foreign Affairs, headed by Ia. D. Ianson, the future head of the so-called independent Far Eastern Republic and later, upon the conclusion of the Soviet-Japanese treaty in 1925, the first Soviet ambassador to Japan (and allegedly also the secret chief representative of the Comintern in that country). Little information about actual revolutionary activities carried on in Irkutsk is available.

Institutions and Individuals Assigned for Propaganda and Study of Asia

We have described the special school for Indian revolutionaries in Tashkent. There were other early efforts along the same lines; for example, a three-month course was set up in the Sverdlov Communist University in Moscow.[36] Attempts were also made to found *Sovpartshkoly,* or Soviet Party Schools, in Turkestan, Bashkiria, the Caucasus, and elsewhere, but no satisfactory results were attained. For one thing, there was an evident lack of suitable instructors, and also there were language difficulties.[37]

In January 1921, the Central Committee of the Russian Communist Party took up the matter of opening a special school for workers from the eastern border regions, and on April 21, 1921, there followed a decree of the All-Russian Central Executive Committee which marked the official establishment of the KUTV. The decree stipulated that the KUTV was to be located in Moscow and was to be under the jurisdiction of the People's Commissariat of Nationalities, which was entrusted with the organization and direction of the projects.[38]

It is clear that from the very first, foreign students were enrolled in the KUTV.[39] According to Stalin in his address to the students of the university on its fourth anniversary, its task was twofold: to train the eastern nationalities

[36] S. Popov, "KUTV—kuznitsa kadrov dlia sovetskogo Vostoka," *Revoliutsionnyi Vostok*, No. 2, 1935, p. 189.

[37] G. I. Broido, "Ocherednye zadachi Kommunisticheskogo Universiteta Trudiashchikhsia Vostoka," *Zhizn Natsionalnostei*, No. 3 (9), March 14, 1922, p. 5. Broido was the first rector of the KUTV.

[38] *Sobranie Uzakonenii i Rasporiazhenii*, No. 36, May 5, 1921, p. 194. It is not known what organization was responsible for the KUTV following the dissolution of the People's Commissariat of Nationalities in 1924. By 1936 the KUTV was under the jurisdiction of the Central Committee of the All-Russian Communist Party (B).

[39] See G. I. Broido, "Kommunisticheskii Universitet Trudiashchikhsia Vostoka," *Zhizn Natsionalnostei*, No. 11 (109), May 28, 1921, p. 1. See also M. N. Roy, "Joseph Stalin, Mephisto of Modern History," *The Radical Humanist* (Bombay), No. 49, December 10, 1950, p. 582.

of the Soviet Union proper, and to provide revolutionary guidance to students from colonial countries.[40]

Beginning with the autumn of 1922, a basic three-year tour of study was inaugurated at the KUTV, and about 800 persons began the course (the number reached 895 by January 1923).[41] The chief sections of the KUTV in 1925-26 were: Leninism and the History of the Russian Communist Party; History; Historical Materialism; Mathematics; Natural Sciences; Philology. The subsections included Physics and Chemistry. Study groups were founded for Leninism and party structure, economic sciences, natural sciences, Eastern studies and colonial politics, history, philology, and education.[42] Instruction was given in English for foreign students. An account of the arrival of Chinese students "from behind the Chinese Wall," written in December 1921, tells how these students looked upon the most elementary postulates of Marxism as the "greatest discovery."[43]

A most illuminating account of the enrollment of foreign students in the above university (known in Japanese as *Kutope*) is provided by a Japanese source. The Communist Party of Japan was ordered by the Comintern to send thirty students a year, but a selection of them was difficult. A total of forty students were sent for the years 1924, 1925, and 1926. They traveled by way of Shanghai under assumed names, all expenses paid. In Shanghai they contacted the Soviet or Chinese Comintern agents, then proceeded to Vladivostok. Upon their arrival in Moscow, they entered *Kutope* for a year of training in Marxism-Leninism, the Russian language, and military service. On finishing their studies at *Kutope*, they were provided with traveling expenses and assigned by Katayama (and later by Kenzō Yamamoto and Sanzō Nozaka) the tasks which they were to carry out in behalf of the Japanese Communist Party after returning to Japan. They returned via Harbin to Shimonoseki, Japan.[44]

Another university for Asians was at first known as Sun Yat-sen University, but later called the Communist University for the Toilers of China. This institution was established in Moscow during September 1925 and opened its doors in November of the same year. Wealthy members of the Kuomintang and overseas Chinese provided the main material support for the university at first, but the Comintern and public organizations in the U.S.S.R. contributed money also. By the middle of 1927, when relations with the Kuomintang were severed, the institution was supported solely by Soviet Russia.

The student received free tuition, board, and room and a monthly stipend of about $10 in rubles for pocket money. The two-year course included natural sciences, economics, economic geography, agrarian problems, mathematics, the history of the revolutionary movement in the East and the West, and classes dealing with Russia, China, and the Communist Party in particular. The theory and practice of Marxism-Leninism as developed in Soviet Russia was also taught. Weekly field trips to Moscow factories, courts, and other institutions gave the students an insight into how the Communist Party directed the eco-

---

[40] Stalin, *Sochineniia*, VII, 133-52; see Document 32.

[41] S. Popov, "KUTV—kuznitsa kadrov dlia sovetskogo Vostoka," *op. cit.*

[42] Information taken from *Ves SSSR*, 1926, Part V, p. 72.

[43] M. Charnyi, "V Kommunisticheskom Universitete Trudiaschikhsia Vostoka," *Zhizn Natsionalnostei*, No. 29 (127), December 14, 1921, p. 2.

[44] Katsunosuke Yamamoto and Mitsuho Arita, *Nihon kyōsan-shugi undō-shi*. Excerpts translated by Travers E. Durkee.

nomic, social, and political life of the U.S.S.R. By 1928, the student body numbered 600 Chinese. Karl Radek was the first rector of this university, a post he held until his fall from favor in 1927, when he sided with Trotsky and Pavel Mif took his place. In 1930 the office of rectorship was abolished.

Sun Yat-sen University can be considered the main source for the Moscow-trained Chinese Communists. The KUTV, although it had some Chinese students, was mostly for non-Chinese Asians; its students came mainly from the eastern nationalities of Russia, and from Japan, India, Korea, and Indonesia.

A third institution for Asian peoples, the former Lazarev Institute in Moscow, became in 1919 the Armianskii Institut (Armenian Institute), and later the Institut Vostokovedeniia imeni Narimanova (Narimanov Institute of Eastern Studies). There was also created the special Vostochnyi Fakultet Voennoi Akademii Rabochei i Krestianskoi Krasnoi Armii (Eastern Faculty of the Military Academy of the Workers' and Peasants' Red Army).

In Leningrad, the Leningradskii Vostochnyi Institut (Leningrad Eastern Institute) trained men for work in the Eastern countries and prepared teaching personnel for other Russian schools for the study of the East. This Institute was divided into sections according to the language in which the subject matter was taught: Japanese, Chinese, Mongol Tibetan, Turkic (Uzbek, Kirghiz, and Tadzhik), Anatolian-Turkish, Persian, Hindustani. E. V. Dumbadze, a Soviet nonreturnee and formerly a student of the Institute, has this to say about its purpose and that of like institutes:

All [these] institutions of learning prepare specialists for work in the East as agents of the Comintern or the G.P.U.[45] Entrance into these institutions involves certain difficulties, and as a rule only the following persons are admitted into them: those who have been members of the Communist Party for at least five years, or those who have been specially recommended by the [Central] Committee of the party. Irrespective of the above it is necessary either to have served in the army, or to have worked in the Cheka. Upon completing the courses in these institutions, the students are attached either to the Comintern (Eastern Section) or to the Foreign Department of the Cheka, which, on their part, give them assignments for the work abroad.[46]

It should be noted also that similar institutes were organized in other cities, among them Baku, Tashkent, Kazan, Samarkand, and Vladivostok, and that special Eastern faculties were added to the universities of various cities.

The training of military men for work in the Eastern countries was not neglected by the Soviet leaders. A so-called Vysshaia Voennaia Shkola Vostokovedeniia (Military School of Higher Learning for the Study of the East) was organized in Tashkent in 1922, taking the place of the previously formed Voennye Kursy Vostokovedeniia (Military Lecture Courses on the East).[47]

The Vysshaia Voennaia Shkola Vostokovedeniia was to prepare specialists for military science and political work in Persia, Afghanistan, India, and China, and to provide responsible workers who knew the language, history, and way of life of the peoples of Turkestan and the neighboring areas. The Arabic, Per-

[45] Gosudarstvennoe Politicheskoe Upravlenie, i.e., the State Political Department, which replaced Cheka, the All-Russian Extraordinary Commission to Fight Counterrevolution and Sabotage.

[46] E. V. Dumbadze, *Na sluzhbe Cheka i Kominterna*, p. 126.

[47] The latter was reorganized in 1920 from the officers' school of eastern languages attached to the military staff of the Turkestan region, which functioned in Tashkent under the tsarist regime.

sian, Uzbek, Urdu, Pushtu, Chinese, Kirghiz, and Turkish languages were taught, and English was obligatory. The history of the Orient and Islam and the geography of areas adjacent to Russia were also taught.[48]

In 1924 the Fifth Congress of the Communist International decided upon an intense "bolshevization" of all communist parties in capitalist countries, and one result of this decision was the founding that year of the Lenin School, known also as the Mezhdunarodnye Leninskie Kursy (International Lecture Courses in Leninism), to provide advanced training for qualified party workers of all countries including those from Asia. Students were selected from among experienced revolutionary workers who were in need of specialized Marxist and Leninist indoctrination and who—according to J. T. Murphy, a former English Communist—were to be engaged in a study "of the strategy and tactical problems of the Comintern, the organizational and political experiences of the communist parties of different countries, as well as in criticism and generalization of the experiences arising from the current work of the Communist International."[49]

One year of academic study in this institution was required and included the following subjects: political economy, history of the Russian Communist Party, history of the labor movement, party construction, and the Russian language. In addition, field work was undertaken, including manual work in factories (eight hours per week), together with a study of relations and management in factories. For this purpose the students were sent to various regions in European Russia and Siberia, and to Tashkent. They were required also to participate in plenums of the Executive Committee of the Communist International, and to take part in celebrations of Russian revolutionary anniversaries. This school was attended by such well-known Chinese Communists as Li Li-san, Chang Wen-t'ien, and Chou En-lai; by the Indonesian Prawirodirdjo Alimin and by Maurice Thorez, L. L. Sharkey, and Earl Browder. Tito, then in Soviet Russia, gave lectures on "trade and union matters" to Yugoslavian students of the institution (at a fee of twenty rubles per lecture).[50] Gustav Holmberg, former head of the G.P.U. in West Sweden and a member of the Swedish Central Committee of the Communist Party, also taught at this school.[51]

But Communist leaders were concerned with more than propaganda in Asia and Asiatic Russia; they also initiated academic studies of these regions. For this purpose the Nauchnaia Assotsiatsiia Vostokovedeniia (Scientific Association for Eastern Studies) was founded on December 12, 1921, to provide a central organization to supervise existing institutions of Eastern learning.[52]

[48] "Vysshaia Voennaia Shkola Vostokovedeniia Turkestanskogo Fronta (Okruga)," *Novyi Vostok*, No. 2, 1922, pp. 730–31; I. Iagello, "Vysshaia Voennaia Shkola Vostokovedeniia," *Novyi Vostok*, No. 4, 1923, pp. 503–4; K. G. Vasilevsky, "Sredne-Aziatskie Kursy Vostokovedeniia R.K.K.A.," *Novyi Vostok*, No. 20–21, 1928, pp. 497–98.

[49] J. P. Murphy, "The First Year of the Lenin School," *Communist International*, No. 14, September 30, 1927, p. 267. For the excerpt of the decision of the Fifth Congress of the Communist International on the training of foreign students in communism, see Document 32; see also circular letter from the Agitation and Propaganda Department of the ECCI, December 2, 1924, to the Central Committee of the British Communist Party (*Communist Papers; Documents Selected from Those Obtained on the Arrest of the Communist Leaders on 14th and 21st October, 1925* (Cmd. 2682), pp. 22–23.

[50] Vladimir Dedijer, *Tito*, p. 103.

[51] Jan Valtin (Herman Krebs), *Out of the Night*, pp. 298, 371.

[52] *Sobranie Uzakonenii i Rasporiazhenii*, No. 80, December 31, 1921, p. 835. See also *Zhizn Natsionalnostei*, No. 30 (128), December 23, 1921, p. 1.

M. L. Veltman (M. Pavlovich), the Russian specialist on Eastern problems, was made the head of the Association. Branches were established in Harbin, Irkutsk, and Vladivostok, and a periodical, *Novyi Vostok* ("The New East"), was issued.

Professor D. Anuchin defined the need for the study of Asia in the first issue of the *Novyi Vostok* in the following words:

> Far back in Russian history, Russia not only possessed Asian territories, but had been to a considerable degree itself an Asian state. This fact on the one hand gives Russia the right to participate in charting the destinies of the Asian countries, and, on the other hand, imposes on her the moral duty of studying Asia, its peoples, and its history, as well as of assisting in the political development and education of the Asian peoples. Before [the revolution] the Asians saw in Russia only a political and material force. We must see to it that in the future, Russia will appear to Asia as a spiritual force enjoying the respect of the Asian peoples and promoting their cultural development.[53]

Evidences of the Radical Movement in Asia

The October Revolution in Russia attracted the attention of many Asian intellectuals, particularly in the Far East. In China, a Society for the Study of Marxism was formed by Li Ta-chao, professor of history at the University of Peking. Separate groups of this society sprang up in various regions of China. On June 24, 1920, the Moscow *Izvestiia* reported that the Chinese Association of Journalists had sent three delegates to Russia to look around.[54] A few months later, *Izvestiia* issued the following information:

> The delegates of the Chinese press (Peking and Shanghai) who are now in Moscow stated that they were the followers of Karl Marx. They greeted the proletariat of Russia, the first country to give practical application to Marxian teaching. The delegates promised to present a true picture of the Russian situation upon their return to China. They also asked to be regularly informed [of the Russian situation].[55]

The Chinese intellectuals' deep dissatisfaction with the conditions emerging from the peace negotiations at Paris as they were to affect China was made evident by the May 4, 1919, students' demonstration in Peking. The general disillusionment with the ideology of the Western democracies intensified their interest in the Marxist experiment in Russia.[56]

Communist influence reached Japan when Eizō Kondo, member of an American radical political group, returned to Japan from the United States in mid-1919 and later made contact with Comintern agents in Shanghai.

In Indonesia, as will be seen later, a communist party was organized in May 1920. As for Korea and India,[57] they were in the grip of dissatisfaction and discontent with their foreign rulers, Japan and Great Britain respectively.

The mood of the East was reflected by a conference held in China in November 1920, which was attended by the representatives of the Left-wing groups of the various Far Eastern countries. It was reported in *Izvestiia* thus:

---

[53] D. Anuchin, "Aziia kak prarodina i uchitelnitsa chelovechestva; ee nastoiashchee i budushchee," *Novyi Vostok*, No. 1, 1922, p. 249.

[54] *Izvestiia*, No. 137, June 25, 1920, p. 2.

[55] *Izvestiia*, No. 26, February 6, 1921, p. 2.

[56] For more on Chinese contact with the Russian Communists, see our pp. 138–42.

[57] For more information on unrest in India, see Part III.

Japanese papers state that in the middle of November a joint conference of the socialists of the Far East took place. The following countries were represented: Japan
by [Toshihiko] Sakai and seventeen others; Korea by three delegates; China by forty
delegates; Formosa by one delegate. All participants represent the extreme-Left
movement. The conference decided to establish on Siberian territory a central bureau
in order to be able to carry on productive work and to conduct it in contact with the
world proletariat. A representative from India will join the bureau in the near
future.[58]

On the following day, *Izvestiia* published an article by V. D. Vilensky
(Sibiriakov) entitled "Rost kommunizma na Dalnem Vostoke" ("The Growth
of Communism in the Far East") which read as follows:

East Asia has laid down a foundation for an organized unification of the revolutionary work among the toilers of China, Korea, Japan, and India, i.e., among almost
all Asian peoples who make up the 800 million population of the East Asian continent.

Vilensky continued:

We know how discontented the millions of East Asian people are with the yoke that
has been pressed heavily upon them by world imperialism. We know that recently,
in connection with the appearance of militant Japanese imperialism on the Asiatic
continent and its attempt to penetrate deeper into Asia, the discontent began to take
shape, and that finally a slogan was launched for struggle against Japanese imperialism. Now this slogan is being put into effect and, as can be seen from the resolution
of the conference, its goal is similar to the one of the world proletariat. It is exceedingly important that the representatives of the Japanese proletariat were present at
the above conference. . . . The desire of revolutionary India to make an organizational contact with East Asia is equally strong. We see in the above unity a desire
to confront the Pan-Asian movement of Japanese imperialism with the formation
of a revolutionary unity of all oppressed Asian peoples for the struggle against imperialism and for the world social revolution.

Vilensky ended his article by stating triumphantly:

The Eastern Hemisphere is on the eve of a tremendous imperialist struggle for the
possession and mastery of the Pacific Basin and the East Asian continent. It is clear
to us that the toilers of East Asia who understand the development of events, have
hastened to organize the alliance among their own forces which is so much needed.
The conference marks the growth of communism in the Far East and the organizational shaping up of communist parties, of which the Chinese Communist Party is
an example.[59] This is a great historical event in the life of the peoples of East Asia.
Let the imperialists of the world know that even without any "evil intention and
participation" by Soviet Russia, the toilers find the ways and means for the struggle
against their oppressors. We can only welcome them, and send our fraternal greetings to the new fighters for the cause of communism.[60]

[58] *Izvestiia*, No. 5, January 11, 1921, p. 3. Chang Kuo-t'ao told Robert C. North in
an interview November 10, 1953, that the Communist International, while dispatching
G. N. Voitinsky (of whom more will be said later) to China, also sent a Korean revolutionary named Kim to Shanghai for the purpose of organizing a group of "socialists."
Kim put himself in touch with members of the Korean provisional government (in exile),
and also numerous Japanese and Chinese. It is conceivable that this gathering may have
resulted from his activities.
[59] For details on the Chinese Communist Party, see our pp. 138–40.
[60] *Izvestiia*, No. 6, January 12, 1921, p. 1.

B. SOVIET DIPLOMATIC AND REVOLUTIONARY EFFORTS IN THE NEAR EAST

The Soviet Diplomatic Front

While the Communist International was opening its campaigns to win allies and supporters among the Eastern masses, the People's Commissariat of Foreign Affairs in Moscow was working on the other phase of the communist approach to the East, that of attempting to establish diplomatic relations with the existing Asian governments of Turkey, Persia, and Afghanistan.

The conclusion of treaties with the Eastern governments would present to Soviet leaders a twofold advantage: the opportunity to consolidate their holdings through peaceful intercourse, and the possibility of further embittering relationships between the colonies and the imperialist powers. In line with this latter intent, Soviet treaties with the governments of Asia were to be in themselves strongly tinged with elements of pure propaganda.

Reporting at the special session of the Communist faction of the Eighth Congress of Soviets in December 1920, G. V. Chicherin, the People's Commissar of Foreign Affairs, spoke of the difficulties which confronted the Soviet government in its relations with the East:

The movements which are taking place in the East are national. The liberation movement in the East is directed against imperialism, but essentially it differs from communism. As Communists, we favor the liberation movement of the peoples of the East. However, there exists a serious difference between them and us, and therefore in our dealings with the East we are confronted with the difficulty of finding a common language, and of advancing together against world reaction. . . . We are conducting negotiations with the government of the Persian Shah, and we are establishing [diplomatic] relations with Turkey. But our [diplomatic] work in the East is extremely complex. A slow process of evolution is taking place there, and we must take this fact into account. Our policy is that of a compromise with the East, a compromise between us and the national states which are struggling for their own independence against the imperialism of the West.[1]

The first major Soviet diplomatic achievements in the Near East were the signing in February and March, 1921, of treaties of friendship and alliance with the governments of Persia, Afghanistan, and Turkey. To the Soviet government these treaties represented an entering wedge in the drive to undermine British interests in the Near East. To the three Near Eastern states they represented potential protection from Western, particularly British, aggression, which they feared at that time; in addition, the treaties were a weapon of no little value in diplomatic sparring with the Western powers.

Early Soviet Efforts to Win Persia

The first of these treaties, the treaty of friendship between Persia and the R.S.F.S.R., was signed in Moscow on February 26, 1921. Its negotiation was

[1] *Vestnik Narodnogo Komissariata po Inostrannym Delam*, No. 1–2, March 15, 1921, p. 11.

91

preceded by a number of events noteworthy because they reveal with some clarity the simultaneous operation of revolutionary intrigue and diplomatic maneuver which was to become characteristic of Soviet foreign relations.

Moscow viewed Persia as a country of paramount strategic significance. Writing in 1918 on the revolution and the East, K. M. Troianovsky, a Russian Communist, not only emphasized the general importance to the revolution of the Muslims living in Russia, but went on to declare:

If Russia is justly considered to be a citadel of world revolution, then India can be definitely called the citadel of the revolution in the East, a revolution which is bound to resound most strongly in the West and in the world in general.

Troianovsky believed that India in the East, like Russia in the West, was to serve as a vanguard of revolution, and of radical agrarian and other reforms; that Persia, Turkey, and Egypt were the gates to the Indian "citadel"; and finally that Russia's first task was to start a revolt in Persia so as to clear the way for revolution "in India and China, and on to the bastions of imperialism—England, America, and Japan."

The ground for the revolution in Persia has been long prepared; it was prepared by the imperialists of England and "Russia"; only a jolt from outside is needed now, only initiative and determination are necessary.

The Persian revolt can become the key to a general revolution. . . . Owing to Persia's special geopolitical position, and because of the significance of its liberation for the East, it must be conquered politically first of all. This precious key to revolutions in the East must be in our hands; at all costs Persia must be ours. *Persia must belong to the Revolution!*[2]

It cannot be said that the Russian Communists in any sense "conquered" Persia during the years immediately following, but diplomatic relations, at least, were firmly established between the two countries.

Soon after coming to power, the Bolsheviks issued an appeal to the Muslims of Russia and the East (December 7, 1917) which concerned Persia as well as the Muslims within Russian territory. For the benefit of the Persians the appeal proclaimed the nullification of the Anglo-Russian treaty of 1907, by which the spheres of influence of the two governments were respectively outlined, and promised a withdrawal of Russian troops stationed in Persia as soon as military operations ended there.[3]

Moscow simultaneously approached Teheran through diplomatic channels. After signing the armistice with the Quadruple Alliance on December 2, 1917, Trotsky, then Commissar of Foreign Affairs, sent a note to the Persian chargé d'affaires in Petrograd on December 6, 1917, offering immediately to open negotiations for the withdrawal of Russian troops from Persia.

On January 27, 1918, Trotsky sent another official note to the Persian government through its chargé d'affaires in Petrograd with the view, as he said, of dispersing any doubt in regard to the Soviet government's attitude to the Anglo-Russian agreement of 1907. "The Council of the People's Commissars," Trotsky stated, "declares that the Anglo-Russian agreement of 1907, which was directed

[2] K. M. Troianovsky, *Vostok i revoliutsiia. Popytka postroeniia novoi politicheskoi programmy dlia tuzemnykh stran Vostoka—Indii, Persii, Kitaia*, pp. 29, 40-41, 47.

[3] J. Bunyan and H. H. Fisher, *The Bolshevik Revolution, 1917-1918; Documents and Materials*, p. 468.

against the freedom and independence of the Persian people, is annulled once and for all. Simultaneously the Council of the People's Commissars declares as null and void all earlier and later agreements which in any way limit or interfere with the right of the Persian people to a free and independent existence."

Trotsky spoke also of the Soviet government's wish to remove from Persia all Russian soldiers and "the old agents of tsarism and the imperialist bourgeoisie who are equally enemies of the Persian and the Russian peoples." He finally noted that the only possible relations between Soviet Russia and Persia were those that were "based on free agreement and mutual respect among peoples."[4]

Because of the civil war in Russia and the fact that an antisoviet regime ruled Azerbaijan, which separated Russia from Persia, these initial moves on the part of Soviet Russia were followed by two years of relatively little diplomatic activity between the two countries. Two unofficial representatives of the Soviet government were sent to Teheran. The first, Karl Bravin, a former employee of the tsarist government, arrived in Teheran on January 12, 1918, with a message from Lenin to the Persian government:

The Workers and Peasants Government of Russia instructs Comrade Bravin to engage in discussions with the Government of His Majesty the Shah of Persia with a view to the conclusion of trade and other friendly agreements the purpose of which is not only the buttressing of good neighbourly relations in the interests of both nations but together with the people of Iran the joint fight against the most rapacious imperialistic Government on Earth—England, the intrigues of which have hitherto disturbed the peaceful people of Iran and destroyed your great country.

The Workers and Peasants Government is prepared to repair the injustice done by the former Government of the Russian Tsar by repudiating all Tsarist privileges and agreements that are contrary to the sovereignty of Persia. The future relations between Russia and Persia will be based upon a free agreement and mutual respect among nations.[5]

This policy was reaffirmed in another official note sent on June 26, 1919, by Deputy Foreign Commissar L. M. Karakhan.

Another appeal was sent from the People's Commissariat of Foreign Affairs to the workers and peasants of Persia on August 30, 1919. This described at length the maltreatment of the Persian people by the tsarist regime and dwelt on British postwar interference in Persian internal affairs. Referring to the recently signed Anglo-Persian treaty,[6] the Soviet appeal stated that "The Russian Workers' and Peasants' Government, which expresses the will of the Russian masses, treats as a slip of paper and considers absolutely illegal the shameful Anglo-Persian Treaty with which the [Persian] rulers have sold themselves and you to the British robbers." The note reiterated that the Soviet government's policy toward Persia was to cancel all tsarist agreements and to refrain from interfering in Persia's internal affairs.[7]

In addition to sending these official messages, Moscow also strove to estab-

[4] *Pravda*, No. 12, January 30 (Jan. 17), 1918, p. 2.

[5] Iranian State Archive; also *Hagigat* (a newspaper), January 21, 1922, as given in Nasrollah Saifpour Fatemi, *Diplomatic History of Persia, 1917–1923*, p. 138.

[6] This treaty was signed on August 9, 1919. Its terms were very favorable to the British, and were so unsatisfactory to the Persians that it was never ratified by the Majlis (the Persian Parliament) and was officially repudiated by the Persian government in 1921.

[7] Kliuchnikov and Sabanin, II, 341–44; see Document 33.

lish its own representative in Teheran. As noted previously, Karl Bravin had been appointed to act as Soviet representative. Soon, however, a much more suitable person, an ardent Bolshevik, was selected for this role. He was I. I. Kolomiitsev, who had served in Persia with General Baratov's army in 1916 and 1917, and after the October Revolution had stayed in Enzeli as secretary of the Bolshevik Revolutionary Committee. In July 1918, he was sent to Teheran as representative of the Moscow Soviet government. This is how Kolomiitsev described his own appointment:

In July, Comrade Shaumian [at that time head of the Soviet government in the Baku Commune] received a telegram signed by Comrade Karakhan that Bravin, the diplomatic agent of Soviet Russia in Persia, was being recalled to Moscow. Karakhan advised Shaumian to select another person to take Bravin's place. Comrade Shaumian offered me the position of ambassador, knowing that I had worked in Persia for more than a year, and that I had command of French and Persian. I declined to accept this position, considering myself not sufficiently experienced, but agreed to act as the first secretary of the Soviet mission, carrying on the duty of ambassador until another person arrived.[8]

Kolomiitsev, accompanied by a Second Secretary, Karakhanian, arrived in Teheran in August, and proceeded to establish himself as a Soviet representative in Persia, actually prior to any official Persian recognition of the Soviet government. His position was naturally ambiguous, since the former ambassador of the Russian Imperial government in Teheran, Von Etter, continued to hold his official position in Teheran, presumably with the approval of the Persian government. British influence, moreover, was still powerful in the Persian court, British armed forces being stationed in that country. Meantime Kolomiitsev busied himself in gaining support and popularity at least among certain groups of the Persian population.

In reporting to Moscow, however, he was obliged to state that although the Persian people as a whole "are disposed very favorably to the Soviet government . . . one cannot dream at present of a radical *coup d'état* in Persia, since Persia is still going through a feudal period having no industrial proletariat or organized peasantry. Those miserable Persians who die daily by hundreds and thousands in the cities of Persia prefer death to revolution, being terrorized and oppressed by religious prejudices and heartless exploitation on the part of khans and officials who hold more than seventy per cent of all the land in the country." He added, however, that "the Persians are enterprising people, and if one made a concerted effort to propagandize them, results might be favorable."[9] Kolomiitsev was not content with exploring the possibilities of communist influence in Persia; he also concerned himself with emphasizing that the Soviet government in Moscow was the true representative government of Russia, and that all the anti-Soviet groupings that had come to exist during the civil war were mere impostors. Kolomiitsev described his efforts in his report to Moscow thus:

On October 26 or 27 [1918] there appeared in the newspaper *Iran* an announcement by the former tsarist ambassador, Von Etter, regarding the formation of the "Ufa

[8] S. Iransky, "Stranitsa iz istorii krasnoi diplomatii," *Novyi Vostok*, No. 8–9, 1925, p. 154.

[9] *Ibid.*, p. 155.

government,"[10] and about the solemn church services to be held in the building of the Russian embassy, and so forth. Whereupon I published in the next number of *Iran* as follows: "In one of the smaller towns of Russia a band of impostors, making use of British bayonets and Allied gold, proclaimed itself to be an All-Russian government. The Russian Soviet mission hereby declares that the only legal [Russian] government is stationed in Moscow, the heart of Russia, and that the recognition of all kinds of impostors, if such a recognition should follow, would be received by the revolutionary democracy of Russia as an unfriendly act on the part of Persia toward Russia.[11]

Kolomiitsev made similar protests against the occupation by Persian forces of Soviet territory (the village of Serakhs in Transcaspia)—he termed this a robbers' act staged by the British—and against the arrest of members of the Bolshevik Military and Revolutionary Committee in Enzeli. At the same time he continued to press for official recognition from the Persian government. After repeated refusals, he reported, he told the Persian foreign minister: "Although your negative answer, Sir Minister, which is dictated by the will of the British ambassador here, dispirits me, nevertheless I find much consolation in the fact that the Persian people, as represented by a number of your public men, recognize me, the proof of which I receive daily."[12]

However, in spite of Kolomiitsev's claim that he enjoyed popularity among the Persian people, his presence in Teheran was offensive to the Persian government. According to the Soviet account cited above, on November 3, 1918, the building occupied by the Soviet mission was broken into by members of the Persian Cossack brigade, allegedly led by the former consul of the Imperial Russian government, Gildenbrandt. Kolomiitsev's assistant and members of both men's families were taken prisoner; Kolomiitsev escaped and made his way on foot to Baku. He was then recalled to Moscow and soon thereafter was instructed by Moscow to return to Persia, this time with an official offer from the Soviet government to open negotiations regarding the signing of a treaty of friendship. He left for Persia in July 1919, but was captured by anti-Bolshevik forces on the island of Ashur-Ade in the Caspian Sea, and shot by them in August 1919.

The Establishment of the Soviet Socialist Republic in Gilan

The sincerity of the friendly Soviet assurances was called into question as early as 1920 as the result of Soviet activities in northern Persia.

On April 28, 1920, a Soviet republic was established in Russian Azerbaijan. This event was considered by Moscow as an important move toward the extension of Communist influence into Persia and neighboring countries:

Red Turkestan has played the role of a revolutionary beacon for Chinese Turkestan, Tibet, Afghanistan, India, Bukhara, and Khiva. Now Soviet Azerbaijan with its old and experienced revolutionary proletariat and its sufficiently consolidated Com-

---

[10] This was one of the anti-Soviet political organizations headed mainly by the former members of the Russian Constituent Assembly dispersed by the Bolsheviks in January 1918.

[11] Iransky, *op. cit.*, pp. 155–56.

[12] *Ibid.*, p. 156.

munist Party (Gummet)[13] will become a revolutionary beacon for Persia, Arabia, and Turkey. It will bear a direct influence on the Transcaspian regions via Krasnovodsk. The fact that the Azerbaijani language can be understood by the Istanbul Turks and the Tabriz Persians and the Kurds, as well as by the Turkic tribes of the Transcaspian region and by the Armenians and Georgians, will only increase the political significance of Soviet Azerbaijan for the East. From there it will be possible to disturb the British in Persia, to stretch a friendly hand to Arabia, to lead the revolutionary movement in Turkey until it takes the form of a class revolution.[14]

The next Soviet move took place in the Persian province of Gilan. Some antisoviet units of General Denikin had fled to the Persian port of Enzeli where they sought British protection. Red naval units under F. F. Raskolnikov pursued the Whites to Enzeli, forced the British to withdraw, and immediately set about supporting the revolutionary movement which was already under way in the Gilan region.[15]

This movement had started in 1915 as a reform program headed by Mirza Kuchuk Khan, Ehsanullah Khan, and a number of other progressively minded middle-class Persians. By 1917, an open rebellion of the people of Gilan (Jangalis) was under way; their program was intensely nationalistic, Islamic, and progressive. Of the two leaders, Kuchuk Khan was more concerned with political and social reform; Ehsanullah was more radical, inclining toward communist ideology and methods.

As early as 1919, the Bolsheviks had considered ways and means of utilizing the rebel movement in Gilan. *Zhizn Natsionalnostei* pointed out that the work of Kuchuk Khan was "closely connected with communism, although it is interpreted by the Persians in a different sense," and that it represented "a seed which, once it is carefully and skillfully cultivated, will produce a good harvest of revolutionary preparedness among the Persian masses."[16]

When in 1919 the Jangali movement was having a particularly difficult time fighting Persian troops sent from Teheran, Ehsanullah urged Kuchuk Khan to seek the support of the Bolsheviks. After considerable hesitation, Kuchuk agreed, and negotiations were ultimately undertaken with Raskolnikov, who landed in Enzeli at the head of Red forces in May 1920. According to Raskolnikov, he immediately urged Kuchuk Khan to advance on Resht.[17]

Encouraged by Moscow's approval and assisted by the Red forces, Kuchuk Khan's forces succeeded in bringing the entire Gilan region under their control. On June 4, 1920, a soviet socialist republic was proclaimed, with the capital at Resht.

[13] Gummet ("Energy") was a social-democratic group organized by N. N. Narimanov in 1904 for political work among the Azerbaijani workers. The Sixth Congress of the Russian Bolshevik Party welcomed Gummet as the first social-democratic organization with Bolshevik orientation in Azerbaijan. In the summer of 1919, the party split; a small group went over to the Mensheviks, while the Bolshevik group affiliated with the Communist Party of Azerbaijan.

[14] M. Sultan-Galiev, "K obiavleniiu Azerbaidzhanskoi sovetskoi respubliki," *Zhizn Natsionalnostei*, No. 13 (70), May 9, 1920, p. 1.

[15] For Raskolnikov's own account of these events, see Document 35.

[16] Ips, "Zadachi i usloviia sotsialisticheskoi propagandy v Persii," *Zhizn Natsionalnostei*, No. 19 (27), May 25, 1919, p. 2; see Document 34.

[17] *Izvestiia*, No. 128, June 15, 1920, p. 2, and No. 129, June 16, 1920, p. 2.

Immediately upon the formation of the soviet government at Resht, Kuchuk Khan sent a special message to Lenin:

Now is fulfilled the long expected and happy act of the formation of the Persian Soviet Socialist Republic, which we proclaim before all the world. We consider it to be our duty to draw your attention to the fact that there are a number of criminals in Persian territory: Persian oppressors, English traders, and diplomats supported by English troops. As long as these enemies of the Persian people are in Persia, they will prove to be an obstacle to the introduction of our just system all over the country. In the name of humanity and the equality of all nations, the Persian Soviet Socialist Republic asks you and all the socialists belonging to the Third International for help in liberating us and all weak and oppressed nations from the yoke of Persian and English oppressors. . . . We have a firm faith that all the world will be governed by the ideal system of the Third International.[18]

Meanwhile an exchange of messages took place between the Persian Revolutionary Council (headed by Ehsanullah) and Trotsky, the latter stating in his message that "the news of the formation of the Persian Red Army has filled our hearts with joy."[19]

These events in northern Persia were greeted enthusiastically by the Soviet press; the *Krasnaia Gazeta* wrote that the formation of the Persian toilers' republic was "not a dream, not an invention, but a fact, and soon its influence will be felt in all the countries of the East."[20]

On the other hand, foreseeing the possible displeasure on the part of the Teheran and other governments at the participation of Russian Red forces in the Gilan revolutionary movement, Radek wrote in *Izvestiia*:

There are no Russian troops in Persia. Our Caspian fleet which appeared at Enzeli in order to destroy the Whites has now returned to Baku, having taken with it the ships that belong to us. It did not fight the Persian people, and did not even touch the British detachments which have retreated to Resht and are now leaving for southern Persia. There are no territorial Soviet forces in Persia. But "Russian" ideas, the ideas of communism, have entered Persia.[21]

The Persian government naturally viewed Soviet Russian influence in Gilan with considerable annoyance, especially since negotiations were already under way in Moscow for the establishment of normal diplomatic and commercial relations between the two countries. To all Persian protests, however, Moscow invariably replied that there were no Russian troops in Persia but simply those of the Azerbaijan Soviet Republic. In his message of July 10, 1920, to Mirza Firouz, Persia's foreign minister, Chicherin stated:

The attitude of the Russian government toward the internal struggles going on in Persia is one of nonintervention, in spite of the similarity in ideas between the government established at Resht and the Russian government. Nonintervention is the principle not only professed, but also carried out by us in Persia, and we apply this

[18] R. Abikh, "Natsionalnoe i revoliutsionnoe dvizhenie v Persii v 1919–1920 gg. (Vospominaniia uchastnika dvizheniia Ekhsan-Ully-Khana)," *Novyi Vostok*, No. 29, 1930, pp. 106–7.

[19] *Izvestiia*, No. 129, June 16, 1920, p. 1; see Document 36.

[20] *Krasnaia Gazeta*, No. 131, June 17, 1920, p. 1.

[21] *Izvestiia*, No. 124, June 10, 1920, p. 1.

principle to both parties, being no more in a position to support the government established at Teheran against that at Resht than to defend the latter against the former.

Chicherin went on to assure the Persian government of the Russian working
masses' friendly wish "that the Persian masses may increase their well-being
by disposing of their own fate in accordance with their desires."[22] Moscow did
agree, meanwhile, to use its influence toward bringing about the withdrawal
from Persian territory of the Azerbaijani forces, but only on the condition that
British forces also evacuate Persian territory.[23]

British forces were withdrawn from Persia in May 1921; Soviet evacuation was begun in June and completed by September 8, 1921. After the withdrawal of the Red forces from the area, the Persian army under Riza Khan
quickly marched into Gilan and wiped out the Jangali forces.

The reason for the Russian withdrawal from Gilan seems to lie in the nature
of the Jangali movement under Kuchuk Khan's leadership. Very shortly after
the proclamation of the new republic in Gilan, A. Voznesensky, the head of the
Eastern Department of the People's Commissariat of Foreign Affairs, analyzed the Gilan government:

We do not conceal the fact that the composition of the new government is far from
communistic. At the present moment it unites those who have risen under the slogans
of "Away with England" and "Away with the Teheran government which has sold
itself to England." The cabinet consists of the democratic petty bourgeois elements
of northern Persia.[24]

The following month, at the Enzeli Congress of the Persian Communist
Party (see below), similar views were expressed:

... apprehension was felt about Kuchuk Khan's intentions to carry out the bourgeois-
democratic revolution by means of drawing to its side various khans, large-scale landowners, and feudal lords on the ground that in the struggle against the Shah and the
British the entire nation was to be united. It goes without saying that the Communist
Party could not approve of such tactics, because it was fully convinced that *every
revolution in a backward agrarian country which did not remove the feudal oppression and would not liberate millions of peasants* was destined to end in failure. The
liberation of the peasants with the help of feudal lords was, of course, an illusion
which the party was obliged to strongly oppose.[25]

After the signing of the Soviet-Persian Treaty and the withdrawal of the
British troops, there seemed to be even less profit in continuing to support
Kuchuk Khan:

The revolutionary movement in Gilan was fed mainly on the slogan "Away with
the British." Once the British troops were evacuated from Persia, the movement
definitely began to slow down. In view of the backwardness and the state of oppression of the Persian peasantry, the movement found no response among them. The
Persian merchants, on the other hand, and the bourgeoisie in general, connected the
betterment of their position with the opening of trade relations with Soviet Russia.[26]

[22] *Soviet Russia*, August 14, 1920, p. 174.
[23] *Ibid.*, March 19, 1921, p. 295.
[24] *Izvestiia*, No. 124, June 10, 1920, p. 1.
[25] A. Sultan-Zade, *Persiia*, p. 86.
[26] S. Iransky, "Sovetskaia Rossiia i Persiia," *Novyi Vostok*, No. 4, 1923, p. 218.

The Formation of the Iranian Communist Party

Concurrently, a communist party was formed in Persia under the name of the Iranian Communist Party. Originating soon after the October Revolution among a group of Persian workers employed in the Baku oil fields, and known under the name of Adalet ("Justice"), the movement soon attracted Persians living in Turkestan and also in Persia. With the invasion of the Gilan territory by Red forces, and the arrival there from Baku of Haidar Khan, a Communist who became a member of the Kuchuk Khan government and was later (September 1921) killed in a quarrel with Kuchuk Khan, the Iranian party took final shape. No less active than Haidar Khan in the organization of the Iranian Communist Party was A. Sultan-Zade, also known as Pishevari, a somewhat mysterious person connected with the Russian People's Commissariat of Foreign Affairs, and also often the representative of the Iranian Communist Party at the congresses of the Communist International.

On June 22, 1920, a congress was held at Enzeli by the Iranian Communists during which the Adalet party was renamed the Iranian Communist Party. At this congress, the plan of the struggle against British imperialism and the Shah's government was outlined and greetings were sent to the Russian Red Army and Fleet and to the Central Committee of the Russian Communist Party. Lenin and Narimanov were elected honorary chairman *in absentia.*[27]

To elucidate the policy that was to be followed by the Iranian Communist Party, Sultan-Zade sought Lenin's assistance:

... because many [Iranian] Communists were in doubt in regard to the tactics to be pursued by the Central Committee of the Iranian Communist Party, [I] was instructed by the Central Committee of the Party and duly approached Lenin in the summer of 1920 asking him to give us directives concerning our future work. I arrived at that time in Moscow to attend the Second Congress of the Communist International. Comrade Lenin was terribly busy at that time in the Congress, but nonetheless he promised to raise this point at the session of the Executive Committee [of the Comintern]. Just at that time, a special commission was discussing his theses on the national and colonial movement in the colonial and semicolonial countries. ... Therefore, Lenin was very much interested in the Persian situation.

According to Sultan-Zade, some of the Communists from Baku, including Ordzhonikidze, were not in favor of pushing for agrarian revolution in Persia in view of the general backwardness of the peasants. "Comrade Lenin listened attentively to the arguments but remarked that 'in backward countries like Persia, where the greater part of the land is concentrated in the hands of the landowners, the slogans of the agrarian revolution have a practical significance for the peasant millions.' "

In the discussions which followed, Lenin was supported by Bukharin, Zinoviev, and others, and Sultan-Zade and Pavlovich were asked to outline the theses that could be applied to the Persian conditions. Sultan-Zade concluded his account of what happened at the Second Congress of the Comintern in so far as the communist tactics in Persia were concerned with the following remark:

[27] *Izvestiia*, No. 147, July 7, 1920, p. 2. Abbreviated minutes of this congress are given in "Pervyi sezd persidskikh kommunistov 'Adalet,' " *Kommunisticheskii Internatsional* No. 14, 1920, pp. 2889–92.

I immediately communicated to Persia, to the Central Committee of the Iranian Communist Party, the opinions of our experienced comrades and also the decision of the Congress [i.e., the "Theses on the National and Colonial Questions" of the Second Congress]. But to our great regret, events developed soon after with such rapidity that the Persian revolution, not being able to withstand the pressure by the British and the Shah's troops, suffered a defeat.[28]

This "defeat" of the Persian revolution, as Sultan-Zade put it, was probably due in no small degree to the changed estimate of the Persian situation by the Moscow leaders. Reporting on the Eastern countries on November 6, 1921, Chicherin had this to say:

In Persia, the third anniversary of the October Revolution coincided with a radical alteration in the political attitude toward Soviet Russia. On October 22, 1920, the Central Committee of the Communist Party of Iran adopted the resolution that the revolution in Persia must still pass through the stage of the bourgeois revolution. An end was thus put to the efforts to introduce the communist regime in Persia, efforts which had started with the local soviet government in Gilan. On October 25, the ambassador of the Persian government, Mochaverol-Memalek, left Baku for Moscow, and there began negotiations for the conclusion of a treaty between the Russian and Persian governments.[29]

At the Third Congress of the Communist International, which met in Moscow June 22–July 12, 1921, the representative of the Iranian Communist Party admitted that "the conquest of power [in Persia] by the toilers may be delayed. It is closely connected with the world proletarian movement and, therefore, only after the victory of the social revolution in a number of European capitalist countries, can the Iranian Communists, jointly with the toiling masses, raise the question of the seizure of political authority, and the creation of workers' and peasants' soviets."[30]

The Signing of the Soviet-Persian Treaty

As indicated earlier, the Moscow government sought a rapprochement with the Teheran government almost immediately it came to power. However, Persia was not willing to negotiate at that time. In 1920, faced with strong British pressure, Teheran was ready to meet Soviet overtures.

In May 1920, the two governments exchanged notes, the initiative having been taken by Teheran. The note to Chicherin said that the Persian government had learned with satisfaction of the Soviet proclamation of 1918 recognizing Persia as an independent state and annulling all treaties between the tsarist government and the Shah. The Persian government offered to send two delegations, one to Baku and one to Moscow. Chicherin replied immediately:

The Soviet government greets the Teheran government's decision to send a diplomatic mission to Moscow, and declares itself ready to immediately re-establish postal and telegraph relations with Persia. We wish to emphasize once more our intention and our firm decision to establish a new basis for our relations with the peoples of the Middle East.[31]

---

[28] A. Sultan-Zade, *Persiia*, p. 86.   [29] *Pravda*, No. 251, November 6, 1921, p. 6.
[30] *Tretii Vsemirnyi Kongress Kommunisticheskogo Internatsionala, Stenograficheskii otchet*, p. 468.
[31] *Izvestiia*, No. 109, May 22, 1920, p. 2.

The result of these negotiations was that on February 26, 1921, a treaty of friendship was signed between the R.S.F.S.R. and Persia.

The treaty with Russia represented a victory within Persian political circles for the sponsors of friendship with Russia over the sponsors of co-operation with Great Britain, and thus marked the first successful challenge by Soviet Russia to British influence in the East.

By the terms of the treaty the Soviet government formally affirmed its previously declared intention of renouncing the policy of unequal treatment carried out by the tsarist government, stating that "all treaties, agreements, and conventions signed between the Tsarist government of Russia and Persia by which the former impaired the rights of the people of Persia are hereby canceled and declared null and void." All treaties concluded between the tsarist government and third powers and tending to limit Persian independence and sovereignty were also declared abrogated, and the refusal of the Soviet government to enter into such treaties in the future was proclaimed, thus creating the impression that the Soviet government intended to back up its condemnation of unequal treaties, a policy designed to win friends among the Eastern peoples.

Both parties agreed to refrain from interfering in each other's internal affairs. A security clause similar to those included in the treaties with the Baltic states[32] was also included: each party agreed to prevent the creation or sojourn upon its territory of any organization or group of persons hostile to the other, and to prevent the transport of arms to be used against the other. Moreover, each government would do everything in its power to prevent the presence on its territory of forces of a third party hostile to the other government.

This provision—apparently directed at the Allies, and in particular at Great Britain—was buttressed by a feature unique to the treaty, namely, that should a third party attempt to send armed forces into Persia, Russia, or the territory of Russia's allies, then Russia might send her troops into Persia for purposes of defense, provided they were withdrawn as soon as the danger was over.

The Soviet government annulled all Persian debts to the tsarist government, ceded the Russian Bank's property and funds in Persia to the Persian government, and turned over to Persia a number of roads, railroad installations, communication lines, steamships, canals, and so forth, built in Persia and owned by the tsarist government, proclaiming that it had rejected the "world-wide efforts of imperialism to construct roads and telegraph lines in other countries for the purpose of insuring its military influence rather than for the cultural development of the nations." Also turned over to the Persian government by the Soviet government were all Russian concessions in Persia. The Persian government, in turn, guaranteed not to grant the property thus restored to any third party.

Russian religious settlements in Persia were declared abolished, with the following statement: "The Soviet government of Russia is ready, in view of the principles which it has declared with respect to the freedom of religious ideas, to stop religious missionary propaganda in the Islamic countries, the secret aim of which is to gain political influence among the masses and to help the vicious Tsarist intrigues."

[32] See the companion volume, *Soviet Russia and the West, 1920–1927.*

The treaty dealt also with the resumption of commercial relations and provided for the exchange of diplomatic representatives.[33]

The arrival in Teheran of the new Russian ambassador, F. A. Rotshtein, was held up, however, by the new government of Persia, which had signed the treaty, although it had not carried on the negotiations leading up to it. The new government, headed by Zia ed-Din and Riza Khan, refused to allow Rotshtein to proceed to Teheran until all Russian troops had left Persian soil. There were still Russian forces in the Gilan area, and the Russian government agreed to arrange for their withdrawal only after all British forces were also withdrawn. These evacuations did not take place until May and September, as described earlier; the Persian government, however, agreed to allow Rotshtein to take up official residence in Teheran in April 1921.

Rotshtein arrived in Persia accompanied by a large staff, and immediately took up residence at the former tsarist embassy. As a properly accredited representative of his government, he was received by the Shah, to whom he conveyed Russia's desire to aid Persia against all foreign influence. As one of the first signs of his "democratic" intentions toward the Persian rank and file he opened the park attached to the embassy for public use once a week.

On June 26, 1921, Rotshtein sent the following message to Moscow:

Today, June 26, a solemn hoisting of the flag over the building of the Russian mission in Teheran took place in the presence of several hundred citizens who constitute the Russian colony in Teheran. A resolution was unanimously adopted by those present: "On this great and solemn day when the flag of the Workers' and Peasants' Republic is hoisted over the building of the former tsarist mission we, the Russian citizens who live in Teheran, send our greeting to the Soviet government which has liberated not only Russian but also Persian people from tsarist imperialism. We express our hope of seeing the success of the great socialist power for the benefit of all humanity."[34]

Rotshtein began at once to encourage the anti-British feeling already strong in some Persian circles, and to propagate revolutionary ideas by means of the press. A number of new newspapers appeared, apparently subsidized by the Soviet embassy; their tenor was antigovernment as well as anti-British.

In addition, the Soviet representative had to work for a more practical end, a commercial agreement between Russia and Persia. Article XIX of the Soviet-Persian Treaty of February 1921 had stated that the "High Contracting Parties will take steps for a renewal of commercial relations within the shortest period of time after the signing of this Treaty."[35] Unfortunately, from the Soviet point of view, the Persian government was controlled by large landowners, who did not want this article put into effect.

The meaning of the behavior of the Persian feudal lords lies in their horror of the possible spreading of Soviet influence in Persia, in their fear for their land holdings and their privileges. This mood of the Persian ruling circles is cleverly made use of by the English in Persia who want to break off the Russo-Persian Treaty of 1921 and to introduce difficulties in Russo-Persian relations . . . in order to make it easier for themselves, in case of future international complications, to intervene through Persian territory in Transcaucasia and Turkestan.[36]

[33] For the full text of the Treaty of Friendship between Persia and the Russian Socialist Federated Soviet Republic, see Shapiro, I, 92–94.

[34] *Izvestiia*, No. 152, July 14, 1921, p. 2.   [35] Shapiro, I, 94.

[36] Iransky, "Sovetskaia Rossiia i Persiia," *Novyi Vostok*, No. 4, 1923, p. 21.

On the other hand, some progress was made, and support found—or created[37]—in the Persian merchant class. The Persian government's objection to Rotshtein's activities was so strong that Moscow was soon obliged to recall him. In September 1922, the new Soviet ambassador, Shumiatsky, was given a banquet by the Teheran Central Chamber of Commerce. Delegates from the Majlis and Persian Muslim leaders were also present. *Pravda* gave a very complimentary and probably not quite accurate report on this affair:

The Chairman of the Teheran Chamber of Commerce stated in his opening speech that Russo-Persian friendship has been transformed from abstract well-wishing into practical friendly relations. The Nizhnii Novgorod Fair, the organization of mixed trading companies, the negotiations regarding the commercial treaty, and the Baku Fair—these were stages in the joint progress along the same path by Russia and Persia.

"Please communicate to the Assistant People's Commissar of Foreign Affairs, Karakhan," the speaker addressed Shumiatsky, "that the Persian merchant class looks hopefully to Soviet Russia for the development of commercial activities in Persia and also for the beginning of the healing of wounds inflicted by the war without recourse to the usual methods of violence practiced by the European countries, but rather by means of fraternal and peaceful co-operation."

In his reply, Shumiatsky promised to convey these words to the Soviet government and thanked the Chamber of Commerce and the deputies of the Majlis for their friendly attitude toward him as the representative of the R.S.F.S.R. He pointed out that without the support of all the business circles of Persia, the Majlis, and the government, the re-establishment of normal economic relations between the two countries would be impossible.

"It would be a mistake," Shumiatsky said, "to explain the slow progress of the development of Russo-Persian relations by subjective reasons only. The difficulties which we meet are rather of an objective character. Thus the [previously established] sea communication [between Russia and Persia] and the attempt to open [new] sea routes for our commercial fleet to the southern Persian ports inevitably meet the muzzles of the guns with which the Entente tries to force your Turkish brothers to give up their independence."

The general mood of the participants was interpreted by the most popular speaker in the Majlis, Hora-Sani, who said, "Please convey to the Russian government and the Russian people our deep gratitude for their support rendered to the peoples of the East, not in words but by deeds. Please tell them that there should unite around the banner of national liberation which the R.S.F.S.R. honorably holds in its strong hands, all peoples of the East, so that they might attain their final liberation."[38]

Actually, the commercial treaty between Persia and Russia was not signed until October 1927.

Treaty with Afghanistan

On February 28, 1921, two days after signing the treaty with Persia, the Soviet government signed a similar treaty with Afghanistan. Communist interest in that country had been evident from the early days of the Soviet government in Russia. Contact with Afghanistan was made difficult, however, by the state of civil war which cut off Turkestan from Central Russia, and also by the British intervention in Transcaspia.

[37] G. S. Agabekov, *O.G.P.U., The Russian Secret Terror*, p. 85.
[38] *Pravda*, No. 216, September 26, 1922, pp. 2–3.

Zhizn Natsionalnostei described Soviet efforts to reach Afghanistan in the following manner:

The English, who had firmly established themselves in the Transcaspian region, put an end to all efforts by our Turkic comrades aiming at raising a revolt in the regions bordering on Persia. On some occasions the refugees from Afghanistan agreed to return to their country with propaganda literature which was prepared in the form of letters. The former military commissar of the Turkestan region, Stasikov, worked for about two months in Afghanistan, and did everything he could to influence the mood of the masses. But the masses remained indifferent.[39]

As with Persia, Moscow sought to establish diplomatic relations with Afghanistan. The initial move in this direction was made by the new ruler of Afghanistan, Amanullah, whose first act in foreign relations was the recognition of the Soviet government in Russia. Amanullah's representative, Muhamed Vali Khan, was sent to Moscow in April 1919 with a letter addressed to Lenin. The Soviet government reciprocated on May 27, 1919, with the recognition of the independent Afghan state. Answering Amanullah's overture, Lenin declared in 1919:

By the establishment of permanent diplomatic relations between the two great peoples, a way will be opened for them to render mutual assistance against any attempt on the part of the foreign vultures to deprive them of their liberty.[40]

By the end of 1919, Ia. Z. Surits was already established in Kabul as Soviet representative in Afghanistan, and in October 1919 an Afghan mission arrived in Moscow for the purpose of establishing treaty relations with Soviet Russia.[41] Meanwhile during 1919 and 1920 the new Afghan government had its share of trouble, first in a war with Britain that ended by a treaty of August 1919, then in putting down a conspiracy against the new ruler, Amanullah, in June 1920. But the establishment of amicable relations between Soviet Russia and Afghanistan continued to remain the goal of the two governments. On September 13, 1920, representatives of the two states outlined a draft agreement in Kabul, and on February 28, 1921, they signed a treaty in Moscow.

The treaty provided, among other things, that each contracting party would recognize the independence of the other and would refrain from entering into any military or political agreement with any third party prejudicial to the interests of the other; that each party would establish legations and consulates on the territory of the other; that Afghanistan would have the right to transport through Russia, free and untaxed, goods purchased either in Russia or abroad; and that each party would recognize the independence of Bukhara and Khiva.

Further, the Soviet government agreed to submit to plebiscite the question of Russia's rights to certain territories held once by Afghanistan and acquired in the nineteenth century by tsarist Russia. In this regard the treaty stated:

In order to accomplish the promise given by the R.S.F.S. Government of Russia through its President, Mr. Lenin, to the Minister of His Majesty's Government of

---

[39] *Zhizn Natsionalnostei*, No. 22 (30), June 15, 1919, p. 1; see also Document 37.

[40] A. Gurevich, *Afganistan*, p. 28. For Emir Amanullah's letter to Lenin, December 1920, promising co-operation in the effort to liberate the Eastern world, see *L'Asie Française*, November 1921, p. 421.

[41] For the welcome given to this mission, see Document 38.

Afghanistan, which promise being to the effect that the Government of Russia agrees to return to Afghanistan all the lands situated in the frontier zone, and which had belonged to Afghanistan in the past century, it is hereby agreed that a separate agreement will be signed by the plenipotentiaries of the High Contracting Parties on the basis of a plebiscite of the nationals living in those lands.[42]

The Aftermath of the Soviet-Afghan Treaty

Upon the signing of the treaty of friendship with Afghanistan in February 1921, the Soviet government, represented now in Kabul by F. F. Raskolnikov, the "hero" of the Enzeli landing, soon became engaged in the familiar diplomatic contest with Britain for influence over the ruler of Afghanistan.

The British government dispatched a mission to Kabul under Sir Henry Dobbs to negotiate a treaty with Afghanistan in January 1921, that is, just at the time when negotiations were taking place between Soviet Russia and that country for a similar treaty. "The Afghans," according to a British writer, "weighed and counterweighed the advantages of a British or of a Russian alliance. In the end they accepted neither the one nor the other."[43] But the Afghan government, while rejecting both possibilities of alliance, ratified in August the treaty with Russia and in November the treaty with Britain.

A certain political aloofness on the part of Emir Amanullah can be best discerned through the fact that, contrary to Russian wishes, he was giving refuge in Afghanistan to the dethroned Emir of Bukhara, who had fled his own country after the Communist *coup d'état*. At the same time Indian revolutionaries were likewise sheltered in that country, much to the perturbation of Great Britain; and Jemal Pasha of Turkey, brought to Afghanistan ostensibly to reorganize the Afghan army, seemed to be stirring up the Afghan frontier tribes, to the dismay of British authorities in India.

The Soviet government appeared to be well satisfied with its progress toward friendly relations with Afghanistan. Chicherin, reporting on Russian foreign relations during 1923, spoke of the successful economic and diplomatic relations with that country. He emphasized the importance of the Afghan government's willingness to permit Russian technical personnel to supervise the erection of a telegraphic line from Kushka to Kabul via Herat and Kandagar by which direct telegraphic connection could be maintained between the two capitals, Kushka being connected with Moscow.

"The only problem which has caused difficulties between the two governments," Chicherin declared, "is the question of the Afghan government's giving refuge to the supporters of the former Emir of Bukhara and the leaders of the Basmachi movement."

However on July 9, Afghanistan's minister of foreign affairs, Muhamed Vali Khan, assured Raskolnikov that the former leaders of the Ferghana Basmachi would be required to return to the U.S.S.R., or in any event to leave Afghanistan. The minister also proposed to act as a mediator in the negotiations

---

[42] For full text of the treaty see Shapiro, I, 96–97. See also Document 39.

[43] W. K. Fraser-Tytler, *Afghanistan: A Study of Political Development in Central Asia*, p. 199.

of the former Emir of Bukhara for his return to the U.S.S.R., and if he decided against returning, to deport him to India.[44] Amanullah's good will toward Russia was also emphasized by Chicherin, who said that when Raskolnikov called on the Emir before his departure from Kabul in compliance with Lord Curzon's ultimatum[45] he "was granted a very solemn audience" and "was presented with the title of High Sirdar of Afghanistan [Afghan Prince] and the corresponding decoration."[46]

Soviet Rapprochement with Kemalist Turkey

On March 16, 1921, the Soviet government signed a treaty of friendship with the nationalist government of Turkey under Mustafa Kemal Pasha (subsequently known as Atatürk).

Soviet efforts to seek Turkey's friendship, along with that of Persia and Afghanistan, had begun almost immediately after the formation of the Soviet government, when the peace decree confirmed by the Second Congress of Soviets declared that all secret tsarist treaties were null and void.

During 1918–19, little communication passed between Russia and Turkey. In September 1919, however, Chicherin, the People's Commissar of Foreign Affairs, made an appeal to the "workers and peasants of Turkey" which was worded similarly to the one he sent the same year to the Persian people:

Your country has always been a military camp. The European Great Powers, considering you a "sick man," have not only failed to offer you a cure, but, on the contrary, have intentionally maintained your condition . . . The salvation of your country and of your rights from alien and domestic vultures is in yourselves. . . . You must be the masters of your land . . . But that is not enough. A union of the toilers of the world against the world oppressors is necessary. Therefore, the Russian Workers' and Peasants' Government hopes that you, the workers and peasants of Turkey, in this decisive and momentous hour will stretch out your fraternal hand to drive out the European vultures by joint and united effort, to destroy and make impotent those within your own country who have been in the habit of basing their own happiness upon your misery.[47]

A few months later the way was open for diplomatic contact between Soviet Russia and the nationalist government of Turkey. The third Turkish people's congress had, on April 23, 1920, declared itself to be the Grand National Assembly of Turkey, although the old Ottoman government was still technically ruling in Istanbul. Three days after the opening of the Grand National Assembly, its President, Mustafa Kemal, sent a letter to Lenin in which he proposed the establishment of diplomatic relations between Turkey and the Soviet gov-

---

[44] *Godovoi otchet za 1923 g. Narodnogo Komissariata po Inostrannym Delam II sezdu sovetov S.S.S.R.*, p. 75 (cited hereafter as N.K.I.D., *Godovoi otchet za 1923 g.*).

[45] The famous ultimatum presented to the Soviet Russian government by Lord Curzon demanded that Russia abstain from communist propaganda in Asian countries and that Raskolnikov be removed from Kabul. For the Soviet response to this ultimatum, see the companion volume, *Soviet Russia and the West, 1920–1927.*

[46] N.K.I.D., *Godovoi otchet za 1923 g.*, pp. 76–77.

[47] *Zhizn Natsionalnostei*, No. 36 (44), September 21, 1919, p. 2; see Document 40.

ernment. He also asked for aid for Turkey in its struggle against the imperialist powers.[48]

Chicherin replied to Kemal Pasha on June 2, 1920, and in the name of the Soviet government welcomed his proposal:

The Soviet government is following with the greatest interest the heroic struggle for independence conducted by the Turkish people, and, in these present painful days for Turkey, it is happy to establish a firm foundation for the friendship which should unite the peoples of Turkey and Russia.[49]

A delegation from the Turkish national government in Ankara arrived in Moscow in July 1920 for the purpose of negotiating a treaty between the two countries. A generally friendly atmosphere seemed to prevail during these early negotiations, a fact which the Soviet press was anxious to emphasize since at the same time another Turkish delegation was in London, threshing out Turkish problems with the Allies.[50] The London conference failed, but the Moscow conference reached a preliminary agreement.

A final agreement was delayed for a few months, partly because of the Turkish-Armenian hostilities of September–December, 1920. In the meantime, a Soviet mission was sent to Ankara; its secretary Upmal (Angarsky) arrived there on November 6.

A Struggle Between Soviet Russia and Kemalist Turkey Over Armenia

The independent Dashnak Armenian Republic, which had come into existence in May 1918, became involved in a war with Turkey in September 1920. The reasons for the outbreak of this war are still obscure, but it should be noted that the Armenian delegates to the Paris Peace Conference in 1919 had advanced a demand for additional territory, for "a great Armenia extended from sea to sea." They maintained these claims at the London and San Remo conferences in 1920, but no definite decision was made on this point by the Allies. However, by the Treaty of Sèvres in August 1920, the Armenian Republic was given *de jure* recognition and it was also decided to submit the question of how much territory was to be detached from Turkey and added to Armenia to the arbitration of the President of the United States. These decisions were bound to have a disquieting effect on Kemalist Turkey, which naturally opposed any Armenian aggrandizement.

Soviet historians claim that the first attack was launched by the Armenians,

---

[48] Since May 1919, the Turkish nationalists had been engaged in the Turko-Greek War (the Turkish War of Independence, 1919–22) as well as in vying with the Ottoman government in Istanbul for recognition as the real government of Turkey; both the Greeks and the Ottoman government had the support of the Allied powers. A brief summary of the letter from Mustafa Kemal to Lenin appears in M. Tanin, *Mezhdunarodnaia politika S.S.S.R. (1917–1924)*, p. 78.

[49] Kliuchnikov and Sabanin, III, 27; also *Pravda*, No. 123, June 9, 1920, p. 2; see Document 41.

[50] I. P. Trainin, "Dve konferentsii," *Zhizn Natsionalnostei*, No. 6 (104), March 4, 1921, p. 1; also A. F. Miller, *Ocherki noveishei istorii Turtsii*, pp. 111–12.

and Turkish spokesmen concur in this. Mustafa Kemal, addressing the Turkish Grand National Assembly in his famous Six-Day Speech in 1926, explained the cause of the Turkish-Armenian fighting as follows:

You will take note that since the Mudros Armistice the Armenians, both in Armenia and in the border districts, have not desisted one moment from killing Turks *en masse*. In the fall of 1920 the Armenians' atrocities reached an unbearable pitch. We decided on [military] action against Armenia. On June 9, 1920, we had proclaimed a provisional mobilization in the eastern sector. We made the 15th Corps commander, Kazim Kara Bekir, commander of the eastern front. In June 1920, the Armenians, in a move against the local Turkish administrative district which had been set up in Oltu, invaded that region. An ultimatum was issued to the Armenians by our Foreign Ministry on July 7, 1920. The Armenians persisted in the same sort of action. Finally, after three and a half to four months of mobilization, the Armenians' military operations against our troops assembled in the Kötek-Bardiz zone amounted to war. The Armenians were successful in a general attack which they made in force on the Bardiz front the morning of September 24, 1920. . . . The Armenians were repulsed. Our army passed to the attack on September 28. . . .[51]

Armenian writers, on the other hand, maintained that Turkey was the aggressor, and that the Turkish attack was actually a joint move between Kemalist Turkey and Soviet Russia directed at depriving Armenia of any significance as an independent state.

Though it was true that both Turkey and Soviet Russia were interested in the final disposition of the territory claimed by Armenian nationalists, their interests were hardly identical, or even complementary. Soviet Russia had plans for a Soviet federation in the whole Caucasian region, including even Anatolian Turkey;[52] Turkey wished to retain within her boundaries the Armenian-populated territory proposed for cession to Dashnak Armenia by the Treaty of Sèvres.[53]

In the autumn of 1920, moreover, Kemalist Turkey had an additional interest in Armenian territory. The war between Greece and Turkey was going on, and Turkey needed material aid from Soviet Russia. This would be greatly facilitated by the unhampered use of the railway line between Erzerum in Turkey and Baku in Soviet Azerbaijan, and the greater part of this line was controlled by the Armenian Republic.

The struggle between the Turks and the Armenians ran in favor of the Turks. As the Armenians began to lose, they appealed to the League of Nations for help, but while the latter deliberated on the Armenian appeal, one town after another was surrendered to the Turkish army of Kazim Kara Bekir. Kars fell on September 30, and Alexandropol on November 7, after which the Armenians sued for an armistice. On November 18, a truce was signed between the two belligerent armies, and on November 26 peace negotiations began at Alexandropol.

Meanwhile, Soviet Russia did not remain inactive. In May and June Bol-

[51] [Gazi Mustafa,] *Kemal Ataturk* (Istanbul, 1934), II, 39. Translated by Eleanor Bisbee.

[52] See Pavlovich's statement on the next page.

[53] The Treaty of Sèvres was signed by the Sultan's representatives for the Ottoman government, but it was never ratified and therefore was never legally in effect.

shevik uprisings took place in certain districts of Dashnak Armenia but were successfully put down by the Armenian government. The Soviet government protested to the Armenian government about the treatment of Communists in Armenia. In July it sent an ultimatum to the Armenian government demanding the acceptance of a draft treaty (which had been presented earlier and rejected) permitting transportation of Russian troops and ammunition to Turkey by way of the Armenian railways.

The nature and extent of Moscow's desire to sovietize Armenia can be gauged from a statement made by Pavlovich during that period:

A Soviet revolution in Armenia will forestall the attack on Baku which is being planned by the joint forces of the Anglo-Persian troops, Dashnak Armenia, and perhaps also Georgia. A Soviet revolution in Armenia will considerably widen as well as strengthen our starting point [*platsdarm*] in Baku; it will put an end to the counterrevolutionary hopes of the Musavatists[54] and of the Georgian government to overthrow the Soviet regime in Azerbaijan and throughout the Caucasus. A Soviet revolution in Armenia will end British influence in Persian Azerbaijan and will create favorable conditions for the spreading of our revolutionary work there. It will destroy the British plan for establishing a Kurd buffer [state] against us, and in general it will do away with all capitalist machinations for a strategic encirclement of Soviet Russia throughout northeastern Persia (Khorasan), Afghanistan, mountainous Bukhara, Russian Pamir, and as far as Basmachi-held Ferghana. The Soviet revolution in Armenia means a breach in the front which capitalist Britain is erecting against us. Finally, a Soviet coup in Armenia will serve as the first step toward the creation of a Soviet federation in the Caucasus, i.e., of Georgia, Armenia, and Anatolian Turkey, a federation which, on its part, will serve as the starting point around which there will soon be united other Eastern states.[55]

On November 28, Soviet armed forces (mentioned in Soviet sources as the N army) were ordered to advance into Armenian territory. On the next day a communist-led revolt broke out in Armenia and a Military Revolutionary Committee was organized in Karavansarai, which proclaimed a soviet government in Armenia. On December 2, an agreement was assigned between the Russian government and the newly formed Soviet Armenian government which stipulated that, if necessary, the Red Army would defend Armenia's independence.

The Dashnak Armenian government continued to exist, in spite of this, in Erivan. The Commander of the Turkish Army ignored the formation of the so-called Armenian Soviet government and continued to negotiate with the Dashnak government in Erivan. On December 2 a treaty was signed in Alexandropol between defeated Armenia and the Turks, and after this the Dashnak government resigned in favor of the Military Revolutionary Committee.

By the Treaty of Alexandropol, Armenian claims to disputed Anatolian territory were renounced, and Armenia was forbidden to have an army of more than 1,500 men. Turkey, on the other hand, was given control over the Armenian railways and the right to conduct war operations on Armenian terri-

---

[54] The Musavat ("Equality") national party of (Russian) Azerbaijan was in control of the Azerbaijani national government from May 1918 till April 1920, when it was overthrown by the Communists.

[55] M. L. Veltman (M. Pavlovich), "Sovetskaia Rossiia i anglo-frantsuzskie intrigi na Vostoke," *Kommunisticheskii Internatsional*, No. 14, November 6, 1920, p. 2947.

tory—concessions amounting, as one Soviet writer put it, to the establishment of a Turkish protectorate over Armenia.[56]

Because of active Soviet intervention in Armenian affairs, the Treaty of Alexandropol never went into effect. Russian officials were worried, however, that a possible rapprochement between Kemalist Turkey and the Western powers might lead to serious trouble in the Caucasus. "A very complicated situation has come to exist in the Caucasus," Lenin wrote, "a situation which it is not easy to understand. [We must bear in mind] that a war may be thrust upon us any day."[57]

Stalin spoke on the Armenian-Turkish situation in more detail:

There is no doubt that the Sèvres Treaty directed against Turkey may be annulled. . . . The routing of Armenia by the Kemalists, with the Entente maintaining an absolute "neutrality"; rumors that Thrace and Smyrna will be returned to Turkey; rumors concerning the negotiations between the Kemalists and the Sultan, who is the agent of the Entente—all these are the symptoms of a serious currying of Kemalist favor by the Entente, and perhaps even of a certain deviation to the Right by the Kemalists. How this game by the Entente will end, and how far the Kemalists will go in their deviation to the Right, it is difficult to say. But one thing is certain: the struggle for the liberation of the colonies started a few years ago will be intensified, and Russia, a recognized leader of that struggle, will support it with all its strength and all the means available. It is also certain that this struggle will lead to victory, *together* with the Kemalists if they do not betray the cause of the oppressed peoples, or *in spite* of the Kemalists if they join the camp of the Entente.[58]

But Russian fears of Kemal's "deviation" were ill-founded; the nationalist Turks continued to negotiate only as equals and to decline any offers which would in any way compromise their struggle for complete independence.

Mustafa Kemal continued to maintain friendship with Soviet Russia. In November 1920, he appointed Ali Fuat Pasha (later Ali Fuat Cebesoy) ambassador to Moscow, and shortly thereafter (November 29) he personally sent a note to the Soviet government expressing the admiration of the Turkish people for the Russian people and their struggle:

Our nation fully understands the greatness of the sacrifice the Russian nation has made in order to save humanity, because our nation has struggled likewise for centuries in the defense of Muslim countries against the designs of European imperialists. I am deeply convinced, and my conviction is shared by all our citizens, that on the day when the toilers of the West and the oppressed peoples of Asia and Africa realize that international capital is using them in order to enslave and destroy them . . . ; on the day when the realization of the criminality of the colonial policy reaches the hearts of the toiling masses of the world—the rule of the bourgeoisie will be over.

Kemal ended his message by expressing his conviction that "the high moral authority enjoyed by the R.S.F.S.R. among the toilers of Europe, and the love of the Muslim world for the Turkish people" will bring the unification of the masses of the world against the imperialists of the West.[59]

[56] B. Dantsig, *Turtsiia*, p. 88.
[57] Lenin, *Sochineniia*, XXV, 487.
[58] Stalin, *Sochineniia*, IV, 411–12.
[59] Kliuchnikov and Sabanin, III, 28; also *Izvestiia*, No. 274, December 5, 1920, p. 1; see Document 42.

The real intent of such Turkish statements, as well as the subsequent Soviet disappointment with the "Turkish revolution," can be better understood in the light of two statements by Turkish leaders about Turkish policy of that period.

In his memoirs, General Ali Fuat Cebesoy, the first nationalist Turkish ambassador to Moscow, writes:

When it was recognized that the Allies, and especially the English, under the veil of an armistice, wanted to enslave and annihilate the Turkish nation, which had to negotiate with the victorious states of World War I, it (Turkey) considered carefully the general structure of the situation and the world at that time, and sought means to join one out of the group of states vying with each other for advantages, and to save its own existence.

In the political situation of that time it was the United States of America which appeared most capable of checking English imperialism and, on the basis of principle and power, best able to cope with the problem of saving Turkey's existence. But America could not see the high position it might hold in world policy of the future and it returned to its old isolationist policy. When the Americans withdrew from the scene . . . Turkey of necessity turned to the Russians, who had for centuries been an enemy but who were making a pretense of devotion to the humanitarian principle which they proclaim. The Russians appeared to accept this appeal sincerely. . . .[60]

Mustafa Kemal also discussed the Turkish attitude toward communism and Soviet Russia in the Grand National Assembly on January 3, 1921:

As we well know that these theories [communism] are irreconcilable with our way of life, it is evident that we must oppose them. And the government will be absolutely right in taking measures against those who would wish to apply these theories to practice.

Our policy is quite clear: we struggle for the independence of the nation within the national boundaries. I am not too well versed in sociology, but I believe that communism does not recognize boundaries. Perhaps, it does not even recognize freedom without certain reservations. And yet for us even a discussion on this subject is not necessary. In our relations with the Russians we exclude the question of the principles of capitalism and communism.[61]

The Treaty with Kemalist Turkey

Negotiations between the Ankara representatives and the Soviet government in Moscow resulted in the signing of a treaty of friendship on March 16,

As finally drafted, the treaty included a preamble which stated that both governments,

sharing as they do the principles of liberty of nations and the right of each nation to determine its fate, and taking into consideration, moreover, the common struggle undertaken against imperialism, foreseeing that the difficulties arising for the one would render worse the position of the other, and inspired by the desire to bring about lasting good relations and uninterrupted sincere friendship between themselves, based on mutual interests, have designed to sign an Agreement to assure amicable and fraternal relations between the two countries.

[60] General Ali Fuat Cebesoy, "Siyasi Hatiralarι," No. 50, in *Vatan*, Istanbul), April 5, 1954. Translated by Eleanor Bisbee.

[61] Quoted by Ferdi in "Kitaiskaia revoliutsii ne dolzhna itti po puti Kemalizma," *Kommunisticheskii Internatsional*, No. 24, June 17, 1927, p. 34.

The treaty also mentioned establishing "contact between the national movement for the liberation of the Eastern peoples and the struggle of the workers
of Russia," and declared that the contracting parties "solemnly recognize the
right of these nations to freedom and independence, also their right to choose a
form of government according to their own wishes."

Other clauses of the treaty dealt with the boundaries of the Turkish state;
with the transfer of the sovereignty of the Batum district, including the city, to
Georgia; with the retention of Kars and Ardahan and Artvin by Turkey; with
the international status of the Black Sea and the Straits, final settlement of which
was to be referred to a future conference of the littoral states; and with the
application of the most-favored-nation principle. Finally, the treaty also pronounced null and void all previous treaties between the two countries which
might not correspond to the interests of either.[62]

On May 2, 1921, Natsarenus was appointed ambassador to Turkey, and he
was received in Ankara by Mustafa Kemal the following July. His friendly
greetings to Mustafa Kemal reaffirmed Russian approbation of the Turkish
nationalist movement, while Mustafa Kemal's response stressed the determination of the Turkish people to be "the supreme masters of their own fate."[63]

Next the government of the R.S.F.S.R. acted as mediator in the negotiation
of a treaty of friendship formalizing the relations of Turkey with the Armenian,
Georgian, and Azerbaijani soviet republics. That treaty, the Treaty of Kars,
signed October 13, 1921, delimited the frontiers of Turkey, Armenia, Georgia,
and Azerbaijan; declared null and void all treaties entered into by governments
previously exercising sovereignty in any of the territories involved (except the
Soviet-Turkish treaty signed seven months earlier); proclaimed the refusal of
the signatories to recognize any peace treaty or other international act which
might be imposed upon any of them from without; called for a conference of
the Black Sea powers to draw up an international statute assuring the freedom
of the Straits [to commercial navigation?]; and included a security clause and a
most-favored-nation clause.[64]

Dashnak Armenia was the loser, since the six provinces in Anatolia [the
vilayets of Erzerum, Sivas, Diyarbekir, Elâziz (Harput), Van, and Bitlis] which
had been claimed under the Sèvres Treaty remained with Turkey. Districts of
Russian Armenia (Kars and Ardahan) went to Turkey, while Soviet Azerbaijan assumed a proctectorate over the district of Nahichevan. A. Skachko,
writing in *Zhizn Natsionalnostei,* had warned Armenia a few months earlier of
the necessity of "national sacrifices" for the sake of the Communist goal.[65]

On January 2, 1922, a treaty was signed between the Ankara government
and the Ukrainian S.S.R. The Ukrainian side was represented by M. V. Frunze,
Moscow military specialist, commander of Soviet troops in the civil war, and the

---

[62] Full text of the treaty appears in Shapiro, I, 100–102.

[63] *Izvestiia,* No. 152, July 14, 1921, p. 2. See Document 43.

[64] Full text of the Treaty of Friendship between the Soviet Socialist Republic of
Armenia, the Soviet Socialist Republic of Azerbaijan, and the Soviet Socialist Republic
of Georgia on one side and Turkey on the other, Kars, October 13, 1921, appears in
Shapiro, I, 136–37.

[65] A. Skachko, "Armenia i Turtsiia na predstoiashchei konferentsii," *Zhizn Natsionalnostei,* No. 6 (104), March 4, 1921, p. 2.

future Commissar of War of Soviet Russia, who was sent to Turkey in charge of the special Ukrainian mission to negotiate the treaty.[66]

Frunze's appointment in the guise of a Ukrainian representative was significant as indicating Soviet interest in, as well as assistance to, Kemalist Turkey in the war that it was waging at that time against Greece. "The most important military secrets were made known to me," Frunze stated in his report on his stay in Turkey to a joint session of the Council of People's Commissars and the Central Executive Committee of the Ukraine. "I became acquainted with the military plans of the Turkish and the Greek armies, as well as with the requirements of these armies, with the number of fighting men, with the quantity and quality of their armament, with the conditions behind the front line, and so forth. I can truly say that I know as much of the Turkish armed forces as I do of the Ukrainian army."[67]

The war waged by Kemalist Turkey against Greece, and its struggle for the complete liberation of Turkey from the influence and domination of the Great Powers, were considered by the Soviet leaders exceedingly important for communist revolutionary aims:

The heroic struggle of the Turkish people against the vultures of world imperialism, inspired by the example of the workers' and peasants' masses of the R.S.F.S.R., will have a tremendous influence on the growth of the revolutionary movement in the East and on the Muslim countries of the Dark Continent. In Persia, India, Afghanistan, Egypt, Morocco, Algeria, Tripolitania, Tunisia, even among the inhabitants of darkest Africa, the gigantic battles fought by the Turkish peasants in the fields of Anatolia will not pass unnoticed.[68]

The Communist Movement in Turkey

In spite of Pavlovich's prediction, the communist movement in Turkey developed inadequately, and the weak Turkish Communist Party was forced underground.

The first Turkish communist group was organized in June 1920. It was soon joined by the Mustafa Suphi group. Suphi, a Turkish socialist, had been interned as an alien in Russia from 1914 until the October Revolution. After his release, he became active in propagating communist ideas among the numerous Turkish prisoners of war, and finally organized a communist group among them. Suphi was assisted in his efforts by a special Turkish section attached to the Central Bureau of the Muslim Organizations of the Russian Communist Party. The Turkish section was engaged in intensive training of agitators to propagate communist ideas among the prisoners of war.

In the spring of 1920, after the establishment of a soviet regime in Azerbaijan, Suphi went to Baku and devoted his time entirely to the development of the communist movement in Turkey. He aimed at uniting the various com-

---

[66] The importance of Soviet assistance to Turkey at this period can be seen in the message from Mustafa Kemal to the Ninth Congress of Soviets on December 21, 1921, regarding the arrival of Frunze in Turkey (Document 44).

[67] M. V. Frunze, *Sochineniia*, I, 359.

[68] M. L. Veltman (M. Pavlovich), "Vostochnyi vopros na III kongresse i perspektivy osvoboditelnogo dvizheniia na Vostoke," *Zhizn Natsionalnostei*, No. 14 (112), July 16, 1921, p. 1; see Document 45.

munist groups which sprang up in Anatolia and Constantinople. In order to centralize the activities of these groups, a Central Bureau of the Turkish Communist Organizations was created in Baku, and in September, a congress of Turkish Communists, held in the same city, resolved to unite all existing communist groups into one Communist Party of Turkey. In addition to these activities, Suphi organized communist groups among the Turkish prisoners of war and workers who were sojourning in southern Russia and the Crimea. Special courses were also given to the Turks in Baku to train them for propaganda work, and finally a regiment was mobilized among the Turkish prisoners of war to proceed to the Turkish front to fight with the Kemalists against Greek forces. In November 1920, Suphi returned to Anatolia and assumed the leadership of the Turkish Communist Party.[69]

The activities of Suphi and his associates naturally did not please the Kemalist leaders, who sought the friendship of Soviet Russia for practical reasons but had no intention of establishing a communist regime in Turkey. To counteract Suphi's propaganda, the Kemalists organized a legal and so-called official communist party of Turkey, a somewhat curious phenomenon known as the Resmi Kommunist Parti. According to the program of this party, the Turkish people were not as yet in a position to accept the communist program, nor could their religion permit them to do so. Therefore, "the propaganda of the communist ideas at present is harmful to the country. When the soldier is told that he has no fatherland, he will not wish to defend it."[70] Since the organization even denied the need of a violent revolution, it goes without saying that the Moscow-sponsored group found no common language for communicating with it.

In January 1921, Suphi and fifteen other Turkish communist leaders met their death by violence. Although the Turkish government denied that it had any part in the murder, general repressions of the Turkish Communist Party followed, and it became evident that the Kemalist government had no desire to tolerate any communist activity in Turkey. When in the autumn of 1922 the congress of the Soviet-sponsored Turkish Communist Party met at Ankara, it was dispersed by the Turkish police.

The resolution adopted by the Turkish Communist Party in 1923 defined its position in Kemalist Turkey in the following words:

The government of the Grand National Assembly born out of the struggle for independence and proclaiming that it is fully for the "National Pact" and against imperialism, has shown during the last three years by its conduct that its policy has been one of betrayal. The following facts are instructive in this respect:

(1) When their relations with the Soviet government were just started the representatives sent by the government to Moscow stated that there was a large Communist Party in Turkey, that this Party had a numerous following among the peasants, and that the peasants' soviets were already functioning in several localities.

(2) In the first period of its existence, trying to deceive Soviet Russia, the government formed under the name of the Green Army a would-be Bolshevik Party consisting exclusively of bourgeois elements.[71]

[69] M. Sultan-Galiev, "Mustafa Suphi i ego rabota," *Zhizn Natsionalnostei*, No. 14 (112), July 16, 1921, pp. 1–2.

[70] M. L. Veltman (M. Pavlovich), *Revoliutsionnaia Turtsiia*, p. 111.

[71] The Green Army was an anomalous organization of religious fanatics and guerilla bands, infiltrated by Communist Turks from Russia. It was eventually suppressed by the Kemalists.

(3) After the arrival of the first Soviet Ambassador at Ankara, the government formed an official Communist Party composed of the remainder of the Green Army, high government officials, and intellectuals.

(4) The delegation sent by the government to the London Conference to please the imperialist powers announced in all the European capitals through which it was passing that a score of Communists, among whom were our brave comrades Suphi and Ehden Nejat, had been slaughtered, and that they were going to put an end to all the other imprisoned comrades so that the plague of Bolshevism would no more infest the country.

(5) The Agreement with the French in 1921 proves that the government is betraying the East, and that it has given away the "National Pact."

(6) Finally, we have the recent persecution directed against the Communist Party and the Turkish Labourers' Union, coinciding with the convocation of the Lausanne Conference.[72]

Moscow, for its part, condemned official Turkish policy toward the Turkish Communists:

It is imperative for the Ankara government to understand that it can save Turkey only if it realizes that there is no other policy for Turkey to pursue except the policy of unification with the proletarian revolution. Such a step would not prevent the Turkish government from concluding peace agreements with the Western imperialists as long as these agreements are to Turkish advantage. But it is imperative for Turkey to remember in all circumstances that a true liberation is possible for her only in a union with Soviet Russia.[73]

The Communist International was even more definite in its criticism and its recommendations to the Turkish government. The appeal of the ECCI to the revolutionary proletariat and peasantry of the world in early 1923 stated in part:

The Communist International has followed with particularly warm feelings the heroic struggle of the Turkish people against the gang of Entente murderers. Continually drawing the attention of the advanced proletariat of the world, and in particular of Soviet Russia, to the revolutionary struggle of the Turkish workers and peasants, the Communist International has urged the proletariat to render them every possible aid. . . . If this aid had not been rendered, the attack by the imperialist robbers would long ago have brought destruction to little Turkey.

The world proletariat had applauded the Ankara government, the Communist International stated, because they believed its struggles to be "practical preparation for the complete liberation of the Turkish toilers," and not merely a matter of national liberation. It then censured the Ankara government for its recent persecution of the Turkish trade unions and the Turkish Communist Party, and warned it not to follow "the path of Poincaré or Mussolini," since such a policy would isolate it from the only sincere friends of struggling Turkey, namely "the world revolutionary proletariat, and its vanguard, the Communist International."[74]

With equal misgivings, Soviet leaders watched British and French efforts— especially at the Lausanne Conference of 1922-23—to influence Turkey and to draw it away from Soviet Russia. In September 1922, even before the convo-

---

[72] *International Press Correspondence*, No. 116, December 22, 1922, p. 971.
[73] Karl Radek in *Izvestiia*, No. 166, July 27, 1922, p. 1.
[74] *Izvestiia*, No. 33, February 14, 1923, p. 2; see Document 46.

cation at Lausanne, the Soviet government proposed that a conference be held by the powers on the Black Sea to discuss the question of the Straits. At those of the Lausanne sessions in which Soviet Russian representatives participated, the British and Soviet positions on this question appeared to be the reverse of the two countries' respective positions before World War I. Russia now demanded that the Straits be closed at all times to all warships, and open to all commercial navigation, and that Turkey be given the right to fortify the coasts of the Straits. Lord Curzon, representing Great Britain, insisted on having the Straits open to all warships, and emphasized that Russia's plan simply expressed Russia's desire "to convert the Black Sea into a Russian lake with Turkey as the faithful guardian at the gates."[75]

Consequently when the Turkish delegates accepted the British draft of an agreement, Soviet delegates, on their part, refused to affix their signatures to the Lausanne Protocol, which had been drawn, as they believed, in the interest of the Great Powers only.[76]

The Soviet treaties with Persia, Afghanistan, and Turkey were viewed by the Communists, nonetheless, as an important victory for Soviet policy in the East over that of Great Britain, and as an important step toward the consolidation of Soviet political influence throughout Asia. In *Zhizn Natsionalnostei* a Soviet commentator wrote of the future: "Thus, advancing along the appointed path, and consolidating our political achievements, we shall bring about the moment of the complete breakdown of the imperialist policy in the East, and at the same time the triumph of the international revolution."[77]

Soviet Trade with the Eastern Countries

Soviet trade with the Eastern countries, developing soon after the treaties were signed between them and Soviet Russia, was characterized by a number of significant concessions which were granted to these countries by the Soviet government. Special regulations on the foreign trade monopoly were introduced in Soviet Russia in 1920 at the time when the Commissariat of Foreign Trade was created.

The adoption of the foreign trade monopoly signified that the state was to exercise the absolute control of foreign trade. This control was to be carried out through the People's Commissariat of Foreign Trade in conjunction with STO (Soviet Truda i Oborony, i.e., the Council of Labor and Defense). All export and import was to be done according to a plan, and the categories and quantities of all merchandise were also regulated.

But trade with Eastern countries was exempted from many of the above-noted rules. To begin with the Vserossiiskaia Vostochnaia Torgovaia Palata (All-Russian Chamber of Commerce) was established in 1922 to supervise So-

[75] *Lausanne Conference on Near Eastern Affairs, 1922–1923. Records of Proceedings and Draft Terms of Peace* (Cmd. 1814), p. 141.

[76] Soviet participation at the Lausanne Conference, which produced a battle of wits between Lord Curzon and Chicherin, is dealt with in greater detail in the companion volume, *Soviet Russia and the West, 1920–1927.*

[77] I. P. Trainin, "K dogovoru s Afghanistanom," *Zhizn Natsionalnostei*, No. 7 (105), March 17, 1921, p. 1; see Document 39.

viet Russia's trade with the East.[78] *Torgovlia Rossii s Vosotokom* ("Russia's Trade with the East") became its official organ. By the decree of STO, joint trading companies were established for trade with the East, and individual Eastern traders were taken into these companies.

The problem of trade relations with the East was discussed at the Second Conference of the Representatives of the People's Commissariat of Trade, held in 1923. "Our political tasks in the East," L. B. Krasin, the People's Commissar of Foreign Trade, said at this conference, "are quite special. I speak of political tasks in general, and not only of our trade policy, because the problems of general policy are decisive for us in all our relations, including our trade relations with the East." Krasin added that Soviet Russia and the countries of the East had two things in common: they were all the targets of Western imperialism, and they all wished to defend the interests and rights of the oppressed and exploited peoples of the East.

In so far as actual trade with the East was concerned, Krasin explained why special rules, inapplicable to the West, could be used in commercial relations with the Asian peoples:

We fear no competition on the part of the East, either in our trade or in our industry. . . . Nor are we afraid of the East as a competitor for our agricultural products. We do not fear it for the simple reason that Eastern production differs from ours because of the differences in climatic conditions and methods of work.[79]

The conference at which Krasin spoke finally adopted the rules for trading with Eastern countries, and stated in the first paragraph of its theses:

Our external commercial policy in the East must be essentially different from that in relation to the capitalistic West, because of the special character of our economic relations in the East and West, and also as a result of those practical problems which confront the U.S.S.R. in the East.[80]

By these regulations the trade exchange between the U.S.S.R. and the Eastern countries was considerably decentralized, and Eastern merchants were permitted to enter Russia in order to transact individual trade. Advantageous terms to Eastern traders and reduced prices on goods exported to the East were also provided for.

British Protest Against Soviet Propaganda in the East

Soviet diplomatic accomplishments in the Near East, along with the increasing communist propaganda throughout Asia, were viewed in Great Britain with considerable disquietude. Finally, in September 1921, the British government charged the Soviet government with infringing the trade agreement signed by

[78] *The* (London) *Times* (January 1, 1923, p. 9) published a most revealing document, ostensibly the translation of the circular note of the Politburo of the Russian Communist Party of November 25, 1922, stating that this Chamber was also charged with the task of propaganda among the Eastern people. It is impossible to verify the authenticity of this document from Russian sources.

[79] L. B. Krasin, *Voprosy vneshnei torgovli*, pp. 332–34.

[80] Complete text appears in Violet Conolly, *Soviet Economic Policy in the East* pp. 140–42.

the two countries six months earlier,[81] by the terms of which the Soviet government had agreed to refrain from inciting any of the peoples of Asia to any action detrimental to British interests, especially in India and Afghanistan.

The British note detailed specific instances of Soviet violation of the agreement, emphasizing in particular the role of the Comintern and its Eastern Secretariat, and quoting from reports to the Third Congress of the Communist International[82] and to the Central Committee[83] by such prominent Soviet leaders as Lenin and Stalin, among others.

Stalin was quoted as having stated in his report to the Central Committee (and in reviewing the work of the Eastern Secretariat from February 1 to June 1, 1921):

The general guiding purpose of the Eastern Secretariat in all its work is to exert pressure upon the political authority of the capitalist powers of Western Europe through their colonies, discrediting them in the eyes of the native population, and simultantously preparing the latter to emancipate themselves from an alien yoke. The problem of the class struggle in the West will be incomparably easier to solve if the external power of France and England can be undermined.

A further quotation from Stalin concerning Soviet propaganda in Afghanistan and India was included, along with quotations from Eliava[84] on anti-British work in Turkestan and India, and from Nuorteva[85] on "supplying Eastern [communist] organizations with all they require." Lenin was quoted on Soviet Russia's place in preparing the revolution in capitalist states, and on the importance of awakening the workers in the colonies and dependencies.

The British note also referred to Moscow's support of the Indian revolutionaries in Europe. Specifically, the note accused V. L. Kopp, the Soviet representative in Berlin, of aiding Virendranath Chattopadhyaya and other members of the Indian Revolutionary Society stationed in Berlin, and charged Soviet agents with "trying to persuade a well-known Indian anarchist, Dr. Hafiz, who has been studying the manufacture of bombs in Vienna, to proceed to Afghanistan to supervise a bomb depot on the borders of India in order to facilitate their importation into India. Dr. Hafiz has now, with the assistance of the Soviet Government, undertaken the task of manufacturing smokeless powder in Kabul, and has received from the Soviet Government the sum of 10,000 kronen for expenses connected with his wife and children."

The British complained also of the Tashkent "propaganda school, the temporary base for Indian work in which emissaries were trained for dispatch to India,"[86] and also mentioned a special allocation of 2,000,000 gold rubles by Moscow to carry on propaganda in the East and particularly on the Indian frontier.

[81] Text of this agreement appears in Shapiro, I, pp. 102–4.

[82] The Third Congress met June 22–July 12, 1921; see our pp. 143–44.

[83] It is not quite clear whether the note referred to the Central Committee of the Russian Communist Party, or whether it mistakenly referred to the ECCI as "the Central Committee."

[84] Eliava was a member of the Turkestan Commission sent to Turkestan from Moscow in October 1919 and later a member of the Presidium of the Council for Propaganda and Action founded at the Baku Congress of the Peoples of the East, September 1920.

[85] No information is available on Nuorteva.

[86] See our p. 84.

Soviet activities in Turkey and Persia were mentioned also. The note spoke of "the real motives underlying the policy of the Soviet Government in supporting the Turkish Nationalists," and stated that "M. Rothstein [Rotshtein], the representative of the Soviet Government in Teheran, is importing large sums of money, much of which he is known to spend on propaganda," and also on subsidizing anti-British propaganda in certain Persian newspapers.

Finally, the British note protested against Soviet activities and policies in Afghanistan, including the Soviet-Afghan Treaty signed earlier that year. Jemal Pasha, at that time in Afghanistan purportedly to train the Afghan army, was actually there with Soviet support in order to stir up trouble among the tribes living on the Indian border, said the note; moreover, he had come to Kabul from Moscow, and was accompanied by and associated with the Indian revolutionary, Professor Barakatullah.[87]

The Soviet government immediately responded with its usual declaration that it could take no responsibility for the activities of the Third International, and, in this case, denied the charges detailed in the British note, claiming in its denial that the British government had been misinformed and misled by forgers.[88]

The British government thereupon sent a second note stating:

His Majesty's Government had not made these charges without a prolonged and careful investigation in each case into the sources of their information. . . . They see no reason to recede from or even to qualify a single one of these charges now. . . .

It is impossible to accept Mr. Litvinof's attempt to dissociate the Russian Government from the Third International. . . . That the Third International, established in Moscow under the protection of the Russian Government, from whom it draws constant support and resources, should include in its executive MM. Lenin and Trotsky, the two most prominent members of the Russian Government, establishes so close an identity between the two bodies that each must be answerable to charges against the other. Moreover, the procedure adopted in this case has long since become familiar. When the Russian Government desire to take some action more than usually repugnant to normal international law and comity, they ordinarily erect some ostensibly independent authority to take the action on their behalf. . . . The process is familiar, and has ceased to beguile.[89]

This second British note then went on to acknowledge one error in the original note—in the date of one of Lenin's speeches—and to declare that contrary to Soviet conjecture, the information upon which the British government had based its charges had come not from forged sources, but from official Soviet publications supplied by the Soviet delegation in London or received directly from Russia.

Over a year and a half passed before the British government again protested against Soviet violation of the Anglo-Soviet agreement of March 16, 1921. The

---

[87] *A Selection of Papers Dealing with the Relations between His Majesty's Government and the Soviet Government, 1921–1927* (Cmd. 2895), pp. 4–12 (cited hereafter as *A Selection of Papers Dealing with the Relations between His Majesty's Government and the Soviet Government, 1921–1927*).

[88] Kliuchnikov and Sabanin, III, 124–27; also *A Selection of Papers Dealing with the Relations between His Majesty's Government and the Soviet Government, 1921–1927*, pp. 12–16. See Document 47.

[89] *A Selection of Papers Dealing with the Relations between His Majesty's Government and the Soviet Government, 1921–1927*, p. 18.

new protest, the famous ultimatum of Lord Curzon, was sent to the Soviet government on May 2, 1923.

Curzon's note took up in great detail the anti-British activities of Soviet representatives in Persia and Afghanistan (Shumiatsky and Raskolnikov respectively). It cited numerous excerpts from dispatches and statements by these representatives, such as (1) a request from Shumiatsky to the Soviet government for funds to help organize a group of workers in Persia "who can act in an anti-British direction with real activity," and (2) several dispatches from Raskolnikov to the Soviet government describing his work among the Muslims. Associating Raskolnikov's machinations with certain events in India, the note stated:

The Soviet Government has also not failed to carry its activities further into India. Already in November 1922, seven Indians, who had been trained as Communist agitators at Tashkent and, after the conclusion of the Russian Trade Agreement, at Moscow, were arrested on their arrival in India from Moscow, whence they had travelled under the charge of Russian civil and military officials by a circuitous and very difficult route, in order to avoid detection.[90]

The note also stated that in June 1921, a number of banknotes, issued through Lloyd's Bank and the Russian Commercial and Industrial Bank in London to N. Klishko, the Soviet government's official agent in London, were later cashed in India "on behalf of a revolutionary Panjabi in touch with other Indian seditionaries who are known to have been closely associated with the Russian representative in Kabul." Therefore, the note concluded, unless the Soviet officials mentioned above "are disowned and recalled from the scene of their maleficent labours, it is manifestly impossible to persevere with an agreement which is so one-sided in its operation."[91]

The true character of Soviet policies toward Asia is suggested by Documents 48, 49, and 50. For reasons indicated in the companion volume,[92] the Moscow government preferred not to quarrel with Great Britain at that time and was conciliatory in its reply to Curzon's ultimatum, although it by no means discontinued its revolutionary efforts in Asia. We shall deal with these efforts in our later pages.

[90] For more on this matter, see our p. 84.
[91] *Correspondence between His Majesty's Government and the Soviet Government respecting the Relations between the two Governments* (Cmd. 1869), p. 9.
[92] *Soviet Russia and the West, 1920–1927.*

C. SOVIET SUCCESSES AND FAILURES IN THE FAR EAST

Moscow and Outer Mongolia

Soviet activity in the East was not limited to the Muslim world. The Buddhist Mongols—the Buriat Mongols and the Kalmuks within Russia as well as their kinsmen across Russia's borders—were also included in Moscow's plans. Thus although *Zhizn Nationalnostei,* official organ of the People's Commissariat of Nationalities, proclaimed that "the nearest, and perhaps the easiest, way from Europe to Asia" lay through the Muslim countries of Persia and Afghanistan, it acknowledged at the same time another way. "There is also a Mongolian-Buddhist route, which starts in the Kalmuk steppes, and leads through Altai, Mongolia, and Tibet, on to India."[1]

The Soviet government, like its tsarist predecessor, soon became enmeshed in the internal affairs of Outer Mongolia. In August 1919, the Soviet government issued a special declaration addressed to the Mongolian people and government, stating in part:

As soon as the Russian workers and peasants seized authority from the tsarist generals, gendarmes, and capitalists on October 26, 1917, they immediately appealed to the toilers of the world with an offer to establish a political order under which no strong state would dare to seize, or to keep by force, small and weak nations.

Simultaneously, the [Russian] Workers' and Peasants' Government annulled all secret treaties with Japan and China by which the tsarist government, under the pretext of autonomy for Mongolia and allegedly in the interests of the Mongolian people, had actually seized Mongolia from China . . . and plundered the wealth of the Mongolian people, passing it on to the Russian merchants and oppressors of the people. . . .

. . . Mongolia is henceforth a free country. . . .

All institutions of authority and law in Mongolia must henceforth belong to the Mongolian people. . . .[2]

Doksan, a Mongol who took part in the Mongolian revolution of 1919–21, stated some time later that this appeal had made a "tremendous impression upon the advanced people of our country and served as one of the driving forces in the organization of a revolutionary group among our herdsmen. This group made it its aim to liberate our country from foreign usurpers."[3]

Mongolian Revolutionary Contact with Moscow

In the autumn of 1919 two underground Mongol revolutionary groups were founded in Urga under Russian influence, one led by Suhe-Bator, and the other

---

[1] Amur Sanai, "Kliuchi k Vostoku," *Zhizn Natsionalnostei,* No. 19 (27), May 26, 1919, p. 2. See Document 51.

[2] V. D. Vilensky (Sibiriakov), *Sovremennaia Mongoliia,* pp. 52–53; see Document 52.

[3] *Sovremennaia Mongoliia,* No. 6, 1936, p. 6; as given in I. Ia. Zlatkin, *Mongolskaia Narodnaia Respublika—strana novoi demokratii,* p. 121. (Hereafter cited as Zlatkin, *Mongolskaia Narodnaia Respublika.*)

by Choibalsan. Both men maintained close contact with the Russian revolutionaries in Urga and were probably considerably influenced by them.[4] The two groups joined forces in January 1920, and issued proclamations calling upon the Mongols to struggle for the liberation of their country. They also set about making plans for an armed uprising and secretly acquiring firearms. In the spring of 1920, the new organization directed a delegation to proceed to Russia and to ask for assistance. According to a Soviet account,[5] this delegation included Suhe-Bator, Choibalsan, Doksan, and others.

With the encouragement of the Soviet representatives in Irkutsk, some members of the Mongolian delegation started off for Moscow, while others returned to Urga. According to a Soviet source, Suhe-Bator carried with him, concealed in his reed stick, a written appeal to the Soviet government for aid to the Mongolian revolutionaries.[6]

Zlatkin described the results of the Mongols' trip as follows:

The delegation, enriched by the contact with the leading men of the Soviet state and of the Comintern, returned home in November 1920, having been promised assistance by the Soviet government in the task of liberating Mongolia from a common enemy, the White Guards. Thereafter the border town of Kiakhta was turned into the center of revolutionary activities. From there threads were spread to all regions of the country, uniting the revolutionary organization with the masses of *arats* [herdsmen]. From Kiakhta along the Mongolian plains slogans were spread calling the people to struggle and to arms. In November 1920, the first issue of a lithographed illegal paper titled *Mongolyn unen* ("Mongolian Truth") was published.[7]

Anti-Bolshevik Russian Activities in Mongolia

The Mongolian revolutionaries, encouraged and assisted by Moscow, were not the only group working for Mongolian independence at this time. Certain Russian anti-Bolshevik leaders in Siberia were making even broader plans for the unification of Mongolia.

Ataman Semenov, a White leader on the Siberian front, himself half Mongol and listing among his troops a Buriat-Mongol division, organized a Pan-Mongolian movement in 1919. His plan was regarded with some favor by the Japanese, who were then occupying sections of Russian Siberia.

Semenov sponsored a Pan-Mongolian congress which was held in Chita, February 25, 1919. Present were fifteen or sixteen representatives from Inner Mongolia, Barga, and Buriatia. Outer Mongolia was not represented.

The congress resolved to create an independent federated Mongolian state to be composed of Inner Mongolia, Outer Mongolia, Barga, and the Russian Buriat-Mongol region; to organize a provisional government of four ministers, one from each of its component territories; and to leave the final decision as to the type of permanent government to a constituent assembly which would be convened after the formation of the state.

[4] It is of interest to note that Choibalsan had attended the Russian school at the Russian consulate in Urga and in 1912 had been sent to Irkutsk to continue his studies. By 1919 he had become an active revolutionary.

[5] Genkin, *Severnaia Aziia*, No. 2, 1928, p. 81; see Documents 54 and 55.

[6] Zlatkin, *Mongolskaia Narodnaia Respublika*, pp. 122–23.

[7] *Ibid.*, pp. 123–24; see Document 55.

The congress also proposed that the new state have its permanent capital in Hailar, and its temporary capital (until Hailar could be occupied) at the railway station of Dauria; that a twenty-year loan be floated abroad for the purpose of constructing railways in the region; that an army be organized; and that a delegation be sent to the Paris Peace Conference and a special appeal made to the President of the United States requesting American support for Mongolian independence.[8]

It appears that Japan and the Allies opposed the plan to send a delegation to the Paris Conference, for the Mongolian delegates never got further than Japan, where they were denied permission by the Allied ambassadors to proceed to France.[9] Toward the end of May a second conference of Mongol anti-Bolshevik leaders, including some Russian Buriats, took place, this time for a discussion of the problem of drawing Outer Mongolia into the proposed federation. It was agreed that a special delegation should be sent to Outer Mongolia for that purpose.[10]

It soon became apparent that Semenov's Pan-Mongolian plan would fail. His influence with the Mongols of Inner and Outer Mongolia and the Russian Buriats, who had at first supported him, gradually diminished, and his guarantees of a loan and other aid failed to materialize, for his influence with Japan proved to be considerably less than he had implied.

But although Semenov's plan was thus thwarted, another scheme for uniting the Mongols was soon under way. This time the sponsor of Mongolian unity was Baron von Ungern-Sternberg, known as the "mad baron," an anti-Bolshevik soldier of fortune who had roamed the Mongolian steppes as early as 1918 attempting to enlist men for his Savage Division.

In October 1920, having retreated into Mongolia, Ungern attempted to capture Urga, the capital of Outer Mongolia, but failed. A second attempt, in February 1921, in which Ungern's troops were reinforced by Cossack and Buriat units, succeeded. A new government of Mongol princes sympathetic to anti-Bolshevik Russia was formed.

Ungern, like Semenov, appears to have believed that he was destined to establish a great Mongolian state. On May 20, 1921, he wrote one of his agents in Peking:

An earnest campaign for the unification of Inner and Outer Mongolia and the bringing into the fold of Greater Mongolia of the tribes of Western and Eastern Mongolia is being carried on with great success, and I am convinced of the ultimate triumph of the Boghdikhan [Bogdo Khan, the Urga Living Buddha] and of my endeavors. Just now the main attention is beind paid to Eastern Mongolian provinces which must serve us as a sure barrier against the aggression of revolutionary China, and afterwards measures will be taken for the annexation of Western Mongolia. . . .

The next stage in the revolutionary movement in Asia, the movement carried out under the watchword of "Asia for the Asiatics," means the formation of a Middle Mongolian Kingdom which must unite all the Mongolian tribes. I have already succeeded in establishing contact with the Chirghises [Kirghiz]. . . . In like manner

[8] A. F. S——kii, "Materialy k istorii interventsii," *Novyi Vostok,* No. 2, 1922, pp. 594–95.

[9] The text of the declaration which the Mongolian delegation was to present to the Peace Conference in Paris appears in *ibid.,* pp. 599–600.

[10] *Ibid.,* p. 601.

you must direct your activities from Peking in[to] Tibet, Chinese Turkestan and in the first place in[to] Sin-tsan [Sinkiang]. . . ."[11]

On November 11, 1920, as Ungern's forces were regrouping outside Urga, Chicherin, the Soviet Russian Commissar of Foreign Affairs, officially informed the Chinese government that the Chinese forces defending Urga had requested Russian help against the "White Guardist gangs," and that the Soviet government was ready to give aid. Chicherin also promised that the Soviet troops would be withdrawn as soon as they fulfilled their mission.[12]

On November 27, 1920, without waiting for the Chinese reply, Chicherin addressed another letter to the Chinese government to the effect that the Chinese forces in Mongolia appeared to be able to cope with the situation, and that the Soviet government deemed it unnecessary to dispatch troops to Mongolia.[13] The Chinese reply to Chicherin's first note was sent somewhat later by the Chinese government through Krasin, the Soviet representative in London. The note called the plan of sending Soviet troops to Mongolia a violation of that country's sovereignty; it maintained, moreover, that the alleged Chinese request for help had never been made, and that Chinese forces could cope with the situation without assistance.[14]

Formation of the Revolutionary Party and the People's Government in Outer Mongolia

The Mongolian revolutionary group with its headquarters in Kiakhta, a Siberian town on the border of Mongolia, continued its activities. On March 1, 1921, a conference of twenty-six Mongolian revolutionaries was held at Kiakhta, in effect the first congress of the Mongolian People's Revolutionary Party. The conference elected a general staff for a People's Army, with Suhe-Bator as commander-in-chief, elected a party Central Committee, and adopted a party platform of ten articles.[15] The conference further declared that although the party was not officially a communist party, it should remain in contact with the Communist International.

Two weeks later a second conference of the People's Revolutionary Party was held in Kiakhta. This time representatives of partisan detachments and of herdsmen from the border regions were also present. At this second gathering a resolution was adopted calling for the organization of a Provisional People's Government of Mongolia and charging that government with the task of carrying out an armed revolt.

The text of the resolution stated: "We charge the Provisional People's Government with freeing the country from Chinese authority, cleansing it of Russian White Guards' bands and Chinese bandits, establishing friendly relations with neighboring states, and convening the Great Hural [Congress] of the People's

[11] *Letters Captured from Baron Ungern in Mongolia.* Typewritten copy from *Pekin and Tientsin Times,* distributed by the Special Far Eastern Delegation, Washington, D.C., 1921, with original orthography and style maintained (Hoover Library, Stanford University), pp. 5–6.

[12] *Izvestiia,* No. 256, November 14, 1920, p. 1; see Document 53.

[13] *Izvestiia,* No. 269, November 30, 1920, p. 2.

[14] *Izvestiia,* No. 3, January 5, 1921, p. 1

[15] Complete text of this platform appears in G. D. R. Phillips, *Russia, Japan and Mongolia,* pp. 32–35.

Representatives of Mongolia which is to establish a permanent government and to confirm the constitution of Mongolia."[16] That there had existed a close association between the revolutionary Mongolians in Kiakhta on the Russian border and the Moscow representatives in Irkutsk at least since 1920 is confirmed by Genkin when he states: "Ia. D. Ianson, who had been in Irkutsk since 1918 in charge of [soviet] foreign affairs, . . . agreed [in 1920] to set up special machinery to promote revolutionary work among the Mongols. The leadership in this work was taken by the Siberian Regional Bureau of the Russian Communist Party."[17]

On April 10, 1921, the newly formed Provisional People's Government in Kiakhta appealed to the Soviet government for armed assistance in a joint attack upon Ungern's forces and the existing regime in Mongolia.[18] During April and May a Mongolian People's Army was organized and trained, and on July 2, together with Russian Red units, their troops attacked Ungern's forces. On July 6 advanced units stormed Urga, and on July 8, the main forces of both armies, together with the Central Committee of the People's Revolutionary Party and officials of the Provisional People's Government, entered the Outer Mongolian capital. The People's Government signed a special agreement with Hutukhtu (the Urga Living Buddha),[19] establishing a limited constitutional monarchy in Outer Mongolia. Thus Soviet tactics already applied in Bukhara and Azerbaijan by Moscow, and to be applied in years to come in Europe, were resorted to once more: military assistance was rendered to a small revolutionary group within a foreign country—ostensibly at the request of the nationals of that country themselves.

In August of the same year, an official request was made, supposedly upon the initiative of the Mongolian government, for Soviet troops to remain on Mongolian territory. This request was quickly granted. In his reply of August 10 to the Mongolian request, Chicherin stated in part: "Soviet troops have entered the territory of autonomous Mongolia for one purpose only: to defeat the common enemy, remove the constant danger which threatens Soviet territory, and ensure the self determination and free development of autonomous Mongolia."

Chicherin emphasized the ties of friendship and common interests which united the Russian and Mongolian peoples and promised that the Soviet units would leave Outer Mongolia "as soon as the danger to the free development of Mongolia is removed and the security of the Russian [Workers' and Peasants'] Republic and the Far Eastern Republic assured."[20] Actually Soviet troops remained in Mongolia until 1925.

As will be seen later, negotiations between Soviet representatives in China and the Chinese government had started about the same time. In these negotia-

[16] "Postanovleniia sezdov, konferentsii i plenumov Ts.K.M.N.R.P.," Ulan Bator, 1946, pp. 46–47, as given in Zlatkin, *Mongolskaia Narodnaia Respublika*, p. 126.

[17] Genkin, *Severnaia Aziia*, No. 2, 1928, p. 81; see Document 54.

[18] Zlatkin, *Mongolskaia Narodnaia Respublika*, p. 128.

[19] In December 1911, when Outer Mongolia proclaimed its independence from China, Jebtsun Damba Hutukhtu was crowned Great Khan of Mongolia; he also remained head of the Lamaist church in Mongolia. With the establishment of the People's Government in Urga, Hutukhtu's power was considerably curtailed. Hutukhtu was also referred to as Bogdo Khan or Holy Khan.

[20] *Izvestiia*, No. 177, August 12, 1921, p. 2; see Document 56.

tions no satisfactory conclusion was reached on the status of Outer Mongolia. The Chinese government looked upon the occupation of Mongolia by the Soviet Red troops as an infringement on Chinese sovereign rights. While officially continuing to recognize China's sovereignty over Mongolia, the Soviets considered it detrimental to both Russia's and China's interests to remove Russian troops from Mongolia. Meanwhile, the Soviet government offered more than once to act as a mediator in the negotiations between Mongolia and China.[21]

The Soviet-Mongolian Treaty

In October 1921, the new Mongolian government sent a special mission to Moscow to open negotiations for the establishment of regular diplomatic relations between the two countries. The delegates of the Mongolian mission were received by Lenin, who admonished them to continue to strive for the development of the principles of the People's Revolutionary Party and to consolidate their achievements. "It goes without saying," Lenin said, "that you cannot at present dream of becoming a great power such as Mongolia [was] . . . in the time of Genghiz Khan, or of being on an equal cultural level with the Western countries. But it will be sufficient for Mongolia to free itself from the reputation of being a backward and insignificant state."[22]

Lenin declared that in case of war the imperialist powers would try to seize Mongolia in order to make it a starting point for military actions against the enemy country. "Therefore, the only correct path for every toiler in your country to take is to struggle for political and economic independence in alliance with the workers and peasants of the R.S.F.S.R. This struggle cannot be waged in isolation."

Lenin further remarked that it was not appropriate for the Mongolian People's Revolutionary Party to be called a communist party since there was no proletariat in Mongolia; and he spoke, too, of the possibility of the gradual emergence of "a new and noncapitalist economic system of the Mongolian *arats* [herdsmen]."[23]

As an outgrowth of Soviet-Mongolian discussions in Moscow, an Agreement for Establishing Friendly Relations was signed November 5, 1921, by the R.S.F.S.R. and the Mongolian People's Government by which each recognized the other as the only legal government in its respective territory. The security clause which had appeared in other Soviet treaties of the period reappeared in the treaty with Mongolia, along with the customary most-favored-nation clause. A commission was to be established to settle border problems, and provisions were made for a separate agreement to regulate postal and telegraphic communications "in order to strengthen the mutual cultural and economic relations."

The Soviet government officially abandoned extraterritorial rights, stating that "the judicial power of each of the Contracting Parties in civil as well as in criminal matters shall apply to citizens of the other Contracting Party residing on its territory." But this provision would be put into practice only "provided that the Parties, being guided by the high principles of civilization and human-

[21] See Document 57.

[22] *Izvestiia Ulan-Bator-Khoto*, No. 6 (350), January 22, 1927, p. 4. Ulan Bator or Ulan-Bator-Khoto is the capital of Outer Mongolia, formerly known as Urga.

[23] "IX sezd Mongolskoi Narodno-Revoliutsionnoi Partii, Ulan Bator, 1934," pp. 32–33, as given in B. Perlin, *Mongolskaia Narodnaia Respublika*, pp. 26–27; see Document 58.

ity, repudiate the use by their judicial, inquisitional or other organs of any punitive or inquisitional measures which might cause physical suffering or lower a person's moral condition."

In addition the Soviet government agreed, apparently for propaganda purposes, to turn over to the Mongolian government without compensation Russian-owned telegraphic equipment in Mongolia: "The Russian Soviet government, wishing to assist the wise measures of the Provisional government of Mongolia in the matter of organization, independent of the predatory interference of world imperialism—indispensable for the cultural development of the laboring masses of Mongolia—turns over without compensation as the full property of the Mongolian people, the buildings of telegraphic offices with the telegraphic equipment therein which belong to the Russian Republic and are located within the boundaries of Mongolia."[24]

Paragraph XI of the treaty indicated what was to be expected from close association between the new Mongolian government and Soviet Russia and suggested that Russian influence in that country was on the upsurge. It read in part: "Taking into consideration the full importance of regulating the questions of postal and telegraphic communications between Russia and Mongolia, as well as the transmission of transit telegraphic correspondence through Mongolia, in order to strengthen the mutual cultural and economic relations which unite the peoples of both countries, the Parties agree that a special agreement on this subject shall be concluded in the shortest time possible."[25] We shall indicate later the nature of this agreement.

Entirely omitted from the treaty between the Soviet government and Outer Mongolia was any reference to Chinese interests in Mongolia, or for that matter to China at all—a fact which was profoundly disturbing to the Peking government and which, as will be observed, was to become a stumbling block in Sino-Soviet negotiations.

The November agreement between Soviet Russia and Mongolia established Soviet Russia's prominent influence in the latter country, though some members of the Mongolian Revolutionary Party and of the government failed to grant it their full approval.

In the two years that followed (1922–23) there were bitter disagreements among prominent Mongolian leaders as to the future policies of their state. To some extent, these disagreements arose from differences in the leaders' backgrounds: the families of Suhe-Bator and Choibalsan were poor herdsmen; Premier Bodo was a former lama; Danzan's father was a petty tradesman; Tseren Dorji belonged to the upper strata.

A peculiar role was played by the Mongolian Youth League, founded in 1921 and inspired by a Russian Communist, A. Starkov, and also by D. R. Rinchino, a revolutionary Buriat.[26] This organization, an independent body quite apart from the Mongolian People's Revolutionary Party, proposed the immediate adoption of collective forms of economy for which Mongolia was little prepared.

The conflict of various groups and tendencies, coupled with personal in-

[24] Full text appears in Shapiro, I, 137–38.

[25] *Ibid.*, p. 138.

[26] At its inception the League had only thirteen members; in 1927 it had more than 10,000.

trigues, led in the autumn of 1923 to the execution by the radical group of the more moderate members of the government, among them Premier Bodo, as counterrevolutionaries.[27]

Soviet Attempts to Contact the Peking Government

For more than a year civil war and intervention cut off Soviet Russia from direct contact with China. But as Kolchak's Siberian forces were driven back, Moscow was able to send emissaries through the lines of civil war. Even before the final defeat of Kolchak, the Soviet government had dispatched a declaration to the Chinese people and the governments at Peking and Canton signed by L. M. Karakhan and dated July 25, 1919, proposing the establishment of diplomatic relations and offering as an inducement (1) the abrogation of all previous Russian treaties limiting Chinese sovereignty, and (2) the abolition of Russian concessions and special privileges in China. The text of this declaration, when it reached the Chinese government in Peking in a translated form, included a paragraph which the Soviet representatives later claimed had not been in the original Russian text.[28] The paragraph in question read as follows:

The Soviet Government returns to the Chinese people without demanding any kind of compensation, the Chinese Eastern Railway, as well as all the mining concessions, forestry, gold mines, and all the other things which were seized from them by the government of Tsars, that of Kerensky, and the Brigands, Horvat, Semenoff, Koltchak, the Russian Ex-generals, Merchants and capitalists.[29]

The importance of this clause is apparent, and, as it proved later, the dispute over it actually led to a deadlock in the early negotiations between the two governments.

The Peking government failed to respond to the Soviet declaration at that time. One year later, however, in September 1920, after Kolchak's forces had been defeated and the remaining anti-Soviet forces driven back to the Pacific, a special military and diplomatic mission arrived in Moscow from Peking. On October 12, the head of the mission, General Chang Shih-lin, was appointed a permanent representative to the R.S.F.S.R.

Within two months, however, the Chinese mission was recalled from Moscow. At a sumptuous party held by the Commissariat of Foreign Affairs for the departing mission on October 31, Chicherin spoke at length of the dark designs of the victorious coalition against China. He concluded by addressing the head of the Chinese delegation, General Chang:

In you, General, Soviet Russia greets its neighbor and friend. The paths of Russia and that of China are different at present, but their goals are the same, namely, the

---

[27] Genkin, *Severnaia Aziia*, No. 2, 1928, p. 89; see also Ma Ho-tien, *Chinese Agent in Mongolia*, pp. 113–14.

[28] For the Russian text, which the Soviet government claimed was the original copy, see A. A. Ivin, *Kitai i sovetskii soiuz*, pp. 103–5. It is worthy of note that there exists one Soviet source in which the complete text is given: V. D. Vilensky (Sibiriakov), *Kitai i Sovetskaia Rossiia*, p. 15. This declaration is usually spoken of as the First Karakhan Declaration.

[29] *The China Year Book, 1924–1925*, p. 869; see also Jane Degras (ed. and comp.), *Soviet Documents on Foreign Policy*, I, 158–61 (cited hereafter as Degras). For a detailed analysis of this controversial matter, see Allen S. Whiting, *Soviet Policies in China, 1917–1924*, pp. 29–33

liberation from interference by foreign forces in the internal affairs of our peoples. In this task, both China and Russia must find a common language and march hand in hand toward their common goal. Let the slogan of China be that of struggle and not of inaction.

General Chang replied: "I came here by the order of my government to establish a rapprochement between China and Russia. Alas! Not two months have passed and I have been instructed to return. What has caused such a change must be evident to you." He promised then to acquaint his government and his people of the true situation in Russia and added:

The slogan of a rapprochement with Russia, as we can see, becomes more and more popular every day. I firmly believe in its success. I also firmly believe that the principles of truth and justice proclaimed by the Soviet government will not perish, but will be victorious sooner or later. I also promise that the slogan of struggle, mentioned by you, sir, the People's Commissar, will remain firmly imprinted in my heart.[30]

On November 2, General Chang was received by Lenin, who said that in spite of their different paths, Russia and China were bound to be unified in their common aims. "The Chinese revolution," Lenin said, "will lead to revolution throughout the entire East, and will bring finally the downfall of world imperialism." In his reply, Chang expressed the hope that Lenin would become the president of a world republic.[31] On February 13, 1921, *Izvestiia* reported that General Chang was back in Peking and spoke favorably of Soviet Russia.[32]

In the course of negotiations, the Chinese mission in Moscow received on October 27, 1920, a memorandum, later known as the Second Karakhan Declaration, in which the basic principles for an agreement between the two countries were outlined. The Declaration referred to the previous Declaration sent more than a year before and suggested a number of points for future agreement betwen the Chinese and Soviet governments.

All treaties by the former governments of Russia were once more declared null and void, and Russia was to restore to China "without any compensation and for ever, all that had been predatorily seized from her by the Tsar's government and the Russian bourgeoisie." China, on her part, was to pledge to sever connection with officials of the former Imperial Russian government claiming to represent Russia.

Article VIII stated that "the Russian and the Chinese governments agree to sign a special treaty on the functioning of the Chinese Eastern Railway with due regard to the need of the Russian Socialist Federated Soviet Republic, and in the conclusion of the treaty there shall take part, besides China and Russia, also the Far Eastern Republic."[33]

On December 31, 1920, *Izvestiia* reported that the Chinese consul (Wen Huang-pin) and his staff were on their way to Moscow; three days later it noted that a diplomatic mission had been sent to Chita, presumably to negotiate with the government of the Far Eastern Republic. In February 1921, the Chi-

[30] *Izvestiia*, No. 251, November 9, 1920, pp. 1–2.
[31] *Ibid.*
[32] *Izvestiia*, No. 32, February 13, 1921, p. 3.
[33] Degras, I, 212–15.

nese consul and his staff duly arrived in Moscow, and on October 24, 1921, A. K. Paikes, a plenipotentiary of the Russian Soviet government, left Moscow for China to negotiate a formal settlement of outstanding problems. He arrived in Peking in December 1921.

Paikes' mission ended in failure. His denial of the Soviet-Mongolian treaty and his lack of authority to make decisions made his presence in China unwelcome. Nor did the Peking government wish to commit itself in any way before the meeting of the Washington Conference. Meanwhile, on December 8, 1921, the Soviet government wired an official protest to the governments of Great Britain, France, Belgium, Japan, Italy, and the United States, stating that the question of the Chinese Eastern Railway, which was to be discussed at the Washington Conference, was a matter of concern only to China and Russia. Although the Russian government had expressed its willingness to hand over the railway to China, the note stated, "such transfer has not taken place, and Russian rights in this railway remain in force."[34]

A. A. Ioffe's Negotiations with the Peking Government

When Paikes returned to Moscow, Soviet negotiations with China were suspended for a few months. But in August of the same year, a new envoy arrived from Moscow, an experienced Soviet diplomat and negotiator of peace with Germany at Brest-Litovsk, A. A. Ioffe. In his memorandum to the Chinese government of September 2, 1922, Ioffe proposed to open negotiations with the Chinese government on the basis of Karakhan's two memorandums. "True to its policy to the end," Ioffe stated, "the Workers' and Peasants' Government is now prepared, as before, to conduct negotiations with China in complete accord with the principles proclaimed by it in the two declarations mentioned above."[35]

But almost immediately upon the beginning of negotiations difficulties arose which finally led to a deadlock. The points of disagreement were (1) the use of the Russian share of the Boxer indemnity, (2) the question of China's sovereignty over Mongolia, and (3) Russia's claim to the Chinese Eastern Railway.

On September 21, Ioffe warned the Chinese government against unauthorized use of the Russian share of the Boxer indemnity. He was also against the contemplated discussion of the plans for the Chinese Eastern Railway independently by the shareholders of this railway.[36] In another memorandum to the Chinese foreign minister (dated November 3, 1922) Ioffe declared that the Chinese Eastern Railway was on the point of a serious financial crisis, and asked that immediate relief measures be taken. The Russian government had a right, he insisted, to interfere in the affairs of the railway because it was more interested in the Railway's future than any other government. Moreover, the Railway had been built with the money of the Russian people, and it was Rus-

[34] Kliuchnikov and Sabanin, III, 155; also Degras, I, 283. It is interesting to note that while negotiations with the Peking government failed, a local agreement was reached between the officials of the Chinese Turkestan and the Russian Soviet authorities in Tashkent dealing with the trade relations between the two regions and known as Ili Agreement of May 27, 1920. Text is given in Degras, I, 483–84.

[35] Pravda, No. 208, September 16, 1922, p. 1; see Document 59. Chinese consent followed on September 7.

[36] Pravda, No. 215, September 24, 1922, p. 2; text appears in Degras, I, 333–34.

sian property until Russia agreed of her own free will [*dobrovolno*] to pass it over to someone else.[37]

In his additional memorandum of November 6, he stated that to avoid misunderstanding he wished to emphasize that although Russia based her policy on the Karakhan declarations of 1919 and 1920 both in general and specifically in regard to the Chinese Eastern Railway,

it cannot be assumed from the above declarations that Russia has given up her interest in the Chinese Eastern Railway. Russia has only given up the policy of violence as it was used by the tsarist government, and has renounced the rights acquired by the tsarist government through violence. But Russia does not surrender her rights in China until all the problems of dispute between China and Russia are settled through a voluntary agreement. . . . Besides, the above declarations do not annul the legal and just interests of Russia and China. In particular, even if, for example, Russia should pass on to China her right to this railway, this fact would not annul Russia's interests in the Chinese Eastern Railway, which comprises a part of the great Siberian Railway connecting one sector of Russia with the other.[38]

As far as Outer Mongolia was concerned, Ioffe had occasion to express Soviet views on November 7, 1922, when a statement by him was read at a banquet in Peking given by the Russian delegation to celebrate the fifth anniversary of the October Revolution:

New Russia has never forced its will on the will of other people, even if it went contrary to Russia's own economic and political interests. New Russia has never hindered the formation of young republics on Russian territory. Other countries, China, for example, would do well to give up their imperialist policies in regard to, let us say, Mongolia. We know that attempts are being made to use the Mongolian problem against us, but the withdrawal of the [Soviet] troops from Urga is impossible because of the interests of both Russia and China. Besides, the Mongolian people have asked us not to withdraw the Russian troops. Russia has given up once and for all the aggressive policy of the former tsarist government, and does not demand anything from China. The only question in which we desire the recognition of Russia's legal interests is the question of the Chinese Eastern Railway.[39]

Finally, Ioffe's memorandum of November 14, 1922, enumerated once more Russia's stand in regard to the Chinese Eastern Railway and in regard to China in general.[40]

The deadlock in negotiations was now complete, and Ioffe soon left for Japan to open negotiations with that country. Before leaving China, however, he stopped at Shanghai, where he signed a very inportant agreement with Sun Yat-sen, the leader of the revolutionary nationalist movement in China.

Moscow's Relations with Japan

Relations with Japan were even harder to establish than relations with China because of Japanese intervention in the Russian Far East and Siberia.[41]

[37] *Izvestiia*, No. 255, November 11, 1922, p. 1.
[38] *Ibid.*
[39] *Ibid.*
[40] See *Russian Information and Review*, December 16, 1922, p. 171.
[41] For the account of the Japanese intervention jointly with the American and British forces, see John A. White, *The Siberian Intervention.*

On January 5, 1920, the United States had resolved to evacuate its forces from Siberia, and on April 1 all Allied troops except the Japanese troops were withdrawn. A few days later, April 5, Japanese troops unexpectedly attacked the Russian garrison in Vladivostok, while skirmishes between Japanese troops and Red partisans also took place in a number of Siberian towns.

On February 24, 1920, despite the tense situation in Siberia, the Soviet government had approached the Japanese government with a proposal to open peace negotiations "in order to ensure for the two peoples peaceful coexistence, friendly neighborly relations, and mutual satisfaction of reciprocal interests." The Soviet note emphasized that the Russian people "cherish no aggressive designs against Japan," and that "the Soviet government has no intention of interfering in the internal affairs of the Japanese people."[42]

The Japanese government left the Soviet note unanswered. The following March 28, in an attempt to stabilize the situation in Siberia by some other means, the Congress of the Toilers of the Baikal Region met in Verkhneudinsk, allegedly on the initiative of the population, and resolved to found an independent democratic and noncommunist Far Eastern Republic with Chita as the seat of its government. This declaration was communicated to the Soviet government in Russia and also to the governments of the Allied countries. On May 14, Chicherin, the Commissar of Foreign Affairs, recognized the newly formed government of the Far Eastern Republic on behalf of Soviet Russia.[43] The Allies remained silent.

On May 31, the Far Eastern government again addressed the Allied countries, calling their attention to three prerequisites for the final establishment of peace and order in the Russian Far East: (1) that the Red Army of Soviet Russia should cease its eastward advance at a certain established point (in fact, its advance had already been completed); (2) that friendly economic relations should be established between the new republic and the Allied countries; (3) that all foreign expeditionary troops should leave the country, thus permitting the resumption of commercial and industrial pursuits.[44] It is clear that the Far Eastern Republic, which actually maintained close ties with Soviet Russia, was to serve as a buffer and go-between for Soviet Russia and Japan. In addition, the establishment of this republic was intended to align Allied sympathies with the Russian Far East and against the Japanese intervention in that region, as well as to initiate and develop commercial and trade relations between the Russian Far East and the Allied countries.

The first outcome of this move was a declaration signed on July 16, 1920, in Siberia between the representative of the Far Eastern government, Shatov, and the representative of the Japanese government. Referring to the Far Eastern Republic, the declaration stated that no such buffer state "could remain isolated from civilized countries possessing highly developed industries. There is a close community of interests between the territory of the Russian Far East and that of Japan, and for that reason the buffer state is bound inevitably to maintain the closest possible relations and communion with Japan. In the develop-

[42] G. Reikhberg, *Iaponskaia interventsiia na Dalnem Vostoke, 1918–1922 gg.*, pp. 77–78; see Document 60.
[43] See Documents 61 and 62.
[44] *Japanese Intervention in the Russian Far East*, pp. 47–48. (Issued by the Special Delegation of the Far Eastern Republic, Washington, D C., 1921.)

ment of the above-indicated principle, both delegations agree that the buffer
state shall not adopt communism as the basis of its social system but shall have
a national and democratic basis."[45]

The actual reason the Russian Communists agreed to a noncommunist Far
Eastern Republic was provided by V. D. Vilensky (Sibiriakov), the Soviet
mouthpiece on Far Eastern questions:

The Red Army, which had halted by Lake Baikal, was confronted with the task of
a further advance eastward in order to put a final end to the counterrevolution in
the Far East. But the carrying out of this task involved a struggle with Japan, since
at that time the latter had occupied the Transbaikal Region with its troops and was
supported by the notorious Ataman Semenov, who had his headquarters in Chita.

Vilensky then went on to say that the Soviet government did not wish a
war with Japan, especially since it was already facing war with Poland.

Soviet Russia [therefore] had soberly evaluated the existing political situation and
had decided to halt its advance eastward, and instead to consolidate its position by
Lake Baikal and to defend Siberia only. In so far as the Far East was concerned, it
wished to advance a project for the establishment of a buffer state . . . which was
a necessity because of Russia's temporarily weak position in the Far East.[46]

Meanwhile, the continuation of the Japanese occupation of the Russian
Far East had been viewed with misgivings by the United States, and was followed by a number of American protests to the Japanese government.[47]

Finally, early in July, 1921, just as Secretary of State Charles E. Hughes
was announcing the convocation of the Washington Conference on Naval Disarmament, an American mission was sent to the Far Eastern Republic. As the
result of American pressure, the Japanese representatives in Chita proposed
to the government of the Far Eastern Republic that a secret conference be convened to settle the problems outstanding between the two governments and to
clear the way for the establishment of normal diplomatic relations between
them.

On August 26, 1921, delegates of the Far Eastern Republic and Japan met
in the Japanese port of Dairen. The Far Eastern delegation proposed that
Japan immediately evacuate Siberia and that representatives of the R.S.F.S.R.
participate in the conference. The Japanese turned these proposals down. Next
the Far Eastern delegation introduced a scheme which called for the evacuation of Japanese troops within a month in return for economic privileges and
concessions. Again the Japanese delegation refused, this time declaring that
Japanese troops would be evacuated only after the satisfactory settlement of the
"Nikolaevsk incident," and within a time limit which they themselves would set.

The "Nikolaevsk incident" to which the Japanese delegation referred had
served as the official Japanese pretext for continuing the occupation of Russian

[45] Kliuchnikov and Sabanin, III, 40. An armistice between the Far Eastern Republic
and Japan was signed at Gongota Station, July 15, 1920 (Kliuchnikov and Sabanin, III,
38–39).

[46] V. D. Vilensky (Sibiriakov), *Rossiia na Dalnem Vostoke*, pp. 35–36.

[47] Memorandum of the Department of State to the Japanese Embassy, Washington,
May 31, 1921 (*Papers Relating to the Foreign Relations of the United States, 1921*, II,
702–5). For the Soviet protest to the Allied governments against the continuation of intervention in Siberia, see Document 63.

territory after the evacuation of the other Allied powers. In March 1920, a Japanese detachment had been destroyed and Japanese citizens killed by Red partisans in Nikolaevsk. According to the Soviet account this had been the result of an attack by the Japanese detachment on Red partisans in the town in violation of a previous agreement. In any case, the incident had served the Japanese government as a pretext for the occupation of Northern Sakhalin.

The Dairen Conference dragged on from August 21, 1921, to April 16, 1922. In October 1921, the Japanese delegation advanced a series of drastic conditions known as the "seventeen demands." Included among them were demands for special privileges for Japanese citizens throughout the territory of the Far Eastern Republic; for prevention by the Far Eastern Republic of activities on its territory hostile to Japan; for a guarantee from the Far Eastern Republic that a communist regime would not be established on its territory and that private property would not be abolished; for demilitarization of the Vladivostok area and for the placing of Vladivostok under foreign control; for an increase in Japanese fishing privileges; for concessions to Japan in Northern Sakhalin as compensation for the Nikolaevsk incident; for neutrality on the part of the Far Eastern Republic in the event of a war between Russia and Japan; and for the privilege of evacuating the Maritime Region at its own discretion and of evacuating Sakhalin only after settlement of the question of concessions there.[48]

These demands the Far Eastern delegation in turn pronounced unacceptable. After further diplomatic maneuvering the Japanese demands were withdrawn and a number of concessions were granted by the Far Eastern Republic. For a time it appeared that agreement was to be reached. But the Japanese refused to indicate a definite date for the evacuation (particularly of Northern Sakhalin), and finally, on April 15, 1922, announced that new instructions had been received from Tokyo.

The next day the conference came to an end, with no agreement having been reached. On April 27 the foreign minister of the Far Eastern Republic, Ianson, approached the Japanese foreign minister with an official note putting the blame for the failure of the conference on the Japanese representatives' inability to settle the question of the evacuation of Japanese troops from the Maritime Region.[49]

Japan and the Far Eastern Republic again met in conference on September 4, 1922, at Changchun, this time with a representative of the R.S.F.S.R., A. A. Ioffe, also present. When the Japanese representatives proposed at this conference to limit the discussions to the consideration of the Far Eastern problems only and to conclude a treaty with the Far Eastern Republic alone, Ioffe spoke in the name of both Soviet Russia and the Far Eastern Republic.

In criticizing the Japanese proposal he said that "to limit the work of the conference to the settlement of the Far Eastern problems alone would mean that only the problems which concern Japan would be solved." He then went on to say that in spite of the inimical policy pursued by the Imperial Japanese government toward the Russian people, the latter did not harbor any ill-feeling toward the Japanese people. "In full accord with the will of their people, the

[48] M. L. Veltman (M. Pavlovich), *Iaponskii imperializm na Dalnem Vostoke*, pp. 71–73; see Document 64.

[49] *Ibid.*, pp. 77–78; see Document 65.

governments of the R.S.F.S.R. and of the Far Eastern Republic are prepared to forget the past and to come to a friendly agreement with Japan, especially since neither government shares the policy of the tsarist government, but, on the contrary, both understand and recognize full well the vital interests of the Japanese people, and are, therefore, prepared to meet halfway, or as far as possible, that people's just and essential requirements."[50]

Since the Japanese representatives continued to insist on their conditions and refused to evacuate Northern Sakhalin, the Chanchung Conference, like the Dairen Conference before it, ended without an agreement's having been reached. Northern Sakhalin was actually evacuated only in 1925 when the Soviet and the Japanese governments signed the Treaty of Peking.[51]

The Japanese evacuation of the Maritime Region on September 10, 1922, provided new conditions under which it was possible to dispense with the Far Eastern Republic. Therefore, the communist leaders arranged for a conference of the Far Eastern representatives to vote for the incorporation of the Far Eastern Republic into the R.S.F.S.R.[52]

The Washington Conference on Naval Disarmament and Far Eastern Affairs, November 12, 1921–February 6, 1922

In seeking to pierce the line of political and commercial isolation in the Far East by gaining recognition from Japan and China, and indirectly from the United States, Soviet leaders could scarcely approve the conference on naval disarmament and Far Eastern problems that was to be held in late 1921 in Washington, D.C. The conference, which was proposed by the United States, was to include representatives of Great Britain, Belgium, Holland, Italy, France, Portugal, the United States, China, and Japan, but not Soviet Russia. The Soviet government interpreted this plan as unfriendly and vigorously protested, declaring that Soviet Russia would not be bound by any decision made at the conference, and that any discussing of affairs of concern to Russia without Russian participation would be taken to imply the existence of secret agreements directed against Russian interests.

The first protest was voiced by the Russian government on July 19, 1921,[53] the second on November 2 in a declaration by the People's Commissar of Foreign Affairs to the governments of Great Britain, France, Italy, Japan, and the United States. "The toiling masses of Russia received with the greatest indignation this new manifestation of a policy of violence and injustice toward their country," read the declaration of November 2. "The Russian Workers' and Peasants' Government declares that the 130 million people of Russia will not permit others to force their will upon them, nor to treat them as the voiceless objects of their decisions." The declaration also noted that the Great Powers were violating the "elementary requirements of decency and respect for Rus-

[50] *Pravda*, No. 205, September 13, 1922, p. 2; see Document 66.
[51] See our pp. 252–53.
[52] For the text of the decree of the All-Russian Central Executive Committee on the unification of the two republics, November 15, 1922, see *Obrazovanie S.S.S.R.*, p. 269; also Kliuchnikov and Sabanin, III, 206.
[53] Text appears in Kliuchnikov and Sabanin, III, 106–8; also Degras, I, 249–51.

sia's sovereign rights" by attempting to settle Pacific problems without Russia, and that they would suffer the consequences when the time came.

Any decisions that the conference might take in regard to Soviet Russia could only be to the detriment of Russia's interests, . . . [and would be] in the same category as the Versailles and Sèvres treaties. But Russia is not a vanquished country. She emerged triumphant from all the trials to which she was subjected by these very same powers who now assume the task of looking out for her interests. The toiling masses of Russia have already demonstrated that they can withstand any attempts at violence directed from abroad, and they will repel every new attempt of a similar nature in the same manner.[54]

The Soviet government addressed a third communication to the governments of the United States, Great Britain, France, Italy, Belgium, and Japan on December 8, protesting specifically against the discussion of the Chinese Eastern Railway at the Washington Conference without the participation of Russia. This note declared the Railway to be the exclusive concern of China and Russia. In 1919, the Soviet government had expressed its willingness to hand over the Railway to China under certain conditions. Pending the conclusion of an agreement on this point between China and Russia, the Soviet government claimed that its rights with respect to the Railway should remain in force and could not be set aside by a conference to which Russia was not a party.[55]

Moscow used the Far Eastern Republic as a means of circumventing the Great Powers' decision not to invite Soviet Russia to the Washington Conference. A delegation representing the government of this republic arrived in Washington in December 1921. Secretary of State Hughes received the delegation, but declined to admit it to the conference. Thereupon the Far Eastern delegation published a series of documents outlining the aims and organization of the Far Eastern Republic, indicating the nature of the possible economic relations between it and the United States of America, and accusing France and Japan of continuing to support Russian anti-Soviet forces and fan civil war in Russia.[56] The French and Japanese, according to the Far Easterners, were conspiring to transfer Wrangel's remaining forces from the Near East to the Far East, there to overthrow the Far Eastern Republic and create a new government fully subordinate to Japan.

Meantime, Soviet leaders continued to denounce the Washington Conference. Pavlovich compared the American project of naval disarmament to the projects of disarmament advanced by the late Tsar, Nicholas II, in 1899, and by the British government in 1906.

Like the "famous" Tsar's project of 1899 on disarmament and the British project on the limitation of naval armament, the American project of 1921 is designed to establish a provisional status quo in the domain of armament until such time as America finds it appropriate to construct gigantic new men-of-war. The Russian project proposed the establishment of a five-year period within which all agreeing powers were not to increase their armies and their armament; the American project

---

[54] Kliuchnikov and Sabanin, III, 144–45; also Degras, I, 272–74.

[55] Kliuchnikov and Sabanin, III, 155; also Degras, I, 283.

[56] For details, see two issues of the Special Delegation of the Far Eastern Republic, Washington, D.C., 1921, entitled (1) *Trade and Industries of the Far Eastern Republic,* and (2) *Japanese Intervention in the Russian Far East*; see also H. K. Norton, *The Far Eastern Republic of Siberia.*

proposes a ten-year period, apparently to allow time for the widening of the Panama Canal or the construction of a new one to allow the passage of men-of-war of larger size than the present superdreadnoughts. By its project for the limitation of armaments, America is trying to consolidate for ten years its present advantageous position as a military and naval power.

It goes without saying that the acceptance of the American project of the limitation of armaments would in no way diminish the danger of war.[57]

Still more bitter criticism of the conference came from the Communist International. On August 15, 1921, the ECCI outlined its theses on the Washington Conference. "The Washington Conference called by the American government," the theses declared, "is another vain effort on the part of the capitalist society to find a way out of the irreconcilable contradictions which the imperialist world war made apparent, and which it failed to solve." The theses then predicted that this attempt, like the arrangements made by the Versailles Treaty and the League of Nations, would fail.

The purpose of the conference, so the theses stated, was actually the capture of the Chinese and the Siberian markets:

In view of the tremendous need for the development of its economic influence, the United States considers China and Russia (particularly Siberia) as large potential markets which must be secured at any cost. . . . Because of the exclusive position of America as the world's creditor, and because of the competition of American industry with Japanese and British interests, the United States is against all special rights and privileges now enjoyed by Britain, France, and Japan in China, as well as any rights these countries may hope to acquire in Siberia.

In short, the conference was "simply an attempt to regulate the interests of the large-scale Anglo-Saxon industries at the cost of China and Russia," and "would only lead to new world conflict." It was imperative to capture power from the capitalist classes and in that way to provide the foundation "for a true world union of the toiling peoples."

In conclusion, the ECCI called upon "the masses of China and Korea and the people of eastern Siberia to join their ranks closely with Soviet Russia, the only state which is trying to establish with the Eastern countries, threatened as they are by world imperialism, relations based on the principles of equality and fraternal aid."[58]

[57] M L. Veltman (M. Pavlovich), "Vashingtonskaia konferentsiia," *Ot Vashingtona do Genui*, p. 11.
[58] *Biulleten Ispolnitelnogo Komiteta Kommunisticheskogo Internationala*, No. 2, September 20, 1921, pp. 47, 49, 51.

D. COMMUNIST PARTIES AND REVOLUTIONARY POTENTIAL IN THE FAR EAST

The Birth of the Chinese Communist Party

In seeking diplomatic rapprochement with the Far Eastern governments, Moscow leaders did not neglect proselytizing the Far Eastern masses in accordance with the principles laid down by the Second Congress of the Comintern. General unrest, revolutionary tendencies, and an interest in the Communist movement in the East called for generous support by Moscow. By 1920 China had become the focus of Communist attention.

The Bolshevik revolution of November 1917 soon had its repercussion in China. As it had in Russia two decades earlier, the Marxian ideology now attracted the attention of some Chinese intellectuals, and in the spring of 1918 a Society for the Study of Marxism was formed.[1]

Two prominent Chinese intellectuals, both connected with the University of Peking, Li Ta-chao and Ch'en Tu-hsiu, were the founders of this group.[2] Both these men were prominently associated with the May Fourth Movement which sprang from demonstrations on May 4, 1919, by Chinese students and intellectuals in Peking expressing their resentment against Japanese encroachments in Shantung, and against the Peking government's pro-Japanese orientation. Discontent with the Western nations because of the treatment of the Chinese problem during the Paris peace negotiations was now strongly apparent among the Chinese intellectuals. Their faith in the democratic ideas of the West and in Woodrow Wilson's principles of self-determination was shaken, and they were now ready to look for and to absorb new political ideals. Moscow leaders, on their part, kept a watchful eye on the developments in China, and they appeared to consider the time ripe for establishing a communist hold in China.

In the spring of 1920 the Far Eastern Secretariat of the Communist International sent two agents to China: (1) Grigorii Naumovich Voitinsky (Zarkhin), who had lived for a time in the United States and Canada as a student and a worker, and (2) an overseas Chinese, Yang Ming-chai, who had lived in Siberia and knew Russian.[3]

In Peking, Voitinsky contacted Li Ta-chao, who gave him a letter of introduction to Ch'en Tu-hsiu, then in Shanghai. In the summer of 1920 Voitinsky was already active in the organization of the first communist cells in Shanghai, Peking, and Canton. One of the first such groups was the Chinese Socialist Youth Group, which held its first meeting in August 1920, and shortly there-

---

[1] Toa Dōbun-kai, *Saishin Shina Nenkan*, p. 1597.

[2] For an analysis of Ch'en Tu-hsiu's influence and of his relationship to Li Ta-chao, see Benjamin Schwartz, *Chinese Communism and the Rise of Mao*, pp. 7–27, and "Bibliographical Sketch, Ch'en Tu-hsiu, Pre-Communist Phase," Harvard University, Committee on International and Regional Studies, Regional Studies Seminar, *Papers on China from the Regional Studies Seminar*, Vol. II.

[3] According to Chang Kuo-t'ao in an interview with Robert C. North, Hong Kong, November 10, 1953, Yang broke with the Chinese Communists in 1923 or 1924.

after began to receive a monthly contribution of $5,000 gold from the Comintern.[4] Communist cells were also established by Chinese students in Japan and in Paris.[5]

During 1921 the Comintern dispatched another representative to China, Maring (Sneevliet), an active participant in the communist congresses held in Moscow, and, as will be indicated later, the founder of the Communist Party of Indonesia. In July of that year a first conference of the Chinese Communists was held in Shanghai with twelve Chinese attending,[6] representing forty-four Chinese Communists (apparently the total party membership). Maring also attended this conference, and probably Voitinsky.[7]

The conference lasted only a few days, but it made several important decisions. It was decided that the newly formed party was to be called the Chinese Communist Party, and that its aim was to organize the Chinese proletariat and lead it to the ultimate goal, i.e., the seizure of power. In later years this conference was referred to by the Chinese Communists as their first congress.

Meantime a Chinese Communist representative, Chang T'ai-lei, had arrived in Irkutsk in the spring of 1921 in order to establish closer contact with the Far Eastern Secretariat, which then instructed him to prepare a report and deliver it at the Third Congress of the Comintern soon to be held in Moscow. A second representative of the Chinese Communists, Yang Ho-te, had also come to Irkutsk, and the two Chinese held a number of conferences with the representatives of the Far Eastern Secretariat, the outcome of which was the establishment of the Chinese Section of the Far Eastern Secretariat of the Comintern. At one of these sessions Chang T'ai-lei outlined the duties of this Section as follows:

1) A Chinese Section of the Far Eastern Secretariat [in Irkutsk] is established to attend to the problems connected with the relations between the Chinese Communist Party and the Comintern; to supply information to the Chinese Communist Party and to the R.S.F.S.R., as well as to pass on the directives of the Executive Committee of the Comintern to the Chinese Communist Party;

2) Two secretaries are in charge of the Section: one is delegated to this work by the Central Committee of the Chinese Communist Party, and the other by the Far Eastern Secretariat;

3) The Section follows the pattern of Comintern organization by which the communist parties of separate countries serve as sections of the Comintern. Likewise, the relations between the Central Committee of the Chinese Communist Party and the Far Eastern Secretariat of the Comintern must be based on the

---

[4] Robert S. Elegant, *China's Red Masters. Political Biographies of the Chinese Communist Leaders,* p. 43. For more on the early communist developments in China, see also Robert C. North, *Moscow and Chinese Communists,* pp. 53 ff.

[5] *Chung-kuo hsien-tai ko-ming yün-tung shih,* I, 2.

[6] For the names of these Chinese, see Conrad Brandt et al., *A Documentary History of Chinese Communism,* p. 30. For an account of the conference, see Ch'en T'an-ch'iu, "Vospominaniia o I sezde Kompartii Kitaia," *Kommunisticheskii Internatsional,* No. 14, 1936, p. 96. Ch'en says only nine Chinese attended; two other sources (Nym Wales, *Red Dust,* p. 39, and Ken'ichi Hatano, "Chūgoku Kyōsan-tō-shi," *Ajia Mondai Koza*) name thirteen, but not the same thirteen.

[7] Tung Pi-wu, who was at the conference, confirms the presence of two Comintern agents, Maring ("we called him Malin in Chinese") and "a Russian whose name I have forgotten"; see Nym Wales, *Red Dust,* p. 39. According to some reports, the Russian was not Voitinsky but another agent named Nikorusky.

similar principle of organizational contact, that is, the membership of the Chinese Section of the Far Eastern Secretariat will consist of the local representatives of the Central Committee of the Chinese Communist Party in the Far Eastern Secretariat, and the Section itself will be subordinated to this Secretariat.[8]

Chang T'ai-lei and Yang Ho-te left Irkutsk in June to attend the Third Congress of the Comintern in Moscow.

Meantime the Chinese Communist Party continued to increase in membership. In June and July of 1922, it held a second congress at which the party program was outlined in a special declaration or manifesto. By that time, according to the report of a participant, "the development, struggle, and entire policy of the Communist Party of China, as well as the organization and consolidation of the Chinese Red Army, proceeded with the support and leadership of the Comintern."[9]

The party program which was outlined by the second congress in its manifesto of June 10, 1922, called upon Chinese Communists to struggle against imperialism and feudal militarism during the transition period for a democratic republic; for freedom of expression, assembly, and the press; for universal suffrage; and for an eight-hour working day, reduction of land rents, and tax revision.[10]

True to the communist concept of the importance of the proletarian leadership in the revolutionary struggle, the Chinese Communists set themselves to the task of advancing the workers' movement in China, and on May 1–5, 1922 (i.e., before the party's second congress), the first congress of the Chinese Workers' Union was held. Soon thereafter a strike of the Peking-Hankow Railway workers took place in which the Chinese workers were victorious. This strike marked the beginning of the rallying of the Chinese workers' forces under communist leadership, and of general workers' unrest during the few years that followed. More will be said about it later.

The Russian Communists and Sun Yat-sen

At the same time that the Soviet government in Moscow was attempting through diplomatic channels to work out a settlement with the Chinese government in Peking, Soviet leaders were also attempting to gain control of the anti-Peking national-revolutionary movement of the Kuomintang in South China.

On January 1, 1918, the Kuomintang, an influential factor in Chinese political development since 1912, held a conference in Canton attended by representatives from seven independent Chinese provinces. At this conference all ties with the Peking government were broken, and a southern constitutionalist government was set up, with Dr. Sun Yat-sen, founder of the party, at its head. Sun had by that time become interested in the Russian revolution. It appears

[8] B. Z. Shumiatsky, "Iz istorii Komsomola i Kompartii Kitaia (Pamiati odnogo iz organizatorov Komsomola i Kompartii Kitaia tov. Chang T'ai-lei)," *Revoliutsionnyi Vostok*, No. 4–5, 1928, p. 216. (Hereafter cited as Shumiatsky, *Revoliutsionnyi Vostok*, 4–5, 1928.)

[9] Ch'en T'an-ch'iu, "Vospominaniia o I sezde Kompartii Kitaia," *Kommunisticheskii Internatsional*, No. 14, 1936, p. 99; see also Wang Ming, "15 let borby za nezavisimost i svobodu kitaiskogo naroda," *ibid.*, pp. 81–95.

[10] Full text of the manifesto as translated by A. E. Khodorov appears in *Novyi Vostok*, No. 2, 1922, pp. 606–12. For the English translation of the manifesto, see Conrad Brandt, *et al.*, *A Documentary History of Chinese Communism*, pp. 54–63.

that a few years before its outbreak he had met some Russian revolutionaries in London, among whom was Chicherin. It is not known whether he met Lenin. Soon after the establishment of the Soviet government in Russia, however, Sun sent personal greetings to Lenin, and on August 1, 1918, it was Chicherin who replied to Sun in a note setting forth the common aims of Russia and China in opposing world imperialism and calling the Chinese people to common struggle along with the Communists because "our victory is your victory, and our doom is your doom."[11]

Although a few years were to pass before a very close association could be established between the Kuomintang and the Russian Communists, Sun's interest continued. In 1920, the Chinese leader, then living at the French Concession in Shanghai, was visited by Voitinsky, the Communist International's emissary to China.[12] Undoubtedly he also corresponded with Soviet leaders. "Beginning approximately in 1920," writes Vilensky, "Sun Yat-sen carried on correspondence with individual representatives of the Soviet state which reveals his exceptional interest in the Russian revolution."[13]

On October 31, 1920, Chicherin wrote Sun that "trade relations between us must be taken up immediately. No opportunity must be lost. Let China resolutely enter the path of good friendship with us."[14] Chicherin wrote Sun again on August 28, 1921.[15]

Also in 1921 Sun talked with Maring, who a year earlier had been instrumental in organizing the Indonesian Communist Party.[16] In 1923 Sun paved the way for further rapprochement with the Russian Communists by his letter to Karakhan, then in Peking, expressing his admiration of Soviet foreign policy in China.[17]

In January 1923, having in the meantime given up hope of getting material aid for his cause from the Western powers, Dr. Sun conferred in Shanghai with the Soviet representative, Ioffe, who was on his way to Tokyo to attempt to negotiate a treaty with the Japanese government. As the outcome of their talk, Dr. Sun and Ioffe issued a joint statement which marked the beginning of close co-operation between the Kuomintang and the Russian Communists.

The statement included confirmation of earlier Soviet declarations regarding China and went on to say:

Dr. Sun Yat-sen holds that the Communistic order or even the Soviet system cannot actually be introduced into China, because there do not exist here the conditions for the successful establishment of either Communism or Sovietism. This view is entirely shared by Mr. Joffe, who is further of the opinion that China's paramount and most pressing problem is to achieve national unification and attain full national independence, and regarding this great task, he has assured Dr. Sun Yat-sen that China has the warmest sympathy of the Russian people and can count on the support of Russia.[18]

[11] *Izvestiia,* No. 53, March 9, 1919, p. 1 ; see Document 67
[12] For Voitinsky's own account of the visit, see Document 68.
[13] V. D. Vilensky (Sibiriakov), *Sun Yat-sen, otets kitaiskoi revoliutsii,* p. 30.
[14] Eugene Ch'en, as quoted in Lyon Sharman, *Sun Yat-sen, His Life and Its Meaning; a Critical Biography,* p. 244.
[15] *Bolshevik,* No. 19, October 1951, pp. 46–48 ; see Document 69.
[16] See our p. 142.
[17] Text appears in Vilensky, *Sun Yat-sen, otets kitaiskoi revoliutsii,* pp. 30–31.
[18] *The China Year Book, 1924–1925,* p. 863.

Finally, in the autumn of 1923, there occurred a meeting that was to consolidate Russian Communist influence in the Kuomintang for the next four
years. Mikhail Borodin (Grusenberg) arrived in Canton with a letter of introduction to Sun Yat-sen from Karakhan. Borodin came officially as the representative of the Rosta[19] news service, but actually as a representative of the
Communist International. A few years later when the Chinese police raided
the Soviet embassy in Peking, the documents which were seized revealed Borodin's close association with the Comintern.[20]

Within a month of his arrival Borodin was appointed by Sun as a special
adviser to the Kuomintang. The story of Sun's acceptance of Borodin's influence and guidance is still somewhat obscure. According to one version by
Eugene Pick, allegedly a former co-worker of Borodin's in China, a certain
Stoianovich, who was a Soviet agent in Shanghai at that time, tried to persuade
Sun to accept Borodin as his adviser. Sun, who was more concerned at that
time with getting material help from Soviet Russia than with engaging an
adviser for his internal policies, was assured by Stoianovich that Borodin would
be followed by military experts with supplies of arms and money from Soviet
Russia. It was after this assurance that Sun agreed to receive Borodin.[21]

Borodin acquired a tremendous influence in the Kuomintang and within
a short time succeeded in bringing about its reorganization along the lines of
the Russian Communist Party. We shall deal later with that phase of Borodin's
presence in China.

The Emergence of the Indonesian Communist Party

While the Chinese Communist Party was shaping up, another Asian group
embraced the teaching of Karl Marx and Lenin. The Indonesian Communist
Party (Perserikaten Kommunis di India) was formally organized on May 23,
1920.

The Indonesian party drew its membership from two older Indonesian
groups: the East Indian Social Democratic Association (known in Dutch as
the Indische Social-Demokratische Vereninging), founded upon the initiative
of Hendricus Sneevliet (Maring) in 1914; and the Islamic League (Sarekat
Islam), a national Indonesian party founded in 1912 and claiming a broad following among the Muslim masses.

Dissatisfaction of the radical members of the Social-Demokratische Ve-
reeninging over policy matters led to a split during that party's seventh congress, in May 1920. Thereupon the radical dissenters formed the Perserikaten
Kommunis di India with Semaoen as party leader. The meeting which was
held by that group on May 23 was later referred to as the first congress of the
Communist Party of Indonesia.[22]

In addition to Semaoen, the newly organized Indonesian Communist Party
included two other men, Tan Malaka and Alimin, who, like Semaoen, were

---

[19] Abbreviation of *Rossiiskoe Telegrafnoe Agentstvo,* the Russian Telegraph Agency.

[20] See our p. 300.

[21] Eugene Pick (pseud.), *China in the Grip of the Reds.*

[22] I. Milgram, "K voprosu o natsionalno-osvoboditelnom dvizhenii v Indonezii," *Tikhii
Okean,* No. 3 (9), 1936, p. 107.

later to play a prominent role in Indonesian Communist affairs. The three men retained their membership in Sarekat Islam in order to undermine that party's authority among the Muslim masses. As a result of their efforts a number of leftist members of Sarekat Islam withdrew from the party and formed a new group, the so-called Sarekat Rakjat ("People's League"), a group which was to work closely with the Indonesian Communist Party, and which was to become one of the most important factors in Indonesian political life.

The struggle for the masses between Sarekat Islam and the Indonesian Communist Party became extremely bitter, particularly after the Second Congress of the Comintern and the Extraordinary Congress of the Communist Party of Indonesia which followed it in December 1920. This Extraordinary Congress met to consider the acceptance of the Twenty-One Points of the Comintern and membership in that organization. On December 24, 1920, the Congress adopted a resolution favoring Comintern membership.

In the years which followed, the party rapidly increased its influence and power among the Indonesian masses and was instrumental in staging a number of large-scale strikes, such as that of railway workers in Java. Dutch authorities in Indonesia eventually became apprehensive of Communist activity, and in 1923 they arrested the leader of the movement, Semaoen, and exiled him. He was granted the right to choose his place of exile, however, and accordingly went to Moscow. His place as leader of the party was thereupon taken by Darsono, and party work continued.

The Indonesian Communist Party was represented at the Second Congress of the Comintern by Maring; at the Third Congress in 1921 by Darsono; and at the Fourth Congress by Tan Malaka. A representative of the Communist Youth of Indonesia and a member of the Indonesian Council of Muslim Revolutionary Organizations also attended the Third Congress.

The Third Congress of the Communist International

The birth of the three Communist parties in the Far East[23] and other signs of revolutionary tendencies and dissatisfaction seemed to call for stepped-up communist action in the East. But the Third Congress of the Communist International (June–July, 1921), despite the presence of representatives from China–Korea, Indonesia, and Japan,[24] concentrated mostly on Western problems, above all on the partial stabilization of capitalism and ways of coping with it.[25] The apparent "temporary" consolidation of capitalist regimes in the Western countries, which had succeeded to some extent in blocking the revolutionary tendencies of the immediate postwar period, called for new communist tactics in the Western countries and for further efforts at stirring up discontent with the imperialist countries among the peoples of the East.

[23] In addition to Chinese and Indonesian communist parties, the Korean party was formed at a congress held by the Koreans in Irkutsk in May 1921. However, the official year for the formation of the Korean Communist Party as given in the latest edition of the Soviet Encyclopedia is 1925.

[24] The Japanese Communist Party was not officially organized until July 1922. See our pp. 152–54.

[25] See the companion volume, *Soviet Russia and the West, 1920–1927*.

For the most part, specifically Eastern questions were relegated to an especially selected Commission on the National and Colonial Questions. According to Shumiatsky[26] the commission was created upon the initiative of the Near Eastern representatives and was to make up for the mistakes made by the Turkish communists and the failure of the Gilan revolution in Persia.

Foreshadowing the future communist policy in China, the theses of the Commission in regard to the communist policies in the Eastern countries in general (of which several drafts were proposed) advanced the principle of a four-class alliance, that is of the bourgeoisie, the petty bourgeoisie (city artisans), the peasants, and the workers. M. N. Roy, who took part in the work of the Commission, was critical of the idea of the four-class alliance, and objected, as he had done at the Second Congress, to the apparent tendency toward considering the problems of all Eastern peoples to be uniform.

Chang T'ai-lei proposed his own theses. He agreed with Roy that there could be no uniform approach to the problems of all Eastern peoples; but in regard to the participation of the bourgeoisie in the national-revolutionary movement, he expressed views that tallied generally with the viewpoints expressed earlier and subsequently by the Russian Communists:

The question of the role of the bourgeoisie in the oppressed countries is purely a tactical problem because, first, it is not the bourgeoisie that defines the course and the outcome of the national-revolutionary struggle, and, second, the bourgeoisie's participation in the so-called "united national front" is only temporary. The bourgeoisie will follow the revolutionary course only in so far as it gains a certain form of government and economic and financial independence that suits its own rule.

Here Chang differed from Roy, who favored keeping up the struggle on two fronts: against the imperialists, and against the national bourgeoisie. Chang continued:

The national bourgeoisie will follow this course until it wins sufficient political, economic, and financial independence to enable it to establish its own domination [over the Chinese toilers] . . . , or until it discovers that the national-revolutionary movement conflicts with its [the bourgeoisie's] efforts to drive out the imperialists and take their place in the exploitation of the population of its own country. . . . [But] the proposal made by Comrade Roy in his theses that in the economically backward countries of the Near East the peasants and the handicraft workers should carry on simultaneously a struggle on two fronts, i.e., against the imperialists and against their own bourgeoisie, is profoundly wrong. Such a policy is not applicable to the economically backward countries of the Near East, or even to China.

The task of the communists of the colonial and semi-colonial countries of the East is as follows: without surrendering their independent program and organization, the communists must gain predominance in the national revolutionary movements; they must draw the participating masses away from the domination of the national bourgeoisie, and they must force the bourgeoisie to follow the movement for the time being under the slogans "away with the imperialists" and "long live national independence." However, when the moment arrives, this bourgeoisie must be cut off from the movement.[27]

26 Shumiatsky, *Revoliutsionnyi Vostok*, No. 4–5, 1928, p. 218.

27 *Ibid.*, pp. 221–22. Since there are no minutes available of the above commission, or of any other commissions at the Third Congress, we have relied on Shumiatsky's account.

The First Congress of the Toilers of the Far East

During the Third Congress of the Communist International, news was received of the proposed conference of Great Powers that was to meet in Washington by the end of the year (1921) to discuss naval disarmament and Far Eastern affairs in general.[28] The Comintern's Executive Committee countered this proposal with a plan of its own. It would hold a simultaneous conference of representatives of the Eastern revolutionary movements, and thus indicate the strength of Eastern opposition to imperialist plans in the East. One advocate of such a conference, Vilensky, had just returned from the Far East, which he had visited upon the instruction of the Eastern Department of the Commissariat of Foreign Affairs. After reporting the great interest in Soviet Russia displayed by Eastern people of various political opinions, Vilensky remarked:

The intentions of imperialists should be met with organized resistance by the peoples of the Far East. We believe, therefore, that now is the time to raise the question of convening an East Asian Conference of the republic of China, Mongolia, other Far Eastern countries, and the R.S.F.S.R. which should advance the interests of these peoples to counteract the interests of the vultures who are planning a conference in Washington.[29]

The initiative for such a convention seems to have come from Sen Katayama, the Japanese Communist then in Moscow, and Chang T'ai-lei.

The invitation to the congress was drafted by Chang, and it read in part:

Comrades of Korea, China, Japan, and Mongolia! The last word is with you. Join your forces with the world struggle of liberation that was started in the never-to-be-forgotten days of four years ago by the Russian proletariat. . . . On November 11, 1921, a surgical operation over the peoples of the Far East, known as the Washington Conference, will be performed. It is on that day that we convene a congress of the Toilers of the Far East in Irkutsk, the purpose of which is to unite the toilers of the East in the face of a new danger. Our slogans are: Peace and independence of the country. Land to those who till it. Factories to the workers.[30]

It was a preliminary conference (and not the congress itself) that actually met in Irkutsk in November, with 125 delegates present: 54 from China, 39 from Korea, 18 from Mongolia, 11 from Japan, and three from Java and other countries. The work of the conference was divided up into Chinese, Japanese, Korean, and Mongolian sections. The conference itself actually met in full session only once, when Chang T'ai-lei had occasion to remark:

Our union is measured not by the strength of the fleet or of the imperialist armies, but by the fact that in the country where the landlord and capitalist have been overthrown, the representatives of the toilers of the Far East have gathered to protest against the mean comedy known as the Washington Conference, and also to work out a plan for a joint struggle.[31]

After the first session of the conference in Irkutsk, its delegates traveled to Moscow and thence to Petrograd, where they were joined by new delegates.

---

[28] See our pp. 135–37.
[29] *Izvestiia*, No. 168, August 2, 1921, p. 1.
[30] Shumiatsky, *Revoliutsionnyi Vostok*, No. 4–5, 1928, pp. 225–26.
[31] *Ibid.*, p. 227.

Their deliberation continued from January 21 to January 27 as the First Congress of the Toilers of the Far East, sometimes spoken of as the First Congress of the Peoples of the Far East.

The Congress was opened by Zinoviev in Moscow on January 21, 1922, and greeted by Kalinin, Chairman of the Central Executive Committee of the Russian Soviets:

Comrades, you are now in the capital of that country on whose boundaries the sun almost never sets. But it is not its size that characterises its difference from the other states. The chief peculiarity of the country in whose capital you now are, comrades, is the fact that this country considers it impossible and does not desire to enrich itself at the expense of the other border peoples. . . . It does not wish to exploit the toil of these peoples, for the toiling masses themselves are in power here.[32]

The Congress gave the Communists another chance to reiterate their attitude toward national-liberation movements. This was opportune, since this Congress, like the one held in Baku sixteen months earlier, was attended by a large number of noncommunist revolutionary nationals.[33]

Safarov, a prominent specialist on the Eastern problem, declared:

. . . in colonial and semi-colonial countries, like China and Korea, which are actually the colonies of foreign capital, the Communist International and the Communist Parties are obliged to support the national-democratic movement. In these countries the Communist Party must advocate the overthrow of imperialist oppression and support democratic demands such as the nationalisation of the land, self-government, etc. At the same time, however, the Communist Parties must not abandon their Communist program, just as they must not abstain from organising the working class in trade unions, independent of bourgeois influence. Neither must they abstain from organising the working class in an independent Communist Party. . . .

We say, quite frankly that we support . . . bourgeois nationalists . . . because Japanese, American and English imperialism is the most reactionary force. . . . On the other hand, however, we definitely demand from these bourgeois-democratic, these radical-democratic elements, that they make no attempt to dominate over the young labor movement of China and Korea . . .[34]

According to Zinoviev, Communist co-operation with the revolutionary nationals in the East was more necessary than ever:

The Communist International is all the time taking a clear account of the fact that the revolution of the toilers can be victorious under the present circumstances only as a world revolution. . . . we know that the decisive victory will be assured only

---

[32] *The First Congress of the Toilers of the Far East*, p. 8; see Document 70. In addition to the English text of the minutes of the congress, there is also a Russian text (*Pervyi sezd revoliutsionnykh organizatsii Dalnego Vostoka. Sbornik*), and a German (Der Erste Kongress der Kommunistischen und Revolutionären Organisationen des Fernen Ostens, Moskau, Januar 1922). Only the English text, however, includes complete minutes of the congress, and we therefore use it in part in spite of its peculiarities.

[33] The promoters of the Congress, i.e., the Moscow Communists, defined the right of participation in it as follows: "Every national-revolutionary socialist or communist organization has the right to be represented at the Congress of the Peoples of the Far East" (*Pervyi sezd revoliutsionnykh organizatsii Dalnego Vostoka*, p. 290). Actually the number of representatives with the right to vote was as follows: Korea, 52; China, 37; Japan, 13; Mongolia, 14; Java, 1; Buriat group, 8; Kalmuk group, 2 (*ibid.*).

[34] *The First Congress of the Toilers of the Far East*, pp. 198–99; see Document 72.

in the event of the struggle not being confined to the European continent alone, when our struggle will rouse the hundreds of thousands, the hundreds of millions of the toiling and oppressed masses in the East.

Zinoviev also spoke of the Comintern's inadequate knowledge of conditions in the East, and said "the Executive Committee of the Communist International will listen with the greatest attention to the reports and information which will be given by you."[35]

The Congress then heard reports from the representatives of China, Japan, Korea, Outer Mongolia, and Java, each speaker outlining in detail the political, economic, and revolutionary situation in his country. In the manifesto adopted at the closing session of the Congress and addressed to the Toilers of the Far East, the representatives of these countries pledged themselves to struggle against the oppressors, declaring:

We desire to become the masters of our own fate and to stop being the playthings of the imperialists' cupidity and greedy appetites. . . . We have met in the Red capitals of the Soviet republic—Moscow and Petrograd—in order to raise our voices from this world tribune against the world executioners and against the Washington union of the four bloodsuckers.[36]

In addition to the First Congress of the Toilers of the Far East, two other important gatherings took place in Moscow. One was the Congress of the Revolutionary Youth of the Far East, and the other, the First Conference of the Toiling Women of the Countries of the Far East.[37]

Growing Importance of the Revolutionary East in the "Decaying" Capitalist System

Strengthened by the additional knowledge of economic and political conditions in the Eastern countries that was supplied by the representatives of these countries at the Congress of the Toilers of the East, the Communists in Moscow turned their attention once more to policies that were to direct their activities in the East. This further elucidation of Communist tasks was done in the light of existing political and economic conditions throughout the world.

The Fourth Congress of the Communist International, which was in session from November 5 to December 5, 1922, confirmed the earlier communist belief that the world capitalist system was in a state of decay, and that the collapse of capitalism was inevitable. For the time being, however, the capitalist countries had succeeded in stabilizing temporarily their position and were definitely on the offensive.

The capitalist offensive which of late has assumed gigantic proportions compels the workers of all countries to adopt measures of self-defense. . . . Closely allied with

[35] *Ibid.*, pp. 3–5; see Document 70.

[36] *Pervyi sezd revoliutsionnykh organizatsii Dalnego Vostoka*, p. 5; see Document 73. For further delineation of the revolutionary situation in the Far Eastern countries by the Moscow Communists, and of the tasks ahead, see Documents 70, 71, and 72. For a detailed account of this Congress, see Allen S. Whiting, *Soviet Policies in China, 1917–1924*, pp. 72–86.

[37] For documentary material on these congresses, see *Pervyi sezd revoliutsionnykh organizatsii Dalnega Vostoka*, pp. 297–314 and 333–42 respectively.

the capitalist offensive in the economic field is the political offensive of the bourgeoisie against the working class which finds its expression in international fascism.[38]

In view of this development, the Communists concentrated on obtaining influence with the majority of the working class. The slogan advanced already at the Third Congress of the Communist International, "To the Masses!," was stressed again at the Fourth Congress. In other words, the tactics of a united front were adopted; Communist forces were permitted to join with those of other radical groups. The theses of the Fourth Congress stated: "Under certain circumstances Communists must be prepared to form a workers' government jointly with noncommunist workers' parties and organizations."[39]

In so far as the Eastern countries were concerned, the Fourth Congress was able to record considerable progress: the revolutionary unrest and strikes in India in 1919–21, directed against the British; the formation of the Chinese Communist Party in 1921, and a number of strikes organized in the newly created Chinese trade unions; the birth of the Indonesian Communist Party in 1920; the attempts to establish a soviet government in the Gilan province of Persia; the Kemalist national revolution in Turkey; the strong anti-Japanese movement in Korea; the unrest against the British in Egypt; and finally, the revolutionary movement in Mongolia and the establishment of the Mongolian People's Republic. However, according to Zinoviev, the chief speaker at the Congress because of Lenin's illness, the Communist parties in the East were still "very small cells." The Communists had a dual task in the East, said Zinoviev, "first, to broaden the nucleus of the proletarian movement, and second, to go forward as the vanguard of the whole antibourgeois liberation movement."[40]

The united front tactics advanced for the European countries and the United States were to be used in the East also, but in different form, as noted in the "Theses on the Eastern Problems" of the Congress:

While in the West, which is in a period of organized accumulation of strength, the United Workers' Front is appropriate, what the colonial East needs is a United Anti-Imperialist Front. The prospect of a prolonged struggle against world imperialism demands the mobilization of all revolutionary elements.[41]

Consequently, the theses state:

Aware that the will of a nation for political independence under varying historical conditions can be expressed by the most diverse groups, the Communist International supports all national-revolutionary movements against imperialism.[42]

Sentiment on this point was no more unanimous, however, than it had been at the preceding two congresses. Roy, who was then publishing in Berlin the communist periodical *Vanguard,* upheld the views he had expressed before, again emphasizing that no uniform rule for communist development could be applied to all Eastern countries.

[38] Excerpt from the "Theses on the International Political Situation" adopted by the Fourth Congress (*Kommunisticheskii Internatsional v dokumentakh,* pp. 296–97).

[39] *Ibid.,* p. 301.

[40] *Protokoll des Vierten Kongresses der Kommunistischen Internationale, Petrograd-Moskau vom 5 November bis 5 Dezember, 1922,* pp. 51–52 (cited hereafter as *Protokoll des Vierten Kongresses der K.I.*).

[41] *Kommunisticheskii Internatsional v. dokumentakh,* p. 322; see Document 74.

[42] *Ibid.,* p. 319.

The countries of the Far East can be divided into three categories. First, those countries which are nearing the most highly developed capitalism. . . . Second, those countries in which capitalist development has taken place but is still on a lower level, and in which feudalism is still the backbone of society. . . . Third, where primitive conditions still prevail, where feudal patriarchism is the social order.

It was the task of the Congress, Roy said, to face the concrete problems in each such country on the basis of the fundamental principles outlined by the Second Congress of the Comintern. "We stand today before the concrete problem of how to accelerate the development of the movement in those countries . . . but because the social structure of these countries is different, the character of the revolutionary movement [in them] is also different." Consequently, communist tactics must be different also.

At first, said Roy, the revolutionary upheavals in the Eastern countries were a spontaneous reaction to the intensified economic exploitation of them by the imperialists during World War I. But now,

as the social and economic context of these [so far spontaneous] movements has become crystallized, the public forces that lead these movements and the social factors that go into them have become clarified also. Consequently we find today that the elements which were active participants in these movements two years ago are gradually leaving them, if they have not already left.

The national bourgeoisie, which once supported the revolution, now found it more convenient to seek imperialist protection. Consequently, Roy asserted,

the national struggle in the colonies, the revolutionary movement for national development in the colonies, cannot be based purely on a movement inspired by bourgeois ideology and led by the bourgeoisie. . . . This fact brings us face to face with the possibility that another social factor may enter this struggle and wrest the leadership from the hands of those who have been leading the struggle so far.

The Eastern masses represent such a factor, Roy asserted, and they must eventually assume leadership in the struggle. Meantime, the Communists must try to utilize all existing factors which promote the struggle. "At the same time we must keep it definitely in mind, that these factors can operate only so far and no further. We must know that they will go to a certain limit and that they then will try to stop the revolution." Basing his arguments partly on the experience of Kemalist Turkey, Roy was foreshadowing the developments which would soon take place in China.

In conclusion, Roy remarked:

The national revolutionary movement in these [Eastern] countries . . . is not going to be successful under the leadership of the bourgeoisie. . . . It is only under the leadership of a political party representing the workers and peasants that the national revolutionary struggle can come to final victory in these countries.[43]

After Roy's argument the most pertinent remarks were made by Tan Malaka, an Indonesian Communist exiled from Indonesia by Dutch authorities and sojourning for the time being in Moscow. He believed that communist co-operation with the Pan-Muslim movement in his country was imperative. He said:

[43] *Protokoll des Vierten Kongresses der K.I.,* pp. 591–97.

The Sarekat Islamists believe in our propaganda. They are with us with their stomachs, to put it colloquially, but their hearts remain with the Sarekat Islam—their heaven. We cannot give them that heaven. . . . At present Pan-Islamism is a national struggle for liberation, because Islam is for Muslim everything. Not only religion, but state, economy, food, and all—and so Pan-Islamism now means the fraternity of all Muslim nations and the liberation struggle not only of the Arabic, but also the Indian, Javanese, and all other oppressed Muslim nations. Practically, this fraternity is now called struggle for liberation not only against the Dutch, but also against the English, French, and Italian capitalists, consequently against world capitalism. . . . Just as we are willing to support a national war, we also want to support the liberation struggle of the aggressive, very active 250 million Moham-medans who are subject to the imperialist powers. . . . Therefore I ask once more: Should we support Pan-Islamism in this sense?[44]

Malaka was supported by Van Ravesteyn (a Dutch Communist) in his re-port to the Fourth Congress on the Western question. Speaking of the historical struggle of Islam for political liberation, he remarked:

It is the duty of the revolutionary proletariat to watch closely and to give the Muslims all possible moral and political support. . . . The chief enemy of the proletariat and also of the Eastern, and especially of the Muslim peoples, is the British Empire, whose world-embracing imperialism is founded (among other things) upon hegemony over India and naval dominance in the Mediterranean and the Indian Ocean. It lies within the power of the Muslim peoples to break down the bridge that sustains British imperialism. Should this bridge fall, the whole structure will collapse, and its overthrow will have such mighty repercussions throughout the East and the Muslim world that French imperialism too will fall in ruins.[45]

But the lengthy theses adopted by the Congress, though they referred to Pan-Islamism, only touched on the belief that the Pan-Muslim slogans could eventually be replaced by political demands:

In Muslim countries the national movement at first expresses its ideology in the religio-political slogans of Pan-Islamism, which enables diplomats and officials of the Great Powers to exploit the prejudices and ignorance of the masses of the peoples to combat this movement (the British imperialists' game of Pan-Islamism and Pan-Arabism, the British plan of transferring the Caliphate to India, and the gambling of French imperialism with "Muslim sympathies"). With the growth and expansion of the national-liberation movement, however, the religio-political slogans of Pan-Islamism are replaced by concrete political demands. The struggle for the separation of the temporal power from the Caliphate which took place in Turkey recently is evidence of this.[46]

The theses accepted by the Congress, partially in response to Roy's influ-ence, were intended to serve as guiding principles for the development of com-munist movements in the Eastern countries. The theses stated:

The dominant classes in the colonies and the semicolonial countries are unable and unwilling to lead the struggle against imperialism as this struggle is converted into a revolutionary mass movement. Only where the feudal-patriarchal system has not decayed to such an extent as to completely separate the native aristocracy from the mass of the people, as among the nomadic and seminomadic peoples, can those upper

44 *Ibid.*, pp. 188–89.
45 *Ibid.*, pp. 589–90.
46 *Kommunisticheskii Internatsional v dokumentakh*, p. 318.

classes take up the active leadership of the struggle against imperialist violence (Mesopotamia, Morocco, Mongolia).[47]

In actuality, the contradiction, so evident at the Second Congress, between Roy's emphasis on class conflict and Lenin's concept of tactical co-operation with nationalist revolutionaries had not yet been resolved.

Thus, the Fourth Congress, while upholding Roy in the theses, was laying plans for tactical co-operation in China with the middle-class Kuomintang. In the words of Liu Jen-ch'ing:

Starting from the premise that in order to exterminate imperialism in China an anti-imperialistic united front will have to be erected, our party has decided to form a united front with the national-revolutionary party, the Kuomintang. The nature of this united front will be expressed in the fact that we, under our own names and as single individuals, will join the party. The reason for it is twofold. In the first place, we want to propagandize many organized workers in the national-revolutionary party and to win them over for us. In the second place, we can only fight imperialism if we combine our forces, the forces of the petty bourgeoisie and the proletariat. We intend to compete with this party [i.e., Kuomintang] in regard to the winning of the masses by means of organization and propaganda. If we do not join this party we shall remain isolated, and we shall preach a communism which holds great and noble ideas, but one which the masses do not follow. The masses would rather follow the bourgeois party, and this party would use the masses for its own purposes. If we join the party, we shall be able to show the masses that we too are for revolutionary democracy, but that for us revolutionary democracy is only a means to an end. Furthermore, we shall be able to point out that although we are for this distant goal, we nevertheless do not forget the daily needs of the masses. We shall be able to gather the masses around us and split the Kuomintang.[48]

The Fourth Congress, like the Second, was trying to resolve the contradiction between class conflict and co-operation with nationalist revolutionaries by entering into both.

The Congress also emphasized the importance of the agrarian question: "Only the agrarian revolution aiming at the expropriation of the large landowners can rouse the vast peasant masses destined to have a decisive influence in the struggle against imperialism."[49] It urged also the development of the workers' movement in the East and its alliance with the proletariat of advanced countries, which was to lead eventually to the formation of an International Federation of Soviet Republics. "The soviet system represents for the backward nations the least painful form of transition from primitive conditions of existence to the highest culture of communism, destined to take the place of the capitalist method of production and distribution all over the world."[50]

Concluding its session, the Congress addressed a letter of greetings to the workers of Turkey, calling them "a living example of a revolutionary movement of independence to the entire East and to all colonial countries subjugated by imperialism." The letter also expressed its sympathies for the Turkish Communists who had been arrested, imprisoned, and allegedly maltreated by the Kemalist government. "Remember, comrades," the letter stated, "that the gloom of dungeons could not obscure the sun of the revolution," and it added

[47] *Ibid.*   [48] *Protokoll des Vierten Kongresses der K.I.*, p. 615.
[49] *Kommunisticheskii Internatsional v dokumentakh*, p. 319.
[50] *Ibid.*, p. 321 ; see Document 74.

that "the Third International considers it an essential duty to do everything in its power to rescue you from the hands of your hangmen."[51]

The Congress also sent a special telegram to the All-Indian Trade Union Congress, then sitting at Lahore. "Comrades," the telegram stated, "while assuring you of our sympathy and in promising you our utmost support . . . , we must at the same time remind you that yours is a very great cause, and that it must not be restricted. The Indian working class does not fight for a fair daily wage only. The economic emancipation of the Indian workers and peasants depends upon the political liberty of the nation."[52]

The Organization of the Communist Party of Japan

At the Fourth Congress of the Communist International an announcement was made of the founding of a Communist Party of Japan, which had grown out of the Japanese socialist movement headed by Sen Katayama and other intellectuals since the beginning of the century.

During 1918–19 Japanese leftists of all varieties were busily engaged in forming an assortment of small socialist study groups. Impressed by the Russian revolution and stirred by the Rice Riots (spontaneous outbursts resulting from food shortages) and the pressures of increased industrialization, these men were confused in their ideology and wholly inept in the techniques of organization. Even their knowledge of the Russian revolution was vague. They did not receive precise information until the spring of 1920 and then circuitously, by way of the United States.

Sometime during 1917, Eizō Kondo, who made a living in the United States selling art supplies, had met Sen Katayama in New York City and had become converted to the latter's radical views. For some time Katayama had been active in the Revolutionary Propaganda League, an illegal organization which, though weak and largely ineffectual, was the forerunner of the American Communist Party. Being in touch with Katayama and other Left-wingers such as Agnes Smedley, John Reed, Louis C. Fraina, and S. J. Rutgers, Kondo developed deep sympathy and admiration for the Russian revolution.[53]

Events in Japan, particularly the Rice Riots, greatly excited Japanese socialists in the United States. Katayama and Kondo decided that one of them should go to Russia for assistance, and the other proceed homeward in order to push the revolutionary movement. Kondo left San Francisco for Japan in May 1919, and on his arrival met immediately with Toshihiko Sakai and Hitoshi Yamakawa, who were the outstanding Japanese socialist leaders at that time. Shortly afterward, Voitinsky, the Comintern representative in Shanghai, sent a Korean revolutionist to Japan inviting Sakai and Yamakawa to attend the meeting of Far Eastern socialists in that city.[54] They refused, apparently doubting the courier's credentials.

During the spring of 1921, Kondo, Sakai, and Yamakawa began preparations for the founding of a communist party. While these preliminaries were

---

[51] *Protokoll des Vierten Kongresses der K.I.,* pp. 531–32

[52] *Ibid.,* pp. 782–83.

[53] Travers Edgar Durkee, "The Communist International and Japan, 1919–1922," an unpublished doctoral dissertation in the Stanford University Libraries, 1953, p. 14. The subsequent account of the Japanese communist movement is based on this work.

[54] See our pp. 89–90.

in progress, a second Korean arrived from Shanghai in order to establish contact between the Comintern and the new Japanese movement. Toward the end of April in the back room of a restaurant in Tokyo, draft regulations were approved for a Japanese branch of the Communist International. Some days later Kondo, disguised as a Nisei merchant, arrived in Shanghai, ostensibly to buy merchandise.[55] There he met with a Comintern committee consisting of twelve Chinese and Koreans presided over by Pak Chin Shum, sent from Moscow,[56] who listened to Kondo's report on the situation in Japan and gave him a small sum of money for organizational and propaganda purposes.

Comintern leaders continued to be aware of Japan's potential importance to the world communist movement. On June 25, 1921, Zinoviev told the Third Congress of the Communist International: "It is most essential that we should have better communication with Japan; we must secure a firm foothold in Japan. The situation in this country is about the same as that of Russia on the eve of 1905. There is a strong revolutionary movement of the masses."[57]

Two Japanese, Tarō Yoshihara and Unzō Taguchi, were present at the Third Congress, though both had proceeded from the United States.

In Japan, the Dawn People's Communist Party (Gyōmin Kyōsan-to) was founded August 20, 1921, but the Comintern did not recognize it.

In October, Voitinsky sent Chang T'ai-lei to Japan to establish closer Comintern contact with the Japanese revolutionaries. There he asked Kondo, Sakai, and Yamakawa to select a number of workers as delegates to the Conference of the Toilers of the Far East scheduled to meet in Irkutsk in November. The only workers available were anarchists, but this circumstance did not disturb Chang, who may have assumed that they could be converted once they reached Russia. Other delegates included Mosaburō Suzuki (a socialist) and Kyūichi Tokuda, who later became one of the big three of Japanese communism.

The Japanese delegates, after stopping off in Shanghai to confer with Maring, reached Irkutsk in mid-November; from there, as was mentioned earlier, they proceeded to Moscow and thence to Petrograd, where they were joined by Sen Katayama, who was already sojourning in Moscow.

The First Congress of the Toilers of the Far East marked the first real contact between high Comintern leaders and the Japanese communist movement, and the first serious Soviet attempt to analyze Japanese society. In its sessions, Japan was characterized as the only imperialist, capitalist oppressor among the nations of the Far East. Said Zinoviev (speaking of the Washington Conference):

This quadruple alliance of bloodsuckers [Japan, the United States, Great Britain, and France], however, cannot postpone the hour of the inevitable war in the Pacific Ocean. . . . As sure as morning follows night, so will the first imperialist war, which ended in 1918, be followed by a second war which will center around the Far East and the problem of the Pacific. . . . It will be possible to avoid this war only if the young working class of Japan rapidly becomes sufficiently strong to seize the Japanese bourgeoisie by the throat, and if parallel with that there will be a victorious revolutionary movement in America.[58]

[55] Durkee, "The Communist International and Japan, 1919–1922," p. 17.

[56] Rodger Swearingen and Paul Langer, *Red Flag in Japan*, p. 11.

[57] G. E Zinoviev, *Report of the Executive Committee of the Communist International for 1920–1921*, p. 51.

[58] *Pervyi sezd revoliutsionnykh organizatsii Dalnego Vostoka*, p. 23.

According to Zinoviev, the fate of several hundred million people in China, Korea, and Mongolia, and in Japan itself, is in the hands of the working class of Japan: ". . . it is the task of the present congress to coordinate the activities of the oppressed, the non-proletarian masses of the entire Far East with those of the industrial and village proletariat of Japan." The presence at the Congress of representatives of the Japanese workers represented the only serious guarantee that the Comintern was on its way to "a true solution of the Far Eastern problem."[59]

When the Japanese delegates returned to their homeland, they found that Kondo and some of his closest associates had been imprisoned and that the Gyōmin Kyōsan-to was no longer in existence. Kyūichi Tokuda and Kiyoshi Takase began meeting secretly with various radical leaders to discuss the carrying out of Comintern instructions for the establishment of an orthodox communist party. In due course, Arahata, Sakai, and Yamakawa agreed to sponsor such a party, and on July 5, 1922, the Communist Party of Japan was founded under the direct guidance and with the assistance of the Comintern.[60]

The first meeting of the Central Executive Committee (or the first Congress, there being some conflict in the records) was held July 15, just ten days after the birth of the party. Some months later (November–December, 1922) the newly formed party was officially recognized by the Fourth Congress of the Communist International as the Japanese branch of that body. Zinoviev referred to the formation of the Communist Party in Japan in the following words:

In Japan there is a small party which has united its forces with the best syndicalist elements with the assistance of the Executive Committee of the Communist International. This is a young party, but it represents a strong nucleus, and it should now provide itself with a program.[61]

Katayama in his report declared that more attention should be paid to the revolutionary movement in his country:

Japan occupies a very important place in the coming socialist revolution. Japan is the only country in the Far East which is really economically and politically independent. Japan is important for the revolutionary movement of the world because in the near future the workers of Japan may rise against the capitalist class. . . . We all know . . . that we must protect the Russian revolution. Soviet Russia is menaced by Japanese imperialism. For this reason alone the Fourth Congress and the Communists of the world should pay more attention to this matter than they have done so far.[62]

The Importance of the Pacific

Moscow was fully aware by 1922 of the importance of the Pacific for both communist plans and "imperialist" designs. From the Washington Conference had emerged the Four-Power Pacific Treaty by which the United States, Great Britain, France, and Japan guaranteed each other's insular possessions in the Pacific; the ending of the Anglo-Japanese Alliance; the Shantung Treaty, by which the Japanese returned Kiaochow to China; the Nine-Power Treaties,

[59] *The First Congress of the Toilers of the Far East*, p. 59.
[60] Swearingen and Langer, *Red Flag in Japan*, p. 14.
[61] *Protokoll des Vierten Kongresses der K.I.*, p. 51.
[62] *Ibid.*, pp. 598–99.

guaranteeing territorial integrity to China and reiterating the "open door" policy; and the Naval Armaments Treaty, providing for a ten-year naval holiday and establishing a ratio for capital ships. All these measures were viewed by Soviet leaders as simply delaying, but not preventing, what they viewed as an inevitable armed conflict among the capitalist powers, particularly the United States and Japan, for control of the Pacific.

"To meet capitalist Japan's plan," wrote Vilensky in *Zhizn Natsionalnostei,* "American capitalism aims at the creation of a capitalist China. This means the advance of capitalism along the entire front of eastern Asia, and the most merciless exploitation of the proletariat of eastern Asia." Vilensky further predicted that the Four-Power Pacific Treaty would actually lead to a "terrible imperialist slaughter in which millions of proletarians in the eastern hemisphere will be thrown into the fight to settle the American-Japanese rivalry for Pacific hegemony."[63]

Pavlovich spoke of the inevitability of a war between Japan and the United States:

Now that the results of the Washington Conference are clear, it is apparent that the Conference did not solve the Pacific problem in the sense of consolidating a permanent state of friendship among the interested imperialist powers. . . .

Hundreds of pages were written . . . during the two or three years before the World War on the subject of the impossibility of a war between Britain and Germany, and yet war broke out between them. . . . A similar situation may occur in the future Japanese-American war. It is possible, nay it is just probable, that America will not fight Japan alone, but in alliance with Britain, Australia, Holland. America may draw China into the orbit of its influence also. . . . Finally, if Japan cannot be brought to its knees by pure strategy, it will be strangled with the help of a blockade as Germany was in the World War.[64]

Writing in a similar vein, Radek cited Marx's statement in 1851 that "the discovery of gold mines in California transfers the center of world development to the shores of the Pacific Ocean." According to Radek, "The United States of America . . . for economic reasons is compelled to obtain a firm foothold on the Asiatic and European continents. It is driven to this by the industrial development of western America, as well as by the awakening of China."

Capitalist development had penetrated deep into China, said Radek, and four hundred million Chinese people were awakening from their political slumber:

The next thirty years will decide the question whether they themselves will govern their land, which possesses the greatest riches in coal, iron, and oil, and produces such a quantity of rice as would feed the whole of Asia, or whether this process [of political awakening] which is taking place at a dizzy speed, will proceed under the leadership of American capital. The United States of America are preparing to play the role, not only of the dictator of Europe but also of the dictator of Eastern Asia. The prediction made by Marx in 1851 regarding the transference of the center of development from the Atlantic Ocean to the Pacific Ocean is now only being realized.[65]

[63] V. D. Vilensky (Sibiriakov), "Vashington i Vostochnaia Aziia," *Zhizn Natsionalnostei,* No. 3 (132), January 26, 1922, p. 1; see Document 75.

[64] M. L. Veltman (M. Pavlovich), *Pered ugrozoi budushchikh voin,* pp. 56, 64-65.

[65] *International Press Correspondence,* No. 53, July 31, 1924, pp. 551-53. See also Document 76.

DOCUMENTS

A. COMMUNIST REVOLUTIONARY STRATEGY AND TACTICS FOR ASIA

23

Stalin: "Do Not Forget the East"[1]

At the time of the rising revolutionary movement in Europe, when old thrones and crowns are tottering and giving place to the revolutionary soviets of workers and peasants, while the people of occupied countries are driving away the creatures of imperialism, the eyes of the world naturally turn to the West. It is there, in the West, that the chains of imperialism which were forged in Europe, and which have been strangling the world, must first be broken. It is there, in the West, that socialism will be first to develop. At such times, the remote East naturally tends to disappear from our field of vision and is even forgotten, the East with its hundreds of millions of population oppressed by imperialism.

And yet the East must not be forgotten by us even for a moment. It must not be forgotten for the reason that it provides inexhaustible reserves and is the most reliable rear base for world imperialism.

The imperialists have always viewed the East as the basis of their prosperity. Has not the enormous natural wealth of the Eastern countries—cotton, oil, gold, coal, other minerals—been the apple of discord among the imperialists of all countries? That is why even the waging of wars in Europe, and the babbling about [the importance of] the West, do not prevent the imperialists from thinking of China, India, Persia, Egypt, and Morocco, because actually the points of dispute among them concern the East.

[The importance of the East for the imperialists] is also the reason for the eagerness with which they support "law and order" in the Eastern countries, since if law and order did not prevail in the remote East no imperialists could be secure there.

. . .

The task of communism is to do away with the century-old slumber of the oppressed peoples of the East, to infect the workers and peasants of these countries with the liberating spirit of the revolution, to rouse them to struggle against imperialism, and in that way to deprive world imperialism of its "most reliable" and "inexhaustible" reserve. Without this, the definite triumph of socialism, complete victory over imperialism, is unthinkable.

The revolution in Russia was the first to rouse the oppressed peoples of the East to fight imperialism. The soviets in Persia, India, and China are a clear symptom that the age-long slumber of the workers and peasants of the East is becoming a thing of the past.

. . .

[1] *Zhizn Natsionalnostei*, No. 3, November 24, 1918, p. 1; also Stalin, Sochineniia, IV, 171–73.

156

It is the duty of the communists to intervene in the growing spontaneous movement in the East and to develop it further, into a conscious struggle against imperialism. . . .

24

The Meeting of the Road: Russia and Great Britain in the East

[A Communist Interpretation][2]

Since the time of the October Revolution, our chief and most dangerous foe has been today's most powerful imperialist nation, Great Britain, who has always seen in a strong, united Russia a threat to her mastery in Persia, Afghanistan, and especially India.

Differing from the United States and France and even from Germany, Britain—both liberal and conservative, the Britain of the Tories and of the Whigs, of Beaconsfield and of Gladstone, of Chamberlain and of Lloyd George—has always been the enemy of a strong Russia, be it a Russia of the serf-owner Nicholas I or of the "liberal" and humanitarian (according to the English press) Alexander II, be it an autocratic Russia or a "constitutional" (Duma) Russia. [Discusses Anglo-Russian conflicts in the nineteenth century.] . . .

In the course of the last century Britain and Russia, both intent on widening their territorial boundaries and developing their defensive and offensive strength, were like two trains moving at full speed on the same track in opposite directions, moving inevitably ever nearer a final and decisive collision. [Discusses Anglo-Russian conflicts along the Indian border.] . . .

The first glance at a map indicating the history of the expansion of the territorial boundaries of both states gives the impression of the inevitability of conflict—Russia aiming in the direction of India, and Britain advancing north by forced march, as if intending to meet her enemy in an open fight as soon as possible, and at the most remote point from the Indian frontier. And actually the entire foreign policy and military history of Russia throughout most of the last century was, to a considerable degree, the history of an Anglo-Russian conflict. In the Crimean campaign, in the Russo-Turkish wars of 1828 and 1877, in the wars with the Caucasus, in all the Central Asiatic campaigns, and, finally, in the last war with Japan, Russia . . . always faced the Britain of Palmerston, Beaconsfield, Chamberlain, Cecil Rhodes, Kipling, Curzon, etc., as an open or a secret enemy. [Continues discussion of history of conflict in India.] . . .

. . . Great Britain fought tsarist Russia whenever the latter threatened British hegemony in Asia by stretching her hand toward Constantinople or India. But the bourgeois Russia of Miliukov and Guchkov, with their Dardanelles and other imperialistic projects, was still more repugnant to Great Britain, which was even prepared to support the rotten tsarism and the regime of Rasputin and others . . . to prevent the transformation of the country with a population of one hundred and fifty million into a powerful bourgeois state organized on the European pattern and liberated from the fetters of the British and French stock exchanges.

Soviet Russia has appeared to Great Britain to be even more formidable. . . .

In the nineteenth century, tsarist Russia fought her way with fire and sword along

[2] M. L. Veltman (M. Pavlovich), *Sovetskaia Rossiia i kapitalisticheskaia Angliia*, pp. 3–5, 20–22, 25–26, 32, 35.

the northern border of India. Numerous Muslim peoples of the Caucasus who had fought for their independence for scores of years, such as [the peoples headed by] Shamil, were finally subdued, as were separate Muslim states, such as Khiva and Bukhara, which were thereupon included within the borders of the Russian Empire. The Russian advance threatened the independence of the remaining unconquered Muslim states in Asia: Turkey, Persia, and Afghanistan. Consequently Russia appeared in the eyes of the Muslim people to be their chief enemy, and a century-old persecutor of Islam and of the Muslim peoples.

Thus, Great Britain retained a firm hold on India not so much because of the splendidly organized Hindu army, her squadrons, her gold, and her world influence, and not simply because of the natural defenses and impassable heights of the Himalayas and Karakoram, and the formidable fortresses of the Khyber and Bolan passes, but also thanks to the fact that in these narrow mountain valleys lived fanatical Muslim tribes who were Britain's faithful watchmen, guarding the high mountain passes from tsarist Russia, which was hated by all the peoples of the East.

However, as soon as the Soviet government was triumphant in Russia, everything changed. The workers' and peasants' Russia, powerful with her multimillion population, with her invincible Red armies, and attractively fairylike in her new guise, now appeared to the Asiatic peoples not as a century-old oppressor, nor as the enemy and competitor of Great Britain in the exploitation of millions of men, but, on the contrary, as a good genie, a powerful knight liberating the chained prisoner from the world executioner, British imperialism.

If the gigantic Russia of the tsars, whose possessions in Asia were continually growing, appeared to Beaconsfield to be the greatest threat to the British Empire, the Russia of the workers' and peasants' soviets is bound to appear all the more dangerous to the present-day British ministers, Lloyd George, Churchill, Curzon, and others . . . for Soviet Russia enjoys tremendous prestige among the awakening peoples of the East, including those of British India with her population of 300 million, who are daily showing more and more hatred for Britain and a desire to throw off the centuries-old British yoke.

In order to retain India for herself, to continue her hegemony in Asia, to strengthen her rule in Constantinople, on the Bosporus and the Dardanelles, in a word, to retain her old positions and also to keep the new conquests which she acquired as the result of the World War and the routing of Germany and Turkey, Britain declared a life and death struggle against the Soviet government. France and the United States fought the workers' and peasants' government in order to re-establish a bourgeois regime in Russia, as well as a legitimate government which would again gather the scattered possessions of the old empire, and create one powerful state. [They hoped that that state,] in turn, could be a reliable ally for France against Germany and would offset both Japan and Great Britain, who have grown too strong for the liking of the United States. The British government, on the contrary, has stubbornly fought Soviet Russia in order to break up the great empire, to divide her into a number of small, continually squabbling, and therefore weak states, which would be unable to play any role in world politics, much less to threaten British hegemony on the Bosporus, the Dardanelles, and the Black Sea, in Persia, and especially in India. [Discusses effect of World War on balance of power and British role in intervention.] . . .

. . . Britain agreed to give Japan a free hand in Manchuria and eastern Siberia, an area rich in grain, coal, gold, and so forth; she assisted Kolchak, Denikin, Wrangel, Yudenich, and Poland, preparing the advance of fourteen states against Russia (Churchill's boast in 1919) simply in order to weaken and to break up Russia, to be able to take a firm hold of the Baltic Sea, the Caucasus, Persia, the Black Sea, the Bosporus, and the Dardanelles, and to do away once and for all with the "Russian" threat to the British possessions in Asia, and particularly in India. In order to prevent the penetration of Bolshevik influence into Turkey and Persia, and from there into India, Great Britain supported the ephemeral governments of the newly created Caucasian states, as represented by the Azerbaijani Musavats,[3] the Armenian Dashnaks,[4] and the Georgian . . . Mensheviks. In order to retain the key to the Straits, she provided ammunition and money to Venizelos' Greece, hoping to make the Greek soldier a guardian of the Straits against possible danger from Russia. [Discusses intervention, particularly in the Caucasus and Caspian area.] . . .

What then were the factors and the reasons which forced the British imperialists to abandon the struggle against Soviet Russia and to sign a trade agreement on March 16, 1921? Apart from the insistence of the British working class, from the beginning of the intervention, that the blockade of Soviet Russia be ended and that peaceful relations and trade be re-established, there were also other factors which prompted imperialist Great Britain to end the fruitless and expensive struggle. [Discusses Soviet counterattacks in the Caspian and the occupation of Enzeli and Resht in Persia by the Red forces.][5]

It goes without saying that our active policy in the struggle against Great Britain's attempts to strangle the Soviet government could not be limited to such successes as the British evacuation of Enzeli or Resht. We could not possibly permit the routing of Kemal's Turkey, nor could we allow Britain to turn Dashnak Armenia and Menshevik Georgia into instruments for the realization of her imperialistic plans in the Caucasus. . . .

The decisive course of our Eastern policy, expressed among other things in the creation of the Council for Propaganda and Action of Peoples of the East,[6] has forced the British government to ponder the question of the inevitability of an agreement with Soviet Russia. Soviet danger in the East had previously prompted the British military party to preach an irreconcilable war against the Soviet federation. But, now, when it has become apparent that "the armed struggle against Bolshevism in the East is destined to be a failure," as has been openly stated by many British newspapers, and as was also declared by the British premier, Lloyd George, when he admitted that an armed struggle against the influence of Soviet Russia in Asia was senseless—now, revolutionary events in the East and the triumph of Soviet ideas among the masses in Turkey, a considerable portion of the Persian population, in Bukhara, and so on, have forced Great Britain to renounce her policy of "war to the end" against Soviet Russia. Furthermore, Soviet military operations on the shores of the Caspian Sea have threatened Britain with the loss of the Persian cotton market and have undermined her position not only in Teheran but also in southern Persia. Events in Bukhara have increased our influence in Afghanistan and could cause serious reverberations in India, where the situation has become increasingly ominous for British interests.

In view of the fact that the armed struggle against Soviet Russia—a struggle led by British expeditionary forces and a British naval squadron, and assisted by Wrangel, Denikin, Kolchak, and others—ended in a complete collapse and consequently only increased Soviet Russia's extraordinary prestige all over the East and accelerated the spread of Soviet ideas in Persia, India, etc., Britain decided to force the Soviet government to renounce its propaganda practice. The Congress of the Peoples of the East at Baku in September 1920 . . . and the formation in Baku of the Council for Propaganda and Action of the Peoples of the East forced the British

---

[3] Musavat ("Equality"), the Azerbaijani national party, formed in 1912.

[4] Dashnaktsutiun ("Union"), the Armenian national party, formed in the 1890's.

[5] See our p. 96.

[6] A decision of the Baku Congress in September 1920; see our p. 82.

military party and the British ruling classes in general to change their Soviet Russian policy hastily. [This was all the more imperative because] the news of the Congress had spread to every Asian country and strengthened the national-revolutionary movements everywhere.

In September 1920, the Congress of the Peoples of the East convened in Baku under the slogan of the struggle with the centuries-old enemy of the peoples of the East, imperialist Great Britain, and by December, the British government offered a draft of a trade agreement between the governments of Great Britain and Soviet Russia.

[Deals with the British draft of the agreement, and with the clauses referring to Soviet nonintervention in the affairs of the East.] . . .

Thus, we see that as in the period of tsarism, fear for India, which has prompted Britain at certain times to wage war against Russia and at other times to come to an agreement with her, has again forced Great Britain, who has been directing the war of world imperialism, and of the entire Russian counterrevolutionary movement against Soviet Russia, to lay down her arms because of the victory of our Red Army, and the success of our revolutionary propaganda in the East. . . .

25

Importance of Turkestan[7] to Revolutionary Propaganda in the East

a

[Lenin's Letter of Advice to the Communists of Turkestan][8]

Comrades! Allow me, as Chairman of the Council of People's Commissars and as Chairman of the Council of Defense, as well as a member of the party, to address you.

The establishment of satisfactory relations with the peoples of Turkestan is for the Russian Socialist Federated Soviet Republic, without exaggeration, of tremendous and world-wide historical significance. The attitude of the workers' and peasants' Soviet republic toward weak and formerly oppressed peoples will have a practical effect upon all the peoples of Asia, upon the colonies of the world, upon hundreds of millions of people.

I request that you pay special attention to this matter, and make every effort to establish friendly relations with the peoples of Turkestan, in order that we may prove in practice the sincerity of our desire to do away with all traces of Great Russian imperialism, and in order that we may struggle in all honesty with the world imperialism headed by the British.

---

[7] Contact between the Central Soviet government and Turkestan, which had been cut off by civil war, was made in September 1919. By the decision of the Central Executive Committee of Soviets and the Council of People's Commissars, a special Commission for the Affairs of Turkestan was formed on October 8, 1919, and sent to the region in order to correct the mistakes made by the Russian Bolsheviks in their policies toward the native population during the period when Turkestan was cut off from the center.

[8] *Petrogradskaia Pravda,* No. 259, November 13, 1919; Lenin, *Sochineniia,* XXIV, 531.

I ask you, therefore, to receive our Turkestan Commission with full confidence and to follow exactly its directives, which come from the All-Russian Central Executive Committee and which are given in the spirit outlined above. . . .

b

[An Article in the Official Organ of the People's Commissariat of Nationalities][9]

. . .

Marx had foreseen the development of events today when he said that the communist revolution must be preceded by a number of national revolutions of the oppressed peoples, and first of all of India and the peoples of the East. . . .

Only through the period of liberation from imperialist oppression, through the phases of national self-determination, will the East disclose its hidden, but favorable, conditions for the development of socialism. . . .

Turkestan has the responsibility of taking all possible steps in order to hasten the process of drawing the East into the orbit of the world socialist movement. . . .

The practical measures for the realization of these responsibilities by Turkestan are as follows:

1. Creation of special battalions from among the Russian Muslims in order to render active assistance to the East in its struggle against the British imperialists;

2. Creation of an apparatus for the organized propaganda of socialist ideas both through literature, and through specially trained emissaries;

3. The establishment of a permanent official contact [with the Eastern countries] by means of the exchange of representatives and agents with all the countries of the East. . . .

Cossacks' spears appearing on the Himalayan summits were Britain's nightmare in the past. Now these will be the spears of the Russian proletarian Muslims who will be coming to the rescue of their brothers in Persia, India, and Afghanistan.

c

[An Editorial by S. M. Dimanshtein][10]

. . . Our temporary loss of the Ukraine[11] has been offset by an advance in the southeast and by a penetration of the ring of hostile forces which surround us. Our frontiers now touch Khiva, Bukhara, and Afghanistan. From Afghanistan the road leads to Hindustan, the possible key to world revolution, for it is from India that Britain draws a great deal of her strength. . . .

Politically, Turkestan is extremely important to us. When the germ of our revolution reaches the starved and oppressed Eastern peoples it will find conditions well suited to its development. The [World] War has so prepared the whole world for a socialist overturn that, no matter where the revolution breaks out, suitable ground for it will be found. This is particularly true in the British colonies. . . .

[9] Paliukaitis, "Turkestan i revoliutsii Vostoka," *Zhizn Natsionalnostei,* No. 19 (27), May 26, 1919, p. 2.

[10] *Zhizn Natsionalnostei,* No. 36 (44), September 21, 1919, p. 1.

[11] In the course of the civil war, the Ukraine was temporarily surrendered to the anti-Bolshevik forces of General Denikin.

26

The Call to Spread Revolution in Asia

[Central Bureau of the Muslim Organizations of the Russian Communist Party
to Muslim Communists and Sympathizers, December 1918][12]

Comrade Muslims! The events which are taking place in the world, the approaching victory of the world socialist revolution, prompt us to give particular attention
to the most backward peoples of the East.

The ideas which have been almost fully assimilated by the more cultured comrades
of the West are but little known to the comrades in the East. It is the duty of all
Communists to come to the aid of their younger brothers.

We, the Muslim Communists, who know better the language and the way of
life of the peoples of the East, who are Muslim in our great majority, are duty-bound
to take the most active part in this sacred work.

With the above in view, the Central Bureau of the Muslim Organizations of the
Russian Communist Party (B) has decided to organize a Department of International
Propaganda.

The Central Bureau has resolved to publish pamphlets, newspapers, and leaflets
in the native tongues of comrades inhabiting the East, as well as to prepare cadres
of propagandists and agitators.

We call on all Muslim Communist organizations in Russia to carry on the most
active work locally, and we offer at the same time to select the most active workers
[from the native population] and to place them at the disposal of the Central Bureau.

At the same time the Central Bureau appeals to all Muslims who sympathize with
the ideas of communism and who wish to work for the liberation of the oppressed
peoples of the East to respond to the call of the Central Bureau.

In common efforts, the Central Bureau hopes to spread the ideas of communism
quickly in the East and to draw all oppressed peoples into the world laboring family.

Long live the World Revolution!

Long live the Government of the Toilers of the World!

Long live the World Soviet Socialist Republic!

RUSSIAN COMMUNIST PARTY (B)
CENTRAL BUREAU OF THE MUSLIM ORGANI-
ZATIONS

27

Organization of the Department of International Propaganda for the Eastern Peoples

[Resolution of the First Congress of the Muslim Communists in Russia,
November 1918][13]

The peoples of the East have until now been exposed to the most brutal and
unscrupulous exploitation by imperialist powers. Nowhere else has the oppression
of man by man been so great as it has been in the East.

[12] *Zhizn Natsionalnostei*, No. 5, December 8, 1918, p. 8.
[13] *Zhizn Natsionalnostei*, No. 5 (13), February 16, 1919, p. 4.

The Russian proletarian revolution has broken the chains of the Eastern peoples within Russia, but in the other Eastern sectors [of Asia], where the brutality of Anglo-Japanese imperialists continues, little change is noticeable. The Russian revolution has been instrumental in stirring the flame of revolutionary consciousness in the huge masses of oppressed Eastern peoples, and it has called them to struggle against their own oppressors and for their better future.

In clear realization of this duty the First Congress of the Muslim Communists has resolved to organize the Department of International Propaganda for the Eastern Peoples. This department will be attached to the Bureau of the Muslim Communist Organizations of the Russian Communist Party. It will conduct agitation among the peoples of the East, explain the Russian and the world revolution [to come], and gradually bring the revolutionary masses to an understanding of the idea of world communism.

In order to carry out its activity more successfully, the department has been divided into the following twelve sections: (1) Arab, (2) Persian, (3) Turkish, (4) Azerbaijani, (5) Bukharan, (6) Kirghiz, (7) [Caucasus] Mountaineers', (8) Kalmuk, (9) Chinese, (10) Korean, (11) Japanese, and (12) Indian. All the above sections will have one headquarters, and will have one common office.

In order to reach its goal, the department will issue newspapers, periodicals, leaflets, appeals, etc., and will train communist Muslims and send them to the Eastern regions to carry on agitation, and to organize communist collective bodies for the purpose of an active struggle against the ruling classes, and for the ideas of communism. . . .

28

Stalin on the Tasks of the Muslim Communists

[Message Delivered at the Second Congress of the Communist Organizations of the Peoples of the East, at Moscow, November 22, 1919][14]

Comrades! The Central Committee of the Communist Party has commissioned me to open the Second Congress of the representatives of the Muslim Communist organizations of the East.

One year has passed since the First Congress met. Comrades! During this period two great events in the history of socialism have taken place. First, the revolutionization of Western Europe and America and the birth of the communist parties in the West. Second, the awakening of the peoples of the East and [the development of] the revolutionary movement among the oppressed peoples of the East.

There, in the West, the proletariat is threatening to rout the vanguard of the imperialist powers, to take the government away from them; here the proletariat is threatening to destroy the rear of imperialism, the East, as the source from which imperialism draws its strength, and to which it expects to retreat if it is defeated in Western Europe. [States that the bridge that joins the West and the East has been constructed.] . . .

I do not doubt, comrades, that this congress, the Second Congress—richer than the first in both the number and the quality [of its representatives]—will be able to continue the work already started in awakening the peoples of the East and in fortifying the bridge between the West and the East, as well as the work of liberat-

[14] *Zhizn Natsionalnostei,* No. 46 (54), December 7, 1919, p. 3; also Stalin, *Sochineniia,* IV, 279–80.

ing the toiling masses from their centuries-old imperialist oppression. Let us hope that the banner raised by the First Congress, the banner of the liberation of the toiling masses of the East, the banner of the destruction of imperialism, will be carried to the last with honor by the workers of the Muslim Communist organizations.

29

An Outline for the Revolutionary Work of the Communist Party in the East

[Resolution of the Second Congress of the Communist Organizations of the Peoples of the East][15]

1. The Congress finds that the problem of the international social revolution cannot be solved without the participation in it of the East as a definite social and economic unit.

2. The Russian Communist Party (B), which, because of its international position, occupies at the present time a leading place in the world communist movement, must take concrete and actual measures for revolutionizing the East.

3. The revolutionary work of the Communist Party in the East must proceed in two directions. One direction is determined by the basic class revolutionary program of the party which, on its part, prompts the necessity of a gradual formation of communist parties in the countries of the East as sections of the Communist International. The second direction is determined by the present political and, naturally, historical, social, and economic position of the East, which necessitates the support in the East, for a period of time, of the national movement directed at the overthrow of the rule of Western European imperialism there—in so far as such a movement does not contradict those class revolutionary aspirations of the international proletariat which are aimed at the overthrow of international imperialism.

4. In view of these aims, it is necessary to develop immediately the most serious and broad activities directed toward the organization of party work in the East on one hand, and toward the organization of anti-imperialist propaganda on the other.

5. This work must be carried out through the central organ of the communist organizations of the peoples of the East. The organizations of the peoples of the East must create from among themselves separate territorial sections and functional departments, and must work under the direct leadership of the Central Committee of the Russian Communist Party.

6. In order to concentrate the revolutionary energy which is to be transmitted to the East and . . . to awaken its revolutionary instinct, it is necessary to centralize the revolutionary work in the East in the existing and the potential Soviet republics of the Eastern peoples (Turkestan, Kirghiz, and others) and to make them the chief base for revolutionary work in the East.

7. With this purpose in view, it is necessary to start outlining immediately concrete plans for the association and co-operation which must be established among these republics if they are to become the starting point of the revolution in the East.

8. In order to carry out all these tasks, the Congress deems it necessary immediately:

    a. To intensify the training of the Soviet Party workers for the East.

    b. To start preparing a cadre of Soviet orientalists for the East.

[15] *Zhizn Natsionalnostei,* No. 47 (55), December 14, 1919, p. 2.

   c. To start the organization of an Eastern Red Army [from among the toilers] as a part of the international Red Army.

   d. To intensify the training of Red Army commanders recruited from the ranks of the proletariat of the Eastern peoples.

[Clause Added by the Turkestan Delegation]

9. In order to co-ordinate the actions of the oppressed Eastern nationalities with the actions of the revolutionary proletariat of the West, the Third International must declare that the national-liberation movement in the East and the social revolution [in the West] pursue one and the same general aim, namely, the overthrow of the yoke of the capitalist-imperialists. The Third International must also announce that India, Egypt, Turkey, and other states which are under the yoke of imperialism, are henceforth regarded [by the International] as sovereign and independent. This declaration will raise the revolutionary spirit [of these oppressed peoples] and will make it known to them that their cause finds support among the revolutionary proletariat of the West. . . .

30

The Baku Congress of the Peoples of the East

[The First Plenary Session of the Congress, September 1, 1920][16]

NARIMANOV [Chief of the Department for the Muslim Near East in the People's Commissariat of Foreign Affairs]: In the name of the Executive Committee of the Communist International, I declare the First Congress of the Peoples of the East open. (*Stormy applause. The "Internationale" is sung.*)

Comrades, I am greatly honored to have been called upon today to open this first, this unprecedented, this unheard-of congress, the Congress of the Peoples of the East.

Our ancient East was the first to enrich mankind with the principles of morality and culture; but today it will speak of its misfortunes, of the deep wounds which have been inflicted upon it by the capitalists of the bourgeois countries. . . .

We shall see displayed before us today a picture of the terrible, oppressive influence of capitalism. This will persuade the peoples of the East to join their forces and by a common effort to break forever the chains [that capitalism has fastened upon them]. . . .

ZINOVIEV: Comrades, my purpose today is to interpret for you the tasks and aims of the present Congress of the Peoples of the East, as understood by the Communist International. . . .

We are exceedingly proud to know that the Communist International has succeeded, for the first time in the history of mankind, in gathering under one roof representatives of more than twenty peoples of the East, who either have lived so far in a state of animosity, or have been little acquainted with each other. Consequently they have thus never had a chance to discuss the burning questions of the day which concern them all. . . .

Comrades, as you know, the present congress was convened by the Communist International, by the party organization. Yet we have at this congress hundreds of delegates who do not belong to the Communist Party, or to any party, just as we have among us members of other parties. . . .

[16] *Pervyi sezd narodov Vostoka,* pp. 27–48, 69–72, 149–51, 183–86, 204–6, 211–13.

When convening this congress, the Communist International did not ask the people who were invited to it: "Do you belong to the Communist International? Do you belong to the Communist Party?" But what it did say was this: "Are you a toiler? Do you belong to the toiling masses? Do you want to put an end to the internecine struggle? Do you want to organize a struggle against your oppressors? This is all that we want to know. We do not require any party membership card. We want to meet with the toilers in order to discuss the problems of the world with them." . . .

We are waging a battle to the death against those persons who forget, even for a moment, their duty to the oppressed nations, to the toiling masses of those countries which are plundered and exploited by capital.

Comrades, I told you that the Communist International wishes to establish a fraternal union with all the peoples of the East, with all oppressed peoples. I believe, comrades, that you, too, desire such a union, and that you cannot help desiring it. The European proletariat cannot help seeing now that the course of historical development has bound the toilers of the East to the workers of the West. We must conquer or perish together. . . .

The first task of our congress is to awaken the millions of peasants—to explain to them . . . that, unless this fraternal union is formed between them and the organized workers of the world, no way out [of the present oppression] will be found and no victory will be won over the plunderers and oppressors of the world, the English and the French, whose oppression you have known for so long; but that if such a union is formed victory is secure. [Discusses oppression of peoples by imperialist capitalists.] . . .

We know that the toiling masses of the East are backward through no fault of their own. They are illiterate; they are imbued with superstition; they believe in goblins; they cannot read newspapers; they do not know what is going on in the world; they do not understand the most elementary rules of hygiene. But only the lackeys of imperialism make fun of these people. This ignorance is not the fault of the unhappy toiling Turks or Persians. It is their misfortune. The "civilized" bourgeoisie of Paris and London is always inventing new ways to keep the Indian peasants and the toiling Persians and Turks in ignorance. . . .

We are convinced that, under the able guidance of the organized workers of the West, the peasants of the East can rise and can raise millions of other peasants, preparing the ground for the true agrarian revolution, and doing away with landlords, slavery, taxes, debts, and all the other clever tricks invented by the rich. The land would then actually pass to the toilers. That is what the Communist International wishes to accomplish.

The proletariat wishes to help you to seize land and to create a free union of all the peoples of the world. Such is the simple and clear program which is written in the heart of every European toiler, and which must now be written in your hearts, you who are representing the toilers of the East. . . .

. . . What will be the future organization of the East? We have come to the conclusion that soviets must be created even in countries where there are no town workers. Soviets of peasant toilers can be established. These soviets will not be the "soviets" juggled with now and then in Turkey. They will be real soviets, to which every peasant toiler may be elected. . . . We must organize such soviets to represent the toiling peasant masses. . . .

We are not concealing anything from you: we tell you clearly that we disagree on some points with the representatives of the present nationalist movement, and we tell you on which points we agree with them. We say to you: [It is true that] the task of the national movement is to help the East free itself of English imperialism. But we too have our own sacred task—to help the toilers of the East in their struggle against the rich, to help them build communist organizations, to explain to them what communism is, to prepare them for the true toilers' revolution, for the state of true equality, for the liberation of man from every oppression. . . .

I tell you we are confronted with the task of kindling a true holy war against the British and the French capitalists. [Discusses oppression of the colonial peoples.]

Comrades! Much has been said in the last few years about a holy war. The capitalists, while conducting their accursed imperialist war, tried to represent that slaughter as a holy war, and they made many people believe it. When, in 1914–16, the words "holy war" were spoken, they were a monstrous lie. But now, comrades, you, who have gathered for the first time in history in a congress of the peoples of the East, you must proclaim a true holy war against the robbers, against the Anglo-French capitalists. Now we must announce that the hour has struck, and that the workers of the world have awakened and will now arouse tens and hundreds of millions of peasants, will create a Red Army in the East, will arm it, will start a revolt in the rear of the British . . . and will cut down every impudent British officer who has been accustomed to being master in Turkey, Persian, India, and China.

Comrades! Brothers! The time has now come when you should begin to organize a true people's holy war against the robbers and the oppressors. The Communist International appeals today to the peoples of the East and tells them: "Brothers, we call you to a holy war to be directed first of all against British imperialism!" (*A storm of applause. Long shouts of "Hurrah." The members of the congress rise and wave their arms. The orator is unable to speak for a long time. All the members stand and applaud. Shouts: "We swear!"*) . . .

RADEK: The Russian peasants and workers understand very well that they must either defeat world capital or be defeated by it; they know that it is impossible for the workers' and peasants' Soviet Russia to exist for any length of time side by side with capitalistic countries. . . . The Russian worker can for a time seek peace and agreements with the British and French capitalists, and [in this way] gain time while the revolution in other countries is ripening. However, no permanent peace is possible between the country of labor and the countries of the exploiters. Therefore, in its Eastern policy, the Soviet government is not simply maneuvering; it is not dragging the peoples of the East into the struggle in order that the Russian Soviet Republic may profit by it. We sacrificed our own territories, our own peasants, and our own workers at Brest-Litovsk, when the German imperialists, armed to the teeth, dictated their conditions to us, for we were not in a position to defend ourselves.

Workers and peasants of the East! There may arise such a moment when we shall advise you [to compromise] and to throw some attractive morsels to the [imperialist] beasts rather than to allow them to tear you to pieces. Such a situation may arise [again] for us also. Nevertheless, your destiny and ours are one; either we and the peoples of the East shall be united and consequently shall hasten the victory of the Western European proletariat [over capital], or we shall perish, and you will become slaves. Therefore, comrades, what is urgently needed is not that we form an alliance today and then each go our own way tomorrow, or become enemies; but, on the contrary, that we carry on a joint struggle for life or death. . . .

Comrades, when the call is sounded for a holy war against the Entente, and first of all against Britain, our victory will not be immediate, but instead our struggle will be long, partly because the development of the peoples of the East is slow. . . . [We must struggle that all peoples may be free,] that no distinctions may be made between men, no distinctions of race or of color, and that all may have equal rights and equal duties to perform.

The capitalists of the world speak of the danger from the East; they say that when 300 million Indian and 400 million Chinese peasants arise, culture and civilization will perish. But we well know the culture of which they speak; we have witnessed it in the shower of shells on the battlefields; we have witnessed it in the sight of ruined homes and cities. Capitalist culture actually means the death of all culture. Capitalism is unable to guarantee us even the life of a well-cared-for animal; and the sooner such a culture perishes, the better. (*Applause.*)

Comrades, when we hand you our common banner in the struggle against our common enemy, we know perfectly well that jointly we shall create a culture which will be a hundred times higher than the culture created by the slave-owners of the West. The Eastern peoples, oppressed by the capitalists and proprietors, have evolved a philosophy of patience. But we appeal to that desire to struggle which once inspired your ancestors, your great leaders, in their advance to conquer Europe. We realize, comrades, that your adversaries will say that we are appealing to the memory of Genghiz Khan, to the memory of the conquests of the great caliphs of Islam. But we are deeply convinced that yesterday, when you unsheathed your swords and raised your guns, it was not for the purpose of conquest, nor for the sake of turning Europe into a cemetery. You raised your swords in order to create jointly with the workers of the world a new culture, a culture of free toilers.

Therefore, when the capitalists of Europe say that a new wave of barbarian invasions is threatening, a new invasion of the Huns, we answer: "Long live the Red East, which, together with the workers of Europe, will create a new culture under the banner of communism!" (*Stormy applause.*)

[Fifth Plenary Session, September 5, 1920]

PAVLOVICH [After a long speech summarizing power relationships in the prewar period, the conflicts of the bourgeois states in the postwar period, and the role of the Soviet state and the Third International]: The Communist International does not recognize any colonial policy. The peoples of the East have accepted this principle laid down by the Third International, and, with arms in their hands, they will apply it to life. There must be no colonies. All nations are equal. British violators—away from India, Egypt, Persia, Mesopotamia! French bandits—away from Syria! Greek bandits—away from Cilicia and Smyrna, and so on and so on! . . .

The fact that the world is still being divided into two groups of nations, the oppressors and the oppressed, is due, first, to the violence with which the bourgeois governments suppress by fire and sword every manifestation of the desire for national self-determination; second, to the differences which exist among the toiling masses of the East; third, to the treacherous conduct of the native rich and landlords, who are quite numerous in every Eastern country. All the landlords and wealthy classes of Morocco, Algeria, Persia, Turkey, India, and Bukhara . . . are the agents of international imperialism and are supporting the rule of foreign capitalists of the international bourgeoisie.

The revolutionary national movement will improve the lot of the masses only if it becomes a decisive step toward a thorough and broad socialist movement.

The chief assurance of the victory of the Eastern peoples in the struggle with the monster of world imperialism . . . lies in the unification of the toiling masses not only of the entire East, but also of the West. This war can end successfully only on the condition that it is waged on two fronts—namely, against foreign capital and against the native bourgeoisie. . . .

In order to create this condition, the revolutionary masses of the East must be organized in peasant soviets, soviets of toilers.

The Eastern masses will be able to win victory in the struggle for freedom only by combining with the toiling masses of the West. How can we hasten this union? The first step is a close union of all the peoples of the East with Soviet Russia, in whom all the international proletariat sees its advance guard, its leader in the world revolution.

The transitional step toward the full unity of the toiling masses of the different nations lies in a federation of the soviet republics of the East for the struggle against both the expansionist plans of the imperialism powers and the machinations of their own domestic enemies.

[Theses on Soviet Government in the East Adopted at the Sixth Session of the Baku Congress, September 6, 1920]

1. The revolution of the peoples of the East against their foreign and domestic oppressors, against the foreign imperialists and domestic exploiters, makes the question of the future government of all the countries of the East the vital problem of the day. Through all sorts of machinations, the European bourgeoisie has for a long time been able to conceal from the poor proletarian and semiproletarian elements of the population the true nature of [its] governments, which serve as instruments for the oppression of the people. On the other hand, the coercive nature of the government authority in the Eastern countries is not even concealed but [is practiced] absolutely openly.

The lives of the poor, who are completely deprived of every right, as well as the products of their labor, are used simply [to enrich] the various sultans, shahs, emirs, and tribal chieftains who belong to the wealthy and bureaucratic element of the population. Such a state of affairs has prepared the ground for the activities of the imperialist exploiters who, through the help of the rulers, high-ranking army men, and officials, have been able to make their deals in the colonies and in the semicolonial countries at the expense of the poor.

2. As in the Western states, the rich and exploiting elements of the population in the Near Eastern countries have [now] tried to make their governments appear to be governments of the people. The introduction of parliamentary methods of government in Turkey and in Persia and the reorganization of Georgia into a democratic republic under the leadership of the Mensheviks, of Armenia under the leadership of the Dashnaktsutiun Party, and of Azerbaijan under the Musavat Party, have been conducted under the slogans of liberty and equality. However, these reorganizations have failed to create even the appearance of popular government. Unbelievable poverty still exists among the masses, side by side with the luxury of the agents of foreign imperialism; the land, as before, belongs to the old owners; the old system of taxation, extremely detrimental to the toilers, is retained; usurping practices are tolerated and even supported by the government against the interests of the poor. All this has revealed the fallacy of the slogans of equality advanced by the Turkish, Persian, and Azerbaijani democratic parties, as well as by the Menshevik Party and the Dashnaktsutiun Party, which are acting under the cover of socialist slogans.

3. The revolution of the toilers of the East will continue even after the destruction of the authority of the foreign imperialists. It will not cease under a regime which, by pretending to be a popular government and under cover of the slogan of equality, tries to retain the authority of the sultans, shahs, emirs, pashas, and beys; which applies the old methods of oppression to the toilers; and which maintains the inequality between the wealthy and the poor, between the taxpayers and those who profit from the taxes. The revolution will not halt at the boundaries of privately owned land which has been declared sacred. The Eastern peasantry, like the Russian peasantry, will develop their revolution into a great agrarian peasant revolution; the land will pass to the toilers, and all the methods of exploitation will disappear. Like the Russian peasantry, who accomplished the agrarian revolution with the support of the industrial workers, under the guidance of the Communist

Party, and united into soviets, . . . the oppressed peasants of the East hope to obtain in their revolutionary struggle the support of the revolutionary workers of the West, of the Communist International, and of the present and future soviet states.

4. The soviet government and the soviet organization [of society] not only represent the [best] organization for the industrial proletariat; they are also the only suitable type of organization for the toiling masses in general, once these masses remove from their governments the privileged and therefore hostile elements (the landlords, speculators, high-ranking officials, and officers) and organize their own future. Only the soviet government will surrender authority exclusively to the toiling poor. [The creation of and] the union of soviets, and the federation of such soviets, is the only means by which peaceful collaboration among the toilers of the various countries, who have so far been cutting each other's throats in the East, will become possible. Such action will help them to destroy by common effort the authority of foreign and local oppressors and to prevent the attempts of the latter to return to the old systems.

5. So-called democratic self-government, in which the administration is concentrated exclusively in the hands of the privileged groups of the population (khans, beys, and so forth), makes it impossible for the toiling masses to administer their own affairs; it deprives the masses of a chance to acquire the knowledge required for such administration. In contrast to this democratic government, the experiences of the peasantry of Soviet Russia, Siberia, the [autonomous] Bashkir and Kirghiz republics, and Turkestan have proved that the peasants of the Eastern countries are capable of managing their own affairs.

6. The victory of the communist parties in the West will put an end to the exploitation of the Eastern peoples. However, this victory will not mean that the East and the West will not need mutual economic co-operation. On the contrary, the victory of the revolution in both the East and the West will bring about a relationship of mutual assistance and support between countries instead of the former exploitation.

After the victory of the communist revolution [in the West], economic relations will continue to exist among countries, and, therefore, economic relations with Eastern countries, if they do not have soviet regimes, would benefit only the interests of a small capitalist group which, having gathered the harvest and raw materials, would carry on trade with the Western soviet states in absolutely the same manner in which it now trades with the imperialist states—by exploiting the toilers of the East for this purpose.

In order to be completely free from imperialist exploitation, in order to be able to transfer the land to the toilers and to liberate them from the rule of the speculators and exploiters, the removal of the non-toiling elements from the government is required, as well as the removal of all foreign colonial elements (generals, higher officials, etc.), and all privileged persons in general. It is likewise necessary to organize the poor on a soviet basis. All the interests of the toiling peoples of the East indicate clearly that the creation of a soviet government [in the East] is imperative.

[Theses on the Agrarian Question Adopted at the Sixth Session
of the Baku Congress, September 6, 1920]

The mere establishment of political independence in the Eastern countries, such as Turkey, Persia, and Afghanistan, and the mere declaration of the political independence of the colonies, such as India, Egypt, Mesopotamia, and Arabia, cannot free the peasants of the East from oppression, exploitation, and poverty. If the capitalist order is retained in Europe and Asia, those countries of the East which are the most backward industrially, even if they become free of political dependence upon the imperialist countries, will inevitably remain in complete economic dependency on these powers, and will continue to be used for the development of the financial capital of the industrial European countries. The peasants and workers [of the East, meanwhile,] will continue to be exploited by the capitalists. Even if complete political independence is attained by the countries and colonies of the East, so long as they retain a capitalist regime their peasants will inevitably go through the painful process of early capitalist accumulation, which will mean their further impoverishment, the loss of their land, and their proletarianization. They will be forced to sell their labor, to become factory workers and agricultural laborers.

The peasants of the East, who are at present marching hand in hand with their own democratic bourgeoisie in the attempt to win the independence of their countries from the Western European imperialist powers, must remember that they have their own tasks to perform, that their liberation will not be attained simply by a conquest of political independence, and that they should therefore persevere in their efforts even after the attainment of political independence. The peasants of the East must move on and continue to struggle against their own landlords and their own bourgeoisie, who will undoubtedly try, once independence is won, to exploit the peasants for themselves.

In order to attain the complete and true liberation of the peasantry of the East from every oppression, every dependence, every exploitation, it is imperative to overthrow the authority of the local landlords and bourgeoisie, and to establish in the countries of the East a peasants' and workers' soviet government. Only the complete destruction of the capitalist regime in the West and in the East will make it possible for the peasants of the East to retain and to develop their own [agricultural] economy, and to escape the most painful process of the first stage of the accumulation of capital. With the help of the working class of the most advanced countries of the world, after passing through a certain period of development, the peasants of the East will then proceed to the communist regime, which will ensure to every peasant complete liberty and the full use of the products of his labor.

. . . Therefore, the peasants of the East who are struggling for their own liberation have no other choice but to walk side by side with the advanced revolutionary workers of the West, and, in a close union with the revolutionary soviet republics created by the proletariat, to launch a struggle against both the foreign capitalist conquerors and their own despots—the landlords, the bourgeoisie, and the other oppressors. They must carry on this struggle until they win complete victory over the world bourgeoisie; achieve a full social revolution; and, finally, establish a communist order, which alone can bring the peoples of the West and of the East liberation from the exploitation of one people by another, and one man by another.

[Seventh Session of the Baku Congress, September 7, 1920: Concluding Remarks of the Chairman and the Establishment of a Permanent Council for Propaganda and Action]

CHAIRMAN [Zinoviev]: I declare the seventh session of the Congress of the Peoples of the East open. We have before us the task of settling one of the most important questions—perhaps the most important question—of our congress; that of creating a permanent executive body of the Congress of the Peoples of the East. After this congress adjourns, we wish to have an organ which will continue the work which has been so magnificently started by our historic congress.

We are convinced that this congress will be not the last but the first, that we shall convene congresses of the peoples of the East at least once a year, and that during the periods between the congresses, the work of revolutionary propaganda and the struggle for liberation of the East will be continued.

We suggest that the First Congress of the Peoples of the East establish a permanent Council for Propaganda and Action of the Peoples of the East. Both factions of the congress [party and nonparty] and the presidium of the congress have discussed this question, and they now suggest that you pass the following resolution:

"The First Congress of the Peoples of the East resolves to establish, as an auxiliary of the Executive Committee of the Communist International, a permanent organ to unify the peoples of the East, to be entitled the Council for Propaganda and Action of the Peoples of the East. [The Council shall include forty-seven elected members.] . . . Those peoples of the East who were not represented at the First Congress shall have the right to send their delegates to the Council.

"The Council for Propaganda and Action shall organize propaganda throughout the entire East, shall publish a magazine entitled *Narody Vostoka* ("The Peoples of the East") in [Russian and] three [additional] languages, shall organize the publication of leaflets and other written material, shall support and unite the movement for liberation throughout the entire East, shall establish a university of social science for the workers in the East, etc.

"The Council for Propaganda and Action of the Peoples of the East shall have its residence in Baku until the meeting of the Second Congress of the Peoples of the East, which meeting must take place not later than a year from this time.

"The plenary sessions of the Council for Propaganda and Action shall be held in Baku not less than once every three months. In the periods between the plenary sessions of the Council for Propaganda and Action, the work shall be carried on by a presidium of seven which shall be elected by the Council.

"The Council shall organize separate sections in Tashkent and other centers as it deems such sections necessary.

"The entire work of the Council shall be conducted under the guidance and control of the Executive Committee of the Communist International, which shall appoint two persons (out of seven) to the presidium of the Council. These two persons shall have the right to veto the decisions taken."

. . . We are assigning to the Council a tremendous task, and we are convinced that tremendous possibilities will open before this organization which we are trying to create. Today it is not as yet a fully centralized organization, but tomorrow and the day after tomorrow, in the measure that the movement for liberation develops in the East, the Council for Propaganda and Action which we are now creating will become a truly great power among the peoples of the East.

[The proposal was then voted upon and unanimously adopted.]

31

Russian Communists' Leadership in the Revolutionary Struggle of Asia

[An Editorial in *Petrogradskaia Pravda*][17]

The Congress of the Peoples of the East which took place in Baku is undoubtedly an event of world historical magnitude, inasmuch as it will further the organized and systematic revolutionary movement which has already been spreading like a fire through Asia and Africa.

There is a great historical significance in the fact that this time the awakening

[17] *Petrogradskaia Pravda,* No. 207, September 17, 1920, p. 1.

of the East and the organization of its forces for the revolutionary struggle proceed under the leadership of Soviet Russia.

The press of the Entente powers has harped for some time upon so-called "Bolshevik imperialism," by which it means the irresistible appeal of communist ideas to the imagination of all the people of the world.

Being greatly perturbed by the penetration of the ideas of communism into the minds of the European and American proletariat, the imperialists are now anxious about the increasing ideological attraction of communism for the toiling masses of the East.

There was a time when capitalist Europe, and the British imperialists in particular, watched with anxiety the ever-growing strength and influence of tsarist Russia in Asia. This was the time of the seizure by Russian troops of the Caucasus, Transcaspia, Turkestan, and the Amur region. With iron and blood, the landlords' and bourgeoisie's Russia was establishing its mastery over the peoples of the East. Russian advance positions approached gradually closer and closer to India, this pearl in the British crown as well as the Achilles' heel of British imperialism. Now the press of the British bourgeoisie sounds alarm over the growing successes won by the new Russia in Asia . . . , over the unprecedented capacity of communist ideas to influence the peasants of the backward Eastern countries.

By new methods and new means, the new Russia is now establishing its influence on the peoples of the East, but these means are much stronger and much more effective than the aggressive policy of old Russia, the colossus on clay feet.

With the help of Soviet Russia, the East, which is awakening from its lethargic slumber, forms a union with the rising European proletariat. Liberated from the capitalist yoke, the workers' and peasants' Russia represents a center for the organization of the struggle against international capital not only for the workers of all countries, but also for the toilers of the colonies and semicolonies of the East. With Russia's mediation the international proletariat and the masses of Asia, oppressed and exploited by the millionaires of Europe and America, now sign an alliance which definitely forebodes the destruction of capitalism. The resolutions taken at the Baku Congress will resound like an alarm bell in the hearts of the workers and peasants of Asia and Africa, but they will be a funeral dirge for the bourgeoisie which is doomed to perish.

In all corners of the earth, the steps of the gravediggers for the bourgeoisie can be heard, the steps of a new historical class, the proletariat, which is coming to replace the bourgeoisie. The toilers of the East extend their fraternal hands to these newcomers.

32

The Training of Communist Theoretical and Practical Propagandists

a

[Decision of the Fifth Congress of the Communist International, July 1924][18]

. . .

In order to satisfy the need of at least the most important parties for qualified theoretical workers, the Communist International resolves that party workers of

[18] *Piatyi Vsemirnyi Kongress Kommunisticheskogo Internatsionala . . . Stenografi- cheskii otchet*, Part II, p. 101. (Cited hereafter as *Piatyi Vsemirnyi Kongress K.I.*)

the German, British, American, Czechoslovak, Italian, French, Eastern, and, if possible, other sections be sent to Moscow for a long period of time to devote themselves exclusively to the study of Marxist-Leninist theory and practice. With this in view, comrades must be selected (preferably workers) who have had general education and who are able to do academic work. . . .

b

[Excerpts from Stalin's Speech at the Communist University of the Toilers of the East, May 18, 1925][19]

.   .   .

[There are] two lines of activity at the university: one, the purpose of which is to train cadres competent to attend to the needs of the soviet republics of the East, and the other, the purpose of which is to train cadres competent to attend to the [revolutionary] needs of the toiling masses of the colonies and dependent countries. Hence the two kinds of tasks that confront the University of the Toilers of the East.

.   .   .

In the University of the Toilers of the East there are about ten different groups of students who have come to us from colonial and dependent countries. We all know that these comrades thirst for light and knowledge. The task of the University of the Toilers of the East is to forge them into true revolutionaries, armed with the theory of Leninism, equipped with the practical experience of Leninism, and capable of conscientiously fulfilling the immediate tasks facing the liberation movement in the colonies and dependent countries.

[19] Stalin, *Sochineniia,* VII, 134, 150–51.

B. SOVIET DIPLOMATIC AND REVOLUTIONARY EFFORTS IN THE NEAR EAST

33

The Appeal of the People's Commissariat of Foreign Affairs to the Workers and Peasants of Persia, August 30, 1919[1]

In the course of the last century the Russian and British governments treated you as enslaved people. They took advantage of the fact that the once powerful Persian people, now bearing the heavy yoke imposed upon them by their despotic shahs and avaricious feudal lords, had fallen into a state of extreme poverty and humiliation.

Aiming at new conquests, the British plunderers and the agents of tsarism intensified their efforts to enslave you, while at the same time they supported your own domestic oppressors. In that way these plunderers made it impossible for you [to throw off your yoke]. Finally the Persian people became absolute slaves paying tributes [to their masters]. Meanwhile, the despotic and autocratic Tsar ruled supreme in Russia, and in Britain a small group of rapacious capitalists was in power. These two kinds of rulers found it to their advantage that you should remain backward and enslaved, that education and economic conditions in your country should be undeveloped, that the strength and talents of your people should stay dormant. The tsarist government concluded a number of secret treaties with your despotic Shah's government, promising him support and making him pledge not to construct railways and not to develop the natural wealth of your country. The two competing plunderers, the Russians and the British, constantly quarreled among themselves over Persia, yet their disputes merely concerned the question of which one would succeed in stripping or oppressing you most efficiently.

However, the time arrived when the Persian masses arose in a courageous attempt to throw off the unbearable and centuries-old chains, both of the Shah's unlimited rule, and of the feudal oppressors and vampires. The Persian people were given fraternal help by the Russian revolutionists, who themselves fought at home against tsarist despotism and barbarian methods of exploitation and oppression of the Russian people. But at that time tsarism was still able to remain in power. Therefore, when the Persian people rose to struggle for their independence, the British and Russian governments, which had been struggling with each other for centuries for the domination of Persia, signed an agreement and divided the Persian territory between themselves. Thanks to the help given by the tsarist troops, and particularly by the bestial Cossacks sent to Persia by the Russian government, the liberation movement in Persia was broken up, and the best fighters for liberty perished on the guillotine in Teheran and later in Tabriz. In the years that followed, the Persian people bore a double oppression, the oppression of their Persian despots, and the oppression of the Russian and British plunderers, who merely saw in the Persian people the objects of their enrichment. . . . The Persian Majlis, which had been the supreme legislative body, now became the tool of Persian princes and

[1] Kliuchnikov and Sabanin, II, 341–44; also Degras, I, 161–64.

capitalists, and later was dispersed altogether upon the demand of the British and Russian governments.

Then came the great Russian revolution, and the toiling masses of Russia overthrew the barbarian and savage tsarism, and for the first time in history liberated the toilers from the rule of capitalism. The toiling masses of Russia took power into their own hands and became masters of their own destiny. One of the first acts which expressed the will of the Russian Workers' and Peasants' Government was the declaration that each nation, whether great or small, and irrespective of where it was found, that is, whether it had retained its independence in the past or had been drawn against its will into some other state, should henceforth be free in its internal life, and that no country had a right to retain such a nation against its will within this country's boundaries.

In regard to Persia, Comrade Trotsky solemnly informed the Persian people on January 14, 1918 [January 27, N.S.], that all treaties which had been signed between Russia and Britain, or between Russia and other states, which concerned Persia, and which violated the rights of an independent country, were henceforth annulled by Russia, and that the Russian people would return to Persia all that was seized from her, or that was plundered from the Persian people by tsarist generals.

The Persian government, on its part, declared such treaties null and void. It would have seemed that now a new and free life awaited the Persian people, leading to a regeneration of the country after centuries of oppression by foreign plunderers.

However, that was not so. In the spring of 1918 British troops gradually began to occupy Persian territory. The English insisted that they would leave Persian territory as soon as the Turks were driven away and that they would recompense the Persians for all acts of robbery committed and requisitions made by British soldiers. The note of the British government of March 12, 1918, giving such promises, was printed on March 14 in the official Persian organ, the *Raab*. The British promised (although unasked) to help the Persian people to restore their ruined economy after the war. But instead of doing it, they made the Persian people their slaves.

The Russian Workers' and Peasants' Government continues to struggle against numerous foes, against the most powerful masters of the world, large-scale capitalists, and against their agents and servants who have been sent [to Russia] in the hope of drowning in blood the revolutionary movement of the toiling masses of Russia. Recently powerful British capital, in alliance with American and French capital, crushed its world competitor, rapacious German imperialism, and then celebrated its victory over the latter. Taking advantage of the favorable situation, British capital finally decided to seize and place under its domination the whole of Persia. Persia has been stricken from the list of free peoples; her own despots and oppressors have become paid servants of Great Britain. These despots, however, continue to oppress the Persian people and will do so in the future while they themselves will remain agents and servants of the greatest vulture, British capital. . . .

At this moment, when the triumphant victor, the British vulture, tries to throw a net over the necks of the Persian people in order to enslave them completely, the Russian Workers' and Peasants' Government solemnly declares that it does not recognize the Anglo-Persian treaty which would make this enslavement possible. The toiling masses of Russia see in the toiling masses of Persia their own brothers and friends, as well as their future comrades in the revolutionary struggle for the complete liberation of the toilers. The Russian Workers' and Peasants' Government, which expresses the will of the Russian masses, treats as a slip of paper and considers absolutely illegal the shameful Anglo-Persian treaty with which the [Persian] rulers have sold themselves and you to the British robbers.

In the face of this most unscrupulous and rapacious act committed jointly by the

British and the Persian governments, we believe it our duty to confirm once more that which was promised by the Russian people to the Persian people, and that which was stated in our note to the Persian government of June 26, 1919, which the mercenary Persian government has no doubt concealed from the Persian people, namely:

All payments due from Persia in accordance with the tsarist agreement are canceled.

Russia ends once and for all every interference in Persia's internal revenues.

The Caspian Sea, once it is cleared of the robbers' ships of British imperialism, will be declared free for navigation for ships carrying the Persian flag.

The boundaries between Soviet Russia and Persia will be established in accordance with the freely expressed will of the people inhabiting the border territories. All former Russian government and private concessions are annulled. Consular jurisdiction is also annulled.

The Account and Loan Bank of Persia, and all railways which were formerly controlled by Russians, as well as all highways, port constructions, postal buildings, and telephone and telegraph lines, are now passed to the ownership and use of the free and independent Persian people. All other institutions or rulings which placed the Persian people in a subordinate position, or interfered with the life of the Persian people, are declared null and void.

The time of your liberation is near. The hour of reckoning will soon strike for British capital, against which the mass revolutionary movement among the toiling masses of Britain is growing. The time is near when the capitalist vultures will fall in all countries under the blows of their own arisen toilers. The powerful revolutionary movement of the Russian toiling masses, who have broken the chains imposed upon them by their own oppressors and exploiters, serves as the most powerful example for the toiling masses of other countries to follow. Against world capitalism and its agents and servants, and against their own counterrevolutionaries, the Russian masses are waging a successful and victorious struggle. Very soon our valiant revolutionary Red Army will be crossing Red Turkestan and will be approaching the boundaries of oppressed Persia.

The Russian working masses extend to you, the oppressed masses of Persia, their brotherly hands. The hour is near when we shall be able to carry out our task in the joint struggle with you against the oppressors, great and small, who have caused your endless suffering.

34

The Nature of the Propaganda to be Carried on in Persia[2]

. . . The significance of Kuchuk Khan's activities lies not in his armed strength and his fight against the British, but rather in the point of a possible contact with him for the purpose of successful revolutionary propaganda in Persia. Kuchuk Khan is important as a socialist agitator not so much because he is a leader of a guerilla war, but because he is a bearer of social slogans, which he advanced even before the coming of the British to Gilan. . . . His work, which is so closely connected with communism, although it is interpreted by the Persians in a different sense, represents a seed which, once it is carefully and skillfully cultivated, will produce a good harvest of revolutionary preparedness among the Persian masses. . . .

Kuchuck Khan's movement not only has affected Gilan but has also found support in neighboring Mazanderan. . . .

[2] Ips., "Zadachi i usloviia propagandy v Persii," *Zhizn Natsionalnostei,* No. 19 (27), May 25, 1919, p. 2, and No. 20 (28), June 1, 1919, p. 1.

In general, as long as the whole country is conquered and is gripped in the steel clutches of the British as it is at present, the revolutionary work in Persia must clearly conform to the conditions of Persian life and Persian psychology.

The work of agitation [in Persia] must inevitably be concentrated at first on the general hatred of the British, which will serve as a starting point for propaganda. Only later the revolutionary material found among the [Persian] people must be used.

In the realization of their hopeless future [if the British remain in Persia] the Party of Unity and Progress[3] will willingly follow the slogans of a revolutionary struggle against their own domestic and British oppressors. . . .

As to the propaganda of socialist ideals in general, and communism in particular, the agitators must lean, of course, upon local cells and the organizations of Persian socialists whose chief center before the European war was found in Azerbaijan. It was from there that [socialist] influence spread to other Persian regions, mainly to the capital and northern cities, in so far as it was possible under the Persian government and the Anglo-Russian regime.

Now, under the influence of the Russian revolution, and also partially owing to the active work of the Russian revolutionary war committees in [northern] Persia before the British occupation, and also thanks to the agents of the Central Committee of the Persian Socialist Democrats in Baku and Astrakhan, these cells naturally increased in number and became more consolidated. They are, therefore, the kernel of the prepared human material [for revolutionary work]. However, these groups are still not very numerous, nor do they represent a socialistically dependable and sufficiently class-conscious element.

35

Soviet Troops on Persian Territory Support Kuchuk Khan, a Persian Revolutionary

[An Interview with F. F. Raskolnikov, Commander of the Red Fleet on the Caspian][4]

[Describes the struggle of the Red fleet on the Caspian against the Russian anti-Soviet forces.] . . .

"When the White fleet entered Enzeli the British military command interned the White crews, believing that if the White ships were placed under British protection our Red fleet would not attack them.

"At this time the British began energetic preparations to convert Enzeli into a base for their rule on the Caspian Sea. They began to send their marines and officers through Mesopotamia and Persia to provide crews for their naval ships at Enzeli. Simultaneously they began to fortify Enzeli and make it ready for defense. They hoped by fortifying Enzeli to transform it into their foremost outpost, one which would cover the approaches to Persia, Mesopotamia, and, what was most important for them, to India.

"After an insurrection had broken out in Baku, and the insurgent workers had called upon the brotherly Red troops and Red fleet to come to their aid, our fleet was sent from Petrovsk to Baku and arrived there on May 1, almost concurrently with the Red Army.

"After the proclamation of the Azerbaijani republic, knowing that Soviet Russia

---

[3] The Party of Unity and Progress is a misnomer since no such party existed in Persia at that time. The author of the article might have meant the Social Democratic Party (Ejtemayun Amiyun).

[4] E. V., "Na Kaspii i v Persii (Beseda s tov. Raskolnikovym)," *Petrogradskaia Pravda*, No. 155, July 15, 1920, p. 1.

and the Azerbaijani republic could not be sure that the British would not make a new attack on Baku from Enzeli, I decided to seize Enzeli and to remove from there all the White ships, thus depriving the British of their mainstay on the Caspian Sea.

"On May 18 [1920], in the early morning, our fleet approached Enzeli and opened fire, bombarding not the city itself but Kazian, where all the staffs and military forces of the British were located. Simultaneous with the bombardment of Enzeli our torpedo boat made a demonstration near Resht, whither the British immediately sent their cavalry.

"To the east of Enzeli, about twelve to fourteen versts [eight to nine miles] from the city, we landed a force which cut off the British from the road to Resht. They thus found themselves in a trap. At first the British tried to offer resistance and sent two detachments of sharpshooters against us. But after a few volleys from our ships' cannons the British troops became disorganized and retreated. Finding the situation hopeless, they sent emissaries to us to ask for an armistice.

"I told the British emissaries they must immediately surrender Enzeli, in view of the presence in the port of ships and military stores belonging to Russia.

"As to the future fate of Enzeli, I told them that this question would be settled through diplomatic negotiations between Russia and Great Britain. My ultimatum was reported to General [H. B.] Champain, who asked for an extension of the two-hour limit, pointing out that he could not obtain a reply so quickly from the Persian government, whose interests he claimed to represent.

"Some time after this, the Governor of Enzeli came to my ship and declared that he came to greet the Russian Red fleet in the name of Persia. He agreed to evacuate Enzeli.

"Since the British could not present an answer from the Persian government before night, I proposed to General Champain to allow the British troops to leave the city if he would turn over to us all the marine stores which he had seized from the Denikin fleet and part of which were still at Enzeli (a part he had already removed from the city). General Champain accepted this demand and gave a formal promise to return all our stores unharmed. Shortly after this, the Sepoys brought thirty-five cannon locks and turned them over to us.

"After this I gave permission for the evacuation of Enzeli by the British troops, but on the condition that they should not take along the Russian Whites. When the British troops were leaving the city we watched carefully that no Denikin officer should slip through with them.

"The morale of the troops (the English, the Turks, and the Sepoys) seemed to be pretty low. When we opened the road from Enzeli to them, they started at a run, apparently eager to get out of Enzeli as quickly as possible. Before the evacuation of Enzeli the British announced to the local population that they were leaving but for a short time, and that they would send an army of a hundred thousand for a new occupation of Enzeli. But watching their hasty evacuation of the city and how submissively they turned over the military stores to us, the local population did not believe their boast.

"Before the British had evacuated Enzeli, we landed troops which occupied the city. The population greeted us with joy. All the streets and squares were packed with people. The whole city was covered with Red flags.

"From the very moment of our entry we announced that we had no intention of interfering in the internal affairs of Persia. The Persian Governor and other official representatives of the Persian authorities welcomed us as liberators from British oppression. The whole populace cursed the British as exploiters.

"In Enzeli we captured an enormous military prize: Denikin's whole fleet, which had been armed by the British and which consisted of armed ships and transports, came into our possession. In addition to this we captured over fifty cannons, 20,000 shells which were brought from abroad, 160,000 puds[5] of cotton which had been removed from Krasnoarsk and sold to the United States, but which is now being sent to Astrakhan, 8,000 puds of copper, 25,000 puds of rails, forty cars, over twenty ship radio stations and three field radio stations, six hydroplanes, and four destroyers. It is impossible to enumerate the smaller materials. We have removed these military stores to Baku and Astrakhan.

"After the occupation of Enzeli we entered into negotiations with Kuchuk Khan, urging him to advance on Resht. When the British heard this, they hastily evacuated Resht and retreated toward Bagdad.

"Kuchuk Khan had been at one time a mullah, but disillusioned by religion and seeing how his people were exploited by the British, he exchanged the cassock for a rifle. Escaping into the mountains, he gathered a small band of reliable men and for seven years waged bitter warfare against the British, struggling for the liberation of Persia. The British repeatedly dispatched much stronger military detachments against him, but to no avail. The local population supported Kuchuk Khan and always notified him of the approach of British troops. After making a sudden attack on the British and inflicting heavy losses, Kuchuk Khan would retreat into the mountains through paths which his pursuers could not use.

"The arrival of the Red fleet at Enzeli enabled Kuchuk Khan to seize Resht and to form there a revolutionary government of Persia. The revolutionary government formed by Kuchuk Khan was greeted with enthusiasm not only by the poor, but also by the landowners and even by some of the khans who had suffered under the British yoke. Kuchuk Khan is an idealist and revolutionist. He will act in co-operation with the wealthy classes until he drives out the bourgeois Persian government and turns over the land to the poor. He does not like to be called khan, declaring that the khans are the oppressors of the people and that he is simply a representative of the people—Mirza Kuchuk."

Comrade Raskolnikov expressed the belief that the struggle of Kuchuk-Khan for the liberation of Persia from the British yoke would be successful, for the Persian government has no real power in the country. The Persian Cossacks and gendarmerie, the best organized troops of the bourgeois government, are in sympathy with Kuchuk Khan and against the British. Knowing that the people of Persia hate them, and fearing a rebellion in India and Mesopotamia, the British will not dare to send any help to the Persian government.

To fight the British, Kuchuk Khan has formed a revolutionary military council, of which he is a member. Kuchuk Khan himself is fairly well acquainted with military operations, but he is more capable in guerrilla warfare than in mass field warfare. But since the topographical conditions preclude anything but guerrilla warfare, Kuchuk Khan's victory seems to be assured.

Kuchuk Khan's government is revolutionary in its composition and is made up of men who, like Kuchuk Khan, have fought for years for the liberation of Persia. Closest to the Communist Party is Comrade Ehsanullah, who is the commander-in-chief of the armed forces of revolutionary Persia and a member of the Persian revolutionary war council.

The government itself acts in close contact with the Communist Party of Persia. The government understands that the Persian revolution cannot be confined within narrow national forms, but must aid also in the liberation of other peoples of the East. The government is in touch with the revolutionary movement in Mesopotamia.

Kuchuk Khan himself is an ardent sympathizer of Soviet Russia. "When I was leaving," concluded Comrade Raskolnikov, "he asked me to give his sincere regards to Comrade Lenin and to tell him that he will act as his disciple, and that the alliance between Soviet Russia and revolutionary Persia will never be broken."

[5] One pud is equivalent to 36.11 pounds.

36

Exchange of Messages Between the Persian Revolutionary Insurgents and Trotsky[6]

a

[The Revolutionary War Council of the Persian Red Army to the Russian Red Army]

The Revolutionary War Council of the Persian Red Army, organized upon the decision of the Council of People's Commissars of Persia, sends its sincere greetings to the Red Army and Red Navy. After passing through great hardships, and undergoing all kinds of privations, we succeeded in crushing our internal counterrevolution, which was merely a hireling of international capitalism. By the will of the toiling people there was organized in Persia soviet power which began creating a Persian Red Army, with the purpose of destroying the enslavers of the Persian people.

Long live the fraternal union between the Russian Red Army and the young Persian Army! Long live the union of the toilers of the world, the Third International.

> Chairman of the Revolutionary War Council,
> MIRZA KUCHUK
>
> Commander of the Armed Forces,
> EHSANULLAH
>
> Member of the Revolutionary War Council . . . ,
> MUZAFER-ZADE

b

[Trotsky's Reply]

The news of the formation of the Persian Red Army has filled our hearts with joy. During the last decade and a half the toiling people of Persia have been struggling hard for their freedom. They have thus proved to all the world their right to this freedom. In the name of the workers' Red Army of Russia I express my firm conviction that, under the guidance of your Revolutionary War Council, Persia will conquer for itself the right to freedom, independence, and fraternal toil.

Long live the free toiling people of Persia in the family of free nations of Asia and the whole world! . . .

37

A Potentially Revolutionary Situation in Afghanistan and India

[Statement by Professor Barakatullah, an Indian Radical, to *Izvestiia* representative, May 5, 1919][7]

I am not a communist or a socialist, but my political program has been so far that of driving the Britons from Asia. I am an irreconcilable foe of European capitalism in Asia, which is represented largely by the British. In this attitude I come close to the communists, and in that respect you and I are natural allies.

I was unable to sojourn within the boundaries of the British domain from 1906

---

[6] *Izvestiia*, No. 129, June 16, 1920, p. 1.
[7] *Izvestiia*, No. 95, May 6, 1919, pp. 1–2.

to 1914. During this time I worked in Japan publishing a propaganda paper entitled "Muslim Unity." After the outbreak of the European war I was obliged to leave Japan, and I went to San Francisco. There I received in 1915 an invitation from the well-known Indian nationalist Protap (he visited Russia soon after the October Revolution) to come to Afghanistan with him. We reached Afghanistan in the same year, and I remained there until March 1919.

Among the secret documents published by the Soviet Russian government in the *Blue Book*, pp. 74–92, there are documents which show that the British demanded that we be deported from Afghanistan and that Emir Habibullah deceived the British by communicating to them that we had already left Afghanistan, for which information he received a generous remuneration from the British.

In March 1919, after Habibullah was assasinated and the throne was occupied by Amanullah, who hates the British, I, as one of the persons most trusted by the Emir, was sent to Moscow as an extraordinary plenipotentiary for the purpose of establishing permanent relations with Soviet Russia. By doing this the new Emir broke the agreement with the British according to which Afghanistan pledged to enter into no diplomatic relations with any country but England.

The first thing the new Emir did was grant complete political amnesty and announce the establishment of a constitutional regime in the country. I believe that these measures represent only the first steps, and that Afghanistan will not stop at this, since the ideas of communism have penetrated deeply into Afghanistan and even India.

Afghanistan, like India, is not a capitalist state, and it is quite possible that the parliamentary regime will not take deep roots there. It is as yet difficult to say what will happen. But I know definitely one thing, and that is that the well-known appeal by the Soviet government of Russia to all peoples, calling them to struggle against capitalists (for us, a capitalist means a foreigner, or rather a Briton), produced a tremendous impression upon us. Still more effective was the annulment of all secret treaties imposed upon the Eastern countries by imperialist powers, and the announcement of the principle of self-determination for all nations irrespective of size.

The above declarations have rallied around Soviet Russia all the exploited peoples of Asia, as well as all the parties who are far from being socialist. They have also predetermined and brought nearer the Asiain revolution. The British immediately noted the consequences that would ensue from the new Russian slogans, and took every measure possible in order to isolate all the ways leading from Russia to India, including Afghanistan, which lives one life with India and covers up the approach from Russia to India. Hence the advance of the British to Merv, the attempt to form an alliance with Bukhara, and finally the establishment by the British of a Ferghana front with the help of the Russian White Guardists for the purpose of checking the spread of Russian Communist influence in eastern China.

However, while it is possible to seize a territory or conquer a small nation, it is impossible to destroy great ideas. I believe that the British measures are already too late. The ideas advanced by the Bolsheviks . . . have already taken root in the Indian masses, and a small spark of active propaganda will be sufficient to set aflame a huge revolutionary fire in middle Asia.

Conditions for a revolution are ripe in India, conditions similar to the ones in Russia in October 1917. India has been living under a military regime in the true sense of the word for the last thirty-three years, while the Indian people are exploited by the British more than are the workers in other countries. Before the war certain Indian provinces starved; now all India is starving because our food supplies have been used for the provisioning of Allied armies. Diseases, and even plague and influenza, took a toll of eight million lives in India in 1918 according to British statistics. During the past year economic strikes and open risings occurred all over India.

Bengali province is the most revolutionary, since it is, so to speak, the intellectual center of the revolution, while the most active people are those of the Punjab province adjoining Afghanistan. There are good reasons to expect that this summer will be a decisive one for the liberation of India.

38

Greetings Exchanged Upon the Arrival of the Official Afghanistan Mission in Moscow, October 10, 1919[8]

NARIMANOV (Representative of the Commissariat of Foreign Affairs): "Welcome! In the name of the [Russian] Workers' and Peasants' Government and the Commissariat of Foreign Affairs I greet in you [both] friendly Afghanistan and its first ambassador in the capital of the Russian Workers' and Peasants' Government. This historic event proves that imperialism, which aims at the enslavement and humiliation of large and small nations, has been given a death blow. In my official capacity I greet you in the Turkish language, in the name of my government, and in the Russian revolutionary capital. This I do in order to prove that the Russian Workers' and Peasants' Government treats with sincere respect all peoples and all languages, and that it is capable of sincere appreciation of friendship. Welcome again."

THE AFGHAN AMBASSADOR: "I am extremely pleased with the reception given me by the Soviet government. I hope that my stay in the capital of the Russian Workers' and Peasants' Government will help to consolidate our friendship even more."

SULTAN-GALIEV (greeting the Afghan ambassador in the name of the Revolutionary Council of the Republic): "Your small but heroic country is struggling now for its liberation from the centuries-old oppression of the East by British imperialism. We realize that you need assistance and support, and you can rest assured that this help will come from Soviet Russia. I declare to you in the name of the Revolutionary Council of the Republic, and in the name of the revolutionary organizations of the millions of Soviet Russian toilers that Soviet Russia will render you assistance, and that they are also waging a struggle against international imperialism and for the rights of the oppressed peoples of the world."

THE AFGHAN AMBASSADOR: "We know that the Muslim people of Russia are now free, and we most firmly hope that with the help of Soviet Russia, Afghanistan and the rest of the oppressed East will be able to become free also."

39

The Significance of the Treaty with Afghanistan for the Triumph of the World Revolution[9]

The recent treaty with Afghanistan will undoubtedly be of great value in the consolidation of our political influence in the East.

Two orientations have opposed each other in the East, and continue to do so: one is the Soviet orientation; the other, the Entente (chiefly the British) orientation.

England, in an attempt to guard her colonies from Bolshevik infection, has done everything possible to turn the Near Eastern states against us. English diplomats

---

[8] *Izvestiia*, No. 229, October 14, 1919, p. 3.

[9] I. P. Trainin, "K dogovoru s Afganistanom," *Zhizn Natsionalnostei*, No. 7 (105), March 17, 1921, p. 1.

in Afghanistan and Persia have spread a net of predatory intrigues against us. England has even tried to send her troops there, with the definite and unmistakable intention of dealing [us] a blow, should the general political situation permit it. . . .

While we were engaged at the [civil war] front, our chances appeared about equal. To the broad masses of the states adjoining [Soviet Russia], our Soviet regime appeared as an enigma. . . . However, the prestige of the Soviet federation in the East has continued to grow, inasmuch as once victorious we made possible the self-determination of the Eastern people united with us, and in so far as it has become clear that we are not interested in the economic exploitation of these people but, on the contrary, are seeking an alliance with them for a struggle against our common enemy, world imperialism.

Since then, and without overestimating [our position], we are proud to say, our Eastern policy has continued to acquire greater weight on the international political scale, so that we are now able to note without exaggeration that the initiative has passed to us.

How else can we explain the fact that Khiva and Bukhara have joined the Soviet camp,[10] or the negotiations which have been carried on concerning the forced withdrawal of the British troops from Persia, or the failure of British policy in Afghanistan, or the ever-growing revolutionary movement in India, particularly evident at the last All-Indian Congress?

The governments of the neighboring Eastern states are orienting their foreign policies toward Soviet Russia. This does not mean that we wish to assume the role of a commanding master, as the English imperialists have done in the past. Nothing of the kind! It simply means that they [the Eastern peoples] have come to realize that, marching shoulder to shoulder with us in their international policy, they can feel freer and can retain their national dignity better than they have been able to do previously.

This fact was clearly demonstrated by the struggle of Kemal's Turkey (which gained more from the struggle against the Entente usurpers than from negotiations with them). Turkey grew stronger in the eyes of the world because of her friendly relations with Soviet Russia.

Now Afghanistan has done the same. To understand the intentions of the British imperialists, it is sufficient to glance at a map. In the past, Afghanistan served as a flank by which the imperialists tried to safeguard India from Soviet influence. . . . But a healthy political instinct, and especially the latest Turkish events in connection with the Treaty of Sèvres, showed Afghanistan that the British required from it a [treacherous] "Cain's policy." Afghanistan has realized that in the interests of the whole East, as well as in its own, it should link its fate with that of the Soviet federation by signing a treaty of friendship with us.

Thus, advancing along the appointed path, and consolidating our political achievements, we shall bring about the moment of the complete breakdown of the imperialist policy in the East, and at the same time the triumph of the international revolution.

40

Soviet Appeal to the Workers and Peasants of Turkey, September 13, 1919[11]

Comrades, workers and peasants of Turkey!

Your country has always been a military camp. The European Great Powers,

---

[10] See our p. 31.

[11] *Zhizn Natsionalnostei*, No. 36 (44), September 21, 1919, p. 2; also Degras, I, 164–67.

considering you a "sick man," have not only failed to offer you a cure, but, on the contrary, have intentionally maintained your condition, because each of these Powers has aimed at driving you away from the European continent, at seizing the Straits, or, at least, at bleeding, weakening, and enslaving you.

Those of you who think that your Fatherland has existed on the European continent up to the present time thanks to your own strength are mistaken.

This is not so.

You have continued your seemingly independent existence on the European continent thanks to the geographical position of your state, and thanks to the squabbles among the vultures who have been attacking you.

Each of the Great Powers which aimed to subjugate you has heretofore been checked by another interested Great Power; and, in this way, the reading of your Fatherland's death sentence has been postponed until a suitable moment.

This moment has now come.

• • •

The way is now open for England to seize the large and small Muslim states, and to subjugate them. England is already the master of Persia, Afghanistan, the Caucasus, and your own country. Since the surrender of the control of the Straits to England by your government, an independent Turkey has ceased to exist; nor is there any longer a national Turkish city of Istanbul on the European continent. There are no longer any independent Ottoman people.

Comrades, workers and peasants of Turkey! In this critical hour for your Fatherland, you are asking yourselves a question: Why is it that you and your Fatherland are in such a desperate situation? Are you not one of the bravest, most militant people of Asia and Europe? You have always shed your blood for your independence; you, too, in desperation, have dethroned a most powerful despot, Sultan Hamid, and have created a constitutional regime. But all these measures have been to no avail; and you are now suffering under the English yoke. How did it all happen?

It happened because you have always entrusted the fate of your Fatherland to a group of avaricious, mercenary people, people who have sold and now are selling your country as well as you, your wives, and children, your rights and honor, to whichever European Great Power gives them the most money. . . .

In this way, your country and yourselves have always been a plaything in the hands of a group of exploiters, the pashas. Your ill-starred parliament is also nothing else but an assembly of such pashas, exploiters, the slaves of gold, of ranks, titles, etc.

Wherein, then, can salvation be found?

The salvation of your country and of your rights from alien and domestic vultures is in yourselves.

Neither your military party nor any of the so-called democratic parties will save you, just as Scheidemann's Social Democratic Party did not save Germany from the capitalist vultures of France and England. Your Ittihad and Itilâf parties[12] not only will fail to save you, but will also further deprive you of your independence.

As long as your country is ruled by mercenary pashas and unprincipled parties, salvation is not yours.

You must understand once and for all that you, the toiling class, are the body and soul of your Fatherland. It is you, the workers and peasants, who provide food for the country, make her rich, and in the hour of danger defend her from the enemy with your own blood.

Therefore, the fate of the country should be in your hands; you must be the masters of your land; and you and only you must make the laws for the country—

[12] Ittihad ve Terakki Firkasi (Union and Progress Party) and Itilâf ve Hürriyet Firkasi (Unity and Freedom Party).

not the exploiters, the parasites, landlords, pashas, factory owners, or your unprincipled and unbalanced parties, which do not care for the happiness of the toiling class.

Comrades, workers and peasants of Turkey! Your brothers, the workers and peasants of Russia—fed up with the meanness of their own domestic vultures and bloodsuckers, who were in the habit of selling Russia to foreign vultures, the European robbers—have now decided to take the government into their own hands. In the course of the last two years they have been fighting for their own government, for the government of the toilers. Indeed, in Soviet Russia the hour is near when a complete triumph of labor over capital will be attained, and then the enemies will cease their attacks.

But that is not enough. A union of the toilers of the world against the world oppressors is necessary. Therefore, the Russian Workers' and Peasants' Government hopes that you, the workers and peasants of Turkey, in this decisive and momentous hour will stretch out your fraternal hand to drive out the European vultures by joint and united effort, to destroy and to make impotent those within your own country who have been in the habit of basing their own happiness upon your misery.

GEORGII CHICHERIN
People's Commissar of Foreign
Affairs

NARIMAN NARIMANOV
Head of the Department for the
Muslim Near East in the People's
Commissariat of Foreign Affairs

41

The Soviet Government Approves the Establishment of Diplomatic Relations with Kemalist Turkey

[Note from Chicherin, People's Commissar of Foreign Affairs of the R.S.F.S.R., to Mustafa Kemal Pasha, President of the Grand National Assembly of Turkey, June 2, 1920][13]

The Soviet government has the honor of acknowledging the receipt of the letter[14] expressing a desire to enter into regular relations with it and to take part in the common struggle against the foreign imperialism which menaces the two countries. The Soviet government notes with satisfaction the fundamental principles of the foreign policy of the new Turkish government, headed by the Grand National Assembly in Ankara, which are as follows:

(1) The Declaration of the Independence of Turkey.

(2) The inclusion within the Turkish state of territories indisputably Turkish.

(3) The proclamation of Arabia and Syria as independent states.

(4) The decision taken by the Grand National Assembly to allow Turkish Armenia, Kurdistan, the territory of Batum, Oriental Thrace, and all the territories of Turco-Arab population to decide their own destiny. It goes without saying that a free referendum will take place in these localities, with the participation of the refugees and emigrants who were previously obliged

---

[13] Kliuchnikov and Sabanin, III, 26–27.

[14] For a brief summary of Kemal's letter to Chicherin of April 26, 1920, see M. Tanin, *Mezhdunarodnaia politika S.S.S.R. (1917–1924)*, p. 78.

to leave their country for reasons independent of their wishes, and who now will be repatriated.

(5) The granting of all the rights allowed to the national minorities of the most liberal states of Europe to the national minorities of the territories forming part of the new Turkish state headed by the Grand National Assembly.

(6) The referring of the problem of the Straits to a conference of the states bordering the Black Sea.

(7) The abolition of the practice of capitulations and economic control by foreign states.

(8) The abolition of spheres of foreign influence of every kind.

The Soviet takes cognizance of the desire of the Grand National Assembly to align its labors and its military operations against the imperialist governments with the noble ideals of the liberation of oppressed peoples. The Soviet government hopes that diplomatic negotiations will permit the Grand National Assembly of Turkey to establish definite frontiers, determined by justice and the right of peoples to self-determination, between Turkey on one side and Armenia and Persia on the other. Upon the invitation of the interested parties, the Soviet government is always ready to act as mediator.

In order to bring about amicable relations and enduring friendship between Turkey and Russia, the Soviet government proposes to enter into diplomatic and consular relations immediately. The Soviet government extends the hand of friendship to all the peoples of the world, remaining invariably faithful to its principle of recognizing the right of all peoples to self-determination. The Soviet government is following with the greatest interest the heroic struggle for independence conducted by the Turkish people, and, in these present painful days for Turkey, it is happy to establish a firm foundation for the friendship which should unite the peoples of Turkey and Russia.

In bringing the above to your attention . . . , I have the honor to offer you, in the name of the federated [Russian] Workers' and Peasants' Republic, our wishes for the success of the peoples of Turkey in their struggle for independence.

42

Mustafa Kemal Favors a Close Union Between His People and Soviet Russia for the Struggle Against the Imperialists of the West

[Telegram of November 29, 1920, from Mustafa Kemal to the People's Commissar of Foreign Affairs of the R.S.F.S.R., Moscow][15]

Sir Commissar:

I have the honor to confirm your letter of June 2, 1920, handed to me by the chargé d'affaires of your mission in Turkey, and to express my sincere gratitude for your complimentary estimation of the struggle which we are conducting against the coalition of Western imperialists.

It gives me great pleasure to inform you of the admiration which the Turkish people feel for the Russian people, who have not been content only with the breaking

[15] *Izvestiia*, No. 274, December 5, 1920, p. 1.

of their own chains, but for over two years have been conducting an unprecedented struggle for the liberation of the whole world, having borne with enthusiasm and unheard-of suffering so that oppression could disappear forever from the face of the earth.

Our nation fully understands the greatness of the sacrifice the Russian nation has made in order to save humanity, because our nation has struggled likewise for centuries in the defense of Muslim countries against the designs of European imperialists.

I am deeply convinced, and my conviction is shared by all our citizens, that on the day when the toilers of the West and the oppressed peoples of Asia and Africa realize that international capital is using them in order to enslave and destroy them in the interests of their masters, the capitalists; on the day when the realization of the criminality of the colonial policy reaches the hearts of the toiling masses of the world—the rule of the bourgeoisie will be over.

The high moral authority enjoyed by the R.S.F.S.R. among the toilers of Europe, and the love of the Muslim world for the Turkish people, provide complete assurance that the establishment of a close alliance between our two countries is bound to bring together against the imperialists of the West all those who so far have given support to the imperialist rule because of their submissiveness, which is based, on its part, on patience and ignorance.

Please accept, Sir Commissar, my sincere assurances of deep regard,

Chairman of the Grand National Assembly of Turkey,
MUSTAFA KEMAL.

43

A Soviet Plenipotentiary Received in Ankara

[Communiqué from Ankara, June 28, 1921][16]

Yesterday, the President of the Grand National Assembly, Mustafa Kemal Pasha, received the plenipotentiary of Soviet Russia, Natsarenus. The diplomatic representative of the R.S.F.S.R. handed to Kemal Pasha his credentials. An exchange of warm greetings followed. Speaking of the past and present relations between the Russian and Turkish peoples, Natsarenus said: "The desire to raise the cross over St. Sophia was not the desire of the Russian people, but a personal idea of an autocratic Tsar and the ideal of the Russian aristocracy. In the course of time the Russian people found it necessary to annul all treaties signed by the tsarist government and to radically change Russian foreign policy.

"Russia now becomes a natural ally of nationalist Turkey, which is fighting for its freedom and independence. The time is not distant when the courageous Turkish people, victorious and free, will start to organize their own life in accordance with their own wishes."

Mustafa Kemal noted in his answer the development of close relations between Russia and Turkey and said: "Our people, who have risen in defense of their own legal rights, have created a government which leans upon the will of the people that put it into power. Thanks to this, the Turkish people are and will be the supreme masters of their own fate. The established form of government fully corresponds to the conditions of our country, social tendencies, and the needs of the people. Thank you for your decisive confirmation of [Russia's] readiness to fully support our legal rights."

16 *Izvestiia,* No. 152, July 14, 1921, p. 2.

44

Frunze in Ankara

[Telegram from the Turkish National Assembly Read at the Ninth Congress
of Soviets, Moscow, December 1921][17]

To Citizen Kalinin, Chairman of the Congress of Soviets of Russia and affiliated
countries.

To Citizen Petrovsky, Chairman of the Congress of Soviets of the Ukraine.

The Grand National Assembly of Turkey was happy to listen to the declarations
made by Comrade Frunze, the Extraordinary Plenipotentiary of the Ukrainian Soviet
Republic, declarations which leave an ineffaceable imprint on the history of our
independence. The members of the Assembly listened with great pleasure to this
declaration, and every sentence of it called for loud cheers, which differed completely
from the artificial demonstrations of approbation, actually full of lies and hypocrisy
and devoid of all sincerity, which usually characterized such meetings at the time of
the rule of the imperialist governments, on the ruins of which we have now proclaimed the right of all peoples to self-determination. The present event has made
it possible for us to witness the deep mutual sympathies of both friendly peoples, an
event which produced a great impression on all members of the Assembly present.
The fact that the government of the Ukrainian republic had chosen, for the conclusion
of the treaty of friendship and for consolidating still further political and economic
ties between the two peoples, Comrade Frunze, who is one of the most prominent
political leaders, and commander-in-chief, as well as one of the bravest generals, of
the victorious Red Army, this fact (and the fact that we heard of his appointment
on the eve of the battle of the Sakaria [river], when our enemies proclaimed to the
world our imminent final rout) aroused a feeling of special gratitude on the part
of the National Assembly. Our Assembly was all the more moved by this fact because it confirmed and proved the deep sincerity of the political relations [between
the two countries]. Among the highly praiseworthy declarations of the citizen
plenipotentiary, his expression of sympathy for our country's suffering from the
cruelty of the savage foe was particularly consoling to us. I believe it my duty to
repeat once more that the precious solidarity between the two countries serves us as
a great strength, and at the same time as an evident and concrete guarantee for the
successful reaching of the goal which we have set before us.

I take this opportunity to send to you the friendly greetings of the Grand National Assembly, the only true representative body of the people of Turkey.

Chairman of the Grand National Assembly of Turkey and Commander-in-Chief
MARSHAL MUSTAFA KEMAL

45

The Revolutionary Importance of the Turkish Movement of Liberation

[Statement by Pavlovich][18]

. . . It is a well-known fact that the world war which killed scores of millions
of people and devastated Europe was waged mainly for the distribution of Asia, for
the division of the East.

[17] *Deviatyi Vserossiiskii Sezd Sovetov*, pp. 212–13.
[18] M. L. Veltman (M. Pavlovich), "Vostochnyi vopros na III kongresse i perspektivy
osvoboditelnogo dvizheniia na Vostoke," *Zhizn Natsionalnostei*, No. 14 (112), July 16,
1921, p. 1.

When this war was over, an intense struggle was started by the Entente powers against Soviet Russia, and the main moving force of this struggle was again the question of the division of the East. Soviet Russia was formidable, and threatening to France, Britain, and Japan, because it had liberated itself from the foreign yoke, and had called the enslaved East to struggle for liberation, not only by its example but also by giving active aid to the enslaved and oppressed peoples in their struggle against rapacious imperialism.

The great role played by Soviet Russia that has aroused the hatred of all imperialist powers, has been admitted on a number of occasions by the official organs of the bourgeois governments. These organs have emphasized many times that the struggle against the arisen East has not been simply a struggle against Turkish nationalists or the defenders of Arab independence, or against the Persians, the Indians, or the Koreans, but mainly a struggle against Soviet Russia, which is the ally and the bulwark of all the countries of the East.

At present a great danger threatens the imperialist powers in the colonial countries. The reason for this threat is not only the successful struggle which Soviet Russia has been waging against world imperialism, but also the successful struggle of revolutionary Turkey against the capitalist rabble who thought that they had already succeeded in dividing that country. . . .

The heroic struggle of the Turkish people against the vultures of world imperialism, inspired by the example of the workers' and peasants' masses of the R.S.F.S.R., will have a tremendous influence on the growth of the revolutionary movement in the East and on the Muslim countries of the Dark Continent. In Persia, India, Afghanistan, Egypt, Morocco, Algeria, Tripolitania, Tunisia, even among the inhabitants of darkest Africa, the gigantic battles fought by the Turkish peasants in the fields of Anatolia will not pass unnoticed.

The defeat of the Entente's plans for Turkey will arouse national feeling among the countries of the yellow and dark continents even more than the defeat of the Entente's counterrevolutionary plans against Soviet Russia. This defeat of the Entente will increase the desire of the enslaved people for a life-and-death struggle directed at their own liberation.

The persistent struggle by the people of India and Egypt against the British yoke; the national-revolutionary movement in Morocco, Tunisia, and Algeria, directed at liberation from the French imperialists; the unending struggle by the Persian people for their complete liberation from British influence; the awakening of the dark tribes of the Sudan, South Africa, and South America—all these movements, in spite of their narrow and national character, undermine the very bases of the capitalist order, which cannot exist without the exploitation and enslavement of colonial and semicolonial countries. These movements will also receive a tremendous impetus from the successful struggle waged by the Anatolian peasantry against the allied armies of the Entente.

Our Eastern comrades have expressed a firm conviction [at the Third Congress of the Comintern] that the proletariat of England, France, Italy, Greece, the United States, Japan, Holland, and other capitalist countries will be influenced by the ideals of the Comintern and will soon understand that their own liberation from the capitalist yoke, their victory over their own oppressors, can be attained only in a close alliance with the oppressed peoples of the dark and yellow continents. The famous slogan "Proletariat and Oppressed Peoples of the World, Unite!," which was advanced for the first time at the historic Congress of the Peoples of the East in Baku, has been sanctioned now by the Third Congress of the Comintern. The realization of this slogan is the basic condition of the victory of the proletariat over the capitalist world, and of the liberation of all oppressed peoples from the imperialists.

46

Indirect Rebuke to the Turkish Government for the Persecution of Turkish Communists

[Appeal of the Communist International to the Revolutionary Workers and Peasants of the World][19]

. . . The Communist International has followed with particularly warm feelings the heroic struggle of the Turkish people against the gang of Entente murderers. Continually drawing the attention of the advanced proletariat of the world, and in particular of Soviet Russia, to the revolutionary struggle of the Turkish workers and peasants, the Communist International has urged the proletariat to render them every possible aid. . . .

If this aid had not been rendered, the attack by the imperialist robbers would long ago have brought destruction to little Turkey. [Therefore] the Ankara government, which directs the revolutionary movement of liberation of the Turkish people, should not lose sight of this aid. Turkish revolutionary victory will be durable and lasting only if it ensures for itself the further support of the world proletariat, and its vanguard, the Communist International.

What is it then that attracts proletarian sympathies to the struggle of the Ankara government? It is its firm conviction that without the overthrow of the imperialist yoke the liberation of the Turkish workers and peasants from enslavement is impossible. The world proletariat views the struggle of the Ankara government not only as the struggle for the national liberation, but also as a practical preparation for the complete liberation of the Turkish toilers. That is why the news of the persecution of the revolutionary workers and peasants, and of their Communist Party, which has been evident recently in Turkey, causes apprehension to the advanced proletariat of the world. The Ankara national government has taken a dangerous path which is bound to lead it to the state of isolation from the only sincere friends of struggling Turkey, namely the world revolutionary proletariat and the Communist International.

[At present] trade unions are dispersed in Turkey; workers' organizations are persecuted. The Turkish Communist Party has been routed. The arrested Communists are tried by military tribunals. They are accused of treason, and are threatened by the Turkish government with extreme measures of punishment. . . .

[The Communist International warns the Ankara government to desist from following the examples of Poincaré and Mussolini.] The Communist International calls upon the revolutionary proletariat of all countries . . . to sound a word of warning to the representatives of the Ankara government in their respective countries. . . .

47

Moscow's Official Denial of Communist Propaganda in Asia

[The Soviet Government's Reply to the British Government, September 27, 1921][20]

A cursory glance over the document on its delivery was sufficient to enable the People's Commissariat of Foreign Affairs to state to Mr. Hodgson that the charges

---

[19] *Izvestiia*, No. 33, February 14, 1923, p. 2.
[20] Kliuchnikov and Sabanin, III, 124–27; also *A Selection of Papers Dealing with the Relations between His Majesty's Government and the Soviet Government, 1921–1927*, pp. 12–16.

contained therein are either unfounded or based on false information and forgeries. However the People's Commissariat of Foreign Affairs did not think it right to follow the example set up by the British Foreign Office in hastily returning notes which contained, in its opinion, *prima facie* baseless charges, but being anxious to remove any causes for misunderstandings between the Russian and British governments, the Commissariat of Foreign Affairs took great pains to have all the charges brought against it most carefully examined and all the facts that might have given rise to these charges investigated.

In accusing the Russian government of having broken its pledges given in the Anglo-Russian Agreement of March 16, the British note refers to activities of the Russian government and its representatives and agents in Eastern countries allegedly directed against British interests. To substantiate the charges the note brings into play the Third International, quoting a number of alleged reports made to its Central (?) Committee by members and officials of the Russian government, as for instance, Messrs. Stalin, Eliava, Karakhan, and Nuorteva, and an alleged speech made by Mr. Lenin on June 8 at the Congress of the Third International. Indeed, these alleged quotations from the speeches form the background to the rest of the charges and are to show that it is the deliberate policy of the Russian government to undermine the influence of the British government in the East, and to stir up revolutionary movements in the colonies and dependencies of Great Britain, and that the Russian representatives in their activities are but carrying out that policy of the Third International, which, as the note asserts, should be identified with the Russian government.

The Russian government wishes to take this opportunity to emphasize once more, as it has done many times before, that the mere facts (1) that the Third International has for obvious reasons chosen Russia as the seat of its Executive Committee as the only land which allows full freedom to the spreading of communist ideas and personal freedom to Communists, and (2) that some of the members of the Russian government in their individual capacity belong to the Executive Committee, give no more justification for identifying the Third International with the Russian government than the Second International, having its seat in Brussels or counting among the members of its Executive Committee Mr. Vandervelde, a Belgian minister, and Mr. Henderson, a British cabinet minister, gave justification for identifying the Second International with the Belgian or British government. Moreover, the Executive Committee of the Third International consists of thirty-one members, among whom are only five Russians, including three who do not belong to the Russian government.

The Russian government is in a position, however, not only to formally reject the charges based on its being identified with the Third International, but also to deny all the charges in substance. . . .

If the British Office had more exact information at its disposal and genuine Russian documents in its possession, it would have been aware of the strict instructions issued after the conclusion of the Anglo-Russian Agreement by the Russian government to its representatives in the East, ordering them to abstain from any anti-British propaganda and to adapt their activities to the new relationship created between the Russian and British governments by the signing of the agreement. The Russian government has no reason to believe that they are not acting in accordance with the instructions, and that they are not confining themselves to the protection of Russian interests without infringing upon British interests. True to the principle of self-determination for all peoples, the Soviet government and its representatives exercise the greatest respect for the independence of the Eastern countries, in giving up all the privileges and concessions forcibly extorted from them by the tsarist governments and rendering some small material and monetary assistance, thus amending the wrongs done to them by prerevolutionary Russia. The Russian government fails to see in what way the help given to Afghanistan openly on the strength of a treaty, which has been brought to the knowledge of the British government by Mr. Krasin, can be construed as an act unfriendly to Great Britain. The charges of the British government in this respect are either vague and unsubstantial or else based on quite imaginary facts, such as, for instance, the setting up by Mr. Rotshtein of a revolutionary committee in Teheran, or his attempts to bring about the dismissal of the Afghan representatives, who, as a matter of fact, are highly praised by him and enjoy his personal friendship. . . .

C. SOVIET SUCCESSES AND FAILURES IN THE FAR EAST

48

The Importance of the Bourgeoisie of the Eastern Countries for the National Struggle Against Imperialism

[A Statement by Politikus (Chicherin?) in an Article Entitled "We and the East"][1]

. . . We must prove to the East that we are prepared to help it in its struggle sincerely and disinterestedly, and that we are ready to give it needed support. We must also prove that we have no claims to present to the East. We have already tried to apply this policy of disinterestedness in our treaties with Persia of February 26, 1921, with Afghanistan of February 26 of the same year, and with Turkey of March 16, 1921. The above three Eastern states have gained new strength by these treaties granting them not only our neutrality but also our friendship . . .

Persia, which was shackled by the British treaty of 1919, freed itself within a brief space of time from the British military instructors and commanders, and soon forced all British troops to leave Persian territory. Persia has also disbanded the police force organized by the British, has sent away the British financial advisers, and finally has torn to shreds the treaty itself.

Afghanistan, now free from Russian pressure, has raised arms against the British. Partly through its own strength, partly through negotiations while all the time drawing support from us, Afghanistan has forced the British to recognize its independence and sovereignty, and thus to abandon their dream of conquering it. The realization of this dream has been blocked in the past only by the counteraction of Britain's rival—Russia.

Finally, Turkey, which we recognized as a sovereign state in spite of the Sèvres treaty and other treaties, was able, thanks to our material assistance, to rise against the victors in the World War, and not only to halt these victors' assault on the independence of the Turkish people, but also to recapture a part of Turkey's territory in Europe, including the city of Constantinople, which had already come to be thought of [by non-Turks] as an "international" port.

It is true that while we were engaged in the Near East and were waging a domestic struggle against counterrevolution and intervention, we were somewhat slow in reaching the shores of the Pacific and China, a country of many millions known for its ancient culture, and now oppressed by the imperialist vultures. However, once we reached China, we launched there a similar policy of repudiating robbery and violence, a policy of rendering true and disinterested assistance. The peoples of the East, who have been accustomed for centuries to distrust foreigners, have already grown confident of us, and therefore, in whatever part of the world an act of imperialist violence takes place now—Mesopotamia, Arabia, India, Korea—hands are immediately stretched to us in supplication by those who are perishing, and calls for help are heard from those who have succeeded in surviving. We are conquering the East morally, and in that way creating conditions that will increasingly undermine chances of the imperialists for expansion and infiltration . . .

[1] Politikus, "My i Vostok," *Kommunisticheskaia Revoliutsiia*, No. 13–14 (52–53), July 15–August 1, 1923, pp. 23–28.

But to strengthen the East in its struggle against the imperialists by giving not only moral but also material assistance, we must pay heed to its economy and its social dynamics. We must acknowledge that only an economically developed country, led by a strong national bourgeoisie, can force foreign imperialism to retreat. A strong bourgeoisie actually means a victory over feudal remnants and over absolutism. It also means the creation of a compact national state capable of meeting all attempts from outside, just as it means the development of the productive forces within the state, which will finally lead to class struggle and the establishment of a communist regime.

We are actually witnessing the development of the Eastern countries in this direction. Never before has Turkey had such a strong national movement, i.e., the movement against foreign imperialist violators, as it does now under the leadership of Kemal Pasha. Turkey has victoriously defended itself in an unequal struggle against the capitalist world; it has radically changed its political regime by doing away with the old Sultanist absolutism and feudal fetters, and it is now wrestling with the basic tasks of the economic development that would ensure for it [Turkey] an independent existence even if foreign capital continues to lend support to its economy. The Turkish bourgeoisie and Turkish bourgeois intelligentsia are the leaders of this national movement.

A similar but less dramatic situation exists in Persia, where the merchant bourgeoisie is recovering from the war and the loss of markets, and is now raising the national banner of struggle against British imperialism.

While it consolidates the central authority to the detriment of feudal lords, the Persian bourgeoisie seeks, and not without success, to do away with the disorganization of national finances that opened a way in the past for the "peaceful" penetration of British imperialism. The merchant bourgeoisie is also feverishly trying to find a new way to develop the country's productive forces, even with the help of foreign capital, which has been rendered harmless now by legislative acts.

In faraway China, the struggle for liberation from foreign imperialism and the creation of a single strong state has been going on for a long time. The Chinese bourgeoisie are the leaders in this movement.

Finally, in India, the bourgeoisie and the bourgeois intelligentsia have been conducting an open warfare for many years by peaceful and violent means against British domination. In addition, the Indian bourgeoisie has succeeded in unifying under one common national banner two historically hostile elements: the Hindus and the Muslims.

Because of all the above, our policy . . . has been to help the bourgeoisie of the Eastern countries to erect a strong barrier against the imperialist designs of the British and other capitalists. By erecting such a barrier, the Eastern bourgeoisie is also helping us in the struggle against imperialism.

Politically, our policy is to support national movements and national groupings; economically it is reflected in our Eastern trade policy, which differs from our Western policy. For example, we have granted the Eastern countries freedom of import and export with certain reservations; in particular, we are prepared to grant Persia a right of transit, that is, a way to reach the world market by way of our territory, a privilege which tsarism stubbornly denied Persia in the past. We grant special privileges in customs to the Eastern merchants who come to our fairs, as well as privileges connected with the export of capital and goods, etc. If we were richer, we would undoubtedly help the Eastern countries develop their own industries; we would build roads and railways for them, and would send them our instructors and specialists. Under present conditions, we . . . encourage the Eastern countries to receive such help from other countries . . . Those of us who know the impediments created in this respect by tsarist imperialism in the past, as well as the difficulties that are being caused Persia now by the British and other imperialists, will fully appreciate the significance of the new policy of new Russia. . . .

To those of us who are not capable of a dialectic argument, the bourgeoisie-oriented stand taken by the [Russian] Workers' and Peasants' Government might appear a betrayal of communist principles. Thus the Populists accused the early Russian Marxists of betraying socialism when the latter, diagnosing the social and economic development of Russia as advancing toward capitalism, insisted that the old illusion regarding the Russian commune should be repudiated and the way for the advancement of capitalism cleared. . . .

At present the Eastern bourgeoisie is the most progressive Eastern class; it is at once a gravedigger for the rotten feudal aristocracy and the leader of the national struggle against imperialism. Let us then clear the way for the advancing bourgeoisie, but let us not join its ranks. As Communists, let us bring together and organize the proletariat which is coming to life while the native bourgeoisie develops as a class. Let us combine the proletariat's class struggle against the bourgeoisie with the national struggle conducted by the bourgeoisie, either so that these two efforts advance side by side, or so that the proletarian struggle will come abreast of the national struggle if the bourgeoisie grows apprehensive in the last stage of the struggle and begins to compromise with foreign imperialists, as has happened more than once in the past.

The conditions which provide for success in the national struggle lead to the conditions that make the class struggle equally successful. Besides, the struggle against imperialism, irrespective of what forms it takes, is also the struggle for our own existence, and for the existence of the oppressed and exploited peoples of the world.

49

The Role of the Comintern in the Preparation of a Revolutionary Struggle, and the Nature of Communist Propaganda in the East

a

[Lenin's Statement at the Third Congress of the Communist International, July 5, 1921][2]

· · ·

I would like to emphasize here the significance of the movement in the colonies. In regard to this question we believe that all old parties, all bourgeois and petty bourgeois parties of the Second and the Second-and-a-Half Internationals, share the old sentimental views when they deeply sympathize with the oppressed colonial and semicolonial peoples. However, they consider the movement in the colonial countries an insignificant, national, and absolutely peaceful movement. Actually that is not so. From the beginning of the twentieth century great changes have taken place in this respect, namely, millions and hundreds of millions, actually the great majority of the population of the globe, have come out as independent and active revolutionary units. It is quite clear that in the coming decisive battles of the world revolution the movement of the great majority of the population of the globe, which will be directed first at national liberation, will turn against capitalism and imperialism, and, perhaps, play a much greater role than we expect. It is imperative to stress the fact that we, for the first time, in our International, have approached the problem of preparation for such a struggle. Of course great difficulties confront us in this

<hr>

[2] Lenin, *Sochineniia,* XXVI, 453.

task, but nevertheless the movement is marching on, and the toiling masses, the peasants of the colonial countries, although they are backward at present, will play a tremendous revolutionary role in the coming development of the world revolution.

b
[Soviet Russia and the Eastern Countries Are Mutually Complementary][3]

. . . It would be very naïve indeed to think that the sympathies [of the Eastern people for Soviet Russia] are the result of our propaganda in the East. The [Great] Powers continually repeat this but they themselves do not believe it. Indeed, Russia has by no means enough agitators to scatter all over the vast territory of Asia. The source of friendly feelings toward us by the Eastern peoples should be looked for in the nature of Soviet authority, in the methods of our foreign policy, in the self-determination proclaimed by us and applied at home without any restrictions, in our slogan of the equality of all nations [and their right] to a completely independent existence—a refusal we expressed when we surrendered to the appropriate countries all wealth and all property acquired by the colonial policy of tsarist Russia. All these facts play the role of propaganda in our favor in the enslaved East. The people of Asia, oppressed by various imperialists, know that in Soviet Russia they will find an ally and a friend.

[On the other hand,] the significance of the East for Soviet Russia is now quite evident. Soviet Russia and the countries of the East are mutually complementary: just as we represent a strong bulwark for the Eastern peoples in their struggle for their own independence, so the Eastern countries are our allies in our common struggle against world imperialism.

50
The Task of Soviet Diplomacy in the East Outlined by
G. I. Safarov, Communist Representative
in Central Asia[4]

In the East, Soviet diplomacy must first of all prepare the way for the Communist International; it must do so not by police measures, but by "sending out Bolshevik agitators" . . . It would be good if the Soviet sphere of diplomatic activity were just as broad as that of the capitalist countries. . . .

The improvement and development of the rural economy in Turkey, Persia, Turkestan, . . . [and] India provide the basic condition for the actual liberation of these countries. However, it is necessary to emphasize that the development of the proletarian revolution *in Europe* is essential to a victorious agrarian and peasant revolution in the East. [He discusses the importance of the example of the R.S.F.S.R.] . . .

It goes without saying that in these [backward and colonial] countries social revolution meets with millions of difficulties. The soviet peasant revolution in the East cannot lead immediately to socialism. In the settlement of the agrarian ques-

[3] Kh. Eidus, "Nasha politika na Vostoke," *Izvestiia,* No. 155, July 17, 1921, p. 1.

[4] G. I. Safarov, *Problemy Vostoka,* pp. 171, 175-77, 181-83. Safarov, a prominent Bolshevik, was an outstanding authority on the nationality problems in the early period of the Soviet regime and a representative of the Comintern for Central Asia. Later he was attacked for deviating from the party line, tried, and executed. His books are no longer circulated in Soviet Russia.

tion the "wakf"[5] lands must be left untouched, inasmuch as the masses . . . [have not yet fully broken away from religion]. The New Economic Policy applied at present in Soviet Russia must also be applied to Eastern countries; doing away with the open markets would only lead to general displeasure. A number of other typical national peculiarities must be taken into account. It is because of the feudal backwardness, the separation and isolation of the countries of the East, that a special caution must be practiced. . . .

The only thing that can speed up the revolutionary development of the East is the practical instruction of the masses. A mechanical application to the East of revolutionary measures applied in advanced countries . . . [would only be harmful].

The great historical significance of Marxism lies in the fact that it provided a theoretical background to the experience of the workers' movement, and supplied a scientific basis for the revolutionary policy of the working class. Similarly, the backward toilers of the East must be led, on the basis of their own experience, toward an understanding of the tasks of the international proletarian revolution. . . . These peoples cannot directly comprehend the point of view of the international proletariat, but they can understand why an alliance with the proletariat of advanced countries is necessary to their own national interests and to the struggle against imperialism and feudal practices. . . . There can be no special "Eastern communism."

. . . Thanks to the proletarian revolution, the way from feudalism to socialism can be shortened for the countries of the East. The victorious proletariat of the advanced countries can and must come to the rescue of the East with its own technique and socialist organization. . . .

The formation of communist parties in all countries of the East (in all eastern Soviet republics of the R.S.F.S.R., local communist organizations have membership in the All-Russian Communist Party; communist parties are active in Persia, Turkey, and the Dutch Indies; in British India a workers' movement is only now being formed) is of tremendous importance. . . .

Taking into consideration the historical development of the countries of the East, the Communists must make it their first and basic task to unite and to organize all proletarian and semiproletarian elements into an independent political party. This is an exceedingly difficult and responsible task. [He refers to the resolution of the Second Congress of the Communist International confirming this point.] . . .

Gradually and skillfully widening the limits of the national revolutionary movement against imperialism and the feudal lords, the communist parties of the East must mobilize the toiling masses for the struggle for their complete liberation. In their tactics, the Eastern Communists must follow the example of the British proletarian revolutionaries of the first half of the nineteenth century, the Chartists, who combined the struggle to democratize the political regime with the special class interests of the proletariat in that struggle.

There must not be a single false step taken in the struggle of the joint national and revolutionary front against imperialism; there must be no slackening in the defense of the proletarian and semiproletarian interests in this struggle.

Successful communist propaganda in the East must be based on a concrete analysis of the moving forces in the development of the East, and on the vital interests of the town and village poor—not on abstract principles. The struggle against national, religious, and tribal superstitions must be similarly carried out.

National revolution, soviet semiproletarian-peasant revolution, a federated union of peasants' soviet republics of the East and proletarian republics of the West—these are the historical stages of the [coming] revolutionary movement in the East. . . .

[5] Wakf, i.e., land belonging to the Muslim community in the form of pious endowment and under a particular property status, i.e., free from taxation, with the profits from the land passed on to the clergy (see *The Encyclopaedia of Islam,* IV, 1096–1103).

51

The Importance of Buddhist Mongolia
to the World Revolution[6]

It is usually believed that the key to the rich East and India is found in the Muslim countries, Persia and Afghanistan. But this is not quite so. It is true that the nearest, and perhaps the easiest, way from Europe to Asia lies through these countries, but this is not the only way. There is also a Mongolian-Buddhist route, which starts in the Kalmuk steppes, and leads through Altai, Mongolia, and Tibet, on to India.

The initial link in this road is found in the Kalmuks, through whom the idea of the soviet government can be transmitted to the millions of Mongol-Buddhist tribes of the East who are related by blood, religion, and language ties to the Kalmuks. . . .

Finally, Tibet, which is connected with Mongolia geographically and also by religious ties, could likewise fall into the sphere of Soviet influence.

Twenty years ago a Buddhist Kalmuk, Narbanov, and a Buriat, Tsibikov, succeeded in reaching Lhassa, where, on behalf of the Russian Geographical Society, they took some very interesting pictures, which appeared later in the European press. Now, when the East is awakening, it will be easier for the Buddhists to enter the forbidden land, but still quite impossible for the Europeans to do so.

On the other hand, Tibet borders on India; this, then, is the way by which India could establish contact with the center of world revolution—Russia.

The Kalmuk intelligentsia has a particularly important task to perform in this tremendous undertaking, a task which can be made easier by such well-known Eastern specialists as Agvan Dorji [Dorzhiev], the founder of the Buddhist temple in Petersburg [some years back] which greatly displeased England, and a supporter of a rapprochement between Mongolia and Russia. . . . He is at present in the Kalmuk steppes carrying on agitation in favor of soviets among the Kalmuks. He is ready to proceed east any time. Britain once offered large sums of gold for the head of this dangerous revolutionary. The temple mentioned above was actually built for political reasons, namely to distract the attention of Mongolia and Tibet from Britain's advances.

In past efforts at rapprochement between Russia and the Buddhist East, representatives of the Kalmuk people have taken an active part. In the past, missions headed by the Captain of the [Russian Imperial] General Staff, Naran Ulanov, and representatives of the Kalmuk intelligentsia were sent to Mongolia and Tibet for the purpose of establishing contact with these countries. Now, the Commissariat of Foreign Affairs can work out practical measures to be taken for the same purpose.

52

The Soviet Government's Declaration to the Mongolian People
and to the Government of Autonomous Mongolia,
August 1919[7]

The Red troops of the [Russian] Workers' and Peasants' Government have defeated the tsarist Admiral, Kolchak, have crossed over the Ural mountains, and have now entered the Siberian plains. These troops are bringing liberation to the

[6] Amur Sanai, "Kliuchi k Vostoku," *Zhizn Natsionalnostei,* No. 19 (27), May 26, 1919, p. 2.

[7] V. D. Vilensky (Sibiriakov), *Sovremennaia Mongoliia,* pp. 52–53.

Siberian workers and peasants, to the Kirghiz, to the Buriats, and to all toiling people. The Soviet government now appeals to the Mongolian people with the following words:

As soon as the Russian workers and peasants seized authority from the tsarist generals, gendarmes, and capitalists on October 26, 1917, they immediately appealed to the toilers of the world with an offer to establish a political order under which no strong state would dare to seize, or to keep by force, small and weak peoples.

Simultaneously, the [Russian] Workers' and Peasants' Government annulled all secret treaties with Japan and China by which the tsarist government, under the pretext of autonomy for Mongolia and allegedly in the interests of the Mongolian people, had actually seized Mongolia from China, established its own adviser in Urga, and plundered the wealth of the Mongolian people, passing it on to the Russian merchants and oppressors of the people.

However, the revolt of the Czechoslovaks in May of last year, and the invasion of Siberia by Japan, made it impossible for us to carry out our plans and to return to the Mongolian people what had been seized from them by the tsarist government. The Japanese, jointly with the Allies, did not permit the representatives of the Workers' and Peasants' Government to come to Urga with the news from Moscow.

Now, when this news is being brought to you by the victorious Red Army, which is driving away the bands of Kolchak, Semenov, and other robbers, the Soviet government again solemnly declares as follows:

The Russian people have renounced all treaties with the Japanese and Chinese governments which deal with Mongolia. Mongolia is henceforth a free country. Russian advisers, tsarist consuls, bankers, and the rich who have mastered the Mongolian people by means of force and gold, and robbed them of their last possessions, must be driven out of Mongolia.

All institutions of authority and law in Mongolia must henceforth belong to the Mongolian people. Not a single foreigner has the right to interfere with Mongolian affairs. In repudiation of the agreement of 1913, Mongolia now becomes an independent country and has the right to contact independently all other peoples without any guardianship whatsoever on the part of Peking or Petrograd.

The Soviet government solemnly proclaims this to the Mongolian people. The Soviet government asks the Mongolian people to enter into diplomatic relations with the Russian people immediately and to send representatives of the Mongolian people to meet the advancing Red Army.

53

The Soviet Government Offers Help to China Against the Russian Anti-Soviet Forces in Mongolia

[Chicherin to the Chinese Foreign Minister in Peking, November 11, 1920][8]

After Semenov's marauding gangs suffered final defeat, some of the beaten and scattered White Guardist detachments began to retreat into the territory of the Chinese republic. They moved mostly into Mongolia, where they seized Urga and joined forces with local elements hostile to the Chinese republic as well as to the Far Eastern Republic, and to Soviet Russia. The Chinese troops in the Urga region are unable, with only their own forces, to annihilate the White Guardist gangs which operate there; therefore they have turned to our military command and also to the command of the Far Eastern Republic asking us to help them combat these gangs of marauders.

[8] *Izvestiia,* No. 256, November 14, 1920, p. 1.

The Soviet government is of the opinion that common interests demand that this invasion of Mongolia be swiftly liquidated; and it is ready to give aid to the Chinese troops for the purpose of annihilating the White bands in Urga. An appropriate order has been given to our Siberian command. The Soviet government guarantees herewith that its troops dispatched to Mongolia are entering the territory in the capacity of China's friends; and that as soon as the White Guardist gangs in Mongolia are annihilated, the Soviet troops will regard their task as accomplished and will leave Chinese territory immediately.

54

The Formation of the Mongolian People's Party with Assistance from the Russian Communists

[A Soviet Account][9]

Toward the close of 1919, when the occupation regime of General Hsü Shu-tseng was suppressing every hint of freedom and independence for Mongolia, and when the Chinese merchants had their net of economic bondage spread wide, a small group of Mongolian *arats* [herdsmen]—that is, the simple folk—began to consider a way out of the existing situation. These men were national patriots who passionately wished to rescue their downtrodden, impoverished country from oppression by the Manchus.

The most active representatives of this group were: the somewhat effusive Lama Bodo, definitely influenced by European culture, who at one time served in the [Russian] consulate at Urga; Lama Chagdorzan [?], who had many connections with the Mongolian theocrats and with the court; Danzan, the petty official, clever in a way, very energetic, and a great hater of theocratic rule; young Choibalsan, who as a boy went to the school in the Lama monastery and to the school in the Troitskosavsk [now Kiakhta]; and finally, the most brilliant of them all, Suhe-Bator, the offspring of the lowest strata of the population, at one time a recruit in the army and later a printer.

If we take into consideration the state of oppression in which the Mongol arats lived, and also the fact that the Mongol intelligentsia was almost exclusively concentrated in the monasteries and imbued with Buddhist mysticism and scholasticism, then the peculiar bloc of offsprings of lamas, plebeians, and petty officials (since there was practically no proletariat element existing in Mongolia) was perhaps the maximum achievement which the Mongol people could produce at that time.

This group, then, was the basis around which developed, in the years to come, the Mongolian People's Revolutionary Party of many thousands of men. Not a small role had been played in the formation of this party by some Russian workers (Kucherenko, Gembarzhevsky, Agafonov, and others) who worked or served at Urga. The chief role among them was assumed by Suhe-Bator's comrade in the printing office, Kucherenko, who came from Irkutsk at the time the Russo-Mongolian printing office was set up in Urga.

While Kucherenko and others were not Communists, they nevertheless systematically preached Soviet principles to Suhe-Bator and his comrades. In the yard of the Russo-Mongolian printing office, and on the bank of the Tola River . . . the Mongolian oppositionists began to meet secretly, listening avidly to the lessons of "polit-grammota" [i.e., political A.B.C.'s] taught them by Kucherenko.

Inasmuch as the Mongolian people—small in number, disarmed, and widely scat-

[9] Genkin, *Severnaia Aziia,* No. 2, 1928, pp. 79–81.

tered with their herds throughout the land—were in no position to resist the Chinese occupants by themselves, the question of assistance from outside was naturally raised. Existing conditions prompted the revolutionary-minded arats to conclude that if, in the past, even tsarist Russia, avaricious and ready to seize new territories, had seen fit to obtain some kind of autonomy for Outer Mongolia from the imperialist Chinese groups (although admittedly for her own interests), then the Workers' and Peasants' Republic was bound to the rescue of that country.

It can easily be seen, therefore, why "Young Mongolia" at once began energetically to seek rapprochement with the leaders of the Far Eastern Siberian Soviet agencies.

The first meeting of the Mongolian delegation (Danzan, Bodo, Suhe-Bator, Choibalsan, Chagdorzan [?], and Doksan) with the representatives of the Soviet government took place in Verkhneudinsk.

In addition to the instructions of their own organization, these Mongolians brought with them a letter addressed to Lenin by Hutukhtu [Urga Living Buddha], lamas, and princes complaining against General Hsü and requesting intercession.

In early 1920 there also appeared in Verkhneudinsk a certain Rinchino, a Maximalist-Populist, and later a "nonparty Communist." In the past, when he had been a student, Rinchino had made contact with Maper, a former Populist and then a Social Democrat, with B. Z. Shumiatsky, a Bolshevik, and with others. He had also contacted representatives of the Siberian *oblastnichestvo* movement[10] and S.R.'s, but he later withdrew entirely from the latter group. He entertained grand ideas [for the Mongols], played a very important role among the Buriats (particularly in 1917–19), and was exceptionally prominent in the work among the Mongols from 1920 to 1925. . . .

In Verkhneudinsk Rinchino met Ia. D. Ianson, who had been in Irkutsk since 1918 in charge of [Soviet] foreign affairs, and urged him to take up the Mongolian problem. Ianson agreed to set up special machinery to promote revolutionary work among the Mongols.

The leadership in this work was taken by the Siberian Regional Bureau of the Russian Communist Party. Soon the latter organized in Irkutsk a Section for the Eastern Peoples, which then assumed the name of the "Asian Bureau," and still later became a Special Department of the Far Eastern Secretariat of the Comintern (Osobyi Otdel Dalnevostochnogo Sekretariata Kominterna). This Special Department included a number of specialists on the Far East, and with their participation, and especially with the assistance of B. Z. Shumiatsky, preliminary work among the Mongols was launched.

[When the Mongolian delegation came to Irkutsk] Rinchino introduced its members to Shumiatsky. . . . The delegation soon started north to attend to a number of new problems. It visited Omsk, where it called on the Siberian Revolutionary Committee and the Revolutionary War Council of the Soviet Fifth Army. After that some members of the Mongolian delegation returned to Urga, while others, together with Rinchino, proceeded to Moscow.

[10] The *Sibirskoe oblastnichestvo* (Siberian regionalism) movement originated in the nineteenth century. It was based on the idea that Siberia represented a region separate and different from Russia. It was a purely Russian and not a minorities movement, and it underwent several stages of development. At first, its promoters maintained that Siberia was a special and definite unit within the Russian Empire, and therefore had the right to develop along its own special path. Later the idea came to prevail that Siberia was a Russian colony, as the United States had once been a colony of the British Empire. Therefore, autonomous administration of Siberia was proposed. In its last stage, the movement came to advocate the separation of Siberia from Russia, again similar to the United States. (See S. G. Svatikov, *Rossiia i Sibir. K istorii sibirskogo oblastnichestva v XIX v.*)

Meanwhile in Moscow, in connection with events that had taken place in Turkestan, Bashkiria, and the Altai and Minusinsk regions, it had become apparent in party circles that corrective measures were needed in the work in the borderlands. After the end of the Baku Congress, the Politburo of the Central Committee of the Russian Communist Party held a special session, in which Lenin, Stalin, and Bukharin participated. Rinchino and Agvan Dorji (the latter known in the tsarist period as an ardent supporter of Russo-Tibetan rapprochement) were invited to this meeting, where the nationalities problem was discussed at full length and the Mongolian question taken up. After obtaining considerable results [in Moscow] the Mongolian delegation started home. . . .

55

The First Personal Contact of the Revolutionary Mongols with Leaders in Moscow, 1920[11]

In June[?] 1919, V. I. Lenin and I. V. Stalin instructed me to hand to the Mongolian people the declaration of the Soviet government.[12] This declaration stated that, as the result of the victorious proletarian revolution, Russia had annulled the treaties with Persia, China, Mongolia, and other oppressed countries by which the tsarist government had enmeshed the toiling masses of these countries. The Soviet government surrendered to the Mongolian people the lands seized from them by the tsarist government; it gave up rights to concessions . . . ; and it no longer wished to receive the usurous payments on former tsarist loans.

This declaration reached Mongolia in the period of the occupation of Mongolia by the Anfu men (i.e., the party of the Chinese military, closely connected with the Japanese), and it served as the first message of the victorious proletariat to the *arats*.

The second statement made by Lenin and Stalin on Mongolia which became known to us, dates back to the summer of 1920. I, with others, had just returned to Moscow from the Far Eastern front. At the same time, a group of Mongolian revolutionaries also arrived there. They asked us to arrange a meeting for them with V. I. Lenin and I. V. Stalin, since they were anxious to know of the position taken by the Soviet government on the question of the national independence of the peoples of the Far Eastern countries.

Vladimir Ilich received the Mongolians in his study at the Kremlin. To their question about his attitude toward their struggle for liberation from the Chinese military, who, on their part, were influenced by the Japanese forces of occupation . . . in the Soviet Far East, V. I. replied with a detailed analysis of the military situation in Mongolia. He pointed out Mongolia's role as a buffer country between the two struggling worlds, East and West, and noted that the only correct attitude for the toilers of their country to take would be to struggle for their own political and economic independence. This struggle, Ilich told the Mongolians, could not be waged successfully unless their forces were united and one political and national organization established.

One of the Mongolian delegates was asked by V. I. how he interpreted the nature of their struggle. When the delegate replied that he viewed it as a merciless destruction of gamins (i.e., Chinese), Lenin dwelt in detail on the question of revolutionary violence, and on the class nature of its goal.

"It is not the gamins," Lenin said, "that you must destroy; it is not against the gamins, the Chinese, that you must struggle, but against the corrupt Chinese mili-

[11] B. Shumiatsky, "Na zare osvobozhdeniia Mongolii," *Pravda*, No. 190, July 12, 1936, p. 5.
[12] See pp. 199–200.

tary and civil politicians, along with the merchants and money lenders who sell the interests of their own people and their own country. Chinese peasants and workers must be your allies. Even when they wear the soldier uniforms of the army of occupation, they are the representatives of the Chinese toiling masses, and, therefore, if you strike at them, you will simply let their mercenary commanders go unpunished. If you appeal directly to these enslaved masses dressed in soldier uniforms, they will understand you and will take it as an expression of your true friendship and brotherly feeling. If you conduct yourselves properly, you will have in them your allies in the struggle against a common enemy—Chinese and Japanese imperialists—and not your enemies.

I. V. Stalin, who was present at this meeting, developed Lenin's idea. He said that the Mongolian leaders should not aim at the destruction of the Chinese population in Mongolia, since that would be merely a sign of despair. He recommended that they direct the energy of the organized toiling masses of Mongolia against the individuals who led to perdition the great Chinese and Mongolian peoples by destroying these peoples' liberty and independence, against those who inspired constant sanguinary internecine wars among the Chinese generals in order to place the Chinese and Mongolian peoples under the yoke of Japanese capital. . . .

56
Russian Armed Forces in Mongolia

a

[The Provisional Revolutionary Government of Mongolia Appeals to the Government of the R.S.F.S.R., August 1921][13]

The People's Revolutionary Government of Mongolia addresses the government of the Russian Socialist Federated Soviet Republic with a request that it should not withdraw Soviet troops from the territory of Mongolia until the complete removal of the menace from the common enemy, who has now fortified himself in the Eastern steppes.

The People's Revolutionary Government finds it necessary to address this request to the government of the R.S.F.S.R. because the Mongolian government has not yet completed the organization of the machinery of the new political authority. The detention of the Soviet troops is dictated by circumstances, the purpose being to ensure the security of the territory of Mongolia and of the frontiers of the R.S.F.S.R.

The People's Provisional Revolutionary Government of Mongolia is confident that the government of the R.S.F.S.R. will realize the seriousness of the situation and the common interest [of the two peoples] in the defeat of the common enemy, and that it will, therefore, accede to the above request.

Members of the People's Revolutionary Government of Mongolia,
BODO
BOLIUK-SAI-KHAN

b

[The Soviet Government's Reply to the Appeal of the People's Revolutionary Government of Mongolia, August 10, 1921][14]

The Russian Soviet government, in alliance with the government of the Far Eastern Republic, has ordered its troops, together with those of the revolutionary

[13] *Izvestiia,* No. 175, August 10, 1921, p. 1.
[14] *Izvestiia,* No. 177, August 12, 1921, p. 2; also Degras, I, 252-53.

army of the provisional government of Mongolia, to deal a crushing blow to their common enemy, the tsarist general Ungern, who has subject the Mongolian people to unprecedented enslavement and oppression, who has violated the rights of autonomous Mongolia, and who has at the same time threatened the security of Soviet Russia and systematically attacked the fraternal Far Eastern Republic. Soviet troops have entered the territory of autonomous Mongolia for one purpose only: to defeat the common enemy, remove the constant danger which threatens Soviet territory, and ensure the self-determination and free development of autonomous Mongolia.

Welcoming the first steps of the People's Revolutionary Government of Mongolia on the road toward creating a new order in its country, now freed from the enemy through common effort, the Russian government notes with great satisfaction the appeal addressed to it by the People's Revolutionary Government of Mongolia, which expresses the desire that Soviet troops should not be removed from the territory of Mongolia until the complete destruction of the common enemy is finally accomplished. Considering this proposal to be a manifestation of the steadfast, close, and friendly bonds which unite the liberated people of Mongolia with the workers and peasants of Russia, who have thrown off the yoke of the exploiters, the Russian government declares that it recognizes fully the seriousness of the situation and the mutual interest of Russia and Mongolia in the destruction of their common enemy. Having firmly decided to withdraw its troops from the territory of autonomous Mongolia—which is bound to Soviet Russia only by the ties of mutual friendship and common interests—just as soon as the danger to the free development of Mongolia is removed and the security of the Russian [Workers' and Peasants'] Republic and the Far Eastern Republic assured, the Russian government, in complete harmony with the People's Revolutionary Government of Mongolia, states that this moment has not yet come. The Russian government announces its decision to comply with the request addressed to it by the People's Revolutionary Government of Mongolia.

The Russian government is convinced that, in the near future, through the united efforts of the two peoples who are struggling against the violence of the tsarist generals and against foreign oppression and exploitation, the free development of the Mongolian people will be secured on the basis of autonomy; and that, as a result of the organization of the machinery of the people's revolutionary authority in Mongolia, this authority will be definitely established and firmly secured there.

CHICHERIN,
People's Commissar of Foreign Affairs

57

The Soviet Government Stresses the Need for Friendly Sino-Mongolian Relations

[Telegram from Chicherin, People's Commissar of Foreign Affairs of the R.S.F.S.R., to Bodo, Chairman of the Council of Ministers and Foreign Minister of the People's Revolutionary Government of Mongolia, September 14, 1921][15]

The toiling masses of Russia, and the Workers' and Peasants' Government which expresses their will, greeted with joy the establishment of the People's Revolutionary Government of Mongolia, and the liberation of the friendly Mongolian people from a foreign yoke and from the bloody rule of the former tsarist general Ungern. The

[15] *Izvestiia*, No. 207, September 17, 1921, p. 3.

glorious Red Army of the Russian Soviet Republic, together with the troops of the friendly and allied Far Eastern Republic, and with the people's revolutionary army of Mongolia, fought against the enslavers of the Mongolian people and assisted in the liberation of the Mongolian people from oppression by the enemies of the workers and peasants of Russia.

The Russian government expresses to the People's Revolutionary Government of Mongolia its gratitude for that government's friendly feelings toward the toiling masses of Russia and toward the Soviet government, and for the confidence expressed in them in Citizen Bodo's Note of September 10.[16] The Russian government shares the conviction of the People's Revolutionary Government of Mongolia concerning the need to establish peaceful and businesslike relations between Mongolia and China. The Russian government hopes that the steps it is taking in this direction, together with the application of the right of the Mongolian people to self-determination, will lead to favorable results in the near future.

More than once the Russian government has approached the government of China, both directly and through the representatives of the Far Eastern Republic who were in communication with China, with offers to begin negotiations on this question. In the near future, the Russian government expects to enter into permanent relations with the Chinese government by means of a trade delegation which is being sent to Peking.

The Russian government notes with joy the readiness of the People's Revolutionary Government of Mongolia to enter into negotiations with China on this question, as expressed in Citizen Bodo's Note of September 10. It hopes that the Chinese government, for its part, will receive this offer favorably and will interpret it in the spirit of good offices, in order to remove the possibility of a conflict between the peoples and the governments of Mongolia and of China.

58

Lenin Interviews the Mongolian Delegates in Moscow, 1921

[Described in the Political Report of the Central Committee of the Mongolian People's Revolutionary Party to the Ninth Congress of That Party, 1934][17]

First question by the Mongolian delegation:
"What is your attitude, Comrade Lenin, to the organization in our country of the People's Revolutionary Party, and what do you consider is the most important for us?"

Comrade Lenin explained to our delegation the international position of our country, and pointed out that, in case of war, owing to the geographical position of the Mongolian People's Republic, the imperialist powers would try to seize our country in order to make it a starting point for military action against the enemy country. "Therefore," said Comrade Lenin, "the only correct path for every toiler in your country to take is that of a struggle for political and economic independence in alliance with the workers and peasants of the R.S.F.S.R. This struggle cannot be waged in isolation; therefore, the establishment of the party of the Mongolian arats is a condition for the success of their struggle."

16 Text of this note appears in *Izvestiia*, No. 205, September 15, 1921, p. 1.
17 *IX sezd Mongolskoi Narodno-Revoliutsionnoi Partii*, Ulan Bator, 1934, pp. 32–33, as given in B. Perlin, *Mongolskaia Narodnaia Respublika*, pp. 26–27.

Second question by the Mongolian delegation:
"Will the national-liberation struggle be successful?"
Comrade Lenin's reply:
"I myself have participated in the revolutionary movement for thirty years, and from my personal experience I know how difficult it is for any people to free themselves from foreign and domestic oppressors. In spite of the fact that Mongolia is a country of herdsmen and that its basic population is nomadic, the Mongolians have been successful in their revolution, and, what is most important, they have consolidated their success by creating their own national-revolutionary party. The task of this party is to become a party of the masses and to make it impossible for foreigners to rule their country."

Lenin's expression "of the masses" did not mean a party of a large number of members. Comrade Lenin meant that our party was to be closely connected with the arat masses and that it was to assume leadership of them in the struggle against the oppressors and in the efforts to consolidate national independence. That is how the expression "of the masses" should be understood.

Third question by the Mongolian delegation:
"Should not the People's Revolutionary Party of Mongolia be transformed into a communist party?"
Comrade Lenin replied:
"I do not recommend it, because one party should not be transformed into another."

In explaining the nature of a communist party as a party of the proletariat, Comrade Lenin said:

"The Mongolian revolutionaries have much work ahead of them in political, economic, and cultural development before the pastoral population can be called proletarian masses. Once this is achieved, these masses will help in the 'transformation' of the People's Revolutionary Party into a communist one. A mere change of signboards is harmful and dangerous."

Comrade Lenin then outlined in a broad sense the possibility and the necessity for a noncapitalist development of the Mongolian People's Republic. He pointed out that the main conditions which would ensure the noncapitalist development of Mongolia would be the consolidation of the work of the People's Revolutionary Party and of the government. If this were achieved, and the influence of the party and the government were consolidated, if co-operative organizations were developed and new forms of economy and national culture were grafted, then the arats would rally around the party and the government to help them in their efforts to develop the country economically and culturally. "Out of such separate efforts in the new economy of the country, adopted under the influence of the party and the new government, there will finally emerge a new and noncapitalist economic system of the Mongolian arats."

59

The Soviet Offer to the Peking Government to Open Negotiations

[Memorandum of the Extraordinary Plenipotentiary of the R.S.F.S.R. in China, Ioffe, to the Chinese government, September 2, 1922][18]

The extraordinary plenipotentiary of the Russian Socialist Federated Soviet Republic, following personal negotiations with the foreign minister on August 23,

[18] *Pravda*, No. 208, September 16, 1922, p. 1; also Degras, I, 329–30.

30, and 31, 1922, has the honor to address the government of the Chinese republic as follows:

The Russian Workers' and Peasants' Government tried from the first moment of its existence to prove to the Chinese people and to the Chinese government its readiness not only to abandon the aggressive imperialist policy of the tsarist government in regard to China, but also to establish relations on an absolutely new basis, and, primarily, on the foundation of the political and economic equality of both countries.

In the Declaration of the Council of People's Commissars to the Chinese people of July 25, 1919, the fundamental principles on which the government of the R.S.F.S.R. was interpreting its new relations with China were outlined.

In the Note of the Assistant People's Commissar of Foreign Affairs, L. M. Karakhan, of September 27, 1920, these principles were expanded in the form of concrete offers which the government of the R.S.F.S.R. proposed to use as the basis of the Russo-Chinese agreement of friendship.

In spite of the fact that such an agreement has not yet been reached, the workers and peasants of Russia have a feeling of exceptional friendliness toward the Chinese people, who are struggling for their liberation. In view of this, the extraordinary plenipotentiary offers once more to open negotiations with the Chinese government on all problems which pertain to the interests of both countries, in order to establish between the two countries neighborly relations corresponding to the feelings which both peoples have for each other.

True to its policy to the end, the Workers' and Peasants' Government is now prepared, as before, to conduct negotiations with China in complete accord with the principles proclaimed by it in the two declarations mentioned above.

If the government of the Chinese republic agrees with the proposal of the extraordinary plenipotentiary of the R.S.F.S.R. outlined above, the latter will expect to receive the views of the foreign minister as to the time and the place that the Chinese government desires that the Sino-Russian conference be held.[19]

60

Soviet Peace Offer to Japan

[Chicherin to the Japanese Foreign Minister, February 24, 1920][20]

Immediately upon its formation, the Soviet Russian government proclaimed the principle of the right of all peoples to self-determination . . . In December 1917, the People's Commissariat of Foreign Affairs entered into semiofficial conversations with M. Ueda on the subject of the revision of all contractual relations between Russia and Japan, and proposed a new commercial and economic agreement called for by the existing [political] situation in the Far East and the Pacific coast. The proposals of the Soviet Russian government were received by the Japanese ambassador for communication to his government. However, no reply was received from the latter.

In the spring of 1918 similar proposals were again made by the People's Commissariat of Foreign Affairs, through the offices of the Japanese consul, Marumo, in Vologda. Again our proposals were received for transmission to Tokyo, but no result ensued.

[19] The Chinese government sent its consent on September 7. Text is given in *Pravda*, No. 208, September 16, 1922, p. 1.

[20] G. Reikhberg, *Iaponskaia interventsiia na Dalnem Vostoke, 1918–1922 gg.*, also Degras, I, 182–83.

In his report to the Fifth Congress of the Soviets, the People's Commissar of Foreign Affairs once again expressed the Soviet government's desire to find a peaceful solution to economic questions in the Far East and on the Pacific coast. The offer of the Soviet government was transmitted by the Japanese consul to his government, but no reply was received.

Desiring to begin peace negotiations with the Japanese government at the present time, when all attempts to crush the power of the workers and peasants of Russia by force of arms have absolutely failed, when the Entente governments are withdrawing their expeditionary forces from Russia, and when various governments have already entered into conversations with the Soviet Russian government, we address the Japanese government once more with a proposal to engage in peace negotiations.

The peoples of Russia cherish no aggressive designs against Japan. The Soviet government has no intention of interfering in the internal affairs of the Japanese people. It fully recognizes the special economic and commercial interests of Japan in the Far East, interests surpassing in several respects those of other countries. It is equally interested in concluding an agreement on this subject which will be useful and beneficial to both parties.

The Soviet Russian government wishes to establish a *modus vivendi* guaranteeing peace between Russia and Japan, and guaranteeing the reciprocal advantages to both countries which would result from the relations to be established between them. Taking into consideration the numerous voices which reach our ears from Japan demanding satisfaction of the needs of the Japanese people by the conclusion of an agreement with the Soviet government, the Russian government expresses the certainty that these needs will in effect be satisfied by the agreement which it desires to conclude with Japan.

The Russian government does not doubt that in view of the deplorable state of affairs which has resulted from the Japanese expedition in Siberia, and in view of the growing opposition among powerful political parties in Japan to this expedition, it will soon be withdrawn.

The People's Commissariat therefore proposes to the Japanese government to engage in peace negotiations, in order to ensure for the two peoples peaceful coexistence, friendly neighborly relations, and mutual satisfaction of reciprocal interests.

61

Decision to Establish the Far Eastern Republic

[A Resolution of the Congress of the Toilers of the Baikal Region, March 28, 1920, Verkhneudinsk][21]

Taking into consideration the complexity of international affairs in the Far East, as well as local tasks, the Congress of the Toilers of the Baikal Region, fully cognizant of its responsibility and of the seriousness of the moment for all of Russia and for the world revolutionary movement, resolves:

1. To consider it expedient and necessary to form an independent autonomous government within the limits of the Baikal region and of the Far East, to include the regions of Baikal, Amur, and Sakhalin, and the neutral zone of the Chinese Eastern Railway.

2. To establish for these regions a democratic government that is representative of all the elements of the population, and to draw into this government, on a coali-

[21] *Izvestiia Irkutskogo Revkoma*, No. 62, 1920, as given in G. Reikhberg, *Iaponskaia interventsiia na Dalnem Vostoke*, pp. 92–93.

tion basis, all the socialist parties, such as the Socialist Revolutionaries, Social Democrats, and Communist-Bolsheviks, and also public organizations, to be represented by the plenipotentiary member of the regional zemstvo.[22]

62
Moscow's Recognition of the Far Eastern Republic

[Chicherin to Krasnoshchekov, Foreign Minister of the Far Eastern
Republic, May 14, 1920][23]

In the name of the government of the R.S.F.S.R., I have the honor to inform you that upon consideration of the declaration of the provisional government of the Far Eastern Republic concerning the formation of an independent democratic republic on the bases indicated in that declaration, the R.S.F.S.R. hereby recognizes the establishment of the above-named democratic republic and the provisional government that stands at its head.

The Soviet government is ready immediately to enter upon official diplomatic relations with the government of the new republic for the purpose of concluding commercial and political agreements.

In notifying you of the above, I consider it my duty to transmit to you, in the name of the R.S.F.S.R., my wish to see the Far Eastern Republic flourish and maintain peaceful relations with its neighboring countries.

63
Soviet Protest Against Intervention in Siberia

[Note Addressed to the Governments of Great Britain, France, and Italy,
June 1, 1921][24]

The struggle of the toiling masses of Russia for peace and for the right to dispose of their own fate independently has entered a phase of new trials. Having gloriously repulsed, by a gigantic effort and miraculous heroism, the combined attacks of counterrevolution from within and the majority of foreign powers from without, the toiling masses have won the right to govern themselves by means of their own soviets of workers and peasants. They had hoped to ensure for themselves an opportunity to devote their forces freely to the internal reconstruction of Russia in co-operation with other countries. Such co-operation would have been possible if each party concerned had attended to its own immediate needs and economic tasks [rather than assailing Soviet Russia's political integrity].

Unfortunately the Russian toilers' hopes have been blasted by a new attempt at external interference, and by a new co-ordinated attack by Russian counterrevolutionaries and foreign governments. Protected by Japanese bayonets, the White Guards of Vladivostok, who constitute but an insignificant group, suddenly seized authority in that city. Similar *coups d'état* have been effected in Nikolsk-Ussuriiskii and also in other localities occupied by the Japanese. Thus, the most open counterrevolutionary regime has been installed by the Japanese armed forces in the occupied territory.

[22] The zemstvos were the provincial administrative assemblies of prerevolutionary Russia.

[23] Kliuchnikov and Sabanin, III, 24.

[24] *Izvestiia*, No. 120, June 3, 1921, p. 1; also Degras, I, 246–48.

The masses of Russian peasants and workers in the Far East have done every-thing in their power to arrange an acceptable peace with Japan. They organized a separate democratic republic in order to make this peace possible, and this independ-ent Far Eastern Republic signed an agreement with Japan with such an end in view. Japan [declared] that once the peace was signed, she was ready to withdraw her troops from this territory and to return freedom to the Russian masses in the Far East. In the name of these masses the government of their republic constantly strove to consummate a complete agreement with Japan, in order to live with her in peace and in friendly and neighborly relations. But the Japanese government replied to these peaceful efforts with a new and cruel attack upon the internal freedom of these masses and upon their external independence.

The bitterest foes of the Russian masses, the extreme reactionaries whose obvious objective is to conquer Siberia with the aid of Japanese bayonets and then to become the subservient agents of the Japanese conquerors, have seized authority by violence in the localities where the Japanese armed forces exercise their control. . . . [More-over,] the Japanese government is distributing fishing rights in the waters of Kam-chatka among its own capitalists, while actually these rights belonged hitherto to the Russian co-operatives and to other Russian citizens. Japan has introduced her own control there and has seized the revenues accruing from the Kamchatka fisheries. This constitutes an act of arbitrary seizure and plunder of Russia's wealth, and is considered by the Russian government to be a violation of the elementary rights of the Russian masses.

At the same time, with the aid of Japanese armed forces, the remnants of the counterrevolutionary bands of Semenov and Kappel retain their positions on the boundaries of China and continue to occupy the Chinese Eastern Railway. Only because of the assistance of Japanese auxiliary troops are Ungern's bands able to terrorize Mongolia and to prepare attacks against the Russian republic.

The agents of Japanese imperialism penetrate even into Central Asia, attempting to stir up an insurrection there, while emissaries from Turkestan's counterrevolution-ary elements flock to Japan in order to work out their plans in common.

The Russian republic has offered peace to the Japanese government on a number of occasions; and yet, in spite of all the Russian efforts to make peace, the Japanese government is at the present time the instigator of a new campaign of intervention directed against the rule of the Russian workers and peasants.

The Soviet government, expressing the will of the Russian masses, warns the Japanese government that the Russian masses have taken their fate into their own hands, and, having repelled all past attacks by their enemies, will be able to conduct this new struggle victoriously, and will make those who have attacked them feel their strength more than sufficiently.

However, the responsibility for these hostile acts cannot be laid at the door of the Japanese government alone. There is proof that the French government, in its irreconcilable enmity toward the rule of workers and peasants in Russia, is another active instigator of this new campaign of intervention—that it has taken part in Japan's plan for conquest in Siberia. Soviet Russia cannot but consider all the powers of the Entente to be morally responsible for this new link in the chain of intervention, which is the result of the collective workmanship of the Entente powers. It considers this to be a manifestation of hostile activity on the part of the British government entirely out of keeping with the Anglo-Russian agreement.

The Russian government protests most energetically against these acts, whether aimed directly against Russia herself or indirectly through the friendly Far Eastern Republic; and it retains the right to draw the inevitable conclusions therefrom.

> CHICHERIN,
> People's Commissar of Foreign Affairs

64

Japan's "Seventeen Demands" Presented to the Far Eastern Republic in October 1921 at the Dairen Conference[25]

Article 1. The government of the Far Eastern Republic shall make Vladivostok a commercial port exclusively, placing it under foreign control; and it shall not adopt any measures which would interfere with trade relations.

Article 2. The governments of the contracting parties shall bind themselves to re-examine, after the signing of the treaty, the Japanese-Russian fishery convention, and to increase the rights of the Japanese fishing merchants and the Japanese right of cabotage along the Russian coast.

Article 3. The governments of the contracting parties shall bind themselves to conclude an agreement concerning postal and telegraph communication, immediately upon the signing of the present treaty.

Article 4. The governments of the contracting parties shall recognize the right of free trade, communication, and navigation for citizens and ships of each respective contracting party, with privileges equivalent to those enjoyed by the third party [i.e., the R.S.F.S.R.].

Article 5. The governments of the contracting parties shall bind themselves to conclude an agreement concerning customs and tariff rules, on the principles outlined in Article 4.

Article 6. The citizens of each contracting party sojourning on the territory of the other contracting party shall be ensured protection, personal safety, and inviolability of property, and shall enjoy favors equivalent to those of the citizens of the third party.

Article 7. Every citizen of one contracting party sojourning on territory of the other contracting party shall be permitted to engage in trade, industry, the production of manufactured goods, trades, and professional occupations, as well as other activities. Such a citizen shall be granted in his commercial and industrial activities favors equivalent to those of the citizens of the third party. As far as the craft industries, professional occupations, and trades are concerned, citizens of the contracting parties shall be ensured the same rights as citizens of the third party.

Article 8. The citizens of each contracting party shall have the right to enter the territory of the other, to travel and to sojourn there in accordance with the laws of each contracting state. When such a citizen shall enter the country of the other party he shall produce his national passport.

Article 9. Each contracting party shall bind itself not to resort to hostile action against the other, and likewise not to conduct any propaganda which might prove dangerous to the other party. Each likewise shall guarantee to adopt measures forbidding the entrance and the sojourn on its territory, and forbidding the activities, of any organization which might be detrimental to the interests of the other party. The order to surrender such persons to the other party shall be defined in a separate agreement.

Article 10. The government of the Far Eastern Republic shall guarantee to the Japanese government for all time concerned not to introduce on its territory a communist regime, and to retain the principle of private property not only in regard to Japanese subjects, but also in regard to its own citizens.

---

[25] M. L. Veltman (M. Pavlovich), *Iaponskii imperializm na Dalnem Vostoke*, pp. 71–73. Also *Novyi Vostok*, No. 2, 1922, pp. 32–34.

Article 11. While acknowledging the principle of the open door policy, the government of the Far Eastern Republic shall cancel all the existing limitations on Japanese subjects in its territory. It shall likewise guarantee not to introduce such limitations in the future in regard to mining industries, agriculture, the lumber industry, and all extractive industry in general, and shall also grant to Japanese subjects complete freedom of trade in general, and craft and other trades in particular, on an equal basis with the citizens of its own state. The government of the Far Eastern Republic shall likewise guarantee Japanese subjects the right to own land and to conduct coast trade freely under the Japanese flag.

The government of the Far Eastern Republic shall guarantee Japanese subjects free navigation under the Japanese flag along the Amur River, and it shall agree to inform the Chinese government of its desire to grant to Japanese subjects the right of navigation under the Japanese flag along the Sungari River. This article shall apply to Japanese subjects alone, and the rights provided by this article shall not be applied to other foreigners.

Article 12. Both contracting parties shall exchange representatives empowered with the rights of ambassadors, and shall also establish the points for the sojourn of commercial consuls.

Article 13. The governments of the contracting parties shall acknowledge all agreements and conventions which were concluded between the Japanese government and the Russian government, and they likewise shall accept all rights acquired by the citizens of both states at the time of the signing of this treaty.

Article 14. The government of the Far Eastern Republic shall pledge itself to remove, and, if necessary, to blow up, its fortresses and fortifications along the entire coastal line in the vicinity of Vladivostok, and on the boundaries of Korea, and, in the future, never to erect such fortification or undertake any military action in the regions adjoining Korea and Manchuria.

The government of the Far Eastern Republic shall acknowledge the official sojourn and travel of special Japanese military missions and of separate Japanese military representatives throughout the entire territory of the Republic.

The government of the Far Eastern Republic shall pledge itself never to keep any naval forces in the waters of the Pacific, and to destroy those vessels which now exist . . .

Article 15. In the settlement of the Nikolaevsk incident, the government of the Far Eastern Republic shall hand over to the Japanese government the northern sector of the island of Sakhalin as a lease for 80 years, as compensation for the damages inflicted upon Japanese subjects at the time of the Nikolaevsk incident.

Article 16. The present agreement shall come into force at the moment of its ratification by the governments of the contracting parties, and shall remain in force until the conclusion of a permanent treaty in the future.

Article 17. The present agreement shall be prepared in the Russian and Japanese languages, and both texts shall be considered authentic.

Secret Clauses

Article 1. In case of an armed conflict between Japan and the third power, the government of the Far Eastern Republic shall maintain strict neutrality.

Article 2. The Japanese government shall evacuate its troops from the Maritime Region at its own discretion, and at a time that it finds suitable and convenient to itself.

Article 3. The evacuation from the Sakhalin region shall take place after the settlement of the question of the lease of the northern sector of the island of Sakhalin, on the conditions outlined in Article 15.

65

Reasons for the Failure of the Dairen Conference

[Note Addressed by Foreign Minister of the Far Eastern Republic, Ia. D. Ianson,
to the Japanese Foreign Minister, April 22, 1922][26]

On April 16, the Japanese delegation informed the delegation of the Far Eastern
Republic in Dairen that, in accordance with instructions received from the Imperial
Japanese Government, it was cutting short the negotiations with the Far Eastern
Republic. Wishing to throw light on the actual facts concerning the breakdown of
the negotiations, the government of the Far Eastern Republic declares that the break-
down was entirely the fault of the Japanese government.

Early in April, complete accord had been reached with regard to a trade agreement, and also on many other points dealing with the relations between the two
countries. Even the wording of the text of the trade agreement, and of all *supplementary clauses* on other points of an economic and political nature, had been outlined. It seemed, therefore, that after agreement had been reached with regard to the
formation of all the official documents, trade co-operation could be established between
the two parties.

The only question regarding which agreement had not been reached was the question of the evacuation of the Japanese troops from the Maritime region. During the
negotiations in Dairen, this question was often discussed. The Japanese delegation
assured us more than once that the matter would be finally settled in a satisfactory
manner, and that the evacuation would be carried out as soon as a convenient moment
might arise when it would be possible to conclude a general agreement between Japan
and the Far Eastern Republic. . . . However, it later became evident that the Japanese government had changed its mind about the necessity of evacuating the Japanese
troops from the Maritime Region. In spite of the fact that the formulation of the
general agreement had already been settled upon by both parties, the Japanese government refused to guarantee, in writing, an evacuation deadline. Instead, the Japanese
delegation proposed that evacuation negotiations be transferred to a special military
commission which would establish in the future, and after the signing of a trade
agreement, the date for the evacuation.

This move would undoubtedly postpone the evacuation indefinitely, since it is
impossible to foresee what date the military commission might propose. Furthermore, there is no assurance that other factors, over which the government of the
Far Eastern Republic would have no control, would not interfere with the commission's work, and further postpone the evacuation for several months, perhaps even
for a year or more.

The above proposal does not coincide with the Imperial Japanese Government's
original declaration that the evacuation agreement should be signed simultaneously
with the trade agreement. The delegation of the Far Eastern Republic cannot agree
to this prolonged stay of Japanese troops in the Maritime Region, which makes it
practically impossible to re-establish economic and trade relations between the Far
Eastern Republic and Japan, and which nullifies the value of the trade agreement.

It is necessary, therefore, to point out that the break in the negotiations between
the Far Eastern Republic and Japan is the result of the intentional refusal of the
Japanese government to settle the question of the evacuation of Japanese troops from
the Maritime Region.

According to the information available, the Japanese army is taking steps to
extend its zone of occupation in the Maritime Region, and Japanese detachments are

[26] M. L. Veltman (M. Pavlovich), *Iaponskii imperializm na Dalnem Vostoke*, pp. 77–78.

advancing beyond the neutral zone. . . . This extension of Japanese-occupied territory, and the Japanese government's refusal to settle the evacuation question during
the negotiations in Dairen, force us to suppose that the Japanese government has
designs on the Maritime Region, despite its assurances that the Japanese army has
"the most peaceful and friendly intentions" toward the Far Eastern Republic.

The government of the Far Eastern Republic considers it its duty to state that
such designs of the Imperial Japanese Government cannot be considered as legal and
just, and that nothing could justify the Japanese in extending their zone of occupation in the territory of the Far Eastern Republic.

The government of the Far Eastern Republic believes that peace in the Russian
Far East and economic co-operation between Japan on one side, and the Russian Far
East and Siberia on the other side, require the complete evacuation of Russian territory by Japanese troops. The government of the Far Eastern Republic will do everything it can to achieve this end, but it declares that further negotiations between the
governments of both countries can bring satisfactory results only if the Japanese
government will co-operate.

66

Ioffe's Declaration in the Name of Russia at the Changchun Conference, September 10, 1922[27]

After having listened to the declaration of the Imperial Japanese Government
concerning the agenda for the Russo-Japanese negotiations, which was read at the
last session by the chairman of the Japanese delegation, the delegations of the
R.S.F.S.R. and the Far Eastern Republic found it necessary to approach their respective governments for their opinions of the agenda, because it differed considerably from the instructions received by the delegations from their respective governments.

The reply of our governments is now at hand, and, therefore, the delegations of
the R.S.F.S.R. and of the Far Eastern Republic wish to declare as follows:

The desire of the Imperial Japanese Government to limit the questions to be
considered by the Russo-Japanese conference to the problems of the Far East was
absolutely unexpected by the governments of the R.S.F.S.R. and the Far Eastern
Republic, as was Japan's wish to conclude a treaty with only the Far Eastern Republic.

The governments of the R.S.F.S.R. and of the Far Eastern Republic have interpreted and are now interpreting the Russo-Japanese negotiations as a means to the
establishment of normal, neighborly relations between the Russian and Japanese
peoples and their governments, as a result of a voluntary examination and a mutually
satisfactory solution to all questions which have so far interfered with the establishment of such relations.

Furthermore, to limit the work of the conference to the settlement of Far Eastern
problems alone would mean that only the problems which concern Japan would be
solved. The delegations of the R.S.F.S.R. and the Far Eastern Republic, consequently, do not see any practical chance that such a plan could be followed. [Examples
given] . . .

In spite of the inimical policy pursued by the Imperial Japanese Government
toward the Russian people during the last few years, the latter do not harbor any
ill-feeling toward the Japanese people. In full accord with the will of their people,
the governments of the R.S.F.S.R. and of the Far Eastern Republic are prepared to

[27] *Pravda,* No. 205, September 13, 1922, p. 2.

forget the past and to come to a friendly agreement with Japan, especially since neither government shares the policy of the tsarist government, but, on the contrary, both understand and recognize full well the vital interests of the Japanese people, and are, therefore, prepared to meet halfway, or as far as possible, that people's just and essential requirements.

But the governments of the R.S.F.S.R. and of the Far Eastern Republic fail to understand the purpose of negotiations which would serve the interests of one party only, and they cannot agree to such negotiations. The governments of the R.S.F.S.R. and of the Far Eastern Republic are likewise unable to agree that the evacuation of the Siberian territories by the Japanese troops and the return of the property seized by the Japanese would constitute sufficient compensation for Russia and the Far Eastern Republic. The above-mentioned property is the property of the Russian people, and, as such, it should be returned to its legal owner, irrespective of the negotiations. As far as the evacuation of Siberia by Japanese troops is concerned, it was a condition preliminary to the present negotiations, and, therefore, not connected with the negotiations which are about to begin.

As far as these problems are concerned, the Russian people rely on their own strength; nevertheless, they cannot help mentioning the fact that the Japanese occupation of Russian territories finds no sympathetic response on the part of America or Europe, and is not even approved by the Japanese people themselves. . . .

While continuing to emphasize, in accord with their earlier declarations, the desirability of first drafting and signing an agreement dealing with questions of a general nature and of principle, and then passing to the discussion of questions which are of more concrete and definite character, the governments of the R.S.F.S.R. and of the Far Eastern Republic nevertheless believe that the above-mentioned general agreement should not be simply a reproduction of the so-called Dairen project, but should be broader in scope, because the negotiations in Dairen were conducted exclusively between the Far Eastern Republic on one side and Japan on the other, whereas negotiations in Changchun are being conducted between the R.S.F.S.R. and the Far Eastern Republic on one side and Japan on the other. Therefore, the treaty which is to be drafted on the basis of these latter negotiations must be a treaty between Russia and the Far Eastern Republic on one side and Japan on the other.

At the same time, the governments of the R.S.F.S.R. and the Far Eastern Republic believe, as they did before, that the negotiations which were conducted in Dairen for eight months should considerably speed up the present negotiations, since there is no need to repeat the debates on questions of principle which took place in Dairen.

In conclusion, the delegations of the R.S.F.S.R. and of the Far Eastern Republic reiterate once more their readiness to come to a quick agreement with the Japanese delegation on the basis of the statements outlined above.

D. COMMUNIST PARTIES AND REVOLUTIONARY POTENTIAL IN THE FAR EAST

67

Early Soviet Approach to Revolutionary China

[Chicherin's Letter to Sun Yat-sen, August 1, 1918][1]

The Council of People's Commissars has charged me with the honorable task of thanking you, esteemed teacher, for the greetings sent by you to the [Russian] Workers' and Peasants' Government from the people of South China. I am charged likewise to greet you as the leader of the Chinese revolution and as the man who, since 1911, has continued under exceptionally difficult conditions to lead Chinese democracy against its enslavers, the North China and foreign imperialist governments.

When you greeted the Workers' and Peasants' Government of Russia, esteemed teacher, you stated that the Russian and Chinese revolutions have common aims, the liberation of the peoples and the establishment of enduring peace based on the common interests of the two great proletariats, the Russian and the Chinese.

This great goal . . . of universal peace based on fraternity among the toiling classes of all peoples on this globe, has inspired all the activities of Russia's Workers' and Peasants' Government ever since authority passed from the bourgeoisie to the toiling people. As you know, esteemed teacher, our program is outlined in the Declaration to the Peoples of the East by the Fifth All-Russian Congress of Soviets.

Like you, we have encountered tremendous difficulties. Surrounded with an iron ring of bayonets by the imperialist governments, the bourgeoisie's hirelings, the Czechoslovak hordes, and the Russian bourgeoisie who are trying to restore monarchy in Russia, we have been cut off from our friends, the proletariat of South China. Contact with you has been severed for the last two months. Meantime false rumors have been circulated about us by our common enemies through the press, which has sold itself to the bankers and capitalists, rumors designed to conceal the truth from the people of South China, namely that the Workers' and Peasants' Government exists, is holding firm, and, although weary of the struggle, is carrying as before the banner of proletarian victory over the world bourgeoisie, the European robbers and invaders.

Our situation is difficult, and our struggle is uneven. In this hour of tribulation, when imperialist governments are stretching their greedy hands from the east, west, north, and south to strangle the Russian revolution and to take away from the Russian peasants and workers what they have won for themselves by a revolution such as the world has never seen before, and when the Peking government, which is the creature of foreign bankers, is ready to join these robbers, the Russian toiling classes appeal to you, our Chinese brothers, and call you to join our struggle. For our victory is your victory, and our doom is your doom. Let us, therefore, close our ranks in the great struggle for the common interests of the world proletariat.

Long live the toiling peasants of China! Long live the Chinese workers! Long live the alliance of the Russian and Chinese proletariat!

[1] *Izvestiia*, No. 53, March 9, 1919, p. 1. Apparently this letter never reached Sun Yat-sen. See our p. 219.

68

Voitinsky Relates His Early Meeting with Sun Yat-sen[2]

It was in the autumn of 1920 in Shanghai when a Chinese, Comrade Ch., offered to introduce me to Sun Yat-sen, who lived at that time in the French concession in a house specially built for him by Chinese émigrés and members of the Kuomintang.

. . .

Sun Yat-sen received us in his library, a huge room filled with bookcases. He gave an impression of a man of 45–47 (actually he was over 54). He was well built and erect, had soft manners and very distinct gesticulations. The modesty and the cleanliness of his attire at once attracted our attention. . . .

Ignoring the general Chinese rules of etiquette, Sun Yat-sen invited us immediately to the table and began to question us about Russia and our revolution. A little later we switched to a discussion of the Chinese revolution of 1911. . . . However, toward the end of our visit, Sun Yat-sen again returned to the problems of Soviet Russia. It was evident that he was greatly interested in the question of how the struggle in South China, which has just been liberated from counterrevolutionary . . . troops in Canton, could be joined with the struggle of faraway Russia. "The geographical position of Canton does not permit us to establish contact with Russia," Sun complained. He asked repeatedly whether it were not possible to place a very powerful radio station in Vladivostok or in Manchuria so that we could communicate with Canton.

Soon after, Sun Yat-sen left for Canton. There disagreements developed between him and his commander-in-chief, Ch'en Ch'iung-ming. Sun wished to continue military operations, to utilize the victory in the South in order to develop a revolutionary movement in central and northern China. He wished to make southern Kwangtung province an example for the whole of China to follow. This example, he argued, would prompt the Chinese people to introduce a similar order throughout all of China.

After Sun's departure from Shanghai to Canton, it so happened that I, too, visited Canton and together with Comrade Ch. called on General Ch'en Ch'iung-ming.

General Ch'en is a general of the revolutionary period of 1911. Formerly a journalist, he had participated in underground work and was a member of the Kuomintang. He gave the impression of a man of great will power and self-control. By the content of his conversation and his manners, he reminded one of a puritan. He spoke with great respect of Sun Yat-sen, but considered him an impractical idealist.

The disagreement between Sun and Ch'en Ch'iung-ming ended badly for Sun. In the autumn of 1921 [1922?], after Ch'en Ch'iung-ming raised a revolt and seized the city, Sun was obliged to flee Canton.

Once more Sun became a political exile in Shanghai. From there he directed the struggle between the generals who supported him and those of Ch'en Ch'iung-ming. In the spring of 1923, Sun returned to Canton where he finally consolidated his power.

My second meeting with Sun took place last summer [1924] in Canton. He then lived in a large house across the Pearl River and could be reached only by crossing the river in a boat.

I went to see Sun Yat-sen together with the governor of the city, an old member of the Kuomintang, Liao Chung-k'ai. He was an ardent follower of Sun.

A guard of honor stood at the gate of the house. We mounted the stairs and on the second floor entered a large, simply furnished room where Sun Yat-sen was

[2] *Pravda*, No. 61, March 15, 1925, p. 2. This article was written on the occasion of Dr. Sun's death on March 12, 1925. The Ch. of whom Voitinsky speaks was presumably Ch'en Tu-hsiu.

awaiting us. He was dressed simply, just as he was five years ago. This time Sun simply showered me with questions about Russia. It seemed that he saw in me a messenger from a country which, while remote, was at the same time "very close" to China, and that he wanted not only to have his questions answered, but also to take note of the voice, clothes, and manners of a person who had come from the U.S.S.R.

Sun was mostly interested in the progress of our economy and the living conditions of our peasantry. He was unpleasantly surprised when he heard that we had not reached prewar production levels, but again became animated when we spoke of our national education, of the growing young generation, the youth of the freest country in the world.

A few days before my visit to Sun Yat-sen, a treaty was signed between us and the Chinese government in Peking.[3] The Kuomintang people in the South were not pleased with this arrangement. It appeared to them that the signing of this treaty was not loyal to the Southern government of Dr. Sun Yat-sen. Canton was in a state of war with Peking, and yet we signed a treaty with the latter.

These critics did not realize that we were friendly to all China, and that by signing a treaty with the North, we diminished the danger for the South. At present this seems clear to everyone, but at the time of my visit to Sun Yat-sen we feared that many Chinese people would fail to understand the situation.

Carefully wording my question, I asked Sun's opinion on this matter. He spoke very openly and made it clear that he understood thoroughly the meaning of the treaty between the U.S.S.R. and the Chinese government, as well as the significance of it for the Chinese people in general.

In the latter part of our talk Sun asked me in detail about the conditions in our country after the death of Lenin. He was also very much interested in the recognition of our government by capitalist countries.

Sun viewed the development of the movement of liberation in China with optimism. He believed that the antagonism between the imperialists in the Pacific area would make it possible for the Chinese people to launch a serious struggle against world imperialism in the near future. This faith remained with him, it appears, to the end of his life, and he passed it on as his heritage to his party, outlining it in his will.

69

Dr. Sun Yat-sen's Letter to Chicherin, August 28, 1921[4]

Dear Chicherin:

I received your letter from Moscow dated October 31, 1920, which arrived here on June 14, 1921. I delayed answering it because first I wanted to meet the messenger who brought this letter from you to Harbin and forwarded it to me from there. But since he has not yet been able to come to Canton to visit me, I decided to send my answer to your fraternal greetings and your offer to restore trade relations between Russia and China.

First, I must inform you that the above letter was the first and only letter which reached me from you, or from anyone else in Soviet Russia. In the course of the last two years statements have appeared in the capitalist press about official offers allegedly made to me from Moscow. I have received no such offers either by letter or by any other form of communication. In case some of your colleagues have sent letters to me, please note that so far none of them have reached me.

---

[3] The treaty was actually signed on May 31, 1924. See our pp. 247–48.
[4] *Bolshevik*, No. 19, October, 1950, pp. 46–48.

I must brief you on the situation in China. Let me return to the years of 1911–12 when my political work found its decisive expression in the revolution that began in October 1911 and spread rapidly throughout the country. This revolution led to the downfall of the Manchu dynasty and the establishment of the Chinese republic. I was elected president. After serving for a short period of time, I surrendered my office in favor of Yüan Shih-k'ai, since my friends, whom I completely trusted and who had a better detailed knowledge of the Chinese international situation than I, advised me that Yüan Shih-k'ai was capable of unifying the country and of ensuring the stability of the republic because he enjoyed the trust of foreign powers. My friends now admit that my retirement was a big political blunder, . . . [comparable to] Lenin's being superseded by Kolchak, Yudenich, or Wrangel. Immediately after assuming office, or very soon thereafter, Yüan began to work for the restoration of monarchy, with himself as emperor. As you know we defeated him at the end.

However, after Yüan's death, the Great Powers supported a number of pseudo-Cromwells and pseudo-Napoleons, both politically and financially. One of them, Chang Tso-lin, is now the head of a gang of murderers. Officially he is commander of the troops, or military governor of Manchuria; but actually he is the master whose biddings are obeyed by the Peking "government." Chang, on his part, obeys Tokyo in all important matters which concern Japan. Peking, then, is Tokyo's tool in all questions of high politics that concern vital Japanese interests. Moscow must take this fact into serious account in all its dealings with Peking. Not before Peking is thoroughly cleansed (and that will be only when I enter it) can Soviet Russia hope for the restoration of favorable relations with China.

Since you wrote your letter to me, I have been elected president of the national government established in Canton. This government is a *de jure* government because:

(a) the source of its power is the provisional constitution accepted by the first constitutional assembly which met in Nanking in 1912, which is the only existing fundamental law of the Chinese republic;

(b) it [i.e., the national government] was created on the basis of . . . the constitution adopted by the legal Chinese parliament. This government now has its seat in Canton.

My government is also a *de facto* government and its authority is accepted by the number of provinces in southwest China, and also in other provinces under its jurisdiction.

Owing to the geographical position of China, it is impossible for me at present to enter into effective trade relations with you. If you look at the map of China, you will see that the territory under the control of my government is situated south of the river Yangtze, and that between this territory and the Manchurian and Mongolian "gates"—through which trade relations can be established—Chang Tso-lin and his allies hold their sway. There are no "gates," nor can there be any, via Chinese Turkestan until a large railway line is constructed which is included in my project of the railway system for China.

Moscow must wait until I put an end to the reactionaries who always appear in every country on the very next day after a successful revolution. Your own experience in the course of the past three or four years will make you understand what kind of "task" I have before me. I have been engaged in this task for the last nine or ten years, and hope to bring it to a successful conclusion within a short time, if no kind of active foreign intervention takes place. No intervention by the Western powers is likely. They appear to be satisfied with Peking.

Meanwhile, I would like to enter into personal contact with you and my friends in Moscow. I am extremely interested in your work, and particularly in the organization of your soviets, your army, and educational system. I would like to know what you and your friends can tell me about these matters, and particularly about education.

In the same way as Moscow has done, I would like to impress deeply the principle of the Chinese republic into the minds of the young generation, the workers of tomorrow.

With best wishes to you, to my friend Lenin, and to all who have done so much for the cause of human freedom.

Sincerely yours,
SUN YAT-SEN

P.S. This letter is being sent via London by way of the Soviet trade mission which is there now. If it arrives safely and without much delay, please inform me so that in the future I can communicate with you in the same manner. I have established contact so as to receive news from Moscow if it is sent to your mission in London.

70

The Greeting of the Congress of the Toilers of the Far East by Zinoviev and Kalinin

[The Opening Session of the Congress, Moscow, January 21, 1922][5]

ZINOVIEV: Comrades, on behalf of the Executive Committee of the Communist International, I declare the Congress of the Toilers of the Far East open. (Cheers, singing of the "International.")

Comrades, the Executive Committee of the Communist International attaches great importance to the present congress. It instructed me to welcome all the comrades assembled here in the name of all Communist workers organised in the International Brotherhood of Toilers, known as the Communist International. Our international brotherhood, since the first days of its existence, takes clear account of the fact, that the complete victory of the proletariat over the bourgeoisie under the present circumstances is possible only on a world wide scale. There is much that distinguishes us from the previous Internationals, but one of the most important features ... consists in the fact that we not only in words, but in deeds are trying to become the organisation not merely of the toilers of Europe, but of the toilers of the entire world. The Communist International is all the time taking a clear account of the fact that the revolution of the toilers can be victorious under the present circumstances only as a world revolution. Too often has the idea of the world revolution been substituted by the idea of a European revolution. Of course, we know quite well what a tremendous significance the labour movement and the general revolutionary movement in Europe possess in themselves. We do not by any means wish to underrate it, but at the same time we know that the decisive victory will be assured only in the event of the struggle not being confined to the European continent alone, when our struggle will rouse the hundreds of thousands, the hundreds of millions of the toiling and oppressed masses in the East. ...

The Third International considers it its greatest task and will do everything possible to hasten the awakening of the toiling peoples of the Far East. ...

At the Baku Conference, the Executive Committee of the Comintern issued the call "Communist Parties of all countries and toilers of all oppressed nations, unite!"

---

[5] *The First Congress of the Toilers of the Far East*, pp. 3–6, 8. No complete record of this congress is available in Russian. Our source for this document and Document 72 was published in English in Soviet Russia; we have kept the original orthography and style.

Zinoviev was chairman of the Communist International; M. I. Kalinin, later president of the U.S.S.R., was chairman of the All-Russian Central Executive Committee of Soviets.

It is this appeal which we now address to the representatives of the Far East, whom it is our greatest joy to welcome to-day in our country. The Communist Parties of all countries and the toilers of the entire world, and of the Far East in particular, will unite under the banner of the Communist International and score the final victory over world imperialism. Long live the Congress of the Toilers of the Far East! (Applause.)

KALININ: On behalf of the All-Russian Central Executive Committee of the Council of Workers' and Peasants' Deputies, I greet the delegates of the peoples of the Far East. Comrades, representatives of the Soviet republic greet you with the greatest joy for . . . [the enlistment of the new members into the revolutionary camp] increases the number of those who [already] fight for the oppressed.

Comrades, you are now in the capital of that country on whose boundaries the sun almost never sets. But it is not its size that characterises its difference from the other states. The chief peculiarity of the country in whose capital you now are, comrades, is the fact that this country considers it impossible and does not desire to enrich itself at the expense of the other border peoples. This is the substance and peculiarity of our country. It does not wish to exploit the toil of these peoples, for the toiling masses themselves are in power here. In accordance with that, all the relations of this state assume quite a different character from those of all other states. . . .

71

Zinoviev's Analysis of the Eastern Situation and of the Tasks in the East

[Second Session of the Congress of the Toilers of the Far East, January 23, 1922][6]

Comrades! It will be my task to present to you the general outline of the international situation as this congress meets, and to chart out the basic tasks of this congress as the Executive Committee of the Comintern conceives them.

. . . [The main feature of the present post-bellum period is the pressing urgency of, not European questions, but Asian and Far Eastern questions.] . . .

We are already in a position to sum up the results of the Washington Conference. It seems to me that the date of December 10, 1921, will remain one of the gloomiest dates in the history of mankind. On that date, in Washington, a treaty was signed between four of the most powerful, most oppressive, and most reactionary imperialist governments of today: England, France, Japan, and America. I believe that this alliance will be referred to from this date on as the alliance of four bloodsuckers, the alliance of four bloodthirsty imperialist powers which, before having a fight among themselves—and they must inevitably fight—have concluded an armistice so as to oppress more successfully the people they have already been bleeding white for many years.

You undoubtedly know the principal promise that was made in Washington. It was to solve the problem of disarmament. Actually, however—and this is quite evident now—it was the problem of armaments that was solved there. . . . The Washington Conference has once more borne out the communist contention that no disarmament is possible under the capitalist system, and that it will be possible to speak seriously of disarmament only when the oppressed nations have been victorious over the imperialist governments. . . .

Let us see now how the problems of the various Far Eastern countries have been

6 *Pervyi sezd revoliutsionnykh organizatsii Dalnego Vostoka*, pp. 8–28.

solved there. Was the Korean problem solved in Washington? We have been informed that even some active members of the Korean movement of liberation had put some hopes in the Washington Conference, thinking that a certain clarification of the Korean problem might follow therefrom. But what has actually happened? Korea was not even mentioned at the Washington Conference, as if Korea did not even exist, as if the powers which had assembled in Washington had never heard of the existence of Korea. In the official discussions at the Conference, at least, not a word was said of Korea, although views about who was to continue to oppress Korea were probably exchanged behind the scenes. No more convincing lesson could have been learned by the Korean people than the one supplied by the official silence on the Korean question in Washington.

The Chinese problem, as you know, was solved entirely in the American spirit. Agreement was reached on the policy of the so-called "open door," which had been advocated by American capitalists for selfish motives. Because of its strength, America was confident of being able to beat all its competitors in the Chinese market in free competition . . . and to extract even greater profits from its trade with China. It would be the saddest mistake imaginable if any simpletons could be found, say, among the representatives of South China, who would seriously take the "open door" policy to mean a democratic policy, and in that way fall into the ruthless capitalist snare. Yet, I must regretfully state that according to the information received by us (I admit we are poorly informed), there are some people among the active revolutionary workers in South China—adherents of Sun Yat-sen and important representatives of his party—who still look now and then somewhat hopefully toward . . . capitalist America, expecting that the benefits of democracy and progress will be showered upon revolutionary China from that country. I believe, however, that the Washington Conference will convince the more farsighted leaders in South China, as well as the Chinese revolutionaries and all those who wish to struggle for the real independence of their country, even if they are not socialists, that the American capitalists are not their friends but their relentless enemies, whose democratic catchwords express nothing but flagrant hypocrisy and political bigotry.

The Mongolian problem was also forgotten at the Washington Conference. Ever since Mongolia was liberated, thanks to some small aid by the Soviet government (the Soviet government will always be proud of this and of any other chance to lend a helpful hand to Mongolia in the future), the Mongolian problem has been tossed back and forth like a shuttlecock by the capitalists. The Japanese imperialists are now trying to make use of Mongolian independence, having bribed certain mercenary Mongolian politicians to sow discord between Mongolia and the Chinese revolutionaries . . . over the question of whether Mongolia should be restored to China. Nothing has been stated openly about Mongolia at the Washington Conference, just as nothing was said about Korea. As you know, the diplomatic shop talk in Washington is still going on, with no definite results achieved. . . . But one thing is certain: the Washington Conference has confirmed what was to be expected, namely that as long as the bourgeoisie plays the leading role in the wealthiest countries of the world (Japan, America, England, and France) the Far Eastern problem is bound to become increasingly acute, and that in no case can a solution of the problem be expected. . . .

Let us now deal with the problems confronting the countries which are represented at this congress.

The Chinese question. For the last decade China has offered the best example of what the rapacious imperialists are capable of when they are faced by a defenseless country, or at least one which is not strong enough to resist them. . . . The task of the Comintern, and of the present congress in particular, is to bring unity into the scattered ranks of the Chinese revolutionaries. The workers who are members of the Communist International must help the divided and oppressed Chinese people carry out its basic task, namely, to drive out of China all its plunderers; to drive out all the oppressors of the Chinese people who cause them so much suffering. . . .

We know perfectly well that the protest which is growing in China against the imperialists is not a communist protest; it is the expression of a spontaneous and natural desire of the people to be the masters of their own fate. We wish to say that the Comintern is prepared to support fully and most devotedly your [China's] innermost wish; that the Comintern believes itself duty-bound to throw all its power and moral authority to the side of the Chinese people in their struggle for basic freedom and independence. The Comintern will help to bring about the day when the Japanese, American, and English bourgeoisie and officers will not be able to mock the masses of China any longer. . . .

The Korean question. Korea's fate was at first closely connected with the competition between the Russian and Japanese imperialists; during the last few years her fate has been principally in the hands of Japanese imperialists. We know very well that at present thousands of Korean revolutionaries are filling the dungeons, we have heard of hundreds and thousands who have fallen in the struggle against Japanese imperialism, we have heard of the insurrection of 1919, and we are following with undiminishing attention the struggle of the Korean people. . . .

[But] the Communist International has noted with surprise and pain the turn in the course of the struggle of the Korean people for freedom that occurred when some of the Korean leaders turned their hopeful eyes to Versailles, believing that they would succeed in ingratiating themselves with the European and Asian imperialists. Therefore, the present congress is obliged to tell all Korean revolutionaries (regardless of their political orientation) . . . that they must once and for all give up any hope (and that they must kill such hope among the Korean people) that the Korean national question can be solved in any other way than by a close union with the advanced revolutionary workers of Europe and America. . . .

The Mongolian question. I said in passing that the question of Mongolia is expected by some people to be solved by placing Mongolia once more under Chinese sovereignty, and that the imperialists play with this problem as with a toy. . . . It would be very sad if some leaders—say, among the leaders of the revolutionary South China—were so doctrinaire on the Mongolian problem as to propose returning Mongolia to Chinese rule. . . . A people trying even so little to oppress others cannot itself be free. No people of the Far East should forget this truth. . . . We believe it our duty to give a word of warning to the Chinese revolutionaries, so that they would not experience in their deal with Mongolia "as you give, so shall ye receive." . . . If you wish the liberation of the Chinese people, if you wish China to be freed from the Japanese and other oppressors, you must not forget that your own policy must be farsighted when it concerns the Mongolian people, whose fate is closely bound with yours.

. . . We have invited to this congress the representatives of the oppressor nations also. The fact that we see here a number of Japanese representatives proves, I believe, that the Comintern is on the way to a true solution of the Far Eastern problem. This solution is not possible without Japan: the Japanese proletariat holds in its hands the key to the solution of the Far Eastern question . . .

The Japanese bourgeoisie rules over and oppresses many millions of people in the Far East, holding in its hands the fate of all that sector of the world. [Therefore] the defeat of the Japanese bourgeoisie and the final victory of the revolution in Japan can alone solve the Far Eastern question. Only after its victory in that country will the Far Eastern revolution cease to be "a storm in a teacup." This makes the responsibility of the young Japanese proletariat particularly great.

Our information is as yet far from complete (this is the first occasion that we have had for a friendly meeting with the Japanese workers), but even the little that we know goes to prove that the Japanese workers' movement has been launched and is being organized.

In many respects it is still passing through the stage of "infantile sickness."[7] Japan has almost three million workers (the students of the Japanese labor movement speak of much higher figures) and five million landless peasants. Japan is experiencing a headlong capitalist development, but its workers' movement is very weak. Class-conscious Communists can be counted there only by hundreds. The number of revolutionaries, syndicalists, and anarchists also amounts only to some hundreds. Since the rice riots in 1918 (that first great spontaneous mass movement), the Japanese bourgeoisie, so it seems, has had no occasion to contend against any large revolutionary movement. If we examine the present situation in Japan from a distance, as it were, the picture is clear: the Japanese bourgeoisie feels that Japan is fortunately able to gather the fruits of an impetuous large-scale development of capitalism. [Occupied with] becoming fabulously rich, the bourgeoisie has so far had no need to look on the reverse side of the medal and does not yet see the clenched fists of the Japanese workers.

The fate of the Japanese revolutionary movement is acquiring an enormous international importance. I have already told you about the alliance of the four bloodsuckers formed in Washington, for the purpose of crushing, torturing, and partitioning the oppressed peoples of the Far East with even greater savagery than hitherto. This quadruple alliance of bloodsuckers, however, cannot postpone the hour of the inevitable war in the Pacific Ocean. This war is inevitable. As sure as morning follows night, so will the first imperialist war, which ended in 1918, be followed by a second war which will center around the Far East and the problem of the Pacific. This war can be avoided only by a victory of the proletarian revolution. It is not possible to say whether this war will break out in 1925 or 1928, a year earlier or later, but it is inevitable. It can no more be avoided than fate. It will be possible to avoid this war only if the young working class of Japan rapidly becomes sufficiently strong to seize the Japanese bourgeoisie by the throat, and if parallel with that there will be a victorious revolutionary movement in America. . . .

The resistance of the American bourgeoisie will be so determined . . . that all we have experienced recently in Russia [during the civil war] will appear a mere child's play. No less determined will be the resistance of the avaricious, adroit Japanese bourgeoisie. . . .

Therefore, we have the right to say that the fate of several hundreds of millions of people living in China, Korea, and Mongolia, and in Japan itself, is in the hands of the working class of Japan. It is the task of the present congress to co-ordinate the activities of the oppressed, the nonproletarian masses of the entire Far East, with those of the industrial and village proletariat of Japan. You, a small group of advanced workers of your countries, voice the thoughts and aspirations of the hundreds of millions of oppressed Far Eastern people. You must . . . co-ordinate the young workers' movement in Japan with nonproletarian mass movements in countries oppressed by Japan. The Communist International will attend to everything else. . . .

The enthusiasm we are witnessing here is not as yet a communist enthusiasm; it is merely a national-revolutionary enthusiasm. Will you be able to effect a union between the national-revolutionary movement and the mighty proletarian movement which aims at a purely communist order? This union is necessary, and it is inevitable. The Communist International has realized it from the first days of its foundation, and it resolved at its Second Congress that the problem of the oppressed nationalities was extremely important.

[7] A reference to Lenin's famous article, "Left Wing Communism, an Infantile Disorder," written in 1920.

. . . The Communist International stated plainly and clearly that the oppressed peoples must unite around one country, Soviet Russia. This decision was not made by one party only, but by the forty-three parties from all over the world represented at the Second Congress. They called upon all the oppressed peoples to rally around the country where for the first time in history the national question had been happily solved. . . .

[Your task is to solve the problem] of co-ordinating the forces of the awakening oppressed peoples who are conducting the struggle for their own emancipation, and not as yet for socialism, with the fighting proletariat of the countries where the proletariat is numerous. . . . We are not doctrinaires, nor are we sectarians. We do not abandon, nor will we abandon, the principles of communism. We will preach communism wherever we meet even a small group of people. On the other hand, we will fight shoulder to shoulder with the many millions who are fighting merely for their own independence. We will advise our comrades, the Chinese, Korean, and Japanese Communists, who represent at present only small groups, not to stand aside and look down loftily upon . . . their fellow men who have not yet become Communists, but to mix up with the millions of people who are fighting for their own national independence and emancipation. . . . This is essential because history has raised the national question quite definitely, and the solution of it is not to be found in Washington, but in the hands of the proletariat, and only in their hands.

To the leaders of the nationalist movement we say: Give up your faith in Versailles and Washington; do not believe the bourgeois intriguers. Remember that history has confronted us with a problem—either you win your independence side by side with the proletariat, or you do not win it at all; either you receive your emancipation at the hands of the proletariat, in co-operation with it, under its guidance, or you are doomed to remain the slaves of an English, American, and Japanese camarilla; either the hundreds and millions of toilers of China, Korea, Mongolia, and other countries understand that their ally and leader is the world proletariat, and once and for all give up all hope in any kind of bourgeois and imperialist intrigue, or their national movements must be doomed to failure, and imperialists will always ride on their backs, sow seeds of civil war, and crush and carve up their countries. This question is not presented in this manner by theoreticians and writers; it is not the fantasy of some leader; it has been so presented by the process of world history, by the development of world imperialism, which presses forward the problem of the Far East to a place of foremost importance. This is what the Communist International says, addressing itself to both sections of this congress—to that section which is composed of conscious Communists and whose function is to organise the working class for victory over the bourgeoisie, as well as to that section which is composed of nonproletarian elements, of the leaders of those toiling masses which are fighting against foreign oppression. An alliance between these two groups is essential, and we will be playing the game of the bourgeoisie if by any means we weaken this alliance. Our congress will acquire universal historical importance if we can solve the problem of co-ordination and co-operation between these two gigantic historical world forces.

. . . This congress, which is not so very strong numerically, but which is important for its quality, meeting as it does under most difficult conditions and while the canting chorus of the hypocrite plunderers assembled in Washington has not yet died away, has a world-wide and historical task before it. . . . Do not forget that you, the many million peoples of the Far East, are today the only sweet morsel that has not yet been divided. Today, the bourgeois of the world are not aware themselves of what is happening, and of what the morrow has in store for them; they know not what awaits them when they awake, and they do not know whether they are on the eve of a new period of prosperity or on the verge of ruin. At this moment you are those whose weight in the scale will be decisive. If this awakening of the Far Eastern peoples will proceed rapidly, in an organized manner, and energetically, if you declare war on your slumbering East, if you who represent the most advanced elements of your peoples lead their struggle without any consideration for the inevitable sacrifices, and if you understand that your true leader is the Comintern, then many among you will live to see the real and final victory of the world revolution. (*Loud cheers.*)[8]

72

The Interrelation Between the National Revolutionary Movement and the Revolutionary Proletarian Movement

[Safarov's Statement at the Tenth Session of the Congress of the Toilers of the Far East, January 27, 1922][9]

Comrades, the fundamental question which is before our Congress is the question of the inter-relations and the right understanding of these inter-relations, between the national-revolutionary movement, on the one hand, and the revolutionary proletarian movement, on the other hand, in the countries of the Far East. The discussions which followed my report have led me to believe that some of the comrades have arrived at a wrong conception of these inter-relations. Thus, for instance, the representative of the Homindan [Kuomintang], Comrade Tao, has asserted that the principles of the Soviet system and the basic demands of the Soviet revolution are nothing new in China. He said, if I am not mistaken, that the Homindan has been propagating these ideas for the last twenty years. Of course, I do not in the least wish to question the revolutionary development of that Party, but, I am convinced that, in order to come to an understanding between the Communists, on the one hand, and the revolutionary nationalists, on the other, it is absolutely necessary for both sides to know each other well. We know that the Party which is at the head of the South China Government is a revolutionary-democratic Party and we do not wish to question this fact. We are convinced that this Party has done great revolutionary work which was absolutely necessary in China, and we hope to fight side by side with this Party in the future. But, on the other hand, we are not so naïve as to imagine that this Party is a revolutionary Communist Party . . . We say: In colonial and semi-colonial countries the first phase of the revolutionary movement must inevitably be a national-democratic movement. We give our support to this movement, as such, to the extent that it is directed against imperialism. We are supporting it, have always supported it, and will do so in the future, but, on the other hand, we cannot recognise this struggle as our struggle, as the struggle for the proletarian revolution. . . . [But] the proletarian and semi-proletarian masses of China and Korea have a greater task to fulfil than that of national emancipation. They are confronted with the task of the *complete* liberation of their countries. In so far as these masses, that is the proletarian and semi-proletarian elements of the city and village, could take upon themselves the task of the social emancipation of the toiling masses of the oppressed countries, it is wrong and fatal to arouse any illusions on this matter. If we, Communists of China or Korea, raise the slogan of a democratic government, of a uniform income tax, of land na-

---

[8] The congress passed a resolution on Zinoviev's report which simply reiterated its main points.

[9] *The First Congress of the Toilers of the Far East*, pp. 192–99. We have maintained the original orthography and style of this source material, published in English in Soviet Russia.

tionalisation, that is the slogans of the democratic revolution, we would thereby show that we are ready to co-operate with all the honest nationalist democratic organisations, if they have the interests of the toiling majority of their country at heart. But on the other hand, the proletarian and semi-proletarian elements must organise independently in their class unions. The unions which are now being formed as guild and craft organisations directly connected with the Homindan cannot be recognised by us as class unions. They do not understand the class principle, they are not the organs of the class struggle of the proletariat for its emancipation. Therefore, in dealing with you, followers of the Homindan, as with our allies, friends and comrades, we at the same time tell you openly and frankly: we are supporting and will continue to support your struggle in so far as it is a matter of a nationalistic and democratic uprising for national emancipation. But at the same time we shall independently carry on our Communist work of organising the proletarian and semi-proletarian masses of China. This is the cause of the proletarian masses themselves, and must be done by the Chinese workers, the Chinese proletariat. In this sphere the Chinese labour movement must develop quite independently of the radically minded bourgeois and democratic organisations and parties. . . . For a definite historical period we can arrange for a division of labour between us, the representatives of the proletarian revolution, i.e. the proletarian class and the semi-proletarian elements among the peasantry on the one hand, and the representatives of the nationalistic radical and democratic elements of awakening China on the other. However, both sides must understand that this division of labour must be based on a voluntary agreement. The proletarian masses need not reject their own views, they need not refrain from organising their own class party. Only under these conditions is co-operation and a voluntary agreement possible. . . . In China, the working class is just learning to walk, just beginning to develop. The peasant masses are brow-beaten and ignorant, and therefore do not put forward their own demands and views. Comrade Tao's statement on the question of the land nationalisation is the best proof of it. According to what he said the Southern Government was considering the nationalisation of land, and this project was not carried out only because this important revolutionary measure requires uniformity, it is necessary that it be carried out throughout the Chinese Republic. Therefore, according to the Homindan, it is necessary first to clear the Chinese territory of imperialists, and the marauding Dudziuns[10] and to establish democracy in China. This is not the correct way of looking upon this question. As long as we want to organise the masses under our banner, and have the majority of the people on our side we must touch upon the vital interests of the masses, in order that these masses may follow us to the end, that they be ready to die for our and their cause. For the Chinese peasants of Southern China the question of land nationalisation is not one that can be settled from above by administrative reforms, for them it is a vital necessity. We must therefore carry out this revolutionary measure even in a small section of the country in order to show to the Chinese peasants living on the territory occupied by the hostile forces that where democratic regime has been established the peasants live a thousand times better, that their interests are a thousand times more secure. Without a clear understanding of this, without a correct attitude on the land question, the great masses cannot be drawn into the struggle on our side. It is not enough to work out a good program, it is not enough to advocate this program in a small circle of so-called educated society, it is necessary to make it the burning demand of the toiling masses. . . .

Comrade Tao spoke here on the Mongolian question. I did not touch upon this question in my report because the fundamental question before us is that of the relations between the national-revolutionary and the Communist movement, and it is natural therefore that the Mongolian question was put aside. As long as the basic

10 Chinese *tu-chün,* "warlord."

economy of Mongolia is cattle raising distinguished by patriarchal tribal features, to preach Communism and the proletarian revolution in Mongolia is ridiculous, for it is quite clear that it is no use putting the cart before the horse, that it is impossible to skip over a number of inevitable historical stages. Our program, i.e. the program of the Comintern with regard to Mongolia consists in supporting the elements striving for national emancipation, those elements which are now in power and whose representatives are present at this Congress on behalf of the People's Revolutionary Party. On the question of the relations between Mongolia and China Comrade Zinoviev gave an adequate answer. . . .

[Let us now consider the position of Japan.] . . . In this question we must discard the narrow nationalistic point of view and must take the position as it really is. Not only the worker and the peasant, but every honest democrat and defender of his people must understand that there are two Japans. There is the Japan of the Mikado and of plutocracy, militarism, imperialism, and coercion. But there is also another Japan—the proletarian and working class to which the future belongs and which will solve the Far Eastern problem. It is imperative to distinguish between these two irreconcilable camps and not to shut one's eyes to existing facts. Emancipation in the Far East and in the whole world can only be achieved by international solidarity. . . .

Without a proletarian movement in Japan none of the Far Eastern countries can achieve their emancipation. But it would be petty-bourgeois and foolish to imagine that the Japanese proletariat will be able to do it all on its own. No, the Japanese proletarian movement is significant in the sense that the first decisive blow against foreign and predatory imperialism and imperialist coercion must be dealt by the Japanese proletariat, as the best organised and strongest force. Organisation is an outcome of industrial development and of factory life. . . .

I do not agree with Comrade Kato who paints too rosy a picture, and represents the Japanese working masses as fully awakened. We must not forget the power that is exercised by petty-bourgeois chauvinistic prejudices. The petty-bourgeois influence is still very strong among the Japanese working class, and the Japanese proletariat must struggle energetically against it. . . .

In summing up, we may say that, in colonial and semi-colonial countries, like China and Korea, which are actually the colonies of foreign capital, the Communist International and the Communist Parties are obliged to support the national-democratic movement. In these countries the Communist Party must advocate the overthrow of imperialist oppression and support democratic demands such as the nationalisation of the land, self-government, etc. At the same time, however, the Communist Parties must not abandon their Communist program, just as they must not abstain from organising the working class in trade unions, independent of bourgeois influence. Neither must they abstain from organising the working class in an independent Communist Party. . . .

We say, quite frankly that we support . . . bourgeois nationalists, bourgeois to the very marrow, because Japanese, American and English imperialism is the most reactionary force. We are not afraid to say frankly that we will support the nationalist bourgeoisie who are striving to emancipate the productive forces of China and Korea from the yoke of foreign capitalism. On the other hand, however, we definitely demand from these bourgeois-democratic, these radical-democratic elements, that they make no attempt to dominate over the young labour movement of China and Korea and that they make no attempt to divert it from its true path and substitute its ideals by radical democratic ideals painted in Soviet colours. We will more easily come to an understanding if we tell each other what we really are. We have every opportunity of coming to a frank understanding and we must take advantage of this opportunity in order that our tasks may be quite clear. Realising these tasks, we may accomplish the great revolutionary aim towards which we are all striving—the great aim of the national emancipation of the colonial peoples and the emancipation of labour from the oppression of imperialism. (*Loud applause.*)

73

Manifesto of the First Congress of the Toilers of the Far East[11]

Toilers of the Far East!
Workers and peasants of China, Korea, Japan, Mongolia, the Pacific Isles, Indochina, and the Dutch Indies!
Enslaved nations of the Far East!

For many years you have been suffering from the robberies and the savage club-law of the European, American, and Japanese vultures. The Japanese oppressors have bespattered Korea with blood from end to end. The Japanese, American, French, and English robbers are plundering and tearing to pieces China, with her four hundred million population, and are building their own welfare on the blood and tears of the Chinese people. They do not look upon the representatives of the oppressed nations as human beings. They want gold that glitters, profits, wealth, and to get them they are ready to sacrifice hundreds of millions of human lives. Chinese and Koreans are not allowed to enter the gardens and other public places in the foreign quarters of Peking, Shanghai, Tientsin, Hong Kong, Seoul, and Chemulpho—on a par with dogs. In these quarters foreign bourgeois, fattened on other men's blood and sweat, ride about in carriages drawn by men-horses, the rickshas, hastening them with kicks and sticks. The most oppressed and browbeaten slave of the rich of the world—the Chinese coolie—works for these parasites to a state of deadly exhaustion. The Chinese peasant toils beyond his strength sixteen and eighteen hours a day at a stretch, only to see his labor enrich the foreign money-lenders and bloodsuckers and their mercenary lackeys. The Korean pauper has no land to work on for his daily bread. The land is in the hands of the Japanese planter, the landowner, and the capitalist, who with their [minions'] guns and bayonets force the refractory to do the work. Every word of protest, every cry of desperation, is smothered by the rattle of mass shootings in the Philippines, on the island of Formosa, in Indochina and the islands of the Dutch Indies, as well as in near-by British India, which has long been a terrible prison for a people of three hundred millions. Millions of people who are toiling on rice, coffee, cotton, and other plantations, are most cruelly exploited. Only recently has Mongolia been able to free herself from Japanese and White Guard clutches. In Japan, where the ruling classes gained the nickname of "hangmen of the Far East," the factory workers and the peasant-laborers—partly daily laborers on rented land—lead an existence fit only for lower animals. The heavy groans of enslaved hundreds of millions are heard everywhere. The oppressors will hear nothing of freedom and independence for the oppressed nations, nor of their human rights. They have met lately in the halls of the American Exchange in Washington, in order to come to an understanding on how to plunder anew the countries of the Far East. There they have signed their alliance of the four bloodsuckers. Korea, the Russian Far East, and Manchuria have been given over to be robbed and pillaged by Japan. The principle of equal rights of robbery in China has been set up, leaving the leading

11 *Pervyi sezd revoliutsionnykh organizatsii Dalnego Vostoka,* pp. 3–5.

role in this base affair to American capital. The consortium of 1918,[12] invented by America, was to make all the Chinese peasants into tributaries of American capital: they were to pay a considerable tax to the American bankers. Chinese industry was to become subordinate entirely to American. Nothing came of this enterprise in 1918 owing to differences among the oppressors and the unanimous protest by the masses of the Chinese people. Now the vultures desire to create a new consortium—an international firm for the military, financial, and industrial robbery of China. Japan, America, England and France have, for the time being, put off a war, which was ready to break out, for domination over the Pacific. They have postponed it (but not given it up entirely) in order to be able to continue to rob in unison a little while longer.

The World War of 1914 has undermined their strength. The workers' revolution has taken them by the throat in Europe on the very spot of their bloody crime. They have struggled for four years against the Soviet republic, the promised land of all the oppressed and exploited, and they now must openly recognize its strength and their own inability to defeat the Soviets. They hope to re-establish their undermined power in the Far East at our expense and at the price of our lives, our blood, and our toil. They bring new chains, new horrors, and a still more terrible enslavement to the patient and resigned peoples of the Far East.

This must not, this shall not be! We desire to become the masters of our own fate and to stop being the playthings of the imperialists' cupidity and greedy appetites.

The Communist International has sent out a great appeal: World proletarians and all oppressed nations of the world, unite!

We will carry this appeal to our destroyed villages, to the slave plantations, to the factories, schools, and barracks.

We have met in the Red capitals of the Soviet republic—Moscow and Petrograd— in order to raise our voices from this world tribune against the world executioners and against the Washington union of the four bloodsuckers. . . .

74

Theses of the Fourth Congress of the Communist International on the Eastern Problem[13]

1. *The Growth of the Revolutionary Movement in the East*

The Second Congress of the Communist International outlined the general principles of the national and colonial problems for the period of prolonged struggle between imperialism and the proletarian dictatorship. The Congress based these principles on the experience gained from the organization of the Russian eastern regions on the soviet principle, and also on the development of the national-revolutionary movements in the colonies.

Since that time the struggle against imperialist oppression in the colonies and semicolonial countries has been considerably intensified owing to the aggravation of the political and economic crisis of imperialism.

The above has been made apparent by: (1) the collapse of the Sèvres treaty on the partition of Turkey, and the possible complete restoration of the national and political independence of that country; (2) the stormy growth of the national-revo-

---

[12] This was a proposal made to the State Department on July 8, 1918, by a group of American bankers that a new China Consortium should be formed by the United States, Japan, Great Britain, and France for floating Chinese loans. The project was ultimately shelved because of disagreements among the four powers concerned.

[13] *Kommunisticheskii Internatsional v dokumentakh*, pp. 317–25.

lutionary movement in India, Mesopotamia, Egypt, Morocco, China, and Korea; (3) the hopeless internal crisis of Japanese imperialism, which is rapidly creating the conditions for a bourgeois-democratic revolution in that country, and conditions for the passing of the Japanese proletariat to an independent class struggle; (4) the birth of the labor movement and the formation of communist parties in almost all countries of the East.

The facts enumerated above indicate a change in the social basis of the revolutionary movement in the colonies. The anti-imperialist struggle is no longer exclusively guided by the feudal and bourgeois elements of the population, who are ready, on their part, to compromise with imperialism.

The imperialist war of 1914–18 and the prolonged crisis of capitalism which followed it, particularly in Europe, have weakened the guardianship of the Great Powers over the colonies. On the other hand, these same circumstances have narrowed the economic bases and spheres of influence of world capitalism and have intensified imperialist rivalries over the colonies. In that way the equilibrium of the entire imperialist world system has been disturbed (the struggle for oil, Anglo-French conflict in Asia Minor, the Japanese-American rivalry over the domination of the Pacific, etc.).

It is precisely this weakening of imperialist pressure in the colonies, together with the increasing rivalry between various imperialist groups, that has facilitated the development of native capitalism in the colonial and semicolonial countries . . . Hitherto the capitalists of the Great Powers have striven to isolate the backward countries from world economic intercourse. But the demand for national and economic independence put forward by the nationalist movements in the colonies actually expresses the necessity for these countries to pass through a period of the bourgeois development. The growth of the native productive forces in the colonies, therefore, conflicts irreconcilably with the interests of world imperialism, the essence of which is to monopolize the world's productive forces with a view to excess profits.

2. Conditions of the Struggle

The backwardness of the colonies is reflected in the motley character of the national-revolutionary movements against imperialism, movements which, in their turn, reflect the varying states of transition from feudal and feudal-patriarchal relations to capitalism. This variety of conditions makes its impression upon the ideology of these movements. Inasmuch as capitalism in the colonial countries arises and develops from feudal bases in a hybrid, imperfect, and intermediary form, which gives predominance, above all, to merchant capitalism, the rise of bourgeois democracy from feudal bureaucratic and agrarian elements proceeds often by devious and protracted paths. This represents the chief obstacle for successful mass struggles against imperialist oppression. . . .

For that reason the dominant classes in the colonies and semi-colonies are unable and unwilling to lead the struggle against imperialism as soon as this struggle is converted into a revolutionary mass movement. Only where the feudal-patriarchal system has not decayed to such an extent as to separate completely the native aristocracy from the mass of the people, as among the nomadic and seminomadic peoples, can these upper classes take up the active leadership of the struggle against imperialist violence—for example, in Mesopotamia, Morocco, Mongolia.

In Muslim countries the national movement at first expresses its ideology in the religio-political slogans of Pan-Islamism, which enables diplomats and officials of the Great Powers to exploit the prejudices and ignorance of the masses of the people to combat this movement (the British imperialists' game of Pan-Islamism and Pan-Arabism, the British plan of transferring the Caliphate to India, and the French imperialists' gambling with their "Muslim sympathies"). With the growth and expansion of the national-liberation movement, however, the religio-political slogans of Pan-Islamism are replaced by concrete political demands. The struggle for the separation of the temporal power from the Caliphate which took place in Turkey recently is evidence of this.

The main task of all national-revolutionary movements is to bring about national unity and achieve political independence. How well this task is accomplished depends on how far a given national movement is capable of attracting the toiling masses, breaking off all connection with the reactionary feudal elements, and including in its program the social demands of the masses.

Aware that the will of a nation for political independence under varying historical conditions can be expressed by the most diverse groups, the Communist International supports all national-revolutionary movements against imperialism. It does not forget, however, that only a consistent revolutionary line of policy based on the active support of the masses, and an unreserved break with all who would compromise with imperialism in the interests of class domination, can lead the oppressed masses to victory. On the other hand, the connection between the native bourgeoisie and feudal reactionary elements enables the imperialists to make wide use of feudal anarchy, the rivalry between various leaders and tribes, the antagonism between town and country, the struggle between castes and national religious sects, etc., to disorganize popular movements—for example, in China, Persia, Kurdistan, Mesopotamia.

3. *The Agrarian Question*

In most Eastern countries (India, Persia, Egypt, Syria, Mesopotamia) the agrarian question is of the greatest importance in the struggle for emancipation from the despotism of the Great Powers. In exploiting and impoverishing the peasant majorities in the backward nations, imperialism deprives them of the elementary means of existence, while the low development of industry scattered among a few junctional points in the country makes it impossible for it to absorb the superfluous agrarian population. And yet, the superfluous peasants have no means of emigrating. Thus the peasants who remain on the land are pauperized and converted into serfs. . . .

Only an agrarian revolution aiming at the expropriation of the large landowners can rouse the vast peasant masses destined to have a decisive influence in the struggle against imperialism. The fear of agrarian slogans and the constant modifications of them by the bourgeois nationalists (India, Persia, Egypt) is evidence of the close ties between the native bourgeoisie and the large-scale feudal and feudal-bourgeois landowners and of the ideological and political dependence of the native bourgeoisie upon the latter. The hesitation and wavering of the bourgeoisie must be systematically criticized by the revolutionary elements; the halfway policy of bourgeois leaders must be exposed. It is precisely this kind of policy that hinders the organization and the rallying together of the toiling masses, as has been proved by the bankruptcy of the tactics of non-cooperation in India.

To succeed, the revolutionary movement in the backward countries of the East must be based on the action of the peasant masses. For that reason the revolutionary parties in all Eastern countries must define their agrarian program, which should demand the complete and final abolition of feudalism. To get the peasant masses to participate actively in the struggle for national liberation, it is necessary to come out for a radical change in the principles of land ownership. The bourgeois national parties must be compelled to adopt this revolutionary agrarian program as fully as possible.

4. *The Workers' Movement in the East*

The young workers' movement in the East is a result of the development of native capitalism during the last few years. Hitherto the working class in the East, even its fundamental nucleus, has been in a state of transition, on the path from small handicraft to large capitalist industry. Because the bourgeois national intelligentsia attracts the revolutionary workers into the struggle against imperialism, it assumes leadership in the [existing] embryonic trade union organizations. At first the [political] movement [led by the national bourgeoisie] does not extend beyond the limits of the "common national" interests of bourgeois democracy (e.g., the strikes against imperialist bureaucracy and administration in China and India). Frequently, as shown at the Second Congress of the Communist International, representatives of bourgeois nationalism, exploiting the moral and political authority of Soviet Russia, and playing to the class instincts of the workers, have masqueraded their bourgeois-democratic strivings in "socialist" and "communist" forms, in order to divert— sometimes unconsciously—the embryonic proletarian groups from the direct tasks of class organization (e.g., the Yesil Ordu, in Turkey, which painted Pan-Turkism in communist colors; the "state socialism" advocated by some representatives of the Kuomintang in China).

In spite of this, the trade union and political movement of the working class in the backward countries has made considerable progress in recent years. The formation of independent proletarian class parties in almost all the Eastern countries is a remarkable fact, although the overwhelming majority of these parties must still undergo considerable internal reorganization. . . . The extremely important fact that the Communist International estimated from the start the potential importance of the workers' movement in the East shows the Comintern's concern with the real international unity of the proletariat of the world under the banner of communism. The Second and Second-and-a-Half Internationals, to this very day, have not found support in a single backward country precisely because they play the part of "servants" to European and American imperialism.

5. *The General Tasks of the Communist Parties in the East*

While the bourgeois nationalists consider the workers' movement important merely as a means for securing victory for themselves, the international proletariat regards the workers' young movement of the East from the point of view of its revolutionary future. Under capitalism the backward countries cannot achieve modern technique and culture except at the cost of their own barbarous exploitation and oppression by the capitalists of the Great Powers. Alliance [of the Eastern workers] with the proletariat of advanced countries is imperative, not only to further the common struggle against imperialism, but because only by a victory of the proletariat of the advanced countries can the workers of the East obtain unselfish aid in developing their productive forces. An alliance with the proletariat in the West will lay the path toward an international federation of soviet republics. The soviet system represents for the backward nations the least painful form of transition from primitive conditions of existence to the highest culture of communism, destined to take the place of the capitalist method of production and distribution all over the world. This is proved by the experience in the development of the soviet system in the liberated colonies formerly comprising the Russian Empire. Only a soviet form of administration is able to guarantee the consistent fulfillment of the agrarian peasant revolution. Moreover, the specific conditions of agriculture in certain countries of the East (artificial irrigation), maintained in the past by a sort of collective co-operation on a feudal-patriarchal basis and disrupted [in recent times] by predatory capitalism, demand a state organization that is able to serve public needs systematically. As a consequence of special climatic and historical conditions, the [existing] corporations of petty producers in the East are bound to play an important role in the period of transition [to soviet order].

The objective goal of the colonial revolution goes beyond the limited task of establishing a bourgeois-democratic regime because the colonial revolution cannot be victorious as long as imperialism dominates the world. At the early stage of the national movement the native bourgeoisie and bourgeois intelligentsia take the lead. But when the proletarian and semiproletarian peasant masses join these movements, and their social interests assume prominence, the large-scale bourgeoisie and bourgeois landlords begin to withdraw from them. The young proletariat of the colonies is still confronted by a prolonged struggle over a whole historical epoch, a struggle not only against imperialist exploitation but against its own ruling classes, which try to monopolize the advantages of industrial and cultural development and to keep the toiling masses in their previous "primitive" state.

The present struggle to influence the peasant masses should prepare the native proletariat for political leadership. Only after having accomplished its own preparatory training and that of the closely related social classes will the proletariat be able to advance against bourgeois democracy. . . .

The refusal of the communists in the colonies to participate against imperialist oppression, on the pretext of an alleged "defense" of independent class interests, is opportunism of the worst kind, which can only discredit the proletarian revolution in the East. The attempt to isolate oneself from the immediate and everyday interests of the working class for the sake of "national unity" or "civil peace" with bourgeois democracy is no less harmful. The communist and working class parties in the colonies and semicolonial countries have a twofold task: (1) to struggle for the most radical solutions of the problems of bourgeois-democratic revolution . . . ; (2) to organize the workers and peasants to struggle for their special class interests, and in so doing to capitalize on antagonism in the bourgeois-democratic camp. In putting forward special demands, these parties stimulate and release revolutionary energy which finds no outlet in bourgeois-liberal demands. The working class in the colonies and semicolonial countries must know that only by intensifying and extending the anti-imperialist struggle can it fulfill its role as revolutionary leader, and that to extend the struggle it needs economic and political organization and political training.

The communist parties in the colonial and semicolonial countries in the East, which are still in a more or less embryonic stage, must take part in every movement that gives them access to the masses. At the same time, however, they must conduct an energetic campaign against patriarchal and craft prejudices and bourgeois influences in the workers' unions, in order to protect these embryonic organizations from reformist tendencies, and to convert them into mass fighting organizations. They must exert all their efforts to organize the numerous agricultural laborers and artisans of both sexes on the basis of defending their immediate everyday interests.

6. *The United Anti-Imperialist Front*

While in the West, which is in a period of organized accumulation of strength, the United Workers' Front is appropriate, what the colonial East needs is a United Anti-Imperialist Front. The prospect of a prolonged struggle against world imperialism demands the mobilization of all revolutionary elements. This mobilization is especially necessary since the native ruling classes tend to side with foreign capitalists against the fundamental interests of the masses. Just as the United Workers' Front in the West aims at exposing the social-democratic betrayal of the interests of the proletariat, so the United Anti-Imperialist Front will expose the wavering of certain bourgeois nationalist groups in the East. This slogan will also help to develop the revolutionary will; it will make the class-consciousness of the toiling masses more definite and bring them into the front ranks of the struggle, not only against imperialism, but against all survivals of feudalism.

The workers' movement in the colonies and semicolonial countries must first of all make itself an independent element in the common anti-imperialist front. Only when its complete independence is recognized and maintained can it agree to a tem-

porary alliance with bourgeois democracy. The proletariat must make partial demands, such as for an independent democratic republic, the abolition of all feudal
rights and prejudices, the enfranchisement of women, etc., since the present correlation of forces does not permit it to carry out its soviet program. At the same time,
it must strive to put forward such demands as will assist in establishing the closest
possible contact between the peasantry and semiproletarian masses and the workers'
movement. To explain to the masses of the toilers the necessity for an alliance with
the international proletariat and the soviet republics is imperative. The colonial
revolution can be victorious and defend its gains only in conjunction with the proletarian revolution in the advanced countries.

The danger of collusion between the bourgeois nationalists and one or more rival
imperialist powers is greater in the semicolonial countries (China, Persia) and in
countries striving to secure political independence by exploiting the rivalry between
the imperialists (Turkey) than in the colonies. Such collusion would make for an
irrational division of power between the native ruling classes and the imperialists,
and under the cloak of a formal independence, would leave the country in the same
position of a buffer semicolonial state subordinate to world imperialism.

Although partial and temporary compromises made to gain respite in the revolutionary struggle against imperialism are permissible and inevitable, the working class
must irreconcilably resist every attempt by the native ruling classes to preserve their
privileges by an avowed or tacit division of power with the imperialists. The insistence [by the Eastern workers] on a close alliance with the proletarian Soviet republic indicates the existence of a united anti-imperialist front. . . .

7. The Tasks of the Proletariat on the Pacific Coast

The necessity for the establishment of an anti-imperialist front is dictated also
by the constant growth of imperialist rivalry. Today this rivalry has assumed such
acute forms that a new world war, the arena of which will be the Pacific Ocean, is
inevitable unless an international revolution forestalls it.

The Washington Conference was an attempt to obviate this danger, but, as a
matter of fact, it succeeded only in rendering the antagonisms between the imperialists more profound and acute. . . .

The task of the communist parties in the colonial and semicolonial countries on
the Pacific Coast is to conduct an extensive propaganda campaign to explain to the
masses the oncoming danger, to call upon them to regard Soviet Russia as the bulwark of the oppressed and exploited masses.

In view of the danger of war, the communist parties in the imperialist countries,
America, Japan, England, Australia, and Canada, must not limit themselves merely
to propaganda against war, but must do their utmost to remove all the disrupting
factors from their ranks and to prevent the capitalists from taking advantage of
national and racial antagonisms.

These factors are the immigration question and the question of cheap colored
labor. . . .

The communist parties of America, Canada, and Australia must conduct an
energetic campaign against anti-immigration laws, and must explain to the masses
in these countries that such laws, by arousing national hatreds, end by damaging
their cause.

On the other hand, the capitalists desire to repeal the anti-immigration laws in
order to maintain the free import of cheap labor, and thus force down the wages of
the white workers. This attempted offensive of the capitalists can be successfully
averted only if the immigrant workers are absorbed into the existing white trade
unions. At the same time, the demand must be put forward for raising the wages of
colored workers to the level of white workers. Such tactics will expose the plans

of the capitalists and, at the same time, clearly show the colored workers that the international proletariat has no racial prejudices.

In order to carry out these tactics, the representatives of the revolutionary proletariat of the Pacific countries should gather at a Pan-Pacific Conference to work out ways and means of uniting the proletarians of all races in the Pacific regions.

8. *The Task of the Communist Parties in the Home Countries*

The great importance of the colonial revolutionary movements to the international proletarian revolution makes it necessary to intensify the work in the colonies, particularly by the communist parties of the imperialist countries. French imperialism is counting on suppressing the proletarian revolutionary struggle in France and Europe by using its colonial slaves as the fighting reserve of the counter-revolution.

British and American imperialism continues to divide the workers' movement by maintaining an aristocracy of labor, to which it promises a share in the excess profits obtained by exploiting the colonies.

Communist parties in countries possessing colonies must offer systematic ideological and material assistance to the labor and revolutionary movement in those colonies. They must fight the quasi-socialist colonizing tendencies prevailing among certain categories of well-paid European workers in the colonies. European communist workers in the colonies must strive to rally around themselves the native proletariat and gain its confidence by making concrete economic demands on its behalf (equal pay for white and native workers, protection of labor, workers' insurance, etc.).

The formation of exclusive European communist organizations in the colonies (Egypt, Algeria) is a concealed form of colonialism, and is an aid to imperialist interests. The formation of communist organizations on national lines is a contradiction to the principle of proletarian internationalism. All parties belonging to the Communist International must unceasingly explain to the masses of toilers the importance of the struggle against imperialist domination in the backward countries. For this purpose, the communist parties working in the imperialist countries should set up special colonial commissions of their executive committees. The first thing the Communist International can do for the communist parties of the East is help them set up presses, to publish journals and periodicals in the native languages. Special attention must be given to work among the European labor organizations and among occupational troops in the colonies. The communist parties in the imperialist countries must not let slip a single opportunity for exposing the predatory policy of their imperialist governments and their bourgeois and opportunist parties.

75

The New Orientation of the Political Forces in the East After the Washington Conference[14]

The Washington Conference has produced a parody of peace in the Eastern Hemisphere; and the "Quadruple Alliance" of America, Japan, Great Britain, and France has promised to support it.

Having signed this provisional alliance for a balance of power at the expense of the vital interests of the toilers of China and Korea, and of the Russian population in the Far East, the international capitalists have drawn in their claws for the time being.

[14] V. D. Vilensky (Sibiriakov), "Vashington i Vostochnaia Aziia," *Zhizn Natsional-nostei*, No. 3 (132), January 26, 1922, p. 1.

The armed conflict on the Pacific has been delayed; but the basic factors which are creating this conflict have not been removed. The struggle for Pacific markets and for control over routes in the Pacific remains, and has even been intensified.

America, supported by France, succeeded in destroying the Anglo-Japanese alliance; and then, having intimidated England by her disarmament policy, forced Japan to sign an agreement in which the latter, in return for the recognition of her rights in Manchuria and the Russian Far East, renounced her dominant interests in China, including the withdrawal of her troops.

The plans of the United States are clear. America does not wish to begin the struggle with Japan before forming an alliance directly in the rear of her enemy. There is no doubt that in the event of an American-Japanese conflict such a rear would be provided by the Asiatic mainland, and, in particular, by China. The latter represents a potential and powerful force for those who undertake to organize her. The United States has undertaken that task. . . .

It is clear that the "open door" policy applied by the United States . . . removes Japan as a force which could claim special and exclusive rights in China. The decision concerning the withdrawal of foreign troops from China completely clips the wings of Japan, so that the United States can now be assured that part of its grandiose plan for pushing Japan out of China has been accomplished.

What was the cost of this achievement? It was necessary to pay Japan. Her desire to acquire sparsely populated lands was recognized as legal by Washington, in view of the overpopulation of her home territory. The right of colonization and economic activities in Manchuria and in the "South-Eastern Sector of Siberia and adjoining Korea and Manchuria" was recognized.

This recognition of Japan's right to economic expansion actually sanctions Japan's right to territory she has already seized; and, in the opinion of Washington, it must serve as sufficient compensation to her for her losses in China.

Thus, the American-Japanese dispute ended in a compromise in Washington. The United States of America officially consolidated the "open door" policy in China, which is to secure the Chinese market for American capital; and, as compensation, Japan was given the right to mastery over Manchuria, Korea, and the Far East. The isolation of Japan has been, so to speak, achieved within the "Quadruple Alliance," and at the same time Japan has been given a "base" for her economic expansion. . . .

There is no doubt that the armament and centralization of China by American capital will be carried out cautiously. America wishes to defeat Japan and her capital, if not entirely by the forces of China, at least with the help of these forces, armed by the United States. But American capital will, of course, look back cautiously, with apprehension, at the growth of the "Chinese peril" which the Americans themselves are creating. However, this is the inevitable contradiction of modern imperialism, which always risks having the bayonets it directs at its enemies turned against itself. It is this that Japan most hopes for; and, in this hope, she will probably reorganize her program.

But what does the new orientation bring to the workers, peasants, and the toilers in general in eastern Asia?

The Japanese proletariat and the toilers of Korea and Manchuria are now groaning under the burden of Japanese capital. The toilers of China and Mongolia are being threatened with another capitalist burden—that of American-Chinese capital, which, to the degree that China becomes consolidated, will increase its pressure on the Chinese workers and peasants.

To meet capitalist Japan's plan, American capitalism aims at the creation of a capitalist China. This means the advance of capitalism along the entire front of eastern Asia and the most merciless exploitation of the proletariat of eastern Asia. . . .

Finally, this plan will lead to a terrible imperialist slaughter. Millions of proletarians in the Eastern Hemisphere will be thrown into the struggle to settle the American-Japanese rivalry for Pacific hegemony.

Such are the prospects which have opened before the toilers of eastern Asia since the formation of the "Quadruple Alliance."

What, then, is the way out of this situation? The organization of the scattered toiling forces of eastern Asia, their consolidation . . . in [national] communist parties, and then their unification under the banner of the Third International; the organization of a powerful trade union movement, . . . and also the organization of a direct struggle to improve the lot of the masses under the conditions of developing capitalism. These are the tasks which confront the congress of the revolutionary and communist parties of the Far East.[15]

The consequences of the Washington Conference, their direct threat to the interests of the Far Eastern proletariat, have brought the latter to Moscow under the banner of the Third International, where the Eastern proletariat hopes to solve the gigantic tasks which confront it in organizing its forces for the forthcoming struggle against capital, which is advancing on the shores of the Pacific Ocean.

76

The Growing Tension in the Pacific After the Washington Conference, and the Tasks of the Communist International

[Statement by Radek at the Fourth Congress of the Communist International, November–December, 1922][16]

. . .

Despite the present economic weakness of Soviet Russia, it is a power on whose attitude may depend the final outcome of the struggle for the Pacific. If it joins the anti-Japanese coalition, the immediate effect may be the loss, for a time, of its access to the Pacific. Nonetheless, if Russia were to join the anti-Japanese coalition, Japan would be defeated, for it would be cut off from Europe, and at the same time be blockaded from the sea by the American fleet. Japan would also be compelled to carry on a land war with Russia. Moreover, the moral significance of Russia as a revolutionary center would strengthen the resistance of China to Japan. . . . This decisive role of Russia in a possible anti-Japanese coalition applies equally to America, i.e., to the converse case of Russia's joining an anti-American alliance. The policy of Soviet Russia may prove to be the decisive factor in the war which is imminent in the Far East.

It goes without saying that Soviet Russia bases its policy exclusively on the interests of the toiling masses of Russia and of humanity in general. Its policy knows neither an absolute anti-Japanese nor anti-American orientation. Any increase of its influence in the Far East will depend on the energy with which it defends its eastern frontiers. Its importance will grow from day to day. The solution of the problem of oil, coal, and iron in the Far East, in which Soviet Russia will play one of the main roles, will be a better key to the hearts and pockets of the financial autocrats of America than all diplomatic notes, all appeals to humanity, all references to the one hundred and fifty million Russians who have no desire to harm anybody, but just want to live.

The conditions under which the new groupings are beginning to crystallize do not allow any inference from the international situation other than that power is the most decisive factor under any combination. If Russia succeeds, now that all

---

[15] That is, the Congress of the Toilers of the Far East.
[16] Karl Radek, *Likvidatsiia Versalskogo mira*, pp. 58–59, 62–64.

the civil wars are ended, in averting the outbreak of a new one; if it is able to improve its agriculture, and to create for itself a solid, though limited, industrial base—then its voice in questions of world politics will be more respected than ever before. And if, in addition to this, the policy of Soviet Russia does not deviate from that line which won for it the sympathies of the proletarian masses of the world, including the Eastern peoples who are now awakening to new life, then its moral reputation will contribute further to a consolidation of its prestige. Consequently, the masses of all countries will see that the world has to deal with a new power which is able to regulate its relations even with the capitalist countries by upholding its own interests and at the same time defending the interests of the workers of the world—the interests of the oppressed.

．　　．　　．

No date can be fixed, nor can a categoric answer be given to the question as to whether, or at what time, the existing antagonistic tendencies will become sufficiently acute to result in a new world war. The bourgeoisie of the world have been so shaken by the last world war, the effects of which have not yet been overcome, that they are in mortal fear of a new world war, which is bound to bring the final victory of the world revolution. Therefore, they seek feverishly for new compromises. But split up in hostile capitalist groups, incapable of subordinating their respective special interests to the general interest, they are continually playing the part of Penelope, destroying the cleverly spun nets of agreement which they had but yesterday accomplished. In the hands of small cliques, helpless and brainless diplomats, and ambitious army generals, the capitalist classes of the world are quite incapable of promoting a policy of economic reconstruction. Hence the bankruptcy of the Versailles Treaty, which is leading not to the relaxation of tension and an agreement between the Great Powers making peaceful progress possible, but to new conflicts for the re-partition of the world. [Speaks of the failure of the working class in the European countries to pursue the right course.] . . .

The Communist International is the only section of the international proletariat which carries on an active revolutionary world policy. By daily mobilizing the working masses for the struggle against the economic consequences of the war, by mobilizing these masses for the revolutionary struggle, the Communist International becomes a proletarian factor in world politics. Its policy of supporting Soviet Russia is a part of that struggle which it wages against the imperialist peace, and for the proletarian reconstruction of the world. . . .

Each day which makes the decomposition of international capitalism more evident, contributes likewise to the growth of Soviet Russia, and drives the proletarian masses into the revolution struggle. Soviet Russia and the Communist International thus become factors of increasing power in international politics. They will use this power for the liberation of the international proletariat and its allies, the enslaved peasant masses of the Near and Far East, and also the Negro races. It is difficult to say how long this struggle will last. The Communist International must reckon with the possibility of slow progress in the world revolution, just as Soviet Russia has been reckoning with such a possibility. This implies temporary defeats and retreats. It requires the employment of various means of warfare, and first a thorough preparation for the struggle. It implies continual analysis of the world political changes if the working class is determined to play an increasingly important political role. The struggle of the Communist International is, therefore, closely bound up with all the fluctuations and changes of world politics. The Communist International must consequently impress upon all its members in various countries the need for a uniform approach to different world events, and awaken in them a passionate desire not only to understand and to interpret the world situation, but also to hasten the historic process, that is, to carry out the revolution. . . .

PART III

Soviet Russian Diplomacy and Revolutionary Guidance in Asia, 1924–1927

PART III

A. NEGOTIATIONS AND DIPLOMATIC ACCOMPLISHMENTS

Between 1924 and 1927 Russian Bolshevik leaders carried out a multilevel offensive in Asia. Officially, the Soviet Union made diplomatic overtures to the incumbent governments of China, Japan, and countries of the Near East. Semiofficially, the Communist International made increasing use of such organizations as the Red Trade Union International (Profintern) and the Peasant International (Krestintern). Unofficially, through subversive channels, the Comintern alienated Outer Mongolia from China, gave assistance to Japanese and Chinese communist groups pledged to the overthrow of their respective governments, and encouraged communist movements elsewhere (notably in Indonesia and India). In India Comintern efforts came into conflict with the Gandhiian movement, which tended to weaken the communist appeal.

Soviet policies toward China were particularly complex and devious. Moscow sent an ambassador to the legal Chinese government in Peking. Concurrently, this representative acted as an agent for the Third International, which was aiding Sun Yat-sen's Kuomintang in an effort to overthrow the government in Peking. And while the Third International was supporting the Kuomintang, Chinese Communists began joining that party in order to win contact with the masses and eventually to capture it or oust it from leadership of the Chinese revolution.

In all these maneuvers the Communists committed serious mistakes, but they also achieved significant gains, and their leaders made startling predictions of events to come.

Significance of the Revolutionary Situation in Asia

In 1924, a small book entitled *Kitai i sovetskii souiz* was published in Soviet Russia. Its author, A. A. Ivin, presaged what was to come in Asia in the following words:

In the very center of Asia, where one of the greatest revolutions is taking place, two worlds are facing each other, two cultures: the bourgeois culture which has reached its zenith and is now becoming a thing of the past, and the young socialist culture of the future which is just spreading its powerful wings. It is here in this immense country, which in the course of centuries has been for Asia what Greece and Rome were for Europe, it is here, and in the struggle between the two irreconcilable worlds for predominance over numberless human masses, that the future of our planet is being settled. Whether we are entering the kingdom of socialism, or are passing to a new and higher stage of capitalism—this fateful question will be answered by Asia, and first of all by China during the process of its evolution in the next decade. . . . One can forsee that the time is not far distant when the concrete problems of our

243

policy in Asia, and in China in particular, will have to be studied in a most thorough manner, because it is here, and probably faster than anywhere else, that a sharp conflict is brewing between Soviet Russia and the entire imperialist world.[1]

A year later, no less a figure than Stalin characterized the forces of the revolutionary movement in China as "immeasurable," and then went on to say of them:

They have not yet come into anything like full development. The future will show how vast they are. The rulers of the West and the East who do not notice these forces, who do not make sufficient allowances for their strength, will suffer the consequences when the time comes. We, as a state, cannot but take such forces into consideration.[2]

At the same time, the temporary stabilization which the Communists claimed to observe in the capitalist world during this period would lead, according to their interpretation, to further upheavals and wars, since, as Zinoviev put it, "as capitalism begins to establish itself in the least degree, it immediately contemplates new wars. Every step toward the 'stabilization' of capitalism is at the same time a step toward a new war."[3] These future wars, the Communists calculated, would be directed primarily against the awakening East for the purpose of, as they put it, a new partition and robbery of Asia.

But the Communists proclaimed that a new factor had now changed the balance of forces. They asserted that as a result of the October Revolution in Russia, the Eastern problem had acquired a new meaning and had become "a matter of a bond, of a union between the advanced Russian Soviet Republic and the advanced workers of all other countries grouping around this republic, on one side, and all the national-liberation movements of the oppressed colonial peoples, on the other side, a union aimed at a joint struggle against the world bourgeoisie."[4] With this in mind, Zinoviev announced a new slogan for the Communists: "Proletarians of all countries and oppressed peoples of the world, unite!"[5]

In reviewing the position of the Far and Near Eastern countries that were "enslaved by imperialists," and emphasizing the friendship and disinterestedness of the Soviet Union, Voitinsky stated in 1924 that "the Chinese people are beginning to understand the duel that is being fought on the territory of China between our Red diplomacy and world imperialism." Alluding to the nature of the struggle that the October Revolution had unleashed, he remarked:

All forms of struggle against oppression are being sanctified by the great idea of the October Revolution . . . These forms of struggle are becoming identified more and more with the struggle of the vanguard of the world proletariat, the Union of Soviet [Socialist] Republics.[6]

---

[1] A. A. Ivin, *Kitai i sovetskii soiuz*, pp. 29, 30.

[2] Stalin, *Sochineniia*, VII, 293.

[3] *Pravda*, No. 145, June 28, 1925, p. 3; see Document 113.

[4] M. L. Veltman (M. Pavlovich), *Revoliutsionnyi Vostok*, p. 5; see Document 78.

[5] *Pravda*, No. 145, June 28, 1925, p. 3.

[6] G. N. Voitinsky, "Oktiabrskaia revoliutsiia i kolonialnye i polukolonialnye narody," *Novyi Vostok*, No. 6, 1924, pp. xiv, xv. See also Documents 77 and 80.

The Need for Normal Relations with Existing Eastern Governments

Soviet leaders were fully aware that normal diplomatic relations with Russia's Near and Far Eastern neighbors were necessary to promote security and to facilitate commerce. Accordingly, they continued to carry on diplomatic discussions and enter into treaty relationships with the existing governments in these areas, while simultaneously and unrelentingly carrying on communist agitation and propaganda.

It will be remembered that Soviet diplomats had succeeded in 1921 in negotiating treaties with Persia, Afghanistan, and Turkey, and that combined Soviet diplomatic and military pressures had resulted in the establishment in Outer Mongolia of a government subservient to Moscow. In their approaches to the governments of China and Japan, however, the Communists had been less successful.

Negotiations and Treaties with China

The establishment of diplomatic relations with the Chinese government in Peking was complicated by conflicts over the Chinese Eastern Railway and by Chinese chagrin at being dealt out of the Mongolian settlement, while the establishment of relations with Japan was delayed by Japanese expansionist aims in the Russian Far East, by the presence of Japanese troops in that area, and by conflicts over commercial rights in the Russian Far East and the North Pacific.[7] In spite of these difficulties, settlements were negotiated with the Peking government and the Japanese government in 1924 and 1925 respectively.

In late 1923 Karakhan, a figure prominently identified with the Soviet declarations to China of 1919 and 1920,[8] was sent to China to pick up the negotiations that had been left in suspense after the departure of Ioffe from Peking in January of the same year. Upon arriving in Peking on September 2, 1923, Karakhan made his first statement on Soviet foreign policy, especially in regard to China. He spoke of Soviet Russia's respect for the sovereignty of all nations and Russia's condemnation of territorial or any other expansion. As for China:

There exist only two kinds of policy in regard to China practiced by all foreign powers: one is applied by the Soviet Union, the other by all other states without exception. . . . The European countries wish to see China weak and disunited, just as Turkey has been. Only the U.S.S.R. would like to see China, known as the "sick man," become strong and united, carrying out its national policy.

In regard to Russia's claims in China, Karakhan added: "At the same time the U.S.S.R. does not relinquish its rights in China as long as these rights do not violate the sovereignty and interests of the Chinese people."[9] This remark definitely hinted at Russia's stand on the Chinese Eastern Railway and Boxer indemnity questions. The next day, speaking at a luncheon given him by the Chinese foreign minister, Karakhan referred to his declarations of 1919 and

[7] See our 131–35.

[8] See our pp. 128–29.

[9] Communication from Peking, September 5, *Izvestiia*, No. 201, September 7, 1923, p. 2.

1920; their principles, he said, remained unchanged. But he was optimistic about the coming negotiations:

China and the U.S.S.R. have a common front of struggle, i.e., the struggle of the oppressed nations against world imperialism. The U.S.S.R. has come out victorious from that struggle, but China is still carrying it on. The above fact unites the two peoples. . . . I definitely refuse to favor following upon the steps of America's Chinese policy. . . . The principles laid down by the U.S.S.R. as the basis of its relations with China are those of complete equality.[10]

Shortly thereafter, negotiations between Karakhan and the Chinese foreign minister, Dr. Wang, were started in all seriousness. In these negotiations the Chinese Eastern Railway appeared to be the main point of disagreement, being additionally complicated by the fact that the Russian version of Karakhan's declaration of 1919 did not correspond with the text of the declaration as it reached the Chinese government.

Karakhan's stand was clarified by V. D. Vilensky (Sibiriakov) in *Izvestiia*, in an article entitled "Soviet Property in China." Vilensky spoke of the tremendous importance of the Chinese Eastern Railway for all Far Eastern countries, and the huge amount of money Russia had spent to build it. Reviewing civil war events affecting the Railway, he criticized the Chinese government for attempting to control it by dividing authority over it between China and Russian "White Guard usurpers." He denounced all claims for the Railway made by the Russian-Asiatic Bank and "its French 'protectors,' " claiming that the Railway question "concerns only the U.S.S.R. and the Chinese republic, because the two parties enjoy equal legal rights and are equally interested in the settlement of this problem without the interference of a third party."[11]

What to do with Russia's share of the Boxer indemnity was the second major question in the negotiations in Peking. In his note of November 15, 1923, Karakhan proposed that the Russian share be used for educational purposes in Chinese universities. Since Karakhan believed that this money had been used so far by the Chinese government for other purposes, he addressed a letter of protest (December 13, 1923) to the Chinese foreign minister, which read in part:

The government of the Soviet Union must protest in the most energetic manner against the illegal appropriation by the Chinese government of the right to dispose unilaterally of the Russian share of the Boxer indemnity on the strength of the declarations of the Soviet government. Nor is the Chinese government right when it says that the Soviet republics have renounced the Russian share of the Boxer indemnity unconditionally.

While admitting that the declaration of 1919 did not contain conditions for the use of the money, Karakhan saw no excuse for the Chinese government's ignoring that declaration altogether, to say nothing of "supporting the White Guards with sums paid out of the indemnity."[12]

Finally, there was the problem of Outer Mongolia to be solved. On January 17, 1924, Karakhan clarified it in the following manner:

[10] *Izvestiia*, No. 202, September 8, 1923, p. 2.

[11] V. D. Vilensky (Sibiriakov), "Sovetskoe imushchestvo na kitaiskoi zemle," *Izvestiia*, No. 206, September 13, 1923, p. 1.

[12] A. A. Ivin, *Kitai i sovetskii soiuz*, pp. 128–29.

Our position in the Mongolian question is sufficiently clear and sincere: we consider that Mongolia is part of China and we are ready to withdraw the Red Army detachment stationed at Urga as soon as the Chinese government will give the necessary guarantees for the security of our frontiers.[13]

As the negotiations dragged on, the status of the Chinese Eastern Railway remained the most troublesome point, since Chinese authorities insisted on the correctness of their own text. To clarify the Soviet position, Karakhan stated in a letter to Wang on November 30, 1923: "Never and nowhere could I have said that all rights over the Chinese Eastern Railway belong to China."

Making it clear that Russia held a right of property over the Railway as a commercial enterprise, Karakhan nevertheless was prepared to discuss the Chinese proposal for the transfer of all rights in the Railway to China. "I can confirm," Karakhan went on to say, "what was said four years ago, namely, that Chinese sovereignty over the territory of the Chinese Eastern Railway is absolutely recognized by us, and that we shall not insist on any privileges which were enjoyed by the tsarist government and which are still enjoyed by other foreign powers in this zone."[14]

Along with his note, Karakhan sent the copies of his supposedly original Soviet declarations of 1919 and 1920. On January 17, 1924, Karakhan referred once more to Chinese insistence on the correctness of the Chinese copy of the declaration of 1919: "I do not know with what purpose the Peking government continues in official correspondence to insist on its favorite but wrong text of the declaration of 1919." He also reiterated his former stand that the Chinese government could hardly have a right to claim the promises given in that declaration. The Chinese government, he said, "did not accept the declaration of 1919 and rejected our offer in a most trenchant manner, namely, by intervention aimed at the overthrow of the Soviet government and continued support of White Guardist armies and organizations." Now, he said, the Chinese government was trying, five years later, to insist on "rights and claims based on a declaration it had once rejected."[15]

In spite of disagreements and bickering between the two negotiators in Peking, a preliminary understanding between Soviet Russia and China was signed on March 14, 1924, and after some further complications[16] there followed the signing on May 31 of the formal agreement known as the *Agreement on General Principles for the Settlement of General Problems, with Six Declarations,* and an appended *Agreement for the Provisional Management of the Chinese Eastern Railway, with Declaration.*

By the terms of the *Agreement on General Principles,* normal diplomatic and consular relations between Russia and China were restored; all treaties between the tsarist government and China, as well as all treaties between the tsarist government and other governments relative to China, were abrogated; both the Russian and the Chinese governments agreed to refrain from entering into trea-

---

13 *Ibid.,* p. 120.
14 *Ibid.,* pp. 114–15.
15 *Ibid.,* pp. 117–18.
16 For details see *The China Year Book, 1924–1925,* pp. 853–90; also R. T. Pollard, *China's Foreign Relations, 1917–1931,* pp. 186–87; Aitchen K. Wu, *China and the Soviet Union: A Study of Sino-Soviet Relations,* pp. 151–57 (cited hereafter as A. K. Wu, *China and the Soviet Union*).

ties with any third power prejudicial to each other's interests; and the U.S.S.R. renounced all Russian concessions in China, the Russian share in the Boxer indemnity, and Russian extraterritorial rights in China.

The security clause usual to Soviet treaties of the period was included, as was a prohibition against propaganda directed against the political and social systems of either party. On paper, the U.S.S.R. made a concession on the Mongolian question by recognizing Outer Mongolia as being an integral part of Chinese territory and by stating that Soviet troops would be withdrawn from that area. In practice, however, Outer Mongolia remained a virtual appendage of the Soviet Union.

The agreement also provided that within one month a conference should be convened to work out details for the withdrawal of Soviet troops from Mongolia, to re-demarcate boundaries between China and Russia, to settle problems relating to navigation of rivers and other bodies of water, to discuss claims for compensation for losses, and to draw up a commercial treaty. Most important, this projected conference was to work out a permanent settlement of the question of the management and operation of the Chinese Eastern Railway.

The *Agreement on General Principles,* besides referring the Railway settlement to a future conference as mentioned above, declared the Railway to be purely a commercial enterprise, provided for its redemption by the Chinese government with Chinese capital, and placed all Railway matters other than those concerning business operations under the jurisdiction of Chinese authorities.

According to the *Agreement for the Provisional Management of the Chinese Eastern Railway,* the Railway was to be managed—until such time as detailed arrangements were worked out—by a Soviet general manager and a ten-man board of directors (five from each country, with a Chinese president and a Soviet vice-president). Other positions on the line were to be equally divided between Chinese and Soviet citizens.[17]

The Sino-Soviet conference, which was to be called within a month of the Sino-Soviet agreement of May 31, 1924, was not held until August 27, 1925, just before the departure of Karakhan for Moscow. Negotiations were then put off until Karakhan's return from Moscow in December. They were duly resumed on December 1, 1925, but soon stalled again in the dispute over the Chinese Eastern Railway. Apparently Karakhan's interest in the continuation of the conference had considerably diminished, and consequently the conference, although it held a few more sessions, was never brought to any fruitful end.[18]

Meanwhile the above-mentioned agreement for the provisional management of the Railway could not immediately be put into effect because the three Manchurian provinces of North China through which the line passed were controlled by Marshal Chang Tso-lin. The Marshal's so-called Autonomous Government of the Three Eastern Provinces of the Republic of China, known as the Mukden government, at that time did not recognize the authority of the weak and impo-

[17] Texts of the above agreements appear in Shapiro, I, pp. 242–44. A touch of propaganda was added by Karakhan to the signing of the above treaties when he said to the students of Peking University on June 7, 1924: "We have driven imperialism out of our country, but only then shall we be satisfied when there will not be a single oppressed nation in the world. When you will be strong enough to start the battle against imperialism, which is oppressing your country, you may be assured of the sympathies with your cause of the people of the Union." (*The China Year Book, 1928,* pp. 1319–20.)

[18] For details see Pollard, *China's Foreign Relations, 1917–1931,* pp. 198–204.

tent Peking government. It was therefore necessary for the Soviet government to negotiate a separate treaty with the Mukden government.

This agreement, signed on September 20, 1924, and known as the Mukden agreement, resembled closely the agreement signed by Karakhan with the Peking government, but had additional clauses concerning the railroad, namely that

(1) the period for the retrocession of the Chinese Eastern Railway was reduced from eighty to sixty years; (2) a commission was to be appointed by the two governments to settle the question of the disposition of the railway profits; (3) affairs concerning the Chinese Eastern Railway were to be settled by the Soviet-Mukden Conference.[19]

In addition, the agreement stated that all Russian employees of the preceding Russian regime still in the employ of the Chinese Eastern Railway were to be dismissed and that the old Russian consulates in the three Manchurian provinces were to be handed over to the Chinese administration.[20]

In spite of this agreement, Soviet relations with the Mukden government were more strained than cordial, mainly on account of the disagreements over the Chinese Eastern Railway. Although a new board of directors of the Railway was constituted in accordance with the terms of the treaties with Peking and Mukden, a bitter dispute flared up within the year of the signing of the agreements when local Chinese authorities, claiming that land jurisdiction should be divorced from the dominion of the Railway administration, closed the land offices.

In retaliation, and as a protest against the use of the line by Chinese troops without prepayment of fares, the Soviet general manager, Ivanov, ordered the complete suspension of traffic along the line. The Chinese thereupon arrested him on January 21, 1926. On the next day Karakhan sent a strongly worded protest to the Peking and Mukden governments.[21] Moscow, likewise, sent an immediate protest. "We expect the Chinese government," Chicherin stated in his ultimatum, "to take the steps necessary to settle the matter in question by peaceful means and to agree to the investigation of the mutual violations of the agreement on the Chinese Eastern Railway. We demand that complete order be restored on the Chinese Eastern Railway within three days, the agreement reinstated, and Ivanov released." Should the Chinese government be for some reason unable to secure a peaceful settlement, "the Soviet government requests the Chinese government to permit the U.S.S.R. to ensure order by its own means."[22]

For a short time, feeling ran high in Manchuria, but on January 24 a compromise was worked out. According to the agreement reached, Ivanov and other Soviet workers arrested with him by the Manchurian authorities were to be released; normal Railway communication was to be restored; the transportation of armaments and of security troops was to be carried on in accordance with the

19 A. K. Wu, *China and the Soviet Union*, p. 174.

20 For complete text, see Shapiro, I, 279–81. The Peking government at first protested this agreement, but later acquiesced. For Soviet Russia's appreciation of the Sino-Soviet agreements, see Documents 79 and 80.

21 A. K. Wu, *China and the Soviet Union*, pp. 178–79.

22 *Pravda*, No. 19, January 24, 1926, p. 1; see Degras, II, 82.

already existing regulations; and the transportation of Chinese troops was to be paid for out of China's share of the profits from the Railway.[23]

On February 5, 1926, *Izvestiia* published Chicherin's analysis of the Chinese Eastern Railway dispute, accusing the enemies of the Soviet Union of instigating the recent disagreement:

During the past year and a half, the system of joint commercial exploitation of the Chinese Eastern Railway by the Soviet Republic and China has had excellent results; its revenues have increased and its technical condition has been improved. The successful operation of this system has naturally aroused among the enemies of the Soviet Republic and of the Chinese people the desire to spoil relations between the two and disrupt their joint work which was running smoothly. A considerable number of White Guards, remaining in Manchuria after the defeat of Kolchak and his accomplices, tried in every way to create difficulties in the operation of the Railway. . . . The last conflict broke out because enemies of the U.S.S.R. succeeded in persuading some local representatives of the Chinese military authorities, who had fallen under influences hostile to us, to commit illegal acts.[24]

Ivanov was duly released by the Mukden authorities, and in April of the same year a representative of the Moscow government, by the name of Shcherbakov, arrived in Mukden to seek an audience with Chang Tso-lin and to try to improve relations between Moscow and the Mukden government. A conference between the two parties opened on May 21, during which the Soviet representative made several proposals and the Mukden government rejected them all.

The Mukden government stuck to its earlier insistence on the recall of Karakhan. The Soviet representative proposed that this request be withdrawn, that all White Guards be dismissed from the employ of the Mukden government and army, and that only Soviet citizens be engaged as advisers for all police, municipal, and other administrative offices. The conference finally bogged down without arriving at any definite result.[25] Soviet interests definitely shifted toward South China and the Southern Chinese government headed by the Kuomintang.

Negotiations and the Treaty with Japan

When A. A. Ioffe left Peking in January 1923, having negotiated fruitlessly with the Peking government, he stopped off at Shanghai. While there, he received an invitation from Viscount Goto, the mayor of Tokyo, to come to Japan for the medical treatment he needed, and to open unofficial negotiations for the establishment of normal diplomatic and commercial relations between their two countries. Ioffe accepted the offer.

On June 5, 1923, *Izvestiia* published a communiqué from Tokyo, dated June 3, to the effect that the Japanese government had now decided to open

[23] Summaries of this agreement are given in *Izvestiia*, No. 21, January 27, 1926, p. 1; Degras, II, 82–83; and A. K. Wu, *China and the Soviet Union*, p. 179.

[24] *Izvestiia*, No. 29, February 5, 1926, p. 1. Text appears in Degras, II, 83–86. A number of officers of the former Imperial Russian Army who had fought against the Soviets in the civil war were engaged later by Chang Tso-lin to train Chinese armed forces. In addition, Russian civilians acted as advisers to the Chinese military authorities. For an interesting account of the service of these Russians in Chang Tso-lin's army, see V. A. Zubets, "Na sluzhbe v kitaiskoi armii" (typescript in the Hoover Library).

[25] For details, see A. K. Wu, *China and the Soviet Union*, pp. 180–81.

official negotiations with Soviet Russia. Vilensky (Sibiriakov) discussed this communiqué in the same issue of *Izvestiia* in an article entitled "On the Eve of the Russo-Japanese Negotiations." "After a long and stubborn struggle within Japanese political circles over the Russian question," Vilensky wrote, "a moment has finally arrived when Japanese government circles are inclined to make a decision on the opening of Russo-Japanese negotiations." This decision, so he explained, was in conflict with the current Russian policies of Great Britain, which was actually on the point of breaking relations with Russia and instituting a new blockade.[26]

The Japanese decision to disagree with Great Britain, Vilensky believed, marked "first of all a far advanced disintegration of the 'League of Nations.'" On the other hand, it could also mean that the Japanese diplomats wished "to make a better bargain with Soviet Russia, or Britain, or both." As for Soviet Russia, its peace policy had been long evident; its diplomats had been trying for several years to re-establish normal relations with Japan. Vilensky's article, which was apparently designed for foreign consumption, concluded that "if the Japanese people and government are now coming to see the need of Russo-Japanese agreement, we, on our part, have no objection to it."[27]

The negotiations between Ioffe and the Japanese government began with a banquet held in Ioffe's honor, at which over 600 persons were present. But within two months—as in the case of negotiations with China—the Russo-Japanese conversations reached an impasse. On August 4, 1923, A. Lozovsky (S. A. Dridzo) spoke in *Pravda* of the "negative results of the negotiations." It was evident, Lozovsky affirmed, that American businessmen were competing with Japan for the Russian markets, and that they hoped to reach Russia with their goods by way of Siberia. The American plan was evident in spite of the official aloofness from Russia on the part of American Presidents Wilson and Harding.[28]

"The American politicians, financiers, and senators," Lozovsky continued in his article, "seek an agreement with us before we sign the agreement with Japan." Lozovsky was surprised, therefore, at the lack of foresight shown by Japan in making exorbitant demands on Soviet Russia, such as to accept responsibility for the Nikolaevsk incident, to recognize Russian debts, to restore

---

[26] This must refer to the strained Soviet-British relations following Lord Curzon's ultimatum of May 1923 to the Soviet government. See the companion volume, *Soviet Russia and the West, 1920–1927*.

[27] *Izvestiia*, No. 122, June 5, 1923, p. 1.

[28] Lozovsky must have been referring to the concessions obtained from Soviet Russia by Harry Ford Sinclair for the exploitation of Northern Sakhalin, although actually it was still occupied by Japanese troops; to the concession given to Charles H. Smith for the development of the Amur River Basin; and to the offer made by Maxim Litvinov, Soviet Assistant Commissar of Foreign Affairs, to the banking firm of Dillon, Read and Company to run Russia's share in the Chinese Eastern Railway. In addition, Senator William Henry King of Utah, Senator Edwin Fremont Ladd of North Dakota, and Congressman James A. Frear of Wisconsin visited Soviet Russia in the summer 1923. For Senator King's account of this visit, see *Congressional Record Proceedings and Debates of the First Session of the Sixty-eighth Congress of the United States of America*, Vol. 65, Part VII, pp. 7019–64. Soviet accounts of this visit appear in *Izvestiia*, No. 175, August 5, 1923, p. 1, and in *Pravda*, No. 175, August 5, 1923, p. 3. See also W. A. Williams, *American-Russian Relations*, pp. 189–90. For later (1925) American efforts to obtain concessions in Soviet Russia, including W. Averell Harriman's attempt to rationalize manganese production in the Caucasus, see Williams, pp. 212–13.

property to Japanese nationals in Russia, and finally to keep in force the Portsmouth Treaty of September 5, 1905. These claims were outrageous when, as Lozovsky put it, Japan herself "in the course of the last few years has been bayoneting Soviet Russia."[29]

Apparently Soviet diplomats were bent on adhering to the policy outlined by Lenin on December 21, 1920, when he spoke on concessions granted to foreign powers by the Decree of November 23, 1920. Lenin advocated at that time taking advantage of the differences between the contending powers, such as the United States and Japan, and trying to prevent an agreement between them. Referring to the concession given to the United States in Kamchatka, Lenin added:

At this moment we are unable to fight Japan. We are giving America a territory which we ourselves cannot utilize because of our absolute lack of naval and armed forces. As a consequence, we increase the animosity between American imperialists on one hand and the Japanese imperialists and bourgeoisie on the other hand.[30]

After negotiations with Japan were suspended in August 1923, Chicherin, taking advantage of President Coolidge's reference to Russia in his message to Congress on December 6, 1923, hastened to address the President in a telegram of December 16, stating that "the Soviet government has always wished to establish friendly relations with the United States of America based on mutual confidence." Chicherin then mentioned previous Russian efforts to establish such relations, as well as the President's message to Congress, saying that "the Soviet government wishes to inform you of its complete readiness to discuss jointly with your government all problems raised in your message, while the basis of such negotiations should be the principle of mutual noninterference in each other's affairs." Chicherin ended his message by saying that the Soviet government "was prepared to do everything that it could consistent with the dignity and interests of the U.S.S.R. in order to reach the desired goal, namely, to establish friendly relations with the United States of America."[31]

Meanwhile, negotiations with the Japanese, which had been interrupted in Tokyo in August 1923, were resumed in September in Peking, this time between Karakhan and the Japanese ambassador to China, Ioshisawa. New difficulties and interruptions followed, but finally on January 20, 1925, a *Convention Embodying Basic Rules of the Relations Between the Two Powers* was signed.

According to B. Semenov, the change in the intransigent Japanese attitude was due in part to the worsening situation in the Pacific, "which had placed Japan against a powerful bloc of Britain and America." This difficulty, intensified by the latest Chinese events, had forced Japan "to feverishly seek the way out of the existing situation, or if not exactly the way out, at least a temporary security for the near future. The quickest possible agreement with the U.S.S.R. provided such a solution."[32]

[29] *Izvestiia*, No. 174, August 4, 1923, p. 1.
[30] Lenin, *Sochineniia*, XXVI, 8; for further details on Soviet concessions, see the companion volume, *Soviet Russia and the West, 1920–1927*.
[31] Kliuchnikov and Sabanin, III, 294. The above overture was declined by the American government.
[32] B. Semenov, "Iapono-sovetskoe soglashenie," *Novyi Vostok*, No. 7, 1925, p. 26. For Ioffe's account of the negotiations with Japan, see A. A. Ioffe, "SSSR i Dalnii Vostok," *Mirovoe Khoziaistvo i Mirovaia Politika*, No. 10–11, 1927, pp. 26–47.

The agreement with Japan established normal diplomatic and consular relations between the two governments; set forth a Soviet acknowledgment that the Treaty of Portsmouth of September 5, 1905, by which Japan had attained Great Power status, would remain in force; provided that all other treaties between the Japanese government and previous Russian governments were to be revised at a subsequent conference; and called for revision of the Fishery Convention of 1907. The agreement also called for a treaty to regulate trade and shipping which would (1) allow citizens of each country the right to enter the other and move about freely on its territory; (2) allow private ownership and freedom to engage in trade, shipping, mining, and other peaceful pursuits to such citizens; (3) guarantee against discriminatory practices; and (4) grant most-favored-nation privileges. Further, the Soviet government agreed to grant "Japanese subjects, companies, and associations concessions for the exploitation of minerals, forests, and other natural resources in all the territories of the Union of Soviet Socialist Republics."

Also included in the treaty with Japan was a security clause providing that

the High Contracting Parties solemnly affirm their desire and intention to live in peace and amity with each other, scrupulously to respect the undoubted right of a state to order its own life within its own jurisdiction in its own way, to refrain and to restrain all persons in any governmental service for them, and all organizations in receipt of any financial assistance from them, from any overt or covert action liable in any way whatsoever to endanger the order and security in any part of the territories of Japan or the Union of Soviet Socialist Republics.

This clause then went on to state that

it is further agreed that neither Contracting Party will permit on the territory under its jurisdiction the presence of:
  (a) Organizations or groups claiming to be the government for any part of the territories of the other Party, or
  (b) Alien subjects or citizens who may be found to be actually carrying on political activities for such organizations or groups.[33]

In Moscow, the signing of the agreements with China and Japan was the signal for jubilation from speaker's rostrum and printed page. The establishment of diplomatic relations with the governments of these countries was hailed as a great diplomatic triumph for Soviet power. According to Chicherin, the treaty with China was "a big step on the road to liberating the colonial and semicolonial peoples from political subordination to the Great Powers," and he went on to declare that

the appearance of the Soviet Union on the coast of the Pacific Ocean as a power friendly to China immediately raises the question of the world importance of the basin of the Pacific Ocean. . . . It is the ocean of the future. The outlook which the resumption of normal, that is to say, friendly relations between the U.S.S.R. and China opens will only gradually become clear to us. Already today we can trace in general outline the enormous importance of this event.[34]

With regard to the treaty with Japan, Chicherin was even more enthusiastic, describing it as "not only the beginning of a period of friendly relations between

---

[33] Shapiro, I, 284; full text *ibid.*, pp. 283–85.
[34] *Pravda*, No. 123, June 1, 1924; see Document 79.

К советско-японскому соглашению.

ДЯДЯ СЭМ ОСТАЛСЯ САМ...

"SOVIET-JAPANESE AGREEMENT." The legend beneath
reads "Diadia Sam ostalsia sam" ("Uncle Sam Is Left Alone"), a
pun in Russian. Izvestiia, No. 20, January 25, 1925.

the peoples of the U.S.S.R. and Japan," but also "a turning point, a complete change in Far Eastern politics and in world politics in general." He further declared that as a result of the signing of the treaty the Russian Far East had entered upon a period of "peaceful development and friendly relations with its neighbors," which for Japan meant the "existence of a friendly power in the rear in case she is threatened by [diplomatic] complications."[35]

At the same time, Karakhan termed the treaty with Japan "a warning to America, which, by refraining from concluding a treaty with us, only makes her own position worse," and went on to declare that "reports received from America go to prove that America is beginning to perceive all the disadvantages of not having normal diplomatic relations with us."[36]

Soviet Infiltration of Outer Mongolia

No such protracted diplomatic bickering as had preceded the successful consummation of the Sino-Soviet and Soviet-Japanese negotiations occurred between Outer Mongolia and Soviet Russia, the former having succumbed almost immediately to the control of the latter. In fact, a pro-Soviet government was established there with Red Army aid as early as 1921, and thus Outer Mongolia became one of the first satellites of Soviet Russia. Moscow's position there was further strengthened by the death of the Living Buddha in 1924, and the consequent abolishment of the office of Hutukhtu. Later that same year Outer Mongolia was proclaimed a republic, this being officially confirmed in the constitution adopted at the first Great Huruldan (Assembly) which took place in November.[37]

Soviet infiltration of Mongolia was carried on through three different channels: (1) by official representatives of the Soviet government in Mongolia; (2) by representatives of the Comintern; and (3) by Buriat-Mongol citizens of the U.S.S.R. who had racial and religious affinity with the people of Mongolia and lived on the territory adjoining them.[38]

So close were the relations between Bolshevik agents and the Mongolian people that the representatives of the Soviet Russian government and of the Comintern were spokesmen at the congresses of the Mongolian People's Republic and the Mongolian People's Party.

Attending the Third Congress of the Mongolian People's Party, August

[35] *Pravda*, No. 18, January 22, 1925, p. 3; see Document 81. Text also appears in Degras, II, 5–7.

[36] *Izvestiia*, No. 20, January 25, 1925, p. 1; see Document 82.

[37] The text of the Mongolian constitution, which in many ways resembles the constitution adopted by the Fifth Congress of Soviets of the R.S.F.S.R. in July 1918, appears in *Novaia Mongoliia . . . Protokoly I-go Velikogo Khuruldana Mongolskoi Narodnoi Respubliki*, pp. 3–4.

[38] After Ataman Semenov's forces and later those of Baron von Ungern-Sternberg, which included in their ranks a number of Buriats, were defeated, the pro-Soviet committee of the Buriat Communists was formed in eastern Siberia. Later two Buriat regions simultaneously were proclaimed autonomous oblasts. On January 9, 1922, a decree of the All-Russian Central Executive Committee established a Mongol-Buriat Autonomous Oblast within the R.S.F.S.R. In the same year a Buriat-Mongol Autonomous Oblast was established within the Far Eastern Republic. The incorporation of the Far Eastern Republic into the R.S.F.S.R. on November 15, 1922, was soon followed by the unification of the two above Buriat oblasts (May 30, 1923) into the Buriat-Mongol Autonomous S.S.R., with Verkhneudinsk (now Ulan Ude) as its capital.

4–31, 1924, Soviet ambassador Vasilev spoke in a paternal fashion to the Mongol audience:

We may say without exaggeration that the international respect which the U.S.S.R. enjoys reflects upon you also. It is no mere words to say that you have been able to gather here only because the Communist International made it possible for you to work freely. Therefore, remember well: the stronger the U.S.S.R. is, the stronger you will be.[39]

Vasilev pointed out also the importance of party work:

You have made in this respect a great step forward; you have now come close to the Comintern, an organization which settles all the problems of the world. You have won many rights for yourselves, but these rights impose on you obligations also. You must conduct your work in such a manner as to be worthy of the organization with which you wish to march forward shoulder to shoulder.[40]

The docility of the Mongol commoners who took part in this congress[41] can best be illustrated by the telegram the congress decided to send to the Executive Committee of the Communist International:

On the day of the opening of its session, the Third Congress of the Mongolian People's Revolutionary Party sends its hearty greetings to the leaders of the toilers of the world, and the only defenders of the oppressed peoples of the world— to the Communist International. The Congress vows that the party will always remain true to the ideas of the Comintern, and will await the signal to participate in labor's last battle against violence and oppression.[42]

The Mongols soon had occasion to feel the strength of their ties with the Comintern. While the Third Congress of the party was still in session, its chairman (also assistant prime minister), the commander-in-chief of the Mongolian republic, Danzan, was accused of treason and of secret dealings with the Chinese by other members of the party. He and his alleged confederate, Bavasan, were arrested and put to death.

Amid general excitement and the disruption of the sessions of the congress, the Soviet ambassador took the platform once again:

Do not be apprehensive. Such incidents occur not only in Mongolia, but in Russia also. You have done absolutely correctly. We are all against the shedding of blood, but sometimes it so happens that it is necessary to shed a little blood in order to prevent a greater shedding of blood. I think that what you have done is correct, and will help the consolidation of the alliance between Mongolia and the U.S.S.R. Your decision is justifiable in all respects. Let then your minds be at rest. Tell your electors to fix their eyes on the North since it is only the North [i.e., Russia] that can bring you salvation [from the attempts on your independence by China and other powers].[43]

The period between the Third (1924) and the Fourth (1925) congresses of the Mongolian People's Party was marked by party purges much like those that were to follow later in Soviet Russia and elsewhere. How guilty the purged

[39] *Tretii sezd Mongolskoi Narodnoi Partii,* p. 5.
[40] *Ibid.,* p. 6.
[41] Out of the 108 delegates, 88 were commoners.
[42] *Ibid.,* p. 15.
[43] *Ibid.,* p. 225.

ones were it is hard to say; it seems clear, however, that they were those who had opposed the ever-increasing communist influence in their country. By September–October, 1925, the 6,200 members of the party had been reduced to 3,200.[44]

Side by side with the Communist guardianship of the Mongolian People's Party and the Mongolian government, Soviet representatives worked for closer diplomatic bonds with Mongolia and for control over the development of the new Mongolian state.

When Ambassador Vasilev arrived in Mongolia in 1924, he brought with him drafts of two treaties, one projecting a Russo-Mongolian Bank, the other a Russo-Mongolian convention, both of which, according to Vasilev, would be beneficial to both countries. The two treaties were soon ratified by the Mongolian and Russian governments.[45] A third agreement, a telegraphic convention, was signed on October 3, 1924.[46]

But the façade of Mongolia's independence from Moscow's control continued to be maintained. Addressing the Fourth Congress of the Mongolian People's Party, September 24, 1925, its chairman, Damba Dorji, declared:

It is no secret to anyone that the militarists try to prove that the Bolsheviks have allegedly taken possession of Mongolia. This is a lie. The militarists wish to make us quarrel and to separate us, and that is all.[47]

A more subtle reference to the nature of Soviet influence on Mongolia was provided by a Soviet writer in an analysis of the congress: "A hundred young Mongols who are now studying in Moscow, Leningrad, and Verkhneudinsk are destined to play a tremendous role in the growth of political consciousness of the Mongols."[48]

In encouraging Mongolian independence, leaders in Moscow were aware at the same time of the complicated problem of Russo-Mongol-Chinese relations. They found it necessary, therefore, to stress in their talk with the Mongols the necessity of "falling back to the second line of defense"—in other words, making the best of the existing political entanglement of the three countries, and abstaining temporarily from insisting on Mongolia's complete independence from China.[49]

Tannu-Tuva Republic

A few words must be recorded about the Uriankhai region, which in the twenties became the allegedly independent Tannu-Tuva or Tuvinian Republic.

[44] I. I. Genking, "Dva sezda Mongolskoi Narodnoi Partii," *Novyi Vostok*, No. 12, 1926, p. 185. When the party was organized in 1921 on Russian territory (Kiakhta) adjacent to Mongolia, it had only twenty-three members.

[45] For details on the Mongolian finances, see L. Zolotarev, "Denezhnaia reforma v Mongolii," *Novyi Vostok*, No. 13–14, 1926, pp. 232–36.

[46] Text appears in Shapiro, I, 281. Allegedly another agreement was also signed by which the U.S.S.R. undertook to build a line between Urga and the Chinese border, with Russia paying two-thirds and Mongolia one-third. Once the line was completed, its protection was to be entrusted to the Soviet Russian government, which was also to decide on railway officials. In fifty years, Mongolia had the right to redeem this railway. The text of this agreement appears in *The China Year Book, 1926–1927,* p. 800, but does not appear in any Russian source. Its authenticity, therefore, cannot be fully verified.

[47] *Chetvertyi sezd Mongolskoi Narodno-Revoliutsionnoi Partii,* p. 14.

[48] Genkin, *Novyi Vostok,* No. 12, 1926, p. 185.

[49] An interview given by Soviet ambassador Vasilev to a newspaper correspondent, printed in the *North China Herald,* March 15, 1924, p. 402. See also Document 83.

This region is situated in Central Asia bordering on Russia to the north and on Outer Mongolia to the southwest, south, and east. The size of the territory is about 170,000 sq. km., or that of Belgium, Portugal, and Switzerland taken together; its population was 58,117 in 1926 and about 65,000 in 1949.

In the past this territory had been considered as belonging to China. It was nominally independent from 1911 to 1914, in which year it was accepted under Russian protectorate, allegedly by request of the inhabitants. Thereafter Russian influence and the authority of Russian government officials in that region became considerable. According to a Soviet writer, the number of Russian settlers increased 300 per cent in the period 1912–18.[50]

The establishment of the Soviet government in Russia had its repercussion in the Uriankhai region also. On March 8, 1918, a congress called by the Russian settlers elected a regional soviet of workers', peasants', and soldiers' deputies. This congress also adopted a declaration addressed to the natives of the Uriankhai region, which stated among other things:

Soviet authority assures you, citizens of Uriankhai, that it will not interfere in the domestic affairs of the Uriankhai natives, allowing them complete freedom of local self-determination and freedom of conscience. The more detailed directives concerning the relations of the new people's authority to the Uriankhai natives will be given by the central Soviet government.[51]

The immediate reaction of the Uriankhai natives to the above declaration is not clear, but three years later (August 13–16, 1921) the first congress of the representatives of the Uriankhai *hoshun*[52] was held. A special eighteen-person delegation from Soviet Russia represented the Siberian Revolutionary Committee at the congress; and a special mission of three persons from the Mongolian People's Revolutionary Government also attended. The sessions were opened by the representative of the Siberian Revolutionary Committee, I. G. Safianov; they closed with decisions for establishing an independent state and confirming the provisional constitution of the new republic. In December, the first Great Huruldan proclaimed the former Uriankhai region (now called Tannu-Tuva) a new republic, with supreme authority vested in the Great Huruldan (and between its sessions in the Small Huruldan) as described in the constitution of Tannu-Tuva Republic. This constitution was finally confirmed by the Fourth Great Huruldan on November 24, 1926.[53]

In late September, 1921, an official declaration of the Soviet government signed by Chicherin outlined Soviet policy toward Tannu-Tuva:

Eight years ago several Tannu-Tuva (Uriankhai) hoshuns, deceived by crafty tsarist officials, declared their desire of the Russian Tsar's protectorship. The tsarist government made use of this expressed wish to assume despotic rule over all Tannu-Tuva (Uriankhai) people and illegally declared Tannu-Tuva (Uriankhai) its own land.

At the present time, when the workers and peasant masses of Russia have overthrown the despotic tsarist government and have removed tsarist officials, the Rus-

---

[50] N. A. Shoizhelov (Natsov), *Tuvinskaia narodnaia respublika; materialy i dokumenty po istorii natsionalno-revoliutsionnogo dvizheniia tuvinskikh skotovodov*, p. 31. (Cited hereafter as Shoizhelov, *Tuvinskaia narodnaia respublika.*)

[51] *Ibid.*, pp. 35–36.

[52] A tribal territorial unit.

[53] For the complete text, see Shoizhelov, *Tuvinskaia narodnaia respublika*, pp. 95–100.

sian Workers' and Peasants' Government, which expresses the will of the toilers, most solemnly declares that henceforth it does not consider the Tannu-Tuva (Uriankhai) region its own territory, and has no designs on it whatsoever.[54]

A Tuvinian People's Revolutionary Party was founded on October 29, 1921, by active Tuvinians, and issued its first manifesto to the Tuvinian people on December 20, 1921. At its second meeting, February 28–March 1, 1922, this party reorganized its organization bureau into a central committee. This meeting is considered to be the first congress of the Tuvinian People's Revolutionary Party. As in Outer Mongolia, a youth group, the Tuvinian Revolutionary Union of Youth, soon came into existence (1924).

The establishment of the independent Tannu-Tuva Republic, with Soviet blessings and encouragement, antagonized certain native Tuvinians, who in 1924 expressed a desire to join Outer Mongolia. This proposal found approval among some Outer Mongolians,[55] but was not acceptable to the Soviet government. The move was interpreted as a revolt of feudal lords and lamas against the existing legal status of the Tannu-Tuva Republic, and Soviet troops were sent to suppress it. When the inclination of Tuvinians to join Mongolia was discussed at the third congress of the Mongolian People's Party, the Soviet government acceded to the sending of a mixed Mongolian-Russian Commission to settle the question. Russia's point of view prevailed, however, and only a very small sector (16,000 sq. km.) of the Tuvinian Republic called Darkhat was ceded to Outer Mongolia.[56]

To consolidate relations between the Tannu-Tuva Republic and Soviet Russia a treaty of friendship was signed in July 1926 between the two countries modeled on the Soviet-Mongol Agreement of 1921.[57] Thereafter Russian power over the Tannu-Tuva Republic remained undisturbed.

Inner Mongolia

The same coupling of popular desire for independence with close Russian tutorship occurred in Inner Mongolia. In 1923 a People's Party was established there, and in the winter of 1924 a party conference was held in Peking. By July 1925, the People's Party of Inner Mongolia had 300 members and 3,000 candidates for membership.

That party's first congress met in Kalgan in early October, 1925. It was attended by representatives of the People's Revolutionary Party of Outer Mongolia, as well as by representatives of the Kuomintang. In a declaration addressed to "Brother Mongols," the congress came out for self-determination for the peoples inhabiting China; for the establishment of national-revolutionary authority in Inner Mongolia as soon as the authority of imperialists and militarists was overthrown in China; and for broad participation of the population of Inner Mongolia in the government of the country. It also demanded the annulment of all feudal privileges, the granting of self-government to the *hoshuns,* and the convocation of the National Assembly, the Great Huruldan of Inner Mongolia, from among the representatives of Mongol people. Finally, it called

---

[54] *Ibid.,* pp. 38–39.
[55] *Ibid.,* pp. 87–88.
[56] G. M. Friters, *Outer Mongolia and Its International Position,* p. 131.
[57] I. Ia. Korostovets, *Von Ginggis Khan zur Sowjetrepublik,* p. 340.

for transfer of all land to the organs of local self-government, the just regulation of colonization, and the annulment of certain debts. The declaration ended with a call to the whole Mongol laboring population, the middle and lower lamas, and the Mongol intelligentsia to join the banner of the party, and under its leadership to wage a struggle for the liberation of the Mongol people.[58]

Soviet Nonaggression and Neutrality Treaties with Turkey, Afghanistan, and Persia

The negotiations started by the Western powers in Locarno in 1925 for the purpose of bringing Germany back into the Western European alliance, and culminating in the Locarno Pact signed in London on October 16, 1925, were interpreted by the Soviet leaders as a move directed against Soviet Russia. Furthermore, the Locarno Pact was to be followed, so the Russians believed, by other and similar treaties between the Western powers and Russia's neighbors. "The German 'Locarno,'" said *Izvestiia,* "appears to be a starting point for another and much more elaborate plan, namely the encirclement of the Soviet Union by states which will consistently pursue an anti-Soviet policy.[59]

Consequently, Soviet diplomats proceeded immediately to take steps to prevent such an "encirclement." On December 17, 1925, a treaty of friendship and neutrality was signed in Paris between Soviet Russia and Turkey. The purpose and aims of this shortly worded treaty were clearly defined in the first two articles. Article One reads as follows: "In the case of military action being taken against either Contracting Party by one or more other powers, the other Contracting Party undertakes to maintain neutrality as towards the first Contracting Party." Article Two:

Each Contracting Party undertakes to abstain from any aggression against the other; it likewise undertakes not to participate in any alliance or agreement of a political character with one or more other powers directed against the other Contracting Party, or in any alliance or agreement with one or more other powers directed against the military or naval security of the other Contracting Party. Furthermore, each of the two Contracting Parties undertakes not to participate in any hostile act by one or more other powers directed against the other Contracting Party.[60]

Commenting on the importance of this treaty, *Izvestiia* stated:

The treaty which was signed in Paris is an anti-Locarno act in the sense that it is signed for the purpose of peace and not of war. All "Locarno" machinations in the Near East have failed. Neither the U.S.S.R. nor Turkey wishes to be drawn into a military combination or any combination, be it political, economic or financial, which would alienate them from each other. This is the actual meaning of the [Paris] treaty. The treaty puts an end to all provocational rumors about secret U.S.S.R. agreements against Turkey, or secret Turkish agreements against the U.S.S.R. This treaty, likewise, precludes any "Locarno" combination in the Near East, inasmuch as such a combination is impossible without Turkey's participation. . . .

By guaranteeing such nonaggression, and by promising to discuss and to come

---

[58] Text appears in Genkin, *Novyi Vostok,* No. 12, 1926, pp. 192–95; see also *Revoliutsionnyi Vostok,* No. 3, 1928, pp. 237–40.

[59] "Anti-Lokarno," *Izvestiia,* No. 294, December 24, 1925, p. 1. For more on the Soviet reaction to Locarno, see the companion volume, *Soviet Russia and the West,* 1920–1927.

[60] Shapiro, I, 313.

to an agreement on the disputable questions which cannot be settled through diplomatic channels, the Paris treaty shows that, on one hand, there can be no recourse to arms in the settlement of conflicts between the U.S.S.R. and Turkey, and on the other hand, there can be in general no serious conflicts between these two countries. The mutual neutrality which this treaty emphasizes follows largely from all other points of the treaty. Thus, without having recourse to the League of Nations, outside the League, and in spite of the League, which legalizes robbery and violence on the part of the strong states against the weak ones, the peoples of the U.S.S.R. and of the East, inspired by exclusively peaceful intentions, and alien to all plans of encroachment, will regulate their relations in the future in the interest of culture and progress. Herein lies the lesson to those peoples whose governments believe that there can be some other way to settle the problem of international relations except the renunciation of "Locarno."[61]

The Soviet government continued, meanwhile, to cultivate its relations with Turkey. An editorial in *Izvestiia* on the fifth anniversary of the first Soviet-Turkish treaty of friendship, said: "At the time when the future of the entire national-liberation movement of Turkey was greatly jeopardized, the Russian Soviet Republic was the only state which stretched out a friendly hand, and gave assistance to Turkey." Now, several years after the formation of the Soviet and Turkish republics, the position of the two countries had changed considerably.

The unfortunate treaties of Brest-Litovsk and Sèvres have now become a thing of the past. The Soviet Union and the Turkish Republic are now recognized by all great powers of Europe and Asia.... Soviet-Turkish friendship, which has been sustained through the past years of trials, now represents a powerful factor in the international policy of peace.[62]

In November 1926, these ties of friendship seemed to have become even stronger when Turkish foreign minister Tewfik Rouchdi Bey arrived in Odessa on the cruiser *Gamidié* to meet Chicherin in person. This meeting aroused curiosity and speculation among the Western powers, there being rumors that a union of Asian peoples under the leadership of the U.S.S.R. was contemplated.

Pompous celebrations followed. At the banquet given by the Commander of the Black Sea Fleet to the Turkish visitors, including the sailors of the *Gamidié,* Chicherin offered this greeting:

We greet today the heroic Turkish sailors who took part in the Turkish people's struggle for political and economic independence from the imperialist yoke. A new life has now dawned upon Turkey. There was a time when Constantinople was greedily coveted by tsarist diplomacy. This time has passed forever. We have broken away from this past, just as the new Turkey has broken away from the principles which guided the Ottoman Empire.... The Turkish and the Soviet peoples are now opposing every attempt to enslave them by world capital.... We greet the young Turkey that has arisen from the verge of complete destruction by world imperialism.[63]

Chicherin emphasized that it was not simply Turkish military might that he was welcoming. In greeting the Turkish sailors, he said he was greeting also the

---

[61] *Izvestiia*, No. 294, December 24, 1925, p. 1. For more on Soviet security treaties, see the companion volume, *Soviet Russia and the West, 1920–1927*.

[62] *Izvestiia*, No. 61, March 16, 1926, p. 1.

[63] For Chicherin's interpretation of Soviet-Turkish friendship, see Document 84.

Turkish workers and peasants whom these sailors represented, and who were actually responsible for their country's increasing well-being.[64]

It was clear, however, that diplomatic as well as commercial considerations entered into the Soviet attitude to Turkey. Communist aims—superficially, at least—receded into the background, and Turkish friendship was sought in spite of the Turkish government's evident disapproval of the communist movement in Turkey.

A severe blow to this movement was dealt on March 5, 1925, when the Turkish government closed down two communist newspapers. In May of the same year Turkish Communists were arrested and condemned to years of hard labor. On August 13, a government decree announced that membership in the Communist Party was a crime.[65] Nonetheless, in the September 1926 issue of *Kommunisticheskii Internatsional* the following statement was made:

The national-revolutionary movement in Turkey is no doubt a progressive factor; it clears the way for the proletarian revolution; it sweeps away all feudal and imperial tendencies; it strikes at the most sensitive points of [international] imperialism. Consequently, it is imperative for our organization to support it to the best of its ability.[66]

On August 31, 1926, the Soviet government signed a treaty of neutrality and nonaggression with Afghanistan, and on November 28, 1927, there followed an important agreement establishing an airline between Kabul and Tashkent, thus linking Afghanistan and Moscow by air. These two agreements marked the consolidation of Soviet-Afghan relations which had been officially established in March 1921,[67] after which Moscow had skillfully continued to play its cards in Afghanistan by taking the Afghan side against Great Britain.

Reporting officially to the Third Congress of Soviets of the U.S.S.R. in 1925 on Soviet-Afghan relations in 1924, Chicherin had this to say:

The Afghan people had the occasion to become convinced of the unchanging friendship of the toiling masses of the Soviet Union during the closing months of 1923. The relations between Afghanistan and Great Britain were seriously troubled at that time, as a result of the British ultimatum to the Afghan government following the assassination of two British officers and one English woman in the summer of 1923 on the territory of the independent Afghan tribes and close to the Indian border. The Soviet press and the peoples of the Soviet republics sided with Afghanistan at that time and against the unjust demands on the part of Great Britain. This fact was duly appreciated by Afghanistan, which became finally convinced that the Soviet Union was a true supporter—not only in words, but also in deeds—of the principle of peaceful and businesslike co-operation with its neighbors. Afghanistan had further proofs of this [i.e., the attitude of Soviet Russia] last spring when in the southwestern sector of its territory a revolt was raised by some backward tribes against the progressive government of the Emir. This revolt was fed with firearms and supplies from India. One time the situation was quite serious; the insurgents had succeeded in advancing deep into Afghan territory, and were actually eighty miles from the

---

[64] *Izvestiia*, No. 265, November 16, 1926, p. 1.

[65] B. Ferdi, "Kommunisticheskoe dvizhenie v Turtsii," *Kommunisticheskii Internatsional*, No. 6 (64), October 22, 1926, pp. 44-48.

[66] B. Ferdi, "Polozhenie rabochego klassa i kommunisticheskoe dvizhenie v Turtsii," *Kommunisticheskii Internatsional*, No. 9 (58), September 1926, p. 130.

[67] See our pp. 103-4.

capital. The situation was saved by the arrival of our fighting planes, which flew over the Hindu Kush and dispersed the insurgents. These planes and their pilots stayed in Afghanistan to serve the Emir, who has been negotiating with us since that time regarding the construction [with our assistance] of a telegraph line, a radio station, and highways.[68]

Like the treaty with Turkey, the 1926 treaty with Afghanistan pledged neutrality if one of the contracting powers became involved in military action with some third power or powers. By Article Two, each of the two contracting parties undertook "to abstain from all kinds of aggression against the other," and not to "join in any boycott or financial and economic blockades directed against the other." Article Three is interesting in view of the Soviet aerial assistance to the Emir described above. This article reads as follows: "The High Contracting Parties, [each] mutually recognizing the sovereignty and integrity of the other, undertake to abstain from all kinds of armed and unarmed interference in the internal affairs of the other Contracting Party and also not to join or assist any other state or states which may take steps against or interfere with the other contracting state."

Finally, as in other Soviet treaties, but this time perhaps in reference to the Basmachi movement or to the Emir of Bukhara, who with some of his supporters had found refuge in Afghanistan some years earlier, Article Three continued: "The Contracting Parties will not permit any groups or individuals on their own territories to establish or to prosecute activities detrimental to the other Contracting Party."[69]

A treaty of nonaggression and neutrality between the Soviet government and Persia was signed on October 1, 1927. Negotiations leading to this treaty were somewhat more laborious and protracted than those leading to the treaties with Turkey and Afghanistan. Reporting on the position of the U.S.S.R. vis-à-vis other powers before the Fourth Congress of Soviets of the U.S.S.R. on April 19, 1927, A. I. Rykov, Chairman of the Council of People's Commissars, spoke of these negotiations:

The development of friendly relations between the U.S.S.R. and Persia continues to be a cardinal aim of Soviet policy. Several times we have already been, so it seemed, on the eve of signing an agreement. But every time, for some reason or other, this has not happened. Why is that so? It is difficult to say whether this may not have been due to the influence of some outside force. The presence in Moscow of the Persian foreign minister, M. Ansari, who has come to the U.S.S.R. for the purpose of carrying on direct negotiations with us, gives us reason to hope that these negotiations will speedily lead to a successful conclusion and that an agreement will at last be signed.[70]

This treaty resembled to a considerable degree the two previously signed treaties. Article Two stated that "Each of the High Contracting Parties undertakes to refrain from any aggression and from any hostile acts directed against

[68] *Godovoi otchet Narodnogo Komissariata po Inostrannym Delam za 1924 g. k III sezdu sovetov SSSR*, p. 94.

[69] Complete text appears in Shapiro, I, 322–23. The text of the November 28, 1927, agreement concerning the mail and passenger service between Kabul and Tashkent, known as an *Agreement Regarding the Kabul-Tashkent Airline*, appears in Shapiro, I, 356–57.

[70] *Izvestiia*, No. 90, April 20, 1927, p. 2.

the other Party, and not to introduce its military force into the territory of the other Party." Should one of the contracting parties be attacked by another power or powers, the other contracting party agreed to observe neutrality throughout the period of conflict.

By Article Three each of the contracting parties agreed to "take no part, whether *de facto* or *de jure,* in political alliances or agreements directed against the safety of the territory or territorial waters of the other Contracting Party or against its integrity, independence or sovereignty." Each party promised, likewise, to take no part in any economic boycott or blockade instituted by another power or powers against the other contracting party. Article Four prohibited propaganda on the territory of the other contracting party : "Should the citizens of either of the Contracting Parties in the territory of the other Party engage in any propaganda or campaign prohibited by the authorities of the latter Party, the Government of that territory shall have the right to put a stop to the activities of such citizens and to impose the statutory penalties."[71]

Development of Trade Relations with the Eastern Countries

The Soviet government continued to cultivate trade relations with the Eastern countries and to make exemptions from its regulations on the state monopoly of foreign trade in so far as those countries were concerned.[72] It was bent, however, on having them adapt their national economy to the economy of the Soviet Union. S. Iransky wrote in 1926:

Now that the Soviet Union is established, the East finds itself at the crossroads between two political systems: the imperialist system of the capitalist states, and the system of the Soviet republics, which aims at the organization of the world economy on a new basis . . . Theoretically it appears absurd, and practically it is impossible, for the East to organize its national economy and at the same time retain its political independence unless it aligns its national economy with the economy of the Soviet republics.

Soviet foreign trade regulations must, therefore, be so planned as to bring the Eastern countries to adopt the above course. Iransky concluded:

We must take into consideration the fact that the near future will show whether the developing economy of the backward Eastern countries will pass through the capitalist stage of development, or will proceed toward superior forms, bypassing the capitalist stage. One of the basic tasks of the institutions which supervise our foreign trade with the East will be to assist the Eastern countries to bypass the capialist stage of economic development.[73]

---

[71] Full text appears in Shapiro, I, 340–41. On November 23, 1927, the two countries signed another agreement, the *Protocol Regarding the Establishment of the Pehlevi-Baku Air Route* (Shapiro, I, 356).

[72] See our pp. 116–17.

[73] S. Iransky, "Novyi etap v sovetsko-vostochnykh torgovykh otnosheniiakh," *Torgovlia Rossii s Vostokom,* October–December, 1926, pp. 3–4.

B. COMMUNIST EFFORTS TO REACH THE ASIAN PEOPLE

Although Soviet treaties with Eastern countries all contained clauses guaranteeing that neither contracting party would interfere in the other's domestic affairs, Moscow in no way curtailed its propaganda or its aid to communist parties throughout Asia. The Communists' methods and agents varied considerably; they worked partly through the Communist International and other communist organizations, partly through organizations which officially were noncommunist.

Since the work of communist agents in Asia was clandestine in nature, detailed information on this work is scarce, although the scarcity is more pronounced for some countries than for others. Since documents are especially scarce, we shall rely heavily upon the pronouncements, decisions, manifestoes, and appeals of various communist congresses and conferences to suggest the general plan of communist work in noncommunist countries. As far as Asian countries are concerned, the execution of the decisions taken at the communist gatherings is best confirmed by the events that happened there only much later, beyond the period with which this volume is concerned.

The League to Struggle Against Imperialism and Colonial Oppression

Early communist maneuvers to gain influence among liberal and pacifist-minded intellectuals were helped greatly by the noncommunist League to Struggle Against Imperialism and Colonial Oppression, which came into existence on February 7–14, 1927. This organization emerged from the League to Struggle Against Colonial Oppression and Cruelty, which had been founded somewhat earlier in Germany by German intellectuals, among them Willi Münzenberg, a communist member of the Reichstag.[1]

The conference of the newly formed League was convened at Brussels in February 1927, and was attended by many prominent men of the liberal camp throughout the world. The honorary members of its presidium included Romain Rolland; a prominent British Labour Party man, George Lansbury; Upton Sinclair; Albert Einstein; Henri Barbusse; Mme. Sun Yat-sen; Jawaharlal Nehru; and Maxim Gorki, the last *in absentia*. There were numerous representatives from the Asian and colonial countries. China's delegates represented the Nationalist Government, the Kuomintang, and the Canton Strike Committee. Nehru represented the All-India National Congress, Semaoen the Communist Party of Indonesia, and Mohammed Hatta the so-called Indonesian Freedom Party. Sen Katayama, a prominent Communist, spoke for Japan. Palestine, Persia, South Africa, Mexico, and Haiti sent representatives also. Soviet Russia's delegates came from the Soviet trade unions and were headed by G. N. Melnichansky. Altogether there were 174 delegates representing 134 organizations.

[1] See Münzenberg's article in *Pravda*, No. 28, February 4, 1927, p. 1.

The agenda of the conference included such items as imperialist oppression in the colonies; the colonial liberation movement and its support by workers' organizations in the capitalist countries; the problem of co-ordinating the struggle of the working class in the imperialist countries with the struggle in the colonies; and the development of the League into a great international organization with the aim of rendering assistance to the colonial liberation movements.[2]

Special commissions discussed possible courses of action for the national-revolutionary movements in Indonesia, Korea, the Philippines, Japan, and China. A program of action for the colonial and dependent countries was agreed upon and a resolution was unanimously adopted for the working class in the imperialist countries, urging it to fight side by side with all national movements for the complete liberation of the suppressed countries. At home, the workers were to oppose all suppression of colonial peoples; to vote against all military, naval, and air force requisitions for the colonies; and to explain to the citizens and soldiers of their own nations the evils of imperialist policy.

The resolution also demanded the immediate withdrawal of foreign land and sea forces from Chinese territory and Chinese waters, and the prevention, by strikes and similar action, of the transport of arms and troops to China and India. The resolution concluded by stating: "We pledge ourselves in the interest of the political and trade union labour movements in England, India and China to work for the realisation of unity and of common action." The resolution was signed by A. Fenner Brockway, Emil Davies, Raymond L. Bridgeman, Harry Politt, M. J. MacManus, Ellen C. Wilkinson, and one Beckett representing the English side, and by Li Han-chün and Jawaharlal Nehru representing China and India respectively.[3]

The conference also issued a manifesto, addressed to the oppressed people of the world, which took the view that "a position, in which hundreds of millions of men are condemned culturally and violently to suffer material and moral stagnation and to remain the involuntary victims of foreign capitalist exploitation, . . . can really no longer be tolerated."

The manifesto went on to describe the "cruel and relentless exploitation of the over-seas Asiatic, African and American peoples and races," the fatal dissensions that World War I had revealed among capitalist countries, and the inevitable colonial reaction:

A mighty wave of the movement for national emancipation passed over the immense regions of Asia, Africa and America. The banner of revolt against slavery and conquest was raised in China and in India, in Egypt and North West Africa, in Indonesia, and also in the Philippines.

Therefore, the manifesto stated, the Brussels conference had decided to found the League to Struggle Against Imperialism and Colonial Oppression, and to appeal to "all who do not profit from the oppression of others and who do not live on the fruits of this oppression, and to all who hate modern slavery and are longing for their own freedom and the freedom of their fellow-men" to join the League and support it. The manifesto ended as follows:

[2] *Pravda*, No. 38, February 16, 1927, p. 1; also *International Press Correspondence*, No. 16, February 25, 1927, p. 324, and *La Vague Rouge*, No. 4, April 1927.
[3] *International Press Correspondence*, No. 14, February 17, 1927, p. 292.

The emancipation of the oppressed colonial peoples and those subjugated by violence will not diminish the great accomplishments and possibilities of the material and spiritual culture of mankind, but will increase them on a scale never yet experienced. And in this sense the oppressed and enslaved nations which represent the overwhelming majority of mankind, like the proletariat, can conquer the world, the world of the future. Oppressed People and Oppressed Nations, Unite![4]

The conference held its last session on February 14, 1927, having become a permanent institution, namely the League to Struggle Against Imperialism and Colonial Oppression, and having elected a bureau, a provisional executive committee, and a special organizational commission to act between congresses. Six months later, August 20–21, 1927, the executive committee met at Cologne to discuss reports on the Indian situation delivered by Nehru and Shapurji Saklatvala, Indian Communist member of British Parliament.[5]

The Profintern, the Krestintern, and the Communist Women's Secretariat

Among communist organizations proper, the Profintern (Communist Trade Union International), the Krestintern (Peasant International), and the Communist Women's Secretariat, a branch of the Communist International, made the greatest issue of Eastern problems and thus succeeded in drawing a number of Eastern toilers into their ranks.

The Krestintern (known also as the International Peasant Council or the Red Peasant International) was founded in Moscow on October 16, 1923, by peasant delegates representing over forty countries; it was to serve as headquarters for the world peasant movement. At the first conference of the group, A. P. Smirnov, president of the R.S.F.S.R., was elected general secretary and Tomasz Dombal, the Polish delegate, became acting general secretary. Nguyen Ai Quoc (Ho Chi Minh) from Indochina became a member of the presidium; other Asian delegates were Ken Hayashi and Sen Katayama representing Japan. During the first session of the conference an Appeal to the Toiling Peasants of the Colonies, to those "suffering from the double oppression of foreign capitalism and national masters," was drafted:

The International Peasant Conference, which has met in Moscow for the first time in order to outline the organization of the struggle which so far the toilers of the land have not had, appeals to your class-consciousness and asks you to join its ranks. ... Peasants of the colonies, unite! Organize yourselves! Join us! Let us struggle together for the common cause![6]

Two years later, on April 17, 1925, the Krestintern appealed once more, this time to "the peasants of Turkey, Persia, Egypt, Eastern Algeria, Palestine, India, Indonesia, China, Korea, and Japan; to the Negroes of America and Africa; and to all peasants and toilers of colonies and semicolonies and those who are oppressed by capitalists and landlords." These "colonial peasants" were now urged to unite in peasant unions."[7]

[4] *International Press Correspondence*, No. 17, March 3, 1927, pp. 353–55.
[5] *International Press Correspondence*, No. 51, September 1, 1927, p. 1152.
[6] *Krestianskii Internatsional*, No. 1, April 1924, p. 174.
[7] *Krestianskii Internatsional*, No. 3–5, March–May 1925, pp. 168–70.

Besides publishing a magazine, *Krestianskii Internatsional*, the Krestintern founded the International Agrarian Institute, with its seat in Moscow, to study the agrarian problem and the peasant movements in various countries.

Work among the women of the East was the province of the Communist Women's Secretariat of the Communist International, founded in December 1924. It was most successful in China, where its sections were duly established in Peking, Shanghai, and Canton. The theses of this group's Fourth International Conference, held May 29–June 10, 1926, declared:

By drawing the women of the East into the struggle against imperialism, an impetus will be given to the national-liberation movement and its success will be ensured. . . . The Fifth Congress of the Communist International insisted on the fact that "Communist work among women is by no means a side-issue for the Communist Parties, but that it constitutes an important and even determining part of the fundamental task of organisation and realisation of the struggles of the revolutionary proletariat."[8]

The Communist Trade Union International, known as the Profintern, was particularly successful in bringing Eastern workers into the communist fold. Almost from the time of its foundation in 1921 the Profintern had stressed the need for international unity among trade unions; Lozovsky, its chairman, spoke on this point repeatedly. It was emphasized anew by speakers at the First Congress of the Toilers of the Far East, held in Moscow and Petrograd in early 1922. The same year, Australian delegates to the Second Congress of the Profintern proposed the convocation of a Pacific trade union conference. The Australian Council of Trade Unions repeated this proposal in 1923.

The first outcome of these efforts was the Conference of the Transport Workers of the Pacific, which met in Canton in 1924 and addressed a manifesto to the toiling masses of the East and the proletariat of Europe and America. "For the first time in the history of the young but growing labour movement of the East," the manifesto stated, "an event has occurred which is pregnant with important consequences. In the territory of revolutionary South China in Canton, representatives of transport workers from South and North China, from Java and the Philippine Islands gathered in [a] conference called by the Red International of Labour Unions."

The manifesto observed that the imperialist powers not only had failed to fulfill their wartime pledges to the colonial and dependent countries, but had actually strengthened their hold on these countries. "In this respect there is no fundamental difference between the policies of all the imperialist states." Since the imperialists would not grant independence to any subject people voluntarily, the manifesto called for an organized struggle "against world imperialists, against native feudalists, militarists, and capitalists who compromise with the imperialists." Finally, the manifesto called on the Eastern masses to organize into labor and peasant unions, and on the transport workers of the East to amalgamate their unions and "affiliate with the revolutionary transport workers of the world."[9]

The importance of the trade union movement in the colonial and dependent countries was emphasized two years later in a resolution passed by the Sixth Enlarged Plenum of the ECCI. After commenting favorably on the trade unions

[8] *International Press Correspondence*, No. 69, October 26, 1926, p. 1196.
[9] *International Press Correspondence*, No. 65, September 11, 1924, pp. 705–6.

of China, the resolution pointed out the need for all colonial unions to affiliate with the Profintern, and observed that these unions were properly seeking help "in Moscow and not in Amsterdam" (the headquarters of the Second or Socialist International). The resolution concluded by outlining the responsibilities of world communism toward the colonial workers' movement.[10]

The Pan-Pacific Trade Union Conference

Another step toward the unification of colonial trade unions was taken at the Pan-Pacific Trade Union Conference held at Hankow, May 20–26, 1927, and attended by Lozovsky and other representatives from Soviet Russia. Delegates came also from China, Japan, Java, France, the United States, and Britain. The Australian delegates were unable to come because of difficulties with their passports, and there were no representatives from India.

Commenting on the revolutionary tasks in the Pacific and the forthcoming Pacific Conference, Lozovsky wrote on November 26, 1926:

We have a huge task before us: to effect a rapprochement between the international workers' movements in the West and the East. . . . There already exists a certain ideological proximity between the trade unions of China and the U.S.S.R. because these organizations are members of the Profintern. We must pay particular attention at present to Japan; we must see that the workers' movement of this highly developed capitalist country does not remain outside the world union movement. The projected conference of the Pacific trade unions in early May, 1927, will serve as a serious step toward the unification of the world trade union movement. Preliminary steps have already been taken in this direction. We have reason to believe that we shall succeed in uniting a considerable number of the countries of the Pacific. At any rate, it is evident that the unification of the workers of the Pacific has a tremendous political significance: first, in order to prevent any possible conflict on the Pacific; and second, as an important step toward the world unification of trade unions. . . .

The conflicts of recent times have confronted us with the immediate task of organizing international strikes and international actions. The internationalization of our tactics and our actions, and the organization of the latter so that they will run parallel and simultaneously in various countries, have become the basic tasks in the present-day struggle.[11]

The conference of Pacific workers was to meet May 1, 1927, in Canton but was delayed and transferred for political reasons to Hankow, where its first session was held on May 20.

Lozovsky delivered a long report on the Chinese revolution and the international workers' movement, and a supplementary report was presented by Li Li-san, representing the All-China Workers' Federation.[12] Reports were then made by the delegates on the labor situation in their respective countries. At the seventh and last session of the conference a number of resolutions were passed, one of which, noting that "the struggle between the imperialist Powers,

[10] *Shestoi rasshirennyi plenum IKKI,* pp. 635–36; also *International Press Correspondence,* No. 40, May 13, 1926, p. 625; see Document 85.

[11] A. Lozovsky, "Itogi i perspektivy raboty Profinterna k VII sezdu profsoiuzov SSSR," *Krasnyi Internatsional Profsoiuzov,* No. 12, December 1926, p. 547.

[12] Texts of these reports appear in *Pan-Pacific Trade Union Conference, Bulletin of Proceedings,* No. 2, May 21, 1927, pp. 1–10 and 11–14 respectively.

particularly between England, Japan and the United States, for hegemony on the Pacific grows every day and inevitably leads to a new imperialist World War," proceeded:

The only way to prevent a new World War, is to transform the threatening imperialist war of races and nations into a WAR OF CLASSES, a war of exploited against the exploiters. To accomplish this, it is necessary to draw into the trade unions millions of workers; to imbue the masses with the spirit of class consciousness and of class war, and to remember that those who preach class peace and class collaboration consciously or unconsciously lead the working masses into a new war and to mutual destruction of nations.[13]

The resolution called upon the workers of all countries to prevent a new world war, and stated that this could be done "if the workers of all countries irrespective of race and nationality will form a solid fraternal alliance and with united forces will establish everywhere the RULE OF LABOR, in place of the rule of Capital."[14]

The conference also formulated a number of demands for the workers of the Pacific: an eight-hour working day; a compulsory continuous forty-two-hour weekly rest; social insurance for workers; no night work for women; equal wages for equal work; freedom of organization and assembly; freedom of the press; freedom to strike; the abolition of corporal punishment, and so forth.[15]

In analyzing this program in a pamphlet published in Moscow in English, Lozovsky remarked: "These . . . demands may seem rather elementary but as a matter of fact not a single country (except the U.S.S.R.) has this programme carried out in its entirety."[16]

The conference also addressed itself in special appeals to the oppressed toilers of China, India, the Philippines, Indonesia, Korea, and Formosa, and pledged its full support to the struggle of these peoples. It created a permanent Pan-Pacific Trade Union Secretariat and charged it with the publication of a periodical, the *Pacific Worker*. Finally, the conference issued a manifesto addressed to the trade unions and workers of the Pacific and the world. The manifesto declared that the Pan-Pacific Trade Union Conference

is not an attempt to create a new trade union international. It is only an attempt to unite the trade unions of the Pacific sector of the world labour movement—not for the purpose of opposing the workers of this part of the world to the workers of the rest of the world, but for the purpose of bringing the workers of the Pacific closer to the problems that confront the world labour movement.

The Pan-Pacific Trade Union Secretariat created at this conference, the manifesto added, would do everything in its power "to unite the trade unions of the Pacific countries and to mobilise all forces for the formation of a single powerful trade union international comprising the trade unions of all countries, all races, and all nationalities."[17]

[13] *Resolutions and Decisions of the Pan-Pacific Trade Union Conference*, p. 6.
[14] *Ibid.*, p. 7.
[15] *Ibid.*, pp. 17–18.
[16] S. A. Dridzo (A. Lozovsky), *The Pan-Pacific Trade Union Conference, Hankow, May 20–26, 1927*, p. 28.
[17] *Resolutions and Decisions of the Pan-Pacific Trade Union Conference*, p. 28.

Decisions of the Fifth Congress of the Communist International, 1924

The Fifth Congress of the Communist International, which met from June 17 to July 8, 1924, was attended by representatives from Turkey, Persia, India, Mongolia, Indochina, Indonesia, China, and Japan. The Eastern representation at the Communist gatherings in Moscow was definitely on the increase. The Eastern Communists elected to seats on the International's Executive Committee were Roy of India, Katayama of Japan, and Semaoen of Indonesia. Moreover, revolutionary movements throughout the East received considerable attention at this Congress. A special commission on national and colonial questions was appointed, and one session of the Congress itself was devoted entirely to these questions.

At this session Manuilsky, recalling that the Second Congress had called for a united front of proletarians and oppressed national groups, reported that the ECCI had wisely handled each such case individually as it came up. This technique, he stated, had "allowed the Communists in Java to take an active part in the work of the local workers' and peasants' party there. It also allowed the Chinese Communists to join the Kuomintang." Manuilsky warned Communists, however, against "losing their proletarian character by collaborating with the petty bourgeoisie."[18] Lastly, he urged the adoption of the principle of the right of secession for backward national groups, declaring:

There is no doubt whatsoever that the bourgeoisie cannot solve the national question within the framework of the capitalist state. But this does not mean that we must postpone the realization of the right of oppressed nations to separation until the social revolution has been victorious throughout the world.[19]

Roy, representing the Indian Communists, urged Western Communists to take account of the divergent nature of the various national movements in the colonial and semicolonial countries. In his opinion, it was necessary for the Communists to adapt their policies to the changing nature of the revolutionary support given by different social groups at different times: "the tactic which was correct in 1920 might not be correct in 1924, and the parties and social groups in the colonies which were allies of the revolutionary proletariat in 1920 might not be capable of fulfilling such a role in 1924." Roy agreed that "nowhere do the theses [of the Second Congress] say that the Comintern must refrain from supporting the national-liberation movement in the colonies," but maintained that the Second Congress had urged "direct contact" with the revolutionary organizations of the working class and the peasantry, and not with the bourgeois nationalists. He believed that the peasant masses of the colonies represented "a powerful revolutionary factor," and that "in every revolutionary liberation movement in the colonies, the peasant masses are destined to play a role of paramount importance."[20]

Representing Indochina, Nguyen Ai Quoc (Ho Chi Minh) called upon the British and French parties for a more active and energetic colonial policy:

[18] *Piatyi Vsemirnyi Kongress K.I.*, Part I, p. 593; see Document 86.

[19] *Ibid.*, p. 595.

[20] *Ibid.*, pp. 604–11; see Document 87.

It is not sufficient to outline long-worded theses and to pass radical resolutions in order to turn them immediately into Archives once the congress ends its sessions, as has been done in the past. On the contrary, it is imperative to take some concrete steps immediately.[21]

In conclusion, the session adopted a resolution and an appeal to the peoples of East Asia. The resolution, which was included in the theses of the Congress, called upon the Comintern to "give support to the movements of all oppressed nationalities directed against imperialism . . . bearing in mind that these movements represent one of the most important phases of that great movement of liberation which alone can lead to the victory of the revolution, not only on a European but on a world scale."[22]

The appeal told the peoples of East Asia that they were not standing alone in their self-sacrificing struggle, but had the sympathy of the revolutionary proletariat of all countries: "Our paths, leading to the overthrow of capitalist penal servitude and imperialist oppression, are identical." Referring to the approaching last battle against capitalism for the establishment of a World Union of Soviet Socialist Republics, the appeal stated that "the real and final emancipation of the oppressed peoples of the East as well as the working class of the West is possible only by establishing a close alliance and joint struggle against world capitalism."[23]

Communist Efforts in Japan

By mid-1924, communist parties were already entrenched in a number of Asian countries. In Japan, however, the communist movement was less deeply rooted than Comintern leaders might well have hoped. Upon the termination of the Fourth Congress of the Communist International, Kyūichi Tokuda had returned to Tokyo with the Comintern's message that, although the Japanese Communist Party was illegal, a formal party congress should be held to decide upon a platform. A congress was consequently called on February 4, 1923, in Ichikawa in order to select officers and revise party rules.

A second meeting was held March 15, 1923, in Shakuji Park in Tokyo, to discuss party strategy and tactics in general and the Draft Bukharin Platform in particular.[24] This document, drawn up in Soviet Russia sometime during 1922 (whether at the First Congress of the Toilers of the Far East or in the Japanese Commission of the Fourth Congress of the Comintern is not clear),[25] represented the first serious attempt of the Communist International to analyze Japanese society and formulate political strategy and tactics for the Japanese communist movement. Because of the semifeudal nature of the Japanese state, the Draft Platform stated, the Japanese government was opposed not only by the workers but also by other strata of Japanese society: the peasants, the petty

---

[21] *Ibid.*, pp. 656–57.

[22] *Piatyi Vsemirnyi Kongress K.I.*, Part II, pp. 46–47.

[23] *Ibid.*, pp. 214–15.

[24] The subsequent account is based on Travers E. Durkee's doctoral dissertation.

[25] According to a Japanese source: "After Mr. Kyūichi Tokuda had seen sent as a delegate to Moscow when the first Japanese [Communist] party was formed in 1922, he brought the theses with him on his return." Takeshi Muramatsu (ed.), *Nyhon Kyōsan-tō teze* ("Japanese Communist Party Theses"), p. 6.

bourgeoisie, and the so-called liberal bourgeoisie. Japanese Communists were to support the bourgeois-democratic revolution temporarily, recognizing that it could be accomplished only with the help of a thoroughly organized proletariat and peasantry.

Borrowing from Lenin,[26] the Draft Platform stated that in Japan

the triumph of the bourgeois revolution will serve as a prelude to the proletarian revolution, which aims at overthrowing bourgeois supremacy and establishing a proletarian dictatorship. . . . Democratic slogans are, therefore, only temporary weapons of the Japanese Communist Party; they are to be used in the struggle against the Emperor's government, and then abandoned as soon as the temporary and immediate tasks of the party have been achieved.[27]

After the Shakuji Park meeting at which the Bukharin Draft Platform was discussed, Kanson Arahata,[28] mentioned by us earlier, left for Moscow, where he met Katayama for the first time in ten years. At the Third Enlarged Plenum of the ECCI (June 1923), he spoke against a proposal by Zinoviev that a legal proletarian party be formed in Japan. Such an action would be premature, he argued, and would alienate militant anarcho-syndicalist elements of the working class:

Japanese comrades are not afraid of persecution and imprisonment. During the last thirteen years they have become accustomed to repressions. But, in my opinion, it is premature to organize a legal political party. Japanese comrades need the support and sympathy of the active elements of the working class. These elements have been indifferent to political problems; they are inexperienced, and their political horizon is very limited. Even the present leaders of the Yūai-kai are beginning to lose their influence on account of their reformist tendencies. Must we form a party and risk losing the support of the active elements in the working class? The syndicalist workers have been against the communist movement for the very reason that the latter became involved in politics. If we form a [legal] party we shall suffer defeat, at least in the course of the next several years. It is important [first] to educate the workers in politics before we organize them into a political party.[29]

Zinoviev did not agree:

We have at our session Japanese comrade Aoki [Arahata], one of the best workers of the young Japanese Communists. He entirely shares the political views of Comrade Katayama. Having just arrived from Japan, he is informed best of the state of affairs within the Japanese Communist Party.

We disagree with this comrade and with the majority of the Japanese Communist Party on this point [i.e., the formation of a legal communist party in Japan]. The Japanese comrades are convinced that only an illegal communist party can continue

---

[26] See our pp. 36–37.

[27] See Document 88.

[28] Arahata is referred to in Soviet Russian sources as Aoki.

[29] *Rasshirennyi plenum Ispolnitelnogo Komiteta Kommunisticheskogo Internatsionala, 12–23 iiunia, 1923 . . .* , p. 82 (cited hereafter as *Rasshirennyi plenum IKKI, 12–23 iiunia, 1923*). Yūai-kai (Fraternal Society), mentioned by Arahata, was organized in 1912 for the purpose of bringing about class co-operation among all Japanese workers. By 1920, it became an important proletarian mass organization. In 1921, it was renamed Rōdō Sōdōmei (Federation of Trade Unions), but in 1923 Arahata still spoke of Yūai-kai. (See Chitoshi Yanaga, *Japan Since Perry*, pp. 474–75; also P. A. Mif and G. N. Voitinsky [eds.], *Sovremennaia Iaponiia*, Vol. I, pp. 96–99.)

for any length of time in Japan. They do not even wish to hear about the organization of a legal party. . . . I realize, of course, that Comrade Aoki knows the Japanese situation much better than we do, but we do know that strong political unrest is now apparent in Japan. A large number of [Japanese] bourgeoisie are in strong opposition to the existing regime. The idea of a rapprochement with Soviet Russia is one of the most popular ideas in Japan. Workers' strikes follow one after another, so that the wave of strikes spreads through the entire country. How can we then imagine that under such circumstances an attempt to legalize the communist movement in Japan is destined to failure? I think that this is hardly so. Therefore, we shall insist that our Japanese comrades learn the lesson from the American Communist Party,[30] and try to organize a legal communist party in Japan.[31]

But about this time news[32] reached Moscow of mass arrests of Communists in Japan, and Arahata prepared to leave for Tokyo. In May 1923, Japanese police had uncovered incriminating communist documents, and the party, certain that trouble would ensue, sent Fumio Sano, Takatsu, and Kondo to the Soviet Union.[33] More than one hundred arrests were made. In Moscow, the ECCI pledged its support to "the Japanese Communists who have been imprisoned for courageously leading the resistance to the bourgeois bureaucratic and military cliques . . ."[34]

Within three months of the June arrests came the Kanto earthquake of September 1, a tragedy which, coupled with an attempt on the life of Prince Regent Hirohito, gave the police ample excuse for rounding up "undesirable elements" in Japan. Comintern authorities viewed the earthquake as a severe blow to Japanese capitalism and hence to the labor movement, since the "Japanese bourgeoisie will attempt to rebuild Japan's economics at the expense of the working class."[35] In Moscow the ECCI called upon Japanese workers to make the most of the opportunity created for them by the earthquake, to create "a mighty Communist Party and powerful trade unions" for leading the whole working class and the peasantry into battle against the government. "From now onward the imperialist government of Japan is not to have a moment's peace."[36]

Arahata hastened back to Japan with Comintern instructions for an earthquake relief movement and an antigovernment protest movement—a combined struggle calculated to strengthen the Communist Party. But on his return to Tokyo, Arahata discovered that all his comrades favored dissolving the party. The organization had been built on personal relationships, they said, rather than on a mass basis. Hence, it was better to dissolve it and encourage each individual ex-member to enlarge and develop the mass movement in his own environment.[37]

[30] The two communist groups formed in the United States in September and October, 1919, respectively, joined forces in May 1921. In December of the same year they affiliated with the newly formed legal Workers' Party. In 1929, the Workers' Party assumed the name of the Communist Party of the United States of America.

[31] *Rasshirennyi plenum IKKI, 12–13 iiunia, 1923,* pp. 30–31.

[32] *International Press Correspondence,* No. 45, June 22, 1923, p. 440.

[33] Durkee, p. 49.

[34] *Rasshirennyi plenum IKKI, 12–23 iiunia, 1923,* pp. 316–17; also *International Press Correspondence,* No. 52, July 23, 1923, p. 541; see Document 89.

[35] *International Press Correspondence,* No. 61, September 20, 1923, p. 676.

[36] *International Press Correspondence,* No. 67, October 18, 1923, pp. 756–57.

[37] Durkee, pp. 52–53.

When the disastrous earthquake struck Japan, Soviet Russia hastened to express its sympathies for the Japanese people in distress. Several Russian ships were dispatched to Japan with food, but the Japanese authorities turned them back. On September 15, the S.S. *Lenin* was ordered to leave the port of Yokohama immediately. Japanese authorities suspected that together with the food supplies, the *Lenin* carried large quantities of communist literature for propaganda purposes. The Soviet Commissar of Foreign Affairs protested immediately, stating that the refusal to permit the Russian ships to dock "produced a painful impression in the Soviet republics. This most unusual decision can find no justification on any ground. The government of the Soviet Union will continue to try to render help to the Japanese people."[38]

Meanwhile, despite Moscow's opposition to the disbanding of the Japanese Communist Party, those in favor of dissolution won out. Less than two years after its formation, the Japanese Communist Party dissolved itself.

Comintern leaders, deeply disturbed, called in May 1924 for the formation of a Japanese workers' and peasants' party independent of the "bourgeois radicals." A special Comintern appeal urged a program demanding democratic government, immediate adult suffrage for men and women without qualification, freedom to strike and the right to collective bargaining, freedom of opinion, the right of assembly (to hold meetings without the presence of police), and "real freedom of the press."

The appeal warned:

You are disfranchised, unemployment and starvation stare you in the face, and your rulers can offer you nothing but increased exploitation and poverty. . . . Organise your forces for the fight for civil liberties. Hasten with the formation of your Workers and Peasants Party by which alone you will be able to conduct your fight for liberty. . . . Demand the release of the political prisoners.[39]

Despite the dissolution of the Japanese party, Comintern circles proceeded to mention it as though it were still in existence. Said Katayama to the Fifth Congress in July 1924, "The Koreans living in Japan have a strong communist group which is directed by the Japanese Communist Party."[40] However, giving a brief account of the revolutionary movement in Japan in the same speech, and referring to the Japanese Communist Party, Katayama remarked:

The party was young and inexperienced and it suffered many defeats, but just at present there has been formed a legal party, the Workers' and Peasants' Party. The Japanese proletariat will soon take a new step forward in the arena of political struggle.[41]

A little earlier, the ECCI report of May 5, 1924, had glossed over the defeats:

In Japan, the Communist Party, under the guidance of the Comintern, perfected its tactics in connection with the work among the masses, the Trade Unions, and the formation of the Workers' and Peasants' Party, which is destined to play a significant role in the life of the country.[42]

[38] *Izvestiia*, No. 217, September 26, 1923, p. 1.
[39] *International Press Correspondence*, No. 29, May 15, 1924, pp. 291–92.
[40] *Piatyi Vsemirnyi Kongress K.I.*, Part I, p. 621.
[41] *Ibid.*, p. 620.
[42] *From the Fourth to the Fifth World Congress. Report of the Executive Committee of the Communist International*, p. 103.

In January 1925 six men came together in an apartment house in the Japanese district of Shanghai. Voitinsky, the Comintern agent, and Manabu Sano had come from Moscow to rendezvous with Tokuda, Arahata, Fumio Sano, and Suekichi Aono, the four representing the Communist Bureau, which had taken the place of the Communist Party in Japan.[43] The group discussed a draft submitted by Voitinsky and adopted it unanimously as the Shanghai January Theses.

The January Theses dealt with the cause of the dissolution of the party and stated that the immediate task of the Japanese Communists was its reorganization. "The former leaders must put an end to all their past practical and organizational errors, and they must pass on from egocentric and impractical methods of solicitation to the practice of recruiting progressive workers and giving them executive positions."

A second meeting produced the Shanghai May Theses, which dealt with trade union problems in Japan. The recruiting of the masses of the workers into the trade unions was urged, and communist indoctrination was to be carried on through appropriate publications. On the other hand, the conquest of the masses was to be achieved "by means of a revolutionary day-by-day struggle based on realistic strategy," and by the "immediate organization of a proletarian political party," i.e., the Workers' and Peasants' Party, similar to the one proposed by the Comintern for India.[44]

Tokuda now had strong Comintern backing. On his return to Japan from Shanghai he delivered a letter of introduction to Ia. D. Ianson, first Soviet ambassador to Japan after the signing of the Russo-Japanese Treaty. Ianson was to play an important role in Japanese communist activities throughout the whole period 1925-28, for, as Travers Durkee notes, although ostensibly a Russian trade representative, he was actually a Comintern and Profintern agent.[45] "From his office in the Russian Embassy," according to Durkee, "Ianson led the Communist movement. He also decided when, and by what methods, Japanese Communists were to go to Russia."[46]

In Stalin's mind, at least, there remained no doubt about the importance of Japan to Communist plans for Asia. "An alliance between the Japanese and Soviet peoples would mark a decisive moment in the task of liberating the East," the Soviet leader told a correspondent of *Nichi-nichi* in the summer of 1925. "There is but one way out—a change in the Japanese political and social regime which would bring it into accord with the interests of the Japanese people...."[47]

In August 1925 Tokuda, with Ianson's backing, met with Arahata, Watanabe, Kitahara, Fumio Sano, and Maniwa to form a Communist Group (the Comintern would not recognize a six-member Communist Party), which formulated organizational and political theses based on the January and May Shanghai Theses.

For purposes of tightening control over Left-wing activities and reorganizing the Japanese communist movement along more orthodox lines, Moscow re-

[43] This bureau was the so-called Zammu Seiri Iin-kai ("Committee to Wind Up the Affairs of the Party").
[44] See Documents 90 and 91.
[45] Durkee, pp. 65-66.
[46] Durkee, p. 67.
[47] Stalin, *Sochineniia*, VII, 228; see Document 92.

quested the Communist Group in Tokyo to send a representative to the Enlarged ECCI Plenum of February 1926. Tokuda was chosen as the delegate. In the ECCI, E. H. Brown, British Communist, was chairman of the Japanese Committee, which also included Voitinsky and L. Geller[48] of the Soviet Union, Roy from India, and Tokuda and Katayama of Japan. It was decided in the Committee that Voitinsky should draft theses for Japan, and that Roy, Tokuda, and Katayama should form a subcommittee to pass on them. These were known as the Moscow Theses.[49]

Once more, the theses emphasized the need of properly reconstructing the Japanese Communist Party "in accordance with the Comintern's policies." In urging the Japanese Communists to develop a single political party, that is, the Workers' and Peasants' Party, the theses added: "Needless to say, the Communist Party should not lose its independence to the new party, but should rather influence the latter by establishing and controlling party cells within it."

Finally, and in accordance with the Draft Platform of 1922, the theses stated that because the revolution to be carried out by workers and peasants was expected "to be readily transformed into a proletarian revolution, the Communist Party must spearhead every progressive and democratic demand of the workers and the peasants, and devote itself to the task of fulfilling these demands."[50]

Armed with the Moscow Theses and with special instructions, Tokuda returned to Japan in order to re-establish the Japanese Communist Party. After his arrival late in June 1926, he reported to the Enlarged Conference of the Communist Group on his trip. Shortly thereafter he was imprisoned; nevertheless preparations for party reorganization continued. On December 4, 1926, at a hotel in Goshiki Hot Springs, the Communist Party of Japan was founded for a second time. But during the preparations prior to the meeting and in the sessions themselves a serious split developed between those closely associated with the Communist International and those espousing "Fukumotoism"—a demand for "separating" the essential elements of Marxism and "crystallizing" them before attempting a mass united front.[51]

Once more the Communist International took no account of real Japanese communist difficulties. Katayama told the Seventh Enlarged Plenum of the ECCI (November 22–December 16, 1926) that capitalism had achieved a temporary stabilization in Japan. The delegation from Yugoslavia, who spoke on the importance of the peasantry to the world revolution and of various steps taken by the Communists to obtain peasant support, commented favorably on the Japanese party's progress toward this end.[52]

Meantime, in Tokyo the intraparty conflict continued, although Ianson tried to work out a compromise between the contending factions. Reports reaching Soviet Russia prompted the Communist International to summon party leaders to Moscow, where a special commission had been convened to deal with the "Japanese problem."[53] Overwhelming changes had taken place in the Moscow leadership, Zinoviev having been removed from office, Trotsky discredited, and

---

[48] Geller was the head of the Eastern Section of the Profintern.

[49] Durkee, p. 75.

[50] See Document 93.

[51] Durkee, p. 83. "Fukumotoism" after Kazuo Fukumoto. See pp. 277, 278, 459.

[52] *Puti mirovoi revoliutsii*, I, 200; see also Documents 94 and 95.

[53] Swearingen and Langer, *Red Flag in Japan*, p. 26.

Bukharin elevated to new responsibilities. It is significant that Bukharin himself headed the special commission, which met with Fukumoto, Tokuda, Watanabe, Fumio Sano, Nakao, and Kawai to help the Japanese party overcome its deviations and take a correct political and organizational course.

During early meetings of the commission, Fukumotoism was the chief subject of criticism, but as the sessions progressed, various phases of the Japanese question were considered—the past history of the party, revolutionary strategy and tactics, and the structure of Japanese society.

The theses which emerged (known as the July Theses and adopted by the ECCI) represented the first full-scale Comintern analysis of the situation in Japan and the role and duties of the Japanese Communist Party. In essence, the argument of the theses was that over recent years Japanese imperialism had transformed the country into a first-class imperialist power in Asia, governed by a bloc of the bourgeoisie and the landlords under the leadership of the bourgeoisie. But, contrary to the Bukharin Draft Platform of 1922, which had urged temporary support of the liberal bourgeoisie, the July Theses stated that "the hope that the bourgeoisie can in any way be utilized as a revolutionary factor, even during the first stages of the bourgeois-democratic revolution, must be abandoned now."

Nor could analogies with China be drawn, because in China the bourgeoisie was fighting for power in the early stages of the Chinese revolution, while in Japan the bourgeoisie was already in power.[54] In Japan, the high capitalist development would contribute indirectly to the transforming of the bourgeois-democratic revolution into a socialist revolution, "a revolution against capitalism itself."

But by analogy with Russia and also with China, the Japanese proletariat was urged to assume leadership in the bourgeois-democratic revolution and to maintain a right policy toward the peasantry. Since Japanese Communists had not yet experienced Mao Tse-tung's success in the organization of peasant soviets, the theses of 1927 stated that "the peasantry can be victorious in its struggle . . . when it places itself under the leadership of the working class. History shows that the peasant movement is always doomed to failure unless it is led by the proletariat." But the role to be played by the peasants was an important one, and "An alliance of the proletariat with the peasantry is absolutely essential in the interests of both classes." The Japanese revolution would be, therefore, a bourgeois-democratic revolution, but the proletariat, which would be the leader in it, "must not lost sight of its own [proletarian] class goal. On the contrary, the prospect of transforming the [bourgeois-democratic] revolution into a socialist one is indeed the decisive factor for the proletariat during all stages of the struggle."[55]

Meantime, an important task of the Japanese Communist Party was to win control of trade unions and mass parties from within, by united front tactics. But the foremost task, the theses continued, was to cry down Japanese intervention in China and preparations for war against the Soviet Union.

By seeking to carry out the July Theses, the Communist Party of Japan brought itself into the open, fully exposed to repressive measures from the gov-

[54] For Stalin's opinion that the Kuomintang bourgeoisie government was the embryo of the future truly revolutionary government of China, see our pp. 352.

[55] See Document 94.

ernment. Already, in April 1927, General Baron Giichi Tanaka, leader of the ultraconservative Seiyū-kai Party, had become premier. As communist activities grew more intense toward the end of the year, a sharp and bitter struggle developed between governmental authorities and the Communists. Government suppression of the party became systematic and thorough.

Communist Upsurge in Indonesia

The communist movement continued to develop in Indonesia, until it reached its peak with two communist-inspired rebellions against Dutch authorities, in Java in November 1926, and in Sumatra in January 1927. Tan Malaka, who had returned from Moscow in 1925, thought the rebellion premature, but Alimin, another Indonesian Communist, pressed for it. Meanwhile, the Comintern in Moscow watched closely the development of events in Indonesia. On November 20, 1926, the ECCI called upon the workers of the world "to hasten to aid the Indonesian fighters," and specifically to "organize demonstrations before Dutch Embassies and Consulates and demand freedom for the Indonesian people and the military evacuation of the country."[56]

On November 25, the Profintern's Executive Committee stated in a manifesto:

The International Proletariat cannot idly look on at the struggle which has broken out in Indonesia. The International Proletariat must actively support the workers and peasants of Indonesia who are carrying on under the most difficult circumstances a fight against Dutch imperialism. . . . Workers of the whole world, come to the aid of Workers and Peasants of Indonesia.[57]

Dutch authorities, however, had little difficulty suppressing the rebellion, whereupon the Indonesian Communist Party, and also *Sarekat Rakjat*, were proclaimed illegal. The leaders of the Communist Party, Tan Malaka, Semaoen, and Darsono, were imprisoned, but later allowed to leave Indonesia. They stayed for a time in Siam, Japan, and China, maintaining contact with remaining communist forces in Indonesia. Later, they proceeded to Moscow, where they remained for many years absorbing communist doctrine and technique. After World War II, this group of hardened Communists returned to their native land to continue Moscow's work.[58]

Ho Chi Minh of Indochina

The Communist Party of Indochina was not formed until 1930, but efforts directed toward that goal were undertaken with the blessing of the Comintern in Moscow a number of years earlier. The formation of the Communist Party of Indochina is so closely connected with the activities of Ho Chi Minh, the present leader of the Indochinese Communists, that some account of his life must be given here.

Ho Chi Minh (Nguyen Ai Quoc), an Annamite, began his socialist train-

[56] *International Press Correspondence,* No. 80, November 25, 1926, p. 1390.
[57] *International Press Correspondence,* No. 84, December 2, 1926, p. 1438.
[58] See Document 95. For additional information see Virginia McLean Thompson, *The Left Wing in Southeast Asia,* pp. 163 ff.

ing as a young man sojourning in Paris. He went to Moscow in 1923 to study Marxism and also to attend the First Congress of the Krestintern; he became a member of the executive committee of this organization. While Ho was in Moscow, a somewhat curiously worded proclamation was issued by the Executive Committee of the Communist International directed to the Annamites of Indochina. It read: "Oh my brothers, direct the destiny of the country, fathom the desires of heaven, and no one will be able to surpass you."

The proclamation went on to explain the Comintern's desire to help "the unfortunate peoples of the colonies, such as the Annamites, whose lot has been a terrible one since the day when the French barbarians arrived there to kill and to loot." The case of Russia was cited:

Up till now there has never been a situation when the workers and the peasants have seized the reins of government, have risen in a united effort together with the workers and peasants of the rest of the world. Yet this is what happened in Russia, where victory has been won. Russia now belongs to the workers, fishermen, and peasants.

Returning to the situation in Indochina, the proclamation went on to say: "Our country is unjustly seized, we are exploited. . . . It is necessary to put an end to these iniquities. That is what the Communist International wants to do."[59]

Two years later, being assigned the task of introducing communism in Indochina, Ho Chi Minh, now calling himself Ly Thuy, left Moscow for Canton in the official capacity of a translator for the Russian consulate there. In Canton he organized the League of Oppressed Peoples[60] and the Association of Young Annamite Revolutionaries (Thanh Nien), but his work was interrupted after Chiang Kai-shek's *coup d'état* of April 1927, and he was obliged to flee with Russian Communists from China.

In Siam he again established contact with his fellow revolutionaries in Indochina, and in January 1930 he was instrumental in convening a congress of the members of this group (which now assumed the name of the Communist Party of Indochina) in Hong Kong.

Organizing the Communist Movement in India

After their early optimism about influencing India through Afghanistan, world communist leaders shifted their attention toward Mongolia and the Far East and relegated the Indian communist movement to a position of low priority in the struggle for Asia. There continued to be a two-way movement of Indian revolutionaries from Bombay, Delhi, and Calcutta to Moscow and back, but the Russian Communists found it difficult to understand and cope with Gandhiism, which did not satisfy the requirements laid down by Lenin for a bourgeois nationalist movement deserving of communist support. Finally, during the late twenties, while the Gandhian movement was growing rapidly, most of the top Russian-trained communist leaders in India were in jail for their part in the Cawnpore Conspiracy,[61] a result of Russian-directed subversion.

---

[59] *L'Asie Française*, No. 230, March–April, 1925, pp. 121–22.

[60] Another and similar league was organized in Peking in 1924 by Chinese intellectuals. For the appeal of this league to the oppressed peoples of the world, see Document 96.

[61] See below.

The upsurge of the national-liberation movement had been evident in India throughout the period 1918–22, especially in 1920–21, when general unrest among workers and peasants had culminated in a series of large-scale strikes. But in spite of these conditions, the Indian communist movement, in its early stages, attracted only a few individuals, largely from the intelligentsia, and remained almost wholly inspired from the outside. Members of this small leadership group in India, moreover, soon became involved with British authorities in the country because of their contact with Moscow and their acclamation of communist principles.

In May 1922, M. N. Roy, an Indian intellectual who, as we have already had occasion to mention, was playing an important role in the Communist International in Moscow, began publication in Berlin of the English-language publication *Vanguard*, which lasted until December 1924, when its place was taken by the Paris journal, *The Masses of India*. Through the publication of these organs and through Roy's contact with individual Communists in India, the Comintern was trying to develop a movement with legal form and yet capable of carrying on concurrently illegal activities directed at the overthrow of British rule.

In mid-1922 Roy sent back to India Nalini Gupta, who had gone to Moscow the previous year in the company of Viren Chattopadhyaya, C. P. Dutt, G. A. K. Luhani, and others. After recruiting in Calcutta a certain Muzaffar Ahmed, Gupta proceeded to Bombay for a rendezvous with a leader of student strikes named Shripad Amrit Dange.[62] Muzaffar Ahmed and Dange later figured prominently in the Cawnpore and Meerut conspiracies, and at this writing are still active leaders in the Communist Party of India.[63] Working together Gupta and Dange laid plans for a weekly, to be named *Socialist*, which later made its appearance in India under Dange's editorship.[64]

During May 1923, Muzaffar Ahmed and Shaukat Osmani[65] were arrested. Muzaffar Ahmed was released after a few days, but Osmani was taken to Peshawar, where the British police tried to connect him with the Tashkent Conspiracy.[66] Failing in this, the police released him, only to arrest him again on new charges. At about this same time Fazl-i-Ilahi Qurban, a leader of the

---

[62] Saumyendranath Tagore, *Historical Development of the Communist Movement in India*, p. 5. At this writing Tagore is living in Calcutta, where he was interviewed September 6 and 12, 1954, by Robert C. North.

[63] Material on the activities of Muzaffar Ahmed and Dange is scattered through the *Judgment* delivered by R. L. Yorke, Esq., I.C.S., Additional Sessions Judge, Meerut, on January 16, 1933, in the Meerut Communist Conspiracy Case. Sessions Trial No. 2 of 1930. King-Emperor *versus* P. Spratt and Others. Charge under Section 121-A, I.P.C. Two volumes (Simla: Government of India Press, 1933). (Hereafter cited as *Judgment in the Meerut Conspiracy Case.*) The authors are indebted to Dr. Joan Bondurant for the loan of her personal copy of the *Judgment*. For biographical materials on Dange and Ahmed see particularly Volume II, pp. 383–98 and 469–85 respectively.

[64] Tagore, *Historical Development of the Communist Party in India*, p. 5.

[65] Shaukat Osmani was one of the thirty-six Indians to meet Roy in Tashkent in October 1920. For biographical material, see *Judgment in the Meerut Conspiracy Case,* II, 431–40. According to this account (which refers in turn to his own book, *Peshawar to Moscow*), Osmani proceeded from Tashkent to Moscow, which he reached in March 1921. After a three months' stay, he returned to Tashkent, then returned to Moscow for the Third Congress of the Communist International in July 1921.

[66] See our p. 84.

Pan-Islamic Muhajirun movement[67] who had just returned to India by sea, was arrested, tried in Peshawar for conspiracy, and sentenced to three years' imprisonment. Years later he joined the Pakistan Communist Party.[68]

Nalini Gupta, who had been reporting, meanwhile, to Roy in Moscow, was arrested on his return to Calcutta along with Muzaffar Ahmed, and on March 4, 1924, Dange was apprehended in Bombay. In the Cawnpore jail, to which the various prisoners were consigned, Osmani, Dange and Muzaffar Ahmed met, along with Gupta, the only one who had known all the others previously. Others accused in the case were Roy (out of reach in Moscow), Singaravellu Chetty (soon released because of advanced age and infirmity), Professor Ghulam Hussain of Lahore (not brought to trial), and Ramcharan Sharma of Pondicherry (who eluded arrest).[69]

The charge against these men was that they had conspired with the Communist International and among themselves to deprive the King of his sovereignty in British India. Osmani, Dange, Gupta, and Muzaffar Ahmed were sentenced to four years of "rigorous imprisonment" each, but only Dange and Osmani served their full terms, the others being released after a year or so on account of ill health.[70]

Until 1924 there seems to have been no formal organization among Indian Communists, but in that year a certain Satya Bhakta in Cawnpore gathered together a group calling itself a communist party. Bhakta, observing that the government's prosecution against the Indian Comintern agents under Roy's aegis had been based on their treasonable designs against the state, considered that a communist party would not be prohibited if it avoided these features. The premise of his Indian Communist Party was announced, therefore, to be that "the present social organization and the government of India should be changed; that all sources of production should come under the possession of the general public, and that they should become masters thereof . . ."[71]

No doubt Bhakta was saved from the fate of the Cawnpore conspirators because he rejected affiliation with the Comintern and determined to evolve an independent doctrine especially suited to Indian conditions as he saw them.[72] Certainly there was a feeling among many of the comrades that Satya Bhakta's party was not really communist;[73] in any case, it was allowed to exist legally until after it had been "captured by the real Communists."[74]

Comintern reaction to this early deviation made itself felt when Bhakta's party called the first All-India Communist Conference in Cawnpore on December 28, 1925. Some 500 delegates attended the conference, which was under

[67] See our pp. 83–84.

[68] Tagore, *Historical Development of the Communist Party in India*, p. 5.

[69] *Ibid.*, p. 6.

[70] In sentencing Muzaffar Ahmed in the Meerut Conspiracy case, the Additional Sessions Judge took into account that the accused, on obtaining an early release in the Cawnpore case, had at once proceeded to resume his role as a conspirator. See *Judgment in the Meerut Conspiracy Case*, II, 675.

[71] *India in 1925–1926* (Indian Bureau of Public Information), p. 196.

[72] For more information see *The Masses of India*, Vol. II, No. 9, September 1926, supplement entitled "National Communism; Beware of False Friends."

[73] *Judgment in the Meerut Conspiracy Case*, I, 76.

[74] *Ibid.*, p. 87.

the chairmanship of Singaravellu Chetty. Various members of the party disagreed with Bhakta's determination to keep the party free from outside influence and support. Forced to resign, he issued a pamphlet in May 1926 denouncing criticisms of his policy by Roy in the columns of *The Masses of India.*[75]

The Cawnpore conference elected an executive committee and two general secretaries and resolved that party headquarters should be transferred to Bombay, whence it was soon shifted to Delhi.[76]

International communist leaders were trying to work out a more indirect course for achieving their objectives. Inasmuch as India was largely an agrarian country, Moscow Communists considered it important to gain influence among the peasantry there. On August 8, 1925, the Krestintern in Moscow addressed a letter to the Swaraj [Home Rule] Party in Calcutta expressing sympathy over the death of C. R. Das, who, with Motilal Nehru (father of Jawaharlal Nehru), had led the new party:

Bowing our heads in sorrow over the loss of your leader, we pledge on behalf of the organised peasantry throughout the world our support in every way to the measures undertaken by you for the attainment of your ultimate goal. We are convinced that the joint efforts of your party and the world's peasantry, whose spokesman is the Krestintern, will bring about the realization of those tasks for which your never-to-be-forgotten leader has fought so devoutly through the whole of his lifetime.[77]

The letter was signed on behalf of the Krestintern's presidium by Ken Hayashi, Japan; Nguyen Ai Quoc (Ho Chi Minh), Indochina; and others.

A month later, on September 20, 1925, the Krestinern informed the British Communist Party in London that "in accordance with the Praesidium of the Krestintern, a special section has been formed for the purpose of carrying out work among the Hindu peasants. . . . Our first task will be to get in touch with all the existing peasant organisations of India, even if the latter, by their programmes, be at variance with our views as to the general aims and methods of our work among the peasants."[78]

Another course that the international Communists decided to take was the formation of a new party in which the communist influence would be predominant. As early as 1923 Roy had been writing to comrades in India about the advisability of forming a "party of Workers and Peasants,"[79] but Communist leaders in Moscow and in India were slow in determining precisely what kind of party they wanted. In subsequent years Roy talked about the possibility of forming also a nationalist People's Party, which would draw its members from a broader class base, but would contain a "Communist Party inside it."[80]

Similarly, in a letter written probably toward the end of November, 1926,

[75] See *India in 1925–1926,* pp. 196–97.

[76] *Judgment in the Meerut Conspiracy Case,* II, 343. Elected to the executive committee were K. N. Joglekar, S. V. Ghate, R. S. Nimbkar, Muzaffar Ahmed, Abdul Majid, Krishna Swamy Iyengar, and J. P. Begerhotta. The general secretaries were Ghate and Begerhotta.

[77] *Communist Papers. Documents Selected from Those Obtained on the Arrest of the Communist Leaders on the 14th and 21st October, 1925* (Cmd. 2682), p. 93. (Hereafter cited as *Communist Papers.*)

[78] *Ibid.,* p. 104.

[79] M. N. Roy, *Political Letters,* pp. 30, 39.

[80] *Judgment in the Meerut Conspiracy Case,* I, 77–78.

the Foreign Bureau of the Indian Communist Party[81] urged the Communists to organize themselves as an illegal faction inside a legal Workers' and Peasants' Party which, in turn, would enter the People's Party. The letter continued, "our object will be gradually to develop the W. and P. P. into a real Communist Party by means of ideological education and political training connected with action," and proposed that the existing Workers' and Peasants' Party of Bengal should be broadened into an all-India party.[82] (On November 1, 1925, a group within the National Congress, dissatisfied with Congress Party and Swaraj Party policies, had formed the Labour Swaraj Party of the Indian National Congress. Some months later, on February 6, 1926, the new party had been reorganized at the All-Bengal Tenants' Conference held at Krishawar as the Workers' and Peasants' Party of Bengal.)[83]

The membership of the new organization consisted largely of young intellectuals, the most prominent among them being Naresh Chandra Sengupta, a well-known novelist; Atul Chandra Gupta, litterateur and Calcutta advocate; Qutbuddin Ahmed, a retired official who later left the party; Nazrul Islam, the Bengali poet, who subsequently became politically inactive; and Hemanta Sarkar, a young man of considerable brilliance who had already achieved recognition as a follower of Muzaffar Ahmed.[84] Both Nalini Gupta and Muzaffar Ahmed were active in the organizational process, but Sengupta was made chairman and Sarkar and Qutbuddin Ahmed secretaries respectively of the peasants' and workers' subcommittees.[85] The poet Nazrul Islam became editor of the party's weekly organ, Langal ("The Plough"); later, under the editorship of Muzaffar Ahmed, Langal became Ganavani ("The Voice of the Masses").

Nalini Gupta and Muzaffar Ahmed considered themselves Communists, of course, but the others tended to be middle-class nationalists who had become dissatisfied with the leadership of the nationalist movement during the mass turmoil of 1920 and 1922.[86]

The financial position of the party was precarious. For an office the executive maintained two small rooms in a mess hall on Harrison Road. Ganavani

[81] According to the so-called Assembly Letter dated December 30, 1927, and believed to have been written by M. N. Roy as a member of the ECCI and dispatched through C. P. Dutt to Muzaffar Ahmed, "The [Foreign] Bureau will have three members, namely the Comrade in Paris [probably M. A. Sipassi], C. P. D. [Dutt] and myself. . . . A resolution of the Party concerning the Foreign Bureau should be sent to the C.I. in order that all possibilities of . . . misunderstanding and conflict . . . will be eliminated in the future." The Foreign Bureau was further described in the same letter as an organ that "unites in itself representation of the CPI [Communist Party of India] and the C.I." See Judgment in the Meerut Conspiracy Case, I, 189.

[82] Ibid., pp. 87–88.

[83] A Call to Action, Being the Resolutions, Theses and Report Presented to the Third Annual Conference of the Workers' and Peasants' Party of Bengal, Bhatpara, 1928, pp. 45–46.

[84] Ibid., p. 46; also Tagore, Historical Development of the Communist Party in India, p. 7.

[85] As listed in A Call to Action, pp. 54–55, the party office holders in 1927–28 were Atul Chandra Gupta (president); Naresh Chandra Sengupta (vice-president); Saumyendranath Tagore and Muhammad Abdur Razzak Khan (general secretaries abroad and acting, respectively); and Dharanti Kanta Goswami (sectional secretary for labor). In 1928 Muzaffar Ahmed became the sole general secretary, with the chairmanship and vice-chairmanship remaining unchanged.

[86] Tagore, Historical Development of the Communist Party in India, p. 7.

was frequently forced to suspend publication, and party members worked in a state of semistarvation. Ideologically, the comrades were also impoverished. Except for the *Communist Manifesto*, Roy's secret letters, his illegal paper *Vanguard*, and a few of his pamphlets, the party had no resources for ideological development.[87]

The Communist International, meanwhile, had been working out a system of contacts between itself and Indian Communists through British party head-quarters in London. Around 1925 a Colonial Department was actually organized within the British Communist Party to establish contact with India, Egypt, Palestine, Syria, South Africa, and so forth. The British party's chain of command for colonial work, strangely enough, was so like the Empire's that certain communist circles criticized it as a species of imperialism.[88] Under this new arrangement the Comintern called to Moscow, trained, and dispatched to India a whole series of British Communists, including Percy E. Glading (alias R. Cochrane), Philip Spratt,[89] George Allison (Donald Campbell), and Benjamin Francis Bradley.

Glading, who arrived in Bombay January 30, 1925, and left India April 10, attended the All-India Trade Union Congress of that winter, but does not seem to have made contact with Communist groups.[90] Allison reached Bombay April 30, 1926, and began working with the Trade Union Congress, with the Congress Party, and especially with the Bombay Provincial Congress Committee, which was responsible for organizing the Congress Labour Party in Bombay (later the Workers' and Peasants' Party of Bombay).[91] Allison was arrested on January 23, 1927, and later convicted for possession of a false passport. After eighteen months of "rigorous imprisonment," he was deported from India.

In Allison's wake the Comintern dispatched Philip Spratt, a young Cambridge University graduate, who landed in Bombay December 31, 1926, ostensibly as the representative of a bookselling firm. "My principal messages," he has recorded in *Blowing Up India*,[92] "were that the Communist Party of India should launch a Workers' and Peasants' Party as a legal cover, and that members should get into the trade unions and obtain leadership of them." During subsequent months he set about organizing in India a labor research organization through which Comintern funds could be distributed,[93] and helped reorganize the Bombay Congress Labour Party as the Workers' and Peasants' Party of Bombay.[94] Subsequently, he was joined by Bradley, who arrived in

[87] *Ibid.*, p. 8. For a communist estimation of the Indian situation, see Document 97.

[88] *Communist Papers,* pp. 85 and 88.

[89] Philip Spratt, who has long since left the Communist movement, is now an editor of *Mysindia*, a journal published in Bangalore, where Robert C. North interviewed him June 22–23, 1954.

[90] *Judgment in the Meerut Conspiracy Case*, I, 56–59; *Communist Papers*, p. 81.

[91] *Ibid.*, pp 92–94.

[92] Philip Spratt, *Blowing Up India, Reminiscences and Reflections of a Former Comintern Emissary*, p. 29.

[93] M. R. Masani, *The Communist Party of India, a Short History*, issued under the auspices of the Institute of Pacific Relations, p. 26. In this book the author relies heavily upon "India and Communism," a confidential report compiled in the Home Department of the Government of India for the information and use of ranking officials and revised up to January 1, 1935.

[94] *Judgment in the Meerut Conspiracy Case*, I, 97.

Bombay September 23, 1927, as an agent for the "Crab Patent Underdrain Tile Company."[95]

In December 1927, Communists who had journeyed to Madras for a conference of the Indian National Congress, gathered also for a meeting of their own under the chairmanship of S. A. Dange.[96] Even now Communist Party activities were largely confined to the calling of party meetings, but individual Communists, including both Indians and the Englishmen Spratt and Bradley, had penetrated trade union organizations, "applying therein the precepts contained in the authorities on Communism,"[97] and were developing the Workers' and Peasants' parties of Bengal and Bombay into instruments for attracting and influencing the Indian masses.

Generally speaking, however, the movement was still weak, and years were to pass before the Communist Party of India was to become an effective organization.

The Communist Movement in China

The communist movements in other Asian countries during these years were of little significance compared with the vast expansion of the Chinese Communist Party under the leadership and instruction of the Comintern.

In June 1923, when the Third Congress of the Chinese Communist Party was held and it was decided, in accordance with the Comintern's instructions, to form an alliance with the Kuomintang,[98] the Chinese Communist Party had about four hundred members. The workers' movement was also in the early stages of its development. The Kuomintang, on the other hand, although it had little influence as yet upon the workers and the peasants of China, enjoyed status as the party of the Chinese government in Canton, which had been headed by Sun Yat-sen since his return to that city in February 1923. So a Communist-Kuomintang alliance offered advantages to both groups.

The Chinese Communists' dual party membership was, it is true, something of an anomaly in view of the centralistic principles characteristic of any communist party organization directed by the Comintern. But Dr. Sun could scarcely have considered the inclusion of a few Communists in the Kuomintang membership at that time as dangerous to the prestige of the Kuomintang.[99]

Borodin was now the chief adviser to the Kuomintang and gaining more and more influence in it; it was he who personally drafted most of the program adopted at the party's first congress in January 1924. Upon Borodin's sugges-

[95] *Ibid.*, p. 162.

[96] According to Saumyendranath Tagore in his *Historical Development of the Communist Party of India*, this meeting adopted a Constitution of the Communist Party of India, passed a decision to affiliate with the Third International, and elected a central committee including Muzaffar Ahmed, Osmani, Dange, S. V. Ghate, Tagore, and "three others." Ghate, according to the same source, was elected general secretary of the party.

[97] *Judgment in the Meerut Conspiracy Case*, I, 167.

[98] For the text of the Comintern's instructions, see Documents 98 and 99.

[99] In 1929, Ch'en Tu-hsiu, now a dissenter, quoted the following statement made by Dr. Sun at that time to a Comintern delegate: "Inasmuch as the Chinese Communist Party joins the Kuomintang, it must subordinate itself to the Kuomintang's rule of discipline, and it must not express any open criticism of the latter. If the Communists refuse to follow these rules, I shall be obliged to expel them from the Kuomintang. If Soviet Russia takes the side of the Communist Party, I shall be obliged to come forward against Soviet Russia." (*Biulleten Oppozitsii*, No. 15-16, 1930, p. 20.)

tion the Kuomintang party structure was generally reorganized along communist lines. Principles of strict party discipline[100] were adopted, as were measures advocating "equalization of the land," "state control of capital," co-operation with the Soviet Union, repudiation of all unequal treaties signed by China, and the repudiation of foreign concessions and extraterritoriality. Also adopted by the congress were a set of party regulations, a manifesto outlining the perspectives of the coming struggle, a program of action, and a statement of principles based on Sun Yat-sen's three principles of "People's Nationalism," "People's Sovereignty," and "People's Livelihood."[101]

Russian influence in Canton was further consolidated when the Kuomintang established a special military school at Whampoa, with Chiang Kai-shek at its head, to train commanders for the newly organized Kuomintang army. Russian military experts, headed by one Galen (Vasilii Blücher), played an important role at Whampoa, and acted also as military advisers for the national-revolutionary army, which was soon to undertake a military campaign against the northern warlords.

A first offensive against northern China, ordered by Sun Yat-sen before the organization of the new revolutionary army was completed, failed, and the Kuomintang troops were forced to return to Canton. We shall see how a second northern expedition progressed far more satisfactorily for the Nationalists.

By 1924, then, close contacts had been established between Moscow and Dr. Sun Yat-sen; Russian Communist influence was definitely in the ascendant. A few years later Stalin would explain Russian Communist—and more particularly Leninist—approval of Sun Yat-sen this way: "After the October Revolution, and particularly in 1920–21, Lenin had special respect for Sun Yat-sen, mainly because by that time Sun had begun to come into close contact and to co-operate with the Chinese Communists." That did not mean, Stalin said, that Sun was a Communist, since Sun's teaching and the communist or Marxist ideas did not harmonize. "If, however, the Chinese Communists co-operate with the Kuomintang members, it can be explained by the fact that Sun Yat-sen's three principles, i.e., democracy, nationalism, and socialism, represent a completely acceptable basis for the joint work between the Communists and the Sun-ists in the Kuomintang at the present stage of development of the Chinese revolution."[102] The Russians saw important advantages in riding Chinese currents.

[100] For the text of the resolution on party discipline taken at the First Congress of the Kuomintang, 1924, see V. D. Vilensky (Sibiriakov), *Sun Yat-sen, otets kitaiskoi revoliutsii*, pp. 172–73.

[101] Leonard Shih-lien Hsü, *Sun Yat-sen, His Political and Social Ideals*, p. 119.

[102] Stalin, *Sochineniia*, IX, 203. Apparently Dr. Sun's principle of People's Livelihood was rendered by Stalin as socialism.

C. CHINA: THE FATEFUL YEARS 1925–1927

The Shanghai Events of 1925

The anti-imperialist May Fourth (1919) Movement, initiated by Chinese students, has been mentioned earlier. In the same year the Chinese workers' movement had begun to take shape also, when the first workers' union was formed in Shanghai. Similar unions sprang up in Canton and Hong Kong. In 1920 Hong Kong workers organized a strike which lasted twenty days. On May 1, 1922, the first All-China Congress of Trade Unions took place in Canton with 162 delegates attending. These delegates represented, according to a prominent Soviet writer, about 270,000 workers from over one hundred different workers' organizations.[1] In 1922 and 1923 Bolshevik organizers were quick to take advantage of unrest among seamen, dockers, railway men, textile workers, and similar groups, and played an important part in strikes that gripped large sectors of the country at that time. The launching of a struggle by the Chinese workers against their foreign employers, who were almost wholly British or Japanese, was made possible, according to the same Soviet writer, because "the working class of China already had its leader, namely the Communist Party."[2] Actually, the direct influence of the Communist Party at that time was smaller than certain students of Chinese affairs boasted.

In the last days of May events occurred in China which communist historians have interpreted as having given a tremendous impetus to the Chinese revolution of 1925–27.

On April 19, 1925, a strike was started by the Chinese textile workers at Tsingtao, and a month later the Japanese factory administration agreed to the workers' demands. However, when on May 25, the workers came to work, they were told by the administration that, according to the instructions received from the factory headquarters in Tokyo, the contract between them and the workers was annulled. When the workers protested, Japanese armed guards fired upon them.

In retaliation the workers of Shanghai, and especially the textile workers, led a demonstration of protest on May 30 before the foreign settlement. They too were fired upon, and some workers were killed.

This episode set off a great mass anti-imperialist movement which demanded the abolition in China of all special privileges for foreigners. It opened with a strike of workers in Shanghai, and soon spread to Hong Kong, Canton, and Peking. At first strikers found support from the Chinese national bourgeoisie, and for a while the latter took part in the joint committee for supervising the strike, which included delegates from the workers, students, and merchants. The chairman of this committee was Li Li-san, a Moscow-trained Chinese Communist, who, according to M. N. Roy, was assigned by Borodin "to Shanghai to organize the antiforeign movement."[3]

[1] G. B. Erenburg, *Ocherki natsionalno-osvoboditelnoi borby kitaiskogo naroda v noveishee vremia,* p. 52.

[2] *Ibid.*, p. 54.

[3] M. N. Roy to R. C. North in an interview in Dehra Dun, India, October 15, 1951.

When on June 23 more shooting of the Chinese workers took place before the foreign concession of Shameen, the strike of the Hong Kong and Canton workers became general, disrupting and paralyzing the brisk trade of these cities. The Hong Kong and Canton strikes lasted for some sixteen months (June 1925 to October–November, 1926), inflicting very serious damage to foreign trading and commercial interests in China. The strike was now led by the Workers' Strike Committee, which was controlled by the Communists.

Bolshevik interest in these Chinese events was demonstrated in Russia by meetings of protest against the action of the imperialists and by the slogan "Hands off China." In their official public pronouncements, nevertheless, Soviet leaders denied any connection with the anti-imperialist movement that was engulfing large sections of China. In July 1925, Chicherin criticized in a press interview the statement made by Lord Birkenhead, Secretary of State for India, who had accused Russia in his speech of "unceasing underground activities throughout the world to destroy the British Empire." Chicherin spoke of such utterances as extraordinary and as a threat to the Soviet Union. He denied absolutely any Russian Communist participation or encouragement of the anti-British sentiment in China:

The first thing that interests the Britons in their relations with China is the development of trade between the two countries. I declare that we have done absolutely nothing that might even in the slightest degree injure China's foreign trade, in particular . . . its trade with England. . . . I do not deny that our government and our people sympathize with the struggle of the Chinese people, . . . but this does not mean intervention in the internal affairs of another state, and our policy carefully and strictly avoids anything that might be interpreted as such intervention.

He denied that Soviet Russia tried to create chaos in China, and added: "On the contrary, we regard with the utmost sympathy the development in China of progressive principles and productive forces, and the close association of the Chinese people with all other peoples."[4]

Signs of Split Within the Kuomintang

By this time, Right-wing elements within the Kuomintang were viewing the Russian influence with increasing apprehension, and an all-out struggle between Right and Left soon materialized. As early as 1925, a Rightist group opposed to the Russian domination organized a plot to set up new leadership, but was discredited and expelled from the Kuomintang. In January 1926, Right-wing voices were again heard demanding an end to communist influence, but the Kuomintang Second Congress of that month voted to continue the alliance with the Communists. Then, on March 20, 1926, Chiang Kai-shek used the occasion of Borodin's temporary absence from Canton to carry out an anticommunist coup, which, for the moment, reduced the power of the Communists within both the Canton government and the Kuomintang.

But with Borodin's return to Canton, a truce was patched up. It was agreed that in return for Russian assistance in a new campaign against northern warlords the alliance of the Kuomintang and the Communists would continue.

[4] *Izvestiia*, No. 148, July 2, 1925, p. 2. Text appears in Degras, II, 51–52. Chicherin's ambiguous statement contrasts with both the preceding communist activities in China and Moscow's increased influence in 1926 and 1927 as suggested on the following pages.

The northern campaign, launched in July 1926, was designed to defeat Wu P'ei-fu, Chang Tso-lin, and other northern militarists, and to unify the Chinese nation. Advanced contingents of Communist-trained propagandists and political agitators helped out by organizing strikes and peasant revolts behind enemy lines and even infiltrated the warlords' armies.

Referring to the advance of the Chinese revolutionary army and the concurrent progress in labor and peasant unionization, Stalin remarked:

The advance of the Cantonese in a northern direction is usually interpreted not as the development of the Chinese revolution, but as a struggle between the Cantonese general and the [northern warlords]. This is a very serious mistake. The revolutionary armies of China serve as the most important factor in the struggle of the Chinese workers and peasants for their own liberation . . . because the Cantonese advance means a blow against imperialism, a blow to its agents in China. It means freedom of assembly, freedom of strikes, freedom of the press, freedom to organize the revolutionary elements in China in general, and the workers in particular.[5]

Military successes in the northern campaign, by bringing Wuhan province under Kuomintang dominion, resulted in a resurgence of communist strength, for Left elements predominated among Wuhan friends of the Kuomintang. Exploiting this advantageous situation to the fullest, Borodin—employing against Chiang the tactics Chiang had previously employed against him—engineered an extraordinary Congress of the Kuomintang in Canton in October 1926. At this gathering Borodin succeeded in obtaining a vote transferring the Kuomintang capital from Canton to Hankow in Wuhan Province, a move which for the time being strengthened the Russian hand.

The Comintern's Line in Regard to the Chinese Communist Party, February–November, 1926

Just as China appeared on the verge of violent revolution across the countryside an old specter rose to plague the Communists, namely, their fundamental indecision whether to throw their support wholly to the bourgeois nationalists or to incite and develop peasant (and working class) rebellion. In trying to do both at the same time, they succeeded in neither.

In their attempt to direct the Chinese communist movement, the Moscow Communists were actually at a disadvantage because they were but slightly familiar with the Chinese situation and with Chinese ways of thinking. Moreover, Lenin was now dead and Stalin, who was gradually gaining the upper hand in the Soviet state, the party, and the Communist International,[6] was not only new to many of his tasks, but also extremely jealous of his much better educated fellow Communists, especially Trotsky.

Soviet leaders could draw on Lenin's teachings and on the Russian revolutionary experiences of 1905 and 1917, but there were no certain answers to such key questions as when soviets should be introduced into an economically backward country like China, and to what extent the peasantry and the national liberal bourgeoisie should be brought into the revolutionary movement.

---

[5] Stalin, *Sochineniia*, VIII, 362.

[6] Stalin actively participated for the first time in the sessions of the Fifth Congress of the Communist International in 1924.

We have already noted Lenin's interpretation of the Russian bourgeois-democratic revolution of 1905 and the stages that this revolution was to pass through, as Lenin had visualized it, before it was to reach a socialist stage.[7] But whereas the various stages of the Russian revolution had occurred rapidly, so that the revolutionary proletariat's union with the liberal bourgeoisie was of but short duration, Stalin, as we shall see, expected to maintain such a union for a much longer period in China, failing to notice the bourgeois nature of the Kuomintang and accrediting it with a revolutionary potential which it did not possess.

Something similar can be said of Stalin's attitude toward the establishment of soviets in China. These bodies in Russia had originated as organizations for mass revolt during distinctly revolutionary circumstances; their goal was to overthrow the existing government, and to establish their own power instead. Stalin believed there were no such circumstances in China:

> The history of the workers' soviets shows us these soviets can exist and develop only if conditions are favorable for the passing of the bourgeois-democratic revolution into a proletarian revolution, in other words, if conditions are favorable for the passing of authority from the bourgeoisie to the proletariat. Perhaps the workers' soviets perished in Leningrad and Moscow in 1905, just as did the workers' soviets in Germany in 1918, because the necessary favorable conditions were lacking.
>
> It is quite possible that had there been in Russia in 1905 a broad revolutionary organization such as the present Left wing of the Kuomintang in China, there would have been no soviets there at that time. However, there could be no such organization in Russia at that time because the Russian workers and peasants were not subject to national oppression, and, on the contrary, the Russians themselves were the oppressors of other nationalities. Organizations such as the Left wing of the Kuomintang can come into being only under the conditions of a national oppression which unites into one broad organization the revolutionary elements of the country.[8]

The estimate among Russian Communists of the revolutionary potential of the Kuomintang was so high that even the most radical of them all, Zinoviev, had this to say before he joined the Trotskyist camp of the communist alliance with the Kuomintang:

> The Soviet republics have at present one front line with China. This is an event of great world-wide historical significance. . . . The growth of the Kuomintang, the party of Sun Yat-sen, which sympathizes with us to a certain extent, is of tremendous importance to the Comintern.[9]

It should be borne in mind, moreover, that Russian Communist support of the Chinese revolution was planned, to a great extent, as a means for undermining the strength of Great Britain and other imperialist countries by depriving them of opportunities for colonial and semicolonial exploitation.

In accordance with their confidence in the bourgeois-democratic revolution of China, and with their interpretation of the Kuomintang as an organization

[7] See our pp. 36–39.

[8] Excerpt from Stalin's speech at the Eighth Plenum of the ECCI, May 24, 1927 (Stalin, *Ob oppozitsii*, pp. 598–99).

[9] Zinoviev's statement at the Fifth Enlarged Plenum of the ECCI, March–April, 1925 (*Rasshirennyi plenum Ispolkoma Kommunisticheskogo Internatsionala, Stenograficheskii otchet*, p. 44).

of a revolutionary liberal bourgeoisie, Stalin and his associates found it expedient to outline in detail how the Communists in China were to deal with the revolutionary situation developing there.

The ECCI's Sixth Enlarged Plenum (February 17–March 15, 1926) laid down a line calling for the Chinese Communist Party to continue building up a four-class alliance of workers, peasants, intellectuals, and urban petty bourgeoisie within the Kuomintang for the struggle against "the foreign imperialists and the whole militarist-feudal order, for the independence of the country, and for a single revolutionary democratic government."

This Comintern executive session interpreted the frustration of Right-wing attempts to oust the Communists from membership in the Kuomintang as "strengthening the revolutionary trend of the activities of the Kuomintang and the Canton government and assuring the Kuomintang of the revolutionary support of the proletariat."

The Comintern consequently called upon the Chinese Communists in the Kuomintang to support the formation of a revolutionary army, and instructed its own members to "make unmistakably clear to the toiling masses of all imperialist countries the significance of the Chinese toilers' struggle against the imperialists."

The Chinese Communist Party and the Kuomintang were further directed to "develop intensive political work, organizing mass activities and support for the struggle of the People's Armies, utilizing internal contradictions in the camp of the imperialists and counterposing to them a single national-revolutionary front of the large strata of the population (workers, peasants, bourgeoisie) under the leadership of the revolutionary democratic organizations."

The Comintern executive body warned the Chinese Communists at the same time against "a formless merging" of their party into a general democratic movement. The peasant movement was declared to be the fundamental problem of the Chinese national-liberation movement, and the Communists were instructed to work among the peasants and with the existing peasant organizations in order to bring the peasants into the movement in co-operation with the workers. Beyond this, the Chinese Communist Party was ordered to open its membership to rank-and-file workers in order to become a mass organization.

This policy—particularly where it called for co-operation with the Kuomintang and penetration into existing Chinese peasant organizations in an attempt to win mass support—was violently criticized by Trotsky and the Left opposition within Russia, who advocated immediate struggle for the establishment of soviets in China. By 1926, however, the Stalin machine was well enough entrenched within the ECCI to get Trotsky's views denounced as "skipping over the revolutionary-democratic stage of the movement straight to the proletarian dictatorship and soviet power, forgetting the most important and decisive factor of all—the peasantry."[10]

There was logic behind the Stalinist view. Trotsky tended to overlook vast

[10] The complete text of the "Theses on the Chinese Question" of the ECCI's Sixth Enlarged Plenum (February 17–March 15, 1926) appears in *Kommunisticheskii Internatsional v dokumentakh*, pp. 619–23; see Document 100. For a somewhat sympathetic analysis of Trotsky's position in regard to communist policies in China, see Harold R. Issacs, *The Tragedy of the Chinese Revolution*, pp. 188–99.

differences between East and West, to assume that what had succeeded in
Russia would succeed equally well in China. Was it not wiser to work through
an indigenous organization, the Kuomintang, in which the masses had faith?
So far, so good. But what about the genie which communist agitators had
already uncorked, peasant revolt in the countryside? Stalin's policy statements
were ambiguous; he seemed to advocate taking two antagonistic courses at
once.

The crux of the matter was this: Many Kuomintang leaders, both political
and military, were landowners who could not contemplate agrarian revolution
with equanimity. The countryside was indeed on the edge of revolt, but in
order to retain the support of Kuomintang armies, the Central Committee of
the Russian Communist Party, now completely dominated by Stalin, at what
was perhaps the crucial moment made a decision. In October 1926 the Kremlin
dispatched a telegram ordering the Chinese Communists to restrain the peasant
movement until Shanghai was taken, in order not to antagonize Kuomintang
generals in command of the northern campaign. Later, under Trotsky's attack
(August 1, 1927), Stalin admitted that the telegram was a "mistake."[11] However, in view of the old Lenin-Roy controversy over fundamental policy, it is
difficult to perceive how he could have gotten off the horns of his dilemma.

Nonetheless in November, a month after the dispatch of this telegram,
Stalin, in both his speech and the theses adopted at the Seventh Plenum of the
ECCI, laid strong emphasis on the importance of the peasant question and a
radical agrarian program, and in that way nullified to a great extent the directive of the previous month.

Speaking before the Chinese Commission of the ECCI's Seventh Enlarged
Plenum on November 30, 1926, Stalin said:

... we might imagine [from reading the various theses] that there is at present in
China no actual imperialist intervention, but only a struggle between the North and
the South, or of one group of generals against another group of generals. In addition, there is an inclination to understand by intervention a condition in which foreign
troops march into Chinese territory; if this does not take place, then there is no
intervention. This is a serious error, comrades. ... In the present circumstances,
... imperialism prefers to intervene against the revolution by organizing civil war
within a dependent country, by financing the counterrevolutionary forces against the
revolution, by moral and financial support of its Chinese agents. ... Intervention
by using other people—that is the kernel of imperialist intervention at present.[12]

Stalin, on the basis of this analysis, saw Kuomintang forces serving as a
major weapon against the Peking warlords and refused to believe that these
same troops could be turned against him. Yet it was in the same speech that
Stalin remarked:

I know that there are certain people among the members of the Kuomintang, and
even among the Chinese Communists, who do not consider it possible to unleash the

---

[11] "I am far from saying that this telegram was correct. I never considered, nor do
I consider now, our Central Committee infallible. Separate mistakes can take place, and
this telegram is unquestionably a mistake." Stalin's statement at the joint session of the
party's Central Committee and Central Control Commission, August 1, 1927 (Stalin, *Marksizm i natsionalno-kolonialnyi vopros*, p. 178).

[12] *Voprosy kitaiskoi revoliutsii*, pp. 43–44.

revolution in the countryside, because they fear that if the peasantry is drawn into the revolution the united anti-imperialist front will be undermined. This is a profound mistake, comrades. The anti-imperialist front in China will be all the stronger and more powerful the sooner and more solidly the Chinese peasantry is drawn into the revolution.[13]

The Seventh Plenum, so it appears, adopted a dual tactic which emphasized peasant revolt but provided at the same time for support of the landholding Kuomintang. "If the proletariat does not put forward a radical agrarian program," the theses of the Plenum declared, "it will fail to attract the peasantry into the revolutionary struggle and will lose hegemony in the national-liberation movement."[14] Yet all this must be accomplished within the Kuomintang, many of whose bourgeois members "would continue to march with the revolution for a certain time."

The Kuomintang government, the Communists reasoned, would provide effective channels for reaching the peasantry. Later, while supporting the Nationalist Left wing against the Right, Communist members of the government could develop the Kuomintang "into a real people's party—a solid revolutionary bloc of the proletariat, the peasantry, the urban petty bourgeoisie, and the other oppressed and exploited strata."[15]

The Seventh Plenum pushed its contradictions even further, calling upon the Chinese Communist Party to consolidate its alliance with the peasantry, even at the risk of alienating sections of the bourgeoisie. The party was to support "the attempt to overthrow the tyranny of the gentry and the rural officials in the villages, to replace this old semifeudal bureaucracy with local revolutionary organizations which will carry out the decrees of the revolutionary government and protect the interests of the principal masses of the peasantry."[16]

In his November 30 speech before the Chinese Commission, Stalin personally had answered Russian Leftist criticism of Comintern policies in China. Declaring the Chinese revolution to be passing through a transitional stage of bourgeois-democratic revolution for national liberation, he argued that the Chinese Communists should not only remain within the Kuomintang but intensify their work in it. The Kuomintang bourgeois-democratic government, so Stalin believed, was the embryo of the future truly revolutionary government of China.

This future revolutionary government in China, according to Stalin, would resemble "the government which was spoken of in our country in 1905, i.e., a dictatorship of the proletariat and peasantry, but with the distinguishing feature that it will be predominantly an anti-imperialist power. It will be a power of transition to noncapitalist, or, to be more exact, to socialist development in China."

Stalin declared that the immediate formation of peasant soviets, as advocated by the Trotskyists, would be premature. Committees should be elected by the peasants, capable of formulating the demands of the peasantry and of

[13] Ibid., p. 51.
[14] Kommunisticheskii Internatsional v dokumentakh, p. 674.
[15] Ibid., p. 676.
[16] Ibid., pp. 674–75.

taking "all the necessary measures for realizing these demands by revolutionary methods." He did, however, call upon both the Chinese Communist Party and the Kuomintang to raise the question of nationalization of the land.

Communists were to take part in the new national-revolutionary government in order to satisfy the peasants' most urgent demands by legal action, "whether by stripping the landowners of their land or by reducing taxation and rents—whatever the circumstances demand."[17] As for the peasants themselves, Stalin declared that their attitude toward the revolution would depend in large measure on the behavior of the army and its readiness to help them.

Stalin called upon the Chinese Communist Party to demand the abolition of unequal treaties; to advocate nationalization of the railways, of the important factories, and of the land; and to devote special attention to political work in the army and the study of military arts.

Lastly, he declared that three factors would facilitate the revolution in China: (1) it would be directed against imperialism; (2) the capitalist bourgeoisie were weak; (3) Soviet experience and aid would be available.[18]

Shortly after Stalin delivered this speech, the Seventh Plenum adopted its above-noted theses on the Chinese revolution. Reflecting Stalin's views, these theses set forth what the Chinese party should do and how it should go about doing it.

A detailed agrarian program called for reduction of rents, abolition of numerous taxes and the introduction of a single progressive agricultural tax, confiscation of monasterial and church lands and land belonging to landholders engaged in fighting the Kuomintang, arming of the middle peasants,[19] co-ordination of all armed forces in rural districts with the revolutionary authorities, low-interest loans to peasants, determined measures to abolish usury, and a guarantee of perpetual leases to tenant farmers.

The Chinese party was directed to increase its work among the industrial proletariat, to work for the creation of mass industrial unions, to strengthen the contact of the Chinese trade union movement with the world trade union movement, to elaborate strike tactics, to organize mutual aid and strike funds, and to support the formation of co-operatives. It was to agitate for complete freedom of activity for the revolutionary peasants' and workers' organizations, for the legalization of trade unions, for enactment of advanced trade union laws and the right to strike, for an eight-hour day and other forms of adequate social legislation, and for withdrawal of all military units and police detachments from the factories.

It was also stated in these theses that "during the last two years, imperialism has suffered heavy defeats in China, the effects of which will contribute considerably to the aggravation of the crisis of world capitalism. . . ." Declaring the Chinese revolution by virtue of its "anti-imperialist character" to

---

[17] *Voprosy kitaiskoi revoliutsii*, pp. 52–53.

[18] Full text, *ibid.*, 41–56; also Stalin, *Sochineniia*, VIII, 357–74; for excerpts see Document 101.

[19] Middle peasant—a term coined by Lenin when he introduced his three-level distinction among peasants: (1) the *kulak*, or rich peasant, employing other people's labor, who was to be exterminated; (2) the *bedniak*, or poor peasant, who was to be helped and drawn into the party; (3) the *seredniak*, or middle peasant (representing in Russia actually the peasant majority), who was to be courted and drawn into the communist orbit.

"LONG LIVE THE REVOLUTION." Shanghai's bourgeoisie and European imperialists are routed by Chinese revolutionary forces. Pravda, No. 65, March 22, 1927.

be an inseparable part of the international revolution, the theses stated that this factor would "determine the history of the Chinese revolution and the alignment of the social forces participating in it."

The theses then analyzed the stages of the Chinese revolution. The first stage had been dominated by the national bourgeoisie. The second (and current) stage had been marked by a shift in the social basis of the revolution toward the proletariat, the peasantry, and the urban petty bourgeoisie, with a section of the capitalist bourgeoisie remaining. In the emerging third stage, "the driving force of the movement will be a bloc of a still more revolutionary nature"—i.e., minus most of the remaining capitalist bourgeoisie.

The theses also warned against Right-wing attempts to wrest leadership of the national-revolutionary movement from the revolutionary bloc, both from within the movement and by new conservative forces which, because of the success of the revolution, could be expected to join forces with it in order to gain leadership.[20]

The Break Between the Right and Left Wings of the Kuomintang

In China, Kuomintang forces were marching toward the mouth of the Yangtze, and uncounted Kuomintang sympathizers revealed themselves as news of the success of the Nationalist armies spread rapidly throughout China and Manchuria. But political differences within the Kuomintang became more intense. The conflict between Right and Left was about to enter a new phase.

Early in 1927, as Kuomintang armies neared Shanghai, the simmering resentments and discontents of the masses boiled over into a powerful movement directed against both foreign imperialism and native conservatism. On February 17, 1927, in celebration of Nationalist victories in Chekiang province, a Communist-inspired general strike was proclaimed. As the Nationalist armies continued to advance, the general strike burst on February 22 into insurrection against the existing regime in Shanghai.

By February 24, the insurrection was put down with great ferocity by the Shanghai garrison and the police of the International Settlement, only to flare up again a little later. The insurrectionists continued to look for help from the approaching Nationalist army under Chiang Kai-shek.

On March 26 Chiang's army entered Shanghai. But, to the consternation of the insurrectionists, Chiang sided—cautiously, as yet—with the anticommunist group in suppression of the insurrection. The uncomfortable alliance of Chinese Nationalists and Chinese Communists erupted into a new small-scale civil war, with the insurrectionists finally suffering defeat.

On March 24 Chiang's Kuomintang forces attacked Nanking. There was looting, and several missionaries and consular officials were killed. The responsibility for these outrages has never been satisfactorily fixed, but it was widely assumed that Communists within the city had organized the antiforeign outburst. Those who remained of the Nanking foreign colony removed themselves to a hilltop and awaited rescue, which was effected under cover of an Anglo-American barrage. In retaliation for the murder of foreigners, the

[20] *Kommunisticheskii Internatsional v dokumentakh*, pp. 668–80; see Document 102.

British and American warships fired a volley upon the city, inflicting considerable damage and killing a number of Chinese. *Pravda* promptly entered an indignant protest:

The slaughter of Nanking has brought a terrible clarity into the situation. Even the blind must now see the real and true nature of the policy of imperialism in China. . . . [The United States] has for a long time played the role of a liberal "well-wisher" toward the Chinese revolution. Now, when everyone has seen the "Anglo-American bloc" in action, it is easy to understand that America is nothing but a wolf in sheep's clothing.[21]

Moscow continued, however, to misunderstand both the position of Chiang Kai-shek and the nature of the revolutionary potential in China. On April 2, 1927, *Pravda* was still confident of the strength of the revolutionary forces in China:

The Chinese revolution has made a tremendous step forward. If it goes on developing this way, it is bound to radically alter the political physiognomy of the globe. The forces of the revolution will gain over the forces of capitalism. The Chinese proletariat is already occupying the foremost position in the great struggle for liberation. . . . The influence of the Communist Party of China is growing.[22]

Ten days later (April 12) Chiang, in an open attack upon both the Chinese Communists and the Communist-led workers, finally severed the last bond between himself and his erstwhile allies. From Moscow's viewpoint this coup dealt a serious blow to the developing Chinese revolutionary movement. Chiang Kai-shek, "The Hangman," was now denounced by Moscow "with indignation and hatred [as] the enemy of the working class movement."[23]

But even at that stage Soviet leaders refused to be alarmed over the situation in China:

The significance of the Shanghai *coup d'état* lies in the fact that it cut another furrow in the history of the great struggle for liberation in China. . . . We sincerely believe that in the coming difficult period of struggle, the Chinese revolutionary camp will have the necessary self-control and self-reliance. . . . Chiang Kai-shek has challenged the masses. The masses will accept his challenge. Defeat is the best teacher. The Chinese workers and peasants, all Chinese revolutionaries, will learn the necessary lesson from the Shanghai tragedy.[24]

Once the Nationalist armed forces had consolidated themselves in Nanking, Chiang Kai-shek, serving now as spokesman for the anticommunist Right-wing Nationalists, officially established on September 19, 1927,[25] a new Kuomintang government with Nanking as its capital. So it came about that there were actually three governments functioning in China: the Kuomintang government in Nanking, the Kuomintang Left government in Hankow, and the coalition of warlords operating out of Peking—all three in violent conflict.

   [21] *Pravda*, No. 69, March 27, 1927, p. 1.
   [22] *Pravda*, No. 74, April 2, 1927, p. 1.
   [23] "Appeal to the Proletariat of the World and the Oppressed People," by the Executive Committee of the Communist International, April 1927 (*International Press Correspondence*, No. 26, April 21, 1927, pp. 525–26).
   [24] *Pravda* (Editorial), No. 85, April 15, 1927, p. 1; see Document 103.
   [25] Malcolm W. Davis and Walter H. Mallory (eds.), *A Political Handbook of the World, 1928*, p. 37.

The Peking Raid on the Soviet Embassy

While opposition to Soviet Russian influence in South China became more and more evident, the Peking government, concerned over communist activities in the north, accused the Soviet embassy in Peking of disseminating communist propaganda and sheltering government-prosecuted Chinese Communists.

The first definite evidence of Soviet propaganda was obtained on March 1, 1927, when Chinese authorities detained in Pukow a Soviet steamer, *Pamiat Lenina,* which was allegedly carrying a cargo of tea. Borodin's wife and other Soviet officials were found on the boat carrying with them a large quantity of communist literature. Although the Soviet government launched an immediate protest, the Chinese government refused to surrender the ship or the arrested Soviet citizens on the ground that the shipment represented a breach of the Sino-Soviet agreement of 1924.

The next move of the Peking government was to carry out a search of the Soviet embassy in Peking. The execution of this plan was somewhat complicated, since, by the Boxer Protocol, Chinese troops were debarred from the Legation Quarter. But after negotiating with the Dutch minister, W. L. Oudendijk, the senior representative of foreign powers in the Legation Quarter, Chinese officials effected a raid on the Soviet premises.[26]

In the process of the search substantial propaganda material was uncovered and several Soviet employees as well as a number of Chinese found in the building were arrested. On April 9, 1927, the Soviet government sent a lengthy protest to the Chinese government, demanding the immediate withdrawal of Chinese troops and police from the Soviet embassy, the release of the arrested Soviet employees, the return of the documents removed, and so forth. On the whole, however, the protest was mild: "The Soviet government limits itself to the above elementary demands, which are in no way calculated to humiliate the Peking government. Any imperialist government whose representatives had been subjected to similar violence would have answered with the sharpest reprisals." The Soviet government realized "that the Peking cabinet has become the instrument of foreign imperialist circles"; nevertheless, it had no intention of doing what imperialist powers would have done in a similar case, since Soviet policy was determined solely by the interests of the toilers of the whole world, including China.[27]

The status of the Chinese revolution was discussed by Rykov in his speeches to the Thirteenth Congress of Soviets of the R.S.F.S.R. on April 10, 1927. Rykov pointed out the temporary coincidence of hostile actions toward Soviet Russia throughout Chinese territory (i.e., in Peking as well as in Shanghai and Nanking), which indicated to him that a large-scale conspiracy against the U.S.S.R. had been worked out in advance by several governments. He

[26] Oudendijk describes this episode in his reminiscences, *Ways and By-Ways in Diplomacy* (London, 1939).

[27] *Pravda,* No. 81, April 10, 1927, p. 1; see Document 104. Toward the end of April, 1927, a special military court tried the prisoners arrested in the Peking raid. Twenty Chinese prisoners, including the leader of the communist group in Peking, Li Ta-chao, were sentenced to death by strangulation. Fifteen Russian prisoners were given a preliminary trial starting the following July 12, and on September 15 were pronounced guilty of having agitated to produce an internal disturbance in China. The case of the Russians was then sent to a higher court.

condemned the Peking raid as absolutely unjustified, and protested that the Soviet Union "has not a single member of the Red Army on Chinese territory to interfere in the internal affairs of China."[28]

Referring in a later speech to Borodin's activities in China, Rykov remarked:

We are blamed for the fact that the Soviet citizen, Borodin, is participating in Chinese affairs. Intrigues against the British are attributed to Borodin's activities. I must declare that Borodin is not our representative in China. He has received no instructions from the government of the [Soviet] Union, and consequently, our government cannot be responsible for his actions. . . . We are, for instance, aware of the fact that Chang Tso-lin has a British military adviser, Sutton. I do not think that this British adviser is manifesting any great energy to awaken the good feelings of Chang Tso-lin for our government. Nevertheless, I am not at all inclined to blame the British and Chamberlain for the fact that Sutton is Chang Tso-lin's adviser.[29]

Other seized documents contradicted Rykov's claims also. N. Mitarevsky, who was associated with a commission appointed by the Chinese government "to examine and translate the documents seized at the Soviet Embassy,"[30] later published a volume of them with special annotations and, in some cases, facsimiles of the original copies. From these documents it appeared that the Soviet military attaché had played an important role in the Chinese revolutionary movement.

In 1926, reporting on the best means of drawing various Chinese generals to the revolutionary cause, the Soviet military attaché had stated: "As previous experience has shown, the chief trump in our hands for establishing our influence in the people's armies is the supply of arms." Another document in this collection dealt with the regulations relating to groups of instructors and advisers for the Canton revolutionary army. Paragraph I stated:

A Chief Military Adviser is attached to the National-Revolutionary government and to the Commander-in-Chief of the National-Revolutionary army. He is at the same time the Chief of the South-China group who directs the whole work of the group and is responsible for it.[31]

Still another document contained instructions for the military attaché in China, presumably from Moscow. The remaining unburnt facsimile of the original reproduced in Mitarevsky's volume and marked "absolutely secret," states as follows:

Enclosed herewith a resolution on the Chinese question carried at the 7th Plenary Session of the Executive Committee of the Communist International.[32] We are sending you herewith an instruction drafted in conformity with this resolution which you shall carry out.

1. Every attention must be paid at present to lend to the revolutionary movement in China an *exclusively* national character. It is therefore necessary to carry on

[28] *Pravda*, No. 82, April 12, 1927, p. 3.

[29] *Izvestiia*, No. 90, April 20, 1927, p. 2. See Document 105, which repudiates Rykov's assertion.

[30] These documents were later published by the Chinese police in photographic reproduction with the English translation of the original Russian text.

[31] N. Mitarevsky, *World Wide Soviet Plots*, pp. 19, 24.

[32] For excerpts from this resolution see our Document 102.

agitation in favor of the Kuomintang as the party for national independence of China. Take full advantage of the events in Hankow[33] and the position taken towards them by England, as a proof, firstly, of the Kuomintang's success in the national work, and secondly, of the indubitable weakness of the European powers in their position to the Chinese revolution.[34]

New Moscow Line: The Three-Class Alliance

In his Theses for Propagandists which appeared in *Pravda* in April 1927, Stalin managed to present the Shanghai coup as a communist victory and as further evidence that the policies of the Communist International were correct. "The attempt made by Chiang Kai-shek in March 1926 to drive the Communists out of the Kuomintang was the first serious attempt of the national bourgeoisie," he said, to bridle the revolution. The Central Committee of the Russian Communist Party, of course, was at that time already of the opinion that "the policy of keeping the Communist party within the Kuomintang must be maintained. . . . The events which followed entirely proved the correctness of this line."[35]

The Chinese upheaval, Stalin declared, even as survivors of Chiang's purges took refuge in Wuhan, had entered a second stage.

There has commenced a turn from the revolution of the *all-national* united front to the revolution of the masses of *workers and peasants* numbering many millions, to the *agrarian* revolution which will increase and strengthen the struggle against imperialism, against the gentry and the feudal landowners, against the militarists, and against the counterrevolutionary group of Chiang Kai-shek.[36]

And yet, when the time came, in late May when the peasants rose in revolt, Stalin would prove unable to make up his mind to use these millions of peasants. In explaining his policy of restraint, Stalin tried to draw a distinction between the Chinese revolution and the October Revolution:

The revolution in China cannot develop at such a rapid tempo [as the October Revolution] because, among other reasons, the international situation is at present less favorable than in the year 1917 (there is no war between the imperialists).[37]

The Trotsky opposition was demanding immediate communist withdrawal from the Kuomintang Left and the formation of Chinese soviets. But Stalin, who was planning upon the elimination of his opponents, pressed his reasoning against the opposition's plan on the basis of early Bolshevik theories and experiences:

What does it mean to set up soviets now? In the first place one cannot set them up at any moment one chooses; they can only be created in a period of a special rise of the revolutionary wave. In the second place soviets are not set up as mere talking shops. They are set up above all as fighting organs against the existing power,

---

[33] This was the seizure by the Chinese insurgents of the British concession in Hankow on January 5, 1927. Soon after, an agreement was signed by the British legal adviser, O'Malley, who came specially from Peking to Hankow, and the Chinese Nationalists' foreign minister, Eugene Ch'en, by which the British relinquished this concesssion to China. The same also applied to the British concession in Tientsin.

[34] N. Mitarevsky, *World Wide Soviet Plots*, p. 147.

[35] *Voprosy kitaiskoi revoliutsii*, p. 125.

[36] *Ibid.*, p. 127.

[37] *Ibid.*, p. 129.

organs of the struggle for power. This was the case in the year 1905, as it was also the case in 1917.

But what would it mean to create soviets at the *present moment* in the sphere of activity, for example, of the government of Wuhan? This would mean issuing the slogan of a struggle against the power of the revolutionary Kuomintang; for in this territory there is at present no other power than the power of the revolutionary Kuomintang. This means confusing the task of creating and consolidating mass organizations of the workers and peasants in the shape of strike committees, peasants' unions, and peasants' committees, trade union councils, factory committees, etc., upon which the revolutionary Kuomintang is already based, with the task of setting up a soviet system as a new type of state power in the place of the revolutionary Kuomintang. This means to fail to understand what stage the revolution in China is passing through at present. . . .

What does the withdrawal of the Communist Party from the Kuomintang [Left wing] mean *at the present moment*? It means to abandon the battlefield and to leave in the lurch its allies in the Kuomintang, to the joy of the enemies of the revolution. This means to weaken the Communist Party, to undermine the revolutionary Kuomintang [Left wing] . . . and to deliver the flag of the Kuomintang, the most popular flag in China, into the hands of the Right-wing members of the Kuomintang. This is precisely what the imperialists, the militarists, and the Right-wing members of the Kuomintang are demanding at the present moment. It follows therefore, that the opposition . . . is playing into the hands of the enemies of the Chinese revolution. . . .[38]

Stalin's view, as he stated it at the Eighth Plenum of the ECCI, May 24, 1927, was that the formation of soviets in China would be premature, and that the Chinese situation did not resemble the Russian situation of 1917, when Russia was "on the eve of the proletarian revolution."[39] Rather the "revolutionary Kuomintang" in Wuhan must be transformed into an organ of "the revolutionary-democratic dictatorship of the proletariat and the peasantry" (a term coined by Lenin in 1905), with the whole power of the country concentrated in its hands. Under Stalin's domination and swayed by his miscalculation of the political nature of the Kuomintang, the Eighth Plenum resolved on continued support for the Kuomintang Left:

The ECCI regards as incorrect the view which underestimates the Wuhan government and denies its great revolutionary role. . . . The Wuhan government, being the government of the Left wing of the Kuomintang, is not yet the dictatorship of the proletariat and the peasantry, but is on the road to it and will inevitably, in the course of the victorious class struggle of the proletariat, discard its radical-bourgeois camp followers and . . . develop toward such a dictatorship.[40]

New Instructions from Moscow to the Wuhan Government

The Eighth Plenum was used by Stalin and his supporters to muffle the protests of the opposition, the sessions of the Plenum being held in an atmosphere of secrecy and restraint.[41] The program for China that was adopted at these

[38] *Ibid.*, pp. 129–31.

[39] Stalin, *Ob oppozitsii*, 596–97 ; see Document 106.

[40] *Kommunisticheskii Internatsional v dokumentakh*, p. 719 ; see Document 107.

[41] Albert Treint, *Documents de l'opposition et la réponse du parti*, p. 65, as quoted in H. R. Isaacs, *The Tragedy of the Chinese Revolution*, p. 240.

sessions endorsed the support of the Kuomintang Left, military operations against the northern warlords, the development of the agrarian revolution throughout the territory of the Wuhan government, and the conduct of an intensive campaign of agitation and disruption within the army of Chiang Kai-shek.

In the following two or three months Soviet leaders continued to uphold the correctness of their course in the Chinese revolution, supporting their stand with quotations from Lenin's statements and referring to their previous revolutionary experiences in Russia. Speaking before the plenum of the Moscow committee of the party on June 4, 1927, Bukharin stated:

We must differentiate between a revolution such as the Russian one of 1905 and a revolution of an anti-imperialist character in the semi-colonies and "independent" countries.... Why? For the simple reason that in such countries [i.e., semicolonial ones] the part played by the liberal bourgeoisie is not the same as its role in Russia in 1905. In 1904, the bourgeoisie still opposed tsarism, but after the October strike of 1905 the liberal bourgeoisie has already become an openly counter-revolutionary force. ... But did it [the Chinese bourgeoisie] play a counter-revolutionary role between 1911 and 1926? Who is in a position to assert this? Now, indeed, it has gone over to the counter-revolutionary camp, but for many years the part it played made it our duty to support it. We were obliged to utilise it, we were obliged to form a bloc with it. ...

In China the liberal bourgeoisie has played an objectively revolutionary role for many years, and has exhausted itself. It has, however, been by no means a political mayfly, living one day only, of the type of the Russian liberal bourgeoisie in the revolution of 1905.[42]

Referring to the Left wing of the Kuomintang, Bukharin remarked that "this organisation is extremely elastic, it possesses great revolutionary traditions, it unites workers, peasants and petty bourgeoisie, and still possesses great power of expansion in every direction. Are we to throw all this aside and search for something else? This is a question that must be answered."[43] Bukharin went even further; emphasizing the necessity for the Communists to maneuver, he maintained that normal diplomatic relations should be retained with the Nanking regime also.[44]

Among the Communists, however, there was no agreement even in the territory of the Wuhan government. Borodin continued to act in the capacity of an adviser, while M. N. Roy, the newly dispatched agent of the Communist International, opposed both Borodin's and the Chinese Communists' conciliatory attitudes toward the landholding Kuomintang. There were disagreements on other points also. Meantime, Moscow continued to rely on its influence over the Kuomintang Left.[45]

Developments reached a climax when a telegram from Moscow outlining the proper course of action in the agrarian unrest reached the Wuhan government in June:

Without an agrarian revolution victory is impossible. Without it the Central Committee of the Kuomintang will be converted into a wretched plaything of un-

[42] *International Press Correspondence*, No. 39, July 7, 1927, pp. 881–82.
[43] *Ibid.*
[44] See Document 108.
[45] "Minutes of the Chinese Subcommittee of the ECCI," *New Militant* (New York), February 8, 1936.

reliable generals. Excesses must be combated—not, however, with the help of troops, but through the peasant unions. We are decidedly in favor of the land's actually being seized by the masses from below. The fears regarding T'an P'ing-shan's visit are not devoid of foundation.[46] You must not sever yourselves from the workers' and peasants' movement, but must assist it in every possible way. Otherwise you will ruin the cause.

Certain of the old leaders of the Central Committee of the Kuomintang are afraid of what is taking place. They are vacillating and compromising. A large number of new peasant and working class leaders must be drawn into the Central Committee of the Kuomintang from below. Their bold voices will make the old leaders more resolute, or throw them into discard. The present structure of the Kuomintang must be changed. The leadership of the Kuomintang must be freshened and reinforced by new leaders who have come to the fore in the process of the agrarian revolution, while the periphery must be enlarged by drawing into local organizations millions from among the working class and peasant unions. Otherwise the Kuomintang runs the risk of becoming divorced from realities and losing all authority.

It is necessary to liquidate the dependence upon unreliable generals immediately.[47] Mobilize about 20,000 Communists and about 50,000 revolutionary workers and peasants from Hunan and Hupeh, form several new army corps, utilize the students of the school for military commanders, and organize your own reliable army before it is too late. Otherwise there can be no guarantee against failure. It is a difficult matter, but there is no other course.

Organize a revolutionary military tribunal headed by prominent noncommunist Kuomintangists. Punish officers who maintain contact with Chiang Kai-shek or who set soldiers on the people, the workers and peasants. Persuasion is not enough, it is time to act. The scoundrels must be punished. If the Kuomintangists do not learn to be revolutionary Jacobins, they will be lost both to the people and to the revolution.[48]

Moscow's Break with the Wuhan Government

When this telegram fell into the hands of the Kuomintang Left leaders, the situation finally exploded, and the Communists were expelled from the Kuomintang Left:

The climax was reached towards the end of June, 1927. . . . Events followed as if previously planned. The Workers' militia was disarmed; trade unions were closed; demonstrations were forbidden on the threat of shooting; Communists were arrested *en masse*.[49]

Moscow agents Borodin and Roy soon left Wuhan territory.[50]

[46] Apparently Moscow was already suspecting T'an, the communist minister of agriculture in the Wuhan government, of deviation from the Moscow policy for China. He was censured and expelled from the Chinese Communist Party at the party's conference in August for incorrect agrarian policy, becoming thereby one of the scapegoats for Moscow's own miscalculation of the situation (see our p. 306).

[47] This sentence appears in different versions in different sources, but there seems to be no need to question the authenticity of the Russian source from which this translation is made.

[48] I. Stalin, *Marksizm i natsionalno-kolonialnyi vopros*, pp. 186–87; also J. Stalin, *Marxism and the National and Colonial Question*, p. 249; see also Document 109.

[49] M. N. Roy, *Revolution and Counter-Revolution in China*, p. 526.

[50] For more on the Wuhan situation, see H. R. Isaacs, *The Tragedy of the Chinese Revolution*, pp. 252 ff.

The responsibility for the communist failure in Wuhan was placed by Moscow on Chinese shoulders. "The Comintern considered it necessary that these errors committed by the Communist Party of China should be made good at once," stated the ECCI.[51]

Moscow Communists, however, still failed to grasp the seriousness of the communist defeat in China. On July 28, 1927, Stalin wrote in *Pravda*:

The opposition apparently tends to the opinion that the revolution in China has collapsed completely. This, of course, is erroneous. That the revolution in China has suffered a temporary defeat, there can be no doubt. The question is, however, what sort of a defeat is it, and how deep is it? Is it possible that it is a defeat which will last approximately as long as the defeat in Russia in 1905, when the revolution was interrupted for twelve years in order to break out again with renewed force in February 1917, . . . or is it possible that the defeat is similar to that suffered by the Bolsheviks in July 1917, when they were betrayed by the Mensheviks and S.R.'s and were forced to go underground, and a few months later the revolution flooded the streets once again in order to sweep away the imperialist government of Russia. The analogy here is, of course, conditional. It is only valid when the differences between the situation in Russia in 1917 and the situation in China today are taken into consideration.[52]

On the subject of soviets for China, which he had opposed, Stalin now had this to say:

Yesterday, a few months ago, the Chinese Communists could not put forward the slogan of soviets because that would have been adventurism like the adventurism of our opposition, since the leadership of the Kuomintang had not yet discredited itself as an opponent of the revolution. If however (if!) in the near future a new revolutionary upsurge wells up, then the slogan for the formation of soviets can be a really revolutionary slogan. Therefore, it is necessary now, and even before the upsurge begins, side by side with the struggle to replace the present Kuomintang leadership by a revolutionary leadership, to conduct a campaign among the broad masses of the toilers to popularize the idea of soviets, without rushing ahead of events and without attempting to organize soviets now, by keeping in mind that soviets can be formed only in conjunction with a powerful revolutionary advance.[53]

Finally, Stalin tried to justify cautious aspects of his policy, as well as to emphasize his persistent support of a radical program, when he spoke at the joint session of the Central Committee and the Central Control Commission of the Russian Communist Party on August 1, 1927. Once more he drew heavily upon Lenin's theoretical statements, and the experiences of the Russian revolution:

Were there ever revolutions without certain stages of development? Did not our revolution have its stages of development? Take Lenin's "April [1917] Theses" and you will see that Lenin discerned two stages in our revolution: first, the bourgeois-democratic revolution, with the agrarian movement as its main axis; second, the October Revolution, with the seizure of power by the proletariat as its main axis. What are the stages in the Chinese revolution? In my opinion there should be three: the first stage was the revolution of the general national united front, the Canton

[51] "Resolution of the ECCI on the Present Situation in the Chinese Revolution," *International Press Correspondence*, No. 44, July 28, 1927, p. 984.

[52] Stalin, *Sochineniia*, IX, 357–58; also *Pravda*, No. 169, July 28, 1927, pp. 3–4.

[53] Stalin, *Sochineniia*, IX, 359.

period, when the revolution was striking chiefly at foreign imperialism and had the national bourgeoisie's support; the second stage is the bourgeois-democratic revolution, starting after the national troops reached the Yangtze River, when the national bourgeoisie deserted and the agrarian movement grew into a mighty revolution of tens of millions of peasants (the revolution is now in this stage); the third stage is the soviet revolution which has not yet come about, but which will come about.[54]

Two new agents were now dispatched by Moscow to China, both young men with little understanding of the Chinese situation: Besso Lominadze, active in the Russian youth movement, and Heinz Neumann, a young German Communist. Lominadze brought instructions for an uprising at Nanchang.

Neumann was instrumental in convening a secret conference of the Central Committee of the Chinese Communist Party on August 1. The manifesto issued by this conference censured the Chinese Communist Party's leaders for "serious opportunistic mistakes," and called the party to correct them:

The proletarian party cannot be afraid of recognizing its own mistakes. . . . The fact that our party insists that these mistakes must be corrected . . . does not show its weakness, but, on the contrary, reveals the strength of the communist movement in China.

In their efforts to solve the most important problems of the revolution, the manifesto stated, the leaders of the party had deviated from the basic principles of the Communist International and the Leninist evaluation of the Chinese revolution by the Comintern.

In emphasizing the importance of the agrarian revolution, which represents "a central problem of the bourgeois-democratic revolution in China," the manifesto censured the minister of agriculture, T'an P'ing-shan, whose ministry "categorically declined to aid the agrarian revolution," and, on the contrary, "tried to lead the peasant movement along the bourgeois-reformist path."

Next to T'an P'ing-shan, the manifesto passed judgment upon the leader of the party, Ch'en Tu-hsiu, for subordinating the party to the Kuomintang, so that "actually it was not the Communist Party that was directing the Kuomintang, but the top party leaders were kept in complete political imprisonment by the Kuomintang."

Finally, the manifesto definitely condemned the plan advocated by some Chinese Communists, to withdraw from the Kuomintang. The Communists were to remain in the Left-wing section of the Kuomintang, "in the truly revolutionary Kuomintang which, similar to the Chinese Communist Party, has been driven underground by the bourgeois reaction."[55]

The Nanchang and Autumn Crop Uprisings

In August 1927, acting upon instructions from Moscow,[56] the Chinese Communist Party came out in open revolt against the Wuhan government. Communist insurgents occupied Nanchang and managed to set up a revolutionary

[54] I. Stalin, *Marksizm i natsionalno-kolonialnyi vopros*, p. 176; also J. Stalin, *Marxism and the National and Colonial Question*, p. 235; see Document 109.

[55] Complete text of this manifesto appears in Russian in P. A. Mif, *Kitaiskaia Kommunisticheskaia Partiia v kriticheskie dni*, pp. 220–239.

[56] *Pravda*, No. 180, August 10, 1927, p. 3; see Document 110.

committee as a provisional government. The Central Committee of the Chinese Communist Party then issued a declaration to the effect that the Kuomintang leaders had become counterrevolutionary and that opposition to agrarian revolution meant betrayal of the struggle against feudalism, without the destruction of which imperialism could not be overthrown. This declaration further asserted the determination of the Communist Party to carry on the fight in close co-operation with the Kuomintang masses, if no longer with its leadership.

By mid-September, the Communist army had penetrated eastern Kwangtung province, captured the port of Swatow, and set up a revolutionary committee in that port city. The Swatow Revolutionary Committee declared war against both the Wuhan and Nanking Nationalist governments, declared itself in favor of the confiscation of land by the peasants, and laid plans to bring the entire province of Kwangtung under its control. But these grandiose plans were soon brought to an end by the arrival of both foreign battleships and Kuomintang armies from Canton. Early in October the revolutionary committee was forced to abandon Swatow.

And yet as late as September 30, 1927, *Pravda* hailed successes before Swatow as a "new revolutionary upsurge," and called for the organization of soviets of workers', soldiers', and artisans' deputies because the revolution was now spreading to the industrial centers.[57]

Organization of soviets now became the Comintern's slogan for China. On September 27, 1927, Stalin, speaking before the ECCI's presidium and the Central Control Commission, reviewed the revolutionary situation in China:

If before in the period of the development of the Kuomintang, no favorable circumstances existed for the immediate formation of soviets, now, when the Kuomintangists have so scandalized and discredited themselves by their connection with the counterrevolution—now, if the movement is successful, the soviets might become, nay, will become, the basic force to rally around them the workers and peasants of China. . . . Only the most ignorant people can think that the Communists could take part in the Kuomintang, if the [Chinese] soviets are organized. To combine these two incompatible situations is simply to fail to understand the nature and the purpose of soviets.[58]

A peasant insurrection led by Mao Tse-tung in Hunan, which later became known as the Autumn Crop Uprising, failed as the Swatow insurrection had.

The Canton Commune

Moscow's domination over the Chinese Communist Party continued. In November 1927 the Plenum of the Central Committee of the Chinese Communist Party passed an important resolution evaluating the existing revolutionary situation in China and planning policies for the future. The revolutionary situation, according to this resolution, was still promising:

. . . In spite of the serious defeats suffered by the revolution, the strength of the revolutionary movement of the toiling masses is not used up. On the contrary, it now begins to reveal itself in the new upsurge of the revolutionary struggle.

The experience of the last few months proves this very clearly. The Chinese revolution has aroused such large masses of workers, peasants, coolies, and the poor

[57] *Pravda*, No. 223, September 30, 1927, p. 1.
[58] Stalin, *Ob oppozitsii*, 709–10.

to an independent political struggle that several months of bourgeois-militarist reaction could not suppress fully the revolutionary strength of people's revolt.

All the above prompts the Plenum of the Central Committee of the Communist Party of China to recognize that there exists at present a direct revolutionary situation in China. The Central Committee does not wish to cherish any illusions concerning the inevitability of a complete victory of the revolution in the very near future. The objective situation in China is such that the duration of the direct revolutionary situation is measured and will be measured not by weeks or months, but by many years. The Chinese revolution is of a prolonged but permanent nature. It is in character what Marx called a "permanent revolution."

. . .

The best confirmation of this "permanent character of the Chinese revolution" is the new upsurge of the peasant risings in all important provinces of China. In September, the peasant risings spread in Kwangtung, Hunan, and Hupeh. In spite of a number of defeats suffered there by isolated peasant actions, the revolutionary movement of the peasantry in these provinces continues. . . . In October peasant risings flare up in Kiangsu and in the north in Chihli [Hopeh] and Jehol. . . . At the same time in the basic proletarian centers—in Shanghai, Canton, and Wuhan—after a period of depression the workers' movement is beginning to acquire an active and revolutionary character. The wave of the peasant risings calls forth a workers' movement which, while still weak, is coming to meet the peasant wave. . . .

To maintain contact between the revolts of the workers and the risings of the peasants—this is the most important task of the party. Without leadership and assistance from the working class, the purely peasant risings cannot lead to complete victory.[59]

In view of this interpretation of the Chinese situation (which the Comintern shared), the leadership in Canton laid plans for an insurrection to take place in that city on December 10, 1927. The prime mover in the Canton uprising, according to Roy, was the Comintern agent in Canton, Heinz Neumann. The uprising lasted three days, but again a combination of foreign naval power and Kuomintang troops restored Nationalist authority in Canton.

The revolt in Canton was started at 3 A.M. on December 11, and within a matter of hours the main Canton institutions—the telegraph office, the post office, and office buildings—had passed over to the Chinese Red Guard. By December 12 almost the entire city was under the control of the insurgents, and during the day a meeting was held in a city park in order to form a Council of People's Commissars. Chang T'ai-lei[60] was elected Commissar of War and Commander-in-Chief. But after leaving the meeting he was met by a detachment of counterrevolutionary soldiers and killed. This was a serious loss to the Cantonese insurgents, since all threads connected with the preparation of the insurrection were concentrated in Chang's hands.

Consisting of nine workers, three peasants, and three soldiers, the soviet government of Canton hastened to issue a number of decrees, one of which provided for the annulment of unequal treaties, another the confiscation without remuneration of land belonging to landlords and the transfer of it to the peasantry. An eight-hour day was proclaimed for workers, and a six-hour day for minors. A resolution was also passed for the organization of the first units of a Chinese Red Army. The new government was characterized in Lenin's words as a "revolutionary-democratic dictatorship of the proletariat and the peasantry."

[59] P. A. Mif, *Kitaiskaia Kommunisticheskaia Partiia v kriticheskie dni*, pp. 245-47, 249.
[60] For biographical sketch, see p. 458.

On December 13, with support from the naval forces of the Great Powers, Chinese anticommunist militarist forces launched an attack on the newly formed Canton Commune, and by the following day the insurrection had been suppressed.[61] The punishment meted out by the victorious Chinese forces to the Chinese insurrectionists was severe, and thousands of people perished. Among the victims were Soviet consular officials, who had assumed active leadership in the insurrection and used the consulate as an insurrectionary headquarters. After his defection from the Stalinist camp, Roy described the Canton events as follows:

The Canton uprising was the most tragic event in the entire history of the Chinese revolution. It was the greatest mistake ever committed because its bloody suppression was inevitable. It was a foolhardy, ill-conceived, dilettantly [sic] prepared offensive; it was a typical adventure. The Nanchang insurrection had its historical significance. It marked the break of the Communist Party from its fateful opportunist past. But since the break took place much too late, it should not have been the starting point for an offensive on the whole front. The mistakes in the past could not be rectified by plunging headlong into a desperate offensive. . . .

The new policy of the Communist Party, initiated since the Nanchang uprising, was based on the theory that, in consequence of the betrayal of the bourgeoisie, the National Revolution must develop directly to a proletarian Socialist revolution. Events proved that the theory was wrong. The masses did not respond to the slogan of the Soviets. In Canton itself hardly ten thousand workers participated actively in the uprising and supported the Commune.[62]

Moscow responded to the failure of the Canton uprising by disclaiming all responsibility and at the same time characterizing the suppression of the uprising as part of a general campaign against the Soviet Union. In *Pravda,* Chicherin declared:

The political actions of the Kuomintang generals against the U.S.S.R. and against its representatives have spread over the whole of South China; the slaughter in Canton was only the worst of many incidents. The political responsibility for these bestial crimes falls, therefore, on the shoulders of all leading persons in the territory of the so-called "national" governments. . . . In this case, however, the responsibility also falls upon the other powers of the world reaction hostile to the U.S.S.R. The campaign of incitement carried on by all the imperialist and White Guardist groups in Shanghai, Hong Kong, and other important centers of colonial policy in China, and the undoubted instigation from London, which was corroborated by the hymns of praise in the British press, played an almost decisive role in the development of the events. British imperialist reaction is to be considered the most important driving force in the Canton slaughter and in the violence, the murders, and the expulsions of the citizens of the Soviet Union.[63]

The purge of Communists from the Wuhan government and the Kuomintang Left had led, meanwhile, to a restoration of surface harmony within Kuomintang councils and to the reorganization of a united Kuomintang government in Nanking in September 1927. Following the Canton events, Chiang Kai-shek ordered the closing of all Soviet consulates throughout territory controlled by the Kuomintang. This reorganization of the Kuomintang without the Communists, the

---

[61] For Communist International appeals to support the Canton Commune, see Document 111.

[62] M. N. Roy, *Revolution and Counter-Revolution in China,* pp. 562–63.

[63] *Pravda,* No. 294, December 23, 1927, p. 1; see Document 112.

closing of the Soviet consulates, the earlier expulsion of the Russian mission from Hankow, and the December events in Canton all combined to bring to an end, for the time being, the open and direct influence of the Russian Communists upon the national revolution of the Kuomintang in China.

Yet Moscow continued to attach the greatest significance to the development of revolutionary events in China. The theses adopted at the Eighth Plenum of the ECCI, May 18–30, 1927 (about six months before the failure of the Canton Commune), stated in this regard:

All contradictions which exist among the capitalist states become secondary before the basic ridge which divides the globe into two camps. In one camp we find the Union of the Soviet Socialist Republics and revolutionary China; in the other—the entire capitalist world. China and the Union of Soviet Socialist Republics represent two junctions of the entire international situation. . . . China and the Union of Soviet Socialist Republics, which occupy the greater part of Asia and half of Europe, and which possess as yet untouched economic resources, and hundreds of millions of population—these are two inexhaustible reservoirs of raw material, as well as huge world markets. The struggle for these two immense markets is a question of life and death for international capital. Such struggle will fill [many] years to come and will continue until the world proletariat puts an end to the rule of the international bourgeoisie.

The significance of the Chinese revolution for the world proletariat is immense, while the victory of the workers' and peasants' Chinese revolution would serve as a most powerful stimulus to revolutionize the world workers' movement, and the British workers' movement in particular. . . . A revolutionary situation would thus be created for the tremendous mass movements throughout the entire world.[64]

The failure of the Canton Commune, however, had a sobering effect on communist leaders in Moscow. The ECCI's Ninth Plenum, which met in Moscow in February 1928, evaluated the past experiences:

The ECCI considers it necessary to take into account the entire experience of the revolutionary movement of China and the discussion of that experience in all party cells. In particular, it is essential to draw a lesson from the experiences of the Canton insurrection. The Canton insurrection having been a heroic attempt of the proletariat to organize a soviet government in China, and having played a tremendous role in the development of the workers' and peasants' revolution, has nevertheless revealed a whole series of blunders made by the leaders: insufficient preliminary work among the workers and peasants, and among the enemy armed forces; incorrect methods of approaching the workers who are members of the yellow trade unions;[65] inadequate preparation of the party organization and the Communist Youth League for the insurrection; complete ignorance of the Canton events on the part of the Chinese party center; weakness in the political mobilization of the masses (absence of broad political strikes, absence of an elected soviet in Canton as an organ of insurrection), for which the direct leaders who are politically responsible to the Communist International (Comrade N[66] and others) are partly to blame. Despite all these blunders in leadership, the Canton insurrection must be considered an example of the great heroism of the Chinese workers, who have now the right to claim their historical role as leaders of the great Chinese revolution.[67]

[64] *Kommunisticheskii Internatsional v dokumentakh*, p. 701.
[65] Trade unions affiliated with the Amsterdam International.
[66] Heinz Neumann.
[67] *Kommunisticheskii Internatsional v dokumentakh*, p. 766.

D. SUMMARY OF THE REVOLUTIONARY SITUATION IN THE EAST IN 1927

Stalin and his Russian and Chinese colleagues maintained, after the fall of the Canton Commune, that although the first revolutionary wave was over, both worker and peasant movements in China were moving toward another "mighty upsurge," which would prepare the way for further communist victories in Asia. At the same time, communist leaders were correlating the Chinese revolution with "imperialist contradictions" in the Pacific area, and were predicting that "China will become a major power on the Pacific to menace the capitalist world of three continents," i.e., America, Asia, and Europe.[1] The inevitable outcome of these contradictions, according to communist prophecy, would be a future war in the Pacific to which Bolshevik strategists must link the coming revolutionary upsurge.

The role of American imperialism in the struggle for the Pacific was analyzed by Manuilsky at the Seventh Plenum of the ECCI:

Objectively speaking, the aggressor on the Pacific is the United States of North America; the defenders are Great Britain and Japan. American imperialism is the most dangerous to the toiling masses of the entire globe. American imperialism is [intricately] bound up with the struggle for world hegemony. In the coming world war, if the fate of humanity is not previously fundamentally remodeled by the proletarian revolution, American imperialism will play the leading role.[2]

Manuilsky went on to analyze American imperialism in China: "American imperialism considers it wise at present, and in contrast to the brutal unadaptable policy of the Britons, to appear in China in white gloves." But the American imperialists were going to miscalculate this time, because they had overlooked the historical role which China was called on to play in Asia and on the Pacific:

. . . Liberated China will become a magnet for all peoples of the yellow race who inhabit the Philippines, Indonesia, and the numerous islands of the Pacific. China will become a major power on the Pacific to menace the capitalist world of three continents. . . . China will fulfill this task among the island inhabitants of the Pacific, not with fire and sword, but in the course of the normal revolutionary progress of the native population.[3]

Returning to the future war and the future in general on the Pacific, Manuilsky added:

The future will show how these systematic preparations for war on the Pacific will end. . . . Revolutionary China, which has become an active factor in Far Eastern politics, can become, in alliance with the U.S.S.R., the greatest world factor in the Far East. China's hinterland, with its 400 million population, and its strategic rear position in the Pacific struggle, cannot be ignored by the imperialist governments. . . . The greatness of the Chinese revolution lies in the progress of an awakened and arisen China, having behind it our strong Soviet Union, joining its

[1] *Puti mirovoi revoliutsii*, I, 430; see Document 114.
[2] *Ibid.*, p. 424.
[3] *Ibid.*, pp. 429, 430.

destinies to the October Revolution of our toiling masses, and advancing along the workers' and peasants' path.

In alliance with the world proletariat, with its vanguard—the Communist World Party—revolutionary China must become and will become the guardian of peace and the fighter against imperialist wars on the Pacific.[4]

This being so, the latest experiences of the Chinese revolution were, according to the Moscow Communists, extremely important to their understanding of the colonial problem as a whole and to their planning for the future.

But Bukharin, speaking at the Fifteenth Congress of the Russian Communist Party on December 10, 1927, prior to the news from Canton, had emphasized the diversity of problems confronting the colonial revolutionary movements and cautioned the Communists to consider regional peculiarities carefully in deciding on concrete political tactics in different Eastern countries. Bukharin believed that "one of the biggest problems confronting the Comintern and our party as a whole" was to define communist tactics for India, and that it would be "unpardonable folly" to base such tactics solely on the party's experiences in China. Thus, for example, the China tactic of prolonged co-operation with the native bourgeoisie was out of the question in India. Summing up that bourgeoisie, Bukharin said, "As far as we are concerned, it is already an actively hostile force." He added:

I could take as an example Egypt, Persia, or any other [Eastern] country: every such country has certain social relations that are peculiar to itself alone, specific individual features that we must analyze attentively and concretely instead of resting content with generalizations about the colonial problem.[5]

The Fifteenth Party Congress, at which Bukharin stressed the social and political peculiarities of each colonial country, emphasized the intensification of differences within the world capitalist system. A resolution, passed by the congress in connection with the report of the Central Committee and delivered by Stalin, referred to the uneven development of capitalist countries and to the resulting struggle "for spheres of economic and political influence and for the redistribution of the world." The resolution also emphasized the intensification of the differences between the European-American capitalist countries and the colonies, and the armed revolts, national wars, and colonial revolutions resulting therefrom. Consequently, the resolution stated, "capitalist development as a whole has revealed a tendency to shorten the historic period of peaceful 'breathing space' [*peredyshka*], and to bring closer a new period of great imperialist wars, as well as to hasten the opening of revolutionary world conflicts."[6]

The approaching period of "great imperialist wars" required, according to B. Z. Shumiatsky, whose communist and diplomatic activities were dealt with on the earlier pages, an adequate preparation for concrete action on the part of international communism:

In accordance with the nature of the new epoch, . . . the forthcoming Sixth Congress of the Communist International[7] must work out and adopt a clear-cut pro-

4 *Ibid.*, p. 435.

5 *XV sezd Vserossiiskoi Kommunisticheskoi Partii (B); stenograficheskii otchet,* pp. 607, 608; cited hereafter as *XV sezd VKP (B)*. See Document 115.

6 *XV sezd VKP (B)*, p. 1280. For Zinoviev's interpretation of the "epoch of wars and revolutions," the phrase advanced earlier by Marx's followers, see Document 113.

7 This congress met from July 18 to September 1, 1928.

gram. . . . [It] must be a revolutionary program, a program of action; that is, it must not only include a theoretical basis for the developing struggle, but . . . outline and define a leading line for world communism's organized entry into the period of wars and revolutions, and for its victorious advance against world capitalism and imperialism.[8]

This program was all the more needed (in the words of L. Geller, the head of the Eastern Department of the Profintern) because of "the greatest event of our time . . . as yet unknown for its breadth," namely the revolutionary movement in the East.

Speaking of the struggle that was to come, Geller said that it "will be long and difficult, and more than once the people of the East who rise in revolt will suffer defeat; more than once imperialism will succeed in dealing heavy blows to the peoples struggling for their own liberation. This is inevitable. But the fall of imperialism is just as inevitable."[9]

Stalin, speaking at the Fifteenth Party Congress on December 3, 1927, also warned of possible temporary setbacks in the East, such as were actually being witnessed in China, but he added:

The fact that the Chinese revolution has not led directly to victory over imperialism is not important. People's revolutions never win to the end in the first round of the fight. They grow and consolidate in ebbs and flows. It happened everywhere, it happened in Russia, and it will be so in China also.

What was most important, in Stalin's view, was the fact that the Chinese revolution had awakened hundreds of millions of exploited and oppressed peoples from centuries-old slumber. Therefore, in spite of the temporary defeat of the Chinese revolution, "Only the blind and the timid-hearted can doubt the Chinese workers' and peasants' advance toward a new revolutionary upsurge."[10]

The next twenty years of revolutionary development in Asia would reveal both the truths and the miscalculations in the bold prophecies of Manuilsky and Stalin.

[8] B. Z. Shumiatsky, "Desiat let borby i ocherednye zadachi," *Revoliutsionnyi Vostok*, No. 3, 1928, p. 6; see Document 115.

[9] L. Geller, "Oktiabrskaia revoliutsiia i narody Vostoka," *Krasnyi Internatsional Prof-soiuzov*, No. 10 (81), October 1927, pp. 306, 313; see Document 117.

[10] Stalin, *Sochineniia*, X, 282–83; see Document 118.

DOCUMENTS

A. NEGOTIATIONS AND DIPLOMATIC ACCOMPLISHMENTS

77

The Development of the Struggle in the East

[Statement by a Communist Expert in the Far East][1]

In the seventh year of the October Revolution its importance for the oppressed peoples of the East is particularly clear. Ten years ago China, with its population of many millions, was rent asunder by world imperialism. Now, in the seventh year of the October Revolution, there is a great revolutionary upsurge among the masses of the Chinese people, who are uniting for a struggle against the intervention of the imperialists of America, Britain, France, Japan, and other countries. With an unprecedented frankness, the great capitalist powers have launched a full-scale attack upon the toiling masses of China, enslaved by the imperialists.

At this moment the only ally of the Chinese masses and of the Chinese people as a whole, the only defender of their interests, is the Union of Soviet Socialist Republics. This fact is now known to the peoples of southern, northern, and central China as well as to the peoples of outer China—Tibet, Chinese Turkestan, and Mongolia.

. . .

At the other end of Asia, the small country of Afghanistan, heroically fighting for its independence, and struggling desperately to rid itself of the remnants of medieval feudalism which weigh heavily upon the Afghan people, finds in the U.S.S.R. a trusty ally and a comrade who is prepared to defend it from the aggression of British imperialism.[2] The insurrections inspired and nourished by the "Labor" government of MacDonald and headed by Prince Kerim Khan, who is aiming at the throne of Afghanistan, are serving still more to unite the Afghan people with the Union of Soviet [Socialist] Republics, which for several years has proved its sincere desire to help the peoples of Afghanistan. . . .

The people of Turkey, who experienced the revolution of 1908, the impulse to which was our revolution of 1905, who lived through the imperialist intervention after the World War, and who, from peasant Ankara, fought for the independence of Turkey, have found a trusty ally and a friend in the U.S.S.R. in every stage of their struggle. With the aid of Soviet diplomacy, and thanks to the firmness of Soviet policy on questions of the Near East, the struggling Turkish people succeeded at the Lausanne Conference in retaining their independence. The Turkish

---

[1] G. N. Voitinsky, "Oktiabrskaia revoliutsiia i kolonialnye i polukolonialnye narody," *Novyi Vostok,* No. 6, 1924, pp. XIII, XIV–XV.

[2] This refers to Emir Amanullah's efforts to free Afghanistan from foreign control. Like Kemal Pasha in Turkey and Riza Shah Pahlavi in Persia, Emir Amanullah tried to introduce and enforce a number of reforms designed to modernize his country. His reforms, however, were resented by a number of Afghan tribes and led in some cases to armed uprisings. Soviet spokesmen, making the most of the opportunity, asserted that these insurrections were inspired by the British government.

people know that their only friend, both in the struggle for political independence and in the future struggle for economic independence, is the Union of Soviet [Socialist] Republics.

Our neighbor, Persia, who for long years was the prey of the imperialist powers of Britain and tsarist Russia, has since the October Revolution entered on the path of national independence. At the present moment, when British imperialism, masked by the flag of the Second International, is instigating insurrections in southern Persia with the object of overthrowing Riza Khan, the leader of the national-revolutionary movement of Persia and the man who succeeded in securing Persia's independence, the mighty influence of the Soviet Union is the wall against which the British schemes of plunder are being smashed.

The innumerable millions of toilers of India have ceased since the October Revolution to feel that they are alone in their fight against the British oppressors. They know that in the North a powerful force has sprung up and is growing, a force capable of inspiring fear in the heart of "invincible" British imperialism. The toilers of India know that the country of the soviets is their one true and unselfish ally. . . .

The meaning of the October Revolution is becoming familiar even to the most backward and oppressed peoples of the Near and Far East.

Korea, a country of "morning calm," with a population of fifteen millions struggling in the iron clutches of Japanese imperialism, has since 1919, and under the influence of the October Revolution, made heroic attempts to liberate herself; she has been swept by a revolutionary wave . . . from the Amur and the Maritime regions. The cry "Hands off China," which is being carried from the country of the soviets throughout the whole world, will without doubt find a response in oppressed Korea, whose fate is so closely bound up with China's, and will serve as a further stimulus to the Korean liberation movement.

The peoples of Arabia and of the African colonies, who are fighting an unequal duel with the armies of the imperialists, are turning their eyes more and more to the soviet republics, feeling that they are their sole friend and protector in the struggles. These peoples have found the way to Moscow, and on the seventh anniversary of the October Revolution the representatives of Arabia will be able to celebrate with us the victory of the working class over the deadly enemy of the peoples of the East, tsarist Russia, and over international capitalism.

Greater and greater detachments of the oppressed sections of mankind are marching under the banner of the October Revolution. All forms of struggle against oppression are being sanctified by the great idea of the October Revolution: the struggle of the revolutionary proletariat in the capitalist countries; the national-liberation movements of dependent peoples; the struggle against theocracy, against religious oppression. These forms of struggle are becoming identified more and more with the struggle of the vanguard of the world proletariat, the Union of Soviet [Socialist] Republics.

78

The New Russian Communist Interpretation of the Eastern Problem[3]

The October Revolution worked a complete change in the relations between the peoples inhabiting the former tsarist empire and the colonial and semicolonial peoples

[3] M. L. Veltman (M. Pavlovich), *Revoliutsionnyi Vostok,* pp. 3–5.

of the non-Soviet East. At the same time, beginning with the October Revolution, the Eastern problem acquired an absolutely new content and a new aspect. . . .

Speaking in general, we can say that before the October Revolution, the Eastern question was interpreted as a problem of . . . the partition of Turkey, and of Asia as a whole, among the great imperialist powers: Russia, Britain, France, Germany, Japan, and America. It was, therefore, an Asia Minor problem as well as a Pan-Asiatic problem.

It is well known that the impossibility of peaceably settling certain Asiatic problems which faced the ruling classes of the Great Powers was an important cause of the World War. In the final analysis, this was the inevitable consequence of the struggle to partition the remaining unpartitioned sectors of the globe.

The October Revolution introduced an absolutely new content into the meaning of the "Eastern problem." As we pointed out earlier in *Novyi Vostok*, No. 1, 1921, "the East is not only the oppressed Asiatic continent; the East also means the entire colonial world, the world of the oppressed peoples of Asia, of Africa, and of South America, that is of that sector of the world by the exploitation of which the capitalist society of Europe and of the United States maintains its power. . . ."

What then were the changes which the October Revolution introduced into the continent of the Eastern problem, what relations did it establish between the peoples of former tsarist Russia and the oppressed peoples of Asia and Africa? [Refers to Lenin's theses adopted by the Second Congress of the Communist International.][4] . . .

The Eastern problem is now no longer a problem of the partition and robbery of Asia, a problem of the further enslavement and exploitation of the backward peoples of Asia and Africa . . . This problem now becomes a matter of a bond, of a union between the advanced Russian Soviet Republic and the advanced workers of all other countries grouping around this republic, on one side, and all the national-liberation movements of the oppressed colonial peoples, on the other side, a union aimed at a joint struggle against the world bourgeoisie. . . .

79

Chicherin on the Agreement Between the Soviet Union and China[5]

Every one of us and also every Chinese person who has the interests of his people at heart will breathe more easily on learning that the absurd wall which separated us from China has at last been torn down. It is high time! China could have no reason whatever for refusing to resume normal relations with us. The Chinese government is not a creditor of the Soviet Union and could not use the question of the recognition of the Soviet Union in an attempt to compel payment of debts by us. It has hesitated so long to recognize the Soviet Union not because it did not itself wish to recognize us. It began the blockade against the R.S.F.S.R. at the beginning of 1918, later rendered service to the intervention, and until recently hesitated to recognize us for one and the same reason: because of the pressure of the Entente powers. Even the present agreement between Comrade Karakhan and the Chinese foreign minister, Wellington Ku, had to be prepared with the greatest secrecy. The diplomacy of the Great Powers blocked our first agreement with China, and would have blocked this one if we had not succeeded in concealing its preparation.

---

[4] See pp. 63–65.
[5] *Pravda*, No. 123, June 1, 1924, p. 1.

The signing of this agreement by the Chinese government is therefore a big step on the road to liberating the colonial and semicolonial peoples from political subordination to the Great Powers. The significance of this expression of the independence of Chinese policy extends far beyond the frontiers of China. It is an historical event in the emancipation of the Eastern peoples. China thereby demonstrates that she is doing what Turkey did in [the battle of the] Sakaria and in Lausanne, what Persia did in 1920, and what Afghanistan did at the beginning of the rule of the Emir Amanullah. The awakening of the peoples of the East, their struggle against imperialist oppression, the consolidation of their complete independence—all are moving steadily and inevitably forward. The forces of the Eastern peoples are gradually growing. Every day they are increasing in political and economic strength.

Thereby their friendly relations with the U.S.S.R. are strengthened. These friendly relations represent one of the most important elements of that historical process which embraces the whole East. These relations become more firm with every success of the Eastern peoples on the road to emancipation: thus, in resuming normal relations with the U.S.S.R., China takes an important step toward emancipation from foreign oppression, and this step in turn will lead to a further strengthening of friendship with the U.S.S.R.

The normal relations between the U.S.S.R. and China are bound to be of the friendliest nature, and this truth has penetrated deep into the consciousness of the broadest masses in China. The peoples of the Soviet Union and the Chinese people will proceed together hand in hand and render each other the fullest support in every respect. The broad masses of China, among whom the name of Lenin has become enormously popular, realize perfectly well that the Soviet republic is their only consistent and entirely disinterested friend. It is precisely because Chinese public opinion recognizes this, that it has exercised such persistent pressure upon the Chinese government, insisting that an understanding with the U.S.S.R. be reached. The undisguised, brutally cynical act of American diplomacy, which endeavored by intimidation and by open pressure to prevent China from coming to an agreement with us, has still further roused Chinese public opinion, and thereby accelerated the favorable solution of the senseless crisis, which had already lasted too long, between the U.S.S.R. and China.

The strengthening of the Eastern peoples, who are winning their liberation, the transference of their whole foreign policy and their domestic life to entirely new lines, is therefore one of the general causes which led to the restoration of normal relations between ourselves and China. Another general cause is the noticeable change, be it only partial, in the international policy of a number of Great Powers. The bourgeoisie of the strongest Western powers has changed, so to speak, from the Right horse to the Left, among other reasons because their old policy in the colonial and semicolonial countries threatened them with imminent disaster. They were obliged to adopt other methods, to resort to compromises, to carry out the policy of peaceful penetration. This new colonial policy of the bourgeoisie of the strongest countries will meet with an essential obstacle; capital seeks and will always seek in the colonies for surplus profit; it will not invest in the colonies for the same rate of interest with which it is content at home. And in order to be able to obtain a surplus profit it will always endeavor to create suitable political conditions.

The Soviet republic alone remains a constant and sincere friend of the Eastern peoples. But the absolute failure of the policy of the mailed fist in the East is compelling the Great Powers to adopt a line of compromise. Even if the new governments in Britain and France will not immediately carry out this new line to its fullest extent, the road ahead is plain to see. The Chinese government has already realized that the change that has set in in the international relations of the

Eastern peoples must find expression in the greater independence of its [the Chinese government's] line of policy.

The appearance of the Soviet Union on the coast of the Pacific Ocean as a power friendly to China immediately raises the question of the world importance of the basin of the Pacific Ocean. Formerly the cultured world was concentrated around the Mediterranean. Now the political and economic interests of the world reach out more toward the Pacific. It is the ocean of the future. The outlook which the resumption of normal, that is to say, friendly relations between the U.S.S.R. and China opens will only gradually become clear to us. Already today we can trace in general outline the enormous importance of this event.

80

The Chinese Eastern Railway—A Highroad for Proletariat Aid to China

[Statement by G. N. Voitinsky][6]

The treaty recently concluded by the U.S.S.R. and the Chinese republic has revealed to the Chinese people that there exists a new and historically unprecedented attitude toward the people oppressed by imperialism, an attitude permeated with the spirit of real equality between peoples. The enslaving and avaricious treaties which were forcefully imposed upon China by the imperialists of all nations, including the former tsarist government, were disclosed to the Chinese masses by the Sino-Soviet Treaty, and the great danger menacing China of further penetrations by imperialists into the country became obvious.

Our treaty, which abolished once and for all the shameful privilege that permitted the tsarist government to have its own streets (extraterritorial concessions) on Chinese territory, its own courts, its own army, and its own laws—aroused a wave of enthusiasm among the Chinese masses. It also intensified the hatred of these masses for the imperialists who still continue to exercise these privileges.

The treaty's annulment of the Russian portion of the "Boxer" indemnity, an imposition of many millions laid upon the Chinese people by the imperialists after their victory over the insurgent Chinese people in 1900–1901, will help tremendously to bring the Chinese masses into the revolutionary movement of the world proletariat.

The Chinese people are beginning to understand the duel that is being fought on the territory of China between our Red diplomacy and world imperialism. In the heart of China, Peking, after a bitter struggle, the Red flag was finally hoisted in the stronghold of the imperialists, the Legation Quarter. The stone wall surrounding the imperialists' quarters in Peking, through the openings of which guns actually menace the Chinese people, has collapsed in that section where the concession of the tsarist government was originally situated; from this side the Chinese people have obtained the right of entry into the stronghold of imperialism. Here the memorial of Lenin, whose name is honored by the entire Chinese people, will serve as an inspiration to the toiling masses of China and as a symbol of our great October Revolution.

The Chinese Eastern Railway, which was constructed by the tsarist government with the object of enslaving the Chinese people, and which later served as the

[6] G. N. Voitinsky, "Oktiabrskaia revoliutsiia i kolonialnye i polukolonialnye narody," *Novyi Vostok*, No. 6, 1924, pp. XIII–XIV.

"highroad" for the plundering adventures of world imperialism, has at last been torn from the clutches of the imperialists, and will henceforth serve as the "highroad" for the victorious proletariat marching to the aid of the oppressed masses of China.

81

Chicherin on the 1925 Treaty with Japan[7]

The signing of the Soviet-Japanese Treaty in Peking on January 20 is much more significant than a mere recognition of the U.S.S.R. by still another government; it is even more significant than the settlement of the points in dispute between the two governments. This is not only the beginning of a period of friendly relations between the peoples of the U.S.S.R. and Japan; it is also a turning point, a complete change in Far Eastern politics and in world politics in general.

For us, the treaty means the end of the whole period of intervention, civil war, and unregulated relations; it is the culmination of the continually progressing general development of our political relations in the Far East. These relations, once they have passed through various stages, will gradually lead to friendship between us and the peoples of the East. The treaty marks a new and indisputable consolidation of our position in the Far East. . . . The Russian Far East has entered a period of peaceful development and friendly relations with its neighbors. For Japan this means the existence of a friendly power in the rear in case she is threatened by [diplomatic] complications, as she may well be. The establishment more than six months ago of friendly relations with the great Chinese people provided new and wide scope for Soviet policy in the development of fraternal relations between the two peoples on the principle of self-determination. To the ever-growing friendship between the U.S.S.R. and the Chinese people, who are engrossed in a broad movement of liberation, there now has been added friendly relations between the U.S.S.R. and Japan. The newly signed treaty is a manifestation of one of the permanent desires of the peoples of the U.S.S.R.

We cannot help recalling that the most farsighted among the leading statesmen of Japan understood long ago the tremendous significance for their country of friendly relations with Russia. In the nineties of the last century, when tsarist policy began to show the most unceremonious aggressiveness in Korea, Japanese political leaders tried persistently and for a long time to find some way to work out a compromise, and thus to retain friendly relations between the two countries. On the twentieth of this month, while expecting a telegram confirming the signing of the Soviet-Japanese agreement, I was reading the memoirs of the Japanese ambassador to Britain, Hayashi, who described in detail the attempts of Japan at the time of Lobanov and Muravev[8] to come to an agreement with the tsarist government. The memoirs of the tsarist ambassador, Rosen, tell the same story, but from a different point of view, and they confirm the persistent attempts of the Japanese government to reach an understanding with Russia. However, the tsarist government, with the greatest lack of formality, violated the agreement on noninterference in Korean affairs, so that finally the Japanese ruling circles abandoned their earlier policy and devoted their efforts toward basing their foreign relations on a prolonged alliance with Britain.

[7] *Pravda*, No. 18, January 22, 1925, p. 3.
[8] These were two consecutive foreign ministers in the tsarist government, 1895–96 and 1897–1900.

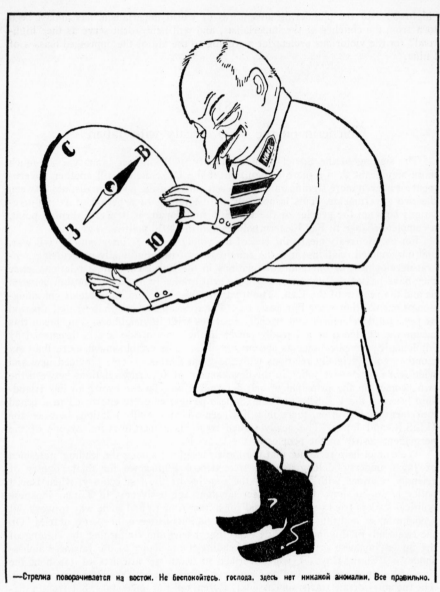

—Стрелка поворачивается на восток. Не беспокойтесь, господа, здесь нет никакой аномалии. Все правильно.

"[Chicherin:] *The needle is turning East. Don't be alarmed, gentlemen; there is no irregularity here. Everything is in order.*" Pravda, *No. 24, January 30, 1925.*

In its policy in regard to Japan, then, the tsarist government pursued its characteristic and greedy designs and was actually the aggressor. However, in the first years of the Soviet regime, which by its very nature aims at peace and fraternal relations between peoples, the Japanese government was the aggressor, and a very active one, even though it did not actually declare war. This period is now over. The exceptionally warm and friendly greetings accorded to the first representative of the U.S.S.R., Comrade Ioffe, have shown how well the Japanese masses understand the necessity and importance of friendship with the U.S.S.R. . . . The Japanese government's attitude toward us has also changed greatly. During the last period of negotiations, the atmosphere was far different from that of the earlier conferences.

But even without waiting for this treaty, we have already had some experience in economic co-operation with Japan. The Far Eastern fisheries have been leased to the Japanese as of old, and the results of this agreement have been very satisfactory. This was the first step taken, and now we can meet other Japanese needs and economic plans. After the successful beginning there will follow a successful continuation.

There exist deeply rooted differences in form between our political regime and Japan's, and consequently the policies of the two states are based on different principles. We are confident, however, that the Japanese government will loyally adhere to the treaty that has been signed. Japan, on its part, can rest assured that we will not violate the treaty, and that, therefore, friendly political relations will be maintained between our two countries. We are also confident that each contracting party will strictly follow the rule of noninterference in the internal affairs of the other.

We are convinced that the agreement signed on the twentieth of January will have an important influence on the existing complex of international relations.

82

The 1925 Treaty Between the Soviet Union and Japan

[Statement by Karakhan in an Interview, January 24, 1925, Peking][9]

Four fundamental questions presented us with difficulties in our negotiations with Japan. First, the question of the handing back of [Northern] Sakhalin; second, the question of the old treaties; third, the question of tsarist debts and the damage we suffered as a result of the intervention; and fourth, the question of coal and oil concessions in Northern Sakhalin.

These questions were resolved in the following manner: Northern Sakhalin will be evacuated by the Japanese as soon as climatic conditions render this technically possible, but in any case not later than May of this year.

The old treaties are to be revised by subsequent negotiations. Only the Treaty of Portsmouth remains in force. We have expressed ourselves as agreed to regard this treaty as of purely historical importance, as its importance for Japan consists in the fact that it confirmed Japan's victory over the tsarist army. This treaty also entitled Japan to the rank of a Great Power. At the same time, while recognizing this treaty, we repudiate in a separate declaration all responsibility for its contents.

The question of tsarist debts, as well as the question of mutual claims, will be dealt with later.

[9] *Izvestiia*, No. 20, January 25, 1925, p. 1; also *International Press Correspondence*, No. 12, February 6, 1925, p. 148.

The most difficult question to resolve was that regarding concessions. From the outset of the negotiations, Japan regarded the concessions as the price to be paid for recognition and for the losses she had suffered, as well as compensation for the evacuation of [Northern] Sakhalin. But in declaring ourselves ready to grant concessions to Japan, we, on our part, made this decision consistent with our general concession policy, and decided not to overstep the limits of the usual conditions in the granting of concessions. The final conditions which were agreed to are the same as those contained in all our concession treaties.

The importance of the concluded treaty goes considerably beyond the points which it actually contains. The treaty with Japan formally liquidates all the remnants of the intervention, which had already been liquidated in practice by the Red Army. The return of Sakhalin almost completes the unity of the regions which had been torn from the U.S.S.R. . . .

The agreement with Japan, which has strengthened our position in the Pacific, serves as a warning to America, which, by refraining from concluding a treaty with us, only makes her own position worse. This agreement, which strengthens us in the Far East, secures at the same time the conditions for our further consolidation on the Pacific and the economic development of our territories in the Far East. Without the establishment of normal relations with Japan it would have been impossible to hope for a complete restoration of our rights to the Chinese Eastern Railway.

For Japan this agreement has at present probably a still greater importance than for us. The threat of isolation which characterizes the present situation of Japan is removed by the existence of a power on the Asiatic continent friendly to Japan. How important this is for Japan can be judged by the indescribable joy which seized the Japanese people after the announcement of the signing of this agreement.

The first stone—the heaviest—of our relations with Japan has been laid. We look forward to extensive economic co-operation with Japan, which will offer us the possibility of developing our productive forces and of supplying Japan with the raw materials without which she is completely dependent upon America and Britain.

Reports received from America go to prove that America is beginning to perceive all the disadvantages of not having normal diplomatic relations with us. It is true these reports express the warning that the negotiations with America will be as prolonged and difficult as were the negotiations with Japan. But I consider this to be incorrect. As a matter of fact, fewer disputed questions separate us from America than separated us from Japan. If America will recognize that our inner political order is our own affair, that she must reconcile herself to this, and that this order guarantees a completely normal and steady economic co-operation with any capitalist country, there will no longer be any obstacle to an understanding.

83

The Tasks of the Mongolian People's Party

[From a Speech by the Representative of the Comintern (Amagaev)
at the Fourth Congress of the Mongolian People's Revolutionary
Party, September 23–October 2, 1925][10]

. . . The present Fourth Congress of the party, which has met in order to settle a number of problems which concern the party and the national constructive

---

[10] *Chetvertyi sezd Mongolskoi Narodno-Revoliutsionnoi Partii, s 23 sentiabria po 2 oktiabria 1925 goda,* pp. 2–3.

work of the country, must outline and emphasize in the clearest and most definite manner the basic tasks which are confronting the party.

Of these tasks two are the most important:

The first task is the establishment of close contact with the Comintern. The People's Revolutionary Party, which is struggling for the political and economic enfranchisement of the arat masses, has acted and has worked from the first days of its existence in absolute agreement with the Comintern. That it has done so is quite understandable. The Communist International is the headquarters of the fighting proletariat and of the oppressed peoples of the East struggling for the liberation of mankind [from capitalist fetters]. The national-revolutionary movement of the arat masses of Mongolia could not have progressed if it had not maintained contact with the Comintern and followed Comintern leadership. In order to bring about a successful national revolution in Mongolia it was imperative to establish and to consolidate close relationship between the People's Revolutionary Party and the Comintern.

After the last [Third] Congress of your party, this association was further consolidated when a representative of the Comintern was appointed by its Executive Committee to maintain this contact with you.[11]

I deem it my duty to tell you at this congress that the joint work of the representative of the Comintern and the Central Committee of your party proceeded very satisfactorily, and that no disagreements or lack of understanding were evident.

Indeed, it is a great honor and a great reward for the party to form in line with the Comintern and to take part in the world revolutionary movement. The congress of your party [I am sure] will state clearly and firmly that the ideological and organizational contact between the party and the Comintern must be maintained and developed, and that the party will not permit, and will mercilessly suppress, every attempt to undermine or weaken this relationship. This is the first task that confronts your Congress.

The second task is the establishment of a closer and direct association between the party and the arat masses. The party must not forget even for a moment that the toiling arat masses represent the driving force of the national revolution, and that the strength of this revolution will be greatly increased if the arat masses are attracted to it. . . .

84

Chicherin on His Meeting with the Turkish Foreign Minister in Odessa, November 1926[12]

. . . Seven years of continuous friendly relations [with Turkey] have borne fruit. The understanding between our two governments is now greater than ever. This was made clear by my meeting with the distinguished and gifted Turkish political leader. It had become necessary for us to sum up, and to systematize the results of our friendly political relations of seven years.

Objective historical forces provided the basis for our relations with Turkey, which were rebuilt on new [political and social] foundations. . . . Almost a year ago [the Turkish Minister and I] met in Paris, and signed a treaty of neutrality of the greatest importance to both countries. We discussed several questions of in-

11 T. R. Ryskulov.
12 *Izvestiia,* No. 272, November 24, 1926, p. 1.

terest to our two governments, but the lack of time restricted our conversations considerably. Meanwhile, the events of the past year made it necessary for us to renew our conversations and to discuss more thoroughly the problems which are confronting us. . . .

[In Odessa] we reviewed all the problems that confront our governments, exchanged views on our relations with other states, and explained our governments' attitudes to the principal political problems of the day. We created no league, Pan-Asiatic or otherwise, and in general we did not draw up any agreements that would be directed against third parties.

As I pointed out in my talk with the Turkish and Soviet sailors in Odessa, our two countries during the past seven or eight years have followed remarkably parallel courses. When Odessa, the city in which we were meeting, was being destroyed [seven years ago] by the imperialist forces of occupation and their White Guard collaborators, young Turkey was exerting its forces to the utmost in fighting the imperialist invaders, the old Sultan's government, and the classes that were supporting this government. The masses of our people and those of Turkey came out victorious, and now they have busied themselves with peaceful work and the internal reconstruction of their respective countries. At the same time the peoples of both the U.S.S.R. and Turkey are warding off, through the gradual strengthening of their own economic positions, the attempts of world capitalists to subject both countries to their domination under the guise of peaceful penetration.

The community of interests which binds our two countries . . . greatly facilitates the reaching of an agreement on our respective policies. Both the U.S.S.R. and Turkey, engaged as they are in peaceful work within their own territories, have no intention of threatening any other country. On the other hand, world imperialists, who are always trying to extend the frontiers of their rule, are threatening both the U.S.S.R. and Turkey. . . .

B. COMMUNIST EFFORTS TO REACH
THE ASIAN PEOPLE

85

The Importance of the Trade Union Movement in the East

[Theses Adopted at the Sixth Enlarged Plenum of the ECCI,
February 17–March 15, 1926][1]

The trade union movement of the colonial and semicolonial countries is a product of the postwar period, and only during the last year has it come forward as an organized force and begun to play an extremely important role in the national-liberation struggle. Of particular importance in this respect is the activity of the trade unions of China and India. The Shanghai, Hong Kong, and Tientsin strikes have revealed such a degree of revolutionary energy and organization as could not have been suspected to exist one or two years ago among the backward and doubly enslaved Chinese proletariat. By this activity the national-liberation struggle of the Chinese people was given a proletarian character and the Chinese proletariat became the lever, the main force of the national-liberation movement of China. Under these circumstances the affiliation of the Chinese trade unions to the Profintern becomes of paramount importance. It shows that the trade unions of all countries enslaved by world imperialism are looking for allies where they have a right to expect to find them—in Moscow and not in Amsterdam. The recent activity of the Chinese proletariat may well be considered the most important historical event since the October Revolution, for it means the further weakening of world imperialism and a further advance of world revolution. Of exceptional importance also are the gigantic strikes which have convulsed India during the last eighteen months. In India the struggle has not yet assumed the same character as in China, but these strikes are the precursors of the imminent political struggles. They show that in India there are sufficiently strong proletarian masses to begin, in the very near future, to play the leading role in the national-liberation struggle just as in China. . . .

All communist parties have a threefold task in relation to the workers' movement in the colonial and semicolonial countries: (1) to establish permanent uninterrupted connection between the various colonial workers' movements; (2) to give complete, unreserved, and wholehearted support to the workers of these doubly oppressed countries in their struggle for national and social emancipation; (3) in countries such as France, which import workers from the colonies, to enlist these workers in the trade unions and devote extensive cultural-educational work to them in order to develop them into fighters for their national and social emancipation.

[1] *Shestoi rasshirennyi plenum IKKI,* pp. 635–36; also *International Press Correspondence,* No. 40, May 13, 1926, p. 625.

86

The Importance of the National Problem
in the Oppressed Countries

[Statement by D. Z. Manuilsky at the Fifth Congress of the
Communist International, June 1, 1924][2]

. . . We have been witnessing lately a very rapid growth of the national and
revolutionary movements in all colonial countries. I have only to remind you of the
strike of Bombay textile workers which lasted several months, and, as you know,
had a very bloody ending, to give a clear idea of the extent of the development of
the revolutionary movement in the colonial countries.

India not so long ago was also the scene of a tremendous outburst of national
indignation among the peasant population in Nakhba [?] province. . . . If time
permitted, I could go on citing for you scores of similar cases in the colonies. . . .

We had three reasons for placing the national question on the agenda of the
Fifth Congress. The first reason is this: Basing ourselves on the rich experience
of Lenin's and Stalin's Russian school of thought, we advanced at the Second Congress, for the first time, the idea of a united revolutionary front for the proletariat
and the oppressed nations and colonies. But we did not put into a concrete form
(nor could we do so, owing to the lack of international experience) the methods
to be used for erecting this united revolutionary front. Now, after four years of
struggle, we have collected sufficient data on this question to be able to come to some
general conclusions.

Second, many mistakes have been made in a number of countries by our young
communist sections in applying the principle of the Red revolutionary front to the
oppressed nationalities, or rather many mistakes have been made in ignoring this
point altogether. The second part of my report will be devoted to an analysis of these
mistakes.

Third, and finally, during the period which has elapsed since the Second Congress
an event of great political importance has taken place. I mean the formation in
Soviet Russia of the Union of Soviet Socialist Republics, which is an experiment
in the solution of the national question under the proletarian dictatorship in a peasant
country made up of many nationalities. . . .

At the Second Congress of the Comintern we put forward two problems. First,
to what extent can the international proletariat make use of national movements . . .
in its mission of liberating mankind from the yoke of imperialism? Second, to what
extent can the oppressed colonial peoples, supported by the international proletariat,
bypass the capitalist phase of development by profiting from the highest forms of
economic development that have already been achieved . . . in the most developed
capitalist countries? By putting the problem in this form, we originated the idea
of the revolutionary front, the details of which have been elaborated by subsequent
decisions of our international congresses. But, as I have already said, at the Second
Congress we were unable to recommend specific methods . . . Only now can we
seriously consider a number of new problems on the basis of our concrete experience. . . .

Lately we have observed in a number of countries a tendency among large masses
of toilers to form workers' and peasants' parties with comparatively radical programs
for the struggle against imperialism. This has happened in the Dutch Indies, and

[2] *Piatyi Vsemirnyi Kongress K.I.*, Part I, pp. 589–95, 603; also *International Press Correspondence*, No. 54, 1924, pp. 570–71, 574.

in particular in Java, and also in China with the organization of the Kuomintang. Finally, purely peasant parties have been organized, such as the Republican Croatian Party in the Balkans under the leadership of Stjepan Radić, whose influence is felt beyond Croatia.

What should be the attitude of the communist sections of the respective countries to such parties? What concrete organizational forms should their common revolutionary front take in the struggle against imperialist oppression? We know that the Comintern has settled these questions as they have arisen. It allowed the Communists in Java to take an active part in the work of the local workers' and peasants' party there. It also allowed the Chinese Communists to join the Kuomintang, where they have promoted a more energetic struggle against international imperialism. But we also know that at the last Plenum of the Central Committee of the Chinese Communist Party, the activities of our comrades in the Kuomintang were severely criticized as "class collaboration." Thus, our sections are faced with a twofold danger: the danger of ignoring the new phenomena which are revolutionizing the East, and the danger of losing their proletarian character by collaborating with the petty bourgeoisie. Still another problem: Is it advisable for the Communists, not only to collaborate with existing parties of this kind, but to take the *initiative* in *organizing* such parties in backward countries? We note that Communists approach this problem with great timidity, with the result that we lose control over the national-liberation movements and surrender them to the native nationalist elements. . . .

We determined at the Second Congress the attitude to be taken by the young communist sections toward national-liberation movements headed by bourgeoisie *on the way to power*. But since then we have been faced with a new situation in the Eastern countries: what to do about the national bourgeoisie which has *already assumed power*. I speak of Turkey and Egypt. In Turkey, after a series of revolutionary wars conducted by Kemal Pasha against foreign armies, the young Turkish bourgeoisie came to power upon the wave of the revolutionary upsurge from below. In Egypt, the British government solved the power problem by "reform from above," i.e., by bringing Zaghloul Pasha back from exile and turning the government over to him. Two types of movement, but both having similar results as far as social-political changes were concerned; both reflected the victory of the native bourgeoisie.

However, in spite of the clarity of the situation, our Turkish comrades have committed serious tactical mistakes. For example, *Aidynlyk*, the organ of the Turkish Communist Party, published a number of articles urging the Communist Party to support the development of national capitalism against foreign capitalism. Here we note among our Turkish comrades the tendency which once upon a time was very clearly expressed in Russia by Mr. Struve's "Legal Marxist" point of view, i.e., that the working class should support the development of capitalism in Russia.[3] Similarly, some of our Turkish comrades seemed at first inclined to confound the interests of the development of the productive forces of the country with the interests of the development of capitalism. Although our Turkish comrades made good their mistakes after it was pointed out to them, we must nevertheless draw up instructions to prevent similar tendencies in other young sections of the Communist International. . . .

There is no doubt whatsoever that the bourgeoisie cannot solve the national

---

[3] Legal Marxism: a political theory upheld by a group of Russian economists and philosophers (P. B. Struve, M. I. Tugan-Baranovsky, S. N. Bulgakov, N. A. Berdiaev, and others) in the closing years of the last century. The representatives of this school of thought denied the necessity of the proletarian revolution, and advanced instead the principle of peaceful evolution toward socialism. As far as Russia was concerned, said Struve, the Russians were "to recognize our backwardness and the need to learn from capitalism."

question within the framework of the capitalist state. But this does not mean that
we must postpone the realization of the right of oppressed nations to separation until
the social revolution has been victorious throughout the world.

. . .

The formation of our Union is a powerful weapon of propaganda in the hands
of our European parties, since it permits them to compare Soviet methods of solving
the national question with those applied by the bourgeois states. That is why our
experience must become the property of all the European proletariat. . . . I am
sure that the commission on the national question to be formed by this Congress will
find practical ways to stimulate the various national movements and impart a revolutionary character to them. The time of declarations of a general character has
now passed; we face now a period of creative revolutionary work in the colonies
and among national minorities. If we fulfill these tasks, we will increase twofold
the prospect of the successful international revolution toward which we all aspire
and of which the Communist International is a guardian.

87

Roy's Insistence on a Better Understanding of the National Movements in the Colonial and Semicolonial Countries

[Statement at the Fifth Congress of the Comintern, July 1, 1924][4]

It is no longer necessary to re-emphasize the importance of the problem of the
colonial and semicolonial countries. Their importance has become almost axiomatic
for the Communist International and its sections. If sufficient application has not
been given to the problem, this is not because its importance has been underestimated,
but rather because the practical background of this problem has not been correctly
understood. The theses of the Second Congress gave us the essential principles on
the national question. We all accepted them, and professed to determine our activities
by them. . . .

I must first point out that the resolution on the report of the Executive Committee [proposed to this congress] contains a clause which does not correspond with
the theses passed by the Second Congress. Nonetheless my amendment to this resolution was rejected on the ground that it was not in accord with these same theses. I
wish to prove to you now that it is actually the [proposed] resolution that is not in
accord . . . I will prove this to you in the light of the experiences acquired by us
since the Second Congress.

Resolutions are passed so as to be carried out; therefore, there must be no
resolutions taken which cannot be carried out. The present resolution says that
"in order to draw the peoples of colonial and semicolonial countries to the struggle
of the proletariat, the Executive Committee must maintain direct contact with the
national-liberation movement. The Executive Committee has always tried, and will
try in the future to maintain this contact."[5] It seems that it has been forgotten here

[4] *Piatyi Vsemirnyi Kongress K.I.*, Part I, pp. 604–11.

[5] The actual text of the quotation in question as it was finally passed by the Congress
read as follows: "In addition to winning the support of the peasant masses and of the
oppressed national minorities, the Executive Committee and its institutions always emphasized the necessity of winning over the revolutionary liberation movements of the colonial
peoples and of all the peoples of the East, so as to make them the allies of the revolutionary

that the attempt at maintaining direct contact with the national movement in the colonies and semicolonies has not always been successful. . . .

First of all, the theses of the Second Congress include a number of points which signify no approval of such a tactic [of contact with the national movements] by the Executive Committee. . . . The theses stated that the Communist Party must render active support to the revolutionary liberation movement, but that the nature of this support must be determined by the existing conditions, which, on their part, must be carefully investigated by the party. . . . In other words, Lenin did not fail to take into account the law of history according to which this or that movement, this or that class which had a revolutionary significance in 1920, might not have this significance in 1924. Therefore, the tactic which was correct in 1920 might not be correct in 1924, and the parties and social groups in the colonies which were allies of the revolutionary proletariat in 1920 might not be capable of fulfilling such a role in 1924. Therefore it was very dangerous to establish a rigid and permanent formula and to be guided by it irrespective of the changing conditions. This mistaken attitude was the reason for the lack of activities on our part which we now lament and which we now wish to remedy. Many colonial peoples have turned their backs on the communists parties of the imperialist countries, because these parties have done nothing or very little for them. Comrades, if we wish to make up for the lack of practical initiative on the part of some parties as regards the national question, we must first of all do away with our basic mistake: we must no longer consider the theses of the Second Congress in a purely mechanical way, or insist on their purely mechanical application.

Now I want to pass to what those theses say about the social groups with which the Communist International must maintain direct contact: "We must apply all our efforts in order to provide a revolutionary nature to the peasant movement, to organize the peasants and all exploited groups into soviets, and in that way to aim at the closest possible contact between the communist proletariat of Western Europe and the revolutionary peasant movement in the colonies and the oppressed countries of the East."

Here, comrades, is indicated quite clearly which social classes in the economically backward colonies represent objectively the most revolutionary elements. Since in the majority of colonies and semicolonial countries capitalism is in the lower stages of development, it would indeed be fantastic to speak of a purely proletarian movement or purely proletarian parties in these countries. But these countries have peasant masses which represent a powerful revolutionary factor. In every revolutionary liberation movement in the colonies, the peasant masses are destined to play a role of paramount importance. Therefore, the theses indicate very clearly that the proletariat of the capitalist countries must establish contact first of all with the peasant masses [of the colonial countries].

I will give one more citation from the theses [of the Second Congress]: "The Communist International is duty-bound to render support to the revolutionary movement in the colonies and in the backward countries exclusively for the purpose of the unification of all forces which will form proletarian parties in the future. The Communist International must educate them [i.e., the peoples of backward countries] to the realization of their task, the task of the struggle against bourgeois and democratic tendencies within these nationalities." The meaning of this statement is quite clear. The task of the Communist International is to unify under its banner,

proletariat of the capitalist countries. This requires not only the extension of the direct contact between the Executive Committee and the national-liberation movements of the East, but also a very close contact between [communist] activities in the imperialist countries and the activities of the colonies of those countries." (*Piatyi Vsemirnyi Kongress K.I.*, Part II, p. 29.)

the banner of advanced proletariat, all social elements which will eventually join the proletarian party. More than that, these elements are called to the struggle against bourgeois-democratic tendencies. . . . Nowhere do the theses say that the Comintern must refrain from supporting the national-liberation movement in the colonies, but instead it is pointed out that, in order to render this support, a "direct contact" is necessary with the revolutionary organizations of the working class and the peasantry and not with the bourgeois nationalists, who themselves have no desire to have anything in common with the Communist International. Yet in our present resolution, not a word is said about it. It simply states that the Executive Committee must maintain direct contact with the national-liberation movement. This is an extremely mistaken generalization. National-liberation movements in colonial and semicolonial countries are not homogeneous.

We must not cram them into a narrow formula. They take different forms in different countries depending on the different social conditions. Most varied strata of population take part in these movements. How can we then expect practical results from the contacts we make if we base our activities on such an indefinite formula? I call the attention of the Congress to this weak side of the tactic which so far the Communist International has followed, and I demand that our position be re-examined.

·   ·   ·

Comrade Manuilsky made a statement yesterday which he would not have made had he been better acquainted with the facts. He said that during the last year there has been a strong revival of the national movement in British India. But, comrades, actually we witness the opposite. The past year is characterized by the worst depression in the Indian national movement. The national movement which was led by bourgeoisie, mainly petty bourgeoisie, reached a tremendous proportion in 1920–21, and struck horror into the hearts of British imperialists because of its great revolutionary potential. But this movement has now passed. If we determine here, at this world congress, our future tactic on the basis of a fictitious picture, we very naturally will fail to reach correct results. . . .

Comrade Manuilsky also spoke of certain sanguinary peasant actions as a sign of the development of the national movement. This is both correct and incorrect. It is correct that the sanguinary events occurred, and that [the revolt] was suppressed by the British imperialism. But it is absolutely incorrect to represent these sanguinary risings as a sign of the increase of the national movement. Actually these risings only prove that the original form of the national struggle belongs already to the past, and that the seeming unity of the national front against foreign rule is actually divided by the growing class conflicts within the ranks of the nationalists. . . .

88

The Japanese Communist Party Platform, 1922

[Said to Have Been Outlined by N. I. Bukharin][6]

While the Japanese Communist Party is obliged to meet the general requirements prescribed for the communist parties of all countries, it must consider the peculiar nature of the development of capitalism in Japan. Capitalism in Japan made re-

[6] Nihon Kyōsan-to-shi Shiryō Iin-kai (Committee for the Compilation of Historical Materials on the Japanese Communist Party), *Nihon mondai ni kansuru hōshin-sho, ketsugi-shū* ("A collection of theses and decisions concerning the affairs of Japan"), pp. 5–11 (cited hereafter as *Nihon mondai ni kansuru hōshin-sho, ketsugi-shū*). Translated by Kay K. Kaneda and Hidemi Fumino.

markable progress during the World War, because the war affected Japan less than other countries. Nevertheless, Japanese capitalism continues to display even today signs of old feudalistic practices. Most of the land is in the hands of wealthy and semifeudalistic landlords, the greatest of whom is the Emperor, who is also the head of the Japanese government. Furthermore, most of the arable land owned by these wealthy landowners is leased to and cultivated by peasants with their own tools. As the result of keen competition for the soil, rents have been constantly rising, and have now become what is known as "starvation rents." While the remnants of the feudal group continue to hold high positions in the state administration, the reins [of government] are now held by a bloc of landowners and commercial and industrial bourgeoisie. The semifeudal nature of the sovereign state is revealed very sharply by the fact that Japanese aristocracy is assigned leading positions by the Japanese constitution. Under these circumstances the forces opposing the present authority of the state come not only from the laboring class, the peasants, and the petty bourgeoisie, but from a wide range of the so-called liberal bourgeoisie as well.

The political demands of the liberal bourgeoisie in Japan are bound to increase in intensity with the development of Japanese capitalism. These demands will center upon universal (manhood) suffrage and the democratization of the national government. At the same time, the steady development of capitalism, which will be accompanied by a bourgeois revolution, will force the wage-earning class and most of the farming population to take up the class struggle. These strata of the population are gradually coming to represent an active and important element in the political life of the nation. The severe postwar economic crisis following the decline of Japanese industrial production has intensified class antagonisms and sharpened the political crisis throughout the country. Under these circumstances everything obviously points to a revolutionary overthrow of the existing political system, and various social forces and classes are now uniting toward this end. [However] the bourgeois revolution in Japan will be accomplished only if it is launched by the thoroughly organized proletariat and the revolutionary-minded peasants. The triumph of the bourgeois revolution will serve as a prelude to the proletarian revolution, which aims at overthrowing bourgeois supremacy and establishing a proletarian dictatorship.

The Japanese Communist Party, which has as its goal the establishment of the proletarian dictatorship, must utilize all the social forces that are capable of combating the present government, because the overthrow of the present government is an inevitable step in the struggle toward a proletarian dictatorship. The Japanese Communist Party is an adversary of bourgeois democracy. Nevertheless, it shall take as its temporary slogans [the slogans of bourgeois democracy, namely] the overthrow of the Emperor's government and the abolition of monarchy. It shall also direct the struggle for the adoption of universal suffrage. In the present phase of the revolutionary movement in Japan, the accomplishment of the above tasks is vital; the proletariat must rally the forces [of opposition] under the communist banner, assume control of these forces, and thus clear the way for the future struggle for soviet government.

The drawing [into the struggle] of the greatest possible number of peasants is particularly important, for the peasants are destined to oppose the government of autocrats. [Inevitably] the liberal and radical bourgeoisie will also try to get the peasant masses on their side. Consequently, the Japanese Communist Party must support all the peasant movements against the landlords. Moreover, by organizing and stimulating such movements, the party shall expose the shortcomings and inconsistencies of the liberal bourgeois reformers. The working people's party must never be an idle spectator of any struggle against the Emperor's government, even if this struggle is carried on under [bourgeois] democratic slogans. The primary tasks of the Japanese Party are to constantly intensify all such struggles, to accentuate the slogans attached to them, and to assume the leading role in the struggle against the existing government.

After these primary and immediate tasks have been accomplished, and after some actual allies of the present government begin to shift to the side of the defeated class or group, the Japanese Communist Party must then make a supreme effort to form, unite, and strengthen proletarian organizations as well as those of the farmers, accelerate the arming of the proletariat, intensify the revolution, and thereby help the workers and peasants seize control of the government with the aid of the Soviet Union. Democratic slogans are, therefore, only temporary weapons of the Japanese Communist Party; they are to be used in the struggle against the Emperor's government, and then abandoned as soon as the temporary and immediate tasks of the party have been achieved. Subsequently, the Japanese Communist Party shall advance the following demands:

A. In political affairs:

　　1. Abolition of the Imperial institution.
　　2. Abolition of the House of Peers.
　　3. Universal suffrage for men and women over eighteen years old.
　　4. Complete freedom for workers to organize themselves.
　　5. Freedom of the press for the workers.
　　6. The right of workers to assemble indoors and out of doors.
　　7. Freedom of demonstration.
　　8. The right to strike.
　　9. Abolition of the present system of the armed services, [civil] police, military police, and secret service.
　10. Arming of the workers.

B. In economic affairs:

　　1. An eight-hour working day.
　　2. Unemployment insurance and other forms of workers' insurance.
　　3. Wages based on the market prices; minimum wage.
　　4. Control of production by factory committees.
　　5. Approval of labor unions by employers and the government.

C. In agricultural affairs:

　　1. Confiscation and nationalization of the land owned by the Emperor and by the wealthy landlords, also of shrines and temples.
　　2. Establishment of a government land fund to support needy farmers, particularly the tenant farmers, who must be given the use of the land they have cultivated with their own tools.
　　3. Progressive (or graduated) income tax system.
　　4. Special taxes on luxuries.

D. In international affairs:

　　1. Abolition of all foreign intervention.
　　2. Withdrawal of troops from Korea, China, Formosa, and Sakhalin.
　　3. Recognition of Soviet Russia.

If the working class of Japan is to succeed in the struggle for proletarian dictatorship [and even] in order to overthrow the present government, it must have a unified and centralized leadership. However, some revolutionary elements (anarchists, syndicalists) object to such leadership because they fail to grasp the inevitable consequences of the class struggle when it reaches a decisive stage. This class struggle will lead sooner or later to a direct collision with the powerfully organized administrative organ of the state. In order to do away with this powerful organ, the revolutionary proletariat must possess extremely well outlined tactics and strategy. These it can have only by consolidating its positive ideology and by organizing its forces.

Therefore, the immediate task which confronts the Japanese Communist Party is to seize control of the labor unions and to establish a firm party influence upon various labor organizations. Above all, the party must eliminate the influence of patriots, social reformers, and yellow socialists[7] within the labor union movements, and in that way win the confidence of the organized workers. The party must also side with the workers in their disputes with the government and the state, and it must play a leading role in every working class movement, even small and insignificant ones. The party must strive for a strong alliance with the workers; under no circumstances must it take an independent stand [away from the workers]. If the party finds that the anarchists and syndicalists are influential within the trade unions, it must become allied with them and form a united front. At the same time, the party must repress their distorted views, which are detrimental to rightful action in the workers' struggle.

The party must also take measures to bring the peasants, especially the large group of destitute farmers, under its own influence. As to the movement which is led by the bourgeois opposition, the party must take advantage of this movement, but it must ruthlessly criticize the inconsistencies of the liberal bourgeoisie and expose the deceptions which they will undoubtedly practice in the face of the growing proletarian movement.

As a branch of the Communist International, the Japanese Communist Party is expected to fulfill its mission in the revolutionary struggle for proletarian dictatorship. For indeed, under the banner of the International, we are now advancing toward the final victory of the world proletarian revolution.

89

Appeal of the Third Enlarged Plenum of the ECCI, June 12–23, 1923, to the Japanese Workers, Peasants, and Youth[8]

The Enlarged Plenum of the Executive Committee of the Communist International expresses its deep sympathy and pledges its complete support to the Japanese Communists who have been imprisoned for courageously leading the resistance to the bourgeois bureaucratic and military cliques' attempts to militarize schools and universities in Japan.

The Enlarged Plenum is fully aware that the Japanese government visits its barbarous policies of inquisition and suppression upon the Communists so as to

---

[7] Members of the Amsterdam International, actually the International Federation of Trade Unions, established in Amsterdam in 1919.

[8] *Rasshirennyi plenum IKKI, 12–23 iiunia, 1923*, pp. 316–17.

crush the proletarian movement and eliminate Japanese radical elements; and that it has sought a pretext to promulgate in the form of an imperial edict (which did not pass last year through the Parliament), a law for the suppression of Communists.

The Enlarged Plenum warns all Japanese workers not to trust the Japanese government's false pretexts for suppressing the Communists, and to resist the government's attempts to discredit the Communists and isolate them from the masses.

The Enlarged Plenum calls upon Japanese workers to carry on the work commenced by the imprisoned Communists who have sacrificed themselves for the cause, and to develop a powerful movement directed against the treacherous plans conceived by the bureaucratic officials and the military.

The Enlarged Plenum appeals especially to Japan's workers, peasants, and student youth, calling the last-named to join the communist movement because it is they who will suffer most of all from the militarization of schools. In the arrested comrades who fell victims of conspiracy on the part of the military clique, Japan's youth must see the advanced fighters for their own cause.

90
The Shanghai January (1925) Theses[9]

At present the Japanese workers' and the peasants' movements, as well as the movement of the revolutionary intelligentsia, have one and the same goal, namely the overthrow of despotims. But there is no organization to bring together all communist[-inclined] elements, and thus the revolutionary movement in Japan as a whole is seriously handicapped. It will be difficult to bring about the revolution in Japan unless the opportunistic notion that a communist party should not be founded until a proper and spontaneous growth of the revolutionary movement is evident, is completely repudiated. The party was dissolved primarily because its former leaders erroneously tried to consolidate the bond among the party members by relying on personal relations and abstract ideological theories, rather than on revolutionary strategy and tactics based on the [economic] condition of the masses.

In addition the above leaders neglected to participate actively in the struggle for democracy and in the daily efforts of the peasants and laborers to improve their lot. They also ignored the directives of the Comintern in regard to the importance of illegal party publications.

Therefore, and in conformity with the Comintern draft platform for the Japanese Communist Party,[10] the Japanese Communists' immediate task is to reorganize the Communist Party. The reorganized party is to assume leadership in the growing social movement directed against despotism, as well as to conduct practical campaigns of propaganda and agitation among the masses in proportion as this struggle against despotism and opportunism develops. The above task will include a tactful fusing of legal and illegal literature and newspapers, the idea being to overcome the liberal ideas of the legal press by the content and spirit of the illegal press. The former leaders must put an end to all their past practical and organizational errors, and they must pass on from egocentric and impractical methods of solicitation to the practice of recruiting progressive workers and giving them executive positions,

[9] *Nihon mondai ni kansuru hōshin-sho ketsugi-shū*, pp. 15–16. Translated by Kay K. Kaneda and Hidemi Fumino.

[10] See Document 88.

thereby reconstructing the party around a core of party members known for their competence.

91

The Shanghai May (1925) Theses[11]

Following the great Kantō earthquake, the aggressive offensive on the part of the capitalists had made it imperative to introduce a change in the labor movement. This was also necessary because the leading Communists were still ignorant of the methods of winning the masses over to the communist side and were unable to oppose the opportunistic leaders effectively. They had also made a mistake in substituting the function of unions for that of the party.

Therefore, it becomes our urgent duty to organize the vast and as yet unorganized masses of the people, especially the Left-wing elements, into the trade unions; to consolidate the trade union movement by accelerating the formation of a national federation [of trade unions]; to support local trade union councils in their independent activities; to stimulate the activities of the factory committees; and thus to contribute to the struggle against the Right-wing [trade union] leaders, as well as to strengthen the trade unions in general.

In order to carry out the above tasks, the Left wing (Kakushin Dōmei) of the Japanese Federation of Labor should not split off from the Federation, but should persistently fight and destroy the Right-wing forces in it from within, as well as attempt to unify all Left-wing forces. Furthermore, so that a direct communist indoctrination program can be carried out side by side with a realistic struggle, a nation-wide trade union paper must be published to agitate and carry on propaganda among the great masses of the workers. In addition, a monthly magazine must be published to help active union members build up their theoretical knowledge and absorb information about international problems. The most important slogans of the day are as follows: (1) the conquest of the masses by means of a revolutionary day-by-day struggle based on realistic strategy; (2) campaigns against unemployment; (3) freedom to organize trade unions; (4) completion of the industrial organizations; (5) establishment of a national federation for [these] industrial organizations; (6) immediate organization of a proletarian political party; (7) condemnation of the coalition between the government and the capitalists; (8) unification of the workers of the Far East; (9) establishment of a single, unified Trade Union International.

92

Stalin's Interest in the Pan-Asian Movement

[Interview with Mr. Futse, Correspondent of *Nichi-nichi*, June or July, 1925][12]

FUTSE: The Japanese people, the most advanced people in the East, are more

---

[11] Tōkyō Chihō Saiban-sho, Kenji-kyoku (Tokyo District Court, Office of the Procurator), *Nihon Kyōsan-to chian iji-hō ihan hikoku jiken yoshin shūketsu kettei-sho* ("Final preliminary decision in the case of the defendants of the Japanese Communist Party involving the breach of the peace preservation law"), pp. 17–18 (cited hereafter as *Nihon Kyōsan-to chian iji-hō ihan hikoku jiken yoshin shūketsu kettei-sho*). Translated by Kay K. Kaneda and Hidemi Fumino.

[12] *Pravda*, No. 150, July 4, 1925, p. 3; also Stalin, *Sochineniia*, VII, 227–31.

interested than any others in the success of the liberation movement of the peoples of the East. They would willingly ally themselves with the U.S.S.R. in the great task of liberating the oppressed peoples of the East from the yoke of imperialism imposed upon them by the Western powers.

However, Japan, as a capitalist state, is sometimes obliged to act against this movement, and to join the ranks of the Western powers. Thus, in accordance with the Anglo-Japanese alliance, Japan was obliged to assist England's efforts to suppress the rebellion in India, and to take joint action with England, America, and France against the Chinese workers during the recent events in Shanghai.[13] What do you think is the best way out of this contradiction between the national desires of the Japanese people and the political and social regime of the Japanese state?

STALIN: It is true that the Japanese people are the most advanced people of the East, and that they are interested in the success of the liberation movement of oppressed peoples. An alliance between the Japanese and Soviet peoples would mark a decisive moment in the task of liberating the East. Such a union would mark the beginning of the end for the great colonial powers, for world imperialism, and it would be invincible.

It is also true that the political and social regime in Japan directs the Japanese people toward imperialism and makes of them an instrument for the enslavement, rather than for the liberation, of the peoples of the East.

You ask the way out of this contradiction between the interests of the Japanese people and the interests of the Japanese political and social regime.

There is but one way out—a change in the Japanese political and social regime which would bring it into accord with the interests of the Japanese people. . . .

FUTSE: You have expressed an opinion that a union of the national-liberation movement of the oppressed peoples of the East with the proletarian movement of the advanced countries of the West would ensure the victory of the world revolution. But we, the Japanese people, have a slogan, "Asia for Asiatics." Do you find a common ground between our desires and your revolutionary tactics in regard to the colonial countries of the East?

STALIN: You ask if there is a common ground between the slogan "Asia for Asiatics" and the revolutionary tactics of the Bolsheviks in the colonial countries of the East.

In so far—and only in so far—as the slogan "Asia for Asiatics" means a call for a revolutionary war against Western imperialism, common ground undoubtedly exists.

But the slogan "Asia for Asiatics" also has another meaning. It contains two distinct ideas which are absolutely irreconcilable with the tactics of the Bolsheviks. First, apparently assuming that Eastern imperialism is better than Western, and, therefore, that there might be no need to struggle against Eastern imperialism, the slogan ignores the question of Eastern imperialism. Second, the slogan makes the workers of Asia suspicious of the workers of Europe; it draws the first away from the second; it breaks up the international connection between the two groups, and in that way undermines the very foundation of the liberation movement.

The revolutionary tactics of the Bolsheviks are directed not only against Western imperialism, but also against imperialism in general, including Eastern imperialism. Bolshevik tactics do not aim at weakening the international contact between the workers of Asia and the workers of other countries, but at broadening and consolidating this contact.

Therefore, in spite of a common ground, there also exist points of disagreement between the slogan "Asia for Asiatics" and the Bolsheviks' tactics in the East.

13 See above, p. 288.

Futse: When talking to me in 1920 and answering my question about whether or not communism would have a better chance of success in the West than in the East, Vladimir Ilich [Lenin] said: "True communism can be successful only in the West. However, the West draws its livelihood from the East; the European capitalist powers grow rich chiefly from their Eastern colonies. At the same time they arm and train the colonials to fight, and by so doing these powers dig their own graves in the East." Do you not think that the events which occur more and more frequently in China, India, Persia, and Egypt, as well as in other Eastern countries, presage the coming of the time when the Western powers will be buried in the graves which they have dug in the East?

Stalin: You ask whether I interpret the development of the revolutionary movement in China, India, Persia, and Egypt, as well as in other countries, to mean that the time is approaching when the Western powers will be buried in the graves which they have dug in the East.

Yes, I do. The colonial countries form the basic rear of imperialism. Revolution in the rear is bound to undermine imperialism, not only because imperialism will be left without a rear, but also because the revolutionization of the East will provide the decisive impetus to touch off the revolutionary crisis in the West. Attacked from both sides—from the rear and the front—imperialism is bound to perish.

93

The Moscow 1926 Theses[14]

In the course of the European war, Japanese capitalism developed so rapidly that the government of the "landlord-capitalist bloc," heretofore under the control of the landlords, has now fallen entirely into the hands of the bourgeoisie. [On the other hand] the bourgeoisie and the landlords have shifted the burden of the [economic] crisis of 1920 and the 1923 Kantō earthquake [disaster] onto the laborers, peasants, and petty bourgeoisie. As a result, the workers and peasants have been reduced to extreme poverty, and many petty bourgeois have moved down into the proletarian group.

As the labor and agrarian movements become more radical, the Japanese Communist group must concentrate its efforts on properly reconstructing the Japanese Communist Party in accordance with the Comintern's policies. It must also unite the workers and peasants into a single political party in order to consolidate all the forces which are in opposition to the bourgeoisie-landlord bloc. Needless to say, the Communist Party should not lose its independence to the new party, but should rather influence the latter by establishing and controlling party cells within it. The Communists should likewise endeavor to enlarge and strengthen the consolidated movements of the Left-wing labor unions by participating actively in these unions' daily struggles and [supporting them in their] demands.

In Japan, the bourgoise revolution will necessarily be carried out by the proletariat and the peasants. Because this revolution is expected to be readily transformed into a proletarian revolution, the Communist Party must spearhead every progressive and democratic demand of the workers and the peasants, and devote itself to the task of fulfilling these demands.

[14] *Nihon Kyōsan-to chian iji-ho ihan hikoku jiken yoshin shūketsu kettei-sho*, pp. 28–29. Translated by Kay K. Kaneda and Hidemi Fumino.

94
Theses of the ECCI on Japan, July 15, 1927[15]

I. *Japanese Imperialism and War*

The great rise in the relative strength of the Far East in world economics and world politics after the war makes the problem of Japanese imperialism a matter of urgent necessity. Furthermore, the strengthening of Japanese imperialism during the last ten years, its growing aggressiveness, and its penetration of China, India, the Near East, the Pacific islands, and the U.S.S.R. are transforming Japan into a first-class imperialist power over the entire Asiatic continent.

Thus, one of the main junctures of the antagonism that is inherent in world capitalism is forming in the Pacific. At the same time, one of the most powerful revolutionary movements of this age, a movement that will have a most profound influence on the advancement of world revolution, is developing in China. The fate of Japanese imperialism is becoming even more closely merged with the fate of world capitalism. Japanese imperialists are playing a most active role in the preparation for the coming war. It may be actually stated that, in so far as Japanese intervention in China is an established fact, Japan is already waging the war.

Therefore, it is impossible to imagine that Japanese capitalists will assume a neutral attitude toward the Chinese revolution, since their direct, vital interests are linked up with those of China. China is the main source of raw materials for Japan with her limited coal and iron deposits. China is the principal market for Japanese industry, and 35 per cent of Japanese export is directed to Chinese ports. China is also the principal field for Japanese foreign investments. . . .

The struggle against the Chinese revolution will force (and to a considerable extent has already forced) the Japanese imperialists to form a bloc with the British imperialists for a joint action against the Chinese workers and peasants, and a joint preparation for a war against the U.S.S.R.

But even if a bloc is formed by the Japanese imperialists with America and Britain for the purpose of struggling against the Chinese revolution and the U.S.S.R., it will not eliminate the profound, constantly increasing differences between them. The interests of Japanese and British imperialists are already clashing sharply in China. Indeed, it is no coincidence that the Japanese press regard the erection of a British naval base in Singapore as a hostile act openly directed against Japan.

The antagonism between Japan and the United States is even sharper. American immigration laws are aimed specifically at Japanese emigrants. At the same time, the United States' own expansion on the Pacific conflicts with Japanese expansionist plans, and in that way brings the inevitable clash between the two powers even closer. The United States, Britain, and Japan are jointly combating the Chinese revolution, and are jointly preparing a war against the U.S.S.R., but they are at the same time arming for a bloody struggle among themselves for the partitioning of the Pacific.

II. *The Internal Situation*

The development of Japanese imperialism, which reached full strength rather late compared with European imperialism (in the 1860's), has been unusually rapid. Japanese capitalism not only was not retarded during the World War and after, but actually made enormous strides during that period. Although Japanese resources and possibilities for the development of capitalism are nothing to those of the United States, capitalistic development of Japan today is undoubtedly on the up-

---

[15] *Nihon mondai ni kansuru hōshin-sho, ketsugi-shū*, pp. 12–36. Translated by Kay K. Kaneda and Hidemi Fumino.

swing, in contrast to the downswing in Britain and the capitalist countries of Europe. . . .

III. *The Driving Forces in the Japanese Revolution*

Japan is now governed . . . by a bloc of the bourgeoisie and landlords, with the bourgeoisie in command. This being so, the hope that the bourgeoisie can in any way be utilized as a primary revolutionary factor, even during the first stages of the bourgeois-democratic revolution, must be abandoned now.

Analogies with China stand no criticism. China was and is an object of imperialist policy, whereas the Japanese bourgeoisie is itself a first-rate imperialist power. In China the "nationalist" bourgeoisie was still fighting for power at the beginning of the revolution, whereas the Japanese bourgeoisie already holds power and is using the government machinery, with all its feudal characteristics and relics, to organize and protect its capitalistic exploitation [of the workers]. Finally, capitalist development in Japan is now at such a high level that it is capable of playing a major part in directly developing the bourgeois-democratic revolution in that country into a socialist revolution, i.e., a revolution against capitalism itself.

The driving forces in the Japanese revolution are the proletariat, the peasantry, and the urban petty bourgeoisie—above all, the proletariat and the peasantry. The Japanese proletariat must unite its own struggle for a socialist revolution with its hegemony in the struggle of all toilers of Japan for a bourgeois-democratic revolution. There are in Japan all the necessary objective prerequisites for the establishment of a revolutionary bloc of workers and peasants to counterbalance the reactionary bloc of landowners and capitalists. It is essential to the success of the revolution in Japan that the working class maintain the right policy toward the peasantry.

[On the other hand] the peasantry can be victorious in its struggle for land, and against the feudal remnants as well as modern capitalistic trusts, only when it places itself under the leadership of the working class. History shows that the peasant movement is always doomed to failure unless it is led by the proletariat. Especially in a country like Japan, where more than half of the population is agrarian, the isolation of the proletariat from the peasantry would be fraught with the greatest dangers, and would place the most effective weapon into the hands of the bourgeoisie. An alliance of the proletariat with the peasantry is absolutely essential in the interests of both classes. But this alliance will be revolutionary and victorious only if the working class will assume the hegemony in it. . . .

Already about 12 per cent of the peasantry are organized in peasant leagues today. The Communists must exert all their energy to bring all these leagues into the Workers' and Peasants' Party under the guidance of revolutionary communist leadership. The reactionary bloc of the landlords and capitalists must be counterbalanced by a revolutionary bloc of the workers and peasants.

.   .   .

VI. . . . *The United Front Problem*

The Communist Party must definitely overcome the principal shortcoming of its leaders, the shortcoming that was the fundamental cause of all its misfortunes in the past, namely, its sectarian spirit. The slogan "To the masses !" is very significant for Japan today.

In this connection, it must be pointed out in particular that the complete absence of activities among the youth of Japan is a most serious error which should be removed as soon as possible. Furthermore, youth activities are becoming unusually important in view of the imminence of war.

Finally, the Communist Party must energetically fulfill its foremost duty as an organization of international revolutionaries,' that is, it must struggle against Japanese intervention in China and against the preparation of war against the U.S.S.R. . . .

95
The ECCI on the Tasks of the Communists in Indonesia[16]

Besides the revolutionary fights in China, the revolt which took place in Indonesia at the end of 1926 and at the beginning of 1927 belong to the most important events which show that the suppressed masses of the East are already drawn into the world struggle between labour and capital. The E.C.C.I. has submitted the lessons of the Indonesian revolt to an extremely careful investigation.

The national-revolutionary movement in Indonesia differs before all from similar movements in the colonies in that, owing on the one hand, to the lack of a native bourgeoisie, and on the other hand, to the existence of concentrated proletarian masses in the big factories of the imperialists, this movement followed another path and the working class succeeded comparatively easily in playing an active role in this movement.

The difficult economic situation of the masses, the deterioration of the petty bourgeoisie and of the intelligentzia, as well as the growth of the Communist Party (the C.P. is the most important political organization of the people) and of the Red trade unions, which accompanied this process—all this characterises the development of Indonesia in the last years. The approach of the mass struggle was no secret for the government of the Dutch slave-holders. It adopted every measure in order to deprive the movement beforehand of its Communist Party and of the trade union movement. The revolt broke out in November 1926, at first on the island of Java and then in Sumatra. Both revolts were bloodily suppressed. But their significance is enormous. They constitute a culminating point in the history of the national-revolutionary movement of Indonesia. These revolts differ from all previous famine revolts, in which the history of this Dutch colony is so rich, in that they constituted a conscious and organized attempt to overthrow the Dutch occupation rule by armed force.

The revolt was carried out under the leadership of the Communist Party. Hundreds of the best Indonesian Communists were shot or thrown into prison. Even before the revolt the best leaders of the Communist Party were arrested. The Party had made great efforts in order to prepare itself for the revolt. The first hours of the revolt showed some signs of technical preparation.

The whole course of the revolt, however, betrayed the lack of an earnest political and organisatory preparation of this movement as a whole. . . .

Dutch imperialism found it comparatively easy to suppress the revolt, but it is powerless when it is a question of abolishing the causes which led to this revolt. The partisan war in Indonesia clearly proves this.

What are now the next tasks of the Communist Party of Indonesia?

The first task of the Indonesian Communist Party is to rebuild the Party as a completely independent organisation, be it at the cost of the greatest sacrifices.

The Party must exert all its forces in order to reorganise the trade unions and to fight for their legalisation. The Communist Party must, by basing itself upon the trade unions, build up a mass workers' party.

Based upon an illegal organisation, the Party must at the same time make use of all the legal possibilities (elections, etc.). The Party must actively work in the national organisations, and before all in youth organisations. It is necessary to establish connections with the Left labour movement of Australia, New Zealand, and Japan, before all, however, with the national revolutionary and labour movement of China.

The Communist Party, by preparing the masses for a new attack upon Dutch

16 *International Press Correspondence*, No. 69, December 8, 1927, pp. 1562–63.

imperialism and for the fight for the national, independent Indonesian Republic, must at the same time educate and organise the masses to fight for the daily demands, such as: amnesty for the political prisoners, withdrawal of the occupation army, freedom of combination, etc., eight-hour day, abolition of the Dutch language as the official language, etc.

96

The Appeal of the League to Struggle Against Imperialism to All Oppressed Peoples of the World, 1924[17]

We are appealing to you, the peoples of India, Korea, Formosa, the Philippines, Siam, Annam, Persia, Egypt, Arabia, and Malaya, and to you, the peoples of the dark race. We are all under the oppression of America, England, Japan, France, and other imperialist countries, and we can liberate ourselves from that oppression only by a joint struggle.

We must take advantage of the present moment, when the policy of seizure and violence in your countries has reached its zenith, to unite all the oppressed peoples of the world, to erect a united front, and to launch an immediate general advance.

We, the oppressed peoples, represent two-thirds of the population of the globe; that is, we are in a great majority. The U.S.S.R. is on our side. Germany, Austria, and Hungary are not against us because the Versailles Treaty has turned them into semicolonies of the Great Powers.

Just think: who is it that is against you, who are your enemies, who is strangling you, who are those bandits that rob you and other Eastern peoples? This is the most important question for all of us, and to it we have already a clear answer. Britain, France, Japan, and America are the chief imperialist powers. The rest, Holland, Belgium, Spain, and so forth, are simply small imperialist barking dogs. Now, don't you know that the population of the imperialist powers does not come even up to 300 million, while the oppressed peoples comprise more than a billion people?[18]

Besides, not all of this 300 million are our enemies; the peasants and workers who make up the great majority of the population in the imperialist countries suffer under the yoke of imperialist governments just as much as we do.

Why, then, in spite of our great numerical superiority, are we too weak to do away with a band of international bandits? Why do they subdue us without much effort? It is because there is no unanimity among us, while our enemies are splendidly organized. Right now the power of the imperialists has reached its highest point. They have forcefully divided among themselves entire countries, and have turned peoples of these countries into their slaves. Thus the Indians and the Burmese are the slaves of Britain, the Philippines are the slaves of America, the Koreans and the Formosan people are the slaves of Japan, the Annamites are the slaves of France, the inhabitants of the Congo are the slaves of Belgium. And if the imperialist powers have not as yet treated our [i.e., China's] four hundred million population in the same manner, they have made them nonetheless the objects of their robbery and violence.

But our patience is exhausted, and we have decided to launch against imperialism a kind of "class struggle," since our demands are not limited to the demand of freedom for ourselves alone. We demand freedom for all those who are weary and oppressed. We are ready to sacrifice our lives in order to free ourselves from the yoke of imperialist powers. In order to do this, all the oppressed peoples of the yellow and dark races, as well as the white race, must organize a united bloc for a decisive struggle against imperialism.

[17] A. Ivin, "Sovremennyi Kitai," *Novyi Vostok*, No. 6, 1924, pp. 16–18.
[18] For somewhat different figures given by Stalin in 1927, see p. 396.

Friends! We, the Chinese, have organized the League to Struggle Against Imperialism. We do not wish to limit membership in this League to Chinese only, but to unify into one organization all those who think as we do.

We know that you too are struggling against imperialist powers, but we know neither your strength nor your methods, just as you do not know ours. This fact is a great hindrance to our common struggle.

We must establish relations with each other, we must share our experience, we must stretch hands of assistance to each other. We ardently desire to come into close contact with you because we deeply believe that in our unified work we shall be able to overcome all hindrances, to put an end to imperialism, and thus to bring about the liberation of all oppressed peoples.

We ask you, therefore, to inform us of the activities of your organizations and of those who ideologically support you. It is imperative only that your information be exact. On our part we shall inform you of our struggle and our methods of struggle.

We are convinced that if we unite we shall march with greater enthusiasm into the struggle against imperialism, for the liberation of the oppressed peoples.

Brothers! Hail to our common union!
Hail to the liberation of all oppressed peoples!
Away with world imperialism!

THE LEAGUE TO STRUGGLE AGAINST IMPERIALISM

97

The Tasks of the Communists in India

[The ECCI's Evaluation of the Indian Situation According to Voitinsky][19]

The problem of participation by the Communists in the [Indian] liberation movement is even more complicated than in China. For one thing, one finds in India a native capitalist class and a considerable industrial proletariat; for another, India is a colony in the true sense of the word, with a strong desire for national independence. Because of class differences within the country, and the antagonism of the Indian people as a whole toward British imperialism, and national differences among the Indian peoples themselves, the Communists must be more cautious [than in China] and adopt a much more complex strategy for the anti-imperialist struggle . . .

The experience gained in the Indian struggle against British imperialism in the course of the last few years provides considerable material for a correct estimation of the problem . . .

The rapid slowing down of the great movement of "passive resistance" headed by Gandhi and of the "boycott" of Britain's government machinery after the great strength of these movements a few years ago; the appearance of the Swaraj Party, and the continuous social differentiation in that party on the basis of class differences, as well as the general weakening of resistance to the British government which has been apparent since last year—all this shows the necessity and the possibility of rallying and organizing the city petty bourgeoisie and revolutionary intelligentsia into an anti-imperialist bloc in support of the national-liberation movement and based on an accelerated struggle against British imperialism.

The resolution of the Enlarged Plenum of the ECCI [1925] on the Indian problem stated as follows:

[19] G. N. Voitinsky, "Kolonialnyi vopros na rasshirennom plenume IKKI," *Kommunisticheskii Internatsional*, No. 4 (41), April 1925, pp. 64–66.

Side by side with the class differentiation within the Swaraj Party, a tendency is evident for bringing together the elements within the national movement which did not join the Swaraj Party. These are the masses of petty bourgeoisie, intelligentsia, students, workers, and peasants. All these elements are now under the yoke of imperialist exploitation, and therefore they must struggle for national liberation. The Swaraj Party failed to exploit the great revolutionary energy of these people because it refused to defend their political and economic demands. At the same time, when the demand for separation from the British Empire became intensified among the ranks of the national movement, the Swaraj Party came definitely to favor local self-government within the British Empire. Its Left wing, which represents more the tendencies of the elements who remained outside the Swaraj Party and who stand for political independence, is not as yet strong enough to struggle against the above viewpoint. . . . But no party in India will be able to unify the forces of the national revolution if it does not come out for independence, for the defense of the economic interests and political rights of the toilers, and for the agrarian revolution.

This makes it clear that in India, more perhaps than in any other country, the Communists will be able to maneuver the liberation movement in the interests of the toiling masses and in the direction of true independence only if they give their attention and energy first of all to the formation of a strong and ideologically mature Communist Party.

Only by working directly with India's workers' movement and supporting all forms of the agrarian movement can the Indian Communist Party take an active part in the organization and leadership of the millions of petty bourgeoisie who are forced to struggle against British imperialism.

The Colonial Commission of the Plenum of the ECCI was obliged to dwell in detail on this problem, because of possible deviations both to the Right—i.e., the overestimation of the revolutionary nature of the existing national parties (Swaraj, National Congress)—and to the Left—i.e., the underestimation of the potential revolutionary strength of the petty bourgeoisie in their desire for independence. . . .

The anti-imperialist bloc must be organized much more carefully in India than in China because the upper Indian bourgeoisie has already become a conservative class, a class that fears revolution within the country much more than it fears national oppression by imperialists.

The difference [between India and China] is very significant for the tactics which should be adopted by the Indian Communists in the liberation movement of their country, and the resolution of the Enlarged Plenum of the ECCI has made this point quite clear.

98

Resolution of the ECCI on the Expected Attitude of the Chinese Communist Party Toward the Kuomintang, January 12, 1923[20]

1. The Kuomintang is the only serious national-revolutionary group in China. It draws support partly from the liberal democratic bourgeoisie and petty bourgeoisie, and partly from the intelligentsia and the workers.

[20] G. S. Kara-Murza and P. Mif (comps.), *Strategiia i taktika Kominterna . . . na primere Kitaia. Sbornik dokumentov*, p. 112 (cited hereafter as *Strategiia i taktika Kominterna*).

2. Inasmuch as the independent workers' movement in the country is still weak, and inasmuch as the national revolution against the imperialists and their domestic feudal agents is the central task for China, and further, inasmuch as the working class is directly concerned with the settlement of this national-revolutionary problem, but is not as yet sufficiently differentiated as an absolutely independent social force—the Executive Committee of the Communist International believes that co-ordinated action is necessary between the Kuomintang and the young Chinese Communist Party.

3. Therefore, under the existing conditions it is expedient for the members of the CCP to remain within the Kuomintang.

4. Membership in the Kuomintang, however, should not be purchased at the price of the effacement of the specific political characteristics of the CCP. The party must retain its own organization with its strictly centralized apparatus. The organization and education of the working masses and the creation of trade unions as a basis for a strong mass communist party are specific and important tasks of the CCP.

In this work, the CCP must act under its own banner and independently of any other political group, trying to avoid, however, any conflict with the national-revolutionary movement.

5. In the realm of foreign policy, the CCP must oppose every Kuomintang attempt to court the capitalist powers and their agents, i.e., the Chinese military governors who are hostile to proletarian Russia.

6. On the other hand, the CCP must influence the Kuomintang in the direction of uniting its efforts with the efforts of Soviet Russia for a mutual struggle against European, American, and Japanese imperialism.

7. While supporting the Kuomintang in all campaigns conducted at the national-revolutionary front—inasmuch as the Kuomintang pursues an objectively correct policy—the CCP must not, however, merge with it, and in the course of these campaigns, it must not fold up its own banner.

99

The ECCI's Directive of Policy to the Third Congress of the Chinese Communist Party, May 1923[21]

1. The national revolution in China and the creation of an anti-imperialist front will necessarily be followed by an agrarian revolution of the peasantry against the remnants of feudalism. The revolution can be victorious only if it becomes possible to draw into the movement the basic masses of the Chinese population, i.e., the peasants with small landholdings.

2. Thus the *peasant problem* becomes the central point of the entire policy [of the Chinese Communist Party]. To ignore this basic point because of other considerations is to fail to understand the full significance of the social and economic foundation upon which alone can be based the victorious struggle against foreign imperialism and the complete destruction of the feudal regime in China.

3. Therefore, the Communist Party, which is the party of the working class, must aim at an alliance between the workers and the peasants. This task can be carried out only by means of continuous propaganda and by the actual application of such slogans of the agrarian revolution as: confiscation of landlords' land, confiscation of monastery and church land, and the passing of this land to the peasants without compensation; abolition of the practice of the starvation lease; abolition of the existing system of taxation, of the practice of the "squeeze"; abolition of the customs barriers be-

[21] *Strategiia i taktika Kominterna*, pp. 114–16.

tween provinces; destruction of the institution of tax-farmers [*otkupshchiki*], abolition of the mandarinate; creation of organs of peasant self-government to take charge of the confiscation of land, and so forth, and so forth.

4. *On the basis* of these requirements, the masses of the peasant poor must be taught the necessity of the struggle against foreign imperialism, utilizing the fact that the tariff income, salt monopolies, etc., are in the hands of foreign capitalists. Only by supplying an agrarian foundation to the slogans of the anti-imperialist front can we hope for real success.

5. It goes without saying that the leadership must belong to the party of the working class. The recent huge strikes have clearly revealed the importance of the workers' movement in China. To consolidate the Communist Party by turning it into a party of the proletarian masses, to gather the forces of the working class into the trade unions—that is the prime duty of Communists.

6. Therefore, while we maintain our earlier position, namely, that the central task for China is "the national revolution against imperialists and their domestic feudal agents,"[22] our basic demand of the Kuomintang must be *unconditional support* of the workers' movement in China, both in the north and in the south.

7. As for the civil war between Sun Yat-sen and the northern militarists, we are supporting Sun Yat-sen, but we require the Kuomintang to create a broad political national movement by means of systematic propaganda and agitation. Such a movement—on the platform of independence, unification, and democratization of the country—will give meaning to the military actions of Sun Yat-sen by drawing the broadest masses possible into the struggle against the northern militarists and foreign imperialists.

8. The Communist Party must continuously influence [*tolkat*] the Kuomintang in favor of the agrarian revolution. In the places occupied by the troops of Sun Yat-sen, it is imperative to insist that confiscation of land be carried out in favor of the poorest peasantry, and that a number of other revolutionary measures be taken. Only thus can we ensure the success of Sun's revolutionary army and its popularity with the peasantry; and only thus can we widen the basis of the anti-imperialist revolution.

8. On the other hand, we must do whatever we possibly can within the Kuomintang to prevent military alliances between Sun Yat-sen and the *militarists,* who are the agents of foreign capital hostile to Soviet Russia. Soviet Russia is an ally of both the Western European proletariat and the oppressed peoples of the East. Combinations between Sun Yat-sen and the militarists would reduce the Kuomintang movement to a movement of one militarist group against others, which would not only lead to the catastrophic disintegration of the national front, but also discredit the workers' organizations and the Communist Party, closely connected as they are with the Kuomintang in the anti-imperialist struggle.

10. In order to prevent the above deviations of the Kuomintang (and in particular of Sun Yat-sen), the Chinese Communist Party must demand the quickest possible convocation of a Kuomintang convention, at which the question of creating a broad national democratic movement must become the central point of discussion.

11. The boycott movement against Japan, which has been started again in China by Chinese insistence on the annulment of the well-known Twenty-one Demands,[23] must be broadly utilized by the party. Our party must broaden its aims and increase its membership until it becomes a general anti-imperialist movement; we must insist on the abrogation of treaties and agreements imposed on China by Britain and Amer-

---

[22] See Document 98.

[23] These were the demands imposed on China in 1915 by Japan, which would have reduced China to a virtual Japanese colony (text appears in John van Antwerp MacMurray (comp.), *Treaties and Agreements with and concerning China, 1894–1919*, II, 1231–34).

ica, as well as by other imperialist powers (extraterritoriality, Boxer indemnities, customs dues, etc.).

12. The Chinese Communist Party must consider the boycott movement against Japan likewise as one of the elements of a united democratic front in the struggle against the northern militarist government, which is cruelly suppressing the workers' and students' movements in order to please the foreign imperialists.

13. Our party must aim at finding suitable means for bringing together large strata of Chinese democracy in the anti-imperialist movement (the committees of action or national committees, etc.). To this task must be drawn, first of all, the Kuomintang and the organizations of revolutionary students.[24]

[24] Some years later Ch'en Tu-hsiu, the organizer of the Chinese Communist Party (who was in the later twenties in opposition to Moscow and the Comintern), had the following to say about the attitude of the Chinese Communists to the Comintern policy in his letter to the members of the Chinese Communist Party of December 10, 1929: "He [Maring, delegate from the Comintern to China] persistently maintained the idea that the Kuomintang was not a bourgeois party, but was a party uniting various classes, and that the proletarian party must join the Kuomintang in order to draw the latter to the side of the revolution. At that time, all five members of the Central Committee of the Chinese Communist Party, Li Ta-chao, Chang T'e-li, Ts'ai Ho-shen, Kao Yü, and I, unanimously opposed this suggestion. Our chief argument was as follows: To join the Kuomintang would mean to mix up the organizations of different classes, and to give up an independent policy. Finally, the delegate of the Third International (Maring) put a question point blank before us, that is, whether we wished to submit to the resolution of the Comintern or not." The leaders of the young Communist Party could do nothing but agree. ("Pismo tov. Ch'en Tu-hsiu ko vsem chlenam kitaiskoi kommunisticheskoi partii," *Biulleten Oppozitsii*, Nos. 15-16 [Paris, 1930], p. 20.) The above statement is also quoted in Ken'ichi Hatano, "History of the Chinese Communist Party" (in Japanese), *Ajia Mondai Koza*, II, 31. Chang T'e-li was a courtesy name of Chang Kuo-t'ao.

C. CHINA: THE FATEFUL YEARS 1925-1927

100

The Chinese Revolutionary Situation and the Tasks of the Chinese Communists

["Theses on the Chinese Question" of the Sixth Enlarged Plenum of the ECCI, February 17–March 15, 1926][1]

1. The Shanghai and Hong Kong political strikes (June–September, 1925) marked the turning point in the struggle of the Chinese people against the foreign imperialists, and the beginning of a tremendous all-national movement under the slogans of national independence and a people's government. The Chinese working class, organized in class trade unions and led by the Chinese Communist Party, appeared as a leading force in the democratic mass movement, as the pioneer and chief fighter for the independence of the country and for the establishment of a people's government. At the same time, this political activity of the Chinese proletariat under revolutionary democratic slogans, and particularly the subsequent economic struggle against the Chinese capitalists, while strengthening the proletarian class organizations, has led to a destratification of the national-liberation movement, to the breaking away of certain elements of the Chinese large trading and industrial bourgeoisie from the movement.

2. The political activity of the proletariat has given a powerful stimulus to all revolutionary and democratic organizations in China, especially to the national-revolutionary party (the Kuomintang) and the revolutionary government in Canton. The Kuomintang, whose principal group has entered into an alliance with the Chinese Communists, represents a revolutionary bloc of the workers, peasants, intelligentsia, and urban petty bourgeoisie by representing their interests in the struggle against the foreign imperialists and the whole militarist-feudal order, for the independence of the country and for a single revolutionary democratic government.

The revolutionary government formed by the Kuomintang in Canton has already been able to establish contact with the broadest masses of workers, peasants, and urban petty bourgeoisie, and with their support it has shattered the counterrevolutionary bands supported by the imperialists. It is now taking steps to revamp the whole political life of Kwangtung province along radical democratic lines. The Canton government, which is the vanguard in the struggle of the Chinese people for liberation, serves as a model for the future revolutionary democratic order of the whole country. . . .

During the last year various elements of the Chinese capitalist bourgeoisie have broken their temporary alliance with the Kuomintang. Others have formed a small Right-wing group within the Kuomintang which openly opposes close alliance with the toiling masses, favors excluding the Communists from the Kuomintang, and opposes the revolutionary policy of the Canton government. The Second Congress of the Kuomintang (January 1926) condemned this Right wing and confirmed the Kuomintang's fighting alliance with the Communists, thus strengthening the revolutionary

[1] *Kommunisticheskii Internatsional v dokumentakh*, pp. 619–23.

trend of the activities of the Kuomintang and the Canton government and assuring the Kuomintang of the revolutionary support of the proletariat.

3. The growth of the mass national-liberation movement in China has still further hastened the enfeeblement, disintegration, and decline of the military-feudal cliques of Mukden and Chihli which serve as the mainstay for the foreign imperialist domination of the country, and which, being constantly supported by the imperialists, comprise the main obstacle to the victory of the Chinese national-liberation movement.

Because of this decline and disintegration, and because of the growing influence of democratic organizations, the Chinese national-liberation movement has begun to form its own military forces . . . The formation of the People's Armies in northern China and their struggle against the military-feudal cliques are a major achievement of the national-liberation movement; from these armies and the Canton Army will be formed a revolutionary democratic army for the whole of China. The Chinese Communists and the Kuomintang should give most decisive support to this work of forming military forces; they should also work hard at revolutionizing both the army's internal relations (its formations, the selection and re-education of cadres, the serious organization of political work) and its mutual relations with the population in bivouac areas.

4. The growth of both national democratic tendencies and proletarian influence in the Chinese national-liberation movement reflects the tremendous moral and political support that movement receives from the world proletarian revolution through the Communist International and the toilers of the Union of Soviet Socialist Republics. The anti-imperialist struggle of the Chinese people and the anticapitalist struggle of the entire world proletariat are developing in close contiguity. The Communist International should make unmistakably clear to the toiling masses of all imperialist countries the significance of the Chinese toilers' current struggle against the imperialists. There should be the most powerful support of this movement. All imperialist efforts to smash it by military intervention or blockade should be resisted with the slogan "Hands off China!" and the demand that China's complete independence be recognized, all unequal treaties abolished, and all troops of imperialist governments evacuated. At the same time, the Chinese Communists should explain to the Chinese toiling masses that only the Communist International is their revolutionary ally in the struggle for emancipation, and that the Second International and Amsterdam,[2] under the mask of benevolence, have actually supported the imperialists against the Chinese people.

5. The imperialists of various countries, struggling to preserve their domination over China, are striving to utilize a certain lull in the development of the mass national-liberation movement for a new attack on China, the main objective of which is to smash the revolutionary democratic centers and organizations. In the face of these new dangers, the Chinese Communist Party and the Kuomintang should develop intensive political work, organizing mass activities in support of the struggle of the People's Armies, utilizing internal contradictions in the camp of the imperialists and counterposing to them a single national-revolutionary front of the broad masses (workers, peasants, bourgeoisie) under the leadership of the revolutionary democratic organizations.

6. The Chinese Communist Party can execute its historical task of leading China's toiling masses in their anti-imperialist struggle only if throughout the whole struggle it continually strengthens its organizations and its influence as the class party of the Chinese proletariat and as a section of the Communist International. That the party

[2] The Amsterdam International, actually the International Federation of Trade Unions, founded in Amsterdam in 1919.

has progressed considerably during the past year is clear from the extensive economic and political strikes it has instigated, but it is far from completely formed. The political independence of the Chinese Communists will develop in the struggle against two equally harmful deviations: *Right-wing liquidationism,* which abandons the independent class tasks of the Chinese proletariat for a formless merging with the general democratic national movement, and *extreme Left moods,* which favor skipping over the revolutionary-democratic stage of the movement straight to the proletarian dictatorship and soviet power, forgetting the most important and decisive factor of all—the peasantry. The tactical problems of the Chinese national-revolutionary movement, despite the peculiar situation, closely resemble the problems which faced the Russian proletariat in 1905. The assimilation by the Chinese Communist Party of the lessons of the Russian revolution of that year, as formulated by Leninism, and the political and organizational consolidation of the party, will help considerably to overcome and avert the above-mentioned deviations.

7. The fundamental problem of the Chinese national-liberation movement is the peasant problem. The victory of the movement's revolutionary democratic tendencies depends upon how many of the 400 million Chinese peasants are drawn, together with the Chinese workers and under their leadership, into decisive revolutionary struggle. . . . In various districts the countryside is covered with a network of the most varying kinds of revolutionary peasant organizations, which from time to time have entered into an armed struggle against the oppressors. But in general the peasantry in China remains split and scattered, and the work of organizing it has scarcely begun. The main task of the Chinese Communists and the Kuomintang is to explain to China's peasants that only by allying themselves with the working class to form an independent revolutionary democratic government can they radically improve their material and political position, and to draw the peasant masses into an active struggle against the militarists and imperialists. Here it should be remembered that all Chinese peasants will act as a unit for a long time yet. Therefore, while taking into consideration the various sorts of peasants, and concentrating their efforts on the proletarian and semiproletarian peasant groups, the Chinese Communists must nevertheless seek to bring together [temporarily] all the existing peasant organizations in a common revolutionary program (see the theses on the peasant question passed by the Enlarged Plenum of the Executive Committee of the Communist International in April 1925)[3] capable of rousing the whole peasantry to an armed struggle against the militarists and against the administrators, middlemen, and gentry who support the semifeudal order in the villages.

8. In the workers' movement the Communist Party of China should extend the fight to improve the extremely hard conditions of the workers, and to strengthen and develop the trade union movement. The trade unions, led by the Communist Party of China, should continue their determined and sustained participation in the whole general revolutionary struggle in China, but at the same time they must become genuine economic organizations, taking keen cognizance of the workers' everyday needs and leading their struggles against foreign and Chinese capitalists. The trade unions must be strengthened, given legal existence, and reorganized on an industrial basis; delegate meetings and factory committees must be arranged. At the same time the party should form its own party factions within the trade unions, thus strengthening its influence in the unions.

9. The Communist Party of China should be particularly alert for signs of international reformism among the Chinese proletariat and in the national-liberation movement. We may look for an offensive of all shades of international reformism against China, from the extreme Right wing in the form of American and Japanese

[3] Text appears in *Kommunisticheskii Internatsional v dokumentakh,* pp. 495–506.

Gomperism[4] right up to the so-called Left wing headed by Otto Bauer.[5] To counteract the "pacifism and democracy" propaganda which these groups will serve up as a screen for the offensive of American capital, the Communist Party of China should launch an extensive campaign to explain the treacherous role of international reformism . . .

10. The Chinese Communist Party must become the mass organization of the Chinese proletariat. Its growth during the past year, in view of the existence of class trade unions uniting hundreds of thousands of workers, has certainly been inadequate. The Chinese Communist Party must outgrow as soon as possible its narrow sectarian views concerning membership of rank-and-file workers in the Communist Party. All superfluous formal obstacles to the entry of workers into the party must be removed. Only by extending and consolidating its ranks can the party be assured of its leadership of the movement.

101

Stalin on the Chinese Bourgeois-Democratic Revolution and the Peasant Question

[Speech to the Chinese Commission of the Seventh Enlarged Plenum of the ECCI, November 30, 1926][6]

. . .

I. *The Nature of the Revolution in China*

Lenin said that the Chinese would soon have their 1905. Some comrades took this to mean that exactly what took place with us in Russia in 1905 would necessarily repeat itself in China. This is wrong, comrades: Lenin certainly did not say that the Chinese revolution would be a copy of the Russian revolution in 1905; he merely said that the Chinese would have their own 1905. This means that apart from the features which the Chinese revolution would have in common with the revolution in 1905, it would have its own specific peculiarities, which would stamp their special features on the whole revolution in China.

What are these peculiarities?

The first peculiarity is that the Chinese revolution, being a bourgeois-democratic one, is also a revolution for national liberation directed against the rule of foreign imperialism in China. . . .

Out of this peculiarity arises another peculiarity of the Chinese revolution, and that is that the capitalist bourgeoisie in China is extremely weak, much weaker than the Russian bourgeoisie in 1905. . . . From this it follows that the initiator and guide of the Chinese revolution, the leader of the Chinese peasantry, must inevitably be the Chinese proletariat, which is better organized and more active than the Chinese bourgeoisie.

---

[4] After Samuel Gompers, conservative labor leader and president of the American Federation of Labor from 1882 to 1884 and again from 1885 to the time of his death in 1924. Gompers consistently opposed socialist movements in the unions, and because of his moderate views was criticized and vilified by the Russian Communists.

[5] Bauer was a prominent member of the Left wing of the Austrian Social Democratic Party. He disagreed with the Russian Communists' interpretation of Marxian philosophy, and was bitterly denounced by them for his "repudiation of revolutionary Marxism."

[6] *Voprosy kitaiskoi revoliutsii*, pp. 41–56; also Stalin, *Sochineniia*, VIII, 357–74; also *International Press Correspondence*, No. 90, December 23, 1926, pp. 1581–84.

Neither should the third peculiarity of the Chinese revolution be overlooked; it is that, side by side with China, there exists and develops the Soviet Union, whose revolutionary experience and help are bound to facilitate the struggle of the Chinese proletariat against imperialism and against the survivals of feudal-mediaevalism in China.

These are the fundamental peculiarities of the Chinese revolution which determine its character and its direction.

II. *Imperialism and Imperialist Intervention in China*

The first defect of the theses[7] before us is that they avoid or underestimate the question of imperialist intervention in China. If we read the theses carefully, we might imagine that there is at present in China no actual imperialist intervention, but only a struggle between the North and the South, or of one group of generals against another group of generals. In addition, there is an inclination to understand by intervention a condition in which foreign troops march into Chinese territory; if this does not take place, then there is no intervention. This is a serious error, comrades; intervention is by no means limited to the entry of troops, and the entry of troops is by no means an essential characteristic of intervention. In the present circumstances of the revolutionary movement in capitalist countries, where the direct entry of foreign troops might lead to a number of protests and to conflict . . . imperialism prefers to intervene against the revolution by organizing civil war within a dependent country, by financing the counterrevolutionary forces against the revolution, by moral and financial support of its Chinese agents . . . The struggle of Wu P'ei-fu and Sun Ch'uan-fang, Chang Tso-lin, and Chang Tsung-ch'ang[8] against the revolution in China would be quite impossible were it not that the imperialists of all countries had inspired these counterrevolutionary generals and supplied them with money, arms, instructors, "advisers," etc. . . . Intervention by using other people—that is the kernel of imperialist intervention at present. . . .

Anyone who evades or undervalues imperialist intervention in China evades or undervalues that which is most important and most essential.

It is said that the Japanese imperialists show a certain amount of "good will" toward the Cantonese and toward the Chinese revolution as a whole. It is said that in this respect the American imperialists are in no way behind the Japanese. This is self-deception, comrades. We must know how to discern the true nature of the policy of the imperialists, including the Japanese and American imperialists, behind their masks. . . . We must make a definite distinction between friendliness and praise addressed to the Canton people, and the fact that the imperialists, who distribute their friendliness most liberally, cling most desperately to "their" concessions and railways in China, from which they do not wish to be "relieved" at any price.

III. *The Revolutionary Army in China*

My second remark in connection with the theses before us concerns the question of the revolutionary armies in China. The point is that the question of the army is evaded or undervalued in the theses. (Voices: "That is correct!") This is their second defect. The northward advance of the Cantonese is generally regarded not as the growth of the Chinese revolution but as a struggle of the Canton generals against Wu P'ei-fu and Sun Ch'uan-fang, as a fight for supremacy of one group of generals against another group of generals. This is a great mistake, comrades.

[7] Stalin refers here to the theses on the Chinese revolution proposed by Petrov and Mif, and to written reports by others which were presented and discussed at the Seventh Enlarged Plenum of the ECCI, November 22–December 16, 1926.

[8] Chinese warlords.

The revolutionary armies in China are the most important factor in the fight of the Chinese workers and peasants for their liberation. Is it then a mere coincidence that until May or June of this year China was regarded as ruled by the reactionaries who had taken over after the defeat of Feng Yü-hsiang's army, but that in the summer of this year it was only necessary for the victorious Canton troops to advance northward and occupy Hupeh in order to change the picture fundamentally in favor of the revolution? No, it was not a coincidence; for the advance of the Canton troops was a blow aimed at imperialism, a blow aimed at its agents in China, a blow for freedom of assembly, freedom to strike, freedom of the press, and freedom to organize for all the revolutionary elements in China in general, and for the workers in particular. In this lies the peculiarity and the greatest importance of the revolutionary army in China. . . .

In China, armed revolution is fighting against armed counterrevolution. This is one of the peculiarities and one of the advantages of the Chinese revolution. This fact also explains the particular significance of the revolutionary army in China.

It is, therefore, an inadmissible defect of the theses before us that they underestimate the revolutionary army.

It follows, therefore, that the Chinese Communists ought to devote special attention to work in the army.

First of all the Chinese Communists must use every means in their power to intensify political work in the army and must succeed in making the army a real and model impersonation of the idea of the Chinese revolution. . . .

Secondly, the Chinese revolutionaries, including the Communists, must make a special study of military art; they must not regard military questions as something of secondary importance, for military questions in China are at present the most important factor in the Chinese revolution. The Chinese revolutionaries, and, therefore, the Communists also, must study military art in order to advance gradually toward leading posts in the revolutionary army. This will guarantee that the revolutionary army of China will follow the right path, directly to its goal. Unless this is carried out, it is inevitable that there should be vacillations in the army.

These are the tasks which the Chinese Communist Party has to fulfill with regard to the question of the revolutionary army.

IV. *The Character of the Future Power in China*

A third defect in these theses is that the character of the future revolutionary power in China is not considered sufficiently, or is altogether disregarded. . . . What is important is not only the bourgeois-democratic character of the Canton government, which forms the nucleus of the future Pan-Chinese revolutionary power; the most important thing is that this power is an anti-imperialist power and can be nothing else, that every advance of this power is a blow aimed at world imperialism and is, therefore, a stroke in favor of the revolutionary world movement. Lenin was right when he said: "Whereas formerly, prior to the epoch of the world revolution, movements for national liberation were part of the general democratic movement, now, after the victory of the Soviet revolution in Russia and the opening of the period of world revolution, movements for national liberation are part of the proletarian world revolution." . . .

I believe that the future revolutionary government in China will, in its character, resemble the government which was spoken of in our country in 1905, i.e., a dictatorship of the proletariat and peasantry, but with the distinguishing feature that it will be predominantly an anti-imperialist government. It will be a government representing the transition to noncapitalist, or, to be more exact, to socialist development in China.

This is the direction in which the revolution in China must develop. The progress of that revolution will be facilitated by three circumstances:

First, the revolution in China, as a revolution for national liberation, will be directed against imperialism and its agents in China;

Second, the capitalist bourgeoisie in China is weak, weaker than the national bourgeoisie was in Russia in 1905, so that the proletariat will have that much less trouble gaining leadership of the Chinese peasantry;

Third, the revolution in China will be able to use the experience and the aid of the victorious revolution in the Soviet Union.

Whether this method will lead to victory fully and finally depends on many circumstances. One thing is clear—that it is the chief duty of the Chinese Communists to fight for this way of development for the Chinese revolution.

From this follows the proper attitude of the Chinese Communists toward the Kuomintang, and toward the future revolutionary government in China. It is said that the Chinese Communists ought to secede from the Kuomintang. This is pure folly, comrades. It would be the greatest mistake for the Chinese Communists to leave the Kuomintang. The whole course of the Chinese revolution, its character, its prospects, undoubtedly indicate that the Chinese Communists ought to remain in the Kuomintang and intensify their work in it. But can the Chinese Communist Party take part in the future revolutionary government? It not only can; it must. The course of the revolution in China, its character, its prospects speak eloquently in favor of the Chinese Communist Party's participation in the future revolutionary government. This is one of the necessary guarantees if the hegemony of the Chinese proletariat is to become a concrete and full reality.

V. *The Peasant Question in China*

My fourth remark concerns the question of the peasantry in China. Comrade Mif believes that we should call at once for the formation of soviets, of peasant soviets, in the Chinese countryside. I believe that this is a mistake. Comrade Mif is in too great a hurry. It is out of the question to form soviets in the countryside and to leave out the industrial centers in China. Yet the question of forming soviets in the Chinese industrial centers has not yet become the order of the day. Furthermore, we must not forget that soviets cannot be considered independently of their connection with the whole situation. It would be possible to organize soviets, i.e., peasant soviets, only if China's peasant movement were reaching its zenith, were breaking down the old power and creating a new one—on the assumption that the industrial centers of China had already broken down the barrier and entered on the phase of forming a soviet government. Can it be said that the Chinese peasantry or the Chinese revolution as a whole has already entered on this phase? No, this cannot be said. Therefore, to speak of soviets now is to try to outpace the situation. At the present moment, we must raise the question not of soviets, but of the formation of peasant committees. I mean committees elected by the peasants, which are capable of formulating the fundamental demands of the peasantry and of taking all the necessary measures for realizing these demands by revolutionary methods. These peasant committees should form the axis around which the revolution in the villages will revolve.

I know that there are certain people among the members of the Kuomintang, and even among the Chinese Communists, who do not consider it possible to unleash the revolution in the countryside, because they fear that if the peasantry is drawn into the revolution the united anti-imperialist front will be undermined. This is a profound mistake, comrades. The anti-imperialist front in China will be the stronger and more powerful the sooner and more solidly the Chinese peasantry is drawn into the revolution. The authors of the theses, especially Comrades T'an

P'ing-shan and Rafes,[9] are perfectly right when they maintain that the immediate satisfaction of the most urgent demands of the peasantry is an essential condition for the victory of the Chinese revolution. In my opinion, it is high time to do away with the inertia and "neutrality" toward the peasantry which is noticeable in the activity of certain elements of the Kuomintang. I think that both the Communist Party of China and the Kuomintang, i.e., the Canton government, ought without delay to pass from words to deeds and immediately take steps to satisfy the most vital demands of the peasantry. What prospects open up in this respect, and up to what limits can and should advance be made? That depends on the course of the revolution. I think that it should finally be carried as far as the nationalization of the land. In any case, we cannot dispense with the slogan of the nationalization of the land.

How are the Chinese revolutionaries to arouse the many million Chinese peasants for the revolution? I think that in present circumstances there are only three alternatives.

First, form peasant committees and have Chinese revolutionaries penetrate them in order to influence the peasantry. . . . However, this way is not enough. It would be ridiculous to suppose that the number of revolutionaries is sufficient to carry this out. The population of China is roughly 400 million. Of these, 350 million are Chinese, and more than nine-tenths of them are peasants. It is a great mistake to assume that a few tens of thousands of Chinese revolutionaries are enough to permeate this ocean of peasantry. Well, then, we must seek other ways.

Second, influence the peasantry through the machinery of the new national-revolutionary government. It cannot be doubted that in the newly liberated provinces a new government will be set up after the pattern of the Canton government. It cannot be doubted that this government will have to satisfy the most urgent demands of the peasantry if it wishes to advance the revolution. The Communists, and the revolutionaries of China in general, must work their way into this new government . . . and help the peasant masses satisfy their most urgent demands by means of its machinery, whether by stripping the landowners of their land or by reducing taxation and rents—whatever the circumstances demand.

Third, influence the peasantry through the revolutionary army. I have already spoken of the extraordinary importance of the revolutionary army in the Chinese revolution. The revolutionary army of China is the force which first penetrates new provinces, which first becomes known among the bulk of the peasantry, and by which the peasant forms his opinion of the new power, of its good or bad qualities. The attitude of the peasantry toward the new power, toward the Kuomintang, and toward the revolution in China as a whole depends in the first place on the behavior of the revolutionary army, on its behavior toward the peasantry and toward the landowners, on its readiness to help the peasantry. If we bear in mind that numerous doubtful elements have joined the revolutionary army in China, that these elements may alter the aspects of the army for the worse, we shall understand the great importance of the political aspect of the army and, so to speak, of its peasant policy in the eyes of the peasants. For this reason the Communists and the Chinese revolutionaries as a whole must take all possible measures to neutralize the elements in the army which are hostile to the peasants, to preserve the revolutionary spirit in the army, and to direct things in such a way that the army helps the peasants and mobilizes them for the revolution. It is said that the revolutionary army in China is welcomed with open arms, but that later, after it has established itself, there is a certain disillusionment. The same thing happened with us in the Soviet Union during the

[9] M. G. Rafes was active in the Ukrainian communist movement in the period of civil war; he later switched his interests to China.

civil war. This is explained by the fact that the army, when it has liberated new provinces and established itself in them, is compelled to maintain itself in some way or other at the expense of the population of the district. We Soviet revolutionaries usually succeeded in making up for these disadvantages by endeavoring to help the peasants against the landowners by means of the army. It is essential that the Chinese revolutionaries should also learn to make up for these disadvantages by carrying out a correct peasant policy with the help of the army.

These are the methods and the points of contact through which it will be possible to carry out a correct peasant policy in China.

VI. *The Proletariat and the Hegemony of the Proletariat in China*

My fifth remark concerns the Chinese proletariat. It seems to me that in the theses sufficient emphasis has not been laid on the role and importance of the Chinese working class. . . . I believe that the Chinese Communists should orientate themselves toward the proletariat, and orientate the active workers in the liberation movement in China toward the revolution. Only then will the question be put in the right way. I know that among the Chinese Communists there are comrades who do not approve of strikes of workers for improving their material and their legal position, and who dissuade the workers from striking. (*Voice*: "That happened in Canton and Shanghai.") This is a great mistake, comrades. It is a serious underestimation of the role and of the prestige of the proletariat in China. This should be recorded in the theses as a decidedly negative phenomenon. It would be a great mistake if the Chinese Communists did not take advantage of the present favorable position to help the workers improve their material and legal position, even though it be through strikes. Why in all conscience have we a revolution in China? A proletariat which allows its members when on strike to be beaten and ill-treated by the agents of imperialism cannot be a leader. This medieval abuse must be abolished so that the sense of power and the sense of its own dignity may be strengthened among the Chinese proletariat, and so that it may thus be made fit to hold the hegemony in the revolution. Unless this takes place, a victory of the revolution in China is not to be thought of. For this reason the economic and legal demands of the working class in China, which aim at a serious improvement of its situation, must be given the place they deserve in the theses. . . .

VII. *Question of the Young People in China*

My sixth remark concerns the young people in China. . . . This question is very important. The young people at the universities (revolutionary students), the young workers, the young peasants—all of them form a force which might drive the revolution forward with giant strides if the young people were brought under the ideological and political influence of the Kuomintang. . . . Youth must also have its place in the theses on the Chinese question.

VIII. *A Few Final Conclusions*

I should like to draw two final conclusions with regard to the struggle against imperialism in China and with regard to the peasant question.

There can be no doubt that the Chinese Communists will now no longer confine themselves to demanding the abolition of the unequal treaties. Even a counterrevolutionary like Chang Hsüeh-liang now advocates this demand. It is obvious that the Chinese Communist Party must go further. It must seek nationalization of the railways, nationalization of the most important factories, and above all nationalization of those undertakings whose owners have distinguished themselves by special hostility and special aggressiveness toward the Chinese people.

Further the peasant question must be given prominence and [its solution] must be connected with the prospect of the revolution in China. In my opinion, the final aim of the whole matter must be the nationalization of the land.

Everything else is a matter of course.

102

The Comintern's Evaluation of the Chinese Situation and Plan of Action for the Chinese Communists

[Theses Adopted at the Seventh Enlarged Plenum of the ECCI, November 22–December 16, 1926][10]

I. *Imperialism and the Chinese Revolution*

1. . . . During the last two years, imperialism has suffered a heavy defeat in China, the effects of which will contribute considerably to the aggravation of the crisis of world capitalism. . . .

The further victories of the revolutionary armies of Canton, supported by the broad masses of the Chinese people, will lead to victory over the imperialists, to the achievement of the independence of China, and to its revolutionary unification, which will consequently increase in numerous ways its power of resistance to imperialism.

The failure of Sun Ch'uan-fang to stop the advance of the Canton Army has convinced the imperialist powers that the traditional method of using the native militarists as instruments to crush the national-revolutionary movement no longer meets the situation. At the same time mutual rivalry does not permit the imperialist powers to unite for open military intervention. Imperialism seeks new methods to meet the new situation. The new policy tends toward recognition of the Canton government. The initiative comes from American imperialism. Even Britain and Japan are considering the recognition of the Canton government as a permissible political measure. These are but diplomatic maneuvers which cover hostile imperialist designs against the revolution.

2. The basic power of imperialism in China is in its monopoly of the entire financial and industrial life of the country (monopoly on the salt tax, mortgage of customs revenue; railways, waterways, mines, heavy industries are mostly owned by foreign capital). If this solid base can be maintained, imperialism will find in China a great help for the stabilization of the capitalist system. . . . Consequently, imperialism will make desperate efforts to crush the Chinese revolution, which threatens to overthrow it. Failing to crush it by the traditional method of provoking a civil war or by eventual armed intervention, imperialism will try to disrupt the movement for national liberation which is developing along revolutionary lines.

In spite of the mutual antagonism among the imperialist powers, the possibility of armed intervention still remains. Foreign intervention takes a peculiar form in China. Under present conditions imperialism prefers to intervene by means of organizing civil war and by financing counterrevolutionary forces against the revolution. . . .

3. From the point of view of its external situation, the Chinese revolution—by the mere fact of its anti-imperialist character—is an inseparable part of the international revolution. Other factors favoring the Chinese revolution are:

[10] *Kommunisticheskii Internatsional v dokumentakh*, pp. 668–80; also *International Press Correspondence*, No. 11, February 3, 1927, pp. 230–34.

(*a*) Mutual rivalries of the imperialist powers in China, which weaken the position of world imperialism;

(*b*) The crisis of world capitalism;

(*c*) The growth of the proletarian movement in Western Europe (an open armed intervention in China is bound to be resisted by the working class in the imperialist countries);

(*d*) The development of national-revolutionary movements in the colonies, which, in their turn, must grow as the Chinese revolution grows;

(*e*) The existence of the proletarian dictatorship in the Union of Soviet Socialist Republics; the proximity of the U.S.S.R. to China; and the remoteness of China from the principal centers of economic, military, and political power of the imperialist states.

4. . . .

The national revolution in China is developing amid peculiar conditions which radically distinguish it from the classical bourgeois revolutions of Europe in the last century, as well as from the 1905 revolution in Russia. The principal difference is China's semicolonial status, its dependence upon foreign imperialism. Moreover, the Chinese revolution is taking place in a period of world revolution and is an integral part of the world-wide movement for the overthrow of the capitalist order. This factor will determine the history of the Chinese revolution and the alignment of the social forces participating in it. . . .

Economically speaking, China's principal feature is its variety of economic forms, ranging from finance capital to the economic survivals of patriarchal and tribal society—the predominant form, however, being merchant capital, and petty trades and home industry in town and countryside.

This to some extent results in a low class differentiation of the Chinese population and explains the inadequate state of organization among the principal social-political forces of the national revolution.

Other factors are the collapse of the central machinery of the government, which has been going on since the interrupted revolution of 1911 and with greater acceleration in the last few years, and the widespread domination of the political organizations of Chinese militarism. . . .

The development of the national-revolutionary movement in China at the present time depends upon the agrarian revolution. . . .

The extreme backwardness of the Chinese economy generally, the manner in which landed property is divided up into minute allotments, the fact that an enormous proportion of the agrarian population are tenant farmers or semi-tenant farmers, the primitive state of technique in both small- and large-scale agricultural enterprises, the extreme agrarian overpopulation, and simultaneously with this the development of commercial agriculture and the process of class differentiation which is going on in the villages, render the general situation in the rural districts extremely complicated and considerably hinder the development of the agrarian revolution in China.

As a consequence of objective circumstances, the class struggle in the rural districts of China reveals a tendency to develop in the following directions—against the survivals of large-scale land ownership, against the gentry, against the merchant-usurer capitalists, and partly against the upper strata of the village kulaks.

5. The successive states of development of the revolutionary movement in China are marked by important realignments of social forces. In the first stage one of the driving forces of the movement was the national bourgeoisie and the bourgeois intelligentsia, which sought support in the ranks of the proletariat and the petty bourgeoisie.

In the second stage, the character of the movement changed—its social basis was shifted to a different class combination. New and more revolutionary forms of struggle developed. The working class appeared in the arena as a political factor of prime importance.

Economic strikes are merging into political struggles against imperialism and are acquiring an exceptionally important world historic significance. The proletariat is forming a bloc with the peasantry, which is actively taking up the struggle for its interests with the petty urban bourgeoisie and with a section of the capitalist bourgeoisie. This combination of forces has found its political expression in corresponding groupings in the Kuomintang and in the Canton government. Now the movement is on the threshold of the third stage, on the eve of a new realignment of classes. In this stage of development the driving force of the movement will be a bloc of a still more revolutionary nature—of the proletariat, peasantry, and urban petty bourgeoisie, to the exclusion of the majority of the capitalist bourgeoisie. This does not mean that the whole bourgeoisie, as a class, will be excluded from the arena of the struggle for national liberation, for besides the petty and middle bourgeoisie, even certain elements of the large-scale bourgeoisie may, for a certain period, continue to march with the revolution.

At this stage, the leadership of the movement passes more and more into the hands of the proletariat.

In this period of transition to a new revolutionary stage, the capitalist bourgeoisie see that under the leadership of the proletariat the anti-imperialist struggle is getting beyond their control, and that it objectively menaces their class interests. They endeavor, therefore, to regain their leadership for the purpose of defeating the revolution. They try to influence the movement with the ideology of bourgeois nationalism as against the ideology of the class struggle.

6. Parallel to this regrouping of the class forces of the revolution, there proceeds the crystallization of the counterrevolutionary forces. This process, in its turn, is closely related to and is influenced by imperialist politics, just as the development of the revolutionary forces is related to and is influenced by the world revolution (the Union of Soviet Socialist Republics and the Western proletariat).

. . . Finding that the militarists are not fully effective instruments for crushing the revolutionary movement, imperialism seeks by reconciliation to gain other allies within the nationalist movement, and to induce the national bourgeoisie to break away from the revolutionary bloc. To strengthen the imperialists' position within the national movement, some sections of the capitalist bourgeoisie and even militarists, who up till now have avoided or condemned the national-revolutionary struggle, have begun to pass to the side of the Canton government. The object of this move is to wrest the leadership of the national-revolutionary movement from the revolutionary bloc of the proletariat, peasantry, and urban petty bourgeoisie, and thereby to stem the tide of the revolution. World imperialism stands behind all these maneuvers of the forces of counterrevolution.

In this transitional period, when the gradual abandonment of the revolution by the capitalist bourgeoisie is historically inevitable, the proletariat must, of course, make good use of such bourgeoisie as remain actively engaged in the revolution.

On the other hand, the proletariat must utilize antagonisms both among the bourgeoisie who are abandoning the revolution and among the various imperialist groups, all without ever losing sight of its principal aims, to which it must subordinate all its strategic maneuvers and tactical moves.

II. *The General Prospects of the Chinese Revolution*

7. Considered from the point of view of class alignment in both camps, the general prospects of the Chinese revolution become very clear. . . . Taking place in the period of capitalist decline, the Chinese revolution is a general struggle for the overthrow of capitalism and the establishment of socialism. The structure of

the revolutionary state will be determined by its class basis. It will not be a purely bourgeois-democratic state, but a democratic dictatorship of the proletariat, the peasantry, and other exploited classes. It will be a revolutionary anti-imperialist government of the period which represents transition to noncapitalist (socialist) development.

The Communist Party of China must exert all its efforts to realize the revolutionary outlook of this transition. Otherwise, i.e., in the event of a bourgeois victory over the proletariat, actual domination over the country will pass into the hands of the foreign imperialists, although this domination may assume new forms.

8. The future of the Chinese revolution depends primarily on the role of the proletariat. The events of the last two years have proved that a revolutionary fighting national front can be organized only under the leadership of the proletariat. The struggle against the hegemony of foreign capital can be successfully carried on only under the hegemony of the proletariat. This is the basic principle determining the tactics of the Chinese revolution.

III. *National Revolution and the Peasantry*

9. In the present transitional stage, the agrarian question is the central question. The class that gives a radical answer to this question will be the leader of the revolution. Under the circumstances in China, the proletariat [is that class] . . .

The power of Chinese militarism lies in its support by foreign imperialism and native landowners. . . . Overthrowing the imperialists, abolishing all survivals of the old feudal relations, national liberation, the revolutionary reform of internal and social relations—these tasks are organically connected with each other and represent the one task of the Chinese revolution.

To overthrow the militarists completely, the economic and political struggle of the peasantry, which constitutes the overwhelming majority of the population, must be developed as a part of the anti-imperialist struggle. The fear that the aggravation of the class struggle in the countryside will weaken the anti-imperialist front is baseless. . . . The refusal to assign the agrarian revolution a prominent place in the national-liberation movement, for fear of alienating the dubious and indecisive co-operation of a section of the capitalist class, is wrong. This is not the revolutionary policy of the proletariat. The Communist Party must be free from such mistakes.

10. In the present transitional situation, the proletariat must choose between allying itself with considerable sections of the bourgeoisie and further consolidating its alliance with the peasantry. If the proletariat does not put forward a radical agrarian program, it will fail to attract the peasantry into the revolutionary struggle and will lose its hegemony in the national-liberation movement. . . .

The national govement of Canton will not be able to retain power in the course of the revolution, and will not gain complete victory over foreign imperialism and over native reaction, unless national liberation is identified with agrarian revolution. . . .

11. Although the Communist Party of China should make nationalization of the land the fundamental plank in its agrarian program, it must make certain concessions to the peculiar economic and political conditions prevailing in China.

On the question of power, which has already been raised by the peasant movement, the Communist Party of China must support the attempt to overthrow the tyranny of the gentry and the rural officials in the villages, and to replace this old semifeudal bureaucracy with revolutionary organizations chosen from the lower strata [of the peasantry], organizations that will carry out the decrees of the revolutionary government and protect the interests of the main peasant masses. The peasants must help establish the local administrations.

The program of the agrarian revolution must produce results in the territories under the authority of the Kuomintang national government. The Communist Party of China and the Kuomintang must immediately carry out the following measures in order to bring over the peasantry to the side of the revolution:

(*a*) Reduce rents to a minimum;

(*b*) Abolish the numerous forms of taxes imposed upon the peasantry and replace them with a single progressive agricultural tax;

(*c*) Regulate and reduce as far as possible the burden of taxation now being borne by the principal masses of the peasantry;

(*d*) Confiscate monasterial and church lands and lands belonging to the reactionary militarists, *compradores*, landlords, and gentry who are carrying on civil war against the Kuomintang national government.

(*e*) Guarantee the tenant farmers perpetual leases of the land they cultivate, and the fixing of maximum rent jointly by the peasant unions and representatives of the revolutionary authorities;

(*f*) . . . render the utmost support to the interests of the peasantry and particularly protect the peasants from the oppression and encroachments of the landlords, gentry, and usurers;

(*g*) Disarm the *min t'uan* [local militia] and other armed forces of squires;

(*h*) Arm the poor and middle peasants and co-ordinate all armed forces in the rural districts with the revolutionary authorities;

(*i*) . . . give maximum support to the peasant organizations, including the peasant unions;

(*j*) Grant loans to peasants at low interest, suppress usury, and support the various peasant mutual aid organizations;

(*k*) Grant state aid to the co-operatives and similar mutual aid organizations.

12. The Communist Party must see that the Canton government enforces these measures as a transition to a more developed stage of agrarian revolution. The instrument of enforcement will be peasant committees under communist leadership. As the revolution develops, these committees not only will assume the authority and power to enforce the above demands but also will intensify the struggle by putting forward more radical demands. The peasants' committees will be the basis of the People's Government and People's Army in the rural districts.

In areas still controlled and dominated by reactionary militarists, the task of the Communist Party is to lead the peasantry against feudalism, militarism, and imperialism. In these areas revolutionary work among the peasantry is of particularly great importance because this will be the surest way to demoralize the reactionary armies. The Communists must utilize such spontaneously created peasant organizations as the "Red Spears" and strengthen their influence among them . . .

13. The attitude of the peasantry toward the revolution is influenced to a great extent by the behavior of the Nationalist armies. . . . It is true that the peasants greet the revolutionary armies with enthusiasm, but it is equally true that this enthusiasm evaporates in time.

The warm support that the peasants have given to the revolutionary armies will be more stable if the Communists and other revolutionary elements who control the movement take steps to compensate the peasants for their hardships by a bold and correct agrarian policy. . . .

IV. *The Communist Party and the Kuomintang*

14. The supreme necessity of winning influence over the peasantry determines the relation of the Communist Party to the Kuomintang and to the Canton government likewise. The machinery of the national-revolutionary government provides

a very effective way to reach the peasantry. The Communist Party must use this machinery.

In the newly liberated provinces [local] governments of the type of the Canton government will be set up. The Communists and their revolutionary allies must penetrate the new governments, so as to give practical expression to their agrarian program by using the governmental machinery to confiscate land, reduce taxes, invest real power in the peasant committees . . .

15. For this reason and many other equally important reasons, the point of view that the Communist Party must leave the Kuomintang is incorrect. The whole process of development of the Chinese revolution, its character and its prospects, demand that the Communists stay in the Kuomintang and intensify their work in it. In order to intensify their activities in the Kuomintang with the object of advancing the revolutionary movement to higher stages of development, the Communists should enter the Canton government. Since its foundation the real power of the Canton government has been in the hands of the Right wing of Kuomintang (five out of the six commissars belong to the Right wing). Even though the Canton government could not exist without the support of the working class, the workers' and peasants' movement in Kwangtung has had to overcome numerous obstacles. Recent events have shown that the Communists must enter the Canton government in order to support the revolutionary Left wing in its struggle against the weak and vacillating policy of the Right. The extension of the Canton government's authority to new areas makes Communist participation in this government still more imperative.

16. The Communist Party of China must strive to develop the Kuomintang into a real people's party—a solid revolutionary bloc of the proletariat, the peasantry, the urban petty bourgeoisie, and the other oppressed and exploited strata—a party dedicated to a decisive struggle against imperialism and its agents. For this the Communist Party must work along the following lines:

(a) Systematic and determined struggle against Tai Chi-t'ao ideology and other Right-wing attempts to convert the Kuomintang into a bourgeois party;

(b) Definite formation of a Left wing in the Kuomintang and the establishment of class co-operation with it, except in the matter of trying to replace its leaders by members of the Communist Party;

(c) Consistent criticism of the Center, which is vacillating between the Right and Left wings, between the further development of the revolution and compromise with imperialism.

V. The Tasks of the Chinese Revolution and the Character of the Revolutionary Government

17. Lenin wrote: "Whereas formerly, prior to the epoch of world revolution, movements for national liberation were part of the general democratic movement, now, after the victory of the Soviet revolution in Russia and the opening of the period of world revolution, movements for national liberation are part of the proletarian world revolution."

The program of the Chinese revolution and the structure of the revolutionary state created by it should be determined from this point of view. The process of class differentiation that follows as the revolutionary movement develops bears out this [Lenin's] conception. The Canton government, in spite of its bourgeois-democratic character, essentially and objectively contains the germs of a revolutionary petty bourgeois state—a democratic dictatorship of the revolutionary bloc of the proletariat, peasantry, and the urban petty bourgeoisie. The petty-bourgeois democratic movement becomes revolutionary in China because it is an anti-imperialist movement. The Canton government is revolutionary primarily because it is anti-imperialist. Being primarily anti-imperialist, the Chinese revolution and the government created by it must strike at the root of imperialist power in China. Repudiation of unequal treaties and abolition of territorial concessions will not be sufficient to weaken the position of imperialism. The blow must be dealt at the economic basis of imperialist power; the revolutionary government must gradually confiscate the railways, concessions, factories, mines, banks, and other business enterprises owned by foreign capital. By so doing it will immediately outstrip the narrow boundary of bourgeois democracy and enter into the stage of transition to revolutionary dictatorship.

Thus, it is a mistake to limit the tasks of the Chinese revolution to (1) the overthrow of imperialism and (2) the liquidation of the remnants of feudalism, on the ground that in its first stage this revolution bears a petty bourgeois nature. The Chinese revolution cannot defeat imperialism without passing over the boundaries of bourgeois democracy. Under the present conditions the proletariat will lead the peasantry to a revolutionary struggle. The movement for the liquidation of feudalism, now led by the proletariat, is bound to develop into an agrarian revolution. Therefore, the tasks of the Chinese revolution become:

(a) Nationalization of railways and waterways;

(b) Confiscation of large-scale enterprises, mines, and banks having the character of foreign concessions;

(c) Nationalization of land, to be realized by successive radical reform measures enforced by the revolutionary state.

VI. *The Communist Party and the Proletariat*

18. To play the dominant role in the revolution the Chinese proletariat must solidify its class organization—political and economic. To organize and train the proletariat for this historic role is the primary task of the [Chinese] Communist Party. The numerical weakness and youthfulness of the Chinese proletariat must be counterbalanced by strength of organization and clarity of ideas.

The general federation of trade unions [i.e., the Profintern], embracing hundreds of thousands of industrial workers as well as the national railwaymen's and seamen's unions, is the basis of the Communist Party. To strengthen these organizations by drawing in broader masses of workers is the immediate task of the Communist Party. In the national-revolutionary struggle of the last two years the working class has displayed tremendous power. In actual struggle it has won the hegemony in the revolutionary movement. On the basis of these traditions and achievements, the working class organizations must be further consolidated and developed along the following lines:

(a) Creation of mass industrial unions, unification of all unions on an industrial basis, strengthening of the All-China Federation of Trade Unions;

(b) Intensification of work among the masses, consolidation of the contact of the leading trade union organs with the wide masses of Chinese workers, unionizing of workers in small enterprises and cultural-educational workers;

(c) Greater attention to the economic struggle of the workers, which should become a political struggle; elaboration of tactics for the strike movement; organization of mutual aid and strike funds; support in the formation of co-operatives, etc.;

(d) Intensified denunciation of the reformists' methods to the masses of the workers;

(e) Strengthening of contact between the Chinese trade union movement and the world trade union movement, especially in the Far Eastern countries.

19. In order to attract the bulk of the working class into the movement and to

strengthen its position in the national revolution, the Chinese Communist Party should agitate for:

(*a*) Complete freedom of activity for the revolutionary peasants' and workers' organizations, legalization of the trade unions, enactment of advanced trade union laws, the right to strike;

(*b*) Labor legislation: eight-hour working day, weekly day of rest, minimum wage;

(*c*) Social legislation: sanitary inspection and sanitary working conditions; housing; insurance against illness, injury, disablement, and unemployment; regulation of labor of women and children, prohibition of night work for women, prohibition of factory labor for children under 14;

(*d*) Institution of factory inspection;

(*e*) Abolition of the system of fines and corporal punishment;

(*f*) Withdrawal of all kinds of military units and police detachments from factory premises;

(*g*) Measures to deal with unemployment: extension of trade union influence over the unemployed, organization of labor exchanges by trade unions.

20. At the present stage of the revolution, an almost untapped source of revolutionary energy is the masses of artisans and handicraft workers who have been ruined by imperialism and are definitely hostile toward foreign capital. The communist vanguard of the Chinese proletariat has the task of organizing these masses and drawing them into the common stream of the national-revolutionary movement. Particularly, the Communist Party must seek, for these workers:

(*a*) The alleviation of tax burdens;

(*b*) The organization of handicraft and artisan workers' unions;

(*c*) The organization of workers' associations.

VII. *The Organizational Tasks of the Communist Party of China*

21. The Communist Party of China is an organized force. It has its leaders; it is establishing its cadres and is leading the masses. Its work has acquired a fairly considerable sweep and a stable form of organization. During the last half year, the party has added many new members, most of them workers.

The peasants' section of the Communist Party is not large numerically, but the party is increasing its activities among the peasantry.

One of the Chinese Communist Party's most important tasks is to widen, intensify, improve, and consolidate the work of party training.

The party has done considerable work in organizing the Young Communist League. . . .

One of the fundamental tasks of the party is to fight for the right to exist openly.

22. Systematic recruiting must be conducted, principally in the industrial districts. The new members must be trained by short-term courses, by special discussions of the party's program and tactics, by everyday work in their respective cells, and ultimately by general party work.

It is necessary to develop collective leadership in the party organizations, from the Central Committee to the factory-street cells.

Persistent and more energetic efforts must be made to draw the best workers into the party leadership, and to strengthen and increase the party's cadres. Special attention must be paid to training cell secretaries, leaders of factions of mass organizations, and the leading personnel of district and regional party committees. The Central Committee and regional committees must choose permanent traveling instructors from the best local party workers.

Cadres of traveling organizers must be established for work in the rural districts. Increased activity and initiative must be encouraged among the lower party organizations, in the cells, at general meetings of party members, etc.

The factions, particularly in the trade unions, in the leading organs of the peasant unions, and in local organizations of the Kuomintang, must be strengthened.

Systematic, firm party guidance of the work of the factions must be maintained.

103

The Shanghai *Coup d'État*, April 1927[11]

Telegrams from Shanghai yesterday and today brought news of tremendous significance for the future of the Chinese revolution. Chiang Kai-shek's command of the Nationalist army has wrought bloody carnage among the Shanghai proletariat. The proletarian fighting detachments and the Shanghai Red Guard have been disarmed. Peaceful workers' demonstrations of protest—Shanghai workers, their wives and children—have been fired upon . . .

The Chinese revolution is being born in hard labor, amid great complications, at a time when relations between the revolution and imperialism have reached the breaking point (Nanking, the preparation of the blockade), and when more and more contradictions are becoming apparent within the hitherto united anti-imperialist front. These contradictions—within the Kuomintang, between the Kuomintang and the military command, and between the working class and the bourgeoisie, which is inclined toward capitulation before imperialism—have been developing with inevitable and inexorable logic.

The realignment of social class forces which the Seventh Enlarged Plenum of the Executive Committee of the Communist International foretold, is taking place. The Comintern indicated the inevitability . . . of a "serious realignment of social forces." In December 1926 the Comintern announced that the Chinese revolution was on the eve of the "third stage" of its development, characterized by "the exclusion of the majority of the capitalist bourgeoisie" from the one revolutionary front. Since then events have happened with great speed and have confirmed the prognosis of the Comintern.

Shanghai, like Nanking, was won from the reactionary militarists. Shanghai was taken from within by the aroused Shanghai workers. Whereupon the imperialists entrenched themselves in the international settlements, and their naval squadrons occupied Chinese ports. Relations with the imperialists became aggravated to the last degree. The masses—the toiling Chinese people—turned rapidly to the Left. The Chinese bourgeoisie, on the contrary, shied away fearfully from the revolutionary banner. The army command, headed by General Chiang Kai-shek, reflected this mood and the liquidationist tendencies of the Chinese national bourgeoisie. The Chinese Communist Party was right when it came out against Chiang Kai-shek. An internal struggle broke out in the Kuomintang, and at the last session of the Central Committee of the Kuomintang the Right wing suffered defeat. Under the pressure of the masses of workers, peasants, petty bourgeoisie, and soldiers, Chiang Kai-shek was obliged to maneuver and to declare that he submitted fully to the directives of the Kuomintang, and to promise to adhere to the revolution and the principles of Sun Yat-sen. But he and his supporters were secretly working toward an agreement with the imperialists. . . . [Then] to please the Chinese bourgeoisie and the imperialists, Chiang Kai-shek fired upon the workers.

Three days ago the crisis resulted in a shameful chastisement of the Shanghai

11 *Pravda* (Editorial), No. 85, April 15, 1927, p. 1.

workers. A counterrevolutionary *coup d'état* was carried out. . . . Chiang Kai-shek became the executioner of the Shanghai proletariat.

The significance of the Shanghai *coup d'état* lies in the fact that it cut another furrow in the history of the great struggle for liberation in China.

The new alignment of forces has been made quite clear. As long as Chiang Kai-shek led the army of the revolution against the northern militarists he was doing revolutionary work. Since the blood of the Shanghai workers fell upon his head, since he treacherously shot 600 proletarians, he has become a Chinese Cavaignac; he and his supporters have become the center, the focal point of the national counter-revolution. Chiang Kai-shek now stands against the revolution and in line with Chang Tso-lin, since he has already hinted at the possibility of a peaceful agreement with the latter. In the eyes of the millions of Chinese people, Chiang Kai-shek has now become a renegade and is on the side of imperialism. . . .

A new situation has arisen in China. The contradictions have been clearly revealed. The menace of the imperialists and of international counterrevolution is now obvious to all revolutionary Chinese. We sincerely believe that in the coming difficult period of struggle, the Chinese revolutionary camp will have the necessary self-control and self-reliance. The Chinese revolution will have strength enough to fling off all renegades and traitors. Chiang Kai-shek has challenged the masses. The masses will accept his challenge. Defeat is the best teacher. The Chinese workers and peasants, all Chinese revolutionaries, will learn the necessary lesson from the Shanghai tragedy. The Chinese will stand closer than ever to the side of the *revolutionary* Kuomintang, the Kuomintang without Chiang Kai-shek. They will organize themselves with still greater persistence; they will prepare themselves for new battles; and they will march on over the Shanghai defeat to final victory.

104

The Soviet Government's Protest Against the "Unprovoked" Raid on the Soviet Embassy in Peking

[Note to the Chinese Representative in Moscow, April 9, 1927][12]

In connection with the raid by armed soldiers of the army of Chang Tso-lin and by the Peking police upon the headquarters of the military attaché of the Soviet Embassy in Peking and upon the living quarters of the employees of the Embassy, I have the honor of requesting you to refer the following to the Peking cabinet:

1. Supplementing the Note of the Chargé d'Affaires of the Soviet Union in Peking, Mr. Chernykh, of April 6 of this year, informing the Peking cabinet of the shameful raid upon the offices of the military attaché and upon the quarters of the employees of the Embassy, and of the fact that the employees were arrested and maltreated, while their living quarters were searched and plundered, it has since been ascertained upon the basis of the information at present in our hands that the apartments and the office of the military attaché were searched, plundered, and partly destroyed by fire, despite all protests. Similarly, the apartments of the employees of the Embassy were demolished and plundered. A number of employees were arrested; some of them were beaten and subjected to other violence and to derision. The names of all the arrested have not yet been ascertained, as the armed police and soldiers permit no one to enter the court where the living quarters of the military

[12] *Pravda*, No. 81, April 10, 1927, p. 1; also *International Press Correspondence*, No. 24, April 14, 1927, pp. 490–91; text also appears in Degras, II, 178–80.

attaché and the employees of the Embassy are situated, and the police have up to the present not announced their names. Armed soldiers and police continue to occupy all quarters, both of the military attaché and of the employees of the Embassy.

2. The raid carried out by the Peking authorities is an unheard-of violation of the most elementary rules of international law. . . . Such violence is absolutely without precedent for two states maintaining official relations with each other.

3. If the Peking government supposed that it was carrying out a raid upon a building which, as was stated in the Note of the Peking government, "was under direct jurisdiction of the Soviet Embassy," then it had not the right to do so without first informing the Soviet Embassy. But the police and the soldiers carrying out the raid did not merely refuse representatives of the Embassy the right to enter the territory which was being searched and plundered, but even refused this right to the Chargé d'Affaires of the U.S.S.R., Chernykh himself.

Such an attitude can be explained only by a desire of the Peking cabinet for the violence and plundering of its agents to take place in the absence of any official [Soviet] representatives. Only the completely improbable and unbelievable statement of the Peking government that during the course of the search weapons and documents were found, proving that an insurrection was being prepared, can explain why the raid upon the quarters of the military attaché and upon the quarters of the employees of the Embassy took place under such extraordinary circumstances. For under such circumstances, when all possibility was removed of even the most elementary control and registration of the confiscated property, etc., there is no guarantee whatever that anything allegedly "found" in these quarters will not be utilized by the hostile foreign powers who inspired and sanctioned the raid of April 6.

4. If the Peking cabinet possessed information that Chinese citizens conducting activity hostile to its interests were present upon the territory directly under the management of the Soviet Embassy, then it could and should have first informed the Embassy of the U.S.S.R. However, as can be seen from your Note, sir,[13] the Peking government considered it more correct in these circumstances to direct itself to the Diplomatic Corps in Peking and, in collusion with the Dutch Ambassador, Oudendijk, to violate the extraterritorial rights of the military attaché, to use violence against employees of the Embassy of the Soviet Union, and to plunder and demolish their living quarters. The co-operation between the soldiers and police of the Peking government and the representatives of the Diplomatic Corps in Peking throws light upon the real motives of that government's unheard-of act of violence and its violation of elementary international rules, and it supplies the best evidence concerning those in whose interests this violence was committed.

The Soviet government emphatically protests against the above-mentioned acts of violence and violation of normal rights, and considers it necessary to insist upon the fulfillment of the following elementary demands:

(a) The Chinese military troops and police must be immediately withdrawn from the quarters of the military attaché, of the employees of the Embassy, and of the Trade Mission.

(b) All the arrested employees of the Soviet Embassy and of the economic institutions of the Soviet Union must be released immediately.

(c) All documents removed from the quarters of the military attaché must be returned immediately.

(d) Personal effects, money, household goods, books, and other objects confis-

13 A note of April 8, from the Chinese chargé d'affaires in Moscow, had informed the Moscow government of the raid, justifying it on the ground that members of the Chinese Communist Party maintained offices in the Soviet embassy building. The text of this note appears in *Pravda*, No. 81, April 10, 1927, p. 1.

За сдельную работу...
(ПОСЛЕ ПЕКИНСКОГО НАЛЕТА).

Первая награда Англии Чжан-Цзо-Лину за его налет составляет 400.000 фунтов стерлингов.

"FOR THE JOB . . . (After the Peking Raid). First British payment to Chang Tso-lin for his raid on the Soviet embassy in Peking, 400,000 pounds sterling." Izvestiia, No. 84, April 13, 1927.

cated or stolen by the police and the military must be returned to their owners immediately.

The Soviet government considers it necessary as a sign of protest to recall its Chargé d'Affaires, Chernykh, and the whole staff of the Embassy from Peking, and to leave only enough staff to carry out consular functions, until the above demands shall have been fulfilled.

The Soviet government limits itself to the above elementary demands, which are in no way calculated to humiliate the Peking government. Any imperialist government whose representatives had been subjected to similar violence would have answered with the sharpest reprisals. The Soviet government, which has sufficient means at its disposal to institute reprisals, declares that it has no intention whatever of taking such measures.

The Soviet government is well aware that irresponsible circles among the foreign imperialists wish to provoke the U.S.S.R. into a war. The Soviet government is well aware that the Peking cabinet has become the instrument of foreign imperialist circles. However, in its policy, the Soviet government has been guided and will be guided in the future only by the interests of the toilers of the whole world, including China. In answer to the Peking provocation, which was intended to aggravate the international situation and to turn into a new world war the *de facto* military operations against China already begun by certain imperialist powers, the Soviet government declares that it will permit itself to be provoked by no one and will defend the cause of peace with all the means at its disposal. The Soviet government does not doubt for one moment that its efforts for peace will receive the unanimous support of the toilers in all countries, including particularly the peoples of China and of the U.S.S.R.

M. Litvinov

105

Borodin's Status in China Confirmed by Moscow[14]

[Extract from a Telegram Sent by the Commissariat of Foreign Affairs at Moscow to the Soviet Representative at Peking, Dated November 12, 1926]

I herewith communicate the department's decision for your execution:—

1. Until a Soviet representative is appointed to Peking, Comrade Borodin is to take his orders direct from Moscow.

2. The Far Eastern Bureau is to be informed that all its decisions and measures regarding questions of the general policy of the Kuomintang in China and of military political work must be agreed on with Comrade Borodin. In the event of differences of opinion arising on these questions, they must be referred to Moscow for investigation. Borodin and the Far Eastern Bureau must keep Moscow's representatives in Peking informed of all their decisions and moves with regard to these questions.

3. Comrade Borodin's appointment as official Soviet representative in Canton is considered inadvisable. Borodin is to remain [?] in charge of the work in the provinces under Canton rule, and an official representative to the Canton government is to be appointed.

[Extract from a Telegram from the Soviet Chargé d'Affaires in London to the Commissariat of Foreign Affairs in Moscow, Dated February 1, 1927]

[14] *Documents Illustrating the Hostile Activities of the Soviet Government and Third International against Great Britain* (Cmd. 2874), pp. 29–30.

It is essential to give a short explanation to the press on Tuesday saying that Borodin is not a Soviet representative and is not even in our service, but is a private citizen in the service of the Chinese government and that the Soviet government is not answerable for his actions.

[Extract from a Telegram from the Soviet Chargé d'Affaires in London to the Commissariat of Foreign Affairs in Moscow, Dated February 4, 1927]

An announcement of Borodin's recent visit to Moscow, where he received instructions, had been previously published. If possible, it would be desirable to contradict this.

106

China on the Eve of the Bourgeois-Democratic Revolution

[Statement by Stalin at the Tenth Session of the Eighth Plenum of the ECCI, May 24, 1927][15]

To organize the soviets of workers' and peasants' deputies now, let us say on the territory of the Wuhan government, would mean to create a diarchy, to launch a struggle to overthrow the Kuomintang Left and form a new soviet authority in China. The soviets of workers' and peasants' deputies are the organs of a struggle to overthrow the existing authority and establish a new one. The appearance of such soviets would simply aggravate the question of who should have full authority. That was the situation in Russia in March, April, May, and June, 1917. At that time there existed the Provisional Government, which held half of the authority—the weightier half, since it was still supported by troops—and the soviets of workers' and soldiers' deputies, who held the other half. The Bolsheviks at that time called for the overthrow of the Provisional Government, and for vesting full authority in the soviets of workers' and soldiers' deputies. None of the Bolsheviks thought at that time of joining the Provisional Government, since one cannot join a government if one works for its overthrow. But can we say that the situation in Russia in March–June, 1917, was analogous to the present situation in China? No, we cannot say it. We cannot say it not only because Russia was then on the eve of the proletarian revolution, while China is on the eve of the bourgeois-democratic revolution, but also because the Provisional Government in Russia was a counterrevolutionary government, whereas the present government in Wuhan is a revolutionary government in the bourgeois-democratic sense of the word. . . .

107

A Communist Attempt to Evaluate the Partial Defeat of the Chinese Revolution

[Resolution on the Chinese Question Adopted at the Eighth Plenum of the ECCI, May 8–30, 1927][16]

1. *The Significance of the Chinese Revolution*

The Plenum of the ECCI states that recent events have entirely confirmed the point of view of the Communist International concerning the Chinese revolution and have brilliantly confirmed Lenin's predictions as to its international role. . . .

[15] Stalin, *Ob oppozitsii*, pp. 596–97.
[16] *Kommunisticheskii Internatsional v dokumentakh*, pp. 717–29; also *International Press Correspondence*, No. 35, June 16, 1927, pp. 727–41.

The Communist International believes that the parties and other organizations which call themselves workers' organizations but which refrain from conducting a decisive struggle against intervention in China, which lull the vigilance of the working class and advocate passivity on this question, objectively (and sometimes subjectively) assist the imperialists. . . .

2. The Crisis in the National-Revolutionary Movement and the New Situation in China

The ECCI notes that events have confirmed the estimate of the driving forces of the Chinese revolution made at the last (Seventh) Enlarged Plenum . . . [especially] concerning the bourgeoisie's inevitable abandonment of the united national-revolutionary front and desertion to the counterrevolution.

Witness the counterrevolutionary *coup d'état* by Chiang Kai-shek and a number of other generals, the formation of the Nanking government, and the secession of the members of the Right wing of the Kuomintang, who have formed, under the banner of Kuomintang, their own counterrevolutionary organization.

. . . The Chiang Kai-shek coup signifies a fundamental realignment of classes, and, consequently, the tactics of the Comintern must be based on this new situation.

Any attempt to base tactics on a possible compromise with Chiang Kai-shek or with the Right wing of the Kuomintang would be nothing less than direct capitulation to Chiang Kai-shek and open betrayal of the interests of the Chinese revolution.

The principal causes for the treachery of the bourgeoisie and of its military leader, Chiang Kai-shek, were (1) the growing mass movement of the working class and peasantry, and the successes won by the Communist Party of China; (2) the increasing pressure of the combined forces of international imperialism . . . Notwithstanding partial defeats and the counterrevolution of Chiang Kai-shek & Co., the revolution has passed to a higher stage; the alliance of the bourgeoisie, the petty bourgeoisie, the peasantry, and the proletariat has collapsed, leaving the proletariat, the peasantry, and the petty bourgeoisie, in which bloc the proletariat is assuming an increasingly dominant role. . . .

The present period is marked by the existence of three camps: Chiang Kai-shek is already shooting down the workers and peasants, but is still fighting against the northern militarists.

The logic of the struggle is converting these three camps into two, but into two new camps, since the capitalist bourgeoisie (led by Chiang Kai-shek, Pai Ch'ung-hsi,[17] & Co.) must inevitably line up more and more closely with feudal reaction and foreign imperialism. Besides, this process will become accelerated. . . .

The ECCI believes that in the period of the revolution which has now passed, the tactics of the bloc with the national bourgeoisie were absolutely correct. . . .

The ECCI emphasizes that Chiang Kai-shek's coup and the radical realignment of classes of which it was the expression must serve as the starting point for the whole of our future tactics, and that these tactics must exclude unity, compromise, or agreement with the bourgeoisie, which has betrayed the national-revolutionary movement and has become an active counterrevolutionary force. . . .

3. The Partial Defeat of the Chinese Revolution and the Principal Forces of the Counterrevolution

The ECCI places on record that the series of bourgeois counterrevolutionary coups (Shanghai, Nanking, Canton, etc.) represents a partial defeat of the Chinese revolution and a real acquisition of strength by the counterrevolutionary bloc.

[17] Pai Ch'ung-hsi, a Kwangsi general, subordinate to Chiang Kai-shek, occupied Shanghai in April 1927.

However, the ECCI regards as incorrect the view that these defeats menace the fate of the revolution as a whole.

This view is wrong because it considers the Chinese bourgeoisie the greatest danger to the revolution, without considering its connections with the forces of imperialism; moreover, it underestimates the powerful and unorganized movement of the toiling masses. . . .

The ECCI imposes upon all its sections the imperative duty of explaining to the working class and the peasantry the fundamental fact that the imperialist troops, which have occupied practically all the important industrial centers of China, are actually the main counterrevolutionary forces in China.

The relatively weak Chinese bourgeoisie would not represent a serious menace to the Chinese revolution if it were not directly and indirectly supported by the foreign interventionists. . . .

It is particularly important to point out the frantic efforts of the imperialists to break up the workers' and communist organizations, to suppress the peasant movement, and to isolate the U.S.S.R.

Offsetting the partial defeat of the revolution, however, we have the fact that it has passed to a higher stage of development and that a more intensive mobilization of the masses has begun. The growth of the peasant movement, the organization of armed forces in the insurgent detachments, the number of victories achieved by the spontaneously organized forces over the armies of the treacherous generals, the preservation of the working class organizations in spite of the terrorist methods of the counterrevolution, the organization of the working class, and the continuous growth of the Communist Party and the Left wing of the Kuomintang are all important symptoms of the further development and intensification of the Chinese revolution.

Generally speaking, the Wuhan government and the Kuomintang Left represent a revolutionary alliance of the urban and rural petty bourgeois masses with the proletariat. Notwithstanding possible and even unavoidable betrayals by various generals, groups of generals, or individual political leaders of the "Left wing" of the Kuomintang, the development of the class struggle will inevitably rouse the masses, whose movement is the pledge of future victories.

The ECCI therefore deems the liquidationist view, that the present crisis in the Chinese revolution is a decisive defeat which creates a new international situation, to be profoundly incorrect. . . .

4. *The Organization of the Workers and Peasants and the Fundamental Tasks of the Communist Party of China*

Because of the enormous difficulties confronting the Chinese revolution—especially imperialist intervention, armed and otherwise, and the inevitable betrayals and desertions of the revolution by vacillating social groupings—the overwhelming masses of the toilers must be drawn into the struggle if victory is to be achieved . . .

To draw the masses into the struggle requires a program of agrarian revolution in the countryside, and of economic and political benefits for the urban workers. The definite abolition of rents paid to the rich; the redistribution of land; the confiscation of all land of landlords, mandarinates, and monasteries; the prohibition of usury; the radical reduction of taxation and the transference of the tax burden to the wealthier sections of the population, etc., must be carried out all over China, and first of all in the territory of the Wuhan government. These measures should rouse the masses against the bourgeois traitors and northern militarists.

Agrarian revolution, which includes the confiscation and nationalization of land—such is the fundamental inner socioeconomic content of the new stage of the Chinese revolution. The "plebian" revolutionary solution of the agrarian problem must be sought from below by the peasant masses themselves, directed by the Communist Party. The Communist Party must prevail upon the government to support the agrarian revolution. There is no other way to establish a true organizational and political center for the workers' and peasants' revolution, an organ of the revolutionary democratic dictatorship of the proletariat and the peasantry. On the other hand, only a policy of agrarian revolution enacted from below [by the masses] and from above [by the government] can provide really reliable armed units and make possible the reorganization of the army on a sound revolutionary basis.

In the towns, efforts must be made to raise the standard of living of the working class, to radically improve the workers' juridical position in the factories and their social position generally, to repeal all laws which place the workers in the position of a disfranchised "class," to institute an eight-hour working day, to raise wages, to get the rights of workers' organizations recognized, etc.

Simultaneously, rapid, bold, and determined efforts must be made to carry out the policy of the mass arming of the workers and peasants, primarily the organized and more class-conscious of them. This policy must be carried out with all necessary firmness.

The ECCI believes that the Communist Party of China must strive hard to carry on, directly and in alliance with the Left wing of the Kuomintang, the work of mobilizing and organizing the masses. . . .

The ECCI calls upon the Communist Party of China to pay close attention to the necessity of strengthening and enlarging as much as possible all the various mass organizations of the workers and peasants, such as trade unions, strike committees, factory committees, and workers' armed units; peasants' committees, peasants' unions, organizations of farm hands, and armed peasants' units; organizations of the urban petty bourgeoisie, organizations of artisans, home craft workers, etc. In all these organizations, propaganda must be carried on for affiliation with the Kuomintang, thus helping to convert the latter into a powerful mass organization of the revolutionary petty bourgeoisie and the working class.

The ECCI resolutely rejects any attempt to oppose the tasks of the national revolution to the tasks of the class struggle of the proletariat. It holds that to contrast the two tasks, as ultra-Left European groups and the Social Democrats do, is to repudiate proletarian hegemony in the Chinese revolution in favor of working class guildism, a form of political opportunism that converts the proletariat into the tail[18] of the democratic kite. As a matter of fact, since the desertion of the bourgeoisie to the counterrevolution, the proletariat has become more and more widely recognized as the leader of the whole national-revolutionary movement. The Chinese revolution cannot develop further or achieve victory unless the working class becomes the leader of the whole of the democratic revolution, which can be brought to its conclusion only in the struggle against the bourgeoisie. . . .

5. The Communist Party and the Kuomintang

. . .

Irrespective of the political situation, the Communist Party must never become merged with any other political organization. It must represent an independent force; it is the organization of a special class, the proletariat, the most consistent and most revolutionary class in the country. For that reason, the Communist Party must never allow itself to be restricted in propagandizing its views and mobilizing the masses under its own banner. It must never abandon its right to criticize the vacillations

[18] Taken from Russian khvostizm, from okhvostie, "lagging behind," a term commonly used by the Bolsheviks. Both words derive ultimately from khvost, "tail."

and hesitations of the revolutionary petty bourgeoisie. On the contrary, only such criticism will drive the petty bourgeois revolutionaries to the Left and to the aid of the working class in the revolutionary struggle.

The Communist Party of China must not, however, interpret its independence as meaning that it must become exclusive and isolate itself from the nonproletarian toilers, and particularly from the peasantry. Thus the ECCI resolutely rejects all demands that the Communist Party leave the Kuomintang or take up a position which would lead to its leaving the Kuomintang. The present moment demands that the proletarian party shall secure the leading role of the proletariat *within* the Kuomintang. In China the Kuomintang is a specifically Chinese form of organization in which the proletariat works directly with the petty bourgeoisie and the peasantry. The proletariat cannot claim the role of leader in the country unless its party, the Communist Party, claims the role of leader *within* the Kuomintang.

The ECCI holds that to underestimate the Kuomintang as a peculiar organizational form of the revolutionary movement is to abandon the Kuomintang's banner to the Right wing. Since that banner is an exceedingly important political factor in the country, the bourgeois leaders, headed by Chiang Kai-shek, strive to march under it. The Communist Party should not screen this political maneuver of Chiang Kai-shek, as it would do if it left the Kuomintang, but expose the bourgeois politicians as traitors to the cause of the national revolution, traitors to the Kuomintang, traitors to the anti-imperialist traditions of Sun Yat-sen, renegades who have joined the camp of the imperialists.

The ECCI considers incorrect the view that the national revolution of liberation (anti-imperialist) has "ended" and that a different kind—a class, a peasants' and workers' revolution—has "commenced." . . .

The ECCI believes that after its bold and determined development of the mass movement, the Communist Party of China must with equal boldness and determination aim at converting the Kuomintang into a genuine mass organization embracing the toiling population of town and countryside . . .

The Communist Party must expose in good time every symptom of vacillation in the direction of alliance with Chiang Kai-shek or with the imperialists, and take corresponding agitational, propaganda, and organizational measures. . . .

. . . The Communist Party of China, as a party of the working class, must assume the leadership of the agrarian movement of the peasantry and ruthlessly combat every effort to restrict the extent of that movement . . .

6. *The Wuhan Government, the Questions of Power, the Army, and the Tasks of the Communist Party in China*

The ECCI regards as incorrect the view which underestimates the Wuhan government and denies its great revolutionary role. The Wuhan government and the leaders of the Left wing of the Kuomintang, by their class composition, represent not only the peasants, workers, and artisans, but also a section of the middle bourgeoisie. Therefore, the Wuhan government, being the government of the Left wing of the Kuomintang, is not yet the dictatorship of the proletariat and the peasantry, but is on the road to it and will inevitably, in the course of the victorious class struggle of the proletariat, discard its radical-bourgeois camp followers and, after overcoming a number of betrayals, develop toward such a dictatorship.

The ECCI holds that the Communist Party of China must take a most energetic part in the work of the Wuhan "Provisional Revolutionary Government." . . .

Participation in the Wuhan government is not like the bourgeois-socialist coalitions in Europe, for the Wuhan government is in fact conducting a revolutionary war against the imperialists and the feudal lords, and now against a considerable section of the bourgeoisie of its own country. . . .

The ECCI reminds the Communist Party of China that it is now more necessary than ever to maintain close contact between the revolutionary government and the masses. Only thus . . . can the revolutionary government's authority grow stronger and its role as the organizing center of the revolution become clear.

The Communist Party of China must see that such a course is followed by the Wuhan government. . . .

. . . Unless these tactics are employed, the participation [of the Communists in the government] will merely bear the character of a political deal between leaders, which will be thwarted by the progress of events and of the great class struggle. To link up and constantly link up the work in the government with the work among the masses is the most imperative duty of the Communist Party of China.

The ECCI believes that in the present circumstances it is a matter of revolutionary expediency to bring about the large-scale democratization of the Kuomintang, to see to it that it embraces the masses and helps their organizations to develop. It is impossible to ignore the specific features of Chinese development which have created such a peculiar organization as the revolutionary Kuomintang, which directly determines the composition of the government. To get broad masses to join the Kuomintang, and there to elect the Kuomintang's governing bodies, and through those bodies to form the national-revolutionary government—this is the task that corresponds to the present stage of the Chinese revolution.

Local differences will at first make for different sorts of local governments: "peasants' committees" and "unions" in the villages, Kuomintang committees, etc. The fundamental task of the Communists is to get the masses of the toilers, the hundreds of thousands and millions of workers and peasants, to participate in the establishment and work of these bodies.

The ECCI considers it inexpedient at present to establish soviets of workers' and peasants' deputies, since to do so (in the Wuhan territory) would be tantamount to proclaiming soviet rule.

At the present stage of the Chinese revolution such a move would unavoidably signify a dual government, and require the overthrow of the Wuhan government; it would mean leaping across the Kuomintang form of state power and organization of the masses directly to . . . the proletarian dictatorship.

As the revolution develops from a democratic revolution into a socialist revolution, soviets of workers', peasants', and soldiers' deputies will become necessary, and the slogan for their formation will become the principal slogan of the party.

The ECCI also considers the reorganization of the army important. . . . Special attention must be given to forming absolutely reliable units from among the revolutionary workers and peasants, recruiting Communists and reliable Left-wing Kuomintangists, clearing the army of counterrevolutionary elements, and creating a Workers' Guard.

7. Some Basic Tactical Problems of Revolutionary Policy in China at the Present Moment

The Communist Party of China is confronted by problems of extraordinary complexity. The interweaving of the struggle against the imperialists and militarists with the struggle against the national bourgeoisie; the presence of large armed imperialist forces on the territory of China; the existing division of China into three zones; the extreme variety of economic and political relations; the existence of a common imperialist front and the antagonisms within that front; the uneven maturing of the revolution in various parts of China; the special "military" forms of the revolution, and the antagonisms within the armies and within the Left-wing front itself, etc., etc.—all these create exceptional difficulties for the development of the revolution.

The ECCI believes that in the face of these difficulties it is quite proper in principle for the Wuhan government to maneuver in its attitude toward foreign imperialism.

The ECCI rejects the view that because the [Wuhan] government is nonproletarian it may not use "Brest-Litovsk" tactics of maneuvering. . . .

The same goes for economic policy; i.e., the government need not necessarily immediately confiscate all foreign enterprises. Here, too, compromise is permissible in principle.

On the other hand, the ECCI considers that the sabotage conducted by the native and foreign bourgeoisie in a number of enterprises (industrial, commercial, and credit), which leads to unemployment and is designed to create economic chaos and paralysis, may compel the government to confiscate and nationalize such enterprises. . . .

Whether to compromise or take the offensive depends on the circumstances. The ECCI in particular believes that the tactics proposed by certain comrades in connection with Chiang Kai-shek's Shanghai coup were absolutely stupid. Those tactics were to anticipate the coup by a rebellion against the imperialists and Chiang Kai-shek, or to give them armed battle on a wide front. But the tactics of rebellion are: having commenced rebellion, advance. Rebellion should only be commenced when there is some chance of success. One cannot "play with rebellion." The tactic of rebellion under all circumstances is not a Leninist tactic. If an extensive armed uprising of the workers in Shanghai had taken place, they would have been cut up by the armed forces of Chiang Kai-shek and the imperialists, and the flower of the proletariat of China would have been wiped out, for there was no chance of success.

The present situation in China calls for the following military-political strategy to be adopted by the Communist Party: support military operations against the North; develop the agrarian revolution throughout the territory of the Wuhan government; and conduct intensive demoralization work in the rear and within the armies of Chiang Kai-shek with the aim of liquidating them, which does not exclude, of course, conducting military operations against them at the appropriate moment. Reliance upon the masses will also have great effect in the civil war. If a proper policy is carried out, the victory of the revolution is assured.

The Communist Party must make it its task to strengthen in every way possible the united front of the workers, peasants, and petty bourgeoisie. In developing the agrarian movement by every means, it will also be necessary to guarantee to the petty bourgeoisie the inviolability of their working property, thus helping them in the struggle against money-lenders' capital. . . .

The creation of strong illegal organizations, beginning with the party and ending with peasant leagues; the organization and leadership of the peasant movement and the movement of the workers; the preparation of mass actions and work among the soldiers—these must constitute the principal tasks of the party.

8. The Attitude of Comintern Sections Toward the Chinese Revolution

As to the significance of the Chinese revolution, the ECCI places on record that:

1. Most of the sections of the Comintern have not sufficiently realized this significance and have inadequately supported the Chinese revolution.

2. The same is true of the Communists belonging to the "Anti - Imperialist League."[19]

The ECCI considers it absolutely essential that these defects shall be speedily

---

[19] The League to Struggle Against Imperialism (see Document 96).

rectified, and to this end calls upon all the sections to take resolute measures in this direction along the following lines:

(a) Agitation and propaganda in the press;

(b) Work in the trade unions and other mass workers' organizations;

(c) Work in the colonies and dependencies of the respective imperialist countries;

(d) Work among soldiers who are to be sent to China.

The ECCI points out that serious preparations must be made to stop the dispatch of troops and arms to China, and requires that its sections conduct energetic work among the imperialist troops, urging them to go over to the revolutionary troops of the Chinese people.

The ECCI instructs the central committees of the various sections to draw up concrete measures in the direction indicated.

The ECCI sends fraternal greetings to its Chinese Section and promises it the warmest support in its great revolutionary struggle.

108

Communist Contact with the Nanking Government to Continue

[Statement by Bukharin, June 1927][20]

. . .

The question may be asked: Is it essential that the Soviet state sever all connection with the Nanking government?

This question must, of course, be answered in the negative. None but the poorest politicians and extremely "naïve" persons imagine that the nature of the proletarian state is such that it has absolutely no connection with the capitalist encirclement. On the contrary, certain relations are indeed desirable. No reasonable person has suggested that the institutions of Soviet diplomacy and foreign trade be completely "abolished" for the sake of the so-called "purity" of our principles. If this Soviet state has its representatives in the bourgeois countries of the West and East, if it maintains relations with the feudal state of Marshal Chang Tso-lin, if it has its representatives in the Fascist paradise of Signor Mussolini, there can be no reason why it should forego relations with the Nanking government. These customary forms of connection should be retained. Still more! If Soviet diplomacy makes use of conflicts of interest between the imperialist powers, why should it not exploit the antagonism between the liberal claimants to China and their imperialist partners, since both plunder China without regard to "form of government"?

The practical distinction between the Comintern and the Soviet government is so absolutely clear in this respect, and we believe we have explained it in so popular a way, that even Chamberlain could understand it. The fact that the proletarian state carries on diplomatic and trade relations with capitalists and feudal exploiters does not signify its "approval" of their policies. The Communist International, on the other hand, conducts neither diplomatic nor trade relations with "other powers." It directly *organizes the revolution*. . . .

[20] N. I. Bukharin, "Tekushchii moment kitaiskoi revoliutsii," *Pravda,* No. 145, June 30, 1927, pp. 2–3.

109
Stalin on the Communist Approach to the Colonial Question

[Excerpts from Stalin's Speech to a Joint Session of the Central Committee and the Central Control Commission of the Party, August 1, 1927][21]

. . .

What is the fundamental position from which the Comintern and the Communist parties generally approach the problems of the revolutionary movement in colonial and dependent countries?

It is a strict differentiation between revolution in imperialist countries, countries that oppress other peoples, and revolution in colonial and dependent countries, countries that suffer from imperialist oppression . . .

The fundamental mistake of the opposition is that they do not understand and will not admit this difference between the two types of revolution. They identify the 1905 revolution in Russia, an imperialist country which oppressed other peoples, with the revolution in China, an oppressed country, a semicolonial country, which is forced to resist the imperialist oppression of other states.

With us in Russia, in 1905, the revolution was directed against the bourgeoisie, against the liberal bourgeoisie, even though it was a bourgeois-democratic revolution. Why? Because the liberal bourgeoisie of an imperialist country is bound to be counterrevolutionary. And that is why the Bolsheviks at that time did not and could not consider temporary blocs and agreements with the liberal bourgeoisie. On these grounds, the opposition assert that the same attitude should be adopted in China in all stages of the revolutionary movement . . .

How does it "happen" that Lenin, who fulminated against agreements with the bourgeoisie in Russia, regarded such agreements and blocs as permissible in China? Perhaps Lenin made a mistake? Of course not. It "happened" because Lenin understood the difference between revolution in an oppressed country and revolution in an oppressor country. It "happened" because Lenin understood that at certain stages of its development the national bourgeoisie in the colonial countries may support the revolutionary movement of its country against foreign imperialism. . . .

Now as to the stages of the Chinese revolution. . . . Were there ever revolutions without certain stages of development? Did not our revolution have its stages of development? Take Lenin's "April [1917] Theses" and you will see that Lenin discerned two stages in our revolution: first, the bourgeois-democratic revolution, with the agrarian movement as its main axis; second, the October Revolution, with the seizure of power by the proletariat as its main axis. What are the stages in the Chinese revolution? In my opinion there should be three: the first stage was the revolution of the general national united front, the Canton period, when the revolution was striking chiefly at foreign imperialism and had the national bourgeoisie's support; the second stage is the bourgeois-democratic revolution, starting after the national troops reached the Yangtze River, when the national bourgeoisie deserted and the agrarian movement grew into a mighty revolution of tens of millions of peasants (the revolution is now in this stage); the third stage is the soviet revolution, which has not yet come about, but which will come about. . . .

What was the nature of the Kuomintang and its government in the first stage of the revolution, the Canton period? They then consisted of a bloc of workers, peasants, bourgeois intellectuals, and national bourgeoisie. Was Canton at that time

[21] Stalin, *Marksizm i natsionalno-kolonialnyi vopros*, pp. 174–87; also J. Stalin, *Marxism and the National and Colonial Question*, pp. 323–49.

the center of the revolutionary movement, the *place d'armes* of the revolution? . . .
Were we right when we supported Canton in China, and, let us say, Ankara in Turkey,
at a time when Canton and Ankara were fighting imperialism? Yes, we were right.
We were right, and we were then following in the footsteps of Lenin; because the
struggle of Canton and Ankara was causing a dispersion of the forces of imperialism,
and enfeebling and undermining imperialism, and was thus facilitating the development of the hearth and home of the world revolution, the U.S.S.R. . . .

But how are we to conceive a united front with the national bourgeoisie in the
first stage of a colonial revolution? . . . A united front can have revolutionary
significance only if and when it does not hinder the Communist Party from conducting its independent political and organizational work, only if it does not prevent it
from organizing the proletariat into an independent political force, rousing the peasantry against the landlords, openly organizing a revolution of workers and peasants,
and thus preparing the conditions necessary for the hegemony of the proletariat. . . .

Comrades Kamenev and Zinoviev have here referred to a single solitary telegram sent to Shanghai in October 1926, stating that for the time being, until Shanghai
is captured, the agrarian movement should not be forced. I am far from saying that
this telegram was correct. I have never considered, nor do I consider now, our Central
Committee infallible. Separate mistakes can take place, and this telegram is unquestionably a mistake. But, in the first place, we ourselves canceled this telegram
a few weeks later (in November 1926). . . . As a matter of fact, it was an isolated,
episodic telegram which was absolutely not characteristic of the line of the Communist International, of the line of our leadership.

·   ·   ·

What was the aim of the Communists in the second stage of the revolution in
China, when the center of the revolutionary movement had been patently transferred
from Canton to Wuhan and when in addition to the revolutionary center in Wuhan
a counterrevolutionary center was set up in Nanking? It was to take full advantage
of every opportunity, for the open organization of the party, the proletariat (trade
unions), the peasantry (peasant unions), and the revolution generally. It was to
impel the Wuhan Kuomintangists to the Left, toward the agrarian revolution. It
was to make the Wuhan Kuomintang the center of the struggle against counterrevolution and the nucleus of the future revolutionary democratic dictatorship of the
proletariat and the peasantry. . . .

The opposition at that time demanded the immediate formation of soviets of
workers' and peasants' deputies. But this was sheer adventurism, an adventurist
sally, for the immediate formation of soviets at that time would have meant skipping
the Kuomintang Left phase of development. Why? Because the Kuomintang in
Wuhan, supporting as it did an alliance with the Communists, had not yet managed
to discredit and expose itself in the eyes of the masses of workers and peasants and
had not yet exhausted itself as a bourgeois revolutionary organization. Because to
have issued the call for soviets and for the overthrow of the Wuhan government, at
a time when the masses had not yet grown convinced from their own experience
of the worthlessness of that government and the necessity for its overthrow, would
have meant to rush ahead, to become divorced from the masses, to forfeit the support of the masses, and thus to bring about the collapse of the cause undertaken. . . .

Why in April 1917 did we Bolsheviks not put forward the practical demand for
the overthrow of the Provisional Government and the establishment of a soviet government, although we were convinced that in the very near future we would be faced
with the necessity of overthrowing the Provisional Government and establishing
a soviet government? Because the masses of the toilers both in the rear and at the
front and, finally, the soviets themselves were not in a position to subscribe to this

demand and still believed in the revolutionary nature of the Provisional Government. Because the Provisional Government had not yet managed to disgrace and discredit itself by supporting counterrevolution in the rear and at the front. Why did Lenin stigmatize the Bagdatiev group in Leningrad in April 1917, which put forward the demand for the immediate overthrow of the Provisional Government and the establishment of a soviet government? Because Bagdatiev's attempt was a risky sally and created the danger that the Bolshevik party might be cut off from the millions of workers and peasants.

The opposition rejoices that the bloc with the Wuhan Kuomintang proved to be short-lived; they moreover assert that the Communist International did not warn the Chinese Communists of the possibility of the collapse of the Wuhan Kuomintang. . . . The opposition apparently thinks that blocs with the national bourgeoisie in colonial countries should be long-lived. But only people who have lost the last remnants of Leninism can think that. The fact that the feudal lords and imperialists in China proved at this stage to be stronger than the revolution, that the pressure exercised by these hostile forces induced the Wuhan Kuomintang to swing to the Right and led to the temporary defeat of the Chinese revolution, can be a cause for jubilation only to people infected with defeatism. As to the opposition's assertion that the Communist International did not warn the Chinese Communist Party of the possible collapse of the Wuhan Kuomintang, this is only one of the usual slanders with which the arsenal of the opposition now teems.

Permit me to cite several documents in refutation of the slanders of the opposition.

The first document, relating to May 1927:

> The most important thing in the internal policy of the Kuomintang now must be to develop the agrarian revolution systematically in all the provinces, and particularly in Kwangtung under the slogan "All Power to the Peasant Unions and Committees in the Rural Districts." This is fundamental for the success of the revolution and of the Kuomintang. This is fundamental for the creation in China of a big and powerful political and military army against imperialism and its agents. Practically the slogan of confiscating the land is quite timely in the provinces infected by a powerful agrarian movement, such as Hunan, Kwangtung, etc. Without this the extension of the agrarian revolution is impossible. . . .
>
> The organization must immediately be undertaken of eight or ten divisions of revolutionary peasants and workers with an absolutely reliable command. This force will serve as a guard for Wuhan both at the front and in the rear for the disarming of unreliable divisions. This must not be delayed.
>
> Work must be intensified in the rear and within the divisions of Chang Kaishek in order to disintegrate them, and assistance must be given to the peasant insurrectionaries in Kwangtung, where the rule of the landlords is particularly intolerable.

Here is a second document relating to May 1927:

> Without an agrarian revolution victory is impossible. Without it the Central Committee of the Kuomintang will be converted into a wretched plaything of unreliable generals. Excesses must be combated—not, however, with the help of troops, but through the peasant unions. We are decidedly in favor of the land's actually being seized by the masses from below. The fears regarding T'an P'ingshan's visit are not devoid of foundation. You must not sever yourselves from the workers' and peasants' movement, but must assist it in every possible way. Otherwise you will ruin the cause.
>
> Certain of the old leaders of the Central Committee of the Kuomintang are afraid of what is taking place. They are vacillating and compromising. A large

number of new peasant and working class leaders must be drawn into the Central Committee of the Kuomintang from below. Their bold voices will make the old leaders more resolute, or throw them into discard. The present structure of the Kuomintang must be changed. The leadership of the Kuomintang must be freshened and reinforced by new leaders who have come to the fore in the process of the agrarian revolution, while the periphery must be enlarged by drawing into local organizations millions from among the working class and peasant unions. Otherwise the Kuomintang runs the risk of becoming divorced from realities and losing all authority.

It is necessary to liquidate the dependence upon unreliable generals immediately. Mobilize about 20,000 Communists and about 50,000 revolutionary workers and peasants from Hunan and Hupeh, form several new army corps, utilize the students of the school for military commanders, *and organize your own reliable army before it is too late. Otherwise there can be no guarantee against failure.* It is a difficult matter, but there is no other course.

Organize a revolutionary military tribunal headed by prominent noncommunist Kuomintangists. *Punish officers who maintain contact with Chiang Kaishek or who set soldiers on the people, the workers and peasants.* Persuasion is not enough, it is time to act. *The scoundrels must be punished. If the Kuomintangists do not learn to be revolutionary Jacobins, they will be lost both to the people and to the revolution.*[22]

110

Moscow's Explanation of the Defeat of the Chinese Revolution and the Call to Organize Soviets

[Excerpt from the Resolution of the Joint Plenum of the Central Committee and the Central Control Commission of the Russian Communist Party on Bukharin's Report, August 9, 1927][23]

. . .

3. *The Problem of the Chinese Revolution*

19. Three main lines of tactics could be laid down for a proletarian party in the Chinese revolution (and three main lines actually have been laid down), all of which must be objectively estimated. Each provides a different estimate of the revolution. The first line of tactics (the Right deviation, which merges directly and immediately into Menshevism) assumes that until the victory over imperialism and the unification of China, it is necessary to maintain the unity of the national "revolutionary" front, including the bourgeoisie, in every stage of development, for which purpose many concessions are to be made—for example, hampering of the agrarian revolution and actual struggle against the "exaggerated demands" of the workers, etc., in order "not to frighten away the bourgeoisie." The second line of tactics (the Trotskyist) rejects on principle (but only recently) the admissibility of entering into any agreements or alliances with the bourgeoisie in general, in any stage of development of the revolution. It assumes that agreements and alliances with the bourgeoisie can

---

[22] The italics are Stalin's.

[23] *Pravda*, No. 180, August 10, 1927, p. 3; also *International Press Correspondence*, No. 48, August 18, 1927, pp. 1074–76.

only weaken the proletariat, etc. Finally, the third line of tactics (the Leninist, carried out by the Comintern) considers agreements with the bourgeoisie of the colonial and semicolonial countries to be necessary, but only in certain stages of development, and under quite definite *conditions*. At the same time it maintains that these agreements are to be *dissolved*, and a determined struggle is to be waged against the former allies, as soon as the conditions of development have changed, the class forces have regrouped themselves, and the like.

20. The Right deviation, of which the leaders of the Communist Party of China were guilty in spite of the instructions of the Comintern, is based upon the entirely wrong conception of a contrast between the national and the agrarian revolutions. The representatives of this deviation assume permanent relations between the fundamental class forces of Chinese society; they do not grasp the complete necessity and inevitability of a development of class antagonisms within the formerly united national-revolutionary front. Nor do they comprehend the complete inevitability of the resultant realignments of the classes, of the struggle between the bourgeoisie and the proletariat for hegemony in the national emancipation movement, and of the transformation of the bourgeois revolution into a bourgeois-democratic revolution, and ultimately into a socialist revolution. . . . The Joint Plenum of the Central Committee and the Central Control Commission is now in a position to state with satisfaction that this Right deviation in the leadership of the Chinese brother party has been liquidated, and the policy of the leadership corrected.

21. The Trotskyist point of view seeks its formal basis in an analogy with the revolution in Russia in 1905, when the Bolsheviks fought determinedly against an understanding with the liberal bourgeoisie, which was advocated by the Mensheviks. The gravest error of the Trotskyist standpoint is the fact that Comrade Trotsky and his adherents (Comrade Zinoviev, etc.) do not grasp the fundamental difference between an imperialist and a colonial country, between revolution in an imperialist country and revolution in a country which unfurls the banner of the struggle against imperialism. Yet Lenin wrote directly on this as follows:

> What is the most important, the main idea of our theses? The difference between oppressed and oppressor countries. We emphasise this difference, ignored by the Second International and the bourgeois democrats. It is especially important for the proletariat, and for the Communist International, in the epoch of imperialism, to ascertain the actual existing economic facts, and to take concrete realities as the point of departure for the solution of all colonial and national problems, and not abstract principles. (Lenin [*Sochineniia*, 1st ed.], XVII, 274.)

Lenin writes further:

> The Communist International must make temporary agreements, and even alliances, with the bourgeoisie democracies of the colonies and backward countries. But it must not amalgamate with them; it must retain the independence of the proletarian movement itself, even its most primitive form. (Lenin [*Sochineniia*, 1st ed.], XIX, 270.)

And finally:

> We Communists must and will support the bourgeois liberation movements in the colonial countries when these movements are really revolutionary and when their representatives do not prevent us from enlightening and organizing the broad masses of the peasantry and the exploited in the spirit of revolution. (Lenin [*Sochineniia*, 1st ed.], XVII, 275–76.)

We see that Lenin's standpoint differs from that of Trotsky. Trotsky's standpoint is a gross distortion of Leninism, based upon a flat disregard of the differences between the countries of imperialism and the colonies; this method is extremely characteristic of the Social Democratic deviation.

22. The basic characteristic of the line taken by the Comintern consists of the analysis of the various stages of the revolution and of the various class alignments. The Comintern favored supporting the national bourgeoisie while the revolution was developing, while the bourgeoisie was still revolutionary, that is: (1) while it was carrying on a real struggle against imperialism; (2) so long as it did not prevent the Communists from educating the working and peasant masses in the spirit of revolution, and from forming revolutionary workers' and peasants' organizations; (3) so long as it did not prevent the formation, consolidation, and expansion of an independent party of the communist proletariat.

These were the conditions during the period of Canton and the northern campaign, up to the treachery of Chiang Kai-shek. His treachery was the outward expression of the defection of the national bourgeoisie from the camp of the revolution into the camp of counterrevolution. During this time not only did the Chinese Communist Party increase its strength, but the workers' and peasants' movement made great progress. . . .

Chiang Kai-shek's *coup d'état* signified a new alignment of class forces. Therefore the Comintern laid down a new line of tactics for this new stage of development. This line consisted of a determined and relentless struggle by the workers, peasants, and petty bourgeoisie against the imperialists and Chang Tso-lin, and at the same time against the bourgeoisie and Chiang Kai-shek. One part of the radical and petty bourgeoisie, which remained in the Kuomintang Left and in the Wuhan government, declared war against Chiang Kai-shek, and made it possible for the Communist Party to continue its work. The Communist Party had to make use of this possibility, in order to organize the defense against the "Cavaignacs" and to mobilize the masses.

The development of the class struggle and the pressure exercised by the imperialists led, however, to a new alignment of forces. The majority of the Wuhan government and of the leaders of the Kuomintang Left deserted the revolution, and the suppression of the workers' and peasants' movement began. This stage again brought with it a corresponding change in Communist tactics and slogans: withdrawal from and declaration of war against the Wuhan government, which had ceased to be "really revolutionary."

23. During all these stages, the Comintern, which had rightly foreseen the transition from one stage to another, considered it necessary to prepare the masses for this transition. The Comintern not only considered it necessary for the independent Communist Party of China to work with the utmost energy, but stressed a far-reaching criticism of all the vacillations of the former allies of this party, including the extreme Left, and a systematic preparation of the forces of the party itself: mass organizations, armed forces, etc., the formation of a suitable point of support, everything to ensure the workers, peasants, and city poor the greatest possible progress of the revolution. The development of the agrarian revolution, the seizure of the land by the peasants from below [i.e., on their own initiative], the development of the workers' movement, the arming of the workers and peasants, the democratization of the Kuomintang and the removal of its vacillating leaders—these were the main slogans of the Comintern.

24. The Comintern drove the revolution forward. But at the same time it was opposed to leaps over stages of revolution which had not yet been properly passed through. It rightly condemned the withdrawal from the Kuomintang, which was a

mass organization, under conditions tantamount to delivering that party into the hands of its Right wing and isolating the Communists from the masses of Kuomintang supporters. It rightly opposed the slogan of soviets when this slogan would have meant breaking with the Wuhan government and the Kuomintang Left while both were still pursuing a revolutionary policy as defined above. At the same time, the Comintern energetically fought against all Right deviations, both among the leaders of the Communist Party of China, who sacrificed the interests of the agrarian revolution and of the workers' movement to their vacillating allies, and within the Communist Party of the Soviet Union itself, where some theoreticians of the opposition preached a perfect apology for the bourgeoisie (Radek with his "Workers' and Peasants' Government" of Canton, etc.), or developed extremely opportunist theories on the Chinese revolution (the "customs" theory of Comrade Trotsky).

25. If the Chinese revolution has suffered a severe defeat in spite of the correct tactics of the Communist International, this has occurred, first, because of the alignment of class forces both in China and internationally; second, because the masses have not yet had time to organize forces powerful enough to defeat the combined forces of the enemy, the forces of foreign imperialism, the feudal elements headed by Chang Tso-lin, and the counterrevolutionary national bourgeoisie; finally, because the working class is not yet strong enough to form a strongly organized mass Communist Party. Moreover, the leaders of the Communist Party of China, in systematically rejecting the instructions of the Comintern, bear partial responsibility for the defeat of the Chinese working class and peasantry.

26. The characteristic features of the present period of the Chinese revolution are this severe defeat and a simultaneous radical realignment of forces: a bloc of the workers, peasants, and city poor is being organized against all the ruling classes and the imperialists. Seen from this aspect, the revolution is striding forward to the highest phase of its development, to the phase of direct struggle for the dictatorship of the working class and the peasantry. . . .

27. . . . The Communist Party must declare that the victory over imperialism, the revolutionary unification of China, and its liberation from the yoke of imperialism are only possible on the basis of the class struggle of the broadest masses of the workers and peasants against the feudal lords and capitalists.

The Communist Party must take all measures possible to retain, consolidate, and expand the workers' trade unions and the peasant organizations (peasant leagues, committees, etc.). Further, the Communist Party must take all measures necessary to arouse the lower strata of the Left Kuomintang against the upper, and must institute an energetic campaign to this end. At the same time, the Communist Party must carry on energetic propaganda for the idea of soviets.

Should the Communist Party's efforts to revolutionize the Kuomintang not meet with success, and should it be found impossible to convert the Kuomintang into a broad mass organization of the workers and peasants, and if at such time the revolution is in the upsurge, then is the time to make the propagandist slogan of soviets a slogan of direct struggle and to proceed at once to the organization of workers', peasants', and artisans' soviets.

Meanwhile, every effort must be made to develop the agrarian movement, to arm the workers and peasants, and to lay the foundations for a really revolutionary workers' and peasants' army. The party must systematically expose the treachery of Chiang Kai-shek and Wuhan, ruthlessly tear every mask from their faces, and act as the real advance guard of the working class, fighting for the hegemony of the working class and marching at the head of the broadest masses of the peasantry and the city poor.

111

The Comintern's Appeal to All Workers, Oppressed Peoples, and Soldiers to Support the Canton Commune, December 14, 1927[24]

In Canton, the immortal city of revolutionary struggles, the workers and peasants have seized power and the banner of soviets, the Red flag of the revolution, has been unfurled over the capital of South China. The unparalleled heroism of the workers of Canton is an event of the greatest importance, an event of really world-wide historical significance.

All the forces of counterrevolution have come into action against the workers and peasants: the foreign imperialists, the bloody hangmen-generals, the counterrevolutionary bourgeoisie of China. These forces are fighting bitterly in Canton. They have surrounded Canton and cut it off from the outside world. Bourgeois telegraph agencies report that Red Canton has already fallen and that mass executions of workers and Communists have begun, but that revolutionary workers' detachments, the Red Army of China, have escaped from the ring.

Should this be true, then the victory of the counterrevolution in Canton can by no means be firm and permanent. In five districts of the province of Kwangtung soviet power is still firm. New struggles are unavoidable. The movement is extending, despite partial defeats. The bourgeois counterrevolutionaries and hangmen-generals will be defeated and the imperialist robbers driven out of China. At the present moment, however, they are swinging the executioner's ax over the heroic Chinese workers' and peasants' revolution.

Hasten to assist the revolution! Help the Chinese soviets! Prevent the transport of soldiers and sailors, of cannons and rifles to crush the Chinese revolution! Refuse to load munitions! Mobilize your forces! Demand the immediate removal of the imperialist troops from China!

Long live the soviet power in China!

Long live the world revolution!

THE EXECUTIVE COMMITTEE OF THE COMMUNIST INTERNATIONAL

112

Moscow's Denial of Responsibility for the Canton Uprising

[Chicherin's Statement, December 22, 1927][25]

The People's Commissariat of Foreign Affairs has already observed on numerous occasions that whenever a revolutionary movement rises in any part of the globe, the adversaries of the U.S.S.R. immediately declare that it was caused by the agents of the Soviet government.

With regard to China, not only the reactionary press, but also members of the governments of capitalist countries, have sought from the beginning to represent the whole nationalist movement as a result of Soviet Union policy and the activity

---

[24] *Pravda*, No. 287, December 15, 1927, p. 1; also *International Press Correspondence*, No. 72, December 22, 1927, p. 1633.

[25] *Pravda*, No. 294, December 23, 1927, p. 1.

of Soviet agents. This is also the path chosen by the counterrevolutionary generals who have drowned the powerful insurrection of the revolutionary workers of Canton in blood. When they piled up the bodies of the tortured workers in the streets of Canton, their hatred was directed primarily against the Soviet citizens there, who are to be found among the first victims.

We have not yet had definite and detailed reports of what happened in Canton. However, we can already say with certainty that a number of Soviet citizens in Canton were maltreated or killed. Reports are at hand from various sources concerning the tragic death of the vice-consul of the Soviet Union, Comrade Khassis. It is difficult to doubt the truth of these terrible reports.

Although the crime of the Canton generals against the U.S.S.R. is atrocious and great, the responsibility for this crime cannot be restricted to Canton.

The political actions of the Kuomintang generals against the U.S.S.R. and against its representatives have spread over the whole of South China; the slaughter in Canton was only the worst of many incidents. The political responsibility for these bestial crimes falls, therefore, on the shoulders of all leading persons in the territory of the so-called "national" governments. Not only Generals Chang Fa-k'uei and Li Fu-lin, who are acting in Canton, but also Li Ting-hsin, Chiang Kai-shek, Pien Shou-ching, and others are the originators of these atrocities.

In this case, however, the responsibility also falls upon the other powers of the world reaction hostile to the U.S.S.R. The campaign of incitement carried on by all the imperialist and White Guardist groups in Shanghai, Hong Kong, and other important centers of colonial policy in China, and the undoubted instigation from London, which was corroborated by the hymns of praise in the British press, played an almost decisive role in the development of the events. British imperialist reaction is to be considered the most important driving force in the Canton slaughter and in the violence, the murders, and the expulsions of the citizens of the Soviet Union.

The toilers of the Soviet Union mourn the tragic death of those comrades who were tortured to death by the hangmen and the instigators of the counterrevolution in South China. However, the blood of these martyrs has not flowed in vain. A people of four hundred millions cannot be indefinitely held up on the way to its liberation, and the militarist cliques, who from leaders of the national movement have become its suppressors, will be swept away. The liberated Chinese people will not forget their friends from the Soviet Union who were murdered by the oppressors of the Chinese people. Their memory and the joint bloodshed of the two great peoples will bind the two states indissolubly together.

In the unheard-of and atrocious crimes of the Chinese counterrevolution and the forces behind it, the government of the Soviet Union sees an attack upon the U.S.S.R. The Soviet Union, although it unswervingly pursues a policy of peace, as expressed in the proposals for disarmament at the conference in Geneva,[26] is at the same time prepared for the worst and will not let itself be taken by surprise.

In the name of the Soviet government, the People's Commissariat of Foreign Affairs protests before the whole world the atrocities of the Chinese counterrevolution. The Soviet government reserves to itself the right to take any measures which it may deem fit in connection with the bloody atrocities committed in South China against the U.S.S.R. These bestial atrocities shall not go unpunished.

[26] See the companion volume, *Soviet Russia and the West, 1920–1927.*

D. SUMMARY OF THE REVOLUTIONARY SITUATION IN THE EAST IN 1927

113

Zinoviev on the "Epoch of Wars and Revolutions"[1]

The phrase "epoch of wars and revolutions" was first made use of at the beginning of this century. At that time the whole Marxist camp agreed that it was the perfect definition of approaching world events . . .

An epoch of imperialist wars, as was demonstrated by Lenin, not only includes but presupposes national wars of liberation (oppressed nations fighting imperialism for their independence). Similarly, an epoch of socialist revolution presupposes revolutionary democratic movements on a large scale (e.g., peasant movements). Such movements, under favorable conditions, gradually develop from bourgeois-democratic into socialist ones. All this is finally the epoch of the world proletarian revolution.

Within this epoch ebb and flow are inevitable. For a few years after the first great victory of the world proletarian revolution in Russia (in 1917), the tide continued to flow. It began to turn in about 1921. When several years without actual war or revolution intervened, the opportunists of the whole world were confirmed in their "conviction" that the epoch of wars and revolutions had ended and had been replaced by an era of "pacifism" and "democracy." . . .

. . . But as capitalism begins to establish itself in the least degree, it immediately contemplates new wars. Every step toward the "stabilization" of capitalism is at the same time a step toward a new war.

If any further proofs are necessary, consider recent events in Morocco[2] and China . . .

The great events in China, which are happening before our eyes, show the advance guard of the European proletariat very plainly what powerful reserves we have in the East. For a whole month now, a movement has been developing in China such as has never been seen before in that country, a movement that is spreading and becoming irresistible in spite of the predatory campaign of the united imperialists.

The events in China will revolutionize the other countries in the East, especially those dependent upon imperialist England. What the Russian revolution of 1905 did for Turkey, Persia, and China, the present great movement in China will do for Indochina, India, etc. The hundreds of millions of oppressed citizens of the East will greedily seize upon every item of news from revolutionary China and will concen-

---

[1] *Pravda*, No. 145, June 28, 1925, p. 3.

[2] From 1924 to 1926, the Rif and Jibālah tribes of the rugged coastal region of Morocco fought to win their freedom from the Spanish Protectorate. Rif and Jibālah successes in 1924 and 1925, and their repercussions in the neighboring French Zone, led to co-operation between France and Spain after August 22, 1925. The combined French and Spanish pressure proved too much for the native tribes, and in May 1926 the Rif leader, Abdul-Karim, surrendered.

trate their thoughts on how they themselves can organize and revolt against the oppressors, the imperialists. . . .

The epoch of wars and revolutions continues and is changing before our eyes into an epoch of imperialist wars and of the socialist revolution. The Communists should understand how to transmit throughout the world from mouth to mouth, from land to land, from continent to continent, the great slogan: "Proletarians of all countries and oppressed peoples of the world unite!"

114

Manuilsky on the Significance of the Pacific Problem and the Future Role of China

[Excerpts from a Report to the Seventh Enlarged Plenum of the ECCI, November 22–December 16, 1926][3]

I should like to direct the Comintern's attention to the Pacific, and to the conflicts brewing there. Three imperialist powers stand face to face on the Pacific: the United States of North America, Japan, and Great Britain.

The armed clash that will occur there within a few years will be of unimaginable violence and enormous consequences. If prior to this clash no decisive battle has taken place between proletariat and bourgeoisie in England and the United States, and if the victory of the revolution in China does not change international relations on the shores of the Pacific, we may witness a war so grim and destructive as to put the great imperialist war of 1914–18 in the shade. . . .

The Comintern devoted little attention to this problem in the past; we were too much of a European International. We were inclined to see all problems of world politics and of the international workers' movement through the prism of European relations. Parties directly involved in the Pacific problem, such as the American and British, have also devoted but inadequate attention to it. Only after the outbreak of the Chinese national revolution did the question of antagonisms in the Far East arouse our interest; since then we have observed events there somewhat more closely. Yet thus far we also have considered the Chinese revolution only in terms of its international development. We ignore its significance to Pacific relations as a whole.

The struggle for China that raged for decades before the World War was part of a struggle for the division of Asia. . . . Until recently China was one of the chief objects of that struggle. China's appearance as an active national-revolutionary state, however, completely overturned all the experts' "analyses" and predictions of the probable grouping of forces in the Pacific. All these people proceeded from the premise of a split-up China, rendered powerless by internal conflicts, a country whose inescapable fate was to be divided up into spheres of influence. They thought in terms of the relations between the United States, Japan, and Britain established by the Washington Conference, without taking into consideration the new, potentially powerful factor of future Chinese policy.

Under certain conditions the Chinese revolution can (1) hasten the armed clash of big powers on the Pacific, "a possibility" bourgeois Pacific experts put off for

[3] *Puti mirovoi revoliutsii*, I, 420–27, 430, 432–35; also *International Press Correspondence*, No. 91, Dec. 30, 1926, pp. 1592–97.

years; (2) exert a revolutionizing influence on all Asia, especially India, whose national-revolutionary movement seems to have ebbed somewhat in recent years. . . .

. . .

Every great colonial movement today must cut deeply into the diplomatic web of international relations of the big capitalist vultures. Every such movement radically changes the relation of forces between them, sharpens their struggles, and stimulates their appetites. The Chinese revolution and the colonial revolutionary movements have prospects of success because they occur at a time in which antagonisms on the Pacific are not lessening, but sharpening. . . .

Finally, the Pacific problem is intensified by changes within the world economy. Since the war, the center of gravity of the world economy has shifted, slowly but uninterruptedly, to the overseas countries. Capitalism has developed tremendously, not only in the United States of North America but also in a whole series of "virgin" countries—Argentina, Brazil, Canada, Australia, etc. In the absence of a great economic crisis, only an armed struggle on the shores of the Pacific can create an immediate revolutionary situation in these countries. . . .

Objectively speaking, the aggressor on the Pacific is the United States of North America; the defenders are Great Britain and Japan. American imperialism is the most dangerous to the toiling masses . . . In the coming world war, if the fate of humanity is not previously fundamentally remodeled by the proletarian revolution, American imperialism will play the leading role. America is already arming now for this war on the Pacific; there is already an extensive literature which discusses this question in detail; and even the very time (1931–33) is set; plans of operations are described; in brief, the picture we had several years before the war in Europe is beginning to resurrect itself. At that time one could find in military literature detailed drafts of the German attack upon Belgium, which were later, in the first days of August, 1914, carried into effect with photographic fidelity.

The whole development of American imperialism in the last twenty to twenty-five years testifies that this relentlessly approaching struggle on the Pacific is in no sense a creation of fantasy. The ruling classes also recognize this. . . .

The notorious Washington Conference (1921) gave rise to certain pacifist illusions, because it put a check on the growth of naval armaments. Yet it eliminated neither the causes nor the chances of the conflict; it merely deferred them. . . .

In its economic program of expansion, American imperialism has passed through three stages:

First, the Monroe Doctrine. This doctrine of "America for the Americans" held sway as long as the markets of North and South America were the highest goal of the American bourgeoisie.

Second, the "Open Door" policy, launched late in the nineteenth century, when the American bourgeoisie first turned its eyes to the Pacific and to the huge Chinese markets. The "Open Door" policy is the policy of every rising young imperialism that comes into the world somewhat belatedly, i.e., when the world is already divided among its capitalist rivals. . . .

Third, dating from the World War and the ensuing economic collapse of Europe, the Dawes Plan, a program aimed at making European industrial countries slaves to American capitalism. No longer content with the countries of Asia, American imperialism invades Europe. In addition to Germany, it "cleans up" Austria, prepares a plan for cleaning up French finances, slinks unobserved into Italy, etc.

Each of these three periods has found its expression in the foreign policy of the United States.

. . .

The American imperialists are going to miscalculate; they are bound to miscalculate because they overlook China's historical role in Asia and on the Pacific. That semiconscious Pan-Asian movement which Japan has thus far endeavored to dominate . . . will turn into a vast movement of the Asian countries oppressed by world imperialism, for their liberation from the imperialist yoke. Japan, which jointly with the White imperialists played an active role in the suppression of the Boxer uprising in 1900, cannot lead such a movement, since it will be directed against Japanese imperialism as well as that of Britain and America; only revolutionary China can lead it.

At the same time liberated China will become a magnet for all peoples of the yellow race who inhabit the Philippines, Indonesia, and the numerous islands of the Pacific. China will become a major power on the Pacific to menace the capitalist world of three continents. China must inevitably clash with American imperialism because the problem of spreading its gigantic population out over the Pacific confronts it even more intensely than it does Japan. China will fulfill this task among the island inhabitants of the Pacific, not with fire and sword, but in the course of the normal revolutionary progress of the native population.

The Kuomintang's most important task at the moment is to foster the revolution by exploiting antagonisms between the powers that encircle China. America's position makes possible greater maneuvering. The plans of American imperialism constitute a terrifying economic and military-strategic menace to Japan.

America's advance in China threatens the very existence of Japanese imperialism. This danger may hasten the armed clash between the United States and Japan . . .

British imperialism is the deadliest, most implacable foe of the Chinese revolution. Whereas America and Japan have not yet ruled in Asia and are only making their imperialist bid for mastery, England is already an "Asiatic" state, and must be driven from its Asian strongholds. This struggle of Asia's toiling masses to oust the British vultures is another factor that may precipitate war in the Pacific. Capitalist England, which in China is already being pressed by America and Japan, and which is beginning to see the possibility of American expansion in India, may make a desperate attempt to provoke a war to be fought by others. The erection and fortification of the Singapore naval base, which took place after England had signed the Washington treaty, proved that the British Admiralty by no means considers impossible such a solution of the present struggle for Asia, for China, and for the Pacific. . . .

While England did tear up its treaty with Japan at the Washington Conference, it made no alliance with the United States. It kept its hands free, stipulating only that complications on the Pacific should be subjected to regulation by a preliminary conference of the four powers which signed the Washington treaty. This position enables England, in case of war, to maneuver to fit the situation. On the one hand, it can sell its neutrality at the highest possible price; on the other, it can urge others into war, in order, when the foes weaken, to seize the fruits of victory for itself. And the Washington treaty gives England the chance, in the event of war between the United States and Japan, either to remain neutral or to enter the war on either side.

The present grouping of forces makes the second possibility the more likely. In siding with Japan, England would immediately lose Canada, Australia, and New Zealand, since Japan's mastery of the Pacific subjects these dominions to a constant threat of attack and England has been valuable to them only as a protection against foreign attacks. Therefore, in case of a Japanese-American war, England would ally itself with the United States. Hence the prospect of a joint attack by England and the United States against Japan seems more likely. England is interested no less than the United States in the elimination of Japanese competition in the Far East, in China particularly. England could combine with Japan for a joint struggle only if the separation process of the Dominions were already so far advanced as to call into question the continued existence of the empire; then British imperialism would have to stake all on a single card.

The United States understands this situation clearly. In America the Singapore naval base is considered a point of support for a future joint campaign of the Anglo-American fleet against Japan. England's strategic obligation to guard its Pacific possessions will probably keep it from starting anything. . . . Rather, it will prefer to remain neutral for a while, as America did in the European war of 1914–18. The present difficulties of the British government also speak in favor of this attitude. England is a country threatened with a social revolution; its ruling classes would have to think seriously before embarking upon a war adventure.

The second phase of the war will be the struggle between England and the United States over Japanese spoils, and for spheres of influence in Asia and the Dominions. Will the capitalist world venture to plunge into this new bloody adventure? Will it not shrink back from the mood of the toiling masses, in whom still lives the remembrance of the devastation of the great imperialist war? There can be no doubt that fear of revolutionary upheavals holds the present capitalist governments within bounds. Yet the Pacific conflict, especially in its first phase, is dangerous for us, the Communists, precisely because it will take place on a front so far distant from Europe. Its participants will be the two countries which suffered least during the imperialist war of 1914–18. The 50,000 American soldiers who fell on the French front are a very small number in comparison with the sacrifices made by the European peoples. America and Japan were affected but lightly by the war; they saw only its victorious side.

And this danger the Comintern must foresee. We are a world party which does not close its eyes to its own weaknesses and its own mistakes. The British General Strike has shown us our weak spots. If the European proletariat did not react sufficiently to such an event, or to the miners' struggle, we are surely ill-prepared for mass action in time of war, when the situation becomes all the more complicated and difficult. A specially responsible task confronts our young communist parties in the Far East at this time, particularly our Chinese comrades. They must even now foresee all the tricks that the imperialist cliques will play upon them in the course of the victorious march of the Chinese revolution.

You will win, comrades; the whole international situation assures us of this. Yet even after you succeed in uniting China, you must not lose sight of the fact that the imperialist bands will stage a rehearsal, maybe several rehearsals, of the Pacific struggle through their own agents in your country, and within your own boundaries. Before the capitalist world plunges into an all-out Pacific struggle, it will probably make an attempt to fight China. The victorious Canton government, which is made strong by the support of the peasant masses, will successfully meet these attempts.

Revolutionary China, which has become an active factor in Far Eastern politics, can become, in alliance with the U.S.S.R., the greatest world factor in the Far East. China's hinterland, with its 400 million population, and its strategic rear position in the Pacific struggle, cannot be ignored by the imperialist governments. What the Second International failed to do during the imperialist war of 1914 can be done by the organized workers' and peasants' state of the Chinese toiling masses. The greatness of the Chinese revolution lies in the progress of an awakened and arisen China, having behind it our strong Soviet Union, joining its destinies to the October Revolution of our toiling masses, and advancing along the workers' and peasants' path.

In alliance with the world proletariat, with its vanguard—the Communist World Party—revolutionary China must become and will become the guardian of peace and the fighter against imperialist wars on the Pacific.

115

Bukharin on the Revolutionary Situation in Colonial and Semicolonial Countries

[Excerpts from a Speech Delivered at the Fifteenth Party Congress, December 10, 1927][4]

The experience of the Chinese revolution is of enormous importance to us, and not only from the point of view of the further successful development of the revolutionary struggle in China. The Chinese revolution has confronted us with the colonial problem in its most concrete form. We have repeatedly approached this colonial problem, and in principle its importance has been clear to us all. But the complicated nature of its social class aspect and of the tasks connected with control over such an enormous colonial revolution have only recently confronted us in their full magnitude. The experience of the Chinese revolution has brought us into actual touch with a diversity of problems of colonial revolutions in general. At the same time, the experience of the Chinese revolution shows very clearly how cautious one must be when deciding on concrete political tactics, how necessary it is to take into careful consideration the peculiarities of development in this or that country.

Drawing a parallel with the Chinese revolution, I want to say just a few words regarding the problem of revolution in India, a problem which will soon be one of the biggest problems confronting the Comintern and our party as a whole. India is also a colonial country, oppressed by British imperialism; India, too, has a national-liberation movement. But it would be unpardonable folly if we tried to mechanically transfer the experience of our Chinese tactics to Indian territory, and to the definition of our tactics in India. Why? Because the correlation of class forces there is utterly different; because from the very beginning we shall be confronted there with an utterly different state of affairs from that in China at the beginning of the Chinese revolution.

· · ·

Is it out of the question in India for proletarians and peasants to co-operate in any way with the native bourgeoisie? I think not. Is it out of the question for us Communists to participate in India, for any length of time, in an organization such as the Kuomintang? I think that such a combination is out of the question for us. Can one contemplate temporary parallel actions or agreements from time to time? I think so. Can one contemplate a prolonged bloc, prolonged support of the Indian bourgeoisie on our part? Certainly not, because from the very beginning our attitude will be extremely critical of the native bourgeoisie . . . , for this bourgeoisie, or at least its most important circles, does not satisfy the conditions laid down by Lenin. First, it has not been carrying on a prolonged struggle against British imperialism. Second, and this is also very important, it is carrying on an active struggle against Communists, interfering with their freedom of action. As far as we are concerned, it is already an actively hostile force. All this goes to show that our attitude here

[4] *XV sezd VKP (B)*, pp. 606–9.

must be quite different. Here is a different combination of classes, and therefore the problems that confront us here are different, in spite of the fact that India, too, is a colonial country.

I could take as an example Egypt, Persia, or any other [Eastern] country: every such country has certain social relations that are peculiar to itself alone, specific individual features that we must analyze attentively and concretely instead of resting content with generalizations about the colonial problem. . . .

Comrades, the colonial problem is assuming an ever-growing importance for us. Its growing acuteness is shown by the fact that this problem is beginning to worry our imperialist opponents more and more, and by the fact that the forces of the growing national-liberation movements are rallying and organizing their ranks, although, of course, this process is not always smooth. . . .

Hence, the Executive Committee of the Communist International has decided— it is as yet only a preliminary decision, but it will probably be endorsed by the Plenum—to place the colonial question in all its magnitude on the agenda of the next international congress of the Comintern. Everyone knows that the colonial question is acute. We have accumulated much experience; the experience of the Chinese revolution is truly inexhaustible; one can and must sum up results in this sphere and adopt a definite line of policy for various other countries. That is why this question will play a major role at the congress of the Comintern next May.[5]

116

The Need for a Communist Program in the Epoch of Wars and Revolutions

[Statement by Shumiatsky][6]

The ten years which have elapsed since the October Revolution now confront us with new tasks. . . . The present stage of the revolution has been spoken of by the Fifteenth Party Congress, which has just ended its sessions, as the epoch of "wars and revolutions." The present world situation calls for the unification of the revolutionary forces of the proletariat and the oppressed forces of the peasantry in the colonies and semicolonies. In striving for this unification we should take into account the experience of the Chinese revolution; we should try to establish one single revolutionary front against imperialism and against the "domestic" bourgeoisie of the colonies and semicolonial countries allied to it.

In order to realize the above historic tasks, and while preparing its forces for the Sixth Congress of the Communist International, international communism should aim at bringing these forces still closer together, organizing and leading them in the attack against the ideological and organizational positions of world imperialism and capitalism, against international reformism and social imperialism.

In accordance with the nature of the new epoch, the epoch of wars and revolutions, the forthcoming Sixth Congress of the Communist International must work out and adopt a clear-cut program. The program must include the characterization of the present epoch and provide a Marxist-Leninist analysis of the correlation of

---

[5] This was the Sixth Congress of the Communist International, July 18–September 1, 1928.

[6] B. Z. Shumiatsky, "Desiat let borby i ocherednye zadachi," *Revoliutsionnyi Vostok*, No. 3, 1928, pp. 5–6.

forces for the years to come; it must draw a general strategic plan of advance against reformism and social imperialism.

This program . . . must be a revolutionary program, a program of action; that is, it must not only include a theoretical basis for the developing struggle, but also provide an estimate and an account of the correlation of the existing forces. It must first of all outline and define a leading line for world communism's organized entry into the period of wars and revolutions, and for its victorious advance against world capitalism and imperialism.

117

The Merging of the Colonial Movements and the European Workers' Movement After October 1917

[Statement by the Head of the Eastern Department of the Trade Union International][7]

The greatest event of our time is the gigantic movement, as yet unknown for its breadth, of the oppressed peoples of the East. Of course, this movement is not absolutely new; its roots go deep into the past. But by its scope and nature the current movement is a natural outcome of our October Revolution, and it differs essentially from what occurred before that revolution.

For centuries history was made by the "white race." Europe, the ruler of the world, dictated its will peremptorily to the many million people of the East . . .

The story of the penetration of the "white race" into colonial countries is, as is well known, a story of endless wars, open robbery, piratic action, violence, and monstrous crimes. This was so at the time of the Spanish and Portuguese conquerors; and it is so today, when imperialism, no longer satisfied with colonial robbery, is importing its own capital into the colonies and mercilessly exploiting native workers for its own enormous profit. . . .

The Russo-Japanese war, in which the "white man," as represented by Russian tsarism, was routed by an Asian Japan, was the first severe blow to white "prestige." A much greater blow was dealt by the imperialist war of 1914–18, when by the imperialists' will hundreds of thousands of "colored" men fought in Turkey, Syria, Palestine, and also France and Belgium. The guns of the Senegal sharpshooters and Indian sepoys which fired by the order of England and France at the Germans in Flanders were also firing at the white man's traditional prestige in the colonies. The colored "slaves" saw that white men differed in no way from themselves; that they could fire upon these white men; that they, the "colored people," were an important factor in helping England and France win the war. This fact increased their self-consciousness and gave them increased confidence in their own strength. Colonial youth gained that confidence also.

Even more important, however, was the economic change in the colonies, which was evident before the war but which the war accelerated considerably, namely the industrialization of the East. . . .

Even before the war small groups of intelligentsia among the middle and petty bourgeoisie of the East protested against colonial robbery, and favored a national-liberation movement. But this "fermentation of minds" failed to reach the masses

[7] L. Geller, "Oktiabrskaia revoliutsiia i narody Vostoka," *Krasnyi Internatsional Profsoiuzov,* No. 10 (81), October 1927, pp. 306–13.

... and served simply to prepare the ground for a truly mass movement. This movement came with the October Revolution.

The October Revolution detonated the huge explosive forces that had accumulated all over the colonial East. Objective conditions were there: huge economic changes caused by industrialization, the growth of cities, the widening gap between the classes, the peasants' pauperization and loss of land, the bankruptcy of petty traders.
. . .

... Certain general characteristics mark the new epoch.

One such characteristic is the scope of the movement. It is no longer a "fermentation of minds" limited to the intelligentsia, but a mass movement. We notice it in China, India, Indonesia, Egypt, and Turkey. The advance of the basic classes—the peasantry and the proletariat—has given this movement impetus, power, political significance, and social direction, thus transforming the national-liberation movement into a nation-revolutionary movement. Herein lies the change in the character, content, and class nature of this movement. . . .

Even before the October Revolution there were Left-wing tendencies in the national movements in India, China, Turkey, and Egypt; in other words, there existed some revolutionary groups. But these groups had no definite goal, and lacked information and social basis. . . . In their pronouncements they did not go beyond political liberalism. They sought no contact with the masses, and their revolutionary spirit was given vent mainly in individual terroristic acts.

The movement acquired quite a different character in the post-October period. Let us take India, Indonesia, China, and Egypt. Everywhere we see the same, the intelligentsia, which still retains leadership, now invites the masses to support the national movement. The peasants reply with the agrarian movement, the workers with strikes. In this way, the national movement, although still directed in the interests of the capitalist bourgeoisie, acquires nonetheless a new class content, becomes revolutionized. Such is a brief picture of the evolution undergone by the national movement throughout the East.

As this movement has developed, it has acquired different characteristics in different countries . . .

The national movement in India, for example, which rose to a great height not long after the October Revolution, and called forth a great agrarian and a powerful strike movement, ebbed considerably in the years that followed, and is now [1927] in a lull. Generally speaking, because of the weak organization of both the peasantry and the workers, and because so much was left up to the middle and petty bourgeoisie, ... this movement has now passed under the control of the large-scale bourgeoisie, which fears the workers' and peasants' movement much more than it fears British imperialism. . . .

Similarly in Egypt. There, too, after a powerful upsurge in 1919–20, marked by a huge strike movement on the part of the proletariat, the Egyptian Wafd Party[8] similar to the Indian Swaraj Party, has moved into the Right-wing camp and is striving to reach an agreement with British imperialism. Consequently, we see the retreat of the masses, who no longer trust their bourgeois leaders, while the movement slackens.

Indonesia is different. There, not only Dutch, but also British, Japanese, and American capital has been active. This "united" powerful foreign capital has seized complete control of the Indonesian economy. Since Indonesia has no native capitalist bourgeoisie, no ground for agreement with imperialism exists there. The movement

---

[8] The Wafd ("Delegation") Party was a nationalist party founded in 1919 by Saad Zaghloul Pasha.

is actually clearly revolutionary, as shown by the latest uprisings; its leaders are true revolutionaries, largely Communists. In this sense the movement in Indonesia is much more mature than in British India. But the united foreign capital there is still sufficiently strong, and therefore the revolutionary movement is forced to retreat; its guerrilla detachments are not yet strong enough to fight successfully against the government troops. Nonetheless, there is no such lull in Indonesia as there is in India. The existence of peasants' and workers' organizations, of a strong communist group (in spite of executions, murders, and mass arrests), and of a close connection between the revolutionary leadership and the peasants, workers, and city poor ensure, despite a temporary defeat, the continuing activity of the movement.

. . . In China, too, the post-October period has been characterized by mass action by the workers, backed by the peasantry and the city poor. The mass character of the movement, the class demands of the workers and the peasants, the retreat of the bourgeoisie—all these are to be found in China, as in Indonesia, but on a much larger scale, expressing themselves in strikes and ruthless civil warfare. Nonetheless, certain features . . . distinguish the Chinese movement from those of India and Indonesia.

Unlike Indonesia, China has a native capitalist bourgeoisie, a group bent on manipulating the national-revolutionary movement in its own interest. Unlike India's workers' and peasants' movement, China's is almost entirely in communist hands. . . .

What does this brief outline tell us? It tells that only the participation of the workers' and peasants' masses in these movements will make them truly national-liberation movements; and that only the leadership of the proletarian party will ensure the correct nature of these movements, by making them irreconcilable to imperialism and by seeing to it that revolutionary methods are used in the struggle for the immediate needs of the peasantry and the workers. . . .

Hence follows another characteristic trait of the post-October period: the oppressed colonial peoples' merging of ranks with the world revolutionary workers' movement, with the U.S.S.R. . . .

Thus the significance of the U.S.S.R. to the national movements of the oppressed peoples of the East becomes particularly clear. . . .

Since the October Revolution, the world, and particularly the Eastern world, has not been what it was before. Look at China, India, Indonesia, Korea, Egypt, Syria, Morocco, the Philippines. Ten years ago imperialism appeared invincible in these countries. It mercilessly exploited hundreds of millions of colonial slaves, and it met with no resistance whatsoever on their part. Now we see in all these countries peoples who have made themselves free; we witness an open struggle between the oppressed and the oppressors, and while some [of these people] have not as yet openly joined the ranks of the fighters, [by their mood of discontent] they are contributing to the breaking out of the revolution in their country. The imperialists are aware of this; they have lost their self-control, which was supported by their strength, their superiority, and their conviction that nothing could threaten them. However, imperialism is far from being conquered as yet. . . . The struggle will be long and difficult, and more than once the peoples of the East who rise in revolt will suffer defeat; more than once imperialism will succeed in dealing heavy blows to the peoples struggling for their own liberation. This is inevitable. But the fall of imperialism is just as inevitable. The oppressed peoples have revolted; they have taken their destiny into their own hands, and they have been consolidating their close ties with the U.S.S.R., with the world revolutionary movement, with communism. The slogan "Proletariat and the Oppressed Peoples of the World, Unite!" is being transferred under our own eyes from a call into a living program of action, into reality. This is the way toward the World October.

118
Stalin on the Coming Upsurge in China

[Excerpt from Stalin's Speech at the Fifteenth Congress of the Russian Communist Party, December 3, 1927][9]

. . . The growth of the revolutionary movement in China, Indonesia, India, and elsewhere is bound to be a decisive blow to world imperialism.

Judge it for yourselves. Out of the world's population of 1,905 million, 1,134 million live in colonies and dependent countries, 143 million in the U.S.S.R., 264 million in the go-between countries, and only 363 million in large imperialist countries . . .

Clearly the revolutionary awakening of the colonial and dependent countries signals the end of world imperialism. The fact that the Chinese revolution has not led directly to victory over imperialism is not important. People's revolutions never win to the end in the first round of the fight. They grow and consolidate in ebbs and flows. It happened everywhere, it happened in Russia, and it will be so in China also.

What is most important is that the Chinese revolution has awakened hundreds of millions of exploited and oppressed people from centuries of slumber; that it has finally denounced the counterrevolutionary nature of the generals' clliques; that it has torn the mask from the Kuomintang lackeys of counterrevolution; that it has consolidated the atuhority of the Communist Party among the masses, raised the movement as a whole to a higher stage of development, and awakened new hopes among the millions of oppressed classes of India, Indonesia, and so forth. Only the blind and the timid-hearted can doubt the Chinese workers' and peasants' advance toward a new revolutionary upsurge.

[9] Stalin, *Sochineniia*, X, 282–83.

CHRONOLOGY

1917

October 27[1] (November 9)	Formation of the Commissariat of Nationalities (Narkomnats) with Stalin at its head.
November 2 (15)	The newly formed Soviet government declares the right to self-determination, including secession, of all peoples of Russia.
November 20 (December 3)	Appeal of the Council of People's Commissars to the Muslims of Russia and the East.
December 31 (January 13, 1918)	Council of People's Commissars declares Russian-occupied Turkish Armenia's right to self-determination, including complete independence.

1918

January 1	Southern Constitutional government under Sun Yat-sen set up at Kuomintang conference in Canton.
January 15 (28)	Third All-Russian Congress of Soviets resolves "to assist in transforming the former Russian Empire . . . into a fraternal union of soviet republics of Russia." The same congress creates the Russian Socialist Federated Soviet Republic.
January 17 (30)	Decree signed by Lenin and Stalin establishing the Commissariat for the Muslim Affairs of Inner Russia to direct work among the Muslims in Russia.
February	Turkestan Red forces rout the "Kokand Autonomy," the native Muslim autonomous government in Ferghana.
February 26	Commissariat for the Muslim Affairs of Inner Russia invites revolutionary Muslims to join the fighting ranks.
March 3	Treaty of Brest-Litovsk, between the R.S.F.S.R. and the Quadruple Alliance.
April 1	Chicherin's letter to Sun.
April 5	Japanese and English forces land at Vladivostok.
April 6	Chicherin's protest to the Allies against Allied intervention.
April 20	Fifth Regional Congress of the Turkestan Soviets establishes the Turkestan A.S.S.R. within the R.S.F.S.R.
April 22	Formation of the independent Transcaucasian Republic.

---

[1] The old-style (Julian) calendar was used in Russia until February 1, 1918 (O.S.). On that date the Gregorian calendar was adopted, the date being changed to February 14.

April 25	Baku Commune established as an independent government under communist leadership.
April 28	Turkey recognizes the Transcaucasian Republic.
May 26	The Transcaucasian Republic dissolved and Georgia's independence proclaimed.
May 28	Armenia's and Azerbaijan's independence proclaimed.
July 31	Fall of the Baku Commune.
August 1	Chicherin's reply to Sun Yat-sen's personal greetings to Lenin.
September 15	Azerbaijani national government established in Baku with Turkish military aid.
November	First Congress of the Muslim Communists in Moscow.

1919

February 25	Pan-Mongolian Conference in Chita, sponsored by Ataman Semenov.
March 2-6	Communist International established at its First Congress.
April 9	Amanullah Khan, Afghanistan's new ruler, contacts Lenin and Chicherin with an offer to establish diplomatic relations.
May	Second Pan-Mongolian Congress sponsored by Ataman Semenov.
May 19	Beginning of Turkish war of independence.
May 27	Lenin and Chicherin reply to Amanullah, recognizing Afghan independence and agreeing to establish diplomatic relations.
June 1	All-Russian Central Executive Committee establishes close military, economic, and financial alliance among the soviet republics.
June 26	Chicherin's appeal to the Mongolian people. Chicherin's note to the Persian government outlining Soviet policy toward Persia.
July 25	First Karakhan declaration to the Peking and Canton governments.
August	Soviet declaration to the Mongolian people and the Mongolian government.
August 19	Chicherin's appeal to the workers and peasants of Persia.
September 13	Chicherin's appeal to the workers and peasants of Turkey.
October	Afghan mission arrives in Moscow.
October 8	Turkestan Commission created in Moscow and ordered to Turkestan.
November 22–Dec. 3	Second Congress of the Muslim Communists in Moscow.

1920

| February | Formation of the Khorezm (formerly Khiva) People's Soviet Republic. |
| February 24 | Soviet government proposes peace negotiations to Japan. |

March 28	Congress of the Toilers of the Baikal Region in Verkhneudinsk decides to establish the Far Eastern Republic.
April 1	Allied troops (except Japanese) withdraw from Siberia.
April 6	Formation of the Far Eastern Republic. Kemal asks the Soviet government for support.
April 27	Red troops occupy Baku.
April 28	Formation of Azerbaijani S.S.R.
May 7	Peace treaty between Soviet Russia and Menshevik Georgia.
May 10	Kemal forms Ankara government.
May 14	Soviet government recognizes the Far Eastern Republic.
May 18	Soviet forces land on Persian territory (Enzeli).
May	Persia offers to establish diplomatic and trade relations with the Soviet government.
May 19	Formation of Bashkir A.S.S.R.
May 23	Formation of Indonesian Communist Party.
May 27	Formation of Tatar A.S.S.R. Ili Agreement, a trade agreement between Soviet Russia and Chinese Turkestan, signed in Tashkent.
Spring	Voitinsky and Yang Ming-chai arrive in China.
June 4	Kuchuk Khan proclaims a soviet socialist republic in Gilan.
June 22	Formation of Iranian Communist Party at its first congress.
July 15	Armistice between Far Eastern Republic and Japan.
July 19–August 7	Second Congress of the Communist International.
August 10	Treaty of Sèvres, between the Ottoman Empire and the Allied powers and others.
August 26	Formation of the Kirghiz A.S.S.R.
September 1-8	Baku Congress of the Peoples of the East.
September 5	Formation of the Bukhara People's Soviet Republic.
September 13	Preliminary treaty between the R.S.F.S.R. and Afghanistan signed in Kabul. Treaty of alliance and economic agreement between the R.S.F.S.R. and the Khorezm People's Soviet Republic.
September–Dec. 2	Turkish-Armenian armed hostilities.
September 30	Treaty of alliance and economic agreement between the R.S.F.S.R. and the Azerbaijani S.S.R.
Autumn	Mongolian delegation in Moscow. Soviet diplomatic mission sent to Ankara.
October	Persian diplomatic mission in Moscow.
October 27	Second Karakhan declaration to the Peking government handed to the Chinese mission in Moscow.
November	Representatives of various Far Eastern Left-wing groups hold conference in China.
November 29	Formation of the Armenian S.S.R.
December 2	Armenian independence recognized by Soviet Russia. Treaty of Alexandropol, between Armenia and Turkey.
Late 1920	Special Department of the Far Eastern Secretariat of the Comintern established in Irkutsk under Shumiatsky.

1921

1921	Establishment of the Profintern (Communist Trade Union International).
January 20	Caucasus Mountaineers A.S.S.R. and Daghestan A.S.S.R. formed; both soon dissolved.
February	Turkish mission arrives in Moscow.
February 25	Establishment of the Soviet government of Georgia.
February 26	Soviet-Persian treaty of friendship.
February 28	Soviet-Afghan treaty of friendship.
March 1	First Congress of the Mongolian People's Revolutionary Party held in Kiakhta.
March 4	Treaty of alliance and economic agreement between the R.S.F.S.R. and the Bukhara People's Soviet Republic.
March 16	Soviet-Turkish treaty of friendship.
March 21	Litvinov's offer to the United States to re-establish diplomatic relations.
March 25	Secretary of State Hughes rejects the Soviet offer.
April 10	Mongolian People's Provisional Government formed in Kiakhta.
April 21	All-Russian Central Executive Committee establishes the University of the Toilers of the East in Moscow.
May	British forces withdraw from Persia.
May 21	Treaty of alliance between the R.S.F.S.R. and Soviet Georgia.
May 26	Japanese-assisted anti-Soviet *coup d'état* in Vladivostok.
June 1	Chicherin's note to Great Britain, France, and Italy protesting against Japanese interference in the internal affairs of the Far Eastern Republic.
June 22–July 12	Third Congress of the Communist International.
July	Chinese Communist Party formally established at its first congress in Shanghai.
July 8	Urga (Ulan-Bator) occupied by Mongolian and Russian Red forces; limited constitutional monarchy established in Outer Mongolia.
July 19	Soviet Russia protests its exclusion from the Washington Conference on Naval Disarmament and Far Eastern Affairs.
August 13–16	First congress of the people of the Uriankhai region.
August 26– April 16, 1922	Dairen Conference between the Far Eastern Republic and Japan.
September 7	British note to the Soviet government concerning Russian Communist activities in the Near East.
September 8	Last Soviet troops leave Persia. All-Russian Central Executive Committee forms the Turkestan A.S.S.R.
September 30	Treaty of alliance between the R.S.F.S.R. and the Armenian S.S.R.
October	Special Mongolian mission to Moscow.

October 13	Treaty of Kars, between Turkey and the Soviet republics of Armenia, Georgia, and Azerbaijan, with the R.S.F.S.R. participating in the negotiations.
October 29	Formation of the Tuvinian People's Revolutionary Party.
November 2	Second Soviet note to Great Britain, France, Italy, Japan, and the United States protesting Russia's exclusion from the Washington Conference.
November 5	Treaty of friendship between Soviet Russia and the Mongolian People's Republic.
November 12– February 6, 1922	Washington Conference on Naval Disarmament and Far Eastern Affairs.
December	Founding of the Tannu-Tuva Republic.
December 12	Founding of the Scientific Association for Eastern Studies under Pavlovich (Veltman).

1922

January 21–27	First Congress of the Toilers of the Far East held in Moscow and Petrograd.
February 22	Signing of the protocol authorizing R.S.F.S.R. representatives to represent the lesser soviet republics also at the forthcoming Genoa Conference.
February 28–March 1	First Congress of the Tuvinian People's Revolutionary Party.
March 12	Formation of the Transcaucasian S.F.S.R.
April 27	Formation of the Yakut A.S.S.R.
June–July	Second Congress of the Chinese Communist Party.
July 5	Founding of the Japanese Communist Party.
September 2	Ioffe's memorandum to the Peking government.
September 4–14	Changchun Conference between Japan and the Far Eastern Republic, with Ioffe participating.
October 25	End of Japanese intervention in the Far East.
November 5– December 5	Fourth Congress of the Communist International, at which formation of Japanese Communist Party was announced.
November 15	Far Eastern Republic incorporated into the R.S.F.S.R.
November 20– July 24, 1923	The Lausanne Conference on Near Eastern problems.
December 26	Tenth All-Russian Congress of Soviets drafts a treaty of union between the R.S.F.S.R., the Ukrainian S.S.R., the Belorussian S.S.R., and the Transcaucasian Federation.
December 30	First Congress of Soviets of the Union of Soviet Socialist Republics declares formation of the U.S.S.R.
1922	Formation of the People's Party of Inner Mongolia. Trial of fifteen Moscow-trained Indians students in Peshawar (Tashkent Conspiracy Case).

1923

January 26	Chinese Communist Party, on ECCI instructions, forms a bloc with the Kuomintang. Sun and Ioffe issue a joint policy statement at a conference in Shanghai.

May 8	"Curzon Ultimatum" accuses Russia of anti-British propaganda in the East.
May 10	Soviet Russia's reply to the "Curzon Ultimatum."
June	Third Congress of the Chinese Communist Party endorses alliance with the Kuomintang.
July 24	Signing of the Straits convention.
September	Borodin arrives in Canton.
September 2	Karakhan arrives in Peking to conduct negotiations with the Peking government.
October 16	Krestintern (Peasant International, also known as the International Peasant Council) founded in Moscow.
December 16	Chicherin's proposal to resume diplomatic relations with the United States.
December 18	Hughes declines Chicherin's offer.

1924

January 20	First Congress of the Kuomintang in Canton.
January 21	Lenin's death.
January 31	Constitution adopted by the Second Congress of Soviets of the U.S.S.R.
March 14	Preliminary agreement in Peking between Soviet Russia and China.
April 9	Dissolution of Narkomnats.
May 31	Resumption of official relations between the Peking and Soviet governments.
Spring	Dissolution of the Japanese Communist Party.
June 17–July 8	Fifth Congress of the Communist International.
August 4–31	Third Congress of the Mongolian People's Revolutionary Party.
August	Insurrection in Georgia suppressed.
September 20	Mukden Agreement, between the Soviet government and Chang Tso-lin.
October 14	Formation of the Tadzhik A.S.S.R.
October 27	Formation of the Uzbek A.S.S.R. First Huruldan of the Mongolian People's Republic adopts constitution. Cawnpore conspiracy trial in India.
December	Establishment of the International Women's Secretariat as a department of the Comintern. Soviet troops withdraw from Mongolia.

1925

January 20	Convention between Soviet Russia and Japan.
March 12	Death of Sun Yat-sen.
April 4	Japanese troops evacuate Northern Sakhalin.
May 30	Shanghai incident; demonstrating Chinese fired upon by British troops.
September	Sun Yat-sen University, later called the Communist University of the Toilers of China, established in Moscow.

September 23–Oct. 2	Fourth Congress of the Mongolian People's Revolutionary Party.
October	First Congress of the People's Party of Inner Mongolia held at Kalgan.
November 1	Foundation of the Labor Swaraj Party of the All-India National Congress.
December 1	Locarno treaties, between the Allies and Germany, signed in London after preliminary negotiations at Locarno.
December 17	Treaty of neutrality and friendship between Soviet Russia and Turkey.
December 28	All-India Communist Conference held in Cawnpore.

1926

February 6	Formation of the Workers' and Peasants' Party of Bengal.
March 20	Chiang Kai-shek closes trade unions and arrests Communist political workers in Canton.
August 31	Treaty of neutrality and nonaggression between Soviet Russia and Afghanistan.
November	Communist uprising in Java.
Mid-November	Chicherin and Turkey's foreign minister meet at Odessa.
November 24	Tannu-Tuva Republic's constitution confirmed by Fourth Great Huruldan.
December 4	Japanese Communist Party formed for the second time.

1927

January	Communist uprising in Sumatra.
February 7–14	League to Struggle Against Imperialism and Oppression of the Peoples of the East founded in Brussels.
April 6	Police raid on the Soviet embassy in Peking.
April 12	Anticommunist coup by Chiang Kai-shek in Shanghai.
April 17	Diplomatic relations established between Soviet Russia and Saudi Arabia.
May 20–26	Pan-Pacific Trade Union Conference held in Hankow.
May 27	Great Britain severs diplomatic relations with Soviet Russia and terminates the trade agreement of 1921.
September 5–18	Autumn harvest insurrection in Hunan, led by Mao Tse-tung.
October 1	Treaty of nonaggression and neutrality between Soviet Russia and Persia.
December 2–19	Fifteenth Congress of the Russian Communist Party.
December 11–14	Communist uprising in Canton.
December 14	Chiang Kai-shek severs relations with Soviet Russia.
December 17	Soviet-Turkish treaty of friendship and neutrality of 1925 renewed.

BIBLIOGRAPHY

The bibliography lists only the materials consulted by the authors in preparing this volume. Except for a few items marked with an asterisk (*), the sources listed below are in the Hoover Library, Stanford, Calif. Each section of the bibliography contains an alphabetical list of books and leaflets, followed by an alphabetical list of articles in periodicals and newspapers. The names of periodicals are given in full, with three exceptions: *K.I.* (*Kommunisticheskii Internatsional*), *N.V.* (*Novyi Vostok*), and *Z.N.* (*Zhizn Natsionalnostei*). Official publications, treaties, and series of periodicals and newspapers are listed separately.

GENERAL

Agabekov, G. S. *O.G.P.U. The Russian Secret Terror.* New York, 1931. Translated from the French.

Agrarnyi vopros na Vostoke. Sbornik statei (The agrarian problem in the East. A collection of articles). Moscow, Mezhdunarodnyi Agrarnyi Institut (International Agrarian Institute), 1933.

Akulinin, I. G. *Orenburgskoe Kazache Voisko v borbe s bolshevikami, 1917–1920* (The Orenburg Cossacks in the struggle against the Bolsheviks, 1917–1920). Shanghai, 1937.

Andrievich, V. K. *Istoriia Sibiri. Chast I: Period ot drevneishikh vremen do ustanovleniia goroda Tobolska i osnovaniia Irkutskogo ostroga* (History of Siberia. Part I: From ancient times to the founding of the city of Tobolsk and the fortress of Irkutsk). St. Petersburg, 1889.

Arsharuni, A. M., and Kh. Gabidullin. *Ocherki panislamizma i pantiurkizma v Rossii* (An outline of Pan-Muslimism and Pan-Turkism in Russia). Riazan, 1931.

Avarin, V. Ia. *Imperializm v Manchzhurii, tom I: Etapy imperialisticheskoi borby za Manchzhuriiu* (Imperialism in Manchuria, Vol. I: Stages of the imperialist struggle in Manchuria). 2d ed. Moscow, 1934.

Balabushevich, V. *Rabochie organizatsii Vostoka* (Workers' organizations in the East). Moscow, 1927. Edited by L. Geller.

Ball, William M. *Nationalism and Communism in East Asia.* Melbourne, 1952. Published under the auspices of the Institute of Pacific Relations.

Barbusse, Henry (comp.). *The Soviet Union and Peace; the Most Important of the Documents Issued by the Government of the U.S.S.R. concerning Peace and Disarmament from 1917 to 1929.* London, 1929.

Barmine, Alexandre. *One Who Survived: The Life Story of a Russian Under the Soviets.* New York, 1945.

Bartold, V. V. *La Découverte de l'Asie. Histoire de l'orientalisme en Europe et en Russie.* Paris, 1947.

———. *Istoriia izucheniia Vostoka v Evrope i Rossii* (The study of the East in Europe and in Russia). Leningrad, 1925.

Bedi, Baba Pyare Lal (ed.). *Muslims in USSR.* Lahore, India, 1947.

Bell, Sir Charles A. *Tibet: Past and Present.* Oxford, 1924.

Bocharov, A. K. *Milli Firka; natsionalnaia kontr-revoliutsiia v Krymu* (Milli Firka [national independence] ; national counterrevolution in the Crimea). Simferopol, 1930.

Bogdanov, M. N. *Ocherki istorii Buriat-mongolskogo naroda* (Essays in the history of the Buriat-Mongol people). Verkhneudinsk, 1926.

Borisov, T. K. *Kalmykiia; istoriko-politicheskii i sotsialno-ekonomicheskii ocherk* (Kalmuk land; historico-political and socio-economic sketch). Moscow-Leningrad, 1926.

Bulletin of Proceedings [of the Pan-Pacific Trade Union Conference], Nos. 1–5. Hankow, May 1927.

Bukharin, N. I. *L'Economie mondiale et l'impérialisme; esquisse économique.* Paris, 1928.

Bunyan, James, and H. H. Fisher. *The Bolshevik Revolution, 1917–1918; Documents and Materials.* Stanford, Calif., 1934.

Carr, E. H. *The Bolshevik Revolution, 1917–1923.* 3 vols. London and New York, 1951–53.

Castagné, Joseph A. *Le bolchévisme et l'Islam* . . . Paris, 1922. Two volumes in one.

Cleinow, George. *Neu-Sibirien (Sib-Krai); Eine Studie zum Aufmarsch der Sowjetmacht in Asien.* Berlin, 1928.

Conolly, Violet. *Soviet Economic Policy in the East; Turkey, Persia, Afghanistan, Mongolia and Tana Tuva, Sin Kiang.* London, 1933.

———. *Soviet Trade from the Pacific to the Levant.* London, 1935.

Contribution à l'étude du problème national en U.R.S.S. Paris, 1948.

Cressey, George B. *Asia's Lands and Peoples. A Geography of One-Third of the Earth and Two-Thirds of Its People.* New York and London, 1944.

———. *The Basis of Soviet Strength.* New York and London, 1945.

Dallin, David J. *The Rise of Russia in Asia.* New Haven, 1949.

———. *Soviet Russia and the Far East.* New Haven, 1948.

Davis, Malcolm W., and Walter H. Mallory (eds.). *A Political Handbook of the World, 1928. Parliaments, Parties and Press as of January 1, 1928.* New York, 1928. Published by the Council of Foreign Relations.

Dedijer, Vladimir. *Tito.* New York, 1953.

Degras, Jane (Tabrisky) (comp.). *Calendar of Soviet Documents on Foreign Policy, 1917–1941.* London, 1948.

———. *The Communist International, 1919–1943; documents* . . . London, 1956–.

———. *Soviet Documents on Foreign Policy.* 2 vols. London and New York, 1951–52.

Dennett, Tyler. *Roosevelt and the Russo-Japanese War. A Critical Study of American Policy in Eastern Asia Based Primarily upon the Private Papers of Theodore Roosevelt* . . . Garden City, N.Y., 1925.

Dennis, A. L. P. *The Foreign Policies of Soviet Russia.* New York, 1924.

Diplomaticheskii Slovar (Dictionary of diplomacy). 2 vols. Moscow, 1948–50.

Dobrov, A. S. *Dalnevostochnaia politika SSHA v period russko-iaponskoi voiny* (The Far Eastern policy of the U.S.A. during the Russo-Japanese War). Moscow, 1952.

Dumbadze, E. V. *Na Sluzhbe Cheka i Kominterna. Lichnye vospomianiia* (In the service of the Cheka and the Comintern. Personal reminiscences). Paris, 1930.

Eidus, Khaim T. *Ocherki rabochego dvizheniia v stranakh Vostoka* (An outline of the workers' movement in the countries of the East). Moscow, 1922.

Eudin, Xenia Joukoff, and H. H. Fisher. *Soviet Russia and the West, 1920–1927, A Documentary Survey.* Stanford, 1957.

Farberov, N. P. *Gosudarstvennoe pravo stran narodnoi demokratii* (Political law of the countries of people's democracy). Moscow, 1949.

Filchner, Wilhelm. *Sturm über Asien, Erlebnisse eines diplomatischen Gegeim-agenten* . . . Berlin, 1924.

Fischer, Louis. *The Soviets in World Affairs. A History of the Relations Between the Soviet Union and the Rest of the World, 1917–1929.* 2d ed., 2 vols. Princeton, 1951.

Florinsky, M. T. *World Revolution and the U.S.S.R.* New York, 1933.

French, F. J. F. *From Whitehall to the Caspian.* London, 1920.

Freund, Heinrich. *Russia from A to Z* . . . Sydney and London, 1945.

Frunze, M. V. *Sobranie sochinenii, tom I: 1905–1923 gody* (Collected works, Vol. I: 1905–1923). Moscow, 1929.

Galkovich, M. G. *S. Shtaty i dalnevostochnaia problema* (The United States and the Far Eastern problem). Moscow, 1928.

Galperin, A. *Anglo-iaponskii soiuz, 1902–1921* (The Anglo-Japanese alliance, 1902–1921). Moscow, 1947.

Gautherot, Gustave. *Le Bolshévisme aux colonies et l'impérialisme rouge.* Paris, 1930.

Gourou, Pierre. *L'Asie.* Paris, 1953. Geography, ethnography with maps.

Grekov, B. D. *Zolotaia Orda i ee padenie* (The Golden Horde and its fall). Moscow, 1950. Introduction by A. Iu. Iakubovsky.

[Gurko-]Kriazhin, V. A. *Natsionalno-osvoboditelnoe dvizhenie na Blizhnem Vostoke. Ch. I: Siriia i Palestina, Kilikiia, Mesopotamiia i Egipet* (The national-liberation movement in the Near East. Part I: Syria and Palestine, Cilicia, Mesopotamia and Egypt). Moscow, 1923.

Gurvich, G. S. *Istoriia sovetskoi konstitutsii* (History of the Soviet constitution). Moscow, 1923.

——. *Osnovy sovetskoi konstitutsii* (The principles of the Soviet constitution). Vol. I. Moscow, 1922.

Hurwicz, Elias. *Der neue Osten; Wandlungen und Aussichten.* Berlin, 1927.

——. *Die Orientpolitik der dritten Internationale.* Berlin, 1922.

Ichihashi, Yamato. *The Washington Conference and After; A Historical Survey.* Stanford, Calif., 1928.

Isaacs, Harold R. *No Peace for Asia.* New York, 1947.

Kantarovich, A. Ia., and L. Ivanov. *Borba za Tikhii Okean; Voenno-morskie sily imperialisticheskikh derzhav* (The struggle for the Pacific; military and naval forces of the imperialist powers). Moscow, 1932.

Kartsov, V. G. *Ocherk istorii narodov severo-zapadnoi Sibiri* (Outline of history of the peoples of northwestern Siberia). Moscow, 1937.

Kerner, R. J. *Northeastern Asia; a Selected Bibliography.* 2 vols. Berkeley, Calif., 1939.

——. The Urge to the Sea. The Course of Russian History. The Role of Rivers, Portages, Ostrogs, Monasteries and Furs. Berkeley, Calif., 1942.

Kohn, Hans. *Geschichte der nationalen Bewegung im Orient.* Berlin, 1928.

Kolarz, Walter. *The Peoples of the Soviet Far East.* New York, 1954.

——. *Russia and Her Colonies.* London, 1952.

Korostovets, I. Ia. *Rossiia na Dalnem Vostoke* (Russia in the Far East). Peking, 1922.

Krasin, L. B. *Planovoe khoziaistvo i monopoliia vneshnei torgovli* (Planned economy and the monopoly of foreign trade). Moscow, 1925.

——. *Vneshtorg i vneshniaia ekonomicheskaia politika sovetskogo pravitelstva* (The Commissariat of Foreign Trade and the foreign economic policy of the Soviet government). Petersburg, 1921.

——. *Voprosy vneshnei torgovli* (Problems of foreign trade). Moscow, 1928.

Krausse, A. *Russia in Asia. A Record and a Study, 1558–1899.* New York, 1899.

Krizis kolonialnoi sistemy. Natsionalno-osvoboditelnaia borba narodov Vostochnoi

Azii (The crisis of the colonial system. The national-liberation struggle of the peoples of Eastern Asia). Moscow, Akademiia Nauk SSSR (Academy of Sciences of the U.S.S.R.), 1949.

Lacoste, Raymond. *La Russie soviétique et la question d'Orient, la poussée soviétique vers les mers chaudes, Méditerranée et Golfe persique.* Paris, 1946.

Langer, W. L. *The Diplomacy of Imperialism, 1890–1902.* 2 vols. New York and London, 1935.

Lattimore, Owen. *Manchuria, Cradle of Conflict.* New York, 1932.

Lenin, V. I. *Imperialism, the Highest Stage of Capitalism.* Moscow, 1947.

———. *Leninskii Sbornik* (Lenin's miscellaneous notes). 35 vols. Moscow, 1924–45. Published under the auspices of the Marx-Engels-Lenin Institute.

———. *Selected Works.* 12 vols. New York, 1935–38.

———. *Sochineniia* (Works). 2d ed., 30 vols., Moscow and Leningrad, 1926–32; 4th ed., 35 vols., Moscow, 1941–50.

Leontiev, K. N. *Sobranie sochinenii, tom VI: Vostok, Rossiia i Slavianstvo* (Collected works, Vol. VI: The East, Russia, and the Slavs). Moscow, 1912.

Lobanov-Rostovsky, Andrei. *Russia and Asia.* New York, 1933.

Lozovsky, *see* Dridzo

Maisky, I. M. *Vneshniaia politika R.S.F.S.R., 1917–1922* (The foreign policy of the R.S.F.S.R., 1917–1922). Moscow, 1922.

Maksimov, A. N. *Kakie narody zhivut v Rossii* (The peoples who live in Russia). Moscow, 1919.

Marx, Karl. *Capital. A Critical Analysis of Capitalist Production.* London, 1889. Translated from the third German edition.

———. *Manifesto of the Communist Party by Karl Marx and Friedrich Engels.* New York, 1935.

Karl Marx and Frederick Engels on Britain. Moscow, 1953.

Materialy po izucheniiu Vostoka . . . nepodlezhashchie oglasheniiu (Materials for the study of the East . . . Restricted use only). 2 vols. St. Petersburg, 1909–15.

Matveev, Z. N. *Chto chitat o Dalne-Vostochnoi Oblasti* (What to read on the Far Eastern region). Vladivostok, 1925.

Mikhailov, N. N. *Across the Map of the U.S.S.R.* Moscow, 1949.

———. *Soviet Geography. The New Industrial and Economic Distributions of the U.S.S.R.* London, 1935.

Millard, Th. F. F. *Our Far Eastern Question: America's Contact with the Orient and the Trend of Relations with China and Japan.* New York, 1916.

Miliukov, P. N. *La politique extérieure des Soviets.* Paris, 1934.

———. *Rossiia na perelome. Bolshevistskii period russkoi revoliutsii* (Russia in a crisis. The Bolshevik period of the Russian revolution). 3 vols. Paris, 1927.

Morse, H. B., and H. F. MacNair. *Far Eastern International Relations.* Boston and New York, 1931.

Muchnik, G. S. *Dvatsat let partiinoi raboty v Sibiri i na Dalnem Vostoke* (Twenty years of party work in Siberia and in the Far East). Moscow, 1935.

Natsionalno-kolonialnye problemy; sbornik materialov (National and colonial problems; a collection of materials). Moscow, Nauchno-Issledovatelskii Institut po Izucheniiu Natsionalnykh i Kolonialnykh Problem (Research Institute for the Study of the National and Colonial Problems), 1937.

Nazarov, P. S. *Moved On! From Kashgar to Kashmir.* London, 1935.

Nikiforov, P. M. *Istoricheskie dokumenty o deistviiakh i zamyslakh mezhdunarodnykh khishchnikov na Dalnem Vostoke* (Historical documents on the activities and plans of the international vultures in the Far East). Moscow, 1923.

Norton, H. K. *The Far Eastern Republic of Siberia,* London, 1923.

Ocherki po novoi istorii stran Srednego Vostoka: Afganistan, Iran, Indiia (An outline of the modern history of the countries of the Middle East: Afghanistan, Iran, India). Moscow, 1951.

Ogorodnikov, V. I. *Ocherk istorii Sibiri. Chast I: Istoriia do-russkoi Sibiri* (An outline of the history of Siberia. Part I: The pre-Russian period). Irkutsk, 1920.

Onraet, René H. de S. *Singapore—A Police Background.* London, 1947.

Ordzhonikidze, G. K. *Izbrannye stati i rechi, 1911–1937* (Selected works and speeches, 1911–1937). Moscow, 1939.

Ot Vashingtona do Genui (From Washington to Genoa). Moscow, Vysshii Voennyi Redaktsionnyi Sovet (Supreme Military Editorial Council), 1922.

Oudendijk, W. J. *Ways and By-Ways in Diplomacy.* London, 1939.

Papukchieva, Maria. *La politique de la Russie à l'égard des Détroits.* Lausanne, 1944.

Parfenov, P. S. *Borba za Dalnii Vostok, 1920–1922* (The struggle for the Far East, 1920-1922). Leningrad, 1928.

Partiia i Komintern; o "staroi" i "novoi" oppozitsii. Sbornik rezoliutsii i postanovlenii (The party and the Comintern; the "old" and the "new" opposition. A collection of resolutions and decisions). 2d enlarged ed. Moscow, 1931.

Partizanskoe dvizhenie v Sibiri (The partisan movement in Siberia). Moscow and Leningrad, Tsentralnoe Arkhivnoe Upravlenie (Central Archives Administration), 1925.

Pasvolsky, Leo. *Russia in the Far East.* New York, 1922.

Pavlovich, *see* Veltman

Payne, P. S. R. *Red Storm over Asia.* New York, 1951.

Phillips, G. D. R. *Dawn in Siberia; the Mongols of Lake Baikal* . . . London, 1943.

———. *Russia, Japan and Mongolia* . . . London, 1942.

Pokrovsky, M. N. *Vneshniaia politika Rossii v XX veke* (Russia's foreign policy in the twentieth century). Moscow, 1926.

Potemkin, V. P. (ed.). *Istoriia diplomatii* (History of diplomacy). 3 vols. Moscow, 1941–45.

Price, Ernest Batson. *The Russo-Japanese Treaties of 1907–1916 Concerning Manchuria and Mongolia.* Baltimore, 1933.

Programmnye dokumenty kommunisticheskikh partii Vostoka (Program documents of the communist parties of the East). Moscow, Marx-Engels-Lenin Institute, 1934.

Radek, Karl. *Likvidatsiia Versalskogo mira; doklad IV kongressu Kommunisticheskogo Internatsionala* (The winding up of the Versailles treaty; report to the Fourth Congress of the Communist International). Petrograd, 1922.

Rapport sur la préparation par le Gouvernement Soviétique des révoltes coloniales. The Hague, The Hague International Colonial Bureau, 193–.

Resolutions and Decisions of the Pan-Pacific Trade Union Conference. Hankow, China, May 1927.

Revoliutsiia na Dalnem Vostoke (Revolution in the Far East). Moscow, 1923.

Romainville, François de. *L'Islam et l'U.R.S.S.* Paris, 1947.

Romanov, B. A. *Ocherki diplomaticheskoi istorii russko-iaponskoi voiny, 1895–1907* (Essays on the diplomatic history of the Russo-Japanese War, 1895–1907). Moscow, Akademiia Nauk, 1947.

———. Rossiia v Manchzhurii (1892–1906); ocherki po istorii vneshnei politiki samoderzhaviia v epokhu imperializma. Leningrad, 1928. An English translation, *Russia in Manchuria (1892–1906). Essays on a History of the Foreign Policy of Tsarist Russia in the Epoch of Imperialism* (Ann Arbor, Michigan, 1952), has been published by the Council of Learned Societies.

Rotshtein, F. A. (ed.). *Mirovaia politika v 1924 godu; sbornik statei* . . . (World politics in 1924; a collection of articles. . . .) Moscow, 1925.

Roy, M. N. *Die Internationalen Verbündeten der Opposition in der KPdSU.* Hamburg, 1928.

———. *The Russian Revolution.* Calcutta, 1949.

Rozhkova, M. K. *Ekonimicheskaia politika tsarskogo pravitelstva na Srednem Vostoke vo vtoroi chetverti XIX veka a russkaia burzhuaziia* (Economic policy of the tsarist government in the Middle East in the second quarter of the nineteenth century and the Russian bourgeoisie). Moscow, 1949.

Rykov, A. I. *Russia's Foreign Policy Outlined by Mr. A. I. Rykov (Chairman of the Council of People's Commissaries) at the Soviet Congress of the Union of Socialist Soviet Republics on April 19th, 1927* . . . London, 1927.

———. *Sotsialisticheskoe stroitelstvo i mezhdunarodnaia politika SSSR* . . . (Socialist construction and the international policy of the U.S.S.R. Report to the Fourth Congress of Soviets). Moscow and Leningrad, 1927.

Safarov, G. *Marx and the East.* New York, 1934.

———. *Osnovy Leninizma* (The bases of Leninism). 2d ed. Leningrad, 1924.

———. *Problemy Vostoka.* (Problems of the East). Petrograd, 1922.

Schmitz, Paul. *Moskau und die islamische Welt.* München, 1938.

Semennikov, V. P. (ed.). *Za kulisami tsarizma. Arkhiv tibetskogo vracha Badmaeva* (Behind the stage of tsarism. Archives of the Tibetan physician Badmaev). Leningrad, 1925.

Semionov, Youri. *La conquête de la Sibérie du IX au XIX siècle.* Paris, 1938. With chronology.

Seton-Watson, Hugh. *The Decline of Imperial Russia.* London, 1952.

Shabad, Theodore. *Geography of the U.S.S.R. A Regional Survey.* New York, 1951.

Shumiatsky, B. Z. *Borba za russkii Dalnii Vostok. Sbornik materialov* . . . (The struggle for the Russian Far East. A collection of materials . . .). Irkutsk, 1922.

Sliozberg, G. B. *Dorevoliutsionnyi stroi Rossii* (Prerevolutionary [political] order in Russia). Paris, 1933.

Stalin, I. V. *Ob oppozitsii; stati i rechi 1921–1927 g.g.* (On the opposition; articles and speeches, 1921–1927). Moscow and Leningrad, 1928.

———. *O politicheskikh zadachakh universiteta narodov Vostoka* (On the political tasks of the University of the Peoples of the East). Leningrad, 1925.

———. *Sochineniia* (Works). I–. Moscow, 1946–.

———. *Voprosy Leninizma* (Problems of Leninism). 11th ed. Moscow, 1947.

———. *Works.* I–. Moscow, 1951–.

Stankevich, V. B. *Sudby narodov Rossii. Belorussia. Ukraina. Litva. Latviia. Estoniia. Armeniia. Gruziia. Azerbaidzhan. Finliandiia. Polsha* (The destiny of the peoples of Russia: Belorussia, the Ukraine, Lithuania, Latvia, Estonia, Armenia, Georgia, Azerbaijan, Finland, Poland). Berlin, 1921.

Sultan-Galiev, M. *Metody anti-religioznoi propagandy sredi musulman* (Methods of antireligious propaganda among the Muslims). Moscow, 1922. Also in article form: Z.N., No. 29 (127), December 14, 1921, and No. 30 (128), December 23, 1921.

Sultan-Zade, A. (pseud.). *Ekonomika i problemy natsionalnykh revoliutsii v stranakh Blizhnego i Dalnego Vostoka* (Economics and problems of the national revolutions in the countries of the Near and Far East). Moscow, 1921.

———. (ed.). *Kolonialnyi Vostok; sotsialno-ekonomicheskie ocherki* . . . (The colonial East; socioeconomic essays . . .). Moscow, 1924.

Svatikov, S. G. *Rossiia i Sibir. K istorii sibirskogo oblastnichestva v XIX v.*

(Russia and Siberia. The story of Siberian regionalism in the nineteenth century). Prague, 1930.

Tamarin, Aleksandr. *Musulmane na Russi* (The Muslims in Russia). Moscow, 1917.

Tanin, M. *Mezhdunarodnaia politika S.S.S.R. (1917–1924)* (International policies of the U.S.S.R., 1917–1924). Moscow, 1925.

————. *10 let vneshnei politiki S.S.S.R. (1917–1927)* (Ten years of U.S.S.R. foreign policy, 1917–1927). Moscow and Leningrad, 1927.

Thompson, Virginia McLean. *The Left Wing in Southeast Asia*. New York, 1950.

———— and Richard Adloff (comps.). "Who's Who in South-East Asia, August 1945–December 1949." Microfilm copy of manuscript cards.

Tompkins, Pauline. *American-Russian Relations in the Far East*. New York, 1948.

Torgovye otnosheniia S.S.S.R. so stranami Vostoka (Trade relations between the U.S.S.R. and the countries of the East). Moscow, 1938.

Toynbee, Arnold J. (ed.). *Survey of International Affairs, 1920–1927*. 7 vols. London, 1925–28.

Trade and Industries of the Far Eastern Republic. Washington, D. C., 1922. Published by the Special Delegation of the Far Eastern Republic to the United States of America.

Treat, P. J. *The Far East: A Political and Diplomatic History*. New York and London, 1928.

Troianovsky, K. M. *Vostok i revoliutsiia. Popytka postroeniia novoi politicheskoi programmy dlia tuzemnykh stran Vostoka—Indii, Persii i Kitaia* (The East and the revolution; an outline of a new political program for the countries of the East—India, Persia, and China). Moscow, 1918.

Trotsky, L. D. *Stalin, an Appraisal of the Man and His Influence*. New York, 1941.

Tsypkin, S. (comp.). *Oktiabrskaia revoliutsiia i grazhdanskaia voina na Dalnem Vostoke. Khronika sobytii 1917–1922 gg.* (The October Revolution and civil war in the Far East. Chronicle of events, 1917–1922). Moscow and Khabarovsk, 1933.

Ukhtomsky, E. E. *K sobytiiam v Kitae. Ob otnoshenii Zapada i Rossii k Vostoku* (The events in China. On the relations of the West and Russia to the East). St. Petersburg, 1900.

Valtin, Jan (Herman Krebs). *Out of the Night*. New York, 1941.

Varga, Eugen. *Lenin i problemy sovremennogo imperializma. Sbornik* (Lenin and the problem of modern imperialism. A collection [of articles]). Moscow, 1934.

————. *The Process of Capitalist Decline; Report to the Fourth Congress of the Communist International*. Hamburg, 1922.

Vashingtonskaia konferentsiia po ogranicheniiu vooruzhenii i tikho-okeanskim i dalne-vostochnym voprosam 1921–1922 g. (The Washington Conference on the Limitation of Armament and on the Pacific and Far Eastern Problems, 1921–1922). Moscow, 1924. Documents translated by A. V. Sabanin.

Veltman, M. L. (M. Pavlovich). *The Foundations of Imperialist Policy; A Course of Lectures Read to the Academy of the General Staff in 1918–1919*. London, 1922. Translated from the Russian.

————. *Imperializm i borba za velikie zheleznodorozhnye i morskie puti budushchago; k voprosu o prichinakh mirovoi voiny* (Imperialism and the struggle for the great railway and sea routes of the future; on the causes of the World War). Moscow, 1925.

————. *Pered ugrozoi budushchikh voin* (Under the threat of future wars). 2d ed. Moscow, 1924.

————. *Sovetskaia Rossiia i kapitalisticheskaia Amerika* (Soviet Russia and capitalist America). Moscow, 1922. Vol III in the series *R.S.F.S.R. v imperialisticheskom okruzhenii* (The R.S.F.S.R. in the imperialist encirclement).

———. *Sovetskaia Rossiia i kapitalisticheskaia Angliia* . . . (Soviet Russia and capitalist England . . .). 2d ed. Moscow, 1925. Vol. II in *R.S.F.S.R. v. imperialisticheskom okruzhenii.*

*Vernadsky, George. *The Mongols and Russia.* New Haven, 1953.

———. *Protiv solntsa. Rasprostranenie russkago gosudarstva k vostoku* (Against the sun. The expansion of the Russian state eastward). Moscow, 1914. Reprint from *Russkaia Mysl* (Russian Thought), 1914.

Ves S.S.S.R. Spravochnaia i adresnaia kniga na 1926 god (The U.S.S.R.: Reference and address book for 1926). Moscow and Leningrad, 1926.

Vilensky, V. D. (Sibiriakov). *Rossiia na Dalnem Vostoke* (Russia in the Far East). Moscow, 1923.

Vlugt, Ebed van der. *Asia Aflame; Communism in the East.* New York, 1953.

White, John A. *The Siberian Intervention.* Princeton, 1950.

Williams, E. T. *Tibet and her Neighbors.* Berkeley, Calif., 1937.

Williams, W. A. *American-Russian Relations.* New York, 1952.

Witte, S. Iu. *Vospominaniia. Tsarstvovanie Nikolaia II* (Memoirs. The reign of Nicholas II). 2 vols. Berlin, 1922.

Yakhontoff, V. A. *Russia and the Soviet Union in the Far East.* New York, 1931.

Zhukov, E. N. (ed.). *Mezhdunarodnye otnosheniia na Dalnem Vostoke (1870–1945 g.g.)* (International relations in the Far East, 1870–1945). Moscow, Akademiia Nauk, 1951.

Altdorffer, H. von. "Die Kongresse der Mohammedaner Russlands in Kazan." *Der Neue Orient,* Band II, No. 1, October 1917, pp. 14–15.

Anuchin, D. "Aziia kak prarodina i uchitelnitsa chelovechestva; ee nastoiashchee i budushchee" (Asia as a birthplace and teacher of mankind; its present and future). *N.V.,* No. 1, 1922, pp. 232–49.

"Appeal to the Proletariat of the World and the Oppressed People, April 1927," by the ECCI. *International Press Correspondence,* No. 26, April 21, 1927.

Berlin, L. "Angliia i Tibet" (England and Tibet). *N.V.,* No. 2, 1922, pp. 355–66.

"Le Bolchévisme et l'Islam." *Revue du Monde Musulman,* LI and LII, October and December, 1922.

Broido, G. I. "Kommunisticheskii Universitet Trudiashchikhsia Vostoka" (The Communist University of the Toilers of the East). *Z.N.,* No. 11 (109), May 28, 1921, p. 1.

———. "Ocherednye zadachi Kommunisticheskogo Universiteta Trudiashchikhsia Vostoka" (The immediate tasks of the Communist University of the Toilers of the East). *Z.N.,* No. 3 (9), March 14, 1922, p. 5.

Charnyi, M. "V Kommunisticheskom Universitete Trudiiashchikhsia Vostoka," *Z.N.,* No. 29 (127), December 14, 1921, p. 2.

Chervonnyi, A. (B. Z. Shumiatsky). "10 let borby i ocherednye zadachi" (Ten years of struggle and the immediate tasks). *Revoliutsionnyi Vostok,* No. 3, 1928, pp. 5–21.

Chicherin, G. V. "Rossiia i aziatskie narody" (Russia and the Asian peoples). *Vestnik Narodnogo Komissariata po Inostrannym Delam,* No. 2, August 12, 1919, pp. 1–7.

———. "Stenogramma obshchego sobraniia chlenov Rossiisko-Vostochnoi Torgovoi Palaty, 12 okt. 1926 g." (Minutes of the general meeting of the Russian Eastern Chamber of Commerce, Oct. 12, 1926). *Torgovlia Rossii s Vostokom,* Oct.-Dec., 1926, pp. 23–31. Speech by Chicherin, pp. 23–24.

Dimanshtein, S. M. "Metody revoliutsionnoi i kommunisticheskoi propagandy na

Vostoke" (Methods of revolutionary and communist propaganda in the East). *Z.N.,* No. 8 (14), April 26, 1922, pp. 2–7.

———. "Nashi protivorechiia i Vostok" (Our contradictions and the East). *Z.N.,* No. 36 (44), Sept. 21, 1919, p. 1.

Ditiakin, V. "Vostochnyi vopros vo vtoroi polovine XIX veka v osveshchenii Marksa i Engelsa" (The Eastern problem in the second half of the nineteenth century as seen by Marx and Engels). *N.V.,* No. 22, 1928, pp. 116–31.

Eckardt, Hans von. "Die Zukunft der Mohammedaner in Russland." *Der Neue Orient,* Band II, No. 1, October 1917, pp. 111–13.

Efendiev, N. (N. Samurskii). "Politicheskie techeniia sredi musulman" (Political tendencies among the Muslims). *Z.N.,* No. 33 (41), August 31, 1919, p. 1, and No. 36 (44), September 21, 1919, p. 3.

Eidus, Kh. "Nasha politika na Vostoke." *Izvestiia,* No. 155, July 17, 1921, p. 1.

Filatin. "Sezd kommunisticheskikh organizatsii narodov Vostoka" (The Congress of the Communist Organizations of the Peoples of the East). *Z.N.,* No. 45 (53), November 30, 1919, p. 1.

Galperin, A. "Obzor mezhdunarodnykh otnoshenii na Dalnem Vostoke s kontsa XVIII v. i do 1918 goda" (A sketch of diplomatic relations in the Far East from the end of the eighteenth century to 1918). *Istorik-Marksist,* No. 4, 1939, pp. 94–118.

Geller [Heller], L. "Borba na Tikhom Okeane" (The struggle on the Pacific). *Krasnyi Internatsional Profsoiuzov,* May 1926, pp. 627–44.

———. "Mirovaia revoliutsiia i sezd narodov Vostoka v Baku, 1–8 sentiabria 1920 g." (The world revolution and the Congress of the Peoples of the East in Baku, September 1–9, 1920). *Voennaia Mysl,* Vol. I, September 1920, pp. 107–19.

———. "Oktiabrskaia revoliutsiia i narody Vostoka" (The October Revolution and the peoples of the East). *Krasnyi Internatsional Profsoiuzov,* No. 10 (81), October 1927, pp. 306–13.

Gertsenberg, I. "Osvobozhdenie Vostoka i baron Wrangel" (The liberation of the East and Baron Wrangel). *Z.N.,* No. 20 (77), July 29, 1920, p. 1.

Godes, M. "Oktiabrskaia revoliutsiia i Vostok" (The October Revolution and the East). *Problemy Marksizma,* No. 9-10, 1932, pp. 19–41.

Grigortsevich, S. "Iz istorii amerikanskoi agressii na russkom Dalnem Vostoke (1920–1922)" (American aggression in the Russian Far East, 1920–1922). *Voprosy Istorii,* No. 8, August 1951, pp. 59–79.

Gurko-Kriazhin, V. "10 let vostokovednoi mysli" (Ten years of Eastern studies). *N.V.,* No. 19, 1927, pp. xxxv–xlvii.

H. A. "Der kulturell-nationale autonome Verband der Mohammedaner Innerrusslands und Sibiriens." *Der Neue Orient,* Band II, No. 1, October 1917, pp. 343–45.

Ia. P. "Aziatskaia i tikhookeanskaia rabochie konferentsii" (The Asian and Pacific Workers' Conferences). *K.I.,* No. 11 (48), November 1925, pp. 175–77.

Iagello, I. "Turkestanskaia Vysshaia Voennaia Shkola Vostokovedeniia" (The Military School for Advanced Eastern Studies in Turkestan). *N.V.,* No. 6, 1924, pp. 515–17.

———. "Vysshaia Voennaia Shkola Vostokovedeniia" (The Military School for Advanced Eastern Studies). *N.V.,* No. 4, 1923, pp. 503–4.

Iransky, S. "Novyi etap v sovetsko-vostochnykh torgovykh otnosheniiakh" (A new trend in Soviet-Eastern relations). *Torgovlia Rossii s Vostokom,* October-December 1926, pp. 3–6.

Iumagulov, Khasiz. "Validovshchina: stranichka iz nedavnego proshlogo Bashkirii" (The Validov movement: A page from the recent history of Bashkiria). *Z.N.,* No. 2 (8), January 17, 1922, pp. 6–7.

"K istorii anglo-russkogo soglasheniia" (The history of the Anglo-Russian agreement [1907]). *Krasnyi Arkhiv*, No. 69-70, 1935, pp. 3–39. Documents.

"K itogam sezda narodov Vostoka" (Résumé of the Congress [of the Communist Organizations] of the Peoples of the East). *Z.N.*, No. 46 (54), December 7, 1919, p. 3; No. 48 (56), December 21, 1919, p. 2; and No. 1 (58), January 4, 1920, p. 2.

"K predstoiashchemu sezdu revoliutsionnykh i kommunisticheskikh partii Dalnego Vostoka" (The coming congress of the revolutionary and communist parties of the Far East). *Z.N.*, No. 2 (131), January 17, 1922.

Kammari, M. "Sozdanie i razvitie I. V. Stalinym marksistskoi teorii natsii (Origin and development of Stalin's Marxist theory of nations). *Voprosy Istorii*, No. 12, December 1949, pp. 65–88.

Karakhan, L. M. "Zadachi vostokovedeniia" (The tasks in the study of the East). *N.V.*, No. 7, 1925, pp. 3–4.

Kotliarevsky, S. "Pravovye dostizheniia Rossii v Azii" (Russia's legal accomplishments in Asia). *N.V.*, No. 1, 1922, pp. 34–44.

Leonov, N. "Uriankhaiskii krai do nachala XX stoletiia" (The Uriankhai region before the twentieth century). *N.V.*, No. 3, 1923, pp. 405–19.

Lesnik, S. "Kommunisticheskii Universitet Trudiashchikhsia Vostoka. K 2-letnei godovshchine ego sushchestvovaniia" (The Communist University of the Toilers of the East. Its second anniversary). *N.V.*, No. 3, 1923, pp. 569–71.

Madiar, L. "Predely revoliutsionnoi roli kolonialnoi burzhuazii v kolonialnykh revoliutsiiakh" (The limits of the revolutionary role of the colonial bourgeoisie in the colonial revolutions). *K.I.*, No. 31-32 (157-158), 1928, pp. 50–61.

Murphy, J. P. "The First Year of the Lenin School." *Communist International*, No. 14, September 30, 1927.

Narimanov, N. "Lenin i Vostok" (Lenin and the East). *N.V.*, No. 5, 1924, pp. 9–12.

Nechkina, M. "K voprosu o formule naimenshee zlo" (On the question of the term "the least evil"). *Voprosy Istorii*, No. 4, 1951, pp. 44–48.

[Nelidov, A. I.] "Zapiska A. I. Nelidova o zaniatii prolivov" (A. I. Nelidov's report on the occupation of the Straits). *Krasnyi Arkhiv*, No. 46, 1931, pp. 179–83.

Pak Chin Shum. "Osvoboditelnoe dvizhenie narodov Vostoka i sovetskaia Rossiia" (The liberation movement of the peoples of the East and Soviet Russia). *Z.N.*, No. 7 (64), February 29, 1920, p. 2.

"Pervye shagi russkogo imperializma na Dalnem Vostoke, 1888–1903 gg." (First steps of Russian imperialism in the Far East, 1888–1903). *Krasnyi Arkhiv*, No. 52, 1932, pp. 34–124. Documents.

Pestkovsky, S. S. "Probuzhdenie Vostoka" (The awakening of the East). *Z.N.*, No. 15 (23), 1919, p. 1.

Politikus. "My i Vostok" (We and the East). *Kommunisticheskaia Revoliutsiia*, No. 13-14 (52-53), July 15–August 1, 1923.

Popov, A. "Rossiia i Tibet" (Russia and Tibet). *N.V.*, No. 20-21, 1928, pp. 33–54.

Popov, K. "Ob istoricheskikh usloviakh pererastaniia burzhuazno-demokraticheskoi revoliutsii v proletarskuiu" (On historic conditions for the transformation of the bourgeois-democratic revolution into the proletarian revolution). *Bolshevik*, No. 21-22, Nov. 30, 1928, pp. 35–42; No. 23-24, Dec. 31, 1928, pp. 70–86; and No. 1, Jan. 15, 1929, pp. 69–85.

Popov, S. "KUTV—kuznitsa kadrov dlia sovetskogo Vostoka" (KUTV—forging the workers for the Soviet East). *Revoliutsionnyi Vostok*, No. 2, 1935.

Pozner, V. "Vysshaia partiinaia shkola v Turkestane" (The Party school of higher learning in Turkestan). *Kommunisticheskaia Revoliutsiia*, No. 11-12 (35-36), October 1, 1922, pp. 182–85.

Prager, P. "K postanovke voprosa o nekapitalisticheskom puti razvitiia otstalykh stran" (On the question of the noncapitalist development of the backward countries). *Proletarskaia Revoliutsiia,* No. 5 (100), May 1930, pp. 55–94, and No. 6 (101), June 1930, pp. 73–102.

"Problemy Dalnego Vostoka: I. Kitai. II. Etapy Koreiskogo revoliutsionnogo dvizheniia: koreiskii kommunisticheskii sezd" (Problems of the Far East: (1) China. (2) Stages of the Korean revolutionary movement: the Korean communist congress). *Z.N.,* No. 14 (112), July 16, 1921, pp. 2–3.

R—de. "Kulturnye zadachi revoliutsii na musulmanskom Vostoke" (The cultural tasks of the revolution in the Muslim East). *Z.N.,* No. 1 (99), 1921, p. 1.

"Rabochee dvizhenie na Vostoke" (The workers' movement in the East). *Z.N.,* No. 15 (23), 1919.

Radek, Karl. "The Face of the Earth After the War." *International Press Correspondence,* No. 53, July 31, 1924, pp. 551–53.

———. "Ocherki mirovoi politiki" (An outline of world politics). *K.I.,* No. 8, 1921, pp. 4557–72.

Rafail, M. "Lenin, 1905 god i Vostok" (Lenin, the year 1905, and the East). *N.V.,* No. 10-11, 1925, pp. 1–14.

Rakovsky, Kh. G. "Lokarno i Blizhnii Vostok" (Locarno and the Near East). *N.V.,* No. 10-11, 1925, pp. XLIII–XLV.

"Revoliutsionnaia propaganda sredi narodov Vostoka" (Revolutionary propaganda among the peoples of the East). *Z.N.,* No. 5 (13), February 16, 1919, p. 4.

"R.K.P. (B), Ts. B. Musulmanskikh Organizatsii k kommunistam musulmanam" (The Central Bureau of the Muslim Organizations of the Russian Communist Party (B) to the Muslim Communists). *Z.N.,* No. 5, December 8, 1918, p. 8.

"Rol Rossii v probuzhdenii Vostoka" (Russia's role in the awakening of the East). *Z.N.,* No. 40 (48), October 19, 1919, p. 2.

Roy, M. N. "Joseph Stalin, Mefisto of Modern History." *The Radical Humanist* (Bombay), No. 49, December 10, 1950.

Ryskulov, T. R. "Komintern i rabota na Vostoke" (The Comintern and the work in the East). *Z.N.,* No. 40 (96), December 15, 1920, pp. 1–2.

S. D. "Lloid-Dzhorzh, Krasin i Vostok" (Lloyd George, Krasin, and the East). *Z.N.,* No. 17 (24), July 9, 1920, p. 1.

Safarov, G. I. "Oktiabr i kolonialnaia revoliutsiia" (The October [Revolution] and the colonial revolution). *Bolshevik,* No. 19-20, October 31, 1930, pp. 39–54.

———. "Vostok i revoliutsiia" (The East and the revolution). *K.I.,* No. 15, 1920, pp. 3127–40.

———. "Vostok i sotsialisticheskaia revoliutsiia" (The East and the socialist revolution). *Pravda,* No. 155, July 16, 1920.

Said-Galiev, S. "Koran i revoliutsiia" (The Koran and the revolution). *Z.N.,* No. 5 (62), February 8, 1920, p. 2.

Sanai, Amur. "Kliuchi k Vostoku" (The keys to the East). *Z.N.,* No. 19 (27), May 26, 1919, p. 2.

Schmidt, A. "Vostokovedenie v Turkestane" (Studies of the East in Turkestan). *N.V.,* No. 6, 1924, pp. 512–14.

"Sezd trudiashchikhsia Dalnego Vostoka. Polozhenie v dalnevostochnykh stranakh" (The Congress of the Toilers of the Far East. The situation in the Far Eastern countries). *Z.N.,* No. 4 (133), January 31, 1922, p. 2, and No. 5 (134), February 9, 1922, p. 3.

Shumiatsky, B. Z. *See* A. Chervonnyi

Sultan-Galiev, M. "Agitatsionno-propagandistskaia rabota partii. Metody antireligioznoi propagandy sredi musulman" (Agitation and propaganda work of the party. Methods of antireligious propaganda among the Muslims). *Vestnik Agitatsii i Propagandy,* No. 22-23, November 1921, pp. 27–32.

————. "K obiavleniiu Azerbaidzhanskoi sovetskoi respubliki" (The proclamation of the establishment of the Azerbaijan soviet republic). *Z.N.,* No. 13 (70), April 9, 1920, p. 1.

————. "Sotsialnaia revoliutsiia i Vostok" (Social revolution and the East). *Z.N.,* No. 38 (46), October 5, 1919, p. 1; No. 42 (50), November 2, 1919, p. 1.

"Tezisy o zadachakh proletarskoi revoliutsii na Vostoke (Polit'otdel poezda 'Krasnyi Vostok')" (Theses on the tasks of the proletarian revolution in the East [by the] political section of the "Red East" train). *Z.N.,* No. 24 (81), July 25, 1920, p. 1.

"Tikhookeanskaia konferentsiia profsoiuzov" (The Pacific Trade Union Conference). *Krasnyi Internatsional Profsoiuzov,* No. 7 (78), July 1927, pp. 127–51.

"Tsarskaia diplomatiia o zadachakh Rossii na Vostoke" (Tsarist diplomacy on the tasks of Russia in the East). *Krasnyi Arkhiv,* No. 18, 1926, pp. 5–17. Documents.

Tiutchev, F. I. *Polnoe sobranie sochinenii.* 3 vols. St. Petersburg, 1913.

Ustrialov, N. V. "Rossiia na Dalnem Vostoke" (Russia in the Far East). *Vestnik Manchzhurii,* No. 1-2, 1925, pp. 12–17.

V—i, S. "Sezd trudiashchikhsia Dalnego Vostoka" (The Congress of the Toilers of the Far East). *Z.N.,* No. 4 (133), January 31, 1922, p. 2, and No. 5 (134), February 9, 1922, p. 3.

Vasilevsky, K. G. "Sredne-Aziatskie Kursy Vostokovedeniia R.K.K.A." (The Central Asian lecture courses on the East for the workers' and peasants' Red Army). *N.V.,* No. 20-21, 1928.

Veltman, M. L. (M. Pavlovich). "K dvukhletiiu Kommunisticheskogo Universiteta Trudiashchikhsia Vostoka" (The second anniversary of the Communist University of the Toilers of the East). *N.V.,* No. 3, 1923, pp. 567–59.

————. "Lenin i narody Vostoka" (Lenin and the peoples of the East). *N.V.,* No. 5, 1924, pp. 3–8.

————. "Lozanskaia konferentsiia" (The Lausanne Conference). *N.V.,* No. 3, 1923, pp. 3–34.

————. "Novaia ugroza na Dalnem Vostoke. Vashingtonskaia konferentsiia i nashe polozhenie na Tikho-okeanskom poberezhie" (A new threat in the Far East. The Washington Conference and our position on the Pacific coast). *Z.N.,* No. 17 (115), September 3, 1921, p. 1.

————. "Revoliutsiia 1905 g. i Vostok" (The revolution of 1905 and the East). *Istorik-Marksist,* No. 1, 1926, pp. 142–53.

————. "Sezd narodov Vostoka v Baku i ego znachenie" (The Congress of the Peoples of the East in Baku and its significance). *Z.N.,* No. 33 (90), October 27, 1920, pp. 1–2.

————. "Sovetskaia Rossiia i anglo-frantsuzskie intrigi na Vostoke" (Soviet Russia and Anglo-French intrigues in the East). *K.I.,* No. 14, November 6, 1920.

————. "SSSR i Vostok" (The U.S.S.R. and the East). *N.V.,* No. 6, 1924, pp. III–XII.

————. "Vashingtonskaia konferentsiia" (The Washington Conference). *Ot Vashingtona do Genui,* Moscow, 1922; also in *Vestnik N.K.I.D.,* No. 9-10, December 15, 1921, pp. 3–12, and No. 1-3, January-March 1922, pp. 3–14.

————. "Vserossiiskaia Nauchnaia Assotsiatsiia Vostokovedeniia" (The All-Russian Scientific Association for the Study of the East). *Z.N.,* No. 1, January 1, 1923, pp. 267–71.

[————]. "Tikhookeanskaia problema" (The Pacific problem). *N.V.,* No. 1, 1922, pp. 16–33. Pseudonym "M. P."

Viktorov, V. "Kommunisticheskii Universitet Trudiashchikhsia Vostoka" (The Communist University of the Toilers of the East). *Z.N.,* No. 1, January 1, 1923, pp. 261–66.

BIBLIOGRAPHY   417

Vilensky, V. D. (Sibiriakov). "Vashington i Vostochnaia Aziia" (Washington and
     East Asia). Z.N., No. 3 (132), January 26, 1922, p. 1.
Voitinsky, G. N. "First Conference of Transport Workers of the Pacific." Inter-
     national Press Correspondence, No. 65, September 11, 1924, pp. 704–6.
————. "Oktiabrskaia revoliutsiia i kolonialnye i polukolonialnye narody" (The
     October Revolution and the colonial and semicolonial peoples). N.V., No. 6,
     1924, pp. xiii–xv.
"Vsem Ugnetennym Narodam i Vsem Ugnetennym Klassam. Manifest Brussels-
     kogo kongressa po borbe s imperializmom" (To All Oppressed Peoples and All
     Oppressed Classes. A Manifesto of the Brussels Congress on the Struggle
     Against Imperialism). N.V., No. 16-17, 1927, pp. 401–5.
"Vysshaia Voennaia Shkola Vostokovedeniia Turkestanskogo Fronta (Okruga)"
     (The Military College for Advanced Eastern Studies in the Turkestan Region).
     N.V., No. 2, 1922, pp. 730–31.
"Zwei Ansichten über das politische Programm des russischen Islam. Berichte und
     Reden von Ahmed Bey Tsalikow und Mohammed Rasulzadeh." Der Neue
     Orient, Band II, No. 1, October 1917, pp. 525–28.

CAUCASUS

L'Action du Parti S. R. Arménien dit "Daschnakzoutioun," 1914–1923; rapport
     présenté au Congrès Socialiste International de Hamburg (Mai 1923). Paris
     and Vienna, 1923.
L'Arménie et la question arménienne avant, pendant et depuis la guerre. Paris,
     Délégation de la République Arménienne, 1922.
Allen, W. E. D., and Paul Muratoff. Caucasian Battlefields. A History of the Wars
     on the Turco-Caucasian Border, 1828–1921. Cambridge, 1953.
Baddeley, John E. Russia's Conquest of the Caucasus . . . London, 1908. With
     maps, plans, and illustrations.
Bagirov, M. D. Iz istorii bolshevistskoi organizatsii Baku i Azerbaidzhana (Bol-
     shevik organization in Baku and Azerbaijan). Moscow, 1946.
Bina, Ali Akbar. La Question au début du XIX siècle des traités de Gulistan et de
     Turkman-Tchai (1813–1828). Paris, 1939.
Baldwin, Oliver. Six Prisons and Two Revolutions; Adventures in Trans-Caucasia
     and Anatolia, 1920–1921. London, 1925.
Beriia, L. P. K voprosu ob istorii bolshevistkikh organizatsii na Kavkaze; doklad
     na sobranii Tiflisskogo partaktiva 21–22 iiulia, 1935 g. (Bolshevik organizations
     in the Caucasus; speech to the Tiflis branch of the party, July 21–22, 1935).
     7th ed. Moscow, 1948.
————. On the History of the Bolshevik Organizations of Transcaucasia. New
     York, 1939.
————. 15 Years of Soviet Georgia. Moscow, 1936.
Borian, B. A. Armenia, mezhdunarodnaia diplomatiia i SSSR (Armenia, interna-
     tional diplomacy, and the U.S.S.R.). 2 vols. Moscow, 1928–29.
Chaikin, V. A. K istorii rossiiskoi revoliutsii (Kazn 26 bakinskikh komissarov)
     (On the Russian revolution. The execution of twenty-six Baku commissars),
     Vol. I. Moscow, 1922.
Dubner, A. Bakinskii proletariat v gody revoliutsii (1917–1920) (The Baku pro-
     letariat in the years of revolution, 1917–1920). Baku, 1931.
Guseinov, Mirza-Davud. Tiurskaia demokraticheskaia partiia federalistov ("Musa-
     vat") v proshlom i nastoiashchem (The Turkic Democratic Federalist ("Musa-
     vat") Party in the past and present). Tiflis, 1927.
Guseinov, Ragim. Ocherki revoliutsionnogo dvizheniia v Azerbaidzhane (Essays
     on the revolutionary movement in Azerbaijan). Vol. I. Baku, 1927.

Guseinov, T. *Oktiabr v Azerbaidzhane* (October in Azerbaijan). Baku, 1927.

Ishkhanian, B. *Narodnosti Kavkaza. Sostav naseleniia, professionalnaia gruppi-rovka i obshchestvennoe razsloenie kavkazskikh narodnostei* (The peoples of the Caucasus. Composition of the population; professional and social grouping of the Caucasian nationalities). Petrograd, 1916.

K trudiashchimsia massam vsego Kavkaza (To the toiling masses of the Caucasus [an appeal of the Caucasus Regional Committee of the All-Russian Communist Party (B)]). Baku, 1919.

Karaev, A. G. *Iz nedavnego proshlogo; materialy k istorii Azerbaidzhanskoi Kommunisticheskoi Partii (B)* (From the recent past; materials on the history of the Azerbaijan Communist Party (B)). Baku, 1926.

Kazemzadeh, Firuz. *The Struggle for Transcaucasia (1917–1921)*. New York, 1951.

Khachapuridze, G. B. *Bolsheviki Gruzii v boiakh za pobedu sovetskoi vlasti* (The Bolsheviks of Georgia in the struggle for the victory of Soviet power). 2d ed., revised and enlarged. Moscow, 1951.

Khatisian, A. "The Origin and Development of the Armenian Republic." Athens, 1930. Microfilm in Armenian.

Krasilnikov, F. S. *Kavkaz i ego obitateli; geografichesko-etnograficheskie ocherki* (The Caucasus and its inhabitants; a geographic-ethnographic essay). Moscow, 1919.

Makharadze, F. I. *Sovety i borba za sovetskuiu vlast v Gruzii 1917–1921* (The soviets and the struggle for soviet government in Georgia, 1917–1921). Tiflis, 1928.

Nikuradze, Alexander (A. Sanders). *Kaukasien, Nordkaukasien, Aserbeidschan, Armenien, Georgien, geschichtlicher Umriss*. München, 1944.

Papazian, K. S. *Patriotism Perverted; a Discussion of the Deeds and the Misdeeds of the Armenian Revolutionary Federation, the so-called Dashnagtzoutune*. Boston, 1934.

Pasdermadjian, Hrant. *Histoire de l'Arménie depuis les origines jusqu'au traité de Lausanne*. Paris, 1949.

Ratgauzer, Ia. A. *Borba za sovetskii Azerbaidzhan; k istorii aprelskogo perevorota* (The struggle for Soviet Azerbaijan; the April *coup d'état*). Baku, 1928.

Samursky, N. *Dagestan* (Daghestan). Moscow, 1925.

Vachnadze, David. *Gruziia mezhdu Severom i Iugom; s drevneishikh vremen do nashikh dnei* (Georgia between North and South from ancient times to the present day). Paris, 1936.

Varandian, Mikael. *History of the Armenian Revolutionary Federation*. Paris, 1932. In Armenian.

Vardanian, S. *Podpole; nabroski po istorii kommunisticheskogo dvizheniia molo-dezhi v Zakavkazii* (The underground; essays on the communist youth movement in Transcaucasia). Tiflis, 1926.

Baikov, B. "Vospominaniia o revoliutsii v Zakavkazii (1917–1921 g.g.)" (Reminiscences of the revolution in Transcaucasia, 1917–1921). *Arkhiv Russkoi Revoliutsii*, No. 9, 1923, pp. 91–194.

Gukovsky, A. I. "Pobeda sovetskoi vlasti v Armenii v 1920 godu" (The victory of the Soviet government in Armenia in 1920). *Istorik-Marksist*, No. 11, 1940, pp. 8–17.

Kuznetsova. "Krakh turetskoi interventsii v Zakavkazii v 1920–1921 godakh" (The failure of the Turkish intervention in Transcaucasia in 1920–1921). *Voprosy Istorii*, No. 9, September 1951, pp. 143–56.

[Ordzhonikidze, G. K.] "Federatsiia Zakavkazskikh Respublik. Iz rechi tov. Ordzhonikidze na obshchegorodskom sobranii Tiflisskoi organizatsii K. P. Gruzii" (Federation of the Transcaucasian Republics. From the speech of Comrade Ordzhonikidze to the Tiflis branch of the Georgian Communist Party). *Z.N.*, No. 31 (129), December 31, 1921, pp. 2–3.

Skachko, A. "Armeniia i Turtsiia na predstoiashchei konferentsii" (Armenia and Turkey at the forthcoming conference). *Z.N.*, No. 6 (104), March 4, 1921, p. 2. Kars Conference in 1921.

CHINA

Aikhenvald, A. *O takticheskoi linii Kominterna v Kitae* (On the tactical line of the Comintern in China). Moscow and Leningrad, 1927.

Badmaev, R. A. *Rossiia i Kitai* (Russia and China). St. Petersburg, 1905.

*Bakulin, A. B. *Zapiski ob ukhanskom periode kitaiskoi revoliutsii (Iz istorii kitaiskoi revoliutsii 1925–1927 g.g.)* (Notes on the Wuhan period of the Chinese revolution, 1925–1927). Moscow and Leningrad, 1930.

Brandt, Conrad, *et al. A Documentary History of Chinese Communism*. Cambridge, Mass., 1952.

——. "Bibliographical Sketch, Ch'en Tu-hsiu, Pre-Communist Phase." Harvard University. Papers on China from Regional Studies Seminar, Vol. II.

Bukharin, N. I. *Problemy kitaiskoi revoliutsii* (Problems of the Chinese revolution). Moscow, 1927.

Chao Kuo-chün (comp.). "The Communist Movement in China; a Chronology of Major Developments, 1918–1950." Typescript. Russian Research Center, Harvard University, 1950.

The China Year Book, 1924–1925; 1926–1927; 1928. Published in Tientsin and Peking.

Chung-Kuo hsien-tai ko-ming yün-tung shih (China's recent revolutionary history). Vol. I–. Yenan, 1941–.

Dalin, Sergei. *Molodezh v revolutsionom dvizhenii Kitaia* (Youth in the Chinese revolutionary movement). Moscow, 1925. Preface by Karl Radek.

——. *V riadakh kitaiskoi revoliutsii* (In the ranks of the Chinese revolution). Moscow, 1926. Preface by Karl Radek.

Dridzo, S. A. (A. Lozovsky) (ed.). *O Kitae* (On China). Moscow and Leningrad, 1928.

——. *Revoliutsiia i kontr-revoliutsiia v Kitae* (Revolution and counterrevolution in China). Moscow, 1927.

Efimov, G. B. *Ocherki po novoi i noveishei istorii Kitaia* (Sketch on the modern and latest history of China). 2d ed. Moscow, 1951.

Elegant, Robert S. *China's Red Masters. Political Biographies of the Chinese Communist Leaders*. New York, 1951.

Erenburg, G. B. *Natsionalno-osvoboditelnoe dvizhenie v Kitae posle Velikoi Oktiabrskoi Sotsialisticheskoi Revoliutsii (1918–1924 g.g.)* (The national-liberation movement in China after the Great October Socialist Revolution, 1918–1924). Moscow, 1950.

——. *Ocherki natsionalno-osvoboditelnoi borby kitaiskogo naroda v noveishee vremia* (An outline of the national-liberation struggle of the Chinese people in recent times). Moscow, 1950.

——. *Sovetskii Kitai* (Soviet China). 2d ed. Moscow, 1934.

Ermashev, I. I. *Svet nad Kitaem* (Light over China). Moscow, 1950.

Fromentin, Pierre. *Mao Tsé Tung, le dragon rouge*. Paris, 1949.

Green, O. Mortimer. *The Story of China's Revolution*. London and New York, 1945.

Hsiung, S. I. *Life of Chiang Kai-shek*. London, 1948.

Hsü, Leonard Shih-lien. *Sun Yat-sen, His Political and Social Ideals* . . . Los Angeles, 1933.

Hu Chiao-mu. *Tridtsat let kommunisticheskoi partii Kitaia* (Thirty years of the Communist Party of China). Moscow, 1952. Translated from the Chinese.

IKKI i VKP po kitaiskomu voprosu; osnovnye resheniia (The ECCI and the All-Russian Communist Party on Chinese problems; basic decisions). Moscow, 1927.

International Commission of Judges. *Report of the International Commission of Judges Appointed to Inquire into the Causes of the Disturbance at Shanghai, May 30, 1925.* Shanghai, 1925.

Isaacs, Harold R. *The Tragedy of the Chinese Revolution.* Revised ed. Stanford, Calif., 1951.

———— (ed.). "Draft Survey of Materials Relating to Communism in China, 1927–1934." Mimeographed.

Ivin, A. A. *Borba va vlast sovetov; ocherki sovetskogo dvizheniia v Kitae* (The struggle for the soviets; a sketch of the soviet movement in China). Moscow, 1933.

————. *Ot Khankou k Shankhaiu* (From Hankow to Shanghai). Moscow and Leningrad, 1927.

————. *Kitai i sovetskii soiuz* (China and the Soviet Union). Moscow, 1924.

————. *Pervyi etap osvoboditelnoi borby v Kitae* (First stage of the liberation struggle in China). Moscow, 1926.

————. *Pisma iz Kitaia; ot versalskogo dogovora do sovetsko-kitaiskogo soglasheniia* (Letters from China; from the Versailles treaty to the Soviet-Chinese agreement). Moscow, 1927.

Kantarovich, A. Ia. *Amerika v borbe za Kitai* (America in the struggle for China). Moscow, 1935.

Kara-Murza, G. S., and P. Mif (comps.). *Strategiia i taktika Kominterna v natsionalno-kolonialnoi revoliutsii na primere Kitaia. Sbornik dokumentov* (Strategy and tactics of the Comintern in the national-colonial revolutionary movement, as exemplified in China. A collection of documents). Moscow, 1934.

Khodorov, A. E. *Kitai v borbe za nezavisimost* (China in the struggle for independence). Moscow, 1925.

Kotenev, A. M. *New Lamps for Old. An Interpretation of Events in Modern China and Whither They Lead.* Shanghai, 1931.

Kuchumov, V. *Ocherki po istorii kitaiskoi revoliutsii* (Essays on the history of the Chinese revolution). Moscow, 1934.

Lattimore, Owen. *Inner Asian Frontiers of China.* New York, 1940. Also introduction to 2d ed.; n.p., 1951.

Mif, P. A. *Heroic China; Fifteen Years of the Communist Party of China.* New York, 1937.

————. *Kitaiskaia Kommunisticheskaia Partiia v kriticheskie dni* (The Chinese Communist Party in critical days). Moscow, 1928.

————. *Uroki shankhaiskikh sobytii* (The lessons of the Shanghai events). Moscow, 1926.

See also Kara-Murza

Mitarevsky, N. *World Wide Soviet Plots as Disclosed by Hitherto Unpublished Documents Seized at the U.S.S.R. Embassy in Peking.* Tientsin, 1927.

Nazonov, N. *La lettre de Shanghai; document inédit caché par Staline.* Paris, 1927.

Neuberg, A. *L'insurrection armée.* Paris, 1931.

Nikiforov, V. N. *Narodnaia revoliutsiia v Kitae; ocherk istorii borby i pobedy kitaiskogo naroda* (People's revolution in China; an outline of the struggle and victory of the Chinese people). Moscow, 1950.

Nilus, E. Kh. *Istoricheskii obzor Kitaiskoi Vostochnoi Zheleznoi Dorogi, 1896–*

1923 g.g. . . . (Historical outline of the Chinese Eastern Railway, 1896–1923). 2 vols. Harbin, 1923.

"Noiabrskii plenum TS.K.KKP; rezoliutsii" (November [1927] plenum of the Central Committee of the Chinese Communist Party; resolutions). *Materialy po Kitaiskomu Voprosu,* No. 1 (10), 1928, pp. 3–22.

Norins, M. R. *Gateway to Asia: Sinkiang, Frontier of the Chinese Far West.* New York, 1944.

North, Robert C. *Moscow and Chinese Communists.* Stanford, Calif., 1953.

Otsuka, R. *The Red Influence in China (Prepared for the 6th Conference of the Institute of Pacific Relations).* Tokyo, 1936.

Pavlovsky, M. N. *Chinese-Russian Relations.* New York, 1949.

Pick, Eugene (pseud.). *China in the Grip of the Reds.* Shanghai, 1927.

Pokrovsky, S. *Voprosy kitaiskoi revoliutsii* (Problems of the Chinese revolution). Leningrad, 1927.

Pollard, R. T. *China's Foreign Relations, 1917–1931.* New York, 1933.

Popov, I. I. *Ot Nebesnoi Imperii k Seredinnoi Respublike. Ocherki po istorii Kitaia, Manchzhurii, Mongolii i Tibeta so statiami: Istoriia torgovykh otnoshenii mezhdu Rossiei i Kitaem, russko-kitaiskii torgovyi dogovor i transmongolskaia zheleznaia doroga* (From the Celestial Empire to the Middle Republic. Essays on the history of China, Manchuria, Mongolia, and Tibet with articles: The history of trade relations between Russia and China, the Russo-Chinese trade agreement, and the Trans-Mongolian railway). Moscow, 1912.

Postanovlenie IKKI o tekushchem momente kitaiskoi revoliutsii (Decision of the ECCI on the existing situation in the Chinese revolution). Moscow, 1927.

The Present Condition of China. N.p., Japanese Foreign Office, 1932.

Rafes, M. G. *Kitaiskaia revoliutsiia na perelome* (The Chinese revolution at a turning point). Moscow, 1927.

Roy, M. N. *Kitaiskaia revoliutsiia i Kommunisticheskii Internatsional. Sbornik statei i materialov* (The Chinese revolution and the Communist International. A collection of articles and materials). Moscow and Leningrad, 1929.

———. *My Experiences in China.* 2d ed. Calcutta, 1945.

———. *Revolution and Counter-Revolution in China.* Calcutta, 1946.

Royal Institute of International Affairs. *China and Japan . . .* London, 1939.

Ruki proch ot Kitaia. Rechi tt. Radeka, Sen Kataiamy, Tsin-Hua i drugikh na mitinge organizovannom Ob-vom "Ruki proch ot Kitaia" (Hands off China. Speeches by Comrades Radek, Sen Katayama, Ishi-Kua [?], and others at a meeting organized by the "Hands Off China" Association). Moscow, 1924.

Savvin, V. P. *Vzaimootnosheniia tsarskoi Rossii i S.S.S.R. s Kitaem* (The relations of tsarist Russia and the U.S.S.R. with China). Moscow, 1930.

Schwartz, Benjamin. *Chinese Communism and the Rise of Mao.* Cambridge, Mass., 1951.

Schwartz, Bruno. *The Hankow Riots of June 11th, 1925.* Hankow, 1925. Clippings from the *Independent Herald.*

Semenov, B. *Novyi etap kitaiskoi revoliutsii* (The new stage of the Chinese revolution). Moscow and Leningrad, 1927.

Serebrennikov, I. I. *Russkie interesy v Kitae* (Russian interests in China). Shanghai, 1934.

Sharman, Lyon. *Sun Yat Sen. His Life and Its Meaning, a Critical Biography.* New York, 1934.

Shishkin, P. D. *Bolshevizm v Kitae. Obzor deiatelnosti severo-manchzhurskoi kommunisticheskoi partii* (Bolshevism in China. An outline of the activities of the North Manchurian Communist Party). Shanghai, 1930.

Simpson, B. L. *Manchu and Muscovite . . . Being Letters from Manchuria written during the Autumn of 1903 with a Historical Sketch Entitled "Prologue to the Crisis"* . . . London and New York, 1904.

Skachkov, P. E. *Bibliografiia Kitaia; sistematicheskii ukazatel knig i zhurnalnykh statei o Kitae na russkom iazyke 1730–1930* (Bibliography of China; a systematic reference volume on books and articles from periodicals in the Russian language, 1730–1930). Moscow, 1932.

Sovety v Kitae; sbornik materialov i dokumentov (Soviets in China; a collection of materials and documents). Moscow. The Communist Academy, 1934.

Soviet Plot in China. Peking, 1928. Documents published by the Peking metropolitan police after a raid on the Soviet embassy in Peking in April 1927.

Stalin, I. V. *O perspektivakh revoliutsii v Kitae; rech v Kitaiskoi Komissii IKKI, 30 noiabria 1926 g.* (On the prospects of the revolution in China. Speech at the Chinese Commission of the ECCI, November 30, 1926). Moscow and Leningrad, 1927.

———. *Revoliutsiia v Kitae i oshibki oppozitsii* (The revolution in China and the mistakes of the opposition). Moscow and Leningrad, 1927.

Sun Yat-sen. *Memoirs of a Chinese Revolutionary, a Programme of National Reconstruction for China*. Taipei, 1955. Translated from the French.

———. *Souvenirs d'un révolutionnaire chinois*. Paris, 1933. Translated from the Chinese.

T'ang Leang-li. *The Inner History of the Chinese Revolution*. London, 1930.

Toa Dōbun-kai. *Saishin Shina Nenkan* (Annual of contemporary China). Tokyo, 1935.

Vilensky, V. D. (Sibiriakov). *Gomindan—partiia kitaiskoi revoliutsii* (The Kuomintang—party of the Chinese revolution). Moscow and Leningrad, 1926.

———. *Kitai i Sovetskaia Rossiia* (China and Soviet Russia). Moscow, 1919.

———. *Sun Yat-sen, otets kitaiskoi revoliutsii* (Sun Yat-sen, father of the Chinese revolution). Moscow, 1924.

Voprosy kitaiskoi revoliutsii (Problems of the Chinese revolution). Leningrad and Moscow, 1927.

Wales, Nym. *Red Dust: Autobiographies of Chinese Communists*. Stanford, Calif., 1952. Introduction by Robert C. North.

Weigh Ken Shen. *Russo-Chinese Diplomacy*. Shanghai, 1928.

Whiting, Allen S. *Soviet Policies in China, 1917–1924*. New York, 1954.

Woo, T. C. *The Kuomintang and the Future of the Chinese Revolution*. London, 1928.

Wu, Aitchen K. (Ai-ch'en). *China and the Soviet Union (A Study of Sino-Soviet Relations)*. New York, 1950.

Yakhontoff, V. A. *The Chinese Soviets*. New York, 1934.

Young, Karl Walter. *The International Relations of Manchuria; A Digest and Analysis of Treaties, Agreements, and Negotiations Concerning the Three Eastern Provinces of China* . . . N.p., Institute of Pacific Relations, 1929.

Zubets, V. A. "Na sluzhbe v kitaiskoi armii" (In the service of the Chinese army). Typescript.

A. A. "Tri shankhaiskikh vosstaniia" (Three Shanghai uprisings). *Problemy Kitaia*, No. 2, 1930, pp. 64–86.

Bandalian. "Oshibki kitaiskoi kompartii" (Mistakes of the Chinese Communist Party). *Izvestiia Ulan-Bator-Khoto*, No. 74 (418), October 1, 1927, p. 3.

Baranovsky, M. "Borba Kitaia za otmenu neravnopravnykh dogovorov" (China's struggle to annul unequal treaties). *Mirovoe Khoziaistvo i Mirovaia Politika*, No. 12, 1926, pp. 98–106.

Borodin, M. M. "Krestianskoe dvizhenie v pr. Khubei (Rech t. Borodina proiznesennaia na krestianskom sezde v g. U-chan)" (The peasant movement in Hupei province: Speech of Comrade Borodin at the peasant congress at Wuhan). *Materialy po Kitaiskomu Voprosu,* No. 9, December 1927, pp. 4–44.

———. "Prichiny porazheniia kitaiskoi revoliutsii" (Reasons for the defeat of the Chinese revolution). *Izvestiia Ulan-Bator-Khoto,* No. 73 (417), September 28, 1927, pp. 3–4.

Bubnov, A. "O kitaiskoi revoliutsii" (The Chinese revolution). *Kommunisticheskaia Revoliutsiia,* No. 8, April 1927, pp. 3–10.

Bukharin, N. I. "Tekushchii moment kitaiskoi revoliutsii" (The present stage of the Chinese revolution). *Pravda,* No. 145, June 30, 1927.

———. "Perspektivy kitaiskoi revoliutsii; doklad . . . Ianvar 1927" (Prospects of the Chinese revolution; report . . . January 1927). *Revoliutsionnyi Vostok,* No. 1, 1927, pp. 3–21.

Ch'en T'an-ch'iu. "Vospominaniia o I sezde Kompartii Kitaia" (Reminiscences of the First Congress of the Chinese Communist Party). *K.I.,* No. 14, August 1936, pp. 96–99.

Ch'en Tu-hsiu. "Pismo tov. Chen-Du-Siu ko vsem chlenam kitaiskoi kommunisticheskoi partii" (Letter of Comrade Ch'en Tu-hsiu to all members of the Chinese Communist Party). *Biulleten Oppozitsii,* No. 15-16, September-October, 1930, pp. 19–23.

"Deklaratsiia priniataia na avgustovskoi konferentsii KKP" (Declaration passed at the August [1927] conference of the Chinese Communist Party). *Materialy po Kitaiskomu Voprosu,* No. 8, 1927, pp. 13–26.

Dimitrov, G. "K piatnadtsatiletiiu Kompartii Kitaia" (The fifteenth anniversary of the Chinese Communist Party). *K.I.,* No. 14, August 1936, pp. 78–80.

"Exchange of Telegrams Between the Comintern, the C.C.P., and the Kuomintang Party." *International Press Correspondence,* No. 20, March 19, 1925, pp. 286–87.

Ferdi, B. "Kitaiskaia revoliutsiia ne dolzhna itti po puti Kemalizma" (The Chinese revolution must not follow the path of Kemalism). *K.I.,* No. 24 (98), June 17, 1927, pp. 33–37.

Galkovich, M. "Amerikanskii imperializm v Kitae" (American imperialism in China). *K.I.,* No. 8 (32), February 25, 1927, pp. 41–46.

———. "Politicheskie posledstviia kantonovskikh pobed" (The political consequences of the Canton victories). *Mirovoe Khoziaistvo i Mirovaia Politika,* No. 12, 1926, pp. 36–42.

Geller, L. "Rabochee dvizhenie v Kitae" (The workers' movement in China). *K.I.,* No. 11 (48), November 1925, pp. 95–104.

Graham, M. W., Jr. "A Decade of Sino-Russian Diplomacy." *The American Political Science Review,* Vol. XXII, No. 1, February 1928, pp. 45–69.

Grimm, E. "Doktrina 'otkrytykh dverei' i amerikanskaia politika v Kitae (ot 1899 do 1921–22 g.g.)" (The doctrine of the "Open Door" and American policy in China from 1899 to 1921–22). *Mezhdunarodnaia Zhizn,* No. 4-5, 1924, pp. 109–32.

———. "Etapy kitaiskoi revoliutsii" (Stages of the Chinese revolution). *Mezhdunarodnaia Zhizn,* No. 7, 1926, pp. 45–61.

———. "Kitaiskii vopros ot Simonosekskogo mira do mirovoi voiny (1895–1914)" (The Chinese question from the time of the Shimonoseki treaty to the World War, 1895–1914). *N.V.,* No. 6, 1924, pp. 43–62.

"Hands off China; Appeal of the International Propaganda Committee of the Transport Workers." *International Press Correspondence,* No. 81, November 27, 1924, p. 923.

Hatano, Ken'ichi. "Chūgoku Kyōsan-tō-shi" (History of the Chinese Communist Party). *Ajia Mondai Koza* (Tokyo and Osaka, 1939), II, 23–46.

Ianson, Ia. D. "Kitai" (China). *Z.N.*, No. 28 (85), September 16, 1920, pp. 2–3, and No. 29 (86), September 24, 1920, p. 1.

Ioffe, A. A. "Amerikanskaia politika v Kitae" (American policy in China). *Mezhdunarodnaia Zhizn*, No. 2, 1927, pp. 3–12.

Iu. An'li [Hu Han-li (?)]. "Kommunisticheskii Internatsional i vozniknovenie kommunisticheskoi partii Kitaia" (The Communist International and the birth of the Communist Party of China). *K.I.*, No. 9-10 (187-188), 1929, pp. 178–84.

Iurievsky. "Iz istorii Kitaisko-Vostochnoi Zheleznoi Dorogi" (Notes on the Chinese Eastern Railway). *Mezhdunarodnaia Zhizn*, No. 11, 1926, pp. 80–84.

Ivin, A. "Kitai i Sovetskaia Rossiia. Pismo iz Pekina" (China and Soviet Russia. A letter from Peking). *Krasnaia Nov*, No. 3 (20), April-May 1924, pp. 183–92.

––––––. "Sovremennyi Kitai" (Modern China). *N.V.*, No. 5, 1924, pp. 357–72, and No. 6, 1924, pp. 1–18. Includes text of the Appeal of the League for the Struggle Against Imperialism to All Oppressed Peoples of the World.

"K poslednim sobytiam v Kitae. Pobeda gen. U-Bei-Fu" (On the latest events in China. Victory of General Wu Pei-fu). *Vestnik N.K.I.D.*, No. 6, 1922, pp. 148–52.

Kara-Murza, G. "Kitai v 1918–1924 godakh" (China in 1918–1924). *Istorik-Marksist*, No. 5–6, (75–76), 1939, pp. 150–67.

Khodorov, A. E. "Chang Tso-lin i Kitaisko-Vostochnaia Zheleznaia Doroga" (Chang Tso-lin and the Chinese Eastern Railway). *Mezhdunarodnaia Zhizn*, No. 10, 1926, pp. 20–36.

––––––. "Epokha vtoroi revoliutsii v Kitae" (The period of the second revolution in China). *N.V.*, No. 19, 1927, pp. 20–39.

––––––. "Kitai i mirovoe khoziaistvo" (China and the world economy). *Mezhdunarodnaia Zhizn*, No. 4, 1926, pp. 47–61.

––––––. "Kitaisko-Vostochnaia Zheleznaia Doroga" (The Chinese Eastern Railway). *Mezhdunarodnaia Zhizn*, No. 1, 1924, pp. 17–33.

––––––. "Novye puti v istorii Kitaia" (New paths in Chinese history). *N.V.*, No. 6, 1924, pp. xxvii–xxxv.

––––––. "Pervye etapy kitaiskoi revoliutsii" (The first stages of the Chinese revolution). *N.V.*, No. 18, 1927, pp. 64–90.

"Kitaiskaia revoliutsiia i zadachi kommunisticheskikh partii" (The Chinese Revolution and the tasks of communist parties). *K.I.*, No. 13 (71), December 10, 1926, pp. 3–8.

"Kitaiskii vopros na Plenume Ts. K. VKP(B)" (The Chinese question at the plenum of the Central Committee of the All-Russian Communist Party (B)). *K.I.*, No. 34 (108), August 26, 1927, pp. 3–8.

"Krestianskoe dvizhenie v Khunani" (The peasant movement in Hunan). *K.I.*, No. 21 (95), May 27, 1927, pp. 22–29.

Lozovsky, A. (S. A. Dridzo). "Kitaiskaia revoliutsiia na perelome" (The Chinese revolution at a turning point). *K.I.*, No. 37 (111), September 16, 1927, pp. 18–23.

Mandalian, T. "Ot russkogo k kitaiskomu Oktiabriu" (From the Russian to the Chinese October). *Krasnyi Internatsional Profsoiuzov*, No. 10 (81), October 1927, pp. 418–23.

"Manifest Ts. K. KKP o politicheskom polozhenii" (Manifesto of the Central Committee of the Chinese Communist Party on the political situation). *Materialy po Kitaiskomu Voprosu*, No. 7, 1927, pp. 34–42. Translated from the Chinese.

Mao Tse-tung. "Krestianskoe dvizhenie v Khunani; pismo s Chansha ot 18 fevralia s.g." (The peasant movement in Hunan; a letter from Changsha, February 18 [1926]). *Mezhdunarodnaia Zhizn*, No. 10, 1926, pp. 20–26. Translated from the Chinese.

Martynov, A. "K peregruppirovke sil kitaiskoi revoliutsii" (The regrouping of forces in the Chinese revolution). *K.I.*, No. 8 (82), February 25, 1927, pp. 9–18.

Mif, P. A. "Kharakter i dvizhushchie sily kitaiskoi revoliutsii" (The nature and moving forces of the Chinese revolution). *Bolshevik*, No. 1, January 1, 1927, pp. 12–26.

———. "Kitaiskaia kommunisticheskaia partiia v kriticheskie dni" (The Chinese Communist Party in critical days). *Bolshevik*, No. 21, November 15, 1927, pp. 63–74; No. 23-24, Dec. 31, 1927, pp. 98–117; No. 5, March 1928, pp. 64–79. Also appears as a separate volume under the same title.

———. "Krestianskii vopros v Kitae" (The peasant problem in China). *K.I.*, No. 10-11 (68–69), November 22, 1926, pp. 26–36; No. 13 (71), December 10, 1926, pp. 20–28.

———. "Spornye voprosy kitaiskoi revoliutsii" (Debatable problems of the Chinese revolution). *Bolshevik*, No. 3-4, February 29, 1928, pp. 108–22.

"Minutes of the Chinese Subcommittee of the ECCI." *New Militant* (New York), February 8, 1936.

"Natsionalno-revoliutsionnoe dvizhenie v Kitae i taktika kitaiskoi partii" (The national-revolutionary movement in China and the tactics of the Chinese [Communist] Party). *K.I.*, No. 11 (48), November 1925, pp. 87–94.

"Ob otnoshenii Gomindana k kommunistam (Reshenie Ts. K. Gomindana)" (On the attitude of the Kuomintang toward the Communists; decision of the Central Committee of the Kuomintang). *Materialy po Kitaiskomu Voprosu*, No. 6, 1927, pp. 58–59.

"Polozhenie vnutri Kommunisticheskoi Partii Kitaia ko vremeni V sezda" (Situation within the Chinese Communist Party at the time of its Fifth Congress). *K.I.*, No. 41 (115), October 14, 1927, pp. 46–47.

"Protiv Suniatsenizma za Leninizm" (Against Sun-Yat-sen-ism, for Leninism). *Materialy po Kitaiskomu Voprosu*, No. 1 (10), 1928, pp. 29–58. Translation of a leaflet published by the Central Committee of the Chinese Communist Party.

Rafes, M. G. "Materialy po istorii Gomindana; II Kongress Gomindana" (Materials on the history of the Kuomintang; the Second Congress of the Kuomintang). *N.V.*, No. 18, 1927, pp. 1–39.

———. "Shankhaiskoe dvizhenie i ego itogi" (The Shanghai movement and its results). *N.V.*, No. 12, 1926, pp. 1–17.

"Resolution of the ECCI on the Present Situation in the Chinese Revolution." *International Press Correspondence*, No. 44, July 28, 1927, pp. 983–85.

"Revoliutsiia i kontr-revoliutsiia v Kitae" (Revolution and counterrevolution in China). *Bolshevik*, No. 7-8, April 15, 1927, pp. 3–12.

"Rezoliutsii V sezda KKP: Politicheskoe polozhenie i zadachi kompartii" (Resolution of the Fifth Congress of the Chinese Communist Party: The political situation and the tasks of the Communist Party). *Materialy po Kitaiskomu Voprosu*, No. 7, 1927, pp. 5–13.

Riutin, M. "Kitaiskaia revoliutsiia i losung sovetov" (The Chinese revolution and the slogan of soviets). *Bolshevik*, No. 11-12, June 15, 1927, pp. 29–41.

Semenov, B. "Borba v Kitae" (The struggle in China). *N.V.*, No. 15, 1926, pp. XVIII–XXXII.

———. "Borba vokrug Shanghaia" (The struggle around Shanghai). *N.V.*, No. 16-17, 1927, pp. XIV–XXIV.

———. "Kanton i Gongong" (Canton and Hong Kong). *Mezhdunarodnaia Zhizn*, No. 5, 1926, pp. 3–15.

———. "Nastuplenie reaktsii v Kitae" (The coming of the reaction in China). *Mirovoe Khoziaistvo i Mirovaia Politika*, No. 4, 1926, pp. 3–14.

————. "Novyi etap kitaiskoi revoliutsii" (The new stage of the Chinese revolution). *N.V.*, No. 18, 1927, pp. LXXV–LXXVIII.

————. "Okonchanie pervogo etapa grazhdanskoi voiny v Kitae" (The end of the
first stage of civil war in China). *N.V.*, No. 6, 1924, pp. XXXVI–XXXX.

————. "Polozhenie v Kitae" (The situation in China). *N.V.*, No. 10-11, 1925,
pp. XLVI–LI.

————. "Tamozhennaia konferentsiia v Kitae" (The customs conference in China).
Mezhdunarodnaia Zhizn, No. 1, 1926, pp. 46–60.

Shumiatsky, B. Z. "Iz istorii Komsomola i Kompartii Kitaia (Pamiati odnogo iz
organizatorov Komsomola i Kompartii Kitaia tov. Chang T'ai-lei)" (On the
Communist Youth and Communist Party of China. In memory of one of the
organizers of the Communist Youth and Communist Party of China, Comrade
Chang T'ai-lei). *Revoliutsionnyi Vostok*, No. 4-5, 1928, pp. 194–230.

Stalin, I. V. "O perspektivakh revoliutsii v Kitae" (On the prospects of the revolution in China). *Bolshevik*, No. 23-24, December 31, 1926, pp. 13–21; also *K.I.*,
No. 13 (71), December 10, 1926, pp. 9–19. Speech to the Chinese Commission
of the ECCI, September 30, 1926. Also published in book form.

————. "Revoliutsiia v Kitae i zadachi Kominterna (rech tov. Stalina na X zasedanii IKKI 24 maia 1927 goda)" (The revolution in China and the tasks of the
Comintern; speech at the tenth session of the ECCI, May 24, 1927). *K.I.* No. 23
(97), June 10, 1927, pp. 12–25.

Sten, Ia. "Kitaiskaia revoliutsiia i taktika Kominterna" (The Chinese revolution
and the tactics of the Comintern). *Kommunisticheskaia Revoliutsiia*, No. 13-14,
July 1927, pp. 28–43.

————. "Voprosy kitaiskoi revoliutsii" (Problems of the Chinese revolution).
Kommunisticheskaia Revoliutsiia, No. 16-17, August-September 1927, pp. 34–43.

Strakhov (Ch'u Ch'iu-pai). "Voprosy kitaiskogo professionalnogo dvizheniia"
(Problems of the Chinese trade union movement). *Problemy Kitaia*, No. 2, 1930,
pp. 28–62. Translated from the Chinese and abridged.

T'an P'ing-shan. "K sovremennomu politicheskomu polozheniiu v Kitae" (The
present political situation in China). *K.I.*, No. 4 (62), October 8, 1926, pp.
17–24.

————. "Uspekhi kantonskoi armii i perspektivy kitaiskoi revoliutsii" (Successes
of the Canton army and prospects of the Chinese revolution). *K.I.*, No. 7 (65),
October 29, 1926, pp. 11–17.

"Tezisy Ts. K. Kitaiskoi Kompartii o politicheskom polozhenii i zadachakh Kitkom-
partii (priniatye na avgustovskoi ekstrennoi partkonferentsii)" (Theses of the
Central Committee of the Chinese Communist Party on the political situation
and the tasks of the Chinese Communist Party, passed at the extraordinary party
conference [August 1927]). *Materialy po Kitaiskomu Voprosu*, No. 8, December 1927, pp. 3–10.

"V sezd Kompartii Kitaia i Gomindan" (The Fifth Congress of the Chinese Communist Party and the Kuomintang). *K.I.*, No. 1 (85), March 18, 1927, pp. 3–8.

Veltman, M. L. (M. Pavlovich). "Borba za Kitai" (The struggle for China). *Z.N.*,
No. 6 (135), February 16, 1922, p. 1.

Vilensky, V. D. (Sibiriakov). "Interventsiia v Kitae" (Intervention in China).
N.V., No. 6, 1924, pp. XVI–XXIII.

————. "Kitaiskaia kommunisticheskaia partiia" (The Chinese Communist Party).
N.V., No. 2, 1922, pp. 604–12. Includes "Deklaratsiia Kitaiskoi Kompartii o
sovremennom politicheskom polozhenii v Kitae" (Declaration of the Chinese
Communist Party on the present political situation in China), June 10, 1922;
translated by A. E. Khodorov with an introduction by Vilensky.

————. "Nakanune obrazovaniia kommunisticheskoi partii v Kitae" (On the eve of the formation of a communist party in China). *K.I.*, No. 16, 1921, pp. 3585–94.

———. "Politicheskie gruppirovki i partii v Kitae" (The political groupings and parties in China). *K.I.*, No. 23, 1922, pp. 6077–6104.

———. "Polozhenie v Kitae" (The situation in China). *N.V.*, No. 12, 1926, pp. LVI–LXIV.

———. "Sovetskoe imushchestvo na kitaiskoi zemle" (Soviet property on Chinese territory). *Izvestiia*, No. 206, September 13, 1923, p. 1.

Voitinsky, G. N. "Borba za Gomindan. Sobytiia na severe i iuzhnoe pravitelstvo" (The struggle for the Kuomintang. Events in the North and the government of the South). *K.I.*, No. 7 (56), July 1926, pp. 35–53.

———. "Gomindan i Kompartiia Kitaia v borbe s imperializmom" (The Kuomintang and the Communist Party of China in the struggle against imperialism). *N.V.*, No. 6, 1924, pp. XXIV–XXVI.

———. "Interventsiia v Kitae" (The intervention in China"). *Bolshevik*, No. 12-13, October 20, 1924, pp. 49–54.

———. "K otsenke polozheniia v Kitae" (An evaluation of the situation in China). *K.I.*, No. 4 (53), April 1926, pp. 5–23.

———. "K voprosu ob oshibkakh kitaiskoi kompartii v revoliutsii 1925–1927 gg." (Mistakes of the Chinese Communist Party in the revolution of 1925–1927). *Problemy Kitaia*, No. 4-5, 1930, pp. 84–104.

———. "Partiia Gomindana i kitaiskaia revoliutsiia" (The Kuomintang and the Chinese revolution). *Bolshevik*, No. 1, April 1, 1924, pp. 119–23.

———. "Politicheskie otnosheniia v Kitae nakanune revoliutsii 1925–1927" (Political relations in China on the eve of the revolution of 1925–1927). *Voprosy Istorii*, No. 7, July 1947, pp. 50–72.

———. "Proletariat i natsionalnoe dvizhenie v Kitae" (The proletariat and the national movement in China). *N.V.*, No. 4, 1923, pp. 280–90. Includes two documents: (1) Manifesto of the Communist Chinese Party concerning the existing political situation, July 1923, signed by the Central Committee of the Chinese Communist Party, and (2) Appeal of the Union of Peking Students, August 31, 1923.

———. "Tendentsiia revoliutsionnogo dvizheniia v Kitae i Gomindan" (The tendency of the revolutionary movement in China and the Kuomintang). *K.I.*, No. 3 (40), March 1925, pp. 153–59.

Wang Ching-wei. "Razlichie mezhdu kommunizmom i Suniatsenizmom" (The difference between communism and Sun-Yat-sen-ism). *Materialy po Kitaiskomu Voprosu*, No. 1 (10), 1928, pp. 23–28. Speech to the students of Shanghai College, December 1927; translated from the Chinese.

Wang Ming. "15 let borby za nezavisimost i svobodu kitaiskogo naroda" (Fifteen years of the Chinese people's struggle for independence and freedom). *K.I.*, No. 14, August 1936, pp. 81–95.

Whiting, Allen S. "The Soviet Offer to China of 1919." *The Far Eastern Quarterly*, X, No. 4 (August 1951), pp. 355–64.

COMINTERN, ECCI, KRESTINTERN, PROFINTERN

Official and semiofficial contemporary publications are listed first, in chronological order by subject. Commentaries and later compilations follow in the usual order.

Comintern

Der I Kongress der Kommunistischen Internationale; Protokoll der Verhandlungen in Moskau vom 2 bis zum 19 März 1919. Petrograd, 1920.

Pervyi Kongress Kommunisticheskogo Internatsionala; protokoly zasedanii v Mo-

skve so 2 po 19 marta 1919 goda (First Congress of the Communist International; minutes of the meetings in Moscow, March 2–19, 1919). Petrograd, 1921.

Pervyi Kongress Kominterna, mart 1919 g. (First Congress of the Communist International, March 1919). Moscow, 1933.

Otchet Ispolnitelnogo Komiteta Kommunisticheskogo Internatsionala Vtoromu Vsemirnomu Kongressu Kommunisticheskogo Internatsionala (Report of the Executive Committee of the Communist International to the Second World Congress of the Communist International). Petrograd, 1920.

The Second Congress of the Communist International; Proceedings of Petrograd Session of July 17th and of Moscow Sessions of July 19th–August 7th, 1920. Moscow, 1920.

Vtoroi Kongress Kominterna, iiul–avgust, 1920 g. (Second Congress of the Comintern, July–August 1920). Moscow, 1934.

Tretii Vsemirnyi Kongress Kommunisticheskogo Internatsionala. Stenograficheskii otchet (Third World Congress of the Communist International. Stenographic report). Petrograd, 1922.

Decisions of the Third Congress of the Communist International Held at Moscow, July, 1921. London, 1922 (?).

Theses and Resolutions Adopted at the Third World Congress of the Communist International (June 22 to July 12, 1921). New York, 1921.

Bulletin des III Kongresses der Kommunistischen Internationale, Nos. 1–24; 24 Juni–20 Juli, 1921. Moscow, 1921.

Chetvertyi Vsemirnyi Kongress Kommunisticheskogo Internatsionala 5 noiabria–3 dekabria, 1922 goda; Izbrannye doklady, rechi i rezoliutsii (Fourth World Congress of the Communist International, November 5–December 3, 1922; selected reports, speeches, and resolutions). Moscow and Petrograd, 1923.

"Communist International IV Congress, 1922." *International Press Correspondence,* No. 106, December 2, 1922.

Postanovleniia IV Vsemirnogo Kongressa Kommunisticheskogo Internatsionala (Decisions of the Fourth World Congress of the Communist International). Petrograd, 1925.

Protokoll des Vierten Kongresses der Kommunistischen Internationale, Petrograd–Moskau vom 5 November bis 5 Dezember, 1922. Hamburg, 1923.

From the Fourth to the Fifth World Congress; Report of the Executive Committee of the Communist International. London, 1924.

Piatyi Vsemirnyi Kongress Kommunisticheskogo Internatsionala, 17 iiunia–8 iiulia 1924 g. Stenograficheskii otchet (Fifth World Congress of the Communist International, June 17–July 8, 1924. Stenographic report). Moscow and Leningrad, 1925. In two parts.

Kommunisticheskii Internatsional pered Shestym Vsemirnym Kongressom; obzor deiatelnosti IKKI i sektsii Kominterna mezhdu V i VI kongressami (The Communist International before the Sixth World Congress; a survey of the activities of the ECCI and the sections of the Comintern in the period between the Fifth and Sixth congresses). Moscow and Leningrad, 1928.

ECCI

Thesen des Executiv-komitees der Kommunistischen Internationale. Hamburg, 1921.

Biulleten Ispolnitelnogo Komiteta Kommunisticheskogo Internatsionala 8 sent.–23 dek. 1921 (Bulletin of the Executive Committee of the Communist International, Sept. 8–Dec. 23, 1921). Petrograd, 1921. Four numbers in one volume.

Deiatelnost Ispolnitelnogo Komiteta i Prezidiuma I. K. Kommunisticheskogo Internatsionala ot 13-go iiulia 1921 g. do 1-go fevralia 1922 g. (The activities of the

Executive Committee of the Communist International and its presidium from July 13, 1921, to February 1, 1922). Petrograd, 1922.

Rasshirennyi plenum Ispolnitelnogo Komiteta Kommunisticheskogo Internatsionala, 12–23 iiunia 1923 goda; otchet ([Third] Enlarged Plenum of the Executive Committee of the Communist International, June 12–23, 1923; report). Moscow, 1923.

Rasshirennyi plenum Ispolkoma Kommunisticheskogo Internatsionala. Stenografi-cheskii otchet ([Fifth] Enlarged Plenum of the Executive Committee of the Communist International [March 21–April 6, 1925]. Stenographic report). Moscow, 1925.

Otchet Ispolkoma Kominterna (aprel 1925 g.–ianvar 1926 g.) (Report of the Executive Committee of the Comintern, April 1925–January 1926). Moscow, 1926.

Shestoi rasshirennyi plenum Ispolkoma Kominterna (17 fevralia–15 marta 1926). Stenograficheskii otchet (Sixth Enlarged Plenum of the Executive Committee of the Comintern, February 17–March 15, 1926. Stenographic report). Moscow and Leningrad, 1927.

Tätigkeitsbericht der Exekutive der Kommunistischen Internationale, Februar–November, 1926. Hamburg and Berlin, 1926.

Puti mirovoi revoliutsii; Sedmoi rasshirennyi plenum Ispolnitelnogo Komiteta Kommunisticheskogo Internatsionala. Stenograficheskii otchet (The paths of the world revolution; the Seventh Enlarged Plenum of the Executive Committee of the Communist International [November 22–December 16, 1926]. Stenographic report). 2 vols. Moscow, 1927.

[Bukharin, N. I.] *Capitalist Stabilization and Proletarian Revolution; Report to the VII Enlarged Plenum of E. C. of the Comintern on Point I on the Agenda: "The World Situation and the Tasks of the Comintern."* Moscow, 1926.

VIII Plenum Ispolnitelnogo Komiteta Kommunisticheskogo Internatsionala, 18–30 maia 1927 goda. Tezisy, rezoliutsii i vozvaniia (Eighth Plenum of the Executive Committee of the Communist International, May 18–30, 1927. Theses, resolutions, and appeals). Moscow, 1927.

Krestintern

1—re Conférence internationale paysanne . . . Paris, 1923 (?).

"Pervaia Mezhdunarodnaia Krestianskaia Konferentsiia. Materialy" (The First International Peasant Conference. Materials). *Krestianskii Internatsional*, No. 1, April 1924, pp. 158–74.

Protokoll vom Ersten Internationalen Bauernkongress, vom 10 bis 16 Oktober, 1923, in Moskau. Berlin, 1924.

Profintern

Profintern i Komintern; vopros o vzaimootnoshenii Profinterna i Kominterna na I-om Mezhdunarodnom Kongresse revoliutsionnykh profsoiuzov (Profintern and Comintern; the problem of relations between the Profintern and the Comintern discussed at the First International Congress of Revolutionary Trade Unions). Moscow, 1921.

Dridzo, S. A. (A. Lozovsky). *Itogi i ocherednye zadachi mezhdunarodnogo prof-dvizheniia (Doklad i zakliuchitelnoe slovo na IV kongresse Profinterna)* (The results and tasks of the day in the international trade union movement: Report and conclusive remarks at the Fourth Congress of the Profintern). Moscow and Leningrad, 1928.

———. "Itogi i perspektivy raboty Profinterna k VII sezdu profsoiuzov SSSR" (Conclusions and prospects for the work of the Profintern at the time of the seventh congress of the trade unions of the U.S.S.R.). *Krasnyi Internatsional Profsoiuzov*, No. 12, December 1926, pp. 535–49.

———. "O nashei dalneishei rabote v profsoiuzakh" (Our future work in the trade unions). *K.I.*, No. 1, January 1926, pp. 82–98.

———. *The Pan-Pacific Trade Union Conference, Hankow, May 20–26, 1927.* Moscow, 1927.

Other Congresses

Pervyi sezd narodov Vostoka, Baku, 1–8 sentiabria 1920 g. Stenograficheskie otchety (The First Congress of the Peoples of the East, Baku, September 1–8, 1920. Stenographic report). Moscow, 1920.

Der Erste Kongress der Kommunistischen und Revolutionären Organisationen des Fernen Ostens, Moskau, Januar 1922. Hamburg, 1922.

Pervyi sezd revoliutsionnykh organizatsii Dalnego Vostoka. Sbornik (First Congress of the Revolutionary Organizations of the Far East. A collection of materials). Petrograd, 1922.

The First Congress of the Toilers of the Far East . . . Petrograd, 1922.

Bantke, S. (ed.). *Borba bolshevikov za sozdanie Kommunisticheskogo Internatsionala; materialy i dokumenty, 1914–1919 g.g.* (The Bolsheviks' struggle to form the Communist International; materials and documents, 1914–1919). Moscow, 1934.

Borkenau, Franz. *The Communist International.* London, 1938.

James, C. L. R. *World Revolution, 1917–1936; the Rise and Fall of the Communist International, 1937.* London, 1937.

Kabakchiev, Kh. S. *Kak voznik i razvivalsia Kommunisticheskii Internatsional (kratkii istoricheskii ocherk)* (How the Communist International was founded and developed. A short outline). Moscow, 1929.

Kommunisticheskii Internatsional i voina; dokumenty i materialy o borbe Kominterna protiv imperialisticheskoi voiny i v zashchitu SSSR (The Communist International and the war; documents and materials on the struggle of the Comintern against imperialist war in defense of the U.S.S.R.). Moscow and Leningrad, 1928.

Kommunisticheskii Internatsional v dokumentakh; resheniia, tezisy i vozvaniia kongressov Kominterna i plenumov IKKI, 1919–1932 (The Communist International in documents; decisions, theses, and appeals of the congresses of the Comintern and plenums of the ECCI, 1919–1932). Moscow, 1933.

Lenin, V. I. *Kommunisticheskii Internatsional; stati, rechi, dokumenty, 1914–1923* (The Communist International; articles, speeches, documents, 1914–1923). 2 vols. Moscow, 1934 and 1937.

Rezanov, A. S. *Le travail secret des agents bolchévistes.* Paris, 1926.

———. *La Troisième Internationale Communiste* . . . Paris, 1922.

Roy, M. N. *The Communist International.* Delhi, 1946.

Tivel, A. (comp.). *5 let Kominterna v resheniiakh i tsifrakh* (Five years of the Comintern in resolutions and figures). Moscow, 1924. Supplement to *Kommunisticheskii Internatsional*, No. 1.

———. *10 let Kominterna v resheniiakh i tsifrakh* (Ten years of the Comintern in resolutions and figures). Moscow, 1929.

Zinoviev, G. E. *Report of the Executive Committee of the Communist International for 1920–1921.* Moscow, 1921.

[Bukharin, N. I.] "Rech tov. Bukharina na Presidiume IKKI (27 sentiabria 1927 g.)" (Speech of Comrade Bukharin to the presidium of the ECCI, September 17 [on China]). *K.I.*, No. 41 (115), October 14, 1927, pp. 8–17.

"Pravaia opasnost v VKP i Kominterne" (The danger of Right deviation in the All-Russian Communist Party and the Comintern). *K.I.*, No. 48 (174), November 30, 1928, pp. 3–6.

Ryskulov, T. R. "Komintern i rabota na Vostoke" (The Comintern and its work in the East). *Z.N.*, No. 40 (96), December 15, 1920, pp. 1–2.

Safarov, G. I. "Natsionalno-kolonialnyi vopros na IV Kongresse Kominterna" (The national and colonial questions at the Fourth Congress of the Communist International). *N.V.*, No. 2, 1922, pp. 58–74.

Veltman, M. L. (M. Pavlovich). "Kolonialnaia i natsionalnaia politika na II-om kongresse III Internatsionala" (Colonial and national policy at the Second Congress of the Third International). *Z.N.*, No. 25 (82), August 1, 1920, pp. 1–2, and No. 26 (83), August 10, 1920, pp. 1–2. Summary of speeches and text of the supplementary theses.

―――. "Voprosy natsionalnoi i kolonialnoi politiki i III Internatsional" (The problems of national and colonial policy and the Third International). *Z.N.*, Nos. 32–40 (except 35), October–December 1920.

―――. "Vostochnyi vopros na III kongresse i perspektivy osvoboditelnogo dvizheniia na Vostoke" (The Eastern question at the Third Congress and the prospects of the liberation movement in the East). *Z.N.*, No. 14 (112), July 16, 1921, p. 1, and No. 15 (113), July 30, 1921, p. 1.

Voitinsky, G. N. "Kolonialnyi vopros na rasshirennom plenume IKKI" (The colonial question at the [Fifth] Enlarged Plenum of the ECCI). *K.I.*, No. 4 (41), April 1925, pp. 63–69. Quotations from the resolutions on communist tasks in India, Java, Egypt, and the American colonies and semicolonies.

"Voprosy revoliutsionnogo dvizheniia na Vostoke na predstoiashchem rasshirennom plenume IKKI" (The problems of the revolutionary movement in the East at the coming [Sixth] Enlarged Plenum of the ECCI). *K.I.*, No. 12 (49), December 1925, pp. 24–39.

INDIA

A Call to Action, Being the Resolutions, Theses and Report Presented to the Third Annual Conference of the Workers' and Peasants' Party of Bengal, Bhatpara, 1928. Calcutta, 1928.

Dutt, R. P. *India Today.* Bombay, 1949.

Limaye, Madhu. *Communist Party: Facts and Fiction.* Hyderabad (Deccan), 1951.

Masani, M. R. *The Communist Party of India, a Short History.* New York, 1954. Issued under the auspices of the Institute of Pacific Relations.

Melman, S. M. *Indiia* (India). Moscow, 1943.

Mohan Das, S. R. *Communist Activity in India (1925–1950).* Bombay, 1951.

Roy, M. N. *The Aftermath of Non-Cooperation.* London, 1925.

―――. *I Accuse; from the Suppressed Statement of M. N. Roy on Trial for Treason Before Sessions Court, Cawnpore, India.* New York, 1932.

―――. *One Year of Non-Cooperation; from Ahmedabad to Gaya.* Calcutta, 1923.

―――. *Political Letters.* Zurich, 1924.

Singh, Rattan. *A Brief History of the Hindustan Gadar Party (Submitted to the Assembly of the League against Imperialism by the Party's Delegate Rattan Singh on the 27th of July 1929 at Frankfort on Main).* San Francisco, 1929.

*Spratt, Philip. *Blowing up India. Reminiscences and Reflections of a Former Comintern Emissary.* Calcutta, 1955.

*Tagore, Saumyendranath. *Historical Development of the Communist Movement* *in India.* Calcutta, 1944. Edited and published by the Politbureau of the Central Committee of the Revolutionary Communist Party of India.

A. T. "Natsionalno-revoliutsionnoe dvizhenie v Indii" (The national-revolutionary movement in India). *Z.N.,* No. 5 (134), February 9, 1922, pp. 2–3.

Achariia, M. "Polozhenie v Indii k nachalu 1922 goda" (The situation in India in early 1922). *Vestnik N.K.I.D.,* No. 1, 1922, pp. 69–75.

"Agrarnoe dvizhenie i propaganda v voiskakh Indii" (The agrarian movement and propaganda among the Indian troops), *Z.N.,* No. 6-7 (12-13), April 14, 1922, p. 19.

[Gurko-]Kriazhin, V. A. "Revoliutsionnoe dvizhenie v Indii" (The revolutionary movement in India). *Z.N.,* No. 14 (71), May 16, 1920, pp. 2–3.

"The International Association of the Oppressed Peoples." *The Masses of India* (Paris), II, No. 9, September 1926, pp. 10–11.

Mio-Kai. "Sovremennoe polozhenie Indii" (The present situation in India). *Mezhdunarodnaia Zhizn,* No. 5, 1926, pp. 46–58.

"National Communism; Beware of False Friends." *The Masses of India* (Paris), II, No. 9, September 1926, supplement.

"Revoliutsionno-natsionalnoe dvizhenie v Indii" (The revolutionary national movement in India). *Z.N.,* No. 26 (124), November 19, 1921, p. 4.

"Rol Rossii v probuzhdenii Vostoka. Mnenie indiiskogo revoliutsionera tovarishcha Mohamed Ibi Abdullah Ensari" (Russia's role in the awakening of the East. Opinion of an Indian revolutionary, Comrade Mohamed Ibi Abdullah Ensari). *Z.N.,* No. 40 (48), October 19, 1919, p. 2.

Roy, M. N. "Klassovaia differentsiia v revoliutsionnom dvizhenii Indii" (Class differentiation in the revolutionary movement in India). *K.I.,* No. 5 (42), May 1925, pp. 149–68.

———. "Manifest Revoliutsionnoi Partii Indii. Vozvanie k britanskomu proletariatu" (The Manifesto of the Revolutionary Party of India. Appeal to the British proletariat). *Z.N.,* No. 24 (81), July 25, 1920, pp. 1–2.

———. "Perspektivy indiiskogo natsionalnogo dvizheniia" (The prospects of the Indian national movement). *K.I.,* No. 3 (77), January 21, 1927, pp. 28–36.

———. "Sotsialnaia revoliutsiia v Indii" (Social revolution in India). *Z.N.,* No. 31 (88), October 10, 1920, p. 2.

Sardar. "Revoliutsionnoe dvizhenie Indii v sviazi s sobytiiami v Kitae" (The revolutionary movement in India in connection with the events in China). *Revoliutsionnyi Vostok,* No. 2, 1927, pp. 96–106.

Tivel, A. "Puti i perspektivy indiiskoi revoliutsii" (Ways and prospects of the Indian revolution). *N.V.,* No. 1, 1922, pp. 104–18.

Trainin, I. P. "Vseindiiskii sezd" (The All-Indian Congress). *Z.N.,* No. 6 (104), March 4, 1921, p. 1.

Zakharia. "Krestianskoe dvizhenie v Indii i indiiskoe krestianstvo" (The peasant movement in India and the Indian peasantry). *Krestianskii Internatsional,* No. 2, May 1924, pp. 58–70.

INDOCHINA AND INDONESIA

Blumberger, J. Th. Petrus. *Le communisme aux Indes Néerlandaises.* Paris, 1929.

———. *De Communistische Beweging in Nederlandsch-Indië.* Haarlem, 1935.

Dingley, S. *Borba krestianstva Indonezii* (The struggle of the Indonesian peasantry). Moscow, 1927. Translated from the French.

———. *The Peasants Movement in Indonesia.* Berlin, 1927.

Ennis, T. E. *French Policy and Developments in Indochina.* Chicago, 1936.

Guber, A. A. *Natsionalno-osvoboditelnoe dvizhenie v Indonezii* (The national-liberation movement in Indonesia). Moscow, 1946.

Kahin, G. M. *Nationalism and Revolution in Indonesia*. Ithaca, N.Y., 1952.

Political Parties and Movements in the Netherlands East Indies. Washington, D.C., 1945.

Vasileva, V. Ia. *Indo-Kitai* (Indochina). Moscow, Institut Mirovogo Khoziaistva i Mirovoi Politiki (Institute of World Economy and Politics), 1947.

Villemotier-Comberomaine, L. *Le mouvement bolchévick et l'intervention en Indochine française, 1925–1940*. 2d ed. Paris, 1944.

A. T. "Natsionalno-revoliutsionnoe dvizhenie v gollandskikh koloniiakh" (The national-revolutionary movement in the Dutch colonies). *Z.N.*, No. 2 (131), January 17, 1922, p. 4.

Darsono, Raden. "Polozhenie narodnogo dvizheniia v Indonezii" (The condition of the people's movement in Indonesia). *K.I.*, No. 9 (67), November 12, 1926, pp. 46–49.

Fratsevich. "Sarekat Islam" (Sarekat Islam). *Revoliutsionnyi Vostok*, No. 4-5, 1928, pp. 307–30. On Indonesian political movements.

Galkovich, M. "Filippiny v borbe za svoiu nezavisimost" (The Philippines in the struggle for their independence). *Mirovoe Khoziaistvo i Mirovaia Politika*, No. 2, 1926, pp. 106–14.

Guber, A. A. "Natsionalno-osvoboditelnoe dvizhenie v Indonezii" (The national-liberation movement in Indonesia). *Revoliutsionnyi Vostok*, No. 3-4 (15-16), 1932, pp. 251–70, and No. 1 (17), 1933, pp. 190–200.

———. "Revoliutsionnoe dvizhenie v Indonezii na sovremennom etape" (The present stage of the revolutionary movement in Indonesia). *Revoliutsionnyi Vostok*, No. 5 (21), 1933, pp. 32–46.

K[allinikov], Anatolii. "Revoliutsionnoe dvizhenie v Indonezii" (The revolutionary movement in Indonesia). *Izvestiia Ulan-Bator-Khoto*, No. 4 (348), January 12, 1927, pp. 2–3.

Milgram, I. "K voprosu o natsionalno-osvoboditelnom dvizhenii v Indonezii" (On the question of the national-liberation movement in Indonesia). *Tikhii Okean*, No. 3 (9), July–September, 1936, pp. 95–114.

Munster, G. J. van. "The Background and History of the Insurrection in Java." *International Press Correspondence*, No. 87, December 16, 1926, pp. 1498–99.

Sedjammo (Sardjono?). "The Labour Movement in the East Indies." *International Press Correspondence*, No. 10, November 22, 1921, pp. 80–81.

Semaoen. "International Imperialism and the Communist Party of Indonesia." *The Communist International*, No. 17, 1925, pp. 75–82; also *K.I.*, No. 11 (48), November 1925, pp. 142–48.

———. "Natsionalnoe dvizhenie i kommunisticheskaia partiia Indonezii . . ." (The national movement and the Communist Party of Indonesia . . .). *K.I.*, No. 5 (42), May 1925, pp. 159–64.

———. "Vokrug vosstaniia na Iave. Organizatsiia vosstaniia i ego uroki" (Around the revolt in Java. Organization of the revolt and its lessons). *Krasnyi Internatsional Profsoiuzov*, No. 1 (72), January 1927, pp. 70–76.

———. "Nakanune novykh bur v Indonezii" (On the eve of new storms in Indonesia). *K.I.*, No. 37 (111), September 16, 1927, pp. 30–35.

———. "Vosstanie na Iave i Sumatre . . ." (The uprisings in Java and Sumatra . . .). *K.I.*, No. 12 (86), March 25, 1927, pp. 28–35, and No. 14 (88), April 8, 1927, pp. 23–33. This and the preceding article were published under the name Kiai Samin.

JAPAN

Colbert, Evelyn S. *The Left Wing in Japanese Politics.* New York, 1952.
Deistviia Iaponii v Priamurskom krae. Sbornik offitsialnykh dokumentov . . . (Japanese actions in the Maritime Province. A collection of official documents . . .). Vladivostok, 1921.
Durkee, Travers Edgar. "The Communist International and Japan, 1919–1922." 1953. An unpublished doctoral dissertation in the Stanford University Libraries.
Eidus, Khaim T. *Iaponiia ot pervoi do vtoroi mirovoi voiny* (Japan from the First World War to the Second). Moscow, 1946.
Hindus, Maurice G. *Russia and Japan.* New York, 1942.
Iaponiia na russkom Dalnem Vostoke. Krovavaia epopeia iaponskoi interventsii (Japan in the Russian Far East. The bloody period of Japanese intervention). Moscow, 1922.
Japanese Intervention in the Russian Far East. Washington, D.C., 1922. Published by the Special Delegation of the Far Eastern Republic to the United States of America.
Langer, Paul F., and Rodger Swearingen (comps.). *Bibliography on Japanese Communism.* New York, 1950. Published under the auspices of the Institute of Pacific Relations.
Mif, P. A., and G. N. Voitinsky (eds.). *Sovremennaia Iaponiia* (Modern Japan). 2 vols. Moscow, 1934.
Mints, I. I. (ed.). *Iaponskaia interventsiia 1918–1922 gg. v dokumentakh* (Japanese intervention, 1918–1922, in documents). Moscow, 1934.
Muramatsu Takeshi (comp.). *Nihon Kyōsan-tō tēze* (Japanese Communist Party theses). Tokyo, 1952.
Nihon Kyōsan-to-shi Shiryo Iin-kai (Committee for the Compilation of Historical Materials on the Japanese Communist Party). *Nihon mondai ni kansuru hōshin-sho, ketsugi-shū* (A collection of theses and decisions concerning Japanese problems). Tokyo, 1950.
Nosaka, T. *A Brief Review of the Labour Movement in Japan.* Moscow, 1921.
Pozdniev, D. M. *Iaponiia, strana, naselenie, istoriia, politika* (Japan, the country, its population, history, and politics). Moscow, 1925.
Reikhberg, G. *Iaponskaia interventsiia na Dalnem Vostoke 1918–1922 gg.*; kratkii ocherk (Japanese intervention in the Far East, 1918–1922; a brief sketch). Moscow, 1935.
Stoklitsky, A. V. *Iaponiia i Kitai* (Japan and China). Moscow and Leningrad, 1928.
Swearingen, Rodger, and Paul Langer. *Red Flag in Japan. International Communism in Action, 1919–1951.* Cambridge, Mass., 1952.
Tōkyo Chihō Saiban-sho. Kenji-kyoku (Tokyo District Court. Office of the Procurator). *Nihon Kyōsan-tō chian iji-hō ihan hikoku jiken yoshin shūketsu kettei-sho* (Decision at the preliminary hearing of the case of the defendants of the Japanese Communist Party involving the breach of the Peace Preservation Law). Tokyo, 1930.
——. *Tokuda Kyūichi hoka sanjūroku-mei chian iji-hō ihan hikoku jiken yoshin shōketsu kettei-sho utsushi* (Transcript of the decision at the preliminary hearing of the case involving the breach of the Peace Preservation Law by Tokuda Kyūichi and thirty-six others). A mimeographed copy of the handwritten original.
Veltman, M. L. (M. Pavlovich). *Iaponskii imperializm na Dalnem Vostoke* (Japanese imperialism in the Far East). Moscow, 1923.
Vilensky, V. D. (Sibiriakov). *Imperializm sovremennoi Iaponii i sotsialnaia revoliutsiia. K voprosu resheniia Dalne-Vostochnoi problemy* (Modern Japanese

imperialism and social revolution. On the solution of the Far Eastern problem). Moscow, 1919.

———. *Revoliutsionnoe dvizhenie v Iaponii; iz pisem iaponskikh rabochikh* (The revolutionary movement in Japan; from the letters of Japanese workers). Moscow, 1919.

Yamamoto, Katsunosuke, and Mitsuho Arita. *Nihōn kyōsan-shugi undō-shi* (History of the Japanese communist movement). Tokyo, 1950.

Yanaga, Chitoshi. *Japan Since Perry*. New York, 1949.

Zhukov, E. M. (ed.). *Iaponiia. Sbornik statei* . . . (Japan. A collection of articles . . .). Moscow, 1934.

Aboltin, N. V. "Kak byl vozvrashchen SSSR Severnyi Sakhalin" (How Northern Sakhalin was returned to the U.S.S.R.). *Severnaia Aziia*, No. 4 (16), 1927, pp. 44–54.

Iamono, K. "Politiko-ekonomicheskoe polozhenie v Iaponii" (The politico-economic situation in Japan). *Revoliutsionnyi Vostok*, No. 2, 1927, pp. 140–50.

Ianson, Ia. D. "Velikaia Iaponiia" (Great Japan). *Vestnik N.K.I.D.*, No. 9-10, December 15, 1920, pp. 7–12. Documented.

———. "Oktiabrskaia revoliutsiia i iaponskii proletariat" (The October Revolution and the Japanese proletariat). *Krasnyi Internatsional Profsoiuzov*, No. 10 (81), October 1927, pp. 415–17. Written under the pseudonym Khaiama (Hayama).

Iaroslavsky, Emelian. "Russko-iaponskaia voina i otnoshenie k nei bolshevikov" (The Russo-Japanese War and the Bolsheviks' attitude toward it). *Proletarskaia Revoliutsiia*, No. 1 (11), 1939, pp. 47–74.

Ioffe, A. A. "Rossiia i Iaponiia (Chanchunskaia konferentsiia)" (Russia and Japan: Changchun Conference). *N.V.*, No. 4, 1923, pp. 1–11.

———. "SSSR i Dalnii Vostok" (The U.S.S.R. and the Far East). *Mirovoe Khoziaistvo i Mirovaia Politika*, No. 10-11, 1927, pp. 26–47.

Katayama, Sen. "Revoliutsionnoe dvizhenie v Kitae i pozitsiia Iaponii" (The revolutionary movement in China and the position of Japan). *K.I.*, No. 1 (75), January 7, 1927, pp. 16–20.

———. "Rōdō Nōmin-tō i proletarskoe dvizhenie" (Rōdō Nōmin tō [the Farmer-Labor Party] and the proletarian movement). *K.I.*, No. 9 (58), September 1926, pp. 115–19.

———. "Rozhdenie sotsialnoi narodnoi partii v Iaponii (*Shakai Minshu-to*)" (The birth of a Social-Democratic people's party in Japan). *K.I.*, No. 4 (78), January 28, 1927, pp. 46–50.

Natsov, S. "Iaponiia v Mongolii i Manchzhurii" (Japan in Mongolia and Manchuria). *Revoliutsionnyi Vostok*, No. 4-5, 1928, pp. 331–47.

Reikhberg, G. "Bolsheviki Dalnego Vostoka v borbe s iaponskoi interventsiei (1918–1922 gg.)" (The Bolsheviks of the Far East in the struggle against Japanese intervention, 1918–1922). *Proletarskaia Revoliutsiia*, pp. 77–114.

Semenov, B. "Iaponiia i panaziatskaia konferentsiia" (Japan and the Pan-Asiatic Conference). *Mezhdunarodnaia Zhizn*, No. 9, 1926, pp. 3–24.

———. "Iapono-sovetskoe soglashenie (Dairenskaia i Chanchunskaia konferentsii)" (Japanese-Soviet agreement; the Dairen and Changchun conferences). *N.V.*, No. 7, 1925, pp. 20–48.

Shlezinger, B. "Puti ekspansii iaponskogo imperializma" (The ways of expansion of Japanese imperialism). *Mezhdunarodnaia Zhizn*, No. 1, 1927, pp. 35–49.

"To the Workers and Peasants of Japan." *International Press Correspondence*, No. 29, May 15, 1924, pp. 291–92. A Comintern message.

Vasilev, B. "Iaponskaia proletarskaia partiia" (The Japanese proletarian party). *K.I.*, No. 11 (48), November 1925, pp. 136–41.

Veltman, M. L. (M. Pavlovich). "Iaponskii imperializm na Dalnem Vostoke" (Japanese imperialism in the Far East). *N.V.*, No. 2, 1922, pp. 3–57. Includes text of the Seventeen Conditions presented by the Japanese delegation to the delegation of the Far Eastern Republic at the Dairen Conference, together with secret clauses.

———. "Tikhookeanskaia problema i zemletriasenie v Iaponii" (The Pacific problem and the earthquake in Japan). *N.V.*, No. 4, 1923, pp. i-xxvi.

Vilensky, V. D. (Sibiriakov). "Imperializm v Iaponii" (Imperialism in Japan). *Z.N.*, No. 3 (101), February 2, 1921, p. 1.

———. "Sovremennaia Iaponiia. Iz vpechatlenii uchastnika 3-go Tikhookeanskogo Nauchnogo Kongressa" (Modern Japan. Impressions of a participant in the Third Scientific Congress of the Pacific Regions). *N.V.*, No. 16–17, 1927, pp. 83–96.

Voitinsky, G. N. "K desiatiletiiu martovskikh sobytii v Koree" (The tenth anniversary of the March events in Korea). *Revoliutsionnyi Vostok*, No. 7, 1929, pp. 31–35.

———. "K semidesiatiletiiu tov. Kataiama" (The seventieth birthday of Comrade Katayama). *Revoliutsionnyi Vostok*, No. 8, 1930, pp. xviii-xxii.

MONGOLIA AND TANNU-TUVA

Tretii sezd Mongolskoi Narodnoi Partii (Third Congress of the Mongolian People's Party). Urga, 1924.

Chetvertysi sezd Mongolskoi Narodno-Revoliutsionnoi Partii, s 23 sentiabria po 2 oktiabria 1925 goda (Fourth Congress of the Mongolian People's Revolutionary Party, September 23–October 2, 1925). Ulan Bator, 1925.

"Shestoi sezd Mongolskoi Narodno-Revoliutsionnoi Partii" (Sixth Congress of the Mongolian People's Revolutionary Party). *Izvestiia Ulan-Bator-Khoto*, Nos. 73–79 (417–423), September 28–October 15, 1927.

Demidov, S. S. (ed.). *Konstitutsiia i osnovnye zakonodatelnye akty Mongolskoi Narodnoi Respubliki* (Constitution and the basic legislative acts of the Mongolian People's Republic). Moscow, 1952. Translated from the Mongolian.

———. *Mongolskaia Narodnaia Respublika* (The Mongolian People's Republic). Moscow, 1952.

Dunn, E. *The Truth About Outer Mongolia.* Shanghai, 1935.

Engelfeld, V. V. *Politicheskaia organizatsiia sovremennoi Mongolii* (The political organization of present-day Mongolia). Harbin, 1926.

Friters, G. M. *Outer Mongolia and Its International Position.* Baltimore, 1949.

Grumm-Grzhimailo, G. E. *Zapadnaia Mongoliia i Uriankhaiskii krai, tom II: Istoricheskii ocherk etikh stran v sviazi s istoriei Srednei Azii* (Western Mongolia and the Uriankhai region, Vol. II: A historical sketch connecting these countries with the history of Central Asia). Leningrad, 1926.

Kallinikov, Anatolii. *Revoliutsionnaia Mongoliia* (Revolutionary Mongolia). Moscow, 192-.

Kervyn, Louis M. *Ourga (1912–1930); La politique chinoise en Mongolie.* Peking, 1932.

Korostovets, I. Ia. *Von Ginggis Khan zur Sowjetrepublik; eine kurze Geschichte der Mongolei unter besonderer Berücksichtigung der neuesten Zeit* . . . Berlin and Leipzig, 1926.

Lattimore, Owen. *Nationalism and Revolution in Mongolia.* New York, 1955. With a translation from the Mongolian of Sh. Nachukdorji's *Life of Suhe-Bator* . . .

"Letters Captured from Baron Ungern in Mongolia." Typescript, taken from the

Pekin and Tientsin Times and distributed by the Special Delegation of the Far Eastern Republic in Washington, D. C., in 1921.

Ma Ho-t'ien. *Chinese Agent in Mongolia.* Baltimore, 1949. Translated from the Chinese.

Maisky, I. M. *Sovremennaia Mongolia. Otchet mongolskoi ekspeditsii . . .* (Modern Mongolia. An account of the Mongolian expedition . . .). Irkutsk, 1921.

Maslennikov, V. A. *Mongolskaia Narodnaia Respublika na puti k sotsializmu* (The Mongolian People's Republic on the road to socialism). Moscow, 1951.

"Mongolskaia Narodnaia Respublika" (The Mongolian People's Republic). *Bolshaia Sovetskaia Entsiklopediia,* XL (Moscow, 1938), 68–89.

Mongolskaia Narodnaia Respublika; bibliografiia knizhnoi i zhurnalnoi literatury na russkom iazyke, 1935–1950 gg. (The Mongolian People's Republic; a bibliography of books and articles in the Russian language, 1935–1950). Moscow, Akademiia Nauk, 1953.

Novaia Mongoliia; ekonomiko-politicheskoe i kulturnoe sostoianie strany. Protokoly pervogo Velikogo Khuruldana Mongolskoi Narodnoi Respubliki (New Mongolia. Economo-political and cultural conditions of the country. Minutes of the First Great Huruldan of the Mongolian People's Republic). Ulan Bator, 1925.

Perlin, B. *Mongolskaia Narodnaia Respublika* (The Mongolian People's Republic). Moscow, 1941.

Phillips, G. D. R. *Russia, Japan and Mongolia.* London, 1942.

Pomus, M. I. *Buriat-Mongolskaia ASSR* (The Buriat-Mongol A.S.S.R.). Moscow, 1937.

Riabukhin, N. M. "The Story of Baron Ungern-Sternberg. Told by His Staff Physician, N. K. Riabukhin (Riba). Typescript.

Ridge, W. S. *China, Mongolia and Russia. A Survey of Their Recent Relations.* Peiping, 1936.

Shoizhelov, N. A. (Natsov). *Tuvinskaia narodnaia respublika; materialy i dokumenty po istorii natsionalno-revoliutsionnogo dvizheniia tuvinskikh skotovodov* (The Tuvinian People's Republic; materials and documents on the history of the national-revolutionary movement of the Tuva cattle breeders). Moscow, 1930.

Skachkov, P. E. *Vnutrenniaia Mongoliia. Ekonomiko-geograficheskii ocherk* (Inner Mongolia. An economo-geographical essay). Moscow, 1933.

Tan, Tennyson. *Political Status of Mongolia.* Shanghai, 1932.

Tsapkin, N. V. *Mongolskaia Narodnaia Respublika* (The Mongolian People's Republic). Moscow, 1948.

Trudy soveshchaniia po voprosam o razvitii russkikh torgovykh snoshenii s Mongoliei sozvannago Irkutskim General-Gubernatorom . . . (Transactions of the conference on the development of Russian trade relations with Mongolia, convened by the Governor-General of Irkutsk . . .). Irkutsk, 1913.

Viktorov, S. *Mongolskaia Narodnaia Respublika* (The Mongolian People's Republic). Moscow, 1936.

Vilensky, V. D. (Sibiriakov). *Sovremennaia Mongoliia* (Modern Mongolia). Kharkov, 1925. Includes text of Soviet-Mongolian agreement.

Zlatkin, I. Ia. *Mongolskaia Narodnaia Respublika—strana novoi demokratii* (The Mongolian People's Republic, the country of new democracy). Moscow-Leningrad, 1950. Includes chronology.

Berlin, L. "Lenin o Mongolii" (Lenin on Mongolia). *Izvestiia Ulan-Bator-Khoto,* No. 6 (350), January 22, 1927, p. 3.

Chang Chih-yi (comp.). "A Bibliography of Books and Articles on Mongolia." *Journal of the Royal Central Asian Society* (London), Parts II and III of Volume XXXVII, 1950.

[Doksom.] "Istoricheskie uroki 15 let revoliutsii; doklad predsedatelia Malogo Khurala Doksoma na iubileinoi 21-i sessii Malogo Khurala . . . " (Historical lessons of the fifteen years of the revolution; report by the chairman of the Small Hural, Doksom, at the jubilee 21st session of the Small Hural). *Tikhii Okean,* No. 3 (9), July-September 1936, pp. 61–94.

Genkin, I. I. "Dva sezda Mongolskoi Narodnoi Partii" (Two congresses of the Mongolian People's Party). *N.V.,* No. 12, 1926, pp. 184–95.

———. "Konets Ungerna i nachalo novoi Mongolii" (The end of Ungern and the beginning of new Mongolia). *Severnaia Aziia,* No. 2 (20), 1928, pp. 75–90.

Iudin, V. "Piat let mongolskogo narodnogo pravitelstva . . . (Five years of the Mongolian People's Government . . .). *N.V.,* No. 13-14, 1926, pp. 465–66.

Kallinikov, Anatolii. "Aratskoe revoliutsionnoe dvizhenie v doavtonomnoi Mongolii" (The arat revolutionary movement in preautonomous Mongolia). *Revoliutsionnyi Vostok,* No. 5, 1934, pp. 138–56, and No. 6, 1934, pp. 43–64.

Mosina, N. "Novyi etap v razvitii Mongolskoi respubliki" (A new stage in the development of the Mongolian republic). *Revoliutsionnyi Vostok,* No. 7, 1929, pp. 70–85.

Natsov, S. "Natsionalno-osvoboditelnoe dvizhenie v Mongolii" (The national-liberation movement in Mongolia). *K.I.,* No. 9 (58), September 1926, pp. 144–54.

Oiratsky. "Mongoliia kak vorota Buddiiskogo Vostoka" (Mongolia, gate to the Buddhist East). *Z.N.,* No. 26 (34), July 13, 1919, p. 2.

Ordosets. "Natsionalno-osvoboditelnoe dvizhenie vo Vnutrennei Mongolii" (The national-liberation movement in Inner Mongolia). *Revoliutsionnyi Vostok,* No. 2, 1927, pp. 48–65.

Pensky, N. K. "Ekonomicheskie vzaimootnosheniia SSSR i Mongolii" (The economic relations between the U.S.S.R. and Mongolia). *N.V.,* No. 10-11, 1925, pp. 163–74.

Popov, A. L., and A. S. Erusalimsky (comps.). "Tsarskaia Rossiia i Mongolia v 1913–1914 g.g." (Tsarist Russia and Mongolia in 1913–1914). *Krasnyi Arkhiv,* No. 6 (37), 1929, pp. 3–68. Documented.

"Postanovlenie 2-go Velikogo Khuruldana po dokladu M. Kh. i pravitelstva" (The decision of the Second Great Huruldan on the report of the Small Hural and the government). *Izvestiia Ulan-Bator-Khoto,* No. 239, December 9, 1925, pp. 2–3, and No. 240, December 12, 1925, p. 3.

Rinchino, E. D. "K voprosu o natsionalnom samoopredelenii Mongolii v sviazi s zadachami Kitaiskoi revoliutsii" (On the national self-determination of Mongolia in connection with the tasks of the Chinese revolution). *Revoliutsionnyi Vostok,* No. 2, 1927, pp. 65–78.

Ryskulov, T. R. "Velikii Khuruldan Mongolii (Pismo iz Mongolii)" (The Great Huruldan of Mongolia: A letter from Mongolia). *N.V.,* No. 8-9, 1925, pp. 215–29.

S—kii, A. F. "Materialy k istorii interventsii: rol Iaponii v 'panmongolskom dvizhenii' " (Materials on intervention: The role of Japan in the "Pan-Mongolian movement . . ."). *N.V.,* No. 2, 1922, pp. 591–603.

Serebrennikov, I. I. "The Tannu Tuva Republic." *The China Journal* (Shanghai), November 1939, pp. 233–39.

Shoizhelov, Siren. "Mongoliia i iaponskii imperializm" (Mongolia and Japanese imperialism). *N.V.,* No. 8-9, 1925, pp. 199–205.

———. "Mongoliia i Tsarskaia Rossiia" (Mongolia and tsarist Russia). *N.V.,* No. 13-14, 1926, pp. 351–63.

———. "Perelomnyi moment v istorii natsionalno-osvoboditelnogo dvizheniia Mongolii (Itogi raboty Plenuma Tsentralnogo Komiteta Mongolskoi Narodno-Revoliutsionnoi Partii)" (The turning point in the history of the national-liberation movement of Mongolia: Results of the work of the plenum of the Central Committee of the Mongolian People's Revolutionary Party). *N.V.*, No. 10-11, 1925, pp. 203–11.

———. "Zapadnaia Mongoliia" (Western Mongolia). *N.V.*, No. 4, 1923, pp. 151–61.

Shumiatsky, B. Z. "Na zare osvobozhdeniia Mongolii" (On the eve of Mongolia's liberation). *Pravda*, No. 190, July 12, 1936.

Staritsina, P. P. "Marshal Choibalsan; iz zhizni i deiatelnosti" (Marshal Choibalsan; his life and activities). *Kratkie Soobshcheniia Instituta Vostokovedeniia*, Moscow, VI, 1952, pp. 3–15.

"Tsarskaia Rossiia i Mongoliia" (Tsarist Russia and Mongolia). *Krasnyi Arkhiv*, No. 37, 1929, pp. 3–68. Documents.

"Vecher pamiati Sukhe-Bator" (A meeting dedicated to the memory of Suhe-Bator). *Izvestiia Ulan-Bator-Khoto*, No. 159, February 24, 1925, p. 3, and No. 160, March 1, 1925, pp. 3–4.

"Vtoroi Velikii Khuruldan" (The Second Great Huruldan). *Izvestiia Ulan-Bator-Khoto*, No. 230, November 11, 1925, pp. 2–3; No. 231, November 14, 1925, p. 3, and No. 232, November 18, 1925, p. 3.

"Vtoroi Velikii Khuruldan Mongolskoi Narodnoi Respubliki" (The Second Great Huruldan of the Mongolian People's Republic). *Mezhdunarodnaia Zhizn*, No. 4, 1926, pp. 78–84.

"Zhizn i deiatelnost tov. Sukhe-Batora" (Life and work of comrade Suhe-Bator). *Izvestiia Ulan-Bator-Khoto*, No. 13 (357), February 19, 1927, p. 2.

NEAR AND MIDDLE EAST

Atatürk [Gazi Mustafa], Kemal. *Die Neue Türkei, 1919–1927; Rede Gehalten von Gasi Mustafa Kemal Pascha in Angora vom 15 bis 20 Oktober 1927*. 3 vols. Leipzig, 1928–29.

———. *Nutuk* (Speech). 3 vols. Istanbul, 1934.

Bina, Ali-Akbar. *La question iranienne au début du XIX siècle. Les traités de Gulistan et de Turkman-Tchai (1813–1828)*. Paris, 1939.

Bisbee, Eleanor. *The New Turks; Pioneers of the Republic, 1920–1950*. Philadelphia, 1951.

Browne, E. G. *The Persian Revolution of 1905–1909*. Cambridge, 1910.

Churchill, R. P. *The Anglo-Russian Convention of 1907*. Cedar Rapids, Iowa, 1939.

Dantsig, B. *Turtsiia* (Turkey). Moscow, 1949.

Dinerstein, Herbert S. "Soviet Foreign Policy in the Near and Middle East, 1917–1923." Harvard University Ph.D. thesis, 1943.

Dranov, B. A. *Chernomorskie prolivy; mezhdunarodno-pravovoi rezhim* (The Black Sea Straits under the rule of international law). Moscow, 1948.

Fatemi, Nasrollah Saifpour. *Diplomatic History of Persia, 1917–1923; Anglo-Russian Power Politics in Iran*. New York, 1952.

Fraser-Tytler, W. K. *Afghanistan; A Study of Political Developments in Central Asia*. London, 1950.

*Gurevich, A. *Afghanistan* (Afghanistan). Moscow, 1930.

[Gurko-]Kriazhin, V. A. *Natsionalno-osvoboditelnoe dvizhenie na Blizhnem Vostoke* (The national-liberation movement in the Near East). Moscow, 1923.

Howard, Harry N. *The Partition of Turkey; A Diplomatic History, 1913–1923*. Norman, Oklahoma, 1931.

Lenczowski, George. *Russia and the West in Iran, 1918–1948; A Study in Big-Power Rivalry*. Ithaca, N. Y., 1949.

Mikusch, Dagobert von. *Mustapha Kemal; between Europe and Asia* . . . London, 1931.

Miller, A. F. *Ocherki noveishei istorii Turtsii* (Sketch on the recent history of Turkey). Moscow, 1948.
Nelson, C. R. "Kemalist Turkey and the Soviet Union, 1920–1926." Stanford University Master's thesis, 1949.
Reisner, I. M. *Afganistan* (Afghanistan). 2d ed. Moscow, 1929. Introduction by F. F. Raskolnikov.
──────. *Nezavisimyi Afganistan* (Independent Afghanistan). Moscow, 1929.
Shotwell, S. T., and F. Deák. *Turkey and the Straits; A Short History.* New York, 1940.
Shuster, W. Morgan. *The Strangling of Persia.* New York, 1912.
Snesarev, A. E. *Avganistan* (Afghanistan). Moscow, 1921.
Sultan-Zade, A. *Persiia* (Persia). Moscow, 1925.
Sykes, Sir Percy M. *A History of Afganistan.* Vol. II. London, 1940.
──────. *History of Persia.* 3d ed., 2 vols. London, 1951.
Turtsiia (Turkey). Tiflis, Zakavkazskaia Palata Vneshnei Torgovli (Transcaucasian Chamber of Commerce), 1933. With bibliography.
Veltman, M. L. (M. Pavlovich). *Persiia v borbe za nezavisimost* (Persia in the struggle for independence). Moscow, 1925.
──────. *Revoliutsionnaia Turtsiia* (Revolutionary Turkey). Moscow, 1921.
──────. *Revoliutsionnyi Vostok* (The Revolutionary East). Part I. Moscow, 1927.
Vere-Hodge, E. R. *Turkish Foreign Policy, 1918 – 1948.* Ambilly - Annemasse, Switzerland, 1950.
Zarevand. *Turtsiia i panturanism* (Turkey and Pan-Turanianism). Paris, 1930.
Ziemke, Kurt. *Die Neue Türkei; Politische Entwicklung, 1914–1929.* Berlin and Leipzig, 1930.

A. N. "Kommunizm v Armenii" (Communism in Armenia). *K.I.,* No. 13, 1920, pp. 2545–50.
Abikh, R. "Natsionalnoe i revoliutsionnoe dvizhenie v 1914–1917 gg. Vospominaniia uchastnika Ekhsan-Ully-Khana" (The national and revolutionary movement in Persia, 1914–1917. Reminiscences of a participant, Ehsanullah-Khan). *N.V.,* No. 23-24, 1928, pp. 234–67, and No. 26-27, 1929, pp. 125–61.
──────. "Natsionalnoe i revoliutsionnoe dvizhenie v Persii v 1919–1920 gg." (The national and revolutionary movement in Persia, 1919–1920). *N.V.,* No. 29, 1930, pp. 88–107.
"Anglo-russkoe sopernichestvo v Persii v 1890–1906 gg." (Anglo-Russian rivalry in Persia, 1890–1906). *Krasnyi Arkhiv,* No. 56, 1933, pp. 33–64. Documents.
Castagné, Joseph A. "Notes sur la politique exterieure de l'Afghanistan depuis 1919 (mission et traités)." *Revue du Monde Musulman,* XLVIII, 1921, pp. 1–25.
*[Cebesoy] General Ali Fuat. "Siyasi Hatıraları." *Vatan,* Istanbul, April 5, 1924.
Ducrocq, Georges. "La politique du gouvernement des Soviets en Perse." *Revue du Monde Musulman,* LII, December 1922, pp. 84–108.
Dzhengeli, I. "Dzhengeliiskoe dvizhenie 1926 goda v Gilane" (The Jangali movement of 1926 in Gilan). *Revoliutsionnyi Vostok,* No. 2, 1927, pp. 193–99.
E. V. "Na Kaspii i v Persii (Beseda s tov. Raskolnikovym)" (On the Caspian and in Persia; a talk with Comrade Raskolnikov). *Petrogradskaia Pravda,* No. 155, July 15, 1920, p. 1.
Efendiev, N. "Mustafa Kemal i von der Golts" (Mustafa Kemal and von der Goltz). *Z.N.,* No. 40 (48), Oct. 19, 1919, p. 1.
──────. "Pora" (It is time). *Z.N.,* No. 1 (58), January 4, 1920, p. 1. On the need for revolutionary work among Turkish prisoners of war in Russia.
──────. "Problemy Vostoka" (The problems of the East). *Z.N.,* No. 41 (49), October 26, 1919, p. 1, and No. 43 (51), November 19, 1919, p. 1.

————. "Revoliutsionnye perspektivy v Persii" (Revolutionary prospects in Persia). *Z.N.*, No. 2 (59), January 11, 1920, p. 1.

Ferdi, B. "Kommunisticheskoe dvizhenie v Turtsii" (The communist movement in Turkey). *K.I.*, No. 6 (64), October 22, 1926, pp. 44–48.

————. "Polozhenie rabochego klassa i kommunisticheskoe dvizhenie v Turtsii" (The position of the working class and the communist movement in Turkey). *K.I.*, No. 9 (67), November 12, 1926, pp. 43–45.

Fuks, A. K. "Germanskaia politika v Persii" (German policy in Persia). *N.V.*, No. 20-21, 1928, pp. 110–29. Up to 1910.

Gurko-Kriazhin, V. A. "Blizhnevostochnaia problema, Chernoe more i SSSR" (The Near Eastern problem, the Black Sea, and the U.S.S.R.). *N.V.*, No. 5, 1924, pp. 44–50.

————. "Borba za prolivy" (The struggle for the Straits). *N.V.*, No. 2, 1922, pp. 83–125.

Ips. "Rossiia i Afganistan" (Russia and Afghanistan). *Z.N.*, No. 27 (35), July 20, 1919, pp. 1–2.

————. "Zadachi i usloviia sotsialisticheskoi propagandy v Persii" (The tasks and the conditions for propaganda in Persia). *Z.N.*, No. 19 (27), May 25, 1919, p. 2, and No. 20 (28), June 1, 1919, p. 1.

Iransky, S. "Russko-persidskie otnosheniia za piat let" (Five years of Russo-Persian relations). *N.V.*, No. 3, 1923, pp. 90–113.

————. "Sovetskaia Rossiia i Persiia . . ." (Soviet Russia and Persia . . .). *N.V.*, No. 4, 1923, pp. 208–29. Continued from *N.V.*, No. 3, 1923.

————. "Stranitsa iz istorii krasnoi diplomatii. Pamiati t. I. I. Kolomiitseva" (A page from the history of Red diplomacy. In memory of Comrade I. K. Kolomiitsev). *N.V.*, No. 8-9, 1925, pp. 151–59.

Kerner, R. J. "Russia and the Straits, 1915–1917." *Slavonic Review*, VIII, No. 24, March 1930, pp. 589–93.

————. "Russia, the Straits and Constantinople, 1914–1915." *Journal of Modern History*, No. 3, September 1929, pp. 400–415.

Kitaigorodsky, P. "Oktiabrskaia revoliutsiia i natsionalno-revoliutsionnoe dvizhenie Turtsii" (The October Revolution and the national-revolutionary movement in Turkey). *Krasnyi Internatsional Profsoiuzov*, No. 10 (81), October 1927, pp. 407–11.

M. A. "K sobytiiam v Afganistane" (Events in Afghanistan). *Z.N.*, No. 17 (25), May 11, 1919, p. 1.

Nezhdanov, V. V. "Afganistan" (Afghanistan). *Z.N.*, No. 21 (119), October 10, 1921, p. 2.

Osetov, V. "Persidskie partii (Pismo iz Tegerana)" (The Persian parties: A letter from Teheran). *N.V.*, No. 1, 1922, pp. 147–53.

"Persiia v kontse XIX veka. Dnevnik Gen. Kosogovskogo" (Persia at the close of the nineteenth century. The diary of General Kosogovsky). *N.V.*, No. 4, 1923, pp. 446–69.

"Pervyi sezd persidskikh kommunistov partii 'Adalat' " (The first congress of the Persian "Adalat" communist party). *K.I.*, No. 14, November 6, 1920, pp. 2889–92.

Popov, A. "Anglo-russkoe sopernichestvo na putiakh Irana" (Anglo-Russian rivalry in the approaches to Iran). *N.V.*, No. 12, 1926, pp. 127–48.

————. "Stranitsa iz istorii russkoi politiki v Persii" (An outline of the history of Russian policy in Persia). *Mezhdunarodnaia Zhizn*, No. 4-5, 1924, pp. 132–64.

————. "Tsarskaia Rossiia i Persiia v epokhu russko-iaponskoi voiny" (Tsarist Russia and Persia in the period of Russo-Japanese war). *Krasnyi Arkhiv*, No. 53, 1932, pp. 3–37.

Rakovsky, Kh. G. "Lokarno i Blizhnii Vostok" (Locarno and the Near East). *N.V.*, No. 10–11, 1925, pp. xliii–xlv.

Raskolnikov, F. F. "Rossiia i Afganistan. Istoricheskii ocherk" (Russia and Afghanistan. A historical survey). *N.V.*, No. 4, 1923, pp. 12–48.

Reisner, I. "Desiat let vneshnei politiki Afganistana" (Ten years of Afghanistan's foreign policy). *N.V.*, No. 22, 1928, pp. 67–86.

Shtiurmer, Kh. "Turtsiia posle Lozanny" (Turkey after Lausanne). *Mezhdunarodnaia Zhizn*, No. 2-3, 1924, pp. 57–78.

Skachko, A. "Nashi otnosheniia s Turtsiei i ikh znachenie dlia mirovoi revoliutsii" (Our relations with Turkey and their significance for the world revolution). *Z.N.*, No. 39 (96), December 8, 1920, pp. 1–2.

"Sovetskaia federatsiia i Turtsiia" (Soviet federation and Turkey). *Z.N.*, No. 6 (135), February 16, 1922, pp. 2–3. Re Frunze's visit to Turkey.

Sultan-Galiev, M. "Mustafa Suphi i ego rabota" (Mustafa Suphi and his work). *Z.N.*, No. 14 (112), July 16, 1921, pp. 1–2.

———. "Polozhenie v Turtsii v poslednee vremia" (The recent situation in Turkey). *Z.N.*, No. 14 (71), May 16, 1920, p. 2, and No. 15 (72), May 23, 1920, p. 1.

Sultan-Zade, A. "Angliiskii imperializm v Persii i sotsialno-ekonomicheskaia priroda monarkhii Reza-Shakha-Pekhlevi" (British imperialism in Persia and the socioeconomic nature of Riza Shah Pahlavi's monarchy). *Revoliutsionnyi Vostok*, No. 3, 1928, pp. 83–111.

———. "Borba za persidskuiu neft" (The struggle for Persian oil). *Vestnik N.K.I.D.*, No. 6, 1922, pp. 58–63.

———. "Ob iranskoi kommunisticheskoi partii" (On the Iranian Communist Party). *K.I.*, No. 13, 1920, p. 2551.

———. "Revoliutsionnoe dvizhenie v Persii" (The revolutionary movement in Persia). *Z.N.*, No. 28 (85), September 16, 1920, p. 1; No. 29 (86), September 24, 1920, p. 1; No. 30 (87), October 1, 1920, pp. 1–2.

———. "Vtoroi sezd iranskoi kompartii" (The Second Congress of the Iranian Communist Party). *K.I.*, No. 50 (124), December 16, 1927, pp. 31–36.

Timofeev, A. "Imperialisticheskoe 'mirnoe' zavoevanie Persii" (Imperialist "peaceful" conquest of Persia). *N.V.*, No. 2, 1922, pp. 254–71.

Torchinsky, G. "Perspektivy revoliutsii v Persii" (Prospects of the revolution in Persia). *Z.N.*, No. 11 (109), May 28, 1921, p. 8.

Trainin, I. P. "Dve konferentsii" (Two conferences). *Z.N.*, No. 6 (104), March 4, 1921, p. 1. On the Turkish problem.

———. "K dogovoru s Afganistanom" (The treaty with Afghanistan). *Z.N.*, No. 7 (105), March 17, 1921, p. 1.

Tsimring, Iu. "Rabochii front arabskogo Vostoka protiv imperializma" (The workers' front of the Arab East against imperialism). *K.I.*, No. 8 (82), February 25, 1927, pp. 47–50.

Veltman, M. L. (M. Pavlovich). "Dogovor mezhdu Rossiei i Turtsiei" (The treaty between Russia and Turkey). *Z.N.*, No. 8 (106), March 27, 1921, p. 1.

———. "Gibel turetskikh kommunistov" (Death of Turkish Communists). *Z.N.*, No. 10 (108), May 14, 1921, p. 1.

———. "Revoliutsionnaia Turtsiia" (Revolutionary Turkey). *Z.N.*, No. 7 (105), March 17, 1921, p. 2; No. 8 (106), March 27, 1921, p. 2; No. 9 (107), April 23, 1921, pp. 1–2.

———. "Revoliutsionnaia Turtsiia i Sovetskaia Rossiia" (Revolutionary Turkey and Soviet Russia). *Z.N.*, No. 40 (96), December 15, 1920, p. 1. Re Kemal's wire to Chicherin of November 29, 1920.

W. "Les Relations russo-turques depuis l'avènement du bolchevisme." *Revue du Monde Musulman*, LII, Decembre 1922, pp. 181–217.

Zakher, Ia. M. "Konstantinopol i prolivy" (Constantinople and the Straits). *Krasnyi Arkhiv,* No. 6, 1924, pp. 48–76, and No. 7, 1924, pp. 32–54.
Zakhmatkesh. "Oktiabrskaia revoliutsiia i trudiashchiesia Persii" (The October Revolution and the toilers of Persia). *Krasnyi Internatsional Profsoiuzov,* No. 10 (81), October 1927, pp. 412–14.

RUSSIAN CENTRAL ASIA

[Antropov, P. G.] *Materialy i dokumenty I-go sezda Kompartii Turkestana* (Materials and documents on the First Congress of the Communist Party of Turkestan). Tashkent, 1934.
Arkhipov, N. B. *Sredne-aziatskie respubliki* (Central Asian republics). 2d ed. Moscow, 1928.
Asfendiarov, S. S. *Natsionalno-osvoboditelnoe vosstanie 1916 goda v Kazakhstane* (The national-liberation uprising in Kazakhstan in 1916). Alma-Ata, 1936.
Bailey, F. M. *Mission to Tashkent.* London, 1946.
Bartold, V. V. *Histoire des Turcs d'Asie Centrale.* Paris, 1945.
———. *Ocherk istorii Semirechiia* (History of Semirechie). Frunze, 1943.
Belotsky, M. *Kirgizskaia respublika; populiarnyi ocherk* (The Kirghiz republic; a popular outline). Moscow, 1936.
Benzing, Johannes. *Das Turkestanische Volk im Kampf um seine Selbständigkeit.* Berlin, 1937.
Bisnek, A. G. *Bibliografiia bibliografii Srednei Azii* (Bibliography of bibliographies of Central Asia). Moscow and Leningrad, 1936.
Blacker, L. V. S. *On Secret Patrol in High Asia.* London, 1922.
Bozhko, F. *Oktiabrskaia revoliutsiia v Srednei Azii* (The October Revolution in Central Asia). Tashkent, 1932.
Brainin, S. *Vosstanie kazakhov Semirechia v 1917 godu* (The revolt of the Kazakhs of Semirechie in 1917). Alma-Ata, 1936.
Briskin, A. *Strana tadzhikov* (The country of the Tadzhiks). Moscow and Leningrad, 1930.
Brun, Alf Harald. *Troublous Times; Experiences in Bolshevik Russia and Turkestan.* London, 1931.
Caroe, Sir Olaf K. *Soviet Empire; the Turks of Central Asia and Stalinism.* London and New York, 1953.
Castagné, Joseph A. *Les Basmatchis; le mouvement national des indigènes d'Asie centrale depuis la révolution d'octobre 1917 jusqu'en octobre 1924.* Paris, 1925.
———. *Les musulmans et la politique des soviets en Asie centrale.* Paris, 1925.
———. *Le Turkestan depuis la révolution russe (1917–1921).* Paris, 1922.
Cherdantsev, G. N. *Sredne-aziatskie respubliki* (Central Asian republics). Moscow, 1928.
Chokai, *see* Tchokaieff
Desiatiletie natsionalno-territorialnogo razmezhevaniia Srednei Azii, 1924–1934. (The tenth anniversary of the territorial delimitation of Central Asia, 1924–1934). Moscow, 1934.
Etherton, P. T. *In the Heart of Asia.* London, 1925.
Filippov, S. T. *Boevye deistviia na zakaspiiskom fronte, 1918–1920 gg.* (Fighting on the Transcaspian front, 1918–1920). Ashkhabad, 1928.
Furmanov, D. A. *Miatezh* (Revolt). Moscow, 1927.
Gafurov, B. G. *Istoriia tadzhikskogo naroda v kratkom izlozhenii* (A short history of the Tadzhik people). Vol. I. Moscow, 1952.
Gaister, A. I. *Sredniaia Aziia; izuchenie sovetskoi Azii* (Central Asia; the study of Soviet Asia). Moscow, 1933.
Galuzo, P. G. *Turkestan-Koloniia (Ocherk istorii kolonialnoi politiki russkogo tsarizma v Srednei Azii)* (Turkestan as a colony. An outline of the colonial

policy of Russian tsarism in Central Asia). 2d ed. Tashkent, 1935.

Glovatsky, O. *Revoliutsiia pobezhdaet; ekonomicheskie i politicheskie predposylki bukharskoi revoliutsii 1920 goda* (The revolution is winning; economic and political reasons for the Bukhara revolution in 1920). Tashkent, 1930.

Goloshchekin, F. I. *Partiinoe stroitelstvo v Kazakhstane; Sbornik rechei i statei, 1925–1930* (The building up of the party in Kazakhstan; a collection of speeches and articles, 1925–1930). Moscow, 1930.

Gusev, N. I. (ed.). *Kazakhstan* (Kazakhstan). Moscow, 1936.

Iz istorii partiinogo stroitelstva v Kazakhstane. Sbornik statei i materialov (The history of the building up of the party in Kazakhstan. A collection of articles and materials). Alma-Ata, 1936.

Khodzhaev, Faizulla. *K istorii revoliutsii v Bukhare* (An historical account of the revolution in Bukhara). Tashkent, 1926.

――――. *Ocherk revoliutsionnogo dvizheniia v Srednei Azii* (An outline of the revolutionary movement in Central Asia). Moscow, 1923.

Khodzhaev, Mumin. *Sotsialisticheskoe stroitelstvo u vorot Industana* (Socialist construction at the gates of Hindustan). N.p., 1932.

Khodzhibaev, Abdu-Rakhim. *Tadzhikistan* (Tadzhikistan). Moscow, 1929.

Kozlov, T. S. *Krasnaia gvardiia i Krasnaia armiia v Turkmenii* (The Red Guard and the Red Army in Turkmenia). Ashkhabad, 1928.

Kratkii bibliograficheskii ukazatel literatury po Turkestanu (A brief bibliographical index to the literature on Turkestan). Tashkent, 1924.

Krist, Gustav. *Alone Through the Forbidden Land; Journeys in Disguise through Soviet Central Asia*. London, 1938.

Ksenofontov, F. A. *Uzbekistan i Turkmenistan; k voprosu ob ikh vkhozhdenii v SSSR* (Uzbekistan and Turkmenistan. The question of their incorporation into the U.S.S.R.). Moscow and Leningrad, 1925.

Kunitz, Joshua. *Dawn over Samarkand; the Rebirth of Central Asia*. New York, 1935.

Kushner, P. *Gornaia Kirgiziia; sotsiologicheskaia razvedka* (Mountainous Kirghizia; a sociological investigation). Moscow, 1939.

Maier, Anatolii. *Boevye epizody; Basmachestvo v Bukhare* (Battle episodes; the Basmachi movement in Bukhara). Moscow and Tashkent, 1934.

Manzhara, D. I. *Revoliutsionnoe dvizhenie v Srednei Azii, 1905–1920 g.g.; vospominaniia* (The revolutionary movement in Central Asia, 1905–1920; reminiscences). Tashkent, 1934.

Marvin, Charles. *The Russian Advance Toward India. Conversations with Skobeleff, Ignatieff, and Other Distinguished Russian Generals and Statesmen on the Central Asian Question*. London, 1882.

Melkumov, Andronik. *Materialy revoliutsionnogo dvizheniia v Turkmenii 1904–1919 g.g.* (Materials on the revolutionary movement in Turkmenia, 1904–1919). Tashkent, 1924.

Melnikov, G. N. (comp.). *Oktiabr v Kazakstane; ocherki i rasskazy uchastnikov grazhdanskoi voiny* (October in Kazakhstan. Accounts and reminiscences of participants in the civil war). Alma-Ata, 1930.

*Muraveisky, S. (V. Lopukhov). *Ocherki po istorii revoliutsionnogo dvizheniia v Srednei Azii* (An outline of the revolutionary movement in Central Asia). Tashkent, 1926. A typescript, taken from the published book and partly translated into English, is in the Hoover Library.

Nazarov, P. S. *Hunted Through Central Asia*. London, 1932.

Nemchenko, M. A. *Natsionalnoe razmezhevanie Srednei Azii* (The national delimitation of Central Asia). Moscow, 1925.

Pipes, Richard. *Moslems of Soviet Central Asia*. Cambridge, Mass., 1954.

Raikhimbaev, A. R. *Tadzhikistan* (Tadzhikistan). Moscow, 1936.

Revoliutsiia v Srednei Azii. Sbornik (The revolution in Central Asia. A collection [of articles]). Tashkent, 1928.

Ryskulov, T. R. *Kazakhstan.* Moscow and Leningrad, 1927.

―――. *Kirgizstan* (Kirghizstan). Moscow, 1935.

*―――. *Revoliutsiia i korennoe naselenie Turkestana. Sbornik glavneishikh statei, dokladov, rechei i tezisov. Chast I: 1917–1919* (The revolution and the native population of Turkestan. A collection of the most important articles, reports, speeches, and theses. Part I: 1917–1919). Tashkent, 1925. A partial typescript, taken from the published book, is in the Hoover Library.

Safarov, G. *Kolonialnaia revoliutsiia. Opyt Turkestana* (The colonial revolution. Experiment in Turkestan). Moscow, 1921.

Said, Alim (Emir of Bukhara). *La voix de la Boukharie opprimée.* Paris, 1929.

Schuyler, Eugene. *Turkistan. Notes of a Journey in Russian Turkistan, Khokand, Bukhara and Kuldja.* 2 vols. New York, 1877.

Servet, Claude. *Le Turkestan soviétique.* Paris, 1931.

Shmakov, T. A. *Pervye gody borby; vospominaniia uchastnika grazhdanskoi voiny v Srednei Azii* (The first years of struggle; reminiscences of a participant in the civil war in Central Asia). Moscow and Tashkent, 1933.

Shteinberg, E. L. *Ocherki istorii Turkmenii* (Essays on the history of Turkmenia). Moscow and Leningrad, 1934.

Sredniaia Aziia v uchrezhdeniiakh Akademii Nauk 1917–1927 (Central Asia in the institutions of the Academy of Sciences, 1917–1927). Leningrad, Akademiia Nauk, 1927.

Steber, Charles. *L'Asie centrale soviétique et le Kazakhstan.* Paris, 1939.

Strong, A. L. *Red Star in Samarkand.* New York, 1929.

Stählin, Karl. *Russisch-Turkestan, gestern und heute.* Königsberg, 1935.

Tchokaieff [Chokai], Mariia. *Iash Turkestan. Sbornik ko dniu 60-letiia so dnia rozhdeniia i 8-letiiu so dnia smerti glavy Kokandskoi Avtonomii i osnovatelia Iash Turkestana, Mustafa Chokai* (Iash Turkestan [Young Turkestan]. A collection of articles on the 60th anniversary of the birth and 8th anniversary of the death of the head of the Kokand autonomy and the founder of Iash Turkestan, Mustafa Chokai). Paris, 1950.

Tchokaieff [Chokai], Moustapha. *Chez les soviets en Asie Centrale . . .* Paris, 1928.

―――. *Turkestan pod vlastiu sovetov. K kharakteristike diktatury proletariata* (Turkestan under the rule of the soviets. The nature of the proletarian dictatorship). Paris, 1935.

Trudy Instituta Vostokovedeniia: Materialy po istorii Turkmen i Turkmenii (Transactions of the Institute for Oriental Studies: Materials on the history of Turkmen and Turkmenia). 2 vols. Moscow and Leningrad, Akademiia Nauk, 1938–39.

Uchreditelnyi sezd sovetov Kirgizskoi ASSR 4–12 oktiabria, 1920 g. Protokoly (The constituent congress of soviets of the Kirghiz [Kazakh] A.S.S.R., October 4–12, 1920. Minutes). Moscow, 1936.

Vaillant-Couturier, Paul. *Free Soviet Tadjikistan.* Moscow, 1932.

Voina v peskakh; materialy po istorii grazhdanskoi voiny . . . v Srednei Azii (War in the sands; materials on the history of civil war . . . in Central Asia). Leningrad, 1935.

Willfort, Fritz. *Turkestanisches Tagebuch; sechs Jahre in Russisch-Zentralasien . . .* Leipzig, 1930.

Zorin, A. N. *Revoliutsionnoe dvizhenie Kirgizii: Severnaia chast* (The revolutionary movement in Kirghizia: The northern sector). Frunze, 1931.

Ananov, I. "K preobrazovaniiu Sredne-aziatskikh respublik" (On the reorganization of the Central Asian republics). *Sovetskoe Pravo,* No. 4 (16), 1925, pp. 132–38.

Antropov, P. "K piatnadtsatiletiiu vtorogo sezda kommunisticheskoi partii Turkestana" (Fifteenth anniversary of the Second Congress of the Communist Party of Turkestan). *Revoliutsionnyi Vostok,* No. 3 (25), 1934, pp. 193–225.

Avetisov, Ter. Pogos. "Bukhara. Vzaimootnosheniia s Bukharoi v proshlom i nastoiashchem" (Bukhara. Relations with Bukhara in the past and present). *Z.N.,* No. 20 (118), October 3, 1921, pp. 2–3.

B—n, L. "Khambo-Agvan Dorzhiev (K borbe Tibeta za nezavisimost)" (Khambo-Agvan Dorzhiev [Aguan Dorji]; Tibet's struggle for independence). *N.V.,* No. 3, 1923, pp. 139–56.

Baitursunov. "Revoliutsiia i kirgizy" (The revolution and the Kirghiz). *Z.N.,* No. 29 (37), August 3, 1919, p. 1.

Broido, G. I. "Materialy k istorii vosstaniia kirgiz v 1916 godu" (Materials on the Kirghiz uprising in 1916). *N.V.,* No. 6, 1924, pp. 407–34.

———. "Turkestanskie problemy" (The Turkestan problems). *Z.N.,* No. 22 (79), July 11, 1922, p. 1, and No. 23 (30), July 18, 1920, p. 1.

"Bukhara v 1917 godu" (Bukhara in 1917). *Krasnyi Arkhiv,* No. 1 (20), 1927, pp. 78–122.

Bunakov, E. V. "K istorii snoshenii Rossii s sredneaziatskimi khanstvami v XIX v" (Russia's contact with the Central Asian khanates in the nineteenth century). *Sovetskoe Vostokovedenie,* II, 1941, pp. 5–26.

D. M. "K Khivinskoi revoliutsii" (The Khiva revolution). *Z.N.,* No. 24 (81), July 25, 1920, pp. 2–3.

[Frunze, M. V.] "M. V. Frunze na Turkestanskom fronte" (M. V. Frunze at the Turkestan front). *Krasnyi Arkhiv,* No. 100, 1940, pp. 37–78. Documents.

Ginsburg, S. "Basmachestvo v Fergane" (The Basmachi movement in Ferghana). *N.V.,* No. 10-11, 1925, pp. 175–202.

Gnesin, F. "Turkestan v dni revoliutsii i bolshevizma, mart–dekabr, 1917" (Turkestan in the days of revolution and Bolshevism, March–December, 1917). *Belyi Arkhiv,* I, 81–94.

Ibragimov, Iu. "Krasnyi Turkestan. Bukhara" (Red Turkestan. Bukhara). *Z.N.,* No. 13 (21), April 13, 1919, p. 1.

———. "Krasnyi Turkestan. Khiva" (Red Turkestan. Khiva). *Z.N.,* No. 14 (22), April 20, 1919, p. 1.

"Iz istorii vosstaniia kirgizov i kazakhov v 1916 g." (The Kirghiz and Kazakh revolt of 1916). *Borba Klassov,* No. 7-8, 1932, pp. 128–39.

K. "Sezd Khorezmskoi (Khivinskoi) Kommunisticheskoi Partii i soiuz malozemelnykh i bezzemelnykh dekhan" (The Congress of the Khorezm Communist Party and the union of poor and landless dekhans). *Z.N.,* No. 4 (10), March 22, 1922, p. 11.

———. "2-i sezd (Kurultai) Bukharskoi kommunisticheskoi partii" (The Second Congress (*Kurultai*) of the Bukharan Communist Party). *Z.N.,* No. 6 (135), February 16, 1922, p. 2.

———. "Znachenie Turkestanskoi respubliki" (The significance of the Turkestan republic). *Z.N.,* No. 31 (39), August 17, 1919, p. 2.

"K istorii vosstaniia kirgiz v 1916 g." (The Kirghiz uprising in 1916). *Krasnyi Arkhiv,* No. 16, 1926, pp. 53–75. Documented.

Khodorov, I. "Natsionalnoe razmezhevanie Srednei Azii" (National delimitation of Central Asia). *N.V.,* No. 8-9, 1925, pp. 65–81.

Khodzhaev, Faizulla. "Delimitation of National Boundaries in Soviet Central Asia." *Communist International,* No. 9, 1925, pp. 73–87. Translated from the Uzbek.

————. "O Mlado-Bukhartsakh" (The Young Bukharans). *Istorik - Marksist*, No. 1, 1926, pp. 123–41.

————. "Voprosy natsionalno-territorialnogo razmezhevaniia Sovetskoi Srednei Azii" (Problems of national territorial delimitation in Soviet Central Asia). *K.I.*, No. 8 (37), 1924, pp. 217–36.

"Kirgiz Intelligentsiia i Alash-Orda" (The Kirghiz intelligentsia and Alash-Orda). *Z.N.*, No. 20 (118), October 3, 1921, pp. 1–2.

M. N. "Pod znakom Islama" (Under the sign of Islam). *N.V.*, No. 4, 1923, pp. 72–97. About the Basmachi movement.

Kulbesherov, B. "Sovetskoe stroitelstvo v Srednei Azii i ego zadachi k 10-letiiu Oktiabria" (Soviet construction in Central Asia, and its tasks on the tenth anniversary of [the] October [Revolution]). *N.V.*, No. 19, 1927, pp. xxiii–xxxiv.

Mashitsky, A. "K istorii revoliutsii v Bukhare" (A historical account of the revolution in Bukhara). *Vestnik N.K.I.D.*, No. 3-4, May 15, 1921, pp. 24–37, and No. 5-6, July 1, 1921, pp. 70–83.

"Materialy po istorii bukharskoi revoliutsii" (Materials on the history of the Bukharan revolution). *Vestnik N.K.I.D.*, April–May, 1922, pp. 122–36. Documented.

Mindlin, Z. "Kirgizy i revoliutsiia" (The Kirghiz and the revolution). *N.V.*, No. 5, 1924, pp. 217–29.

Narimanov, N. "Nasha politika v Turkestane" (Our policy in Turkestan). *Z.N.*, No. 9 (66), March 21, 1920, p. 1.

Nemchenko, M. A. "Natsionalnoe razmezhevanie Srednei Azii" (National delimitation in Central Asia). *Mezhdunarodnaia Zhizn*, No. 4-5, 1924, pp. 67–92.

Paliukaitis (? pseud.). "Turkestan i revoliutsii Vostoka" (Turkestan and the revolutions of the East). *Z.N.*, No. 19 (27), May 26, 1919, p. 1.

Pestkovsky, S. "Turkestan i mirovaia revoliutsiia" (Turkestan and the world revolution). *Z.N.*, No. 20 (28), June 1, 1919, p. 1.

"Revoliutsionnoe dvizhenie v Khive" (The revolutionary movement in Khiva). *Z.N.*, No. 9 (66), March 21, 1920, p. 1.

Ryskulov, T. R. "Iz istorii borby za osvobozhdenie Vostoka: Vosstanie tuzemtsev Turkestana protiv tsarizma v 1916" (From the history of the East's struggle for liberation: The revolt of the Turkestan natives against tsarism in 1916). *N.V.*, No. 6, 1924, pp. 267–70.

————. "Sovremennyi Kazakhstan" (Modern Kazakhstan). *N.V.*, No. 12, 1926, pp. 105–20.

Safarov, G. I. "Kolonialnaia revoliutsiia. Opyt Turkestana" (The colonial revolution. Experiment in Turkestan). *K.I.*, No. 14, 1920, pp. 2761–67. Later expanded and published in book form.

Sherk-Ugly. "Revoliutsionnoe dvizhenie v Khive" (The revolutionary movement in Khiva). *Z.N.*, No. 9 (66), March 21, 1920, p. 1.

Skalov, G. "Khivinskaia revoliutsiia 1920 g." (The Khiva revolution of 1920). *N.V.*, No. 3, 1923, pp. 241–57.

————. "Sotsialnaia priroda Basmachestva v Turkestane" (The social nature of the Basmachi movement in Turkestan). *Z.N.*, No. 3-4, 1923, pp. 56–61.

Soloveichik, D. "Revoliutsionnaia Bukhara" (Revolutionary Bukhara). *N.V.*, No. 2, 1922, p. 272–88.

Sotsialisticheskii Komitet Partii Mladobukhartsev (Socialist Committee of the Young Bukharan Party). "Vozvanie k Narodam Vostoka" (Appeal to the People of the East). *Z.N.*, No. 7 (15), March 2, 1919, p. 1.

"V Turkestane. Borba s Basmachestvom" (In Turkestan. The struggle with the Basmachi). *Z.N.*, No. 2 (119), October 10, 1921, p. 3.

V. K. "Basmacheskii front" (The Basmachi front). *Z.N.*, No. 16 (73), June 2, 1920, p. 1.

Vasilevsky. "Fazy basmacheskogo dvizheniia v Srednei Azii" (Phases of the Basmachi movement in Central Asia). *N.V.*, No. 29, 1930, pp. 126–41.

"Vosstanie v 1916 v Srednei Azii" (The [Kirghiz] uprising in 1916 in Central Asia). *Krasnyi Arkhiv*, No. 34, 1929, pp. 37–94.

THE SOVIET UNION AND ITS NATIONALITIES

Ananov, I. N. *Ocherki federalnogo upravleniia SSSR* (An outline of federal administration in the U.S.S.R.). Leningrad, 1925.

Arkhipov, K. A. *Sovetskie avtonomnye oblasti i respubliki* (Soviet autonomous oblasts and republics). Moscow, 1927.

Bochkov, A. I. *Tri goda sovetskoi vlasti v Kazani. Khronika sobytii 25 oktiabria 1917–1920 g.g.* (Three years of Soviet rule in Kazan. A chronology of events, October 25, 1917–1920). Kazan, 1921.

Broido, G. I. *Natsionalnyi i kolonialnyi vopros* (The national and colonial question). Moscow, 1924.

Buriat-Mongolskaia Avtonomnaia S.S.R. Ocherki i otchety 1924–25 (Buriat-Mongol Autonomous S.S.R. Surveys and accounts for 1924–25). Verkhneudinsk, 1926.

Chugaev, D. *Obrazovanie S.S.S.R.* (The formation of the U.S.S.R.). Moscow, 1951.

Genkina, E. B. *Obrazaovanie S.S.S.R.* (The formation of the U.S.S.R.). Moscow, 1947.

Hrdlicka, Ales. *The Peoples of the Soviet Union.* Washington, D.C., 1942.

Iakubovskaia, S. I. *Obedinitelnoe dvizhenie za obrazovanie S.S.S.R. (1917–1922)* (The unification movement for the formation of the U.S.S.R., 1917–1922). Moscow, 1947.

Ignatev, V. I. *Sovet Natsionalnostei Tsentralnogo Ispolnitelnogo Komiteta SSSR* (The council of nationalities of the Central Executive Committee of the U.S.S.R.). Moscow, 1926.

Kantor, E. D. (Davydov). *Natsionalnyi vopros na XII sezde R.K.P.* (The nationalities question at the Twelfth Congress of the Russian Communist Party). Moscow, 1923.

Khavin, A. *Sotsialisticheskaia industrializatsiia natsionalynkh respublik i oblastei* (Socialist industrialization of national republcs and oblasts). Moscow, 1933.

Kirimal, E. *Der Nationale Kampf der Krimtürken; mit besonderer Berücksichtigung der Jahre 1917–1918.* Emsdetten, 1952.

Kohn, Hans. *Nationalism in the Soviet Union.* London, 1933.

Kotliarevsky, S. A. *S.S.S.R. i soiuznye respubliki* (The U.S.S.R. and the Union republics). 2d ed. Moscow, 1926.

Lamont, Corliss. *The Peoples of the Soviet Union.* New York, 1946.

Lenin, V. I. *Izbrannye stati po natsionalnomu voprosu* (Selected articles on the nationalities question). 2d ed. Moscow, 1925.

———. *Natsionalnyi vopros, 1910–1920 g.g.* (The nationalities question, 1910–1920). Moscow, 1921.

Matiushkin, N. *Druzhba narodov S.S.S.R.—istochnik sily sovetskogo gosudarstva* (Friendship of the peoples of the U.S.S.R.—a source of strength for the Soviet state). Moscow, 1947.

Mende, Gerhard von. *Der nationale Kampf der Russlandtürken; ein Beitrag zur nationalen Frage in der Sowjetunion.* Berlin, 1936.

Miliukov, P. N. *Natsionalnyi vopros. Proiskhozhdenie natsionalnosti i natsionalnye voprosy v Rossii* (The nationalities question. The origin of nationalities and the nationalities question in Russia). Prague, 1925.

Natsionalnaia politika VKP (b) v tsifrakh (Nationalities policies of the All-Russian Communist Party (B) in figures). Moscow, 1930.

Pipes, Richard. *The Formation of the Soviet Union; Communism and Nationalism, 1917–1923.* Cambridge, Mass., 1954.

Popov, N. N. *Natsionalnaia politika sovetskoi vlasti; kurs lektsii chitannykh na kursakh sekretarei ukomov pri Ts. K. VKP (b)* (The nationalities policy of the Soviet government. A course of lectures . . .). Moscow and Leningrad, 1927.

———. *Oktiabrskaia revoliutsiia i natsionalnyi vopros* (The October Revolution and the nationalities question). Moscow and Leningrad, 1927.

Raimov, R. M. *Obrazovanie Bashkirskoi A.S.S.R.* (The formation of the Bashkir A.S.S.R.). Moscow, 1952.

Stalin, I. V. *Marksizm i natsionalno-kolonialnyi vopros. Sbornik izbrannykh statei i rechei.* Moscow, 1935. Translation: *Marxism and the National and Colonial Question. Articles and Speeches.* New York, 1935.

———. *Sbornik statei. I. Marksizm i natsionalnyi vopros. II. Oktiabrskii perevorot i natsionalnyi vopros. III. Politika sovetskoi vlasti po natsionalnomu voprosu* (A collection of articles: 1. Marxism and the nationalities question. 2. The October Revolution and the nationalities question. 3. The policy of the Soviet government on the nationalities question). Tula, 1920.

Tougouchi-Caiannée, Marc. *U.R.S.S. face au problème des nationalités.* Liége, 1946.

Trainin, I. P. *S.S.S.R. i natsionalnaia problema po natsionalnym respublikam i oblastiam Sovetskogo Soiuza* (The U.S.S.R. and the nationalities problem in the national republics and oblasts of the Soviet Union). Moscow, 1924.

———. *Trud tovarishcha Stalina "Marksizm i natsionalnyi vopros"* (The work of comrade Stalin on "Marxism and the nationalities question"). Moscow, 1940.

Alymov, A., and S. Studenikin. "Sovetskii federalizm i demokraticheskii tsentralizm" (Soviet federalism and democratic centralism). *Sovetskoe Gosudarstvo,* No. 1-2, 1933, pp. 13–20.

Broido, G. I. "Likvidatsiia Narkomnatsa i ocherednye zadachi nashego gosudarstvennogo stroitelstva" (The liquidation of the Narkomnats and the immediate tasks of building up our Soviet state). *Vlast Sovetov,* No. 5, 1924, pp. 12–14.

Dimanshtein, S. M. "Desiat let natsionalnoi politiki partii i sovvlasti" (Ten years of the nationalities policy of the party and of the Soviet government). *N.V.,* No. 19, 1927, pp. iii–xxii.

———. "Marksistskie korni razresheniia natsionalnogo voprosa" (Marxist roots in the settlement of the nationalities problem). *Revoliutsiia i Natsionalnosti,* No. 5-6, 1933, pp. 46–58.

Eudin, Xenia J. "Soviet National Minority Policies, 1918–1921" *Slavonic and East European Review,* No. 21, 1943, pp. 31–55.

Gurvich, G. S. "Avtonomizm i federalizm v sovetskoi sisteme" (Autonomism and federalism in the Soviet system). *Vlast Sovetov,* No. 1, April 1924, pp. 24–29.

Hula, E. "The Nationalities Policy of the Soviet Union." *Social Research* (New York), XI, No. 2, May 1944, pp. 168–201.

Ivanov, L. "Natsionalnye menshinstva posle mirovoi voiny" (National minorities after the World War). *Mezhdunarodnaia Zhizn,* No. 1, 1925, pp. 18–43.

Khodorov, A. E. "Lenin i natsionalnyi vopros" (Lenin and the nationalities question). *N.V.,* No. 5, 1924, pp. 14–43.

Krylov, S. B. "Istoricheskii protsess razvitiia sovetskogo federalizma" (Historical process of the development of Soviet federalism). *Sovetskoe Pravo,* No. 5 (11), 1924, pp. 36–66.

Mansvetov, N. "Velikaia oktiabrskaia sotsialisticheskaia revoliutsiia i sozdanie Narodnogo Komissariata po Delam Natsionalnostei" (The great October socialist revolution and the formation of the People's Commissariat of Nationalities). *Voprosy Istorii*, No. 8, August 1949, pp. 9–29.

Pestkovsky, S. "Kak sozdavalsia Narkomnats" (How the Narkomnats was organized). *Z.N.*, No. 1, January 1923, pp. 272–73.

Popov, N. N. "Ocherednye zadachi partii v natsionalnom voprose" (The immediate tasks of the party in the nationalities question). *Kommunisticheskaia Revoliutsiia*, No. 12 (51), July 1, 1923, pp. 65–78.

———. "Soiuz sotsialisticheskikh sovetskikh respublik i natsionalnaia politika sovetskoi vlasti" (The U.S.S.R. and the nationalities policy of the Soviet government). *Kommunisticheskaia Revoliutsiia*, No. 4 (43), February 15, 1923, pp. 34–36.

Raimov, R. M. "K istorii obrazovaniia Bashkirskoi Avtonomnoi Sotsialisticheskoi Sovetskoi Respubliki" (The formation of the Bashkir A.S.S.R.). *Voprosy Istorii*, No. 4, April 1948, pp. 23–42.

Solovian. "Znachenie natsionalnykh komissariatov" (The significance of the nationalities commissariats). *Z.N.*, No. 19 (27), May 26, 1919, p. 1.

Trainin, I. P. "Piat let natsionalnoi politiki sovetskoi vlasti" (Five years of the nationalities policy of the Soviet government). *Z.N.*, No. 1, January 1923, pp. 14–22.

OFFICIAL PUBLICATIONS AND TREATIES

Great Britain. Foreign Office. *Communist Papers; Documents Selected from Those Obtained on the Arrest of the Communist Leaders on the 14th and 21st October, 1925.* Cmd. 2682. Accounts and Papers, 1926, Vol. XXIII. London, 1926.

———. *Correspondence between His Majesty's Government and the Soviet Government Respecting the Relations between the two Governments.* Cmd. 1869. Accounts and Papers, 1923, Vol. XXV. London, 1923.

———. *Documents Illustrating the Hostile Activities of the Soviet Government and Third International against Great Britain.* Cmd. 2874. Accounts and Papers, 1927, Vol. XXVI. London, 1927.

———. *Lausanne Conference on Near Eastern Affairs, 1922–1923. Records of Proceedings and Draft Terms of Peace.* Cmd. 1814. Accounts and Papers, 1923, Vol. XXVI. London, 1923.

———. *A Selection of Papers Dealing with the Relations between His Majesty's Government and the Soviet Government, 1921–1927.* Cmd. 2895. Accounts and Papers, 1927, Vol. XXV. London, 1927.

*India. Government of India. *Judgment in the Meerut Conspiracy Case.* 2 vols. Simla, 1933.

———. Home Department. *India in 1925–1926. A Statement prepared for presentation to Parliament in accordance with the requirements of the 26th Section of the Government of India Act* . . . Calcutta, 1926.

———. *India in 1926–1927* . . . Calcutta, 1928.

Japan. Ministry of Foreign Affairs. *Relation of Japan with Manchuria and Mongolia.* N.p., 1392.

Russia

Academy of Sciences of the U.S.S.R. Institute of History. *Obrazovanie S.S.S.R., sbornik dokumentov, 1917–1924* (The formation of the U.S.S.R.; a collection of documents, 1917–1924). Moscow, 1949. Edited by E. B. Genkina.

All-Russian Communist Party (B). *Desiatyi sezd R.K.P.(B), Mart 1921 g.* (Tenth Congress of the Russian Communist Party (Bolshevik), March 1921). Moscow, 1933. Stenographic report edited by N. N. Popov.

———. *Dvenadtsatyi sezd Rossiiskoi Kommunisticheskoi Partii (Bolshevikov).*

Stenograficheskii otchet 17–25 aprelia 1923 g. (Twelfth Congress of the Russian Communist Party (Bolshevik). Stenographic report, April 17–25, 1923). Moscow, 1923.

———. *History of the Communist Party of the Soviet Union (B). Short course.* . . . New York, 1939. Translated from the Russian (see next entry).

———. *Istoriia Vsesoiuznoi Kommunisticheskoi Partii (Bolshevikov). Kratkii kurs. Pod redaktsiei Komissii TSK VKP(B), odobren TSK VKP(B), 1938 g.* (History of the All-Union Communist Party (Bolshevik). Short course. Edited by a commission of the Central Committee of the party, and authorized by the Central Committee, 1938). Moscow, 1938.

———. [Bukharin, N. I.] *Otchet delegatsii VKP(B) v IKKI XV sezdu VKP(B). Mezhdunarodnoe polozhenie i zadachi Kommunisticheskogo Internatsionala; doklad i zakliuchitelnoe slovo 9–12 dek. 1927 g.* (Report of the delegation of the All-Russian Communist Party (B) on the ECCI to the Fifteenth Party Congress: The international situation and the tasks of the Communist International, report and final remarks, December 9–12, 1927). Moscow, 1928.

———. *XV sezd Vsesoiuznoi Kommunisticheskoi Partii (B). Stenograficheskii otchet* (Fifteenth Congress of the All-Union Communist Party (B). Stenographic report). 2d ed. Moscow and Leningrad, 1928.

———. *XV Congrès de P.C. de l'U.R.S.S. décembre 1927. Compte rendu abrégé.* Paris, 1928.

———. *Sotsialnyi i natsionalnyi sostav VKP(B). Itogi partiinoi perepisi 1927 goda* (Social and national composition of the All-Union Communist Party (B) according to the party census of 1927). Moscow, 1939.

———. *Tretii ocherednoi sezd Rossiiskoi Sotsial-Demokraticheskoi Rabochei Partii; polnyi tekst protokolov* (Third Congress of the Russian Social Democratic Workers' Party; complete text of minutes). Geneva, 1905.

———. *Trinadtsatyi Sezd Rossiiskoi Kommunisticheskoi Partii (Bolshevikov). Stenograficheskii otchet, 23–31 maia 1924 g.* (Thirteenth Congress of the All-Russian Communist Party (Bolshevik). Stenographic report, May 23–31, 1924). Moscow, 1924.

———. *Vsesoiuznaia Kommunisticheskaia Partiia (B) v rezoliutsiiakh i resheniiakh sezdov, konferentsii i plenumov Ts. K.* (The All-Union Communist Party (B) as seen in the resolutions and decisions of its congresses, its conferences, and the plenums of its Central Committee). 5th ed., 2 vols. Moscow, 1936.

———. Vtoroi ocherednoi sezd Rossiiskoi Sotsial-Demokraticheskoi Partii; polnyi tekst protokolov (Second Congress of the Russian Social Democratic Workers' Party; complete text of minutes). Geneva, 1903.

Communist Academy. [Dimanshtein, S. M.] *Revoliutsiia i natsionalnyi vopros; dokumenty i materialy po istorii natsionalnogo voprosa v Rossii i SSSR v XX veke, tom 3: 1917, okt.–dek.* (The revolution and the nationalities question; documents and materials on the history of the nationalities question in Russia and the U.S.S.R. in the twentieth century, Vol. III: October-December, 1917). Moscow, 1930.

Ministry of Foreign Affairs. *Sbornik diplomaticheskikh dokumentov po mongolskomu voprosu 23 avgusta 1912 g.–2 noiabria 1913 g.* (A collection of diplomatic documents on the Mongolian question, August 23, 1912–November 2, 1913). St. Petersburg, 1914.

People's Commissariat of Foreign Affairs. [Adamov, E. A. (ed.)] *Konstantinopol i prolivy. Po sekretnym dokumentam b. Ministerstva Inostrannykh Del* (Constantinople and the Straits. According to secret documents of the former Ministry of Foreign Affairs). 2 vols. Moscow, 1925–26.

———. [Adamov, E. A. (ed.)] *Razdel Aziatskoi Turtsii. Po sekretnym doku-*

mentam b. Ministerstva Inostrannykh Del (The partition of Asiatic Turkey. According to secret documents of the former Ministry of Foreign Affairs). Moscow, 1924.

————. *Godovoi otchet N.K.I.D. k VIII sezdu sovetov, 1919–1920 gg.* (Annual report of the People's Commissariat of Foreign Affairs to the Eighth Congress of Soviets [of the R.S.F.S.R.], 1919–1920). Moscow, 1921.

————. *Godovoi otchet za 1923 g. Narodnogo Komissariata po Inostrannym Delam k II sezdu sovetov S.S.S.R.* (Annual report for 1923 of the People's Commissariat of Foreign Affairs to the Second Congress of Soviets of the U.S.S.R.). Moscow, 1924.

————. *Godovoi otchet Narodnogo Komissariata po Inostrannym Delam za 1924 g. k III sezdu sovetov SSSR* (Annual report for 1924 of the People's Commissariat of Foreign Affairs to the Third Congress of Soviets of the U.S.S.R.). Moscow, 1925.

————. *R.S.F.S.R. i Gruzinskaia demokraticheskaia respublika. Ikh vzaimootnosheniia* (The R.S.F.S.R. and the Georgian democratic republic. Their mutual relations). Moscow, 1921. Documents.

People's Commissariat of Justice. *Report of Court Proceedings in the Case of the Anti-Soviet "Bloc of the Rights and Trotskyites" Heard Before the Military Collegium of the Supreme Court of the USSR,, Moscow, March 2–13, 1938.* Moscow, 1938. The case of Faizulla Khodzhaev *et al.*

People's Commissariat of Nationalities. *Izvestiia Petersburgskogo Komissariata po Delam Natsionalnostei* (News of the Petersburg [Petrograd] Commissariat of Nationalities). Petersburg, 1920.

————. [Pesikina, E. I.] *Narodnyi Komissariat po Delam Natsionalnostei i ego deiatelnost v 1917–1918 gg.* (The People's Commissariat of Nationalities and its activities in 1917–1918). Moscow, 1950.

————. Dimanshtein, S. M. (ed.) *Natsionalnaia politika sovetskoi vlasti za dva goda. Sbornik* (The nationalities policy of the Soviet government during the [last] two years. Collection of materials). Moscow, 1920.

————. *Natsionalnyi vopros i Sovetskaia Rossiia* (The nationalities question and Soviet Russia). Moscow, 1921.

————. *Otchet Narodnogo Komissariata po Delam Natsionalnostei za 1921 god* (Report of the People's Commissariat of Nationalities for 1921). Moscow, 1921.

————. *Politika sovetskoi vlasti po natsionalnym delam za tri goda, 1917 - XI - 1920* (Three years of the Soviet government's nationalities policy, November 1917– November 1920). Moscow, 1920.

————. *Spravochnik Narodnogo Komissariata po Delam Natsionalnostei* (Reference book of the People's Commissariat of Nationalities). Moscow, 1921.

Deviatyi Vserossiiskii Sezd Sovetov Rabochikh, Krestianskikh, Krasnoarmeiiskikh i Kazachikh Deputatov. Stenograficheskii otchet, 22–27 dekabria 1921 goda (Ninth All-Russian Congress of Soviets of Workers', Peasants', Red Soldiers', and Cossacks' Deputies. Stenographic report, December 22–27, 1921). Moscow, 1922.

————. *Tretii Vserossiiskii Sezd Sovetov Rabochikh, Soldatskikh i Krestianskikh Deputatov* (Third All-Russian Congress of Soviets of Workers', Soldiers', and Peasants' Deputies). Petersburg, 1918.

Sobranie Uzakonenii i Rasporiazhenii Rabochego i Krestianskogo Pravitelstva (Laws and regulations of the workers' and peasants' government of the R.S.F.S.R.), 1917–. Moscow, 1919–. Title varies.

United States. *Congressional Record. Proceedings and Debates of the First Ses-*

sion of the Sixty-eighth Congress of the United States of America, Vol. 65, Part VII.

————. Department of State. *Papers Relating to the Foreign Relations of United States 1918[-1919]. Russia . . .* 4 vols. Washington, D.C., 1931–37.

————. *Papers Relating to the Foreign Relations of the United States, 1921*, Vol. II. Washington, D.C., 1936.

————. Division of Biographical Information. *Far Easterners in the Comintern Structure.* Unclassified typescript, 1950.

————. Office of Strategic Services. *The Communist Party of India.* Washington, D.C., 1945.

Treaties

Adamov, E. A. (ed.). *Sbornik dogovorov Rossii s drugimi gosudarstvami, 1856–1917* (A collection of treaties between Russia and other states, 1856–1917). Moscow, 1952.

Dogovory o neitralitete, nenapadenii i o soglasitelnoi protsedure zakliuchennye mezhdu Soiuzom S.S.R. i inostrannymi gosudarstvami (Treaties of neutrality, nonaggression, and procedure for reaching agreement between the U.S.S.R. and foreign states). Moscow, 1934.

Grimm, E. D. *Sbornik dogovorov i drugikh dokumentov po istorii mezhdunarodnykh otnoshenii na Dalnem Vostoke (1842–1925)* (A collection of treaties and other documents dealing with international relations in the Far East, 1842–1925). Moscow, 1927.

Kliuchnikov, Iu. V., and A. V. Sabanin (eds.). *Mezhdunarodnaia politika noveishego vremeni v dogovorakh, notakh i deklaratsiiakh . . .* (International policies in modern times as expressed in treaties, notes, and declarations . . .). Moscow, 1925–28. In three parts.

MacMurray, John van Antwerp (comp.). *Treaties and Agreements with and concerning China, 1894–1919 . . .* 2 vols. New York, 1921.

————. *Treaties and Agreements with and concerning China, 1919–1929.* Washington, D.C., 1929.

Martens, F. F. de (comp.). *Recueil des traités et conventions conclus par la Russie avec les puissances étrangères publié d'ordre du Ministère des affaires étrangères.* 15 vols. St. Petersburg, 1874–1909.

Outer Mongolia. Treaties and Agreements. Washington, D.C., 1921.

Sbornik dogovorov s Kitaem 1689–1881 gg. (A collection of treaties with China, 1689–1881). St. Petersburg, Ministry of Foreign Affairs, 1889.

Shapiro, Leonard (comp. and ed.). *Soviet Treaty Series: A Collection of Bilateral Treaties, Agreements and Conventions, etc., Concluded between the Soviet Union and Foreign Powers*, Vol. I: *1917–1928.* Washington, D.C., 1950.

Treaty of Peace with Turkey signed at Sèvres, August 10, 1920. Cmd. 964. London, 1920. With maps.

NEWSPAPERS AND PERIODICALS
Newspapers

Izvestiia (News). Petrograd, Moscow. Organ of the Central Executive Committee of Soviets. Daily. Subtitle varies.

Izvestiia Ulan-Bator-Khoto (News of Ulan Bator). Ulan Bator, Mongolia (formerly Urga). Daily. A Russian-language newspaper for the Soviet Russian colony in Ulan Bator.

Krasnaia Gazeta (Red Gazette). Petrograd. Daily.

Petrogradskaia Pravda (Petrograd Truth). Petrograd. Daily. Continued as *Leningradskaia Pravda* (Leningrad Truth).

Pravda (Truth). Moscow. Organ of the All-Russian Communist Party (B) Daily.
Voennaia Mysl (Military Thought). Tashkent. Organ of the Revolutionary War
   Council of the Turkestan Front in 1920 and 1921.
Zhizn Natsionalnostei (The Life of the Nationalities). Moscow. Organ of the
   People's Commissariat of Nationalities. Superseded by the periodical of the
   same name.

Periodicals

L'Asie Française. Paris. Organ of the Committee for French Asia.
Belyi Arkhiv (White Archives). Paris.
Biulleten Ispolnitelnogo Komiteta Kommunisticheskogo Internatsionala (Bulletin
   of the Executive Committee of the Communist International), Nos. 1-4, Sep-
   tember 8-December 23, 1921. Moscow.
Biulleten Oppozitsii (Bolshevikov-Lenintsev) (Bulletin of the Bolshevik-Leninist
   Opposition). Paris, Berlin, New York. Trotskyite organ.
Bolshevik. Moscow. Organ of the Central Committee of the All-Russian Com-
   munist Party (B).
Borba Klassov (The Class Struggle). Moscow. Organ of the Institute of History
   of the Soviet Academy of Sciences. Superseded by *Istoricheskii Zhurnal.*
Communist International. Leningrad, London, New York. Organ of the ECCI.
   Also appeared in Russian, French, and German.
International Press Correspondence. Vienna, Berlin, London. Superseded by *World
   News and Views,* January 1, 1954. Appears in English, French, German, and
   Spanish.
Istoricheskii Zhurnal (History Journal). Moscow. Organ of the Institute of His-
   tory of the Soviet Academy of Sciences. Preceded by *Borba Klassov.* Absorbed
   Istorik-Marksist in 1941. Superseded by *Voprosy Istorii,* July 1945.
Istorik-Marksist (Marxist Historian). Moscow. Organ of the Institute of History
   of the Soviet Academy of Sciences. Absorbed in 1941 by *Istoricheskii Zhurnal.*
Kommunisticheskaia Revoliutsiia (Communist Revolution). Moscow. Organ of
   the Central Committee of the All-Russian Communist Party (B).
Kommunisticheskii Internatsional (Communist International), 1919-43. Moscow.
   Organ of the ECCI. Also appeared in English, French, and German.
Krasnaia Nov (Red Virgin Soil). Moscow. Organ of the Union of Soviet Writers.
Krasnyi Arkhiv (Red Archives). Moscow. Organ of the Chief Office of Soviet
   Archives.
Krasnyi Internatsional Profsoiuzov (Red Trade Union International). Moscow.
Krestianskii Internatsional (Peasant International). Moscow.
The Masses of India. Paris. Preceded by *Vanguard of Indian Independence.*
   Berlin.
Materialy po Kitaiskomu Voprosu (Materials on Chinese Problems). Moscow.
   Organ of the Scientific Research Institute for the Study of China, attached to
   the Sun Yat-sen University of the Toilers of the Far East.
Mezhdunarodnaia Zhizn (International Life). Moscow. Organ of the People's
   Commissariat of Foreign Affairs.
Mirovoe Khoziaistvo i Mirovaia Politika (World Economy and World Politics).
   Moscow. Organ of the Institute of World Economy and Politics of the Soviet
   Academy of Sciences. Changed to *Voprosy Ekonomiki* in 1948.
Novyi Vostok (The New East). Moscow. Organ of the All-Russian Association
   for Eastern Studies.
Pan-Pacific Worker. Hankow. Organ of the Pacific Trade Union Secretariat.
Problemy Kitaia (Chinese Problems). Moscow. Organ of the Scientific Research
   Association for the Study of the National and Colonial Problems.
Problemy Marksizma (Problems of Marxism). Moscow. Organ of the Leningrad
   Section of the Communist Academy.

Proletarskaia Revoliutsiia (Proletarian Revolution). Moscow. Organ of the Marx-Engels-Lenin Institute.

Revoliutsionnyi Vostok (The Revolutionary East). Moscow. Organ of the Scientific Research Association for the Study of the National and Colonial Problems.

Revue du Monde Musulman. Paris.

Russian Information and Review. London. Organ of the Russian trade delegation in London. Superseded by *Soviet Union Review* in 1925.

Severnaia Aziia (North Asia). Moscow. Organ of the Society for the Study of the Ural Region, Siberia, and the Far East.

Sovetskoe Gosudarstvo, see Sovetskoe Gosudarstvo i Pravo

Sovetskoe Gosudarstvo i Pravo (Soviet State and Law). Moscow. Organ of the Institute of Law of the Soviet Academy of Sciences. Title varies: 1930, *Sovetskoe Gosudarstvo i Revoliutsiia* (Soviet State and Revolution); 1931–38, *Sovetskoe Gosudarstvo* (Soviet State). Publication suspended May 1941–December 1945.

Sovetskoe Vostokovedenie (Soviet Eastern Studies). Moscow. Organ of the Institute of Eastern Studies of the Soviet Academy of Sciences.

Soviet Russia. New York, Chicago. Official organ of the Friends of Soviet Russia. After being renamed *Soviet Russia Pictorial,* it was combined in 1924 with *Labor Herald* and *Liberator* to form *Workers' Monthly.*

Tikhii Okean (Pacific Ocean). Moscow. Organ of the Pacific Section of the Institute of World Economy and Politics.

Torgovlia Rossii s Vostokom (Russia's Trade with the East). Moscow. Organ of the Russian Chamber of Commerce.

La Vague Rouge. Paris.

Vestnik Agitatsii i Propagandy (Agitation and Propaganda Messenger). Moscow. Organ of the Central Committee of the All-Russian Communist Party (B).

Vestnik Manchzhurii (Manchurian Messenger). Harbin. Organ of the Chinese Eastern Railway.

Vestnik Narodnogo Komissariata po Inostrannym Delam (Messenger of the People's Commissariat of Foreign Affairs). Moscow. Referred to as *Vestnik N.K.I.D.*

Vestnik 2-go Kongressa Kommunisticheskogo Internatsionala (Messenger of the Second Congress of the Communist International). Petrograd and Moscow, 1920.

Vlast Sovetov (Soviet Power). Moscow. Organ of the All-Russian Central Executive Committee of Soviets.

Voennaia Mysl (Military Thought). Tashkent, 1920–21. Organ of the Revolutionary War Council of the Turkestan front line.

Voprosy Istorii (Problems of History). Moscow. Organ of the Institute of History of the Soviet Academy of Sciences. Superseded *Istoricheskii Zhurnal.*

BIOGRAPHICAL NOTES

We give here biographical notes on persons mentioned in this volume regarding whom the generally available information in non-Russian sources is either inaccurate or scant. For many others we mention, notably most of the Indian revolutionaries, we have found no important information beyond what appears in our text. For biographies and biographical sketches of men not included here, see the following: CHINA: Robert S. Elegant, *China's Red Masters. Political Biographies of the Chinese Communist Leaders*, New York, 1951; Robert C. North, *Moscow and Chinese Communists*, Stanford, Calif., 1953; Benjamin Schwartz, *Chinese Communists and the Rise of Mao*, Cambridge, Mass., 1951; Nym Wales, *Red Dust. Autobiographies of Chinese Communists*, Stanford, Calif., 1952. JAPAN: Rodger Swearingen and Paul Langer, *Red Flag in Japan. International Communism in Action, 1919–1951*, Cambridge, Mass., 1952. SOUTHEAST ASIA: Virginia Thompson, *The Left Wing in Southeast Asia*, New York, 1950. See also United States Department of State, Division of Biographic Information, *Far Easterners in the Comintern Structure* (unclassified).

ARAHATA, KANSON (b. 1887). Japanese Communist, referred to by Russian Communists as Aoki. Originally a syndicalist; later one of the organizers of the Japanese Communist Party; attended Fourth Congress of the Comintern, 1922; imprisoned for one year in 1924; with other Japanese Communists met Comintern representatives in Shanghai, 1925, to discuss trend to dissolve Japanese Communist Party; arrested, 1926; released, 1928; broke with party in the thirties; no longer politically active.

BLÜCHER, VASILII KONSTANTINOVICH (1889–1938?), known also as Galin, Galen, and Galents. Soviet general and military expert, at one time thought to be a German officer and prisoner of war in World War I. As a youth worked in a railway-car plant; arrested and sentenced to over two years' imprisonment for participation in strike, 1910; after 1914 sergeant in Russian army; seriously wounded and discharged; worked in shipbuilding plant at Sormovo, near Moscow, and other plants; joined Bolsheviks, 1916; after October Revolution worked on Samara Revolutionary Committee, and later commanded several Red detachments against Dutov; first man to receive Order of the Red Banner, 1918; commanded a division against Kolchak; later sent to southern front to fight Wrangel; commander-in-chief and minister of war for the Far Eastern Republic, 1921–22; later commander of an army corps and war commissar for the Leningrad fortified region; special member of Revolutionary War Council, 1924; in China, 1924–27, training Chinese at Whampoa Military Academy, and active in field during Kuomintang's northern campaign; commander of the Soviet Union's Eastern Special Army, formed in August 1929 at a time of serious conflict with China over Manchuria; dismissed from his duties in 1938; mysteriously disappeared.

BORODIN (GRUSENBERG), MIKHAIL MARKOVICH (1884–1953). Born in Vitebsk province; joined revolutionary movement in his youth, belonging first to the Bund (All-Jewish Workers' League of Lithuania, Poland, and Russia);

457

worked among Latvian Social Democrats under name of Loro; attended Stockholm Conference of Russian Social Democratic Labor Party, 1906; emigrated to United States and studied at Valparaiso University; became a teacher; founded "Progressive Preparatory School" for emigrés in Chicago; joined Socialist Party of America and was treasurer of Society to Assist Russian Political Prisoners, organized in 1909; went to Moscow, 1918; visited Mexico; arrested in Glasgow, Scotland, in August 1922 for communist propaganda; sentenced to six months' imprisonment on condition of leaving Great Britain after his release; left for Russia; went to China in 1923 upon Karakhan's suggestion, approved by Sun Yat-sen, soon becoming Kuomintang's most influential adviser; stayed with Kuomintang until summer of 1927; left for Russia, traveling with other Russian Communists and Anna Louise Strong by auto across northwest China and Mongolia; was editor of *Moscow Daily News* in the thirties.

CHANG T'AI-LEI (1898–1927). Chinese Communist. Member of students' circle for "social reconstruction," 1919; in Tientsin, organized socialist youth group, which later became Communist Youth League; took part in meeting held in August 1920 by Voitinsky and Ch'en Tu-hsiu in the Shanghai office of the socialist youth group for purpose of organizing Chinese Communist Party; reported in spring of 1921 to Comintern's Far Eastern Secretariat in Irkutsk and was designated secretary of the Secretariat's Chinese Section; in summer of 1921 attended Third Congress of the Comintern in Moscow with Yang Ho-te, and helped draft that Congress's theses on national and colonial questions; secretly visited Japan, 1921; attended Congress of the Toilers of the Far East, 1922; returned to China, 1923; active in communist movement; organized Hong Kong strike in 1925; headed Canton Commune, 1927; killed in street during uprising.

CHANG WEN-T'IEN (b. 1896), known also as Lo Fu. Chinese Communist, and leading Chinese Marxian theoretician and writer. Son of a wealthy farmer; participated in May Fourth Movement, 1919; left for Shanghai and became editor of a commercial newspaper; spent six months in Japan, 1920; proceeded to San Francisco, where he worked for a year and a half on a Chinese-language newspaper and attended University of California; returned to China, 1922, and taught in several schools in Szechwan; joined Chinese Communist Party in Shanghai, 1925; went to Moscow, 1926, and remained for four years, first studying at Sun Yat-sen University and later teaching at the Institute of Red Professors and the Lenin School; returned to China in 1930, traveling with P. A. Mif, newly appointed Comintern representative for the Far East; together with other Chinese Communists opposed the Chinese Communist Party leadership under Li Li-san; after Li's overthrow in January 1931, was elected to party's Politburo; worked at party's Shanghai headquarters; fled to Kiangsi Soviet in 1933, becoming People's Commissar of Propaganda there and one of the party's most prominent leaders in the thirties.

CHOIBALSAN (CHOI BAL SAN) (1895–1952). Mongolian revolutionary. Son of a poor herdsman; sent to a monastery at age 13, but fled from there in 1912; worked as a laborer in Urga, 1912–14; with assistance of Russian and Buriat friends, entered Russian consulate school in Urga; a year later was sent to Irkutsk for further studies; remained there until 1918, witnessing revolutionary upsurge in Siberia; returned to Urga, 1918; organized a secret revolutionary group, 1919; merged his group with Suhe-Bator's similar but larger group, 1920; elected in June 1920 by the Urga revolutionary group to proceed with other delegates to Soviet Russia; elected to Central Committee of Mongolian People's Revolutionary Party and named commissar of Mongolian People's Army, 1921; fought with Soviet troops against anti-Bolshevik forces, notably

Ungern-Sternberg's, in Urga; soon after capture of Urga from Ungern, became assistant minister of war and acting commander of Mongolian People's Army; awarded Order of the Red Banner, 1922; in Moscow studying, 1923–24; active in suppressing alleged conspiracy in Urga headed by Danzan, 1924; continued to hold high offices in government and party; minister of the interior from 1936 and prime minister and minister of war from 1937; personally directed military operations against Japan after 1939; awarded the Russian Order of Suvorov in 1945.

DORJI, AGVAN (1853–1924?), known also as Dorzhiev or Dorjieff. A Buriat and a Russian subject; entered Tibet monastery in 1873, and graduated from school of divinity there; later, as chief councillor on faculty of divinity, appointed educator of the young Dalai Lama; instrumental in lessening Chinese influence in Tibet, and advised Dalai Lama to seek Russian assistance against British attempts to gain influence there; on Dalai Lama's instructions, proceeded to St. Petersburg, traveling via China in the guise of a Chinese, and was received by Nicholas II; later acted as intermediary between the Russian court and the Dalai Lama; fled with Dalai Lama to Urga, 1904, when British forces entered Lhasa; accompanied Dalai Lama to Peking, 1906; returned to St. Petersburg in 1912 with gifts from Dalai Lama for Buddhist temple the erection of which Dorji had promoted; during and after civil war in Russia, carried on religious work among Russian Buriats and Kalmuks.

FRUNZE, MIKHAIL VASILEVICH (1885–1925). Old Bolshevik; active in revolutionary movement, 1905–7; often arrested, spent seven years in prison at hard labor; twice sentenced to death, sentence both times commuted to hard labor; escaped from prison, 1915; active in October Revolution; commander of Soviet forces on eastern and Turkestan fronts, 1918–19; directed military operations and defeated Wrangel's forces in Crimea, 1920; commander of Ukrainian army, 1920–24; chairman of Revolutionary War Council of the Soviet Union and People's Commissar for Military and Naval Affairs, 1925; instrumental in reorganization of Soviet armed forces; awarded Order of the Red Banner and other decorations; died after an unsuccessful operation.

FUKUMOTO, KAZUO. Japanese communist intellectual, well versed in the writings of Marx and Lenin; returned to Japan from extended travel through Europe and America in early 1920's; responsible for the communist "deviation" known as Fukumotoism, which by requiring thorough study of Marxism from every member of a communist party would have made party membership inaccessible to the working masses; censured and branded a Trotskyite, 1927, after discussing his theory with a special committee in Moscow, the committee that later drafted the July Theses (see our Document 94); recanted and returned to Japan; arrested, 1928; arrested again, 1932, and sentenced to ten years' imprisonment; returned to active participation in party work in 1950.

IANSON, IAKOV DAVIDOVICH (b. 1886), known also as Hayama. Latvian by birth; member of the Riga Committee of the Russian Social Democratic Labor Party (B); active in revolutionary movement, 1905–7; arrested and sentenced to six years' imprisonment; exiled to Siberia, 1914, as an undesirable Latvian; active in Irkutsk after February revolution; chairman of regional executive committee of party's Eastern Siberian branch, and representative of People's Commissariat of Foreign Affairs in Irkutsk, 1918–20; foreign minister of Far Eastern Republic, 1921–22; member of Collegium of People's Commissariat of Foreign Trade, 1923; member of Soviet delegations seeking trade agreements with Italy, 1923–24, with Great Britain, 1924, and with Germany, 1925; first Soviet trade representative in Japan, 1925–28, and reputedly Comintern agent there; chairman of Russian Trading Corporation (Arcos) in London, 1930–32; chairman of Soviet Board of Trade and member of board of the U.S.S.R. Council of the Institute of Pacific Relations (formed in 1934).

IOFFE (JOFFE), ADOLF ABRAMOVICH (1883–1937), known also as Viktor Krymsky. Soviet diplomat. Son of a wealthy businessman, physician by training; Menshevik from 1903, working mainly abroad; with Trotsky, edited *Pravda* in Vienna, 1908–12; returned to Russia and was arrested; imprisoned, 1912–17; joined Bolsheviks in 1917 together with Trotsky; headed Soviet delegation to Brest-Litovsk, 1918; Soviet ambassador to Berlin, April–November, 1918; headed delegations to conduct peace negotiations with Estonia, Lithuania, Latvia, and Poland, 1920 and 1921; participated in Genoa Conference, 1922; conducted peace negotiations with China in Peking, 1922–23; negotiated unofficially with Japan for a peace treaty, 1923; later Soviet representative in Austria; sided with Trotsky, 1925–27; committed suicide.

KARAKHAN, LEV MIKHAILOVICH (1889–1937). Soviet diplomat. Menshevik from 1904; joined Bolsheviks, July 1917; secretary to Soviet delegation at Brest-Litovsk, 1918; member of Collegium of People's Commissariat of Foreign Affairs after 1918, later Assistant People's Commissar of Foreign Affairs; Soviet ambassador to Poland, 1921, to China, 1923–26, to Turkey, 1934–37; purged.

KHODZHAEV, FAIZULLA (1896–1938). Uzbek Communist. Son of a rich Uzbek merchant; active in Young Bukharan movement after 1914; participated in armed uprising against Emir of Bukhara, 1917; sentenced to death, but escaped from Bukhara; after October Revolution made contact with Bolsheviks; took part in Turkestan Red Army's unsuccessful campaign against the Emir in early 1918, becoming chairman of Young Bukharans' revolutionary committee; escaped to Soviet Turkestan, and in late 1919 became chairman of Young Bukharans' bureau and editor of their paper; participated in successful *coup d'état* against the Emir, September 1920; joined Communist Party of Bukhara and became a member of its Central Committee; fought against Enver Pasha; became chairman of Council of People's Commissars (and later chairman of Central Executive Committee) of Uzbek S.S.R. and a member of Uzbek Communist Party; from 1922, member of Central Asian Bureau of Central Committee of Russian Communist Party; awarded Orders of the Red Banner and the Red Star; suspected of nationalist deviation in the thirties, and tried in 1938; admitted active participation in Uzbek nationalist "Group of Eighteen"; executed.

MANUILSKY, DMITRII ZAKHARIEVICH (b. 1883), known also as Bezrabotnyi. Old Bolshevik; active in revolutionary movement, 1903–5; arrested for participation in revolt of Kronstadt soldiers and sailors, 1906, and exiled to Yakutsk region; escaped and carried on illegal work in Kiev; emigrated, 1907; obtained law degree from Sorbonne, 1911; carried on illegal work in Moscow and St. Petersburg, 1912–13; emigrated again; returned to Russia, May 1917; after October Revolution active in Ukrainian government and party work; member of Central Committee of Russian Communist Party, 1923–39; elected to ECCI's presidium in 1924, and served as its secretary, 1928–43; appointed acting chairman of Council of People's Commissars and People's Commissar of Foreign Affairs of Ukrainian S.S.R, 1944; acting chairman of Council of Ministers of the U.S.S.R., 1946–53; head of Ukrainian delegation at United Nations Conference in San Francisco, 1945; participated in Paris Peace Conference, 1946, and active in General Assembly of the United Nations; member of Academy of Sciences of Ukrainian S.S.R.; awarded Orders of Lenin and of the Red Star.

MARING (HENDRICUS SNEEVLIET) (1883?–194–). Dutch Communist. Revolutionary agitator in Java before World War I and instrumental in organizing Indonesian Communist Party in 1920; attended Second Congress of the Comintern, 1920; active in China, 1921; leader of Dutch Transport Workers' Federation and member of Profintern's presidium, 1922; Comintern representative in Holland, 1923; later broke with Comintern and headed a Left-wing Socialist group in Holland; killed by Nazis during World War II.

NARIMANOV, NARIMAN N. (1872–1925). Physician by profession; founder of the Persian party Gummet ("Energy") in Baku, 1904; head of Near Eastern Department of People's Commissariat of Foreign Affairs, 1919; later acting People's Commissar of Nationalities; one of initiators of Baku Congress, 1920; chairman of Council of People's Commissars of Azerbaijan S.S.R., 1920–22; member of Central Executive Committee of the U.S.S.R. and its chairman in 1925; rector of Institute for Eastern Studies; wrote dramas and comedies reflecting national-revolutionary tendencies and depicting nationalist and religious prejudices of his fellow citizens.

PAVLOVICH, see VELTMAN.

RASKOLNIKOV (ILIN), FEDOR FEDOROVICH (1892–1938?). Member of the Russian Social Democratic Labor Party from 1910; wrote in *Pravda, Zvezda*, and *Prosveshchenie*; drafted into the navy, 1914; chairman of Kronstadt soviet, 1917; acting commissar of the navy, commander of Volga flotilla, and member of Revolutionary War Council of the eastern front, 1918; commander of Caspian flotilla, 1919–20; commander of Baltic fleet, 1920–21; Soviet ambassador to Afghanistan, 1921–23; editor of *Krasnaia Nov*; member of Collegium of People's Commissariat of Education; Soviet plenipotentiary in Estonia, 1930; charged with deviation from party line and purged.

ROY, MANABENDRA NATH (1898–1954). Indian Communist. Son of a well-known Brahmin family in Bengal; joined revolutionary movement at age 14; participated in Indian revolutionary plot to obtain arms in Germany; married an American, Evelyn Trent; arrested in United States because of political activities; absconded bail, escaped to Mexico, and organized a Mexican communist party; left with his wife for Germany, 1919; figured prominently at Second Congress of the Comintern in Moscow, 1920; member of Comintern's three-man Turkestan Bureau, sent to Tashkent in 1920 to foment revolution in India and the Near East; instrumental in enrolling Indian revolutionaries in a special training school in Tashkent, and later in transferring them to Communist University of the Toilers of the East in Moscow; published a revolutionary periodical, *Vanguard*, in Berlin, and later another, *The Masses of India*, in Paris; sent instructions and money to his revolutionary comrades in India; expelled from Germany and lived in Switzerland and France, continuing to play an important role in Comintern gatherings in Moscow; sent to China by Comintern, 1926; clashed with Borodin and returned to Moscow, 1927; disagreed with Stalin's policies and returned to Berlin; returned to India; arrested in 1931 on 1924 Cawnpore charge and sentenced to six years' imprisonment; retained communist views, but bitterly denounced Stalin's actions in his writings.

RYSKULOV, TURAR RYSKULOVICH (1894–1938?). Kazakh Communist. Son of a poor Kirghiz nomad; arrested in 1916 for revolutionary activities; joined Bolsheviks, 1917; active in Turkestan, 1917–20, and later in Kirghiz (Kazakh) republic, 1922–24; chairman of Council of People's Commissars of Turkestan; member of presidium of Baku Congress, 1920; acting People's Commissar of Nationalities of R.S.F.S.R., 1921–22; accused in the thirties of deviation from party line and purged.

SAFAROV, GEORGII IVANOVICH (1891–1938?). Bolshevik from 1908; active in workers' centers in St. Petersburg; arrested and exiled to Arkhangelsk, 1910; emigrated; returned to Russia with Lenin, 1917; active in civil war; worked with Central Executive Committee's Turkestan Commission, 1919–21; in charge of

Comintern's Eastern Department, 1921–22; editor of *Petrogradskaia* (later *Leningradskaia*) *Pravda*, 1922–26; secretary of Soviet embassy in China, 1926; with Soviet embassy in Turkey, 1927; in opposition to party line and finally purged; author of a number of theoretical works.

SEMENOV, GRIGORII MIKHAILOVICH (1890–1946), known as Ataman Semenov. Siberian Cossack of Mongolian descent; officer in Russian army, 1911; fought with great distinction on Austro-German front, 1914–17; after February revolution, sent by Provisional Government to Far East to form volunteer detachments to fight Bolsheviks; began anti-Soviet activities in Harbin, December 1917, and actively opposed Soviet rule throughout Transbaikal region and Russian Far East, acting independently of Kolchak and drawing support from Japan; attempted to promote Pan-Mongolian movement; after failure of anti-Soviet forces in Siberia and Far East, lived in Japan; came to United States in the twenties, but was deported as an undesirable alien and returned to Japan; after Japan's defeat in 1945, captured in Manchuria by Soviet forces and hanged.

SHAUMIAN, STEPAN GEORGIEVICH (1878–1918). Armenian by birth; joined Russian Social Democratic Labor Party, 1901; expelled from technical institute in Riga for revolutionary activities; went to Berlin to study philosophy; met Lenin and Plekhanov in Switzerland, 1903; published *Kavkazskii Rabochii Listok*, 1905; later directed publication of *Bakinskii Rabochii*; arrested and exiled; back in Baku after February revolution; chairman of Baku soviet; chairman of Council of People's Commissars in Baku Commune, 1918; one of twenty-six Baku Commissars shot near Krasnovodsk in September 1918, allegedly upon the order of British occupation authorities in Transcaspia.

SHUMIATSKY, BORIS ZAKHARIEVICH (b. 1886), known also as Andrei Chervonnyi. Old Bolshevik; in Krasnoiarsk, member of Bolshevik Party Committee, member of strike committee, and an organizer of railway workers' uprising in December 1905; arrested, but escaped and conducted illegal party work elsewhere in Siberia; a leader of the workers' rising in Vladivostok, 1907; after a short period of emigration, again active in revolutionary work; soon rearrested and tried for his 1905 activities; recruited into the army; after February revolution, again active in Krasnoiarsk and chief editor of *Sibirskaia Pravda*; edited workers' magazines in Petrograd, 1917; delegate to Sixth Party Congress; after October Revolution returned to Siberia and became chairman of Central Executive Committee of the Soviets of Siberia; active in civil war, 1918–19; member of Siberian Bureau, later of Far Eastern Bureau, of Central Committee of Russian Communist Party; continued to hold high posts in Siberia and simultaneously in the Soviet government, the party, and the Comintern; member of Revolutionary War Council of the Fifth Red Army, active in Outer Mongolia, 1920–21; plenipotentiary of People's Commissariat of Foreign Affairs for Siberia and Mongolia; headed Comintern's Far Eastern Secretariat in Irkutsk, and Council of Ministers of Far Eastern Republic; Soviet ambassador and trade representative to Persia, 1922–25; rector of Communist University of the Toilers of the East in Moscow, 1926–28; awarded Order of the Red Banner by Mongolian government, 1931.

SUHE-BATOR (1893?–1923). Mongolian revolutionary. Son of a poor herdsman; worked as agricultural laborer and later as stagecoach driver between Kiakhta and Urga; in army of autonomous Mongolia, 1912; later typesetter in first Russo-Mongolian printing office at Urga, where he came into contact with revolutionary-minded Russian co-workers; organized a revolutionary group, 1919; merged this group with Choibalsan's, 1920; presided at first congress of Mongolian People's Revolutionary Party, 1921; commanded a detachment against

Chinese and Ungern-Sternberg; appointed war minister of Mongolian revolutionary government in Urga; reportedly poisoned by his enemies.

UNGERN-STERNBERG, ROMAN NICOLAUS VON (1887–1921). A Baltic baron; officer in Russian Imperial Army; instructed by Provisional Government to form Buriat regiments; after October Revolution, carried on independent struggle against Bolsheviks in Siberia and Mongolia; at one time collaborated with Ataman Semenov, but was censored by Kolchak, head of Siberian anti-Soviet government; defeated by Chinese troops near Urga, 1920; occupied Urga, 1921, advancing a plan to re-establish a great Mongolian kingdom under protection of Manchu dynasty; advanced on Siberia, May 1921; defeated and captured by Soviet forces, June 1921; shot, September 1921. A sadistic psychopath, nicknamed the "mad baron," Ungern was known for his extreme cruelty; he conceived some extraordinary ideas of liberating Russia from the influence of the decaying West with the help of the primitive Asian peoples, notably the Mongols, whose religion and language he had embraced.

VELTMAN (PAVLOVICH), MIKHAIL LAZAREVICH (1871–1927). Revolutionary publicist, economist, and historian. Joined the revolutionary movement young; arrested in 1892 in Odessa and charged with propagandizing that city's workers and sailors; after eighteen months in prison, exiled to Siberia for five years; upon release, left for Paris, where he joined Menshevik group, 1903; wrote in *Iskra* under name of Volonter, chiefly on Russo-Japanese War; returned to St. Petersburg, 1905, and edited with Antonov-Ovseenko an illegal paper, *Kazarma*; arrested, but released; emigrated and continued writing for Russian, German, and French magazines, first on imperialism and international relations, later chiefly on Eastern countries, especially India, Persia, and China; after February revolution, returned to Russia, and after October Revolution, joined Bolsheviks; worked in People's Commissariat of Foreign Affairs, and participated in peace negotiations at Brest-Litovsk, 1917–18; represented Revolutionary War Council on southern front of the civil war, 1919–20; at Baku Congress, 1920, and elected to Council of Propaganda and Action; appointed to Collegium of People's Commissariat of Nationalities, and named head of the newly organized Scientific Association for Eastern Studies, 1921; helped found Institute for Eastern Studies in Moscow and became its rector; helped organize other institutions for Eastern study; lectured on imperialism at the Red Army's Military Academy; editor of *Novyi Vostok*, and author of many workers on imperialism and Eastern problems.

VILENSKY, VLADIMIR DMITRIEVICH (b. 1888), known also as Sibiriakov. In revotionary movement from 1903; active in the social-democratic organization in Tomsk, 1905; arrested in 1908 and sentenced to hard labor in Nerchinsk, where he remained until 1912; later settled in Yakutsk region; after February revolution, chairman of the Yakutsk Central Executive Committee of Soviets of Siberia; worked in Siberian underground during Kolchak period; plenipotentiary of R.S.F.S.R. in Far East, 1920; participated in negotiations with Japan at Dairen Conference, 1920; member of Soviet diplomatic mission to Peking, 1922; returned to Moscow and devoted his time to writing; one of the editors of *Izvestiia*, founder of *Katorga i Ssylka* and *Severnaia Aziia*; wrote articles and books on China, Japan, Mongolia, and the revolutionary movement in Siberia; expelled from party in 1927 for deviation.

VOITINSKY (ZARKHIN), GRIGORII NAUMOVICH (b. 1893). Emigrated to America, 1913; lived in a number of cities in United States and Canada as student and worker; returned to Russia, 1918; joined Communist Party and worked in Krasnoiarsk soviet; worked underground and participated in abortive Omsk rising against Kolchak, 1919; sent to Vladivostok to conduct underground work;

arrested, May 1919, and sentenced to life at hard labor in Sakhalin; in January 1920, staged a revolt with other political prisoners and seized power on the island; worked for Comintern's Far Eastern Secretariat; helped organize first communist cells in Shanghai, Peking, and Canton, 1920; later worked with Chinese Communist Party, especially as its liaison man with Sun Yat-sen; from Shanghai, advised and financed Japanese revolutionary groups trying to organize a Japanese communist party; later head of Department of Public Affairs in Institute of World Economics and World Politics; first vice-president of the U.S.S.R. Council of the Institute of Pacific Relations.

YAMAKAWA, HITOSHI (KIN) (b. 1880). Originally an anarchist; one of the organizers and theoretical leaders of the Japanese Communist Party; arrested, 1923; leader of group that favored dissolution of party, 1925; expelled from party, 1929; political writer and social critic.

INDEX

Adalet, *see* Iranian Communist Party
Afghan War (1919), 83, 104
Afghanistan: Activities of Jemal Pasha in, 105, 119; Afghan mission in Moscow (1919), 83, 182; agreement establishing Kabul-Tashkent airline (1927), 262, 263 n.; Barakatullah on situation in (1919), 182; British treaty with (1921), 105; diplomatic relations with Soviet government established, 104; nonaggression and neutrality treaty with U.S.S.R. (1926), 262–63; relations with U.S.S.R. in 1924, Chicherin on, 262–63; Soviet activities in, protested by Britain, 117–18, 119, 120; Soviet treaty with (1921), 91, 103–6, 116, 119, 183–84, 192–93, 194; Voitinsky on Soviet influence in (1924), 314
Ahmed, Muzaffar, 281, 282, 283 n., 284
Ahmed, Qutbuddin, 284
Alexandropol, Treaty of (1920), 108, 109–10
Alimin, Prawirodirdjo, 88, 142, 279
All-China Congress of Trade Unions, 288
All-China Workers' Federation, 269, 362
All-India Communist Conference (Cawnpore, 1925), 282–83
All-Indian Trade Union Congress, 152, 184, 285
All-Russian Central Executive Committee of Soviets: on counterrevolution in the western borderlands, 23; decrees close alliance of the soviet republics (1919), 33; different from ECCI, 192; establishes Communist University of the Toilers of the East, 85; *see also* All-Union Central Executive Committee of Soviets
All-Russian Chamber of Commerce, 116–17
All-Russian Communist Party, *see* Russian Communist Party
All-Union Central Executive Committee of Soviets, 59 n.: declaration of causes and purposes of U.S.S.R. (1923), 60–62; formed, 35
Allison, George (Donald Campbell), 285
Amagaev, Comintern representative in Mongolia, 322
Amanullah, Emir of Afghanistan, 83, 104, 106, 182, 314 n., 317
American Communist Party, 152, 236, 274
Amsterdam International (International Federation of Trade Unions), 310 n., 333 n., 348
Anglo-Persian treaty (1919), 93, 176
Anglo-Russian agreement of 1907, 5, 92–93
Anglo-Soviet trade agreement (1921), 117–18, 119, 120, 159, 160, 192, 211
Ansari, Persian foreign minister, 263
Anuchin, Dmitrii Nikolaevich (1843–1923), 89

Aoki, *see* Arahata, Kanson
Aono, Suekichi, 276
Arahata, Kanson (Aoki), 273, 274, 276, 457
Armenia: agreement with R.S.F.S.R. (1920), 109; Bolshevik uprisings in, 24, 108–9; Dashnak Armenian Republic, 107–9, 112, 159, 169; delegation at Paris, London, and San Remo conferences (1919–20), 107; hostilities with Turkey, 24, 107–10; loyalty to Provisional government, 11; made a constituent republic (1936), 36 n.; occupied by Red Army, 24–25, 109; relation to R.S.F.S.R., etc., Ordzhonikidze on (1921), 56–58; Treaty of Alexandropol (1920), 108, 109–10; Treaty of Kars (1921), 112; *see also* Transcaucasia
Armenian Institute (formerly Lazarev Institute), 87
Asia: areas of Russian interest, 5; communist activity in (1924–27), 265–310, 325–85; communist parties and revolutionary potential in the Far East (1920–23), 138–55, 217–40; communist policies toward, revised in light of capitalist stabilization, 143, 147–48; communist propaganda in, *see* Propaganda; communist revolutionary strategy for (1918–23), 75–90, 156–74; documents best indicating over-all Soviet policies toward (1921–23), 194–98; main routes of Soviet drive in, 17, 75, 121; major ethnic groups, 4; outline for communist work in (1919), 164–65; Russian communist arrangements for propaganda in, 82–89; Russian institutions for study of, 87–89; Russian leaders on revolutionary future of (1927), 386–96; significant events in, during Russian civil war, 11–12; Soviet diplomacy and subversion in the Near East (1920–23), 91–120, 175–93; Soviet diplomatic accomplishments in (1924–27), 243–64, 314–24; Soviet successes and failures in the Far East (1920–23), 121–37, 194–216; Soviet trade relations with, 116–17, 195–96, 264; Soviet two-edged policy in, 75; Stalin on importance of (1918), 156–57; summary of revolutionary situation in (1927), 311–13; theses on, of Comintern's Fourth Congress, 231–37; three centers for communist organizational work in, 82
Association of Young Annamite Revolutionaries, 280
Autonomous Government of the Three Eastern Provinces of the Republic of China, *see* Mukden government
Autumn Crop Uprising, 307
Azerbaijan: Gummet party, 95–96; made a constituent republic (1936), 36 n.; military and economic alliances with R.S.F.S.R.

465